The Transformation of the Classical Heritage
Peter Brown, General Editor

AMBROSE

NEIL B. McLYNN

AMBROSE OF MILAN

Church and Court in a Christian Capital

UNIVERSITY OF CALIFORNIA PRESS

Berkeley · Los Angeles · London

University of California Press
Berkeley and Los Angeles, California

University of California Press, Ltd.
London, England

© 1994 by The Regents of the University of California

Library of Congress Cataloging-in-Publication Data

McLynn, Neil B., 1960–
Ambrose of Milan : church and court in a Christian capital / Neil B. McLynn.
    p.   cm. — (The Transformation of the classical heritage : 22)
Includes bibliographical references and index.
ISBN 0-520-08461-6 (alk. paper)
1. Ambrose, Saint, Bishop of Milan, d. 397. 2. Church and state—
Rome. 3. Church history—Primitive and early church, ca. 30–600.
4. Rome—History—Empire, 30 B.C.–476 A.D. I. Title. II. Series.
BR1720.A5M37 1994   270.2'092—dc20   [B]   94-2261
    CIP

Printed in the United States of America
9 8 7 6 5 4 3 2 1

CONTENTS

LIST OF FIGURES

ABBREVIATIONS

For most ancient sources the conventions in *PLRE* are followed. Abbreviations for periodical titles in the footnotes follow the conventions of *L'Année Philologique*, supplemented where necessary by those of *Patrology*, vol. 4, ed. A. di Bernardino (1986). Note also the following:

AASS: Acta Sanctorum, ed. Société des Bollandistes. Paris/Rome, 1863–.

CCL: Corpus Christianorum Series Latina. Turnholt, 1954,–.

Chron. Min.: Chronica Minora, ed. T. Mommsen. Monumenta Germaniae Historica, Auctores Antiquissimi. Berlin, 1892–1898.

CSEL: Corpus Scriptorum Ecclesiasticorum Latinorum. Vienna, 1886–.

GCS: Die griechischen christlichen Schriftsteller der ersten drei Jahrhunderte. Leipzig/Berlin, 1897–.

ILCV: Inscriptiones Latinae Christianae Veteres, ed. E. Diehl. Berlin, 1925–1931.

ILS: Inscriptiones Latinae Selectae, ed. H. Dessau. Berlin, 1892–1916.

PG: Patrologiae cursus completus, series Graeca, accurante J.-P. Migne. Paris, 1857–1866.

PL: Patrologiae cursus completus, series Latina, accurante J.-P. Migne. Paris, 1844–1864.

PLRE: The Prosopography of the Later Roman Empire. Vol. 1 (A.D. 260–395), ed. A. H. M. Jones, J. R. Martindale and J. Morris. Cambridge, 1971. Vol. 2 (A.D. 395–527), ed. J. R. Martindale, Cambridge, 1980.

PLS: Patrologia Latina: Supplementum. 1958–1974.

SCh: Sources chrétiennes. Paris, 1942–.

The letters of Ambrose are cited from the new Vienna edition (*CSEL* 82, ed. O. Faller and M. Zelzer, 1968–1990); for convenience, a reference to the older Maurist edition (*PL* 16, 913–1342) is added in brackets. The work referred to as the *Apology* of Palladius is edited by R. Gryson, *Scolies Ariennes sur le concile d'Aquilée* (*SCh* 267, 1980), pp. 264–325, 'Fragments du Palladius'; the same enumeration of chapters (81–140) is followed here.

ACKNOWLEDGEMENTS

This book took shape between Oxford and Japan, with numerous debts incurred along the way.

A happy decade at Lincoln College, Oxford, was crowned by election to a Shuffrey Junior Research Fellowship, which enabled me to plan the work on its present scale; I benefitted much throughout from the kind tutelage of Nigel Wilson. John Matthews supervised the thesis from which this book descends with unstinting cheerfulness and frequent injections of good sense, and has continued to lend robust support since. Argument with Peter Heather and Mark Vessey, often heated but never ill-tempered, was always instructive. Fergus Millar and David Hunt, my thesis examiners, made several important suggestions which I have striven to incorporate. For many years I have leaned heavily, for support both logistical and moral, upon Madeline Littlewood.

In the relative isolation of Japan I have missed the wisdom of these people and the resources of the Bodleian Library; delays and frustration have ensued. But I have derived much stimulation from exploring a familiar field made strange; much pleasure from collaboration with Atsuko Gotoh and other scholars; and much satisfaction from the congenial environment provided by Keio University. All this—and the dedication of the young classicists of Tokyo University who have sacrificed their Saturdays for excursions into late antiquity—has left an imprint upon the present book. I am indebted also to Todd Breyfogle, Philip Beagon, and Stefan Rebenich for supplying references and materials, and especially to the generosity and sympathy of Rita Lizzi. Peter Brown intervened to rescue a project that seemed moribund, and his attentive criticism has prompted many improvements. Neither he nor the others mentioned here have been able to tame my wilfulness or save me from error.

A skittish author learned his paces under the genial aegis of Colin Haycraft and has been steered towards publication with patient efficiency by Mary Lamprech and Richard Miller. Of the many others to whom I owe less obvious but equally significant debts, I mention only Richard Pryor, whose comments when we first stared in teenage astonishment at the tomb of Saint Ambrose remain stubbornly lodged in my memory, and my long-suffering but always supportive family: above all Fusa, who has shared the full pain of my labours but all too little of the joy. To her I dedicate this final fruit of the struggle.

INTRODUCTION

Ambrose conquered three emperors in his cathedral at Milan, and each victory was more spectacular than the last. He preached eloquently to Gratian upon the faith; blockaded himself against Valentinian II in a triumphant campaign of defiance; and brought Theodosius to his knees to make an unprecedented act of public penance. All three are reported to have died with the bishop's name on their lips. It is a record quite without parallel. Other combative bishops, Athanasius or Lucifer, fought their rulers from a safe distance: sustained proximity even to a sympathetic emperor proved fatal to John Chrysostom at Constantinople, and Gregory of Nazianzus, baffled and embittered, resigned from the same see after a matter of weeks. Ambrose's unique record sets him apart from contemporary churchmen and defines him historically. His biography is studded with generals, courtiers and Roman senators, and his name carried weight in a world normally considered theirs. Ambrose was venerated by Persian nobles, Frankish chieftains and a German queen: his diplomatic reach extended as far as the Roman empire's.[1]

But for all his fame, Ambrose is strangely inaccessible. Augustine, whose arrival in 384 as an ambitious rhetorician 'to Milan, to Ambrose the bishop' marks a turning-point both in his own life and in the course of western Christianity, draws a tellingly one-sided picture of his first encounter with the celebrated bishop. In his response to Ambrose's 'fatherly' welcome and the flattering interest that he evinced in the journey

1. Paulinus *V. Amb.* 25, 30, 36.

which had brought him (travelling 'first class' by the imperial postal service) to Milan, one can sense the prickly egoism of the talented provincial: the young man immediately 'began to love him' as 'a man who was
kind to me'.[2] The scene brings Augustine vividly to life; but Ambrose
remains inscrutable behind his 'properly episcopal' demeanour, the
kindness which so stirred Augustine being no more than an aspect of
this routine politeness. The bishop's impeccable manners, moreover, appear to have kept his admirers at a proper distance. Augustine's knack
for making friends had taken him far in his highly competitive profession, but he never became intimate with the bishop who opened his eyes
to the truths of Christianity and baptized him into the faith. Nor did the
rhetor's sharp-eyed scrutiny of Ambrose's calm surface for traces of uncertainty and weakness underneath, or for clues to the sources of his
serenity, yield any results.[3] It is almost as if Ambrose's stature put him
beyond the reach of his contemporaries.

This is of profound significance to the historian, whose most reliable bearings upon the leaders of the fourth-century church are taken
from their peers. The frictions and tensions generated within their close-
knit and jealous world are always richly informative: Gregory of Nyssa
can be approached through his domineering brother Basil, and Basil
through his aggrieved friend Gregory of Nazianzus. The squabbling between Jerome and Augustine reveals much about both men. But when
Jerome turned his critical fire upon Ambrose there followed nothing to
match either his ponderous and carping correspondence with Hippo, or
the furious salvos that he exchanged with Rufinus. Against Ambrose
Jerome said much less, for once, than he might have: Ambrose appears
to have said nothing at all. He weathered the hostility of Jerome as impassively as he did the admiration of Augustine.

Ambrose's impassivity is a still more striking feature of his participation in the 'search for the Christian doctrine of God', the great Chris-
tological and Trinitarian debates that echoed across the fourth-century
Christian world.[4] 'Debate', while hardly a satisfactory term for the often

---

2. Aug. *Conf.* 5.13.23: 'Suscepit me paterne ille homo dei et peregrinati-
onem meam satis episcopaliter dilexit. Et eum amare coepi primo quidem . . .
tamquam hominem benignum in me'.

3. *Conf.* 6.3.3.

4. It is beyond the scope of the present book to provide an introduction to
the fearsomely complex doctrinal disputes of the fourth century; the nine hundred pages of R. P. C. Hanson, *The Search for the Christian Doctrine of God* (1988),
give an outstanding survey of the intellectual basis of the controversies and the
historical circumstances that conditioned their course.

crude exchanges through which these issues were resolved, is useful as a metaphor to suggest the almost physical immediacy conveyed by the records of these encounters. From transcripts of set-piece debates, spare summaries of church councils or the interlocking arguments of rival pamphleteers, one obtains a vivid and precise sense of how the contestants fought out their battles, circling warily around each other before lunging at a suspected weakness. It is often possible also to re-create an audience, for whose benefit important points are underlined and whose sympathies are carefully taken into account; these spectators are sometimes sceptical experts, sometimes attentive neutrals, and sometimes partisans whose passions the speaker or writer sets out to inflame. Ambrose's contributions to this debate, however, seem to float free of their context.

Ambrose produced a series of doctrinal treatises for the attention of a highly select audience. The five imposing books of his *De fide* and the three-volume work *De spiritu sancto* were addressed to—and had been commissioned by—the emperor Gratian himself. These works are certainly polemical, but fail to engage any particular enemies or set of beliefs: the principal target named is Arius himself, the Alexandrian presbyter who had died before Ambrose was born, and the doctrines attacked are constructed (from a number of intermediate sources) from those of several different, and mutually incompatible, opponents of the creed of Nicaea.[5] Much of the material, moreover, proves not to have been composed for the emperor's benefit at all but extracted from the bishop's sermons to his people. But the real puzzle of these derivative and unfocused works is why the emperor should have wanted them in the first place, and it says much for the enduring power of Ambrose's reputation that this question was not addressed until the present generation. It has now been convincingly argued that Ambrose had actually been invited to justify his *own* teachings in the face of criticisms and twisted the terms of his commission in order to produce instead this sonorous *pièce d'occasion*. Ambrose's text was not, like most doctrinal polemic, produced for hand-to-hand combat; *De fide* vaults lightly over the complexities of the battlefield to make its impact far behind the lines, at the imperial headquarters.

The same applies to the one set-piece 'debate' in which Ambrose did participate, the council of Aquileia in 381. He and his supporters re-

5. The peculiarities of Ambrose's polemical style are best appreciated by comparison with such contemporary works as Gregory of Nazianzus' *Theological Orations* or Gregory of Nyssa's *Contra Eunomium*; an instructive contrast can also be drawn with the close and careful argument of the anti-Arian treatise *De Trinitate* presented by the Luciferian presbyter Faustinus to the empress Flaccilla.

mained at cross-purposes throughout with two bishops who held steadfastly to their homoean (in Ambrose's terms, 'Arian') positions, but the
transcript shows Ambrose dictating the pace: it is his agenda, and only
his, which appears in the formal record. The opposing case is preserved
only in the margins of a single fifth-century manuscript, and only recently, through the magnificent work of its editor, has it become possible
to appreciate its strength.[6] But the devastating commentary upon the
proceedings at Aquileia by Palladius, one of the two victims, is fundamentally a tribute to Ambrose's masterful elusiveness. The frustration
which runs through the text, culminating in a vehement but fruitless
challenge to a rematch under fairer conditions, is powerful testimony to
the difficulty of gaining purchase upon the bishop.

Ambrose's inaccessibility is easily taken for granted, as an aspect of
his personality. He can appear a somewhat aloof and overbearing, but
refreshingly uncomplicated and secure figure in a nervous and introspective age. The contrast is nevertheless false, for self-revelation was
conditioned by context as well as by character. The inner lives so brilliantly re-created in Augustine's *Confessions* or Jerome's correspondence
embody, at least in part, a claim to an explicitly personalized authority;[7]
isolation from an audience, pressure of competition or the inapplicability of more conventional approaches could help to shape such claims.
So too could failure: forced retirement (a fate Ambrose himself only narrowly escaped) and not autobiographical compulsion provoked Gregory
of Nazianzus' massive, searing poem *De vita sua*. Ambrose's impersonal,
peculiarly elusive solidity is also a function of self-presentation; and
indeed, if we know him less than his Christian contemporaries, it is
because he was more thorough in his work than they. For perhaps no
body of patristic literature is as carefully controlled as Ambrose's. We
see him sending his work to a friend to be combed for any 'barrister's
pleasantries';[8] even the exegetical treatises that he compiled from his
preaching are collated rather than transcribed, creating considerable controversy over their 'original' core. With Ambrose there is never the sustained immediacy of Augustine's or Chrysostom's sermon transcripts,
which bring their pastoral routines vividly to life, or of Jerome's hasty
and intemperate polemics. Nor do his letters, the prime sources for his
confrontations with successive emperors, escape his editorial control.

6. R. Gryson, *Scolies Ariennes sur le concile d'Aquilée* (1980); the text is reproduced, with different enumeration of chapters, in *Scripta Arriana Latina I* (*CCL*
87 [1982]).

7. For Jerome's self-portraiture, see now M. Vessey, 'Jerome's Origen: The
Making of a Christian Literary *Persona*', *SP* 25 (1993), 135–145.

8. *Ep*. 32 [48].3.

The bishop has recently been revealed as the 'Christian Pliny', with his correspondence organized into a collection of ten volumes, nine 'private' and one 'public', to match his model.[9] None of his contemporaries shows such constant attention to the form in which their writings were issued. We might catch an echo of Ambrose's experience as advocate and administrator in the imperial service in his abiding consciousness of the status of a published text; he never forgot that his books would have to 'speak for themselves'.[10] They were therefore designed not to open a dialogue with friends or opponents but to deliver a self-sufficient, final word.

Ambrose's editorial hand extends even beyond his death, to shape the biography which was commissioned from his former secretary, Paulinus, by Augustine.[11] For Paulinus stood too close to his subject to bring independent judgement to bear, as did his model, Sulpicius Severus, upon his subject, Martin, and too far beneath him to allow the intimacy that suffuses Possidius of Calama's portrait of Augustine.[12] Perhaps the most revealing passage of the *Vita* shows Paulinus interrupted while taking the bishop's dictation by the appearance of a small flame that crept across Ambrose's head and entered his mouth 'like a householder his home', while his face turned 'as white as snow'. Paulinus was momentarily too amazed to write; but he was spared the embarrassment of having to ask his master to repeat himself, since the passage concerned was a quotation from Scripture. Nor apparently did he discuss the incident with Ambrose, going instead to the deacon Castus to report it and seek an explanation.[13] Paulinus' reverence for the bishop precluded any out-of-turn approach; it is therefore no surprise to find his account of the great events of Ambrose's career remaining within the 'official' framework defined by the bishop himself. The biography, much of which consists of glosses on Ambrose's own writings, therefore serves to extend and promote an existing picture.[14] In this it resembles another

9. M. Zelzer, '*Plinius Christianus:* Ambrosius als Epistolograph', *SP* 23 (1989), 203–208.

10. *Ep.* 32 [48].3.

11. On the *Vita Ambrosii,* see the useful work by E. Lamirande, *Paulin de Milan et la "Vita Ambrosii"* (1983).

12. For Sulpicius (invoked at *V. Amb.* 1.1) and his treatment of his subject, see C. Stancliffe, *St. Martin and His Hagiographer* (1983). Possidius recalls his 'familiaria conloquia' with Augustine at *V. Aug.* 31.1 and concludes his account with a moving tribute: 'cum quo ferme annis quadraginta Dei dono absque amara ulla dissensione familiariter ac dulciter vixi' (*V. Aug.* 31.9).

13. *V. Amb.* 42.

14. The most obvious paraphrases are at *V. Amb.* 19 (*Ep.* 30 [24].9); *V. Amb.* 22 (*Ep.* 74 [40]); *V. Amb.* 23 (*Ep. extra coll.* 1 [41]); *V. Amb* 26 (*Epp.* 72–73 [17–18]).

venture recently attributed to Paulinus, the publication of the first group of *Epistolae extra collectionem*, ten letters to emperors which supplement the tenth book of the correspondence.[15] The biography is likewise an appendix to Ambrose's own work, offering neither a privileged glimpse into his private life nor an independent perspective upon his public career.

This leaves the modern scholar little room for manoeuvre. No more able than Paulinus to presume upon any intimacy with Ambrose, we are constantly reduced, like him, to taking the bishop's dictation; and, like Palladius, we can only engage Ambrose upon his own prepared ground. The biographical approach, which has done so much to illuminate his contemporaries Augustine and Jerome, is therefore doomed to failure with Ambrose. To attempt it risks mistaking studio portraits of the bishop for snapshots, in much the same way that a stylized fifth-century mosaic (depicting him with five other men from the historical and legendary past of the Milanese church, each of them individuated by the artist) has been mistaken for an 'authentic' representation.[16]

This book is an attempt instead to relate the form and conventions of Ambrose's 'portraiture' to the vicissitudes of his career. His writings develop a carefully crafted public persona: the emphasis will be on the circumstances and forces which helped to mould this facade, rather than on a search for the 'inner man' behind it. Ambrose's intricate dealings with the emperors, and with the magnates who dominated their courts and his congregation, reveal much about the workings of late Roman politics; his responses to the recurrent emergencies to which his environment exposed him clarify the options available to a bishop in the 'Christian empire' of the fourth century. For Ambrose, so elusive among his introspective fellow-churchmen, becomes more intelligible beside the great public figures of his day. One of his Roman contemporaries, for example, left a vast corpus of letters—organized, just like his, into nine books of personal and one of 'official' correspondence—which no historian would ever dream of using as a 'biographical' source. After

15. See M. Zelzer's remarks in her edition of these letters, *CSEL* 82.3 (1983), at p. lxxxv.

16. See G. Bovini, 'I mosaici di S. Vittore "in ciel d'oro" di Milano', *Corsi di cultura sull'arte ravennate e bizantina* 16 (1969), 71–81, establishing a date in the late fifth century. Scholars have consistently exaggerated the naturalism of this portrait in comparison with the others in the chapel (note the attempt to add scientific rigour by adducing the features of Ambrose's skull: A. Ratti, 'Il più antico ritratto di S. Ambrogio', in *Ambrosiana* [1897], 5–74); but the Ambrose is no more a likeness than are the Protasius and Gervasius flanking him.

long and almost dismissive neglect, Symmachus has in recent years been given credit for his astute tactical sense and his skill in exploiting the formulae with which he worked. It is in relation to men like him, rather than Augustine or Jerome, that Ambrose can most usefully be approached.

Nearly sixty years have elapsed since the publication of the last major study of Ambrose in English, F. Homes Dudden's two-volume *Life and Times of Saint Ambrose* (1935). Much of value can still be learnt from this calm and judicious survey, but its easy rhythms never properly engage the problems inherent in the evidence: by allowing Ambrose to speak for himself, it reproduces the terms which he himself set for the issues in which he was involved.

Homes Dudden built upon solid foundations laid by contemporary continental scholarship. In 1929 Hans von Campenhausen had produced a dazzling reinterpretation of the bishop's political activity. His principal focus was upon the nuances of Ambrose's relations with popes and emperors, but the *aperçus* scattered throughout the book illuminate every aspect of his career, while the close attention to problems of chronology announced the bishop's first systematic exposure to the rigours of modern historical method.[17] Only four years later, von Campenhausen's work was capped by the comprehensive study by J.-R. Palanque, *Saint Ambroise et l'empire romain*, which has remained the basis for all subsequent historical assessments of the bishop's career; debts will be apparent upon almost every page of the present work. Palanque's subtitle, *Contribution à l'histoire des rapports de l'église et l'état à fin du IVe siècle*, well defines his scope: he presents the dealings between Ambrose and successive emperors, then discusses the ideals and principles that underpinned these transactions. Ambrose's works are examined scrupulously and critically, each assessed upon its merits and fitted within a comprehensive chronological scheme that—although in many places since superseded—was one of the book's greatest achievements. For all that, however, Ambrose is allowed to dictate the pace. Neither his credentials as a representative of the church nor his claims upon the state are subjected to any serious scrutiny; the real world is assumed throughout to correspond, essentially, to the terms imposed upon it in the bishop's pronouncements.

Palanque succumbs, moreover, to a biographical fallacy common in studies of Ambrose. From the bishop's various confrontations with

17. *Ambrosius von Mailand als Kirchenpolitiker* (1929).

the authorities, a unifying principle of ecclesiastical autonomy is constructed; his actions are then taken to reflect a single-minded commitment to this ideal, which is in turn explained in terms of his personality. An Ambrose of immense energy is therefore produced, fairly blazing his way through Palanque's pages. In the introduction alone we are alerted to 'sa flamme oratoire . . . signe d'une âme ardente', 'l'ardeur irrésistible qui assurera ses triomphes' and 'son caractère ardent'.[18] And the belief that Ambrose's works are fundamentally transparent—that is, that their contents illustrate their author's character—allows Palanque to discern another, more sensitive and tender, side to the bishop. This combination of different traits makes his Ambrose a complex and credible human being: 'un coeur avide d'affection, un esprit ouvert aux aspirations humaines, il est aussi un chef soucieux de son autorité: l'ardeur même de sa nature le pousse à commander.'[19]

Such terms are echoed, with slight variations, in many other accounts. Angelo Paredi, in his learned and sympathetic biography (1941), produced a character formed from *Romanitas* and Christian otherworldliness.[20] A variety of personalities can be constructed from the different genres in which Ambrose wrote: an influential portrait has shown him exhibiting the contradictions inherent in the fourth-century church, a 'man of action' able 'to grasp and hold power in a ruthless society', who nevertheless betrays a 'feminine intensity' by his delight in the imagery of kissing and in music.[21]

The enticing complexities of Ambrose's inner life are now taken for granted: 'we are dealing with a man whose imaginative world was a tensile system'.[22] Ironically, this false trail has gained its current respectability through what has undoubtedly been the most significant achievement in postwar Ambrosian studies. Pierre Courcelle and his disciples in France have revealed in Ambrose's exegetical treatises an unexpected depth of acquaintance with the Alexandrian Jew Philo and, more surprisingly, the Neoplatonist philosopher Plotinus. Fresh studies continue

18. *Saint Ambroise*, 20, 21, 24. Von Campenhausen makes a similar move from an assumption of consistency to psychological inference in his conclusion (*Ambrosius von Mailand*, 263–271).

19. *Saint Ambroise*, 392. Compare the 'puissance indéfinissable de séduction' allegedly discernible in 'le regard dominateur' of the mosaic (*Saint Ambroise*, 20).

20. *S. Ambrogio e la sua età*, 2d ed. (1960), 520–521, matching 'tutta l'energia dei romani antichi' with 'il suo disinteresse, il suo amore alla croce'. This work was translated into English as *Saint Ambrose* in 1964.

21. P. R. L. Brown, *Augustine of Hippo* (1967), 81–83.

22. Peter Brown, *The Body and Society* (1988), 347.

to demonstrate the subtlety and originality of Ambrose's writings,[23] but despite the claims of their more enthusiastic publicists, these discoveries do not open a window upon Ambrose's mind. The texts concerned share the peculiar opacity which characterizes all the bishop's writings: because he does not argue with his sources (as Augustine, for example, argues with the 'Platonists' in the *Confessions* or with Porphyry in the *City of God*), his response to them remains mysterious. But there is no compelling reason to suppose that Ambrose's reading ever gave him more than material with which to adorn his sermons.[24]

But if we can say less about Ambrose's life than Homes Dudden and his successors have believed, the opposite is true of his times. The later Roman empire is now recognized as a far richer and more complex world than it seemed a half-century ago. The massive, uniform and forbidding structures suggested by the *Codex Theodosianus* and the *Notitia Dignitatum* have taken on more jumbled contours as historians have come to accept a model of an intrinsically passive imperial government; the stark outline of these texts has been blurred further by recognition of the overlaps between central state authority and 'unofficial' sources of power, and of the limited scope of the former.[25] At the same time, studies of the fourth-century church increasingly emphasize the sheer effort required by its leadership to assert an identity for their organization (and ensure their own predominance within it) in the face of both traditional practices and the pressures of the wealth and high public profile bequeathed by Constantine.[26] As bishop of an imperial capital,

23. The key texts are P. Courcelle, *Recherches sur les "Confessions" de saint Augustin*, 2d ed. (1968), 106ff; H. Savon, *Saint Ambroise devant l'exégèse de Philon le juif* (1977); G. Madec, *Saint Ambroise et la philosophie* (1974). The coherence of Ambrose's method of argument has been vindicated by Savon, 'Maniérisme et allégorie dans l'oeuvre d'Ambroise de Milan', *REL* 55 (1977), 203–221, and G. Nauroy, 'La structure du *De Isaac vel Anima* et la cohérence de l'allégorèse d'Ambroise de Milan', *REL* 63 (1985), 210–236.

24. With Ambrose there is never an 'off-the-record' citation, to compare with Augustine's deathbed quotation of Plotinus to his unsuspecting friends (Poss. *V. Aug.* 28.11).

25. There is a fine study of the mechanics of fourth-century decision-making in John Matthews, *The Roman Empire of Ammianus* (1989), 232–278; cf. J. Harries, 'The Roman Imperial Quaestor from Constantine to Theodosius II', *JRS* 78 (1988), 148–172. For the flaws in the system, see R. MacMullen, *Corruption and the Decline of Rome* (1988).

26. See Peter Brown, *Power and Persuasion in Late Antiquity* (1992), 71–158. There is much useful material on the tensions faced by the leaders of the fourth-century church in E. C. Hobbs and W. Wuellner, eds., *The Role of the Christian Bishop in Ancient Society* (1980).

Ambrose operated for much of his career at close quarters to the court, an environment where the clerical leadership was often discomfited by the expansive piety of a wealthy Christian elite. His public activities— whether the construction of churches or the incorporation of philosophical gobbets in his sermons—belong to this general background and should be related to the pressures it generated.

The complexities of Ambrose's world have been well described by modern historians. The unstable and shifting environment of the imperial capital where he operated has been articulated with particular skill by Lellia Cracco Ruggini and her disciples in Italy;[27] an important physical dimension has been added to these studies by a series of archaeological discoveries which have illuminated the city's topography and Ambrose's own contributions to it.[28] From a slightly different perspective, Ambrose has been set against the political background of the Italian court, and in relation to the western aristocracies who sought to dominate it, by John Matthews.[29]

But despite this new understanding of the intricacies and vagaries of fourth-century Milan, Ambrose remains a solid figure radiating massive certainties. The present book is intended to provide a fresh perspective upon aspects of his career which have been taken largely for granted. It is not, to repeat, a biography, nor is the primary concern Ambrose's theological or pastoral work. The purpose is rather to locate him more exactly within his society, and in particular to reassess his relationships and dramatic confrontations with successive emperors. This will involve a fundamental re-reading of the evidence, most of which is supplied by Ambrose himself and which has too often been treated as if it were descriptive rather than prescriptive. Too many scholars have therefore allowed Ambrose to impose his own interpretation upon events, conjuring elaborate ideologies and strategies from his slogans. The present discussion will be confined largely to the tactical level, to allow a more realistic understanding of the constraints under which Ambrose operated and a better appreciation of his achievement in overcoming them. The bishop belongs ultimately within the rough-and-tumble of political life, not above it.

27. See especially Ruggini's *Economia e società nell' "Italia Annonaria"* (1961) and her 'Ambrogio di fronte alla compagine sociale del suo tempo', in *Ambrosius Episcopus* (1976), 1:230–265.

28. For a fully illustrated survey, see M. Mirabella Roberti, *Milano Romana* (1984). The historical significance of the developing Christian architecture of Milan is discussed by R. Krautheimer, *Three Christian Capitals* (1983).

29. J. F. Matthews, *Western Aristocracies and Imperial Court* (1975), esp. 183–222.

These concerns explain the shape of the book. Chapter 1 examines the circumstances of Ambrose's episcopal election, for which the sources are especially problematic: the episode will therefore be approached with reference to Ambrose's own responsibilities as provincial governor, and to the character of the electorate, the Christian communities of Milan. Chapter 2 will trace Ambrose's early years in office, the least well documented phase of his career. Examination of the available sources will suggest the pressures that operated upon him; the same texts will show him forging in response to these a distinctive episcopal identity. Chapter 3, on Ambrose's dealings with Gratian, is the most complex of the book. The relationship can only be understood in its wider context: the need to take account of Gratian's relations with Theodosius, and Ambrose's with his doctrinal opponents, will involve the reader in an elaborate quadrille between Trier, Milan, Sirmium and Constantinople. The reward will be a comprehensive reappraisal of what has been perhaps the most seriously misunderstood phase of Ambrose's career; this will include a new approach to the council of Aquileia, the transcript of which gives us our most sustained close-quarter view of Ambrose in action. Chapter 4 treats Ambrose's celebrated collision with young Valentinian II and his mother, Justina. Here too the broader political context will provide a basis for revising conventional views: analysis of the character of Valentinian's regime, and of Ambrose's claims upon it, will permit a fresh reading of the texts which embody the bishop's version of the affair. In chapters 5 and 6 the focus shifts to the social and religious forces operative in imperial Milan. Chapter 5 explores Ambrose's relations with his congregation and his style of leadership, discussing in particular his construction of churches and his preaching; chapter 6 shows his connexions with members of the social and political elite, and with the Italian episcopate. His dealings with Theodosius are discussed in chapter 7, in relation to the latter's designs in the west (which were much less straightforward than has generally been realized) and the variables represented by Valentinian II and the reluctant usurper Eugenius. A short final chapter explores the circumstances of his last years and the development of his reputation in the subsequent generation.

The Ambrose who will emerge is in many respects very different from the man who captivated Augustine with his kindness. The welcome he extended to the young rhetor, however, belongs within a pattern of social relations typical of the age. It was probably only a few years earlier that an equally impressive welcome was given to another *peregrinus,* at Rome this time, but the effusions proved misleading. Ammianus Marcellinus never once mentions Ambrose in his history, which takes its coverage of western events to the year after the bishop's election; he will nevertheless be as constant a point of reference in the following pages as Augustine. Ammianus shared with Ambrose the experience of living in the shadow of an imperial court, a world of menace but also of rich possibilities. His heroes are men who retain their dignity among the dangers and temptations which such a life offered; the poise Ambrose retains throughout his career should be seen in the same perspective, as the fruit of constant effort. Ammianus shows us Symmachus' father, a match for his son in his studied calm, missing out upon a prestigious appointment through nepotistic intrigue at court; he shows also how allegations of a private, but grossly insensitive, remark provoked the indignant populace of Rome to burn down his mansion and cause him to flee the city.[30] We would never have guessed the circumstances from Symmachus' own allusions. These were nevertheless the forces which swirled and eddied through the fourth century. The smooth facades Ambrose presents to us might be seen as the product of erosion, after long exposure to such blasts; it is not always appreciated that considerable qualities—and considerable luck—were required merely to weather these storms. The Ambrose of this book is, above all, a survivor. The achievement, if less spectacular than the victories of church over state with which he has so often been credited, should not be underrated.

30. Amm. Marc. 21.12.24, 27.3.3; Matthews, *The Roman Empire of Ammianus*, 270, 416–417.

CHAPTER ONE

THE RELUCTANT BISHOP

SNATCHED FROM THE JUDGEMENT SEAT

Ambrose never lingered over the circumstances of his election, even while preaching to his people on the anniversary of his consecration, 'when my priesthood seems to begin again'. 'You are my fathers and mothers', he reminded them, recalling how they had made him their bishop; but within a sentence he had marched to their converse role as sons and daughters, and he devoted the remainder of the sermon to their filial obligations.[1]

Equally brisk and purposeful are Ambrose's other allusions to the election. In *De officiis* he explains his deficiencies as a teacher with a striking phrase: he had been 'snatched into the priesthood from the magistrate's tribunal and my robes of office'. But exactly the same expression—'raptus de tribunalibus'—is repeated in another work in relation to his former devotion to the 'vanities of the world'.[2] Even the apparent spontaneity of an exclamation, 'How I resisted being ordained!', which interrupts a disquisition about the qualities necessary for the episcopate, is deceptive. The outburst is part of an elaborate argument, and

1. *Exp. Evang. sec. Luc.* 8.73.
2. *De off.* 1.4; *De poen.* 2.72. The repetition of the formula becomes especially noteworthy with acceptance of the early date argued for this section of *De officiis* by M. Testard, 'Etude sur la composition dans le *De officiis ministrorum* de saint Ambroise', in *Ambroise de Milan*, ed. Y.-M. Duval (1974), at 155–156; this would separate the two works by more than a decade.

serves to forestall the objection that by accepting ordination immediately after his baptism, Ambrose had breached his own requirement that a bishop should 'uphold in himself the precepts of the law'.[3]

These snippets are, moreover, less informative than they might initially appear. Other authors use similar expressions to describe experiences which scarcely justify their urgency. Paulinus of Nola, like Ambrose a former magistrate, wrote asking Augustine to help him with his religious studies, since he was 'unskilled, only just emerging after my many shipwrecks from the waves of the world'; he describes himself elsewhere as having been 'dragged by force' into his ordination as a presbyter and 'captured from the forests of the world'. But both Paulinus and Augustine, who had used similar language to claim what amounted to a period of study leave immediately after his ordination, had advertised themselves as potential recruits for the church by renouncing their careers and professing ascetic vocations.[4] When Gaudentius, whom Ambrose made bishop of Brescia, recalled to his people his unsuccessful resistance—'I tried with all my strength to refuse'—they would have understood his modesty in its context: as a prominent presbyter of his church and a favourite disciple of the previous bishop, Gaudentius had long been marked out as a future leader.[5]

If Ambrose were our only source, we would probably bracket him with these men as a victim of an overly public commitment to his faith. The only significant indication of anything unusual is Ambrose's claim—prompted by the most serious crisis of his career—that the emperor had 'guaranteed' him security of tenure if he accepted the post.[6] But this does not prepare us for the account of the election by Rufinus of Aquileia, which shows Ambrose literally being dragged from the tribunal of his provincial governorship of Aemilia and Liguria:

> When Auxentius, the bishop of the heretics at Milan, had died, the people of the two parties clamorously supported their different claims. The grave dissension and dangerous unrest of the parties threatened to produce immediate destruction for their own city if they failed to fulfil

3. *Ep. extra coll.* 14 [63].65.

4. Paul. Nol. *Ep.* 4.3; Aug. *Ep.* 21. P. R. L. Brown, *Augustine of Hippo* (1967), 139, characterizes Augustine's ordination as the kidnapping of a passing 'star'; Paulinus was seized by a congregation that knew of his plans for ascetic renunciation and so 'believed themselves to be on the brink of a massive windfall': W. H. C. Frend, 'The Two Worlds of Paulinus of Nola', in *Latin Literature of the Fourth Century*, ed. J. W. Binns (1974), at 112.

5. Gaud. *Tract.* 16.2.

6. *Ep.* 75 [21].7.

their mutually contradictory aims. Ambrose was at that time governing the province. When he saw the disaster that lay in store for the city, he hastened, in accordance with his rank and duties, to enter the church, to calm the disturbance among the people. When he had there concluded a long speech, in accordance with the laws and with public order, a shout and a single cry suddenly arose among the people who were fighting and quarreling among themselves: 'Ambrose for bishop!' They shouted that he should be baptized immediately (he was a catechumen) and be given to them as bishop, and that there was no other way that they could become a single people sharing a single faith, unless Ambrose were given to them as bishop. Although he demurred and resisted fiercely, the desire of the people was referred to the emperor and the order came to implement it with all speed. For the emperor said that it was thanks to God that this sudden conversion had restored the divided beliefs and antagonisms of the people into a single shared consensus and inspired a unanimous proposal. Shortly afterwards, Ambrose obtained the grace of God and was both initiated in the sacred mysteries and made bishop. (*HE* 11.11)

Rufinus provides rich flesh indeed for the bones of Ambrose's reminiscences. He shows him drafted, unlike the other famous conscripts to the fourth-century church, directly from the reserved occupation of the imperial service. Still more dramatic is the information that the people of Milan, Ambrose's 'parents in the priesthood', had been divided into two factions which were reconciled only in the act of creating him their bishop. Their quarrel was no trifle: as 'catholics' and 'Arians', they stood on opposite sides of the great fault line that cut through the church of the fourth century.[7]

At the time of Ambrose's consecration, in December 374, Rufinus had already begun the ascetic career that would keep him away from Italy until the very moment of the bishop's death in the spring of 397.[8] But when composing his history at Aquileia he had ready access to

7. The party labels applied by Paulinus and Rufinus are propagandist; more accurate are 'Nicene' and 'homoean' (referring respectively to adherence to the doctrine of one substance shared by Father and Son, as embodied in the creed of Nicaea, and rejection of this concept in favour of a doctrine that the two Persons were similar, *homoioi*), although neither term designates a united and organized party.

8. The year of Ambrose's consecration is established as 374, against the argument for 373 originally proposed by von Campenhausen and followed by Palanque and Homes Dudden, in O. Faller, 'La data della consacrazione vescovile di sant'Ambrogio', in *Ambrosiana* (1942), 97–112. F. X. Murphy, *Rufinus of Aquileia* (1945), 232–233, assigns Rufinus' departure from Italy to 373 and his return to 397; slightly earlier dates have been proposed by A. D. Booth, 'The Chronology of Jerome's Early Years', *Phoenix* 35 (1981), at 250.

information. He wrote at the request of the local bishop, his old friend
Chromatius, a correspondent of Ambrose who had probably been consecrated by him; other knowledgeable informants were also available.[9]
But Rufinus gives us not merely his own well-informed interpretation
but the 'official' version of the Milanese church. Ambrose's biographer,
Paulinus, writing a decade later, echoed his account almost exactly: riot,
speech, acclamation, resistance and imperial intervention follow one another in the same sequence, the only difference being Paulinus' elaboration of Ambrose's ruses to avoid consecration. These details make it
unlikely that he was copying Rufinus, whom he fails to use for other
important episodes like the clash with Justina and the penitence of Theodosius. On the other hand, Paulinus' account does not betray any con-
fidences obtained directly from the bishop. The two reports should
therefore be seen as parallel versions of a tradition which had already,
at the time of Ambrose's death, achieved uniformity.[10]

It is difficult to make historical sense of this remarkable sequence of
events. Reducing the episode to a charade—orchestrated either by Ambrose himself (his reluctance therefore being nothing more than the conventional 'rite of refusal') or by his political superiors (in an attempt to
ensure a reliable tenant for this important see)[11]—fails completely to
account for its most extraordinary feature: nowhere else are homoeans
and Nicenes ever reported to have turned so suddenly from strife to
harmony. Most historians therefore stress Ambrose's personal (or political) attractiveness, which is argued to have appealed across party barriers. Milanese Christians, according to one highly influential account,
were 'sensible to the humane qualities of their governor', attracted by

9. Rufinus' account is analyzed by F. Thélamon, *Païens et chrétiens au IVème
siècle* (1981), 337–341. His own attitude towards popular elections is revealed in
a gloss upon Eusebius' account of a similarly deadlocked contest: 'alius de alio,
ut fieri solet ⟨in⟩ talibus, conclamaret' (*HE* 6.29.1).

10. Paulin. *V. Amb.* 6–9. The parallels with Rufinus are noted, and dependence argued, in M. Pellegrino's edition, *Paolino di Milano: Vita di S. Ambrogio*
(1961), pp. 16–18; but cf. J. Fontaine, *REL* 50 (1962), 332. Paulinus' somewhat
distanced account (esp. *V. Amb.* 6.1, 9.3: 'fertur') can be contrasted to Possidius'
references to Augustine's reminiscences about his election at Hippo (*V. Aug.* 4.2:
'ut nobis ipse retulit'; 4.3: 'ut ipse retulit').

11. The former is implied for Ambrose's resistance by J. Béranger, 'Le refus
du pouvoir', *MH* 5 (1948–49), at 191, and argued explicitly for the entire episode
by H. von Campenhausen, *Ambrosius von Mailand als Kirchenpolitiker* (1929),
26–29 (for the tendentiousness of which see Palanque, *Saint Ambroise*, 16–17).
For the latter view, see C. Corbellini, 'Sesto Petronio Probo e l'elezione episcopale di Ambrogio', *RIL* 109 (1975), 181–189.

his judicial mildness and sober lifestyle.[12] A subtle variant makes Ambrose a compromise candidate, whose opportune arrival provided an acceptable solution to both sides after each had failed to secure the election of their own first choice. The homoeans looked not only to his personal qualities but also to his likely fidelity to Valentinian I's policy of religious neutrality.[13]

But any homoeans who expected their governor to protect their community from doctrinal extremism were mistaken. Ambrose would immediately prove, by insisting upon baptism from a 'catholic' bishop, that he was no neutral. Nor, as we shall see, were his allegiances likely to have been a secret. More fundamentally, the explanations cited above assume that Ambrose's qualities were visible to the Christians in the basilica, that the bishop could already be recognized beneath the magistrate's mask. But the government of a province offered little scope for the exercise of the Christian virtues. During his short term of office a governor was closely circumscribed by his responsibilities for enforcing the law, supervising the collection of taxes and maintaining order.[14] Besides, his was a much harsher role than the bishop's: he represented the savage and relentless face of the late Roman judiciary, the 'terror of public administration' which left little room for manoeuvre.[15]

There happens to survive a contemporary, if somewhat overwrought, account of a *consularis* of Aemilia and Liguria in action.[16] During an assize at Vercelli, the governor (who made regular tours of his province) heard a charge of adultery brought by a jealous husband. Routine interrogation ('as the bloodstained hook tore at his livid flesh and the truth was sought through the pain in his ravaged sides' [Jer. *Ep.* 1.3]) duly extracted a confession from the alleged lover, but the wife steadfastly failed to oblige. 'Thereupon the *consularis*, his eyes gorged with slaughter, like a wild beast which having once tasted blood ever thirsts

12. Y.-M. Duval, 'Ambroise, de son élection à sa consécration', in *Ambrosius Episcopus*, ed. G. Lazzati (1976), 2:243–283, at 255. Cf. A. H. M. Jones, *The Later Roman Empire* (1964), 151, on the appeal of Ambrose's 'strength of character'.

13. M. Meslin, *Les Ariens d'Occident* (1967), 44–45; cf. J.-R. Palanque, *Saint Ambroise* (1933), 31.

14. The best evidence for the office of the provincial governor comes from Syria, thanks to the writings of Libanius. See P. Petit, *Libanius et la vie municipale d'Antioche* (1955), 253–258, and J. H. W. G. Liebeschuetz, *Antioch* (1972), 111–114.

15. The phrase is Ambrose's: *De poen.* 2.67.

16. Jerome *Ep.* 1, composed soon after Auxentius' death (alluded to at 15: 'Auxentium . . . sepultum paene ante quam mortuum'). It is highly unlikely, but not altogether impossible, that the governor referred to was Ambrose.

for more, orders the tortures to be doubled, and gnashing his teeth in rage threatened a similar penalty for the torturer himself unless the weaker sex should be made to confess what masculine strength had been unable to keep secret' (1.4). When the torturer finally retreated in baffled exhaustion, the governor ('stirred with sudden rage') resolved the impasse by delivering a verdict of guilty on the couple on the strength of the one confession, summing up with the proposition that 'adultery takes two' (1.6). The whole population streamed out to watch the execution, supervised by the governor's minions: both the implacability of the legal process and the consent that underpinned it are illustrated by the chief official's successful prevention of an attempt to rescue the woman by protesting that this would only lead to his own execution (1.10). But beneath the exuberant rhetoric, the episode represents a perfectly ordinary example of the judiciary in action; nor, for all the lurid colours in which he paints the *crudelis iudex*, does Jerome suggest that he could have acted very differently. He concludes by condemning not the individual but the system. 'After these great miracles (the woman's survival after seven swipes of the executioner's sword), the laws continue to run their savage course' (1.14).

The crowds who attended trial and execution did not come to protest or to express their sympathy with these victims of legal savagery; they made their half-hearted rescue attempt only when the spell of authority was temporarily broken by the executioner's incompetence. The fulminations of the *consularis* were fed with at least the tacit consent of his people, including the Christians.[17] At Milan, too, churchgoers may well have approved of the manner in which Ambrose enforced the stern morality of the Christian empire; but their assessment of his performance at the tribunal will have been conditioned by the gruesome, polluting instruments that surrounded him.[18] It is especially difficult to envisage the grim figure of a Christian judge, the sword-wielding 'avenger of God against those who do wrong', being hailed as a peacemaker by two parties each convinced that their opponents were criminals.[19] The

17. In Jerome's account the clergy supervise the woman's recuperation in secret (*Ep.* 1.13–14); their worries of 'suspicions' aroused by the doctor's visits to the church imply distrust of the congregation.

18. Paulinus' claim that Ambrose did not under normal circumstances use torture (*V. Amb.* 7.1) is implausible: below, n. 167. For Ambrose's own unremittingly negative view of his former office, see A. Lenox-Conyngham, 'The Judgement of Ambrose the Bishop on Ambrose the Roman Governor', *SP* 17 (1982), 1:62–65.

19. 'Vindex Dei in eos qui male agunt': Amb. *Ep.* 50 [25].1.

pattern of relations attested elsewhere between provincial governors and their Christian subjects will suggest a very different interpretation for the scene.

The acclamation is central to Rufinus' account. The contents are recorded in full to emphasize the unity which it represented: the word *one* appears five times in three sentences. Historians have therefore been encouraged to envisage Ambrose being nominated upon an overwhelming wave of popular support, an authentically—and exceptionally—'democratic' candidate.[20] But this is to be overimpressed by a phenomenon that was a quite ordinary feature of episcopal elections, and of public life in general. All acclamations, moreover, were by their nature 'unanimous'.[21] Nor was there anything unusual about the report to Valentinian, the second hinge upon which Rufinus' account turns. For want of a more reliable index of popular feeling, acclamations were recorded and dispatched to the court as legitimate testimonials to the quality of a governor's administration.[22]

The stress which Rufinus puts upon these aspects suggests instead the polemical or apologetic use made in other election narratives of the people's unanimous support for a candidate. The biographers of Cyprian and Martin castigate, respectively, the 'certain men' who opposed Cyprian and the fastidious bishops of Gaul by invoking against them the 'spiritual desire' or 'divinely inspired assent' which united the people behind their chosen leader.[23] In these cases the dissent masked by the demonstration of popular unity endured beyond the bishop's death to influence the shape of the biography. Although Ambrose did

20. For this view, see F. L. Ganshof, 'Note sur l'élection des évêques', *RIDA* 4 (*Mélanges Visscher* 3, 1950), at 478–479, 497–498; cf. R. Gryson, 'Les élections épiscopales en Occident au IVe siècle', *RHE* 75 (1980), at 269–271.

21. See the excellent discussion by C. Roueché, 'Acclamations in the Later Roman Empire', *JRS* 74 (1984), 181–199; also Liebeschuetz, *Antioch*, 209–219 (with some splendid examples of the abuses that the system created). Philostorgius *HE* 9.10.14 reports a dissenting counteracclamation at the election of Demophilus of Constantinople ('unworthy' instead of 'worthy'): we can be confident that this did not appear upon the church's official record of the occasion.

22. *CTh* 1.16.6.

23. Cyprian: Pontius *V. Cyp.* 5.6 (with G. W. Clarke, *The Letters of St. Cyprian of Carthage* [1984], 1:266–268), for the opposition at Carthage; for the polemical purposes of Pontius' biography, see *V. Cyp.* 1.2. For Martin, see Sulp. Sev. *V. Mart.* 9.3–7, with commentary by J. Fontaine (*Sulpice Sévère: Vie de saint Martin* [SCh 134, 1968], 2:641–661); cf. C. Stancliffe, *St. Martin and His Hagiographer* (1983), 71–85, for the context.

not face the same posthumous pressures, the account of his election seems just as much designed to confer legitimacy. Rufinus is scrupulously evenhanded about assigning responsibility for the initial affray: both heretics and orthodox contributed to the 'grave dissension and dangerous unrest' which 'threatened immediate destruction for the city'. But the apologist is betrayed in the emphasis upon the propriety of Ambrose's reaction. The governor's visit to the church, prompted by anxiety to avert the disaster that lay in store for the city, accorded with his rank and duties ('pro loco et officio suo'); his long speech conformed with the laws and with public order ('secundum leges et publicam disciplinam'). Yet Rufinus protests too much, for Ambrose had chosen an extremely unorthodox method of keeping the peace.

Magistrates regularly confronted mobs, but appeasement of this sort was reserved for the most desperate emergencies. The usual practice was described in a celebrated passage of Ammianus, where the prefect of Rome, Leontius, calmed an angry crowd by singling out an individual, Peter Valvomeres, for exemplary punishment.[24] The only recorded attempt to employ rhetoric to restore order was when a later urban prefect, Tertullus, faced a hungry mob who blamed him for a bread shortage. The 'impending doom' which he faced, however, was not his city's but his own; his melodramatic gesture of offering his children to the mercy of the populace suggests the extremities to which he was reduced.[25] Ecclesiastical disputes could be serious and even bloody affairs, but they threatened neither the vital interests of the state nor the lives (or reputations) of its representatives. Faced with the notorious papal election of 366, the prefect Viventius (a Christian) proved 'able neither to repress nor to calm the disturbances' and withdrew to the suburbs until the bloodletting subsided: this behavior did not affect his standing in the eyes either of Ammianus, who praised him as 'sensible and honest', or of the emperor, who rewarded him with further promotion.[26]

The contest in Milan had apparently not yet resulted in actual violence, and in any case it lacked the ambitious candidates who had fuelled the carnage at Rome. That Ambrose had a 'duty' to intervene at this stage is therefore doubtful, but his method of restoring order was also peculiar. Leontius' arrest of Peter Valvomeres can be taken as a

24. Amm. Marc. 15.7.4.
25. Amm. Marc. 19.10.1–4.
26. Amm. Marc. 27.3.11: 'prudens et integer'; cf. *PLRE* 1, p. 972, for his subsequent tenure of the prefecture of Gaul. The supporters of the defeated papal candidate were less impressed with Viventius, claiming that he had been bribed: *Collectio Avellana* 1.6.

paradigm of normal procedures. Social disturbance involved criminal activity, and the magistrate's duty was to identify and punish the offenders. This is the bleak doctrine enshrined in the *Digest* of Justinian: 'The good and serious-minded governor should take care that the province which he rules is peaceable and quiet. He will attain this without difficulty if he acts diligently to free his province of wicked men and to hunt them down' (1.18.13: Ulpian). All that was required, therefore, was the proper application of coercion.

Disturbance of the religious peace received similar treatment. The natural state of affairs was concord, which according to the emperor Valentinian I ought to prevail both inside church buildings and in ecclesiastical issues. Any interference with this concord betrayed the urgings of an 'unquiet spirit' and therefore deserved the utmost severity: a rescript of the same emperor decreed that offenders should not be deemed Christians at all, but were 'cut off from the terms of the laws and of religion'.[27] Theoretically, then, magistrates involved themselves in ecclesiastical disputes merely to lend their authority (and coercive powers) to the beleaguered representatives of authentic Christianity. An equally narrow view of official responsibilities is implied by Ossius of Corduba's alleged outburst to a *vicarius* of Spain: 'Your mandate is not to investigate but to enforce'.[28] Both the demand made of the vicar and his subsequent abdication of responsibility, although fictional, ring true. Precisely this background explains the imperial edict addressed to the provincial governors of Africa two generations later, accusing them of negligence in pursuing the outlawed Donatist schismatics (and therefore of connivance in the harm done to Catholics) and ordering that the offending Donatists be identified and executed.[29]

Ambrose's sermon upon law and order was therefore unusual. But still more curious than the governor's appeal to the two parties, or even their sudden unity, was their initial presence together in the basilica. 'Contested' elections, especially when doctrine was at issue, seldom saw the rival parties assemble together to match numbers—or vocal cords.[30] All elections were unanimous, and were conducted in an atmosphere designed to give the appointee a mandate: rival candidates would be acclaimed by their supporters at separate assemblies, *after* which they

27. *Coll. Avell.* 5.1–2; 11.3.
28. *Coll. Avell.* 2.36: 'non cognitio tibi mandata est sed exsecutio'.
29. *Sirm.* 14.
30. This point is well made by R. Lane Fox, *Pagans and Christians* (1986), 511.

would compete for recognition.[31] At Milan in 374, the homoeans had a clear advantage in this process. For twenty years the cathedral had been held by Auxentius, and it was his presbyters and congregation who assembled there to appoint a successor. When the Nicenes arrived, they came as intruders; if the fracas that ensued was indeed sedition, they were the culprits. The governor's plea for tranquillity was therefore no simple demand for a compromise. It was a highly controversial assertion of the equal status of the two groups.

Ambrose's intervention therefore served at least implicitly to assist one party in the contest against the other, not to bring a neutral and impersonal authority to bear upon the situation. This would have been less difficult for the people assembled there to grasp than it has been for modern historians. For if the mask of power in the Roman world was terrible in aspect, it was worn by men of various interests and susceptibilities which were expected to condition their conduct in office. Governors were judged not by reference to transcendent moral standards but by the company they kept and the causes they sponsored.

The clearest evidence for the difference that allegiances could make in the behaviour of governors (and to the responses they elicited) comes from the representative of a particularly articulate interest group: Libanius, the rhetor of Antioch. In his autobiographical oration he dwells on the unsatisfactory attitude of men like Tisamenus, *consularis Syriae* in 386, who (unlike his grandfather, who had 'always shown respect for me, as befitted a man of eloquence') snubbed Libanius and his oratory—and also turned down a request for a 'trifling but perfectly proper favour'.[32] Eustathius (*consularis* in 388) also proved disappointing, despite a promising start: after showering Libanius with professional compliments and attentions, he severed ties upon receiving a request on behalf of one of the orator's pupils.[33] Much more satisfactory were men like the praetorian prefect Musonianus, who insisted that Libanius call upon him each evening (apparently finding these visits more relaxing than his bath), allowed the orator to bring deserving cases to his attention, and paid him the signal honour of commissioning a panegyric for

31. The opposition to Demophilus at Constantinople in 370 (above, n. 21) came from disgruntled members of his *own* community. A parallel election was held (in secret) for the Nicene Evagrius: Socrates *HE* 4.14; Sozomen *HE* 6.13. At Rome in 366, Damasus and Ursinus were acclaimed in separate churches, the Basilica in Lucinis and the Basilica in Sicininis: for documentation and discussion see C. Pietri, *Roma Christiana* (1976), 408–412.

32. Lib. *Or.* 1.251.

33. Lib. *Or.* 1.271–272.

delivery on the rhetor's own chosen ground, in the council chamber.[34] A professed devotion to culture therefore reflected well upon a government official and gave him a point of contact with an important part of his constituency; it also involved him in particular allegiances and created expectations of concrete favours.[35]

The Christian churches inevitably drew governors into similar commitments. Libanius describes, unsympathetically but plausibly, how a known Christian would attract interfering 'advisors'. The *consularis Syriae* Protasius had already been prejudiced against Libanius before taking up his appointment at Antioch by his Christian friends, who 'appointed one of their clique to accompany him on his journey here, to keep the panic alive within him'.[36] This man's principal task was probably to steer Protasius toward the correct congregation, there being at least three claimants to the Antiochene see; two of these factions, the Paulinians and Meletians, were at roughly the same time engaged in vigorous competition for the support of another influential visitor to Antioch, the former *comes* Terentius.[37]

Protasius' successor, moreover, was also a creature of his Christian friends, consorting only with 'human garbage' and keeping his headquarters closed to 'all those from whom he might have learned something'.[38] This exclusive intimacy between pious governors and local Christian lobbies naturally created suspicions of collusion and improper influence. Hostile sources sometimes verge on paranoia: Julian even surmised secret visits by bishops and presbyters to a pagan magistrate's residence, to explain the latter's punishment of a pagan priest.[39]

There were nevertheless solid grounds, in the case of committed Christian officials, for such suspicions. Attendance at divine service, for example, might expose a magistrate to ambush. Gregory of Nazianzus once preached a sermon in the presence of the local governor, who was in the city to impose a collective punishment upon it. In a masterly performance, he first honours the magistrate with membership in the congregation, as a 'sheep' of his 'flock', before preaching upon the rewards

34. Lib. *Or.* 1.106–108.

35. For the complex relationship between *paideia* and power, see Peter Brown, *Power and Persuasion in Late Antiquity* (1992), 35–58.

36. Lib. *Or.* 1.167.

37. For Terentius, see Basil *Ep.* 214 (late 375); the best guide to the tangled ecclesiastical politics of Antioch in this period is still F. Cavallera, *Le schisme d'Antioche* (1905).

38. Lib. *Or.* 1.169.

39. Julian *Ep.* 88 (Bidez-Cumont), 450C.

to be won, in this world and the next, from clemency.[40] Similar pressures can be detected in the petitions with which fourth-century churchmen bombarded those officials who recognized their authority. Gregory appealed to Olympius, another *praeses Cappadociae*, by invoking not only the suppliant's conventional grey hairs but also 'the priesthood, for which you have often shown reverence'.[41] The full force of such appeals is suggested by the prayer addressed to Olympius when he in his turn was preparing to penalize Gregory's city, that the governor might eventually receive judgement from God in the same terms as those in which he dispensed it to the citizens of Nazianzus.[42]

Personal commitment and sectarian pressure could also induce a governor to participate in disputes between Christians. In 375 Basil of Caesarea greeted the *vicarius* Demosthenes ingratiatingly: 'We are always very grateful to God and to rulers who have care over us, whenever we see the government of our country entrusted to a man who is not only a Christian but also upright in character, and a strict guardian of the law according to which we regulate human affairs'.[43] But Demosthenes, as Basil knew, was actually the wrong sort of Christian. 'Whether the man is at heart inclined to heresy', he wrote to his friend Eusebius, 'I am not sure (for I think that he is inexperienced in all reasoning, and has neither interest nor practice in such things; for I see that he is fully taken up, body and soul, in other matters both day and night), but yet he is friendly with heretics, and no more friendly to them than he is full of hate towards us'.[44] He manifested this hatred in a conventional way, applying the strict letter of the law against curials improperly enrolled in Basil's clergy; his informants were probably his 'heretical' associates, the party led by Basil's former friend Eustathius of Sebaste.[45] Demosthenes subsequently accompanied Eustathius to the city of Nicopolis to attend the election of a successor to Bishop Theodetus. To Basil's disgust, this suffrage proved effective and the presbyter Fronto 'disgracefully betrayed both the faith and himself, and received as a reward for the betrayal a name of infamy', the title of bishop.[46]

40. Greg. Naz. *Or.* 17; J. Bernardi, *La prédication des pères Cappadociens* (1968), 121–124 (cf. 131–139, on *Or.* 19, another sermon delivered before an official). The best example of overt pressure applied in such circumstances is a sermon preached by Ambrose to Theodosius: below, p. 303ff.

41. Greg. Naz. *Ep.* 140.

42. Greg. Naz. *Ep.* 142.3.

43. Basil *Ep.* 225.1.

44. Basil *Ep.* 237.2.

45. For similar tactics in Africa, see *CTh* 16.2.1.

46. Basil *Ep.* 239.1; also *Ep.* 247, where he expresses his intention to write about the matter to the imperial court.

This episode returns us conveniently to Ambrose and his arrival, the previous year, at the basilica of Milan. Like Demosthenes at Nicopolis, he will have been acknowledged by both parties as a Christian; but his intervention is no more likely than the former's to have been seen as the routine behaviour of a conscientious magistrate. Two rival groups had been claiming the Milanese see for two decades, during which the full weight of civil authority had been at the disposal of the homoean bishop Auxentius against the seditions of his Nicene opponents. Ambrose came not to suppress this latest riot and preserve the status quo but to legitimize the Nicenes' interruption of the official 'Auxentian' succession ceremony. It is neither necessary nor particularly plausible to attribute to him any intention of pressing his own candidacy. But the Nicenes reacted all too enthusiastically to this long-awaited demonstration of official support. To Ambrose's dismay—and quite likely a reaction from their opponents compounded of surprise and gratified recognition of the governor's discomfiture—they raised the cry, 'Ambrose for bishop!'

MILAN DIVIDED: CONSTANTIUS II AND THE COUNCIL OF 355

To understand what was at stake between the groups fighting over the succession to Auxentius, we must briefly go back to the circumstances of the latter's accession two decades earlier. The arrival in the west in 352 of the emperor Constantius II had inaugurated a particularly tortuous passage of what has well been described as 'the search for the Christian doctrine of God'.[47] The emperor's determined efforts to steer his bishops, who had spent much of the previous decade exchanging anathemas between the two halves of a divided empire, towards a formula capable of expressing their shared faith unleashed a complicated struggle over the agenda of this reunification process. Two principal groups can be discerned, although these are far smaller, less solid and less organized than the catholic and Arian parties invented by contemporary polemic and perpetuated in much modern writing. The bishops

47. R. P. C. Hanson, *The Search for the Christian Doctrine of God* (1988); Constantius' dealings with the western churches are described at 315–347. The revisionist account by H.-C. Brennecke, *Hilarius von Poitiers und die Bischofsopposition gegen Konstantius II* (1984), although its central thesis is ultimately untenable (see the reviews by J. Doignon, *RHE* 80 [1985], 441–454, and Y.-M. Duval, *REAug* 32 [1986], 195–197), raises many important questions. The present sketch, although differing on several points of interpretation, is greatly indebted to both these works.

travelling in the imperial entourage, led by Ursacius and Valens, had earned Constantius' confidence by their loyalty and ability and shared with him a fierce hostility to Athanasius of Alexandria, but their court position was strictly unofficial and they could not count on unconditional imperial support in legislating for their own beliefs.[48] The western 'opposition' clung to certain allegiances quite unacceptable to Constantius (particularly in their support of Athanasius) but enjoyed the considerable advantage of operating upon their own ground.[49] Auxentius' appointment to Milan, after a stormy council held there in 355, was a by-product of this struggle. The congregation of Milan played a pivotal role in the events that ended with his consecration: the two parties that contested the succession to Auxentius in 374 derived their identities from their conflicting responses to the council of 355.

The principal item on the agenda of the council of Milan was ratification of the condemnation of Athanasius.[50] Sulpicius Severus, our only complete narrative source, describes how a proposal to link this matter to a discussion of doctrine so dismayed the Arian leaders Ursacius and Valens, who relied upon dissimulation and stealth, that they fled to the imperial palace, 'not daring to make public their blasphemies because of their fear of the people, who maintained the catholic faith with outstanding zeal'. The heretics then attempted to intimidate the populace with a letter 'sent out in the emperor's name' (presumably an edict), which was read out inside the church but to no effect. Finally the local bishop, Dionysius, was expelled from Milan for dissent; Auxentius, Sulpicius reports laconically, was 'immediately installed in his place' by the Arians.[51]

48. The provisional nature of the ascendancy enjoyed by Ursacius and Valens is well brought out by E. D. Hunt, 'Did Constantius II Have "Court Bishops"?', *SP* 19 (1989), 86–90.

49. Modern scholarship has consistently underestimated the prospects of this group by identifying Constantius too closely with the views of Ursacius and Valens. But the only basis for ascribing a specific doctrinal programme to the emperor is the difficulty of otherwise accounting for the western 'resistance' (Hanson, *The Search*, 329–331); the 'purge' of traitorous bishops invented by Brennecke is essentially a response to the same difficulty. I will argue elsewhere my view that the western leaders had genuine room for manoeuvre at Constantius' councils.

50. The council of Milan and its associated problems are discussed by Brennecke, *Hilarius von Poitiers*, 147–184; G. Gottlieb, 'Les évêques et les empereurs dans les affairs ecclésiastiques du IVe siècle', *MH* 33 (1976), 38–50; Hanson, *The Search*, 329–334.

51. Sulp. Sev. *Chron.* 2.39.3–6. Sulpicius wrote some fifty years after the event but followed the contemporary account by Hilary of Poitiers; for his use of

This episode, and especially the role assigned to the people of Milan, has a crucial bearing upon Ambrose's election. If Sulpicius' account is accepted, the sudden unanimity of the Milanese Christians in 374 can be interpreted as a reassertion of their 'outstanding zeal' for the 'catholic faith' in 355. For Sulpicius should imply that Milan was still a fundamentally catholic city at Auxentius' death (apart from the few misguided or opportunist converts the interloper had won); most of the Arians at Ambrose's election can therefore be seen as conformists who had aligned themselves behind the heretical bishop in a spirit of unhappy dissimulation, 'collaborators' naturally at odds with the Nicene 'resistance' which had kept faith with Bishop Dionysius after his exile in 355. Hence the vehemence of the consensus around Ambrose, an outsider recognized by both parties as the man they needed to lead them back to their original catholic unity. Ambrose was, on this view, a genuine victim of his people's unanimous resolve, and his election was but one of a series of popular initiatives that had begun with this episode in 355 and would culminate in another mass protest against imperially sponsored Arianism in 386.[52]

But the Milanese people cannot bear the explanatory weight that this thesis places upon them. The level of popular involvement in ecclesiastical controversy has been much exaggerated by modern scholarship; the doctrinally innocent west of the mid-350s is a particularly unlikely place to find a congregation capable of discovering heresy in the confession of a Valens.[53] Even Sulpicius, who of course assumed an anachronistic division between the defenders of an established Nicene faith and their 'heretical' opponents, gives no instance elsewhere in his account of the resistance to the 'Arian conspiracy' of any initiative by the laity. A small deviation between Sulpicius and his source acquires considerable importance against this background. Hilary of Poitiers, whose account gives every indication of being derived from a firsthand

---

this source, see G. K. van Andel, *The Christian Concept of History in the Chronicle of Sulpicius Severus* (1976), 86–89.

52. The connexion is developed at some length by Duval, 'Ambroise, de son élection', esp. 252–256 ('j'insiste sur la liaison 355–374–386': 256n251) and in his conclusion at 383.

53. The pervasive modern assumption that ordinary Christians were passionately involved in doctrinal questions is criticized in my 'Christian Controversy and Violence in the Fourth Century', *Kodai* 3 (1992), 15–44. Brennecke rightly excludes any familiarity among the Milanese congregation with the Nicene creed (*Hilarius von Poitiers*, 181); for Valens' ability to placate even a hostile and suspicious audience, see Jerome *Dialogus Orthodoxi et Luciferiani* 18 (describing the council of Rimini).

source, like Sulpicius describes the heretic leaders rejecting a demand for a doctrinal discussion (which he attributes to Eusebius of Vercelli, not Dionysius of Milan) and withdrawing to the palace because of the 'fear' that the people inspired among them, but does not involve the congregation directly in the action; it was only *after* Eusebius' attempt to introduce doctrine to the agenda had been suppressed that 'the matter, after much shouting, was brought to the attention of the people'.[54] Hilary's text fails us shortly after this point, but the implication is clear. The catholic people of Milan did not rise against the heretics themselves but were somehow brought into play at a crucial point in the proceedings.

Hilary's account also confirms that the occasion in question was not the council of Milan itself but a supplementary session convened shortly afterwards for the benefit of Eusebius of Vercelli; this explains the congregation's apparent absence from the actual scene of the meeting.[55] A group of letters from Eusebius' correspondence further clarify the situation. An important ally of Liberius of Rome (the leader of the western campaign to deflect Constantius from his current ecclesiastical strategy, whose petitions to the emperor had led to the summons of the council in 355), Eusebius had not been invited to Milan for the council itself; the exclusion was almost certainly deliberate, to ensure a minimum of conflict and so further the council's declared objective of 'informing' the westerners about developments in the east.[56] In the immediate aftermath, however, a small embassy from the council arrived at Vercelli with a letter reporting the bishops' condemnation of Athanasius and two other notable pariahs, Marcellus of Ancyra and Photinus of Sirmium, and inviting Eusebius in the strongest possible terms to declare his assent.[57] Enclosed was a note from the emperor, conveying his 'encour-

54. Hil. *Appendix ad Coll. Antiar. Par.* 2.3 (*Liber I ad Constantium* 8 [*CSEL* 65, p. 187]): 'res post clamorem multum deducta in conscientiam plebis'. The shift from Eusebius to Dionysius in Sulpicius' account is discussed by L. A. Speller, 'A Note on Eusebius of Vercelli and the Council of Milan', *JThS*, n.s., 36 (1985), 157–165.

55. Hilary locates the episode in the cathedral ('ad ecclesiam', 'e dominico'); we should envisage a meeting held in a sacristry or annex, as at Aquileia in 381. Sulpicius' mention of a condemnation of Lucifer and Eusebius (*Chron.* 2.39.3) is probably a garbled reference to the council proper; the ten-day wait imposed on Eusebius before his 'summons' in Hilary's account can be interpreted as the interval before his request for this additional session.

56. Constantius (*Ep. ad Eus.* 3 [*CCL* 9, p. 120]) describes the council as a platform organized especially for 'eos . . . qui alibi gesta possint facile revelare'.

57. Council of Milan *Ep. synodica ad Eus.* (*CCL* 9, p. 119); the character of the bishops' message is well conveyed by their references to their 'infinite patience'

agement and advice' that Eusebius should not delay to attach himself to the consensus of his brothers.[58]

Eusebius' reply shows that he was not, as Hilary has it, the victim of a conspiracy but rather the instigator of one. For when he announced his decision to come to Milan, in fulfillment of his 'duty' to obey Constantius, he was interpreting a metaphor literally; his additional remarks about the inability of the council's delegates to explain themselves betray his disingenuousness.[59] Eusebius' summons had actually come from another quarter entirely: Liberius' defeated representatives at the council. In the third of the letters to reach Eusebius from Milan, Bishop Lucifer of Cagliari and two junior associates had urged him to come, assuring him that 'upon your arrival Valens will be driven out and the devices of the blaspheming Arians split apart and utterly wrecked'.[60] The sequel shows, moreover, that this group had recruited another important ally. When the bishops had finally reconvened, Eusebius suddenly produced a copy of the Nicene creed which he invited them to sign; at once Dionysius of Milan, who had already subscribed to the condemnation of Athanasius at the council proper, took the document and began to write.[61] One does not have to be a cynic to suspect prearrangement; although the reasons for Dionysius' volte-face escape us, this highly dramatic scene cannot have been unrehearsed.[62]

Eusebius' production of the creed (which must have come as a com-

---

in consulting Eusebius and to their resolve to take appropriate steps if he decided to act 'alias quam optamus'.

58. Constantius *Ep. ad Eus.* 5: 'hortamur pariter ac moneamus, ut consensui fratrum tuorum adhaerere non differas'.

59. Eus. Verc. *Ep.* 1 (to Constantius): 'sed quia pleniter mihi ratio reddi non potuit et debui tuae clementiae parere, hoc necessarium duxi, ut Mediolanum venire properarem'. There is likewise no suggestion in the council's synodical letter that Eusebius should come in person; he was asked to listen to the delegates and 'communicato pariter cum his consilio definiat, quod . . . totus prope definivit orbis' (*Ep. synod. ad Eus.* 2). Hilary's claim that Eusebius was 'ordered' to Milan is therefore false.

60. *Ep. legatorum sedis apostolicae* (CCL 9, p. 120).

61. Hil. *App. ad Coll. Antiar. Par.* 2.3.2 (CSEL 65, p. 187). Dionysius' condemnation of Athanasius is reported by Lucifer *De Athanasio* 2.8; this explains his presence in the list of thirty signatories from the original council, a document which Brennecke treats with excessive scepticism (*Hilarius von Poitiers*, 165–166).

62. The theatrical character of the incident is well analyzed by J. Doignon, *Hilaire de Poitiers avant l'exil* (1971), 444–454. Brennecke's arguments against its authenticity (*Hilarius von Poitiers*, 178–182) prove only the oddity of Eusebius' gesture and its failure to ignite an immediate response.

plete surprise to the bishops who had gathered to hear—and answer—
his professed difficulties about the rationale of their earlier proceedings)
can therefore be interpreted as an attempt to bounce the meeting into a
declaration of support for the Nicene formulae. This was not an attempt
to rally the bishops behind a coherent theological position but a tactic
designed to derail Ursacius and Valens, who had until then controlled
the agenda.[63] But Eusebius' bold attempt to seize the initiative was
thwarted by the speed of Valens' reactions. Wresting the pen from Dionysius with an angry shout, he was able to close the meeting and usher
the bishops to the security of the palace before the populace could be
brought to bear against them.[64] The context implies that the people
had been mobilized as a further means of exerting pressure upon the
meeting; but it was a dangerous last resort, for it left Eusebius and his
friends the no doubt somewhat reluctant leaders of a demonstration
against the legitimate ecclesiastical authorities, and soon against the emperor himself.

The affair ended dramatically. Constantius, having addressed a letter to the dissidents to no effect, eventually lost patience and dispatched
soldiers, who cleared a path through the people inside the church 'with
the utmost savagery' and dragged the ringleaders from the sanctuary of
the altar; the three bishops were duly marched from the church, 'surrounded by weapons, hedged in by an army'.[65]

The 'pious people' thrust aside by Constantius' soldiers correspond
neatly to the 'plebs' who had rallied to defend the faith from Valens'
attack and the 'populus' who shouted down the emperor's letter, implying mass participation throughout the whole episode. But our sources
all derive from Hilary's apology for Eusebius, which for all its vividness
is designed to establish the latter as the innocent victim of Ursacius' and
Valens' machinations: the role attributed to the people, and especially

63. Gottlieb's chivalrous denial of any 'mobiles tactiques' here ('Les évêques',
at 47) is misplaced. Western bishops had used a similar device, from a position
of strength, at a previous church council at Milan, in 345, when they refused to
give audience to an eastern delegation unless they repudiated an Arian *sententia*
(Hil. *Coll. Antiar. Par.* A.vii.4). The same council had also extracted from Ursacius and Valens an explicit disavowal of their hostility to Athanasius (*Coll. Antiar. Par.* B.ii.5–7; Hanson, *The Search*, 312–313).

64. Hil. *App. ad Coll. Antiar. Par.* 2.3.2, for Valens' shout that 'non posse
fieri ut aliquid inde gereretur' ('that won't get us anywhere'). Hilary's argument
here requires him to make *all* the bishops at the council, not just Ursacius and
Valens, party to his 'plot' against Eusebius.

65. Hil. *In Const.* 11; Amb. *Ep. extra coll.* 14 [63].68.

their rejection of the emperor's letter,[66] conferred valuable legitimacy upon Eusebius and his friends, whose arrest must have been connected with their explicit defiance of imperial authority. But in reality, only the hardiest of those who rallied to their bishop at the shouted news of the 'attack' on the faith will have stood beside him as the affair escalated into a headlong confrontation with the emperor. Dionysius had done little to prepare the Milanese people for this clash. He had assented to the condemnation of Athanasius a few weeks earlier, and he was acknowledged as the emperor's 'friend'.[67] This friendship will have involved dealings with the alleged heretics Ursacius and Valens, whose long stay at Milan must have brought them into regular (and presumably well-publicized) contact with the local clergy.[68]

There is, moreover, an eyewitness account of this second phase of the incident which suggests that Sulpicius' abrupt reference to popular 'aversion' to the emperor's letter is misleading. In his pamphlet *De non conveniendo* Lucifer of Cagliari describes an 'eloquent and forceful' edict issued by Constantius during the struggle, probably identical to Sulpicius' imperial letter, which urged 'peace' upon the dissidents.[69] The bishops were roundly denounced as 'enemies of peace, hostile to unity, opponents even to brotherly affection', and also—an unmistakable thrust at Dionysius—as betraying the emperor's friendship.[70] But the most significant feature of Lucifer's account is the use of the first person throughout: he and his fellow bishops are shown confronting the emperor alone, without the slightest hint that a popular rebellion was afoot. In the struggle over the allegiance of 'individual catholic

66. We only have Sulpicius' version of this crucial scene (*Chron.* 2.39.5–6), but his laboured and inconsequential account of the letter's composition seems to reflect a concern (in his source, Hilary?) to deny the document's validity as a genuine expression of the emperor's wishes.

67. *Coll. Avell.* 2.23: 'Constantio regi . . . familiaris'; Amb. *Ep. extra coll.* 14 [63].68, 'imperatoris amicitiam'.

68. Compare Sozomen *HE* 8.10, illustrating the tensions that could arise between the bishop of an imperial capital and visiting prelates, but more importantly how an appearance of harmony could be orchestrated from the palace.

69. *De non conv.* 9.62: 'eximiis verbis pulcherrimisque sensibus conscriptum edictum'; 3.75: 'pacem volo firmari in meo imperio' (cf. 5.68, 6.1, 10.13). Gottlieb, 'Les évêques', 43–46, analyzes Lucifer's text and convincingly reconstructs the edict as an appeal for unity and calm.

70. *De non conv.* 1.4, 'nos fuisse atque esse inimicos pacis, hostes unitatis, adversarios etiam fraternae caritatis'; 15.2, 'dicis nos facere inique . . . quod non tecum . . . aeternae fuerint fixae amicitiae'.

bishops' the people become mere spectators, to whom Constantius' machinations were 'revealed'.[71]

Constantius' readiness to send in his troops to dislodge the protesters provides some corroboration of the small numbers of their supporters. What is more, this delicate operation was apparently accomplished without bloodshed. Neither Hilary nor Ambrose, for all their emphasis upon the use of weapons and the 'terror' that this caused, cited any actual fatalities. The silence is telling, for martyrs were too precious a commodity to ignore. Those Milanese Christians still present to witness Dionysius being dragged from the church might therefore more reasonably be counted in scores than in hundreds; the rest of the city saw the dissidents being brought to trial and subsequently dispatched into an exile which, in the circumstances, must have appeared amply justified.[72]

A replacement for Dionysius was swiftly found: the Cappadocian presbyter Auxentius, who had formerly served in Alexandria. Auxentius continues to be presented by historians as an alien, unable throughout his career even to address his flock in Latin.[73] But this misunderstanding derives simply from a hostile caricature, Athanasius' gibe in 358 that Auxentius could not *yet* speak the language properly; six years later, however, he would show an impressive command of the subtleties of Latin word order.[74]

Nor should the new bishop be dismissed as an interloper. True, he owed his appointment to the emperor rather than the clergy and people of Milan; but by 355 Constantius was anything but a stranger in the city. Since his original arrival there three years previously—a period that had already given the Milanese their most prolonged access to the imperial power in a generation—a whole cycle of ceremonies had helped establish his patronage: victory celebrations, imperial anniversaries and con-

71. *De non conv.* 1.2–3 for the 'machinamenta . . . cuncto dei populo revelata'; 3.80 for Constantius' objective: 'singulos catholicos episcopos communioni iungere Arrianorum'. At 3.77 Lucifer notes without comment the emperor's desire 'scindere . . . populum dei'.

72. Lucifer *Moriendum esse pro filio* 4.7–12 describes his defiance before a body of *iudices* while Constantius listened inside the *velum* (cf. 1.50–57). It is possible but unlikely that this refers to an interview *before* the arrest, where the use of force was threatened; in this case we might imagine a period of negotiation before the final assault.

73. R. Krautheimer, *Three Christian Capitals* (1983), 72, dismisses Auxentius as lacking 'broad popular support'.

74. Athan. *Hist. Ar.* 75; cf. below, p. 26. For Auxentius, see Meslin, *Les Ariens*, 41–44.

sular accessions all involved him in dealings with the populace.[75] The conspicuously Christian character of his court, moreover, ensured him as high a profile in the church of Milan as in the city as a whole.[76] His 'friendship' with Dionysius was simply one aspect of a comprehensive embrace. It was therefore natural that Constantius should have taken the lead in appointing a successor to the disgraced bishop. His search so far afield (Auxentius was allegedly eighty days' journey from Milan at the time) demonstrated to the Milanese both the seriousness with which he took his responsibility and the awesome reach of the imperial power that he was putting at their disposal.[77] Auxentius owed his appointment to his ability to meet the high standards set by Constantius' pious court; their presence in Milan for nearly two years after his accession gave him ample time to consolidate his position and set the tone for his episcopate.

Dionysius' remaining loyalists, confirmed in opposition to Constantius by their treatment at his soldiers' hands, had cut themselves off from the 'official' church of Milan.[78] Their opposition to Auxentius was muted and indirect: no successor, for example, was nominated when Dionysius died in exile. Auxentius, moreover, was soon sufficiently confident of himself to take the lead in suppressing less formal chal-

75. The emperor's most recent *adventus* to Milan, after a victory over the Lentienses, had come immediately before the council: Amm. Marc. 15.4.13. The cycle of imperial festivities under Constantius is conveniently presented in the codex-calendar of 354: see now M. R. Salzman, *On Roman Time* (1990), esp. 137–140. The emperor assumed the consulate at Milan in 353 and 354; for the atmosphere of these occasions see M. W. Gleason, 'Festive Satire', *JRS* 76 (1986), esp. 108–113. It can also be assumed that both the consuls of 355, Constantius' *magister equitum* Arbetio and Lollianus, *PPO Illyrici* from July 355, had been at court to receive their consulates in January.

76. T. D. Barnes, 'Christians and Pagans in the Reign of Constantius', in *Entretiens Hardt* 34 (1989), 301–337, emphasizes the difference between the number of Christian office-holders at the courts of Constantius and his brother Constans (at 318–321).

77. 'Eighty *monai*': Athan. *Ep. ad episc. Aeg. et Lib.* (*PG* 25, 553B). The figure (perhaps nominal: Auxentius is bracketed with another of Constantius' appointees in Italy, Epictetus) corresponds almost exactly to the distance from Cappadocia to Milan reported in the itineraries.

78. If Ambrose's allusion to a military presence at Auxentius' installation (*De spir. sancto* 3.59) is taken literally to apply to his consecration, rather than to the previous affray, it probably relates to the perceived danger of disturbance by Dionysius' partisans. The purpose was therefore to reassure law-abiding citizens, not to impose the new bishop by force.

lenges. In about 357 the Pannonian ex-soldier Martin arrived at Milan to found a monastery, which was probably intended (given Martin's background as a disciple of Hilary) as a focus for opposition to the bishop. His biographer laconically records the outcome: 'Auxentius, the leading spirit and chief of the Arians, persecuted him with the greatest severity, and after heaping many injuries upon him drove him from the city'.[79] Whether these injuries were dealt by indignant clerics or—as is more likely—with the aid of the secular authorities, the peremptory treatment handed out to Martin shows the strength of Auxentius' position. Martin's mission, meanwhile, can only have reinforced the impression created in 355 that the 'Nicenes' were obstinate troublemakers.

The respective positions of the two groups were consolidated in subsequent years. This is of the utmost importance for an appreciation of the situation in 374: the 'orthodox' group in the contest for the succession to Auxentius were heirs to the protesters of 355, and therefore to a record of disorder and schism. Ambrose's intervention did not ensure a hearing for the authentic voice of the 'people', but advanced the interests of a faction.

THE AGE OF AUXENTIUS

After Constantius' final departure from Italy in 357 for a series of fresh crises on the frontiers, Milan remained the principal focus of western ecclesiastical politics as the headquarters of the praetorian prefect Taurus. The enormous logistical operation which in 359 saw some four hundred western bishops converge on Rimini—far more than at any previous council in the region—was presumably organized from the city, before Taurus departed to supervise the proceedings in person. The council and its eastern counterpart at Seleucia were untidy and stormy affairs which provoked charges of fraud and coercion, but the final outcome was accepted by the majority and represented a considerable personal triumph for Constantius (who was directly involved in the preliminary arrangements at Sirmium and the final negotiations at Constantinople): the new homoean creed was the first to which the bishops of both halves of the Christian empire had given their combined assent.[80]

79. Sulp. Sev. *V. Mart.* 6, with Fontaine, *Sulpice Sévère: Vie de saint Martin*, 2:590–599.
80. The complex proceedings of 357–60 are covered by Hanson, *The Search*, 343–380; Y.-M. Duval, 'La "manouevre frauduleuse" de Rimini', in *Hilaire et son*

Auxentius of Milan, who had apparently escaped the anathemas hurled about by the 'opposition' during the debates at Rimini, emerged as an eloquent spokesman for the council's homoean creed and the 'unity of six hundred bishops' which it and Seleucia together represented.[81] But Constantius' settlement was undermined within two months of the signing of the new creed, when the proclamation of Julian at Paris created an alternative source of legitimacy for the opponents of Rimini. Hilary of Poitiers, who had followed the 'confessors' of Milan into exile, returned in early 360 and took immediate advantage of the new situation.[82] His council of Paris proclaimed support for the Nicene *homoousion* in a letter to the friends whom he had made during his exile in the east, opening up (if only for propaganda purposes) a new ecclesiastical axis. The first name on the list of those 'excommunicated' at the easterners' request was Auxentius.[83]

By the end of 361 Constantius was dead and Julian the undisputed master of the empire. But any hopes raised among Hilary and his friends by the usurper's previous courtship of the Gallic church (which had seen him celebrate Epiphany in the cathedral of Vienne before marching against Constantius)[84] were dashed with the unmasking of his pagan beliefs. No attempt was made under the new regime, therefore, to enforce Auxentius' excommunication by the council at Paris. The bishop of Milan was also able to survive the return of the exiles of Constantius' reign. Eusebius of Vercelli, assisted by Hilary, 'worked continually' among the bishops of northern Italy 'to recall each individual church to the true faith'.[85] But this campaign to persuade the bishops who had

---

temps, ed. E. R. Labande (1969), 51–103, offers an ingenious interpretation of the controversial course of the council of Rimini. For the role of Taurus and the scale of the preparations, see Sulp. Sev. *Chron.* 2.41.1–4.

81. The criticism of Auxentius reported by Athanasius (*De synod.* 10) appears in a translated document which in its original Latin version does not include his name: Hil. *Coll. Antiar. Par.* A.v.1.2 (parallel texts at *CSEL* 65, p. 82).

82. Y.-M. Duval, 'Vrai et faux problèmes', *Athenaeum,* n.s., 48 (1970), 251–275.

83. The council of Paris is known only from its own publicity, the letter to the eastern Nicenes: Hil. *Coll. Antiar. Par.* A.i (*CSEL* 65, pp. 43–47). Saturninus of Arles, target of the only concrete initiative there reported, was perhaps still at Constantinople (cf. Hil. *Ad Const.* 2.2), which would make the council's redoubled excommunication of him as empty a gesture as their confirmation of the easterners' condemnations of Auxentius and the other 'Arian' leaders.

84. Amm. Marc. 21.2.5.

85. Ruf. *HE* 10.30–31. Duval's claim ('Vrai et faux problèmes', 268) that this work involved the convocation of councils is unlikely. I follow Duval's date for

attended Rimini to 'renounce their perfidy' was limited in scope: Eusebius' accommodation with Germinius of Sirmium, one of the 'disruptors' responsible for presenting the 'novel proposals full of perverse teachings' at Rimini, suggests that he required only a denial of Arianism.[86] Auxentius' willingness to condemn Arius publicly as a heretic allowed the northern Italian bishops to avoid the difficult choice between the renascent faith of Nicaea and the creed they had themselves helped formulate at Rimini (from which they had probably derived considerable local prestige), and to remain in communion with both Eusebius and Auxentius himself.[87]

A potentially more serious threat to Auxentius from Eusebius was disruption inside Milan. Julian's policy was to show no preference for any single Christian leader in a city, and Mamertinus, the new praetorian prefect of Italy, who arrived directly from the new court at Constantinople, was an enthusiastic supporter.[88] Eusebius and Hilary took advantage, to develop a community inside Milan that 'confessed the true Godhead of Christ, his equal divinity and consubstantiality with the Father':[89] they presumably taught the remnants of Dionysius' supporters to express their opposition to Auxentius in doctrinal terms, setting the revived slogans of Nicaea against those of Rimini. But they appear to have had little success in winning converts from Auxentius' congregation, and the credentials of their dissident supporters could be questioned. In a public statement that Hilary quoted without denial or comment, Auxentius claimed that those Milanese who were now calling him a heretic 'had never communicated, even with those who have been

---

the return of Eusebius, despite S. Rebenich, *Hieronymus und sein Kreis* (1992), 58–61.

86. Germinius reports his dealings with Eusebius at *Altercatio Heracliani* 136 (*PLS* 1, 346); the Nicenes at Rimini record their complaints against him in their letter to Constantius (Hil. *Coll. Antiar. Par.* A.v.1.2 (*CSEL* 65, p. 82). Germinius' subsequent commitment to the 'dated creed' of May 359 (below, p. 95) involved a clarification, not a disavowal, of the Rimini settlement.

87. The ten bishops who heard Auxentius at Milan in 364 allowed him to rest his case on Rimini and a denial of Arianism: Hil. *Contra Aux.* 13–15. Hilary's refusal to criticize them (and the lack of any other evidence for 'court bishops' in Valentinian's entourage) suggests that they were local; if so, they constituted a large proportion of the regional episcopate (cf. below, p. 278).

88. See Amm. Marc. 21.12.20, 22.3.1, for Mamertinus' services to Julian; 22.5.4, for Julian's approach to Christian conflicts.

89. Hil. *Contra Aux.* 7.

bishops before me'.[90] This ought strictly to imply that these opponents had *refused* to hold communion with Dionysius or his predecessors, and were thus an extremist group quite separate from the mainstream of Milanese Christianity. A more plausible interpretation is that they had not been baptized members of Dionysius' community, but had received the sacrament (if at all) only since his dismissal. But the core of Dionysius' congregation, the baptized faithful, appear in either case to have remained true to their recognized bishop Auxentius.

The weakness of the Nicene counteroffensive in Milan soon became apparent when, in the summer of 364, a new emperor arrived in Milan. Valentinian I remained in the city for a whole year, issuing a stream of laws that indicate the damage wreaked upon the economy and the armed forces by Julian's disastrous Persian adventure.[91] By his presence in Milan, Valentinian, a pious Christian, also brought the issue of religious diversions to a head. He immediately put the campaign against Auxentius in its official perspective, publishing a 'grievous edict' which, Hilary lamented, threw the 'true church' into disarray. This probably urged the people to rally behind their legitimate bishop, like Valentinian's other proclamations of concord and peace as the special attributes of a Christian community.[92] Hilary responded with an 'importunate interpellation', a formal statement to the emperor accusing Auxentius of blasphemy, of being an 'enemy of Christ', and (more specifically) of holding beliefs at variance with those of Valentinian and 'everyone else'.[93] This last charge concerned a question of fact, which the emperor therefore ordered investigated by two of his senior officials, with a panel of about ten bishops to assist them.[94]

This affair is known only through Hilary himself, who later pub-

---

90. Quoted at Hil. *Contra Aux.* 13.

91. There is a good survey in A. Piganiol, *L'empire chrétien (325–395)*, 2d ed. (1972), 190–192.

92. Hil. *Contra Aux.* 7. The edict perhaps echoed the terms of that issued by Constantius II in 355 (n. 69 above). *Coll. Avell.* 2.57 laments the power of the 'speciosum nomen pacis' to deceive 'regias aures'; compare Valentinian's own pronouncement upon the importance of securing peace 'ubi maxime debet esse concordia, scilicet in ecclesiae vel sede vel causa' (*Coll. Avell.* 5.2).

93. *Contra Aux.* 7. Eusebius' conspicuous absence from the ensuing proceedings perhaps reflects the prudence of a near neighbour; Auxentius nevertheless used the hearings to score some effective points off him (*Contra Aux.* 13, 15).

94. *Contra Aux.* 7. The same pair, the Illyricans Ursacius and Viventius, had earlier been deputed to investigate the causes of Valentinian's illness at Constantinople (Amm. Marc. 26.4.4).

lished an elegant booklet (*Contra Auxentium*) to show how Auxentius had resorted to a semantic dodge in order to dissemble his real beliefs.[95] Auxentius is presented as being on the defensive throughout, unable without danger to disagree with Hilary's formula (presumably intended to represent the beliefs of the emperor and 'everyone else') that Christ was 'of one divinity and substance with the Father' (*Contra Aux.* 7). When Auxentius assented to this proposition, Hilary presented a dossier containing a transcript of the hearing to the *quaestor* (one of the presiding officers) for the emperor's attention. Auxentius was then instructed to produce a written statement confirming this, and he used the opportunity to 'deceive' Valentinian by professing Christ as 'deum verum filium'—meaning 'God, a true son' rather than 'the Son, truly God' (8). Hilary attaches Auxentius' profession to his pamphlet to prove the point (13–15).

But although Auxentius' document does indeed contain the offending phrase, if taken as a whole it cannot be reconciled with Hilary's interpretation. The issue is patently not that of the Son's full consubstantial divinity. Auxentius answers two charges, of being an Arian and of refusing to admit that Christ is (without the crucial qualifications 'real' or 'consubstantial') God.[96] His creed is simply 'what I have believed from infancy, just as I have been taught, receiving it from the Holy Scriptures' (14): there is no pretence of it being Nicene. Auxentius ranges himself instead with the six hundred bishops of Rimini and (not to be outdone by Hilary in loading the emperor with paperwork) offers Valentinian the acts of the council, requesting that 'you should order them to be read' (15). If this is a deception, it is an extraordinarily brazen and somewhat incompetent one, since these papers contained an explicit rejection of the term 'substance', which Auxentius was ostensibly pretending to support.[97] But Hilary has misrepresented the matter in making it hinge upon Auxentius' acceptance of a Nicene formula to satisfy a Nicene emperor. Valentinian required only a repudiation of Arius, something nearly every so-called Arian had long been ready (in all good con-

---

95. For Hilary's *Contra Auxentium*, see M. Meslin, 'Hilaire et la crise arienne', in *Hilaire et son temps*, ed. E. R. Labande (1969), at 39–41.

96. These charges are recorded by Auxentius in his memorandum, cited at *Contra Aux.* 13.

97. The letter of the western bishops from Rimini (*Coll. Antiar. Par.* A.vi [*CSEL* 65, pp. 87–88]; cf. Hanson, *The Search*, 379n123) hailed the rejection of 'substance' terminology; both the 'dated' creed of 359 and that of Nice (360) formally excluded its use.

science) to give. It was Auxentius' success in escaping Hilary's attempt
to tar him with the Arian brush, rather than a false profession of adherence to Nicaea, that was the basis of the official conclusion 'that he did
not disagree with the opinion of the faith which I had expounded' (9).
Valentinian's church was simply too broad for Hilary's offensive to work.

The emperor, who was probably the first baptized Christian to attain the purple, then gave Auxentius a concrete, public endorsement:
'After this the king came to communion with him, in the sincerity of his
faith' (9).[98] The people of Milan could hardly have been shown a clearer
lead. Hilary's persistence in protesting against Auxentius' 'deception'
must therefore have smacked of petulant mischief-making, his claim
that 'it was all a misrepresentation' and that 'God and men were being
tricked' (9) merely bearing out the bishop's charge that he was a troublemaker who 'tried to form schisms everywhere' (15). Valentinian, always
alert to such matters, soon lost patience. Hilary was compelled to leave
Milan: 'There was no freedom for me to remain there against the king's
will' (9).

Neither the circumstances of Hilary's expulsion nor the episode as a
whole can have done his cause any credit, and the subsequent publication of Contra Auxentium looks like an exercise in damage limitation.
This work was addressed to his 'most beloved brothers who remain true
to their fathers' faith and who loathe the Arian heresy, the bishops and
all the peoples'—particularly, one suspects, the Italian bishops among
whom Hilary and Eusebius had been working and from whom the bishops present at the hearing had probably been drawn.[99] Hilary's presentation of Auxentius as a lackey of the court who had prevailed by evad-
ing the 'real' issue of the Son's consubstantiality was therefore designed
to confuse an issue that probably appeared all too clear. But he had little
success in his efforts to isolate Auxentius. An almost casual remark at
the end of his tract—'let him summon as many synods as he wants
against me' (12)—shows that Auxentius could count on the support of
his neighbours.

The 'people' addressed by Hilary included the congregation of Milan,
the innocent victims of Auxentius' duplicity: he addressed them with

98. Amb. Ep. 75 [21].5 describes Valentinian as 'baptizatus in Christo'. It is
possible, but unlikely, that Valentinian was baptized after his accession, like his
brother Valens (cf. Theodoret HE 4.12.4).

99. It would be interesting to know where Jerome came across this tract (De
vir. ill. 100: 'elegans libellus'): Rome, Trier or Aquileia?

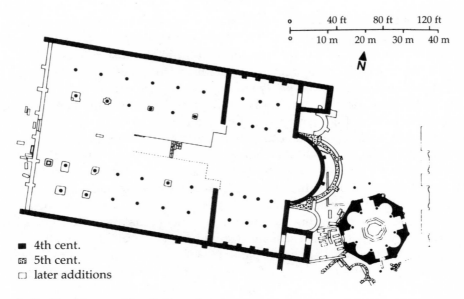

1. Basilica Nova and baptistery, plan.
Reproduced by kind permission of Professor R. Krautheimer.

particular emphasis in his peroration. But he only betrayed his frustration at the strength of their allegiance to Auxentius: 'One thing I warn:
beware the Antichrist. For it is wrong that love for walls has seized you,
wrong that you adore the Church of God in its ceilings and buildings,
wrong that you repeat the name of peace inside these. Is there any doubt
that it is in these places that the Antichrist will sit?' (*Contra Aux.* 12).
These words have been given a particular resonance by the discovery of
the remains of a splendid fourth-century church, identified with the Basilica Nova later mentioned by Ambrose, beneath the Piazza del Duomo
in the centre of Milan. The massive scale of this building (its dimensions,
80 by 45 metres, approach those of Constantine's gigantic church of
Saint John Lateran at Rome), the quality of its construction, and its lavish decoration set it apart from anything else known in northern Italy at
this time.[100]

100. M. Mirabella Roberti, *Milano Romana* (1984), 106–111; R. Krautheimer,
Three Christian Capitals (1983), 74–77. The fullest description is by A. de Capitani
d'Arzago, *La chiesa maggiore di Milano, Santa Tecla* (1952). Even after a fourth-
century enlargement, the cathedral complex of Aquileia was still substantially
smaller.

The magnificent setting available to Auxentius for the performance of his duties must have raised his stature in the community as a whole. The evidence precludes certainty, but it is entirely likely that he was the first bishop of Milan to enjoy the use of this cathedral, whether construction began under Constantius while he resided in the city or during the reign of Constans.[101] It gave him a considerable advantage when confronting strangers. The discussion with Hilary may well have taken place inside this church: besides impressing upon the audience the solidity of the bishop's position, it would have given the challenger an opportunity to see for himself the hold that walls and ceilings exercised upon the people of Milan.

Against this, Hilary could only appeal to the puritanism traditionally invoked by excluded Christian minorities. The authentic church, he insisted, was that of the persecution, coming together in 'secret meetings' in mountains or forests. Even without the melodramatic colour and the exotic locations, this language indicates nicely the status of Auxentius' opponents. The emperor's stance made open conflict with the bishop impossible, but Valentinian's surviving rescripts on ecclesiastical affairs show a tolerance for schisms that caused no disturbance.[102] The Milanese dissidents were therefore relegated to impotent obscurity upon the margins of the city.

An incident that can plausibly be associated with this group is briefly and obliquely mentioned by Ammianus as an example of Valentinian's ungovernable temper. Diodorus, a retired *agens in rebus*, had lodged a civil suit against a *comes*, who turned to the emperor for help when the judge ordered three officials to summon him just as he was departing on official business. Whatever the basis of the original charge, the timing of the arrest was maladroit, given the emperor's insistence on administrative efficiency. Diodorus could be suspected, moreover, of employing the less dangerous procedures of civil law in order to bring what amounted to a criminal charge. So, at least, Valentinian appears to

101. The assumption that this church housed the council of 355 (e.g., Krautheimer, *Three Christian Capitals*, 77) is based on two errors: acceptance of Socrates' and Sozomen's vastly inflated figure of three hundred for the participants of the council, and reliance upon an adjective in Ambrose's account of the expulsion of Dionysius and Eusebius (*Ep. extra coll.* 14 [63].68: 'cum raperentur de ecclesia maiore') now shown to be a medieval insertion (M. Zelzer, *CSEL* 82.3, p. 271).

102. Compare *Coll. Avell.* 5, readmitting the Ursinians to Rome with the proviso that 'si aliquid spiritu iterum gesserint inquieto, quo tranquillitas reformata turbetur, severissima in eos sententia promoveri'.

have interpreted the matter: treating it as a criminal case, he executed both Diodorus, for *calumnia*, and the three officials, presumably for collusion.[103]

'The Christians venerate their memory at Milan even to this day, and call the place where they are buried *Ad Innocentes'*. This cult has been interpreted as a generalized protest by the Christians of Milan against the cruelty of Valentinian's government.[104] But this assertion is based on an inaccurate conception of Valentinian, whose 'terror' was reserved for a tiny minority of the population. Besides, Diodorus, who had tried to exploit a legal technicality to escape the dangers of a normal prosecution, was hardly an obvious martyr. We should consider instead the circumstances of 365 (much the most convincing date), when Valentinian was residing in Milan and Auxentius was 'glorying in worldly attentions' from him.[105] The bishop was hardly likely to condone a public pronouncement of the government's injustice.

But others could. Hilary had urged his followers to remain separate and to congregate outside the city, in their 'secreta coenabula'. This was the area belonging to the dead and reserved for their veneration, which notoriously resisted episcopal efforts to impose control. The four victims, presumably members of the Christian community,[106] provided a valuable focus for the dispossessed Nicenes. By tending their graves and celebrating their memory they could demonstrate that they, unlike the time-serving bishop, were more concerned to honour Milanese citizens than to keep favour with the palace, and were also able to express their resentment against a regime that had been so drastically mistaken in its doctrinal choices. The cult therefore helped sustain the identity, and advertise the opposition status, of the Nicene Christians. It was to endure, and even to escape the influence of Ambrose. Despite his keen interest in bringing the peripheries of Milan, and the worship of the dead conducted there, under his direct patronage and control, the Innocents seem to have remained outside his scope. They are never once

103. Amm. Marc. 27.7.5. The legal issues are discussed by M. Martroye, 'Un passage d'Ammien Marcellin', *Bull. de la soc. nat. des antiqu. de France* (1922), 165–172.

104. H. I. Marrou, 'Ammien Marcellin et les "Innocents" de Milan', *RecSR* 40 (1952), 179–190.

105. Hil. *Contra Aux.* 4: '[ecclesia] diligi se gloriatur a mundo'; cf. 'at nunc . . . divinam fidem suffragia commendant', '[ecclesia] pendet ad dignationem communicantium' (a likely reference to Valentinian and his court's participation in the mass).

106. Ambrose's supporters would include both retired officials and serving members of the palace staff; see below, pp. 181, 221.

mentioned in his works, although Ammianus says explicitly that they were still being venerated fifteen years into Ambrose's episcopate.

The establishment of a Christian cult so clearly intended to condemn the government brings out the polarity between the two congregations in Milan, and also the marginal character of the opposition to Auxentius. Only when the bishop died, ten years after Hilary's defeat, did this group finally make an open challenge. There is no evidence, however, that Auxentius' position within the city had been eroded during the last decade of his life. This returns us to the problem of Ambrose's intervention. Nothing in the recent history of Milan suggested that the Nicenes had any claim to the governor's attention and goodwill. At least one Nicene troublemaker, indeed, had been beaten and expelled in the recent past, probably by a previous *consularis*. Ambrose's plea for 'peace' was not, as we have seen, a 'natural' official response to the situation he encountered at the basilica. To explain his behaviour, we must therefore explore the governor's own background, and the attitudes and prejudices he brought with him to his office.

AMBROSE THE ROMAN

Ambrose had been 'educated in the liberal studies' at Rome.[107] His associations with the city made a lasting impression upon contemporaries: Rome was his 'own territory' to his biographer, his 'motherland' to his most dangerous enemy.[108] This was mistaken (he was born at Trier), but the error itself helps suggest the strength of Ambrose's identity as a 'Roman of Rome'. It remains strong and continues to sow misapprehensions. Modern historians invariably assume Ambrose's *Romanitas* to mean specifically that he belonged to the 'aristocratic cousinhood', the top drawer of senatorial society.[109] The evidence is tenuous. Both in his sole claim to noble ancestry at Rome, and in his purported family connexion with the orator Symmachus, dubious testimony has been interpreted in the light of Ambrose's unmistakably aristocratic demeanour as a bishop.[110] But this is less a reflection of real social eminence than a

107. Paulin. *V. Amb.* 5.1.
108. Paulin. *V. Amb.* 9.4: 'proprium solum'; Palladius *Apol.* 139: 'genetrix'. Basil of Caesarea saluted Ambrose, upon his election, as a 'man from the royal city' (*Ep.* 197).
109. Palanque, *Saint Ambroise*, 6–8; S. Mazzarino, *Storia sociale del vescovo Ambrogio* (1989).
110. See below, chap. 6, pp. 263–275, for the relationship between Ambrose and Symmachus.

trick of perspective: the modest backgrounds of his episcopal colleagues made it easy for Ambrose to shine among them.[111]

Aristocratic life at Rome, besides, embraced a broad spectrum of ranks. The gregarious nobles of the ancient capital offered their hospitality generously (if erratically, to the embarrassment of those who misread the relationship thus signalled). During his student days the blueblooded millionaire Pammachius consorted on apparently equal terms with Jerome, a provincial of limited means and obscure lineage preparing for a career in the imperial administration.[112] The educational background that Ambrose shared with these two friends, almost the only detail recorded of his 'Roman' upbringing, therefore gives only the vaguest of clues to his social position.

The bishop was born, according to his biographer, 'while his father Ambrose was placed in the administration of the prefecture of the Gauls'.[113] It follows from this, and from the probability that he was born in 339, that Ambrose's homonymous father was praetorian prefect at the court of Constantine II, who ruled the western provinces from 337 until 340.[114] The office conferred enormous power but again distances the family from the noble clans of Rome. The prefects of the Constantinian dynasty tended (except in Italy, where the great landed families sought office to protect their own interests) to be proven servants of the dynasty, often from very humble backgrounds, who had earned their promotion by long years of service at court.[115] Moreover, the elder Ambrose died prematurely; the timing suggests a connexion with Constantine's disastrous invasion of the Italian territory of his brother Constans in 340.[116] If so, his dependence on a particular regime sets him apart from

111. See especially F. D. Gilliard, 'Senatorial Bishops in the Fourth Century', *HTR* 77 (1984), 153–177, for the curial background of most bishops.

112. Jerome hails Pammachius as his 'condiscipulum quondam et sodalem et amicum' (*Ep.* 49.1). For the perils of reading too much into the warmth of a Roman noble's greeting, see Amm. Marc. 14.6.12–13.

113. *V. Amb.* 3.1: 'posito in administratione praefecturae Galliarum patre eius Ambrosio'.

114. The date depends upon identification of the 'barbarici motus' which marked the passing of Ambrose's 'annum tertium et quinquagensimum' (*Ep.* 49 [59].4). These were probably, as argued by Palanque (*Saint Ambroise*, 480–482), the raids that in 392 induced panic at Milan. For the father's office, see *PLRE* 1, p. 51; cf. Mazzarino, *Storia sociale*, 75–82.

115. Neither of the two prefects of Gaul recorded immediately before the elder Ambrose's proposed tenure appears to have been of particularly distinguished extraction: see *PLRE* 1, Tiberianus 4 (pp. 911–912) and especially Saturninus 9 (p. 806).

116. This aspect is explored by Mazzarino, *Storia sociale*, 10–12.

those aristocrats who could distance themselves from the failures of the rulers they served, like Vulcacius Rufinus, who made himself indispensable to Constans, Magnentius and Constantius in succession.[117]

It is also noteworthy that Ambrose's parentage is known only from Paulinus; the bishop never even hints at his father's identity. Perhaps, indeed, the biographer—who wrote two full generations after the elder Ambrose's death—was only guessing. He gives the information to introduce his first miracle, a swarm of bees that descended upon the infant Ambrose to presage his honey-tongued fluency. His source was clearly Ambrose's elder sister, to whom he must also have owed the detail that the incident occurred in the courtyard of the *praetorium*.[118] Perhaps this was all that Marcellina had said, and Paulinus, reluctant to press so venerable an informant but fully prepared to fill out incomplete information, drew his own conclusions from the setting; his subject's constant dealings with prefects made the inference logical enough.[119] But a father's court office did not, in any case, guarantee his son a position in the Roman elite.[120] Ambrose belongs rather to the margins of aristocratic society at Rome, where the nobleman's studied poise was an achievement rather than a birthright.

His *Romanitas* itself was perhaps more acquired than innate. Rome was a generous foster-mother; above all, it made a natural retirement home for courtiers deracinated by long years on the move with the emperors.[121] Ambrose's mother and sister, whose presence in the *praetorium* of Trier suggests that they had followed the father on his nomadic career, may well have felt a similar attraction, especially if their position at Trier had been compromised by the civil war of 340. The family nevertheless seem first to have spent several years on their estates. The decisive impulse for the move to Rome was perhaps the educational needs

117. *PLRE* 1, Rufinus 25 (pp. 782–783).

118. Marcellina, mentioned in the account of the episode at *V. Amb.* 3.3, is cited as an informant at 1.3.

119. Similar explanatory glosses by Paulinus are evidently inferred from Ambrose's writings: note *V. Amb.* 22.1 ('posito Theodosio imperatore Mediolanii') and the gross error at 26.1 ('Valentiniano augusto intra Gallias posito'). 'Praetorium' is used of the headquarters of a *magister officiorum* at *V. Amb.* 37; praetorian prefects appear at 5.1, 8.3, 26.3, 31.2, 31.5, 34.1.

120. See J. F. Matthews, *Western Aristocracies and Imperial Court* (1975), 42n7, for one case where the progeny of a successful bureaucrat apparently struggled. The dynasties established in Constantinople by the families of the disgraced prefects Ablabius and Taurus (both of whom had risen from humble backgrounds) reflect the very different character of the new capital's aristocracy.

121. Ammianus (himself an excellent specimen of the type) mentions the admirable eunuch Eutherius: 16.7.7.

of Ambrose and his brother, but religious factors were also involved: shortly after their arrival, in the early 350s, Ambrose's sister, Marcellina, made a formal profession of virginity.[122] The mother might also have looked to the powerful Roman church and its increasingly sophisticated administration for more practical help: as a widow of property, she belonged to a species notoriously vulnerable to predators.[123]

The only recorded family connexion with Rome is Christian. A martyr, the 'noble virgin' Soteris, appears twice in Ambrose's works as his sister's 'ancestor' and his own 'personal exemplar'.[124] Soteris throws important light upon the family background; but despite Ambrose's breezy allusions to the 'consulates and prefectures' of her forebears, she supplies better evidence of assertive religiosity than of noble ancestry. Her tomb on the Appian Way is not recorded until the Middle Ages, and the only other evidence from antiquity (a reference to her feast on a gravestone) is dated 401, after Ambrose's death. It is inconceivable that the Christian aristocrats of fourth-century Rome, whose hunger for appropriate models is well attested, would have consigned an authentically noble martyr to such neglect.[125] Nor is Ambrose's own relationship to Soteris clear. Since the physical ancestry implied by his language is excluded by her vocation, she has been assumed to be a great-aunt or suchlike;[126] but Marcellina's vaunted 'succession' to an 'inherited' chastity suggests that the connexion was obtained by that most characteristic (and flexible) Roman institution, testation.[127] Perhaps it was only with

122. The date of Marcellina's consecration (despite Palanque, *Saint Ambroise,* 482–483) might be anywhere between 353 and 356. The circumstances of her ascetic formation, 'constituta in agro nulla socia virgine, nullo informata doctore' (*De virg.* 3.37), should exclude any prolonged tutelage at Rome beforehand. Paulin. *V. Amb.* 4.1 puts Ambrose at Rome 'cum adolevisset'.

123. Ambrose details the perils to which widows were exposed: *Exp. Ps. 118* 6.20 (invasion of property); 8.58 (fraud); 16.6–7 (vexatious litigation); more prosaically, *Ep.* 24 [82].7. The wife and daughter of the executed prefect Rufinus retired to Jerusalem (after most of his property had been plundered): Zosimus 5.8.2–3.

124. *De virg.* 3.38: 'auctor . . . generis'; *Exh. virg.* 82: 'domesticum piae parentis exemplum'.

125. The evidence—such as it is—is noted by Pietri, *Roma Christiana,* 533, 614n3. Soteris' absence from the *Depositio martyrum* of 354 (*Chron. Min.* 1, pp. 71–72), a decidedly 'senatorial' source, is particularly telling. So too, perhaps, is the fact that Ambrose claims noble rank for her only in *Exh. virg.,* delivered in 394, by which time few could have questioned his assertions (and at a moment when he needed urgently to promote himself).

126. Palanque, *Saint Ambroise,* 5: 'grande-tante ou collâterale'.

127. *De virg.* 3.37; cf. 2.2 for a similar expression applied to himself.

their mother's burial beside Soteris that Ambrose and Marcellina's link with the martyr was sealed and the promotion of her cult begun.

However it was acquired, the family's privileged claim upon the memory and the grave of a martyr sets them firmly within the society of Christian Rome. Pope Liberius himself conferred the virgin's veil upon Marcellina at a well-attended ceremony for the feast of Christmas, in the new basilica of Saint Peter's.[128] One of the consecrated virgins who 'vied for her company' duly joined the household as her companion, and they embarked upon a pious routine in which visits from clergymen appear to have provided the social highlights. Without a father to initiate him into masculine society Ambrose shared the same milieu, and his biographer shows him habitually mimicking these guests by presenting his right hand to be kissed by the women of the family; the gesture, striking testimony to the influence of clerical mannerisms upon the household, might perhaps be interpreted as a teenager's self-assertion in the most authoritative manner he knew.[129]

Ambrose's family thus join the entourage of Pope Liberius beside the other female supporters attested archaeologically and in the literature, although Theodoret's charming account of the noblewomen of Rome lobbying Constantius (and their own reluctant menfolk) on the pope's behalf must be treated with caution.[130] But the story does reflect the important fact that the Christians of Rome were given much more sustained exposure to, and became much more deeply engaged in, the issues debated at the council of Milan than the Milanese congregation who actually witnessed the event. Liberius wrote to his legates immediately after the council declaring his unconditional support for their intransigence; and for a year thereafter he maintained a highly conspicuous defiance of the council's verdict, even rejecting a gift from Constantius to Saint Peter's. For his part, the emperor organized a propaganda campaign against the pope, whose targets included aristocrats, women and ascetics.[131] But Liberius' following remained solid, and the emperor

---

128. *De virg.* 3.1: 'quantus ad natalem Sponsi populus convenerit'. For the occasion, see J. Fontaine, ed., *Ambroise de Milan: Hymnes* (1992), 266.

129. Paulin. *V. Amb.* 4; 9.4.

130. C. Dagens, 'Autour de pape Libère', *MEFR* 78 (1966), 327–381; Theodoret *HE* 2.17.1–6. For female asceticism in Rome during the 350s, see R. Lizzi, 'Ascetismo e monachesimo nell'Italia tardoantica', *Codex Aquilarensis* 5 (1991), at 56–58.

131. Athan. *Hist. Ar.* 37–38. Liberius' letter to his legates: Hil. *Coll. Antiar. Par.* B.vii.2 (*CSEL* 64, pp. 164–166: with the admission at p. 165 that he lacked accurate knowledge of 'quae gesta sunt in ipsa congressione').

eventually arranged a nighttime kidnapping rather than risk a conventional arrest. After Liberius' exile it proved impossible to rally his people behind Felix, the deacon who supplanted him.[132]

Ambrose, entering manhood against this background (he was about sixteen at the time of the council of Milan), will have been alive to these events and will probably have known about the events in Milan that had precipitated the pope's removal: the 'confession' of Dionysius and its sequel. His family had access to informed gossip upon ecclesiastical affairs through their clerical visitors, who could learn about developments in Milan from the regular traffic between the two Italian capitals and also from at least one victim of Auxentius' repression, Martin of Tours.[133]

Some clerics from the Milanese church may have also removed to Rome rather than serve Auxentius or take the extreme step of forming a schism. Simplicianus, a presbyter of Milan and, in extreme old age, Ambrose's successor as bishop of the city, was in Rome during the mid-350s to help inspire the spectacular conversion of the rhetor Marius Victorinus. The circumstances of his sojourn are unclear, but Simplicianus' apparent lack of a formal position in the Roman church (and the unlikelihood that he joined the Milanese church *after* this point, during Auxentius' tenure) fits such an interpretation.[134] Direct contact between Simplicianus and Ambrose at Rome cannot necessarily be inferred from his later role as Ambrose's 'father in receiving grace';[135] more important is the general environment, in which a household like Ambrose's is unlikely to have remained indifferent to the issues and personalities that divided the church.

The later 350s saw a progressive hardening of the battlelines. The creed issued at Sirmium in 357 provoked a strong reaction at Rome, as elsewhere, and even if the convert Victorinus' contributions to the de-

132. Felix was 'notatus a senatu vel a populo': *Coll. Avell.* 1.3; cf. Pietri, *Roma Christiana*, 249–251. Liberius' arrest is described at Amm. Marc. 15.7.6–10, specifically in connexion with his refusal to subscribe to the *Acta* of the council of Milan.

133. Martin in Rome: Sulp. Sev. *V. Mart.* 6.7. Contacts between the two cities are likely to have been especially frequent while Constantius' court was at Milan, until 357.

134. Aug. *Conf.* 8.2.3–5: Simplicianus' direct involvement seems to have ended when he introduced Victorinus to the clergy who would prepare him for baptism. Note also the presence in Rome c. 372 of another opponent of Auxentius, a deacon of the Milanese church: below, p. 41.

135. *Conf.* 8.2.3: 'patrem in accipienda gratia'.

bate were reserved for a learned minority, his watchword of the Nicene *homoousion* entered the popular vocabulary.[136] Liberius returned from exile somewhat compromised, but after Constantius' death he reasserted his authority over the Italian church by leading a campaign against the settlement of Rimini. At exactly the time that he was urging 'those who had acted through ignorance at Rimini' to return to their allegiance to Nicaea and to 'unleash their anger with particular vehemence upon the authors of the Arian poison',[137] Auxentius was proclaiming to Valentinian the 'unity of the six hundred bishops' achieved at Rimini; there could be no room for compromise between this Arian *auctor* and the pope.

Such was the theological baggage that Ambrose took with him when he left Rome to begin his career as an advocate in the praetorian prefect's court at Sirmium on the Danube.[138] Though such positions carried considerable prospects and were jealously sought by ambitious lawyers, Ambrose's choice of career nevertheless confirms his place on the margins of the Roman elite. Even for those nobles without the means or inclination to pursue the Symmachan ideal of leisured detachment from public affairs, the advocate's profession was an unnecessarily roundabout path to promotion, as they could avail themselves of court connexions to secure preferment directly. Nor can the careers of those men who began by combining the tenure of the traditional republican magistracies with service at the bar provide parallels to establish an aristocratic tradition of forensic practice; their activities were confined to Rome itself, where their work on their senatorial colleagues' behalf bore directly upon their own advancement.[139] The business that came before

136. For the importance of 357 as a turning-point, see Hanson, *The Search*, 343–347. Ambrose betrays no sign of acquaintance with Victorinus' anti-Arian works, produced at Rome in the later 350s: another sign, perhaps, of distance from the aristocratic milieu for which these texts were presumably intended, although Peter Brown, *The Body and Society* (1988), 346, suggests that upper-class study groups 'had been an element in Ambrose's culture during his early years as a senator'.

137. Hil. *Coll. Antiar. Par.* B.iv.1 (*CSEL* 65, pp. 156–157). This letter is discussed by Pietri, *Roma Christiana*, 264.

138. Paulin. *V. Amb.* 5.1.

139. The evidence collected by C. Lécrivain, 'Note sur le recrutement des avocats', *MEFR* 5 (1885), 276–283, is often cited in reference to the bar in general; but the careers of men like Ragonius Vicentius Celsus (who held the traditional republican magistracies before becoming *praefectus annonae*: PLRE 1,

the praetorian court was more diverse; though more significant for the empire as a whole, it rarely engaged the interest of the grandees of the ancient capital.[140]

Ambrose's career therefore evokes comparison with Jerome's rather than Pammachius'. Indeed, it recalls that of a contemporary who can by no means be included in the polite society of Rome: Maximinus, the 'hellish judge' who terrorized the city's nobility in the latter years of Valentinian's reign. The black language in which Ammianus describes Maximinus' rise to power is very different from the lustre that Paulinus gives Ambrose, but the pattern is not dissimilar: fortified by an omen (involving birds rather than bees) interpreted by his father, who had served in the lower ranks of the administration, Maximinus moved from a 'mediocre' education in the liberal arts to an 'inglorious' career at the bar, which in turn brought a series of provincial governorships.[141] Ambrose did not start so low, nor did his rise attract the same rumours of sorcery and blackmail; his career nevertheless paralleled Maximinus' exactly.

The turning-point of Ambrose's career was his appointment as assessor by the praetorian prefect Petronius Probus, who took office in the spring of 368.[142] Probus, ten years Ambrose's senior, could boast one of the most distinguished pedigrees of the age. But despite his awesome wealth (and the attractions of his magnificent mansion at Rome) he retained an appetite for office unmatched among his peers: this was the third of four prefectures he held during his lifetime. Between postings he 'wasted away' (according to Ammianus) 'like a fish out of its natural element', although even in office he was plagued by a succession of minor ailments. Probus is presented by Ammianus as seeking office not for his own enjoyment or aggrandizement but because he was thrust forward by pressure from his numerous dependents, who wanted his protection while they pursued their own ends. The historian accuses him only of condoning such activity, and while deploring the devasta-

---

p. 195) and Postumianus (*PLRE* 1, pp. 718–719) did not take them outside Rome itself.

140. Symmachus' letters to praetorian prefects rarely concern litigation. One of few examples, *Ep.* 4.68 (concerning an estate let out by a *clarissima femina* at Aquileia), stresses that recourse to the 'iudicium praetoriani culminis' was a last resort. Moreover, such cases (cf. *Epp.* 2.66, 75, 87, all to Flavianus) seem to have been dealt with by direct appeal to the prefect.

141. Amm. Marc. 28.1.5–7.

142. Paulin. *V. Amb.* 5.1.

tion wrought to the provinces of Illyricum under Probus' tenure, he also maintains that this was the result of excessive obedience to the harsh fiscal policies of the emperor.[143]

The character of Probus' administration is relevant to the 'splendid conduct of cases' that brought Ambrose to the prefect's attention and the evidently satisfactory service that he gave as advisor. But promotions usually depended as much on connexions as merit, and if (as is likely) Ambrose's brother, Satyrus, also benefitted from Probus' favour some sponsorship might reasonably be surmised.[144] Although their Roman roots gave them acquaintances in common with Probus, the brothers' distinctive family background—and the distinctly 'clerical' impression that Ambrose's demeanour apparently made on the prefect— invites the suggestion of backers from the church of Rome.[145] Probus became more visible within the Christian community of Rome after his death, in his majestic tomb on the Vatican abutting that of Saint Peter, than he had probably been in life.[146] His religion nevertheless left him susceptible to the pleas of the clergy, who might therefore be included among his notoriously clamorous legions of dependents. His formidable wife, Proba, was (besides being exposed to the attentions of importunate clergymen) a devout admirer of dedicated virgins.[147] Hence Ambrose's initial claim upon the prefect's attention may not have been as the son of a long-dead court official but as the younger brother of the virtuous Marcellina.

When Probus departed for Illyricum in 368 there was a new pope in Rome, more systematic than his predecessor in exploiting his connexions with his aristocratic parishioners and far more adroit in his dealings

143. Amm. Marc. 27.11.1–7; cf. *PLRE* 1, pp. 736–740. Probus is discussed by Matthews, *Western Aristocracies*, 37–38; cf. D. M. Novak, 'Anicianae domus culmen, nobilitatis culmen', *Klio* 62 (1980), 473–493.

144. Satyrus served a term as provincial governor, which Ambrose implies was simultaneous with his own: *De exc. frat.* 1.25.

145. It might be noted that Ambrose had received no preferment from the Roman aristocrat who had preceded Probus, the pagan Rufinus. Probus' lighthearted command that Ambrose govern his province 'like a bishop' (Paulin. *V. Amb.* 8.3) implies something of how he perceived him.

146. See Matthews, *Western Aristocracies*, 195–197.

147. Jerome *Ep.* 130.7; see *Ep.* 22.28 for the attentions paid to Christian matrons (of whom Proba was among the wealthiest and most distinguished). For references to Proba's subsequent involvement in the controversies over Pelagius and John Chrysostom, and her bequests to the Roman church, see *PLRE* 1, Proba 3, pp. 731–732.

with the government. Damasus survived a turbulent inauguration to assert the authority of the Roman see with unprecedented vigour at home and abroad, laying particular stress upon its apostolic roots and tradition of doctrinal purity as the leader of a united orthodox west.[148]

The presence of an unrepentant Auxentius in Milan was an irritating impediment to the pope's pretensions upon this last count. Athanasius of Alexandria expressed surprise at the heretic's survival, supplying information about his criminal past in the Alexandrian presbytery as if to bestir Damasus to action.[149] But his hands were tied by the emperor. Valentinian's endorsement of Auxentius still stood, and he showed no inclination to countenance the comprehensive doctrinal settlement that alone could overrule the creed of Rimini from which the bishop of Milan derived his legitimacy.

Damasus had a flair for publicity. Denied the opportunity to settle accounts directly with Auxentius, he nevertheless created the impression of decisive action. Some ninety bishops gathered in Rome in (probably) 371 to discuss Auxentius, broadcasting the results of their deliberations in the synodal *Confidimus quidem*.[150] The preamble (in one of the two versions of the text that survive)[151] announces that the council had been convened 'ex imperiali rescripto', which must mean that it had been sanctioned by Valentinian himself. How this permission was obtained from a ruler notorious for his reluctance to disturb the religious status quo is unclear. The text, however, suggests that a certain amount of subterfuge and misrepresentation was involved. The council's letter begins with a reference to a *relatio* from the bishops' 'brothers in Gaul and Venetia', who had written to report the doctrinal confusion being sown in their region through the acceptance of false teachings by certain unsophisticated bishops, and the condemnation of Auxentius for propagating these errors. Valentinian's rescript is most plausibly seen as a response to this same *relatio*, originally submitted by its authors to the court; by inviting them to correct their wayward colleagues, the emperor was in effect refusing to act upon their resolutions and (given the likely

148. For a sympathetic sketch, see C. Pietri, 'Damase, évêque de Rome', in *Saecularia Damasiana* (1986), 31–58. Damasus' propaganda is described by Pietri, 'Concordia apostolorum et renovatio urbis', *MEFR* 73 (1961), 295–322; cf. J. M. Huskinson, *Concordia Apostolorum* (1982).

149. Athan. *Ep. ad Afros* 10.

150. The discussion of the council and its proceedings by Pietri, *Roma Christiana*, 733–736, 791–800, is now fundamental.

151. The Latin version is preserved in the collection of Theodosius the deacon; cf. below, p. 41.

refusal of Auxentius' 'victims' to cooperate) ensuring a stalemate. This would accord with Valentinian's well-attested practice of leaving bishops to resolve their disagreements independently, but the phrasing of imperial rescripts often left the recipients scope to interpret and apply them to their own convenience.[152] It was probably by such means that Valentinian's authority was invoked to summon the largest western council since Rimini and to authorize the bishop of Rome to pronounce upon the condition of the northern Italian church.

The bishops were careful not to provoke the emperor by presuming too much upon the authority conveyed by the rescript, confining themselves in their synodal letter to a report, without comment, of the previous judgement by the 'Gauls and Venetians' against Auxentius. No practical measures were announced: the document is principally concerned to hail the Nicene creed as the true standard of orthodoxy and to refute the pretensions of Rimini on the novel grounds that the bishop of Rome had lent his approval to the former and not the latter. This declaration neither endangered the stability of the Italian church nor required any response from the imperial authorities, presenting Auxentius with no more immediate threat than the confident pronouncement that it 'would not be long' before he was stripped of his episcopate.

The council served principally as a vehicle for the propaganda of the Roman church. The letter that it produced has survived under two headings, one of them (preserved in a Greek translation by the historians Sozomen and Theodoret) addressed to the bishops of Illyricum and therefore, we may surmise, one of a series of copies circulated among the western provinces.[153] More interesting is the Latin version, addressed to the 'catholic bishops of the east'; this text played a fleeting but significant role in ecclesiastical history when Meletius of Antioch and no fewer than 152 other bishops subscribed to it in 379, to establish their bona fides with the Roman church.[154] The document was first brought to Alexandria by the council's legate, Sabinus, 'deacon of Milan'—presumably therefore

152. See Amb. *Ep.* 75 [21].5, for Valentinian's policy; cf. below, p. 125, for the manipulation of a rescript at the council of Aquileia (with the connivance of the praetorian prefect).

153. Soz. *HE* 6.23.7–15; Theod. *HE* 2.21.2–12.

154. The text was eventually included in the archive reproduced in the *codex Veronensis;* an edition and discussion (arguing for the priority of this Latin version) are provided by M. Richard, 'La lettre *Confidimus Quidem* du pape Damase', *AIPhO* 11 (1951), 323–340. For criticism of this position, and the case for Sozomen's text as the original, see F. Scheidweiler, 'Besitzen wir das lateinische Original der römischen Synodalschreibens vom Jahre 371?', *AIPhO* 13 (1955), 572–586.

a dissident at odds with Auxentius' clergy—to offer a riposte to Athanasius' previous demand for action against Auxentius.[155] The impression that it created, of the successful elimination of the last pockets of
heresy, was promoted extensively by Sabinus, who subsequently travelled (probably on private initiative) to visit Basil of Caesarea.[156] Basil
gave him several letters to take back to Italy, acknowledging his value as
an informant who had 'accurately described the happy state of affairs
among you'. The western bishops were invited to contrast this with the
difficulties (which Sabinus could describe to them at first hand) endured
by the eastern Nicenes. Basil's lament—'The evil of heresy spreads almost from the borders of Illyricum to the Thebaid'[157]—suggests that Sabinus had presented the western position somewhat optimistically, for
he shows no awareness that his guest's city was still occupied by a Cappadocian heretic as incorrigible as his own neighbours.

But this comforting version of the situation was reserved solely for
export. The council of Rome could not touch Auxentius, the security of
whose position was demonstrated when the presbyter Filastrius, an energetic controversialist who specialized in the detection of heresy, set
himself up at Milan as the 'able guardian of the lord's flock'. 'Subjected
to blows', he soon retired to a more sympathetic environment to evoke
admiration by his status as a victim of persecution and his scars.[158]

It was the *consularis* to whom the established church appealed to
suppress such troublemakers. Perhaps Filastrius was lucky: at Sirmium
in 367 the spokesmen of the Nicene minority who sought to 'cause sedition and make two peoples out of one' were met with the crowd's
shout of 'let them be handed over to the *consularis* and put to death!'.[159]
But by the end of Auxentius' life, the secular authorities at Milan could
no longer be relied upon to uphold the rights of the established church.
Ambrose took up the post of *consularis* of Aemilia and Liguria in about
372/3.[160] It is tempting to associate his appointment with the council of

155. Sabinus' name appears at the bottom of the Latin text: 'ego Sabinus
diaconus Mediolanensis de authentico dedi'. For his mission, see M. Richard,
'Saint Basile et la mission du diacre Sabinus', *AB* 67 (1949), 179–202.

156. Sabinus conveyed a personal message to Basil from Valerian of Aquileia (Basil *Ep*. 91); Basil also implies, in *Ep*. 90.1, that only Athanasius had been
addressed directly by the Roman council.

157. Basil *Ep*. 92.2.

158. Gaud. *Tract*. 21.6–7. After mentioning Filastrius' experiences at Milan,
Gaudentius speaks of him as having remained 'non exiguo tempore' at Rome.

159. *Altercatio Heracliani, PLS* 1, 350.

160. The only reason Palanque gives for dating Ambrose's appointment to
c. 370—and thus assigning him an exceptionally protracted term in office—is to

Rome, or at least the campaign to undermine Auxentius that had inspired it. Not all the letters sent to Illyricum, perhaps, were addressed to bishops: Christian office-holders were regularly lobbied by their pastors to help in the fight against heresy, and Probus, who could make his own appointments to the provincial governorships of Italy, was in an ideal position to assist the cause.[161] The fate of Filastrius had shown that effective opposition to Auxentius was impossible while the bishop still enjoyed official support, so it was necessary to install a governor prepared to neglect his duty. Probus' final words as he saw his appointee off—'go, act as a bishop, not as a judge'—could be read as an invitation to do precisely that.[162] But Ambrose is unlikely to have needed such advice. For ten years, the Roman church had been denouncing the council of Rimini and its representatives. Neutrality was therefore not a practical possibility for the pious catechumen, who can only have recoiled from Auxentius' church and from the 'diversa consilia' preached there. If he did not seek out the opposition group himself, he can hardly have escaped their attention. We need not suspect him of conspiracy with them to secure the see for himself. But the irruption of these Nicenes into Auxentius' great basilica—a building that few of them had entered before—reflects their confidence that the usual stern punishments for public disorder would not be imposed against them.

That confidence proved well founded. The governor duly arrived at the church; once there, however, he sought not to disperse the troublemakers but to assume control of the proceedings. His speech might indeed have urged peace and order, but this was no plea for moderation or compromise. Ambrose was in effect insisting that the intruders be given a say in the appointment of the new bishop; the franchise was to be extended by decree to a group who had been isolated from the main community for twenty years and were tainted by a reputation for rebellion and disorder. He had come, then, to help these people regain their voice within the church, and perhaps to assist them in claiming a more significant role than their numbers warranted. But he seems to have overestimated their discipline or underestimated their resourcefulness. Their response to the first demonstration of official support that they

---

account for the growth of the 'universal popularity' he assumes must explain the election: *Saint Ambroise*, 483–484.

161. For prefects appointing governors, see Jones, *The Later Roman Empire*, 372, 391. Liebeschuetz, *Antioch*, 111–112, provides documentation for the appointment of some *consulares Syriae*.

162. Paulin. *V. Amb.* 8.3: 'Vade, age non ut iudex sed ut episcopus'.

had received since 355 was to claim their governor for themselves, with the cry, "Ambrose for bishop!"

FROM ACCLAMATION TO CONSECRATION

Rufinus describes Ambrose's reaction to the people's cry in just five words: 'obluctante illo et plurimum resistente' (Ruf. *HE* 11.11), 'he struggled and put up a great deal of resistance'. But Paulinus, who until this point had echoed Rufinus almost exactly, gives full details of Ambrose's resistance. 'When he realized what was happening, Ambrose left the church and ordered his tribunal to be set up. Then, contrary to his usual practice, he ordered some people to be put to the torture'. The people refused to be deterred from their desire to see him consecrated, persisting in their acclamations when he successively announced his intention of becoming a philosopher, invited prostitutes to his house and attempted to flee Milan altogether.[163]

These episodes were until recently disregarded as hagiographical exaggeration or fantasy. But Paulinus' credit has now been substantially restored. It has been convincingly argued that his account of Ambrose's manoeuvres is too circumstantial, and provides too much potentially damaging material against the bishop, for them to be classified with other examples of the 'refus préalable'; nor, given the clumsiness of Paulinus' exegesis, can they have been invented to allow pious disquisitions upon their typological significance.[164] Besides, public life was sufficiently theatrical to make the events themselves quite plausible: a fourth-century governor could expect to be acclaimed even at his tribunal and in his residence.[165] But Paulinus misrepresents one central aspect of the situation, as in his preceding account: the 'populus' who pursued their governor so energetically were not the two Christian congregations of Milan, fused together by their common enthusiasm for Ambrose, but the same group of Nicenes who had hailed him in the basilica.

What Paulinus describes is the process by which Ambrose's nomination assumed the *appearance* of unanimity. The governor went to his tribunal, abandoning the ungrateful Nicenes and protecting himself

163. Paulin. *V. Amb.* 7–8.
164. Duval, 'Ambroise, de son élection'.
165. See A. Cameron, *Circus Factions* (1976), 240, for acclamations to a governor 'outside his residence or in his audience hall'.

from the grave risks that his abortive intervention had incurred. He could not know whether the bishops and presbyters supervising the occasion would take steps against him, but the emperor's notorious intolerance of official misconduct gave ample cause for anxiety.[166] Ambrose's resumption of his official routines should therefore be seen as an attempt to downplay the fracas in the basilica and to distance himself from it. He duly began his next case, ordering the customary torture to be applied.[167]

In doing so he incidentally demonstrated his ineligibility for the episcopate, for it was agreed that even an upright judge was inevitably tainted by his responsibility for administering the cruelties of the law.[168] But Ambrose's supporters would not desist. Having followed him from the church, they responded to his order with a shout of 'Your sin upon our heads'. The immediate effect was to complicate his attempts to disown them; at the same time, probably by accident, they were redefining the issue. The acclamation at the tribunal, recorded by the *exceptores* who attended the governor, could be presented as the 'authentic' voice of the Christian people. Unlike the cheers in the basilica, it provided the basis for a credible candidacy; it also established an initiative that the Nicenes would not relinquish.

'Disturbed', Ambrose departed for home with the crowd in attendance. The acclamations continued outside his residence, but with a significant change: Ambrose now began a dialogue with his admirers. He was first 'induced to refrain' from his intention of becoming a philosopher, deferring to their authority. His subsequent invitation of prostitutes to his home (strictly for show, says Paulinus, who in this instance can readily be believed) prompted the same refrain as the earlier tor-

166. A proconsul of Africa had previously been fined—and exposed to subsequent hounding—for an act of 'charity' during a famine, suggesting the risks attached to any departure from official norms: Amm. Marc. 28.1.17–18.

167. Paulin. *V. Amb.* 7.1; the claim that this was 'contra consuetudinem' is highly implausible, given its routine use in criminal cases (Jones, *The Later Roman Empire*, 519–520; cf. the bland remarks in the schoolbook edited by A. C. Dionisotti, 'From Ausonius' Schooldays?', *JRS* 72 [1982], 83–125, at secs. 74–75). Those magistrates who deliberately avoided bloodshed (e.g., Paul. Nol. *Carm.* 21.375–376) did so by deferring any capital sentences until after their term, but torture was unavoidable unless the judge refused to hear any criminal cases.

168. A contemporary papal decretal bluntly excludes all former magistrates from the priesthood, explaining of them that 'immunes a peccato esse non posse manifestum est. Dum enim et gladius exeritur aut iudicium confertur iniustum aut tormenta exercentur pro necessitate causarum . . .' ([Siricius] *Ep.* 10.5 [*PL* 13, 1190–1191]: for the attribution to Damasus, see Pietri, *Roma Christiana*, 764–772).

tures: 'Your sin upon our heads'. But by now Ambrose could not seriously have expected any other response. When the cry had first been
raised at the tribunal, he had still been free to ignore the interruption
and continue with his duties; now he was acting for the crowd's benefit,
supplying them with their cues.

Two distinct purposes were fulfilled by these gestures, besides the
opportunity that the attendant negotiations afforded Ambrose—for the
first time since his arrival at the basilica—to consult directly with his
partisans. The first was to put himself publicly at odds with these
people. The suspicions of collusion raised by the governor's earlier behaviour became less compelling with the spectacle of his vehement opposition to the pleas of the besieging Nicenes. But Ambrose's initiatives,
by focusing attention upon each of the points that disqualified him from
the episcopate, at the same time invited the people to overrule them.[169]
He had not sought the nomination at the basilica, and had done his
utmost to disavow it in the immediate aftermath. But the persistence of
his supporters, as well as the encouraging failure of the Auxentians to
take any countermeasures, appear to have persuaded him that the legitimacy of a reluctant candidacy offered the best hope of salvaging himself from the wreckage of this extraordinary day.

In presenting his 'sins' for popular judgement Ambrose underwent
the first of the transformations that would make him a churchman. The
next step was to make himself the people's prisoner. Attempting to flee
to Pavia by night, he left by the appropriate gate, only to be discovered
the next morning at a *different* gate of Milan and taken into custody by
his people. It is difficult to accept that this was simply bad luck and that
Ambrose was making a genuine bid to escape.[170] Those contemporaries
who fled to avoid ordination or consecration, like Gregory of Nazianzus
or Evagrius of Pontus, were men already dedicated to the religious life
who wanted to continue their contemplation of God;[171] Ambrose, on the

169. The 'philosophy' project served to advertise Ambrose's background in
'saecularis pompa' (Paulin. *V. Amb.* 7.2), which appears to have been used
against him by Jerome (*Prolog. in Comm. in Eph.*); the arrival of the women allowed an informal equivalent to the *inspectio morum*. These episodes are discussed with much illustrative material by Duval, 'Ambroise, de son élection',
263–274, and interpreted as genuine efforts to escape.

170. *Pace* Duval, 'Ambroise, de son élection', 277.

171. Gregory fled to his ascetic friends to compose his *Apology*: cf. J. Bernardi, *SCh* 247 (1978), 29ff; Evagrius is shown meeting the Egyptian monk Am-
monius while in hiding from Theophilus: Socrates *HE* 4.23.75–76.

other hand, could not hope to find peace by flight. His abrupt departure, even had his enemies failed to exploit it against him, could easily be construed as a tacit admission of wrongdoing. His objective was more limited: to escape from a situation at his house which could not be sustained indefinitely, and to allow his 'capture'. The Porta Romana, where he was discovered, was the main triumphal route into Milan, adorned with the obligatory colonnade and other trappings.[172] Ambrose therefore returned to the city in a variant of the *adventus* ceremony. The spectacle of the governor humbled by capture, but also exalted by the divine intervention which had thwarted his plans, could hardly fail to provoke curiosity and baffle criticism.

The flight is plausibly to be assigned to the night immediately following the election. In the space of twenty-four hours, the *consularis* had therefore been divested of the trappings of his secular authority, and the circumstances of his initial involvement in the election blurred by the fast-moving events that had followed. The pace now slowed, with Ambrose imprisoned in his house but still obstinately refusing his 'destiny'. It would require the intervention of a higher authority to break the deadlock that had been contrived.

According to both Paulinus and Rufinus, Ambrose's fate was decided by a *relatio* to Valentinian: the *consularis* abandoned his resistance when the emperor ordered that the Milanese people's decision be put into effect.[173] Ambrose himself recalled the episode to Valentinian II in 386, reminding him that the people had 'asked' the emperor's father for him and that the latter had 'promised peace if the man elected should take up his episcopate'.[174]

This emphasis upon the emperor's intervention has misled historians to assume that there were serious negotiations between candidate and court. Several, taking their cue from Ambrose's remark, have imagined him presenting the emperor with his terms for accepting the episcopate.[175] But this is to misunderstand the purport of Valentinian's rescript and of the original *relatio*. Rufinus' version of the rescript plau-

172. Mirabella Roberti, *Milano Romana*, 93–95.
173. Paulin. *V. Amb.* 8.2–9.2 (esp. 9.1: 'praeceptum'); Ruf. *HE* 11.11 ('iubetur').
174. Amb. *Ep.* 77 [21].7.
175. Duval, 'Ambroise, de son élection', 278–282: 'il cherche à ne pas s'engager tant qu'il n'a toutes les garanties et autorisations nécessaires'; cf. Corbellini, 'Sesto Petronio Probo', 187–188.

sibly has the emperor attributing the people's 'sudden conversion' to unanimity to the will of God: there are no promises here, nor even a hint of the candidate's reluctance or at his imprisonment by his people. Valentinian seems as blithely unaware that there was a question to be addressed in Paulinus' account, which reports his 'joy' that a judge under his orders should be sought as bishop.

Both authors are probably citing the actual rescript, preserved in Milan as Ambrose's certificate of legitimacy. When the bishop quoted it to Valentinian II in 386 he appears to have blurred one important point in his précis: to judge from Rufinus, Valentinian had not *promised* peace but had *predicted* it. In doing so he was merely echoing the terms of the 'desiderium populi' that had been forwarded to him, the claim that the Christians of Milan would not be 'one people and one faith' unless Ambrose were given to them as their bishop. To Valentinian the case was therefore as simple as that which the prefect of Rome reported to his son in 385: the unanimous election of Siricius as Damasus' successor. The response on that occasion consisted of a summary of the prefect's message—the acclamation for Siricius and against Ursinus—and an expression of satisfaction at the result.[176] Valentinian's rescript will similarly have paraphrased a report of Ambrose's nomination and added the pious self-congratulation reported by Paulinus.

Valentinian, therefore, was deceived. Acclamations in Ambrose's favour were certainly available—from the basilica, law courts and streets—but they did not represent an authentic 'desiderium populi'. The presentation of the issue to the emperor in these terms was possible because of the yawning information gap between a fourth-century emperor and his subjects. Communications on ecclesiastical matters were not immune from manipulation. Athanasius of Alexandria was alleged to have secured recognition of his election by forging a letter to Constantine from the city's *koinon*; two years after acclamations against Ibas of Edessa had been reported to the emperor and had secured his dismissal, they were discovered to have been the work of a small minority who could command the services of a claque.[177] In Ambrose's case, too, the emperor was given a seriously distorted picture of the situation in Milan.

Valentinian's information is unlikely to have come from the bishops supervising the election, who were neither required to make such re-

176. *Coll. Avell.* 4.
177. For Athanasius, see Philost. *HE* 2.11, discussed by Hanson, *The Search*, 247–249; for Ibas, see Liebeschuetz, *Antioch*, 217–218.

ports nor sympathetic to Ambrose's cause.[178] Those of Auxentius' colleagues whose support he had retained into the 370s were the ones most likely to come to Milan to attend his deathbed and oversee his burial and succession; as familiar faces at Milan, they were also the likely recipients of invitations (and appeals for support) from the city's clergy, the group most directly interested in the proceedings.[179] Ambrose's intervention in 'their' election (which was evidently disruptive enough to prevent its resumption after his departure) and subsequent antics will hardly have appeared to them as signalling a 'divine conversion' of the Nicenes to doctrinal unity. The surprise is rather their failure to present their own version of the situation. Probably, however, the course of events leading to Ambrose's 'imprisonment' had created genuine confusion among these provincial prelates, and it was dangerous to mount a direct challenge at the faraway court against men with powerful connexions.[180]

Ambrose's connexions are the key to the eventual outcome. The most likely author of the report was the *vicarius*, the prefect's deputy in Milan.[181] His attitude to Ambrose is unknown; but there was a further link in the chain between Milan and the emperor. In Paulinus, Valentinian's 'joy' at the receipt of the report is juxtaposed with the 'delight' felt by the prefect Petronius Probus.[182] But Probus' happiness will have preceded the emperor's, for aggrandizing prefects tended to divert their vicars' business through their own offices.[183] He was therefore able to influence the manner in which the affair was presented to Valentinian. Probus, as Ambrose's patron, had his own interest in the outcome and was, besides, notoriously indulgent to the transgressions of his sub-

---

178. Soc. *HE* 4.30 ascribes the *relatio* to the bishops but explains it by Ambrose's refusal, after accepting baptism from them, to agree to consecration. He could only make sense of his source, Rufinus, by assuming, against the latter's explicit testimony, that Ambrose had been made eligible for the episcopate at the time of the *relatio*.

179. Compare the gathering of Ambrose's friends at his deathbed in 397: below, p. 367. For the clergy's role, cf. Greg. Naz. *Epp.* 40–43 on the election of Basil.

180. The fate of the critics of Romanus in Tripolis provided a contemporary object-lesson: Amm. Marc. 28.6.8.

181. The vicar received the emperor's reply: *V. Amb.* 9.1. His responsibility for examining the 'sub se iudicum flagitia ac super his referendi' is set out at *CTh* 1.14.2.

182. *V. Amb.* 8.3: 'Laetabatur etiam praefectus Probus'.

183. In 378 Gratian was to criticize one of Probus' successors for his failure to ensure that appeals from vicars reached the imperial court: *CTh* 1.15.8.

ordinates: 'His sense of honour extended so far as never to order a
client . . . to break the law, but if he discovered that any had committed
a crime he would defend him without any regard for truth and decency,
even if justice herself was crying out against him'.[184] One method of
'protection' is described by Ammianus, who reports how embassies
from Probus' provinces to the imperial court were supplied with a prepared text praising his administration. Only when the protocol of one
such ceremony was broken, after Valentinian had recognized an ambas-
sador from Epirus as an old friend and engaged him in private conversation, did the real feelings of the provincials emerge.[185] Probus, clearly,
was well practised in the arts of information management.

Ambrose was well protected, but there remained a considerable element of uncertainty. Irregular appointments, even when they were supported by the influence of the greatest men in the empire, risked exciting
Valentinian's suspicions and anger. When the general Theodosius applied on behalf of Africanus (like Ambrose, an advocate who had obtained a provincial governorship) for a further term in another province,
he received the brusque reply to 'change' the man's head instead—and
so Africanus paid with his life for 'striving, like many others, towards
higher things'.[186] With his fate placed in such unpredictable hands, Ambrose went into hiding on the estate of an aristocratic friend, Leontius,
and awaited developments there.[187] But his removal from Milan also
achieved a more positive result. As the captive of the Nicenes, Ambrose
was still the creature of a party. If he were to take the place of Auxentius,
he needed to assert a less partisan identity. Escape was therefore a further step in his transformation, turning him from the minister of the
state's terrible justice to a fugitive from it. This was a much more effective footing upon which to enter the church than amid the pomp of
secular pride that had previously surrounded him.

When Valentinian's reply finally arrived, informing the Milanese
that the emperor had discerned the voice of God in the acclamations that
had been reported to him, the *vicarius* published a stern edict to force
the fugitive from hiding.[188] Delivered over to the church (that is, the
established community of Auxentius, who still represented the 'official'

184. Amm. Marc. 27.11.4.
185. Amm. Marc. 30.5.4–10.
186. Amm. Marc. 29.3.6.
187. Paulin. *V. Amb.* 9.1.
188. *V. Amb.* 9.1. The edict was from the vicar rather than Valentinian, who
knew nothing of Ambrose's adventures and had simply issued the vague instructions 'ut insisteret rebus perficiendis'.

face of Milanese Christianity), Ambrose did not look like an ambitious opportunist or an agent of sectarian factionalism.

There was only one discordant note, ominous for the tenor of Ambrose's episcopate: his insistence that he would not receive baptism 'except from a catholic bishop', which strongly suggests that he had rejected the bishop originally proposed by his new church as heretical.[189] But once the terms of the ceremony had been arranged to the candidate's satisfaction, everything proceeded smoothly and in a manner designed to emphasize publicly the complete integration of the new bishop into his community. The process lasted a whole week, with Ambrose being baptized on one Sunday and then admitted in turn into each of the grades of the clergy—from doorkeeper to presbyter—before receiving his episcopal consecration on the next. There was nothing superficial about this procedure, which seems to have been an invention designed to attract publicity rather than an expedient to satisfy canonical regulations.[190] It served to identify Ambrose with each of the groups in his church and provided a gathering liturgical momentum for his approaching consecration. The occasion, his biographer records, was duly invested with 'the utmost grace and rejoicing among everyone'.[191]

Not everyone, however, was so impressed with this, the first of the many spectacular public relations coups that became the distinctive mark of Ambrose's episcopate. In 381, the bishop was to organize the peremptory deposition of the venerable Palladius of Ratiaria. Meditating upon the matter in a subsequent pamphlet, Palladius wondered whether Ambrose might not have learnt this casual attitude to the episcopal office from the circumstances of his own 'easily obtained, muddled and ill-considered' promotion.[192] The words seem to point to the ceremony of 7 December when Ambrose finally received his formal nomination and consecration to the episcopate. The staging of the event obviously left the presiding bishops no opportunity to conduct their traditional examination of the candidate. Palladius' tone implies that he blamed the bishops for their negligence, but he saw clearly enough that their presence was incidental to a ceremony that bypassed the disciplines of the church.

Two years before making these remarks, Palladius had already la-

189. *V. Amb.* 9.2.
190. *V. Amb.* 9.3. R. Gryson misses the point of this elaborate ceremony when he pronounces (*Le prêtre selon saint Ambroise* [1968], 225n18) that 'une pareille succession d'ordinations faites seulement pour la forme est assez invraisemblable dans le cadre de l'époque'.
191. *V. Amb.* 9.3: 'ordinatus est summa gratia et laetitia cunctorum'.
192. Pall. *Apol.* 120: 'facilem ac passivam et non libratam'.

mented that despite 'sinning against religion', Ambrose had won favour because of 'a previous error from a judge and an emperor' and was now protected from conviction for his crime by the lapse of time.[193] The passage is obscure but can be interpreted to fit the reconstruction suggested here. Ambrose's 'crime' would be his interference with the original election, which because of two 'erroneous' official responses (the vicar's misleading *relatio* and Valentinian's unconsidered reply) had been rewarded rather than punished.

But Palladius was also to offer a much more explicit analysis of how Ambrose had secured his position. Where Valentinian had detected the hand of God, he saw much more mundane forces at work. 'You were appointed irregularly and unworthily, by the good graces of your friends and through human patronage'.[194] The patronage had come from neither the people of Milan nor the careless bishops who conducted the consecration, but the machinery of the imperial administration whose subsequent deployment on Ambrose's behalf was to be a principal cause of Palladius' own downfall.[195] Palladius knew his enemy well, and although he interpreted Ambrose's accession in retrospect as the result of a successful conspiracy rather than an improvised response to a botched coup, his verdict is fundamentally correct.

193. *Apol.* 84: 'etenim in religionem peccando praeeuntis tam imperialis quam iudicarii erroris tibi conciliasti faborem, interim securus de crimine indulgentia temporis'.
194. *Apol.* 120: 'sed amicali gratia suffragio t[. .] humano passim crearis indigne'.
195. Palladius uses almost exactly the same terms in the following paragraph to describe Ambrose's collusion with a praetorian prefect: 'aeclesias Dei per humanum patrocinium . . . vasteres' (*Apol.* 121).

- CHAPTER TWO -

CONSOLIDATION

OPENING GAMBITS

Ambrose had been bishop for more than two years before he wrote his first book.[1] *De virginibus* begins with an elaborate and somewhat tangled apology. He was writing, he claimed, through fear: 'Mighty necessity' compelled him, as a bishop and therefore a 'trustee' of God's eloquence, to 'invest' that eloquence in the minds of his people; he preferred to do so in writing to spare himself embarrassment, 'for a book does not blush' (*De virg.* 1.1).

Even allowing for the self-deprecation expected from a literary novice, the images into which Ambrose tumbles seem excessive.[2] The bishop presents himself as an ass labouring under a burden of worldliness and as a thorny bush (1.2); he had remained for three years beneath a fig tree that had borne no fruit, still in the shadow of the itch of worldly pleasure: his place was a lowly one, fragile, soft and barren (1.3). There follows a more dramatic justification for his book than shyness. Ambrose was 'mute', 'unable to speak', and had taken recourse to the pen in order to overcome this disability, just as John the Baptist's father, Zechariah, had recovered his powers of speech by writing his son's name; the reader should therefore not be surprised at his 'audacity'

1. Ambrose describes himself at *De virg.* 2.39 as 'nondum triennalis sacerdos', implying a date in the summer or autumn of 377, when his third anniversary was already in sight.

2. The conventions are set out by T. Janson, *Latin Prose Prefaces* (1964), esp. 116–161.

(1.4).[3] A further defensive barrage is laid down at the opening of the second volume.

The remarkable diffidence that kept Ambrose tongue-tied for two years can be explained by the difficulties he faced in adjusting to his new office. Characteristically, he allows only the briefest glimpse of his problems, in a remark made twenty years after *De virginibus:* he noted Dionysius' good fortune in escaping by his death in exile the 'confusion' spread among the people and clergy by the teachings and practices of the heretics.[4] When Ambrose became bishop, 'heretical' teachings had had thirteen more years to become ingrained, and he possessed none of the training or experience necessary to combat them.

His 'unanimous' election had not guaranteed Ambrose the support of either Auxentius' congregation or his clergy. The latter naturally remained in place.[5] Ambrose had been appointed (and approved by the emperor) as Auxentius' successor and therefore lacked the authority to replace the existing order wholesale, which the emperors Theodosius and Valens gave, respectively, to Gregory of Nazianzus at Constantinople in 380 and the homoean Lucius at Alexandria in 373.[6] As a novice, Ambrose depended greatly on his clergy; as a Nicene, he did what he could to distance himself from Auxentius' 'establishment'. The presbyter Simplicianus, friend of Marius Victorinus at Rome and (perhaps) émigré from Auxentius' Milan, returned in time to become Ambrose's 'father in receiving grace', an enigmatic expression which seems nevertheless to refer to baptismal preparation (if not baptism itself).[7] The favour shown him by Ambrose, who 'truly loved him as a father', and the preferment granted to other dissidents helped give a new face to the

---

3. The argument is curious in view of Ambrose's responsibilities as a preacher; it might be associated with his emphasis upon the positive value of silence at *De officiis* 1.5–22, especially if the passage dates to the beginning of his episcopate.

4. *Ep. extra coll.* 14 [63].70.

5. The only explicit reference is the late but well-informed Severus of Antioch, *The Sixth Book of the Select Letters,* ed. E. W. Brooks (1904), 2:2.304, citing a letter from Theophilus of Alexandria to Flavianus of Antioch; for the reliability of the testimony, see Y.-M. Duval, 'Ambroise, de son élection à sa consécration', in *Ambrosius Episcopus* (1976), 2:243–283, at 254n44.

6. For the circumstances of Gregory's accession, see Socrates *HE* 5.7–8; Sozomen *HE* 7.5; and Gregory's own account, *Carmen de sua vita* 1325ff. There is a highly coloured account of Lucius' purge of the Alexandrian clergy in Theodoret *HE* 4.22.

7. Aug. *Conf.* 8.2.3. For *gratia* in a baptismal context, cf. *Conf.* 8.2.5 and esp. 9.5.13 (Augustine's preparations for baptism, 'quo percipiendae tantae gratiae paratior . . . fierem'); but cf. p. 51 above, for Ambrose's baptism by a bishop.

clergy; but otherwise Ambrose had to make the best of the available materials. Reshuffles were necessarily limited. One priest whom Ambrose had 'found in the clergy' was forbidden ever to walk in front of the bishop, having offended him by his 'insolent gait'; he continued to serve until, threatened with a summons before Ambrose's episcopal tribunal, he prudently 'denied that he was ours'.[8] The episode conjures up a convincing, if unpleasant, atmosphere of indirect pressure and manoeuvre.

Ambrose's concern for the dignity of his processions is nevertheless significant. At the outset he could offer the people of Milan little except gestures, but these were precisely his forte. Clergy and people, for example, benefitted from the gold and silver Ambrose bestowed upon 'the church and the poor', apparently on the occasion of his consecration.[9] This donative did not involve any imprudent liquidation of his assets: although 'given to the church', the bishop's property, which included a substantial holding in Africa, remained under his personal management. Close supervision was required, for the bishop's resources were modest in comparison to the dizzying sums available to certain aristocratic contemporaries. But the income was invested in Milan and helped to fund a building programme whose results remain impressive today. Although Ambrose's churches took years to complete, the city must have felt the bustle of the construction work from the beginning of his tenure.[10]

In thus imposing himself upon Milan, Ambrose seems to have resorted to some questionable tactics. One especially significant sleight of hand is recorded in De officiis. Recalling criticism from 'Arian' opponents for his sale of church plate, Ambrose pleaded the overriding importance of raising cash to ransom prisoners.[11] The use of church treasure for such purposes was honourable and sanctioned by tradition;[12] but this was

8. De off. 1.72. This man is to be distinguished from the deserter to the Arians during the conflict of 386, who was never a member of the clergy (below, p. 185).

9. Paulinus V. Amb. 38.4: 'in tempore quo episcopus ordinatus est'.

10. For Ambrose's churches see chap. 5; for a building already under construction in 378, see n. 92 below.

11. De off. 2.136. Another response to these criticisms, at 2.70, specifies the context: 'Illyrici vastitate et Thraciae'. This is clearly a reference to the Gothic war; but the Goths took prisoners from the outset of their rising in 376 (Amm. Marc. 31.6.7–8, 8.7–8), so Ambrose's interventions did not necessarily follow the battle of Adrianople in 378. There were also prisoners to be ransomed in Illyricum in 374/5: Amm. Marc. 29.6.6 describes an imperial princess's narrow escape from capture.

12. W. Klingshirn, 'Charity and Power: Caesarius of Arles and the Ransoming of Captives in Sub-Roman Gaul', JRS 75 (1985), 183–203.

probably not the basis of the complaints. Ambrose also mentions some less conventional outlets for the proceeds of his sales. The poor of Milan, the 'treasures of the church', seem also to have benefitted.[13] A still more dubious use is mentioned as an afterthought: 'Nobody can condemn the construction of a temple of God'. Subsequent remarks regarding burial sites confirm that the churches concerned are cemetery basilicas, like the Basilica Ambrosiana that the bishop built to house his own remains.[14] His opponents were therefore not being petulant but expressing an understandable suspicion that church funds were being diverted to enhance the bishop's personal stature. Even the ransoming of prisoners might well have smacked of opportunism: there can have been but few Milanese *cives* among the beneficiaries, and the gesture of 'smashing' the plate probably made more of an impact at Milan than did any subsequent transactions at the impromptu sales held by the Goths. The bishop's contribution might perhaps be seen as equivalent to the removal, in more recent times, of park railings in Britain in the name of a 'war effort': the symbolic sacrifice of a conspicuous public amenity. Ambrose claimed the credit personally, while using the proceeds to fund distributions to parishioners and to supplement his own means for his building programme. As a further bonus, the liquidation of the church's treasure helped dismantle the legacy of Auxentius and Constantius, who had probably supplied many of the items involved.[15]

There is a similar combination of the spectacular and the tentative, with an admixture of guile, in *De virginibus*. The book soon belies its hesitant introduction. Ambrose launches into a blood-curdling rendition of the martyrdom of Agnes, followed by an exuberant demolition of the claims of pagan virgins, a highly wrought contrast between the estates of matrimony and virginity (much to the latter's advantage) and a series of further set-pieces; a full range of biblical references gives substance to the rhetoric. But much of this dazzling exhibition, it is now known, is derivative: an Athanasian text has been shuffled and interwoven with reminiscences from Cyprian. Ambrose nods to the latter but gives no hint of his indebtedness to his Greek source, which was only revealed by a papyrus found in the present century.[16]

---

13. *De off.* 2.141. Ambrose's charity caused controversy again in 386: *Sermo contra Aux.* 33.

14. *De off.* 2.142: 'nemo potest indignari, quia humandis fidelium reliquiis spatia laxata sunt'.

15. Peter Brown, *Power and Persuasion in Late Antiquity* (1992), 96 (with the contrasting case of Rabbula of Edessa).

16. There is a fine study of Ambrose's use of his sources, with a sympathetic appreciation of his own contributions, by Y.-M. Duval, 'L'originalité du "De

There was nothing disreputable in publishing translations: Evagrius of Antioch had rendered another of Athanasius' ascetic texts, *Vita Antonii*, into Latin during a recent visit to northern Italy. Nor were they beneath a bishop's dignity: Eusebius of Vercelli had produced a version of Eusebius of Caesarea's commentary on the Psalms.[17] Ambrose's decision not to acknowledge his debts is best explained by his need to establish his own authority as a teacher. Through *De virginibus* he created a public voice of his own, learned and weighty; the later application of the same formula in adaptations of Philo, Origen and Plotinus should not blind us to the audacity of the project.

Ambrose's credentials were based ultimately upon his knowledge of Greek. His fluency in the language has been questioned, but there were few to test him in late fourth-century Italy: nobody would take up the charges of plagiarism and ineptitude subsequently voiced from abroad.[18] On the other hand, Ambrose had to meet the standard set by Auxentius, a native speaker of Greek whose service to a learned bishop at Alexandria had given him a good grounding in contemporary theology; the Milanese congregation will therefore have had certain expectations. But Ambrose worked hard at his studies, poring in silence over complicated texts during his brief hours of leisure. What is more, he was *seen* to do so. The custom of admitting visitors to these sessions of silent scholarship, attested a decade later, can plausibly be extended to the beginning of his episcopate: the people of Milan were allowed (in a somewhat contrived manner) to observe the progress their bishop, a man compelled to 'teach and learn at the same time', was making with his studies.[19] The process was driven by competition; the defensiveness with which *De virginibus* bristles suggests how hard Ambrose had to struggle to win acceptance for his theological credentials.

Ambrose also had to deal with considerable open opposition. He found it necessary to thank the emperor Gratian effusively, a full six years after his election, for 'shutting the mouths of the heretics'. A hostile

---

virginibus" dans le mouvement ascetique occidental: Ambroise, Cyprien, Athanase', in *Ambroise de Milan: dix études*, ed. Y.-M. Duval (1974), 9–66. See also G. Rosso, 'La "lettera alle vergini": Atanasio e Ambrogio', *Augustinianum* 23 (1983), 421–452.

17. Evagrius' version of the *Vita Antonii* (c. 370) is placed in a northern Italian context by J. N. D. Kelly, *Jerome* (1975), 33. Eusebius' translation is known only from Jerome *De vir. ill.* 96.

18. For reservations about Ambrose's Greek, see S. Giet, 'De saint Basile à saint Ambroise', *RecSR* 33 (1944), 95–128.

19. Aug. *Conf.* 6.3.3.

source presents this as an ordinance obtained by Ambrose specifically to muzzle those 'catholic' teachers who sought to speak out against him, so that he could escape exposure as a heretic.[20] Two notable controversialists were present in Milan during the early years of the bishop's career. An 'alliance' between Ursinus, the candidate for the papacy defeated in the bloody election of 366, and the homoean cleric Iulianus Valens is mentioned in a letter sent to Gratian by the council of Aquileia in 381.[21]

On the basis of this text, Ursinus and Valens are generally held to have established an Arian church together at Milan.[22] But although Valens' role as a homoean champion is secure, Ursinus makes an unlikely collaborator. His main platform against Damasus had been his uncompromising resistance to 'Arian heretics' during Constantius' reign; furthermore, his papal candidacy has plausibly been associated with the extreme champions of Nicaea at Rome, the Luciferians.[23] The fall from grace implied by his alleged cooperation with the Arians eight years later is inherently improbable, for Ursinus continued to enjoy enough popular support at Rome to encourage a prefect of the city in 381 to make a renewed appeal on his behalf. It was this situation which occasioned the letter from Ambrose and his colleagues. To preempt the appeal they recalled for the emperor's benefit the one Ursinian enormity which they had themselves witnessed.[24] On inspection the allegation hardly amounts to much. Ursinus had been

> coupled and conjoined with the Arians at that time, when he set about disrupting the church of Milan in his unholy alliance with Valens, sharing secret counsels in front of the synagogue doors or in the homes of the Arians, and joining his followers with them; and because he could not himself openly attend their congregations, he offered instruction and information on how the peace of the church might be disturbed.

20. *Ep. extra coll.* 12 [1].2; Palladius *Apol.* 84.

21. *Ep. extra coll.* 5 [11].3; translated below. The episode must have occurred between Ursinus' release from banishment in Gaul in 372 (*Coll. Avell.* 12.2) and his confinement to Cologne, which was long established in 378 and was probably associated with the measures taken against the 'amentia Ursini' in 376 (*Coll. Avell.* 13.2–4).

22. J.-R. Palanque, *Saint Ambroise et l'empire romain* (1933), 43–44.

23. *Coll. Avell.* 1.1; M. R. Green, 'The Supporters of the Antipope Ursinus', *JThS* n.s. 22 (1971), 531–538.

24. *Ep. extra coll.* 5 [11].6: the people of Rome had been left in suspense 'post relationem praefecti urbis'. The episode at Milan is placed firmly in the past (3: 'eo tempore . . . quo moliebatur'), which excludes the suggestion that it belonged to 381 and that long exile had made Ursinus an 'inveterate intriguer' (Green, 'The Supporters of the Antipope Ursinus', 357).

He drew strength from the Arians' frenzy, inasmuch as he was providing supporters and allies for them. (*Ep. extra coll.* 5 [11].3)

The one clear implication is that Ursinus had *not* publicly attended any
Arian assemblies. The only 'proof' of his presence at private meetings,
moreover, was the Arians' success in building up support, which was
assumed to reflect the veteran guerrilla's expert advice. This is nothing
but a smear, intended to compromise Ursinus' case for clemency by associating him with the heretics condemned by the council of Aquileia
and (at least implicitly) by the emperor himself.[25]

Ursinus' activity in Milan should instead be associated with the traditional Luciferian constituency, the uncompromising puritans who rejected a church built upon 'basilicas gleaming with gold and clothed
in the finery of expensive marbles, or raised high by magnificent columns.'[26] This reflects exactly the character of the Nicene opposition
group at Milan, the source of the disturbances that led to Ambrose's own
election. An intriguing possibility therefore emerges. The new bishop,
for all his anti-Arian credentials and the gesture of refusing baptism
from a heretic, had not allowed ideology to interfere with the practical
business of organizing his see. Retention of Auxentius' presbyters made
sound administrative sense, but one can understand the disappointment among the Nicenes when, having waited twenty years for their
restoration, they saw their victory amount to so little. Ambrose's pragmatism could be represented as betrayal, and Ursinus was by 374 the
most famous western champion of the victims of compromised ideals.

This hypothesis, constructed from a single sentence of a letter written some half-dozen years after the event, can only suggest the possible
scope of Ambrose's early difficulties. But the letter's failure to cite any
official action against Ursinus for his previous mischief-making in Milan,
despite the boost it would have given to a somewhat unconvincing case,
is also telling. We might infer that Ursinus' activities in Milan had gone
unpunished and that the exile to Cologne in 375/6, which must have
been a great relief to Ambrose, was occasioned by the excesses of his
followers in Rome.[27] For Ambrose had been in no position to take the

25. *Ep. extra coll.* 5 [11].1, reminding the emperor of his anti-Arian statutes;
accusations against Valens had been made in the council's previous letter (*Ep.
extra coll.* 4 [10].10). The charge might also have served to undermine the legitimacy of the homoean community of Milan, which was still active in 381.

26. *Coll. Avell.* 2.121 (from a 'Luciferian manifesto' published in 383); the
language shows striking similarities to Hilary *Contra Aux.* 12.

27. Ursinus' original confinement to Gaul in 368 was also perhaps a response to the disturbances caused by his followers in Rome; the references to
their 'turbulenta seiunctio' at *Coll. Avell.* 8–10 do not mention Ursinus himself.

initiative against him: as a professed Nicene trying to take over an Arian administration intact, he could not afford to provoke an ideological confrontation.

CONCERNING VIRGINS

Given his lack of theological training, Ambrose's reluctance to confront his doctrinal opponents directly was prudent. Besides, by playing too overtly to the Nicene group that had propelled him to office, he risked alienating the 'Auxentian' majority in his congregation and clergy. By addressing himself instead in his first book to 'holy virgins'—and meanwhile 'singing the praises of virginity every day' at Milan—Ambrose found an alternative theme, and in doing so he became, almost by accident, one of the principal spokesmen for a movement that was changing the western church.[28]

Ambrose hesitates to claim any authority over the virgins. In his 'second prologue' to De virginibus, almost as painful as the first, he confesses himself to be 'too weak to teach, unequal to the task of learning', but willing nevertheless to respond to a request from certain virgins that he write: he could offer them only affection, instead of the magisterial authority of Cyprian's classic treatise De habitu virginum, but would nevertheless do his best to 'ingratiate himself' (De virg. 2.1–4).[29] But of all possible episcopal roles, there was none for which Ambrose's upbringing as the son of a pious widow and the brother of a consecrated virgin had better qualified him. He puts due emphasis upon his background in De virginibus, where his boast of the family tie with the virgin martyr Soteris (which had bequeathed him an association with asceticism 'by a sort of inherited experience of ancestral virtue') stands out in sharp relief against his diffidence concerning his qualifications and professional status.[30] But above all, he had Marcellina. The final book of De virginibus is addressed directly to his sister, recalling her consecration at the hands of Pope Liberius and Soteris' gift of a 'succession to an inheritance of

28. Fundamental to the following section is Peter Brown, The Body and Society (1988), esp. chap. 12, 'Daughters of Jerusalem', 259–284. For the economics of asceticism, see R. Lizzi, 'Una società esortata all'ascetismo', Studi storici 30 (1989), 129–153.

29. Cf. De virg. 2.39–43, where Ambrose resumes the same theme in slightly more positive terms: 'licet usu indoctus, sed vestris edoctus moribus'. For Ambrose's use of Cyprian, see Duval, 'L'originalité du "De virginibus"', 21–29.

30. De virg. 2.2: 'haereditario quodam paternae virtutis usu in nos est successione transfusum'.

chastity, inspired by what a parent martyr has instilled'.[31] Marcellina, in turn, advertised her brother's book to a receptive audience at Rome.[32]

Ambrose's ascetic credentials were therefore firmly anchored in Rome. So too, perhaps, was his language. In no other Christian community of the age were women of such high status so prominent; Ambrose's imagery, in which virgins hold sway like queens, soar aloft to meet Christ and enjoy the protection of an army of angels—so different from his avowed master Cyprian's hectoring watchword, 'discipline'— seems to evoke such imperious contemporary heroines as Melania and Marcella. A more precise debt to Rome is also suggested by his dependence upon an Egyptian source. At exactly the time of his election to Milan, an invigorating wind from the desert was blowing through the city, as the exiled Peter of Alexandria, Athanasius' successor, arrived with a company of monks to teach the pious ladies of Rome the 'discipline of virgins and widows'.[33] The only recorded connexion between Marcellina and Marcella, Peter's most famous disciple, is admittedly indirect and hypothetical, but ascetic society was small and intimate.[34] It is therefore reasonable to look for an echo of recent developments at Rome in Ambrose's preaching.

Much in Ambrose's message, and especially in the style in which it was conveyed, was new to northern Italy. Female asceticism was not foreign to the region, but the prevailing pattern was for domestic, ancillary arrangements.[35] At Aquileia, for instance, the widowed mother and virgin sisters of two clergymen maintained a 'blessed household',

31. De virg. 3.37: '[soror] quam haereditariae castitatis inspirata sucessio parentis infusione martyris erudivit'.

32. Jerome's reference in 384 to the 'opuscula quae ad sororem scripsit' (Ep. 22.22) suggests how the De virginibus was marketed at Rome. Ambrose himself claims that the book was commissioned by 'pleraeque absentes' (De virg. 2.5; cf. 2.3, 'rogantibus virginibus'), behind whom we can plausibly imagine Marcellina.

33. Jer. Ep. 127.5. Cf. Kelly, Jerome, 92–94, for Peter's influence upon the aristocratic Marcella. For the impact of Melania's arrival in Egypt to fund the monks' resistance to the Arians, see Brown, The Body and Society, 280.

34. Jer. Ep. 46.7 asks Asella to convey his regards to Marcella and to a Marcellina who is plausibly to be identified with Ambrose's sister, whose ability to remember a childhood incident from c. 340 (Paulin. V. Amb. 3.3) suggests that she was a close contemporary of Asella, age fifty in 384 (Jer. Ep. 24.4). S. Rebenich, Hieronymus und sein Kreis (1992), 158n90, leaves the question open.

35. The contours of female asceticism in Italy are sketched by Duval, 'L'originalité du "De virginibus"', 54–56; see also F. E. Consolino, 'Il monachesimo femminile nella tarda Antichità', Codex Aquilarensis 2 (1989), 33–45; R. Lizzi, 'Ascetismo e monachesimo nell'Italia tardoantica', Codex Aquilarensis 5 (1991), 55–76.

a private glory to sustain their menfolk's 'public confession' against the Arians.[36] Ambrose's innovation was to parade the commitment of the daughters of his well-to-do parishioners in public. Their fellow-Christians were invited to inspect the 'signs of their prudence and the proof of their deeds' and to admire them for their victories over the prince of the world (*De virg.* 1.19); he even provided them with the necessary concomitants of aristocracy, a *patria* and lineage (1.20). His enthusiasm betrays the salesman.[37] To offer a daughter to the church, he insisted, was an investment for the whole family, whose sins would be redeemed by her merits; she would meanwhile continue to live with her parents, sparing them the pain of loss and the expense of a dowry (1.32–33).

There was room for considerable misunderstanding here.[38] For all his emphasis upon family solidarity, Ambrose was teaching the young women of Milan to repeat the heady language of their aristocratic counterparts at Rome and to resist their parents' efforts to use them as matrimonial pawns. He recalled for them the case of one girl, 'noble as the world sees it', who had taken refuge at the altar to hurl defiance at her family. 'Why do you still trouble yourselves to search for a marriage? I have long since had one arranged. You offer a bridegroom? I have found a better. Tell tall tales of a fortune, vaunt a pedigree, extol his power; I have someone with whom nobody can compare' (1.65–66). The moral of this story was that such cases could be resolved happily: the girl retained her inheritance. But tensions clearly existed, which the bishop's occasional penchant for the language of confrontation can have done nothing to defuse. Ambrose complained of his problems in finding recruits: even pious widows were refusing to allow their daughters to come forward and volunteer themselves for Christ (1.58). These overprotective mothers were urged to respect their daughters' right to a free choice in love (1.58). But however scrupulous he was in these efforts to conciliate anxious parents, Ambrose's whole enterprise necessarily led to a dangerous trespass upon the territory of the family.

The most potent source of tension concerned the status of the girl

36. Jer. *Ep.* 7.6: 'ad privatem gloriam publica haec accessit et aperta confessio'.

37. Cf. Duval, 'L'originalité du "De virginibus"', 54, on Ambrose's much lesser emphasis than his Egyptian source on the obligations of commitment.

38. F. E. Consolino, 'Modelli di comportmento e modi di sanctificazione per l'aristocrazia femminile d'Occidente', in *Società romana e impero tardoantico*, ed. A. Giardini (1986) 1:273–306, at 277–278, comments upon the contradictions implicit in the programme of Ambrose's *De virginibus*.

who had been dedicated to virginity. As far as the church was concerned, she was theirs, but the family tended to think otherwise. After
all, the ceremonies of taking vows and receiving the veil, for all their
parallels to betrothal and marriage, lacked any formal status and left the
girl physically in her parents' hands. It was therefore not surprising that
they could be tempted to reassert their authority over her if a change in
circumstances so required, or that the girls themselves might sometimes
change their minds. The penalties devised against those who revoked
their commitments show the church's helplessness to enforce its claims.[39]
Ambrose, whose own family background had not prepared him for such
conflicts (and probably left him unsympathetic to the genuine problems
that might occasion them) was obdurate in the face of defections. Soon
after the publication of De virginibus, a match was arranged for one of
his protégées, against her own will. Ambrose, a second John the Baptist,
thundered out an uncompromising message in her support: 'It is not
permitted that you should have her'.[40]

The Herods of Milan seem not to have appreciated such posturing.
We are given a fascinating glimpse of the tensions at work in Milan
when Ambrose faced these critics at the festival of saints Peter and Paul
in June 378. His sermon, which entered circulation as an appendix to De
virginibus, is conveniently (if somewhat misleadingly) labelled De virginitate.[41] The text presents him squaring up defiantly to his opponents: 'I
am not bringing any public charges against anyone, but come simply to
defend myself. For accusations have been made against me, and unless
I am mistaken it is from among you that my accusers are drawn' (De
virgt. 24). The 'defence' is a masterpiece of evasion. Ambrose's talents
as advocate and exegete harmonized perfectly, dissolving the serious

39. The problem is beautifully presented by Brown, The Body and Society,
260–262. The council of Valence, in the year of Ambrose's election, could only
delay the penance (and subsequent readmission to the congregation) of girls
'quae se voverint, si ad terrenas nuptias sponte transierint' (CCL 148, p. 39);
Pope Damasus less realistically declared the marriage of a 'virgo velata' to be
tantamount to adultery, while demanding that those who had not yet been formally veiled do penance, to redeem with tears and fasting their 'crimen admis-
sum' ([Siricius] Ep. 10.1.3–4: PL 13, 1182–1184).

40. De virgt. 11. The situation must be inferred from the text: at 10–11 Ambrose accuses the father of trying to renege upon a vow made to the church
(presumably in offering his daughter); he affirms the daughter's desire to remain
faithful to her vocation at 26.

41. The manuscript history is conveniently summed up in Cazzaniga's 1954
edition, xvii–xxii. Note that no incipit actually gives the title De virginitate; most
texts treat the work as a further instalment of De virginibus.

charge of interference in the affairs of family and property into a sustained display of biblical imagery which drenched his audience in the dizzy perfumes of the spiritual life. The material world was allowed no purchase upon this. In reply, for instance, to a complaint that he was inducing girls to dedicate themselves too young, he declared that their years should be calculated by the maturity of their modesty and the grey hairs of their *gravitas* (39). These resonant but imprecise phrases are typical of the bishop's generalized defence of asceticism (with which, as good Christians, his audience could hardly disagree); this then melts into a soaring panegyric of the virgin's life, organized as a running commentary of the Song of Songs. Upon these terms he was unassailable, and the attack necessarily rebounded: 'I fear that I might have appeared to have hired my critics to collude in a sham trial and to heap praises upon me which should belong to others' (25).

The sheer confidence of Ambrose's tone, so different from *De virginibus* of at most a year earlier, shows how much progress he had made in settling into his new role. So does the studious ease with which he deploys the fruits of his reading, the effortless dismissal of Plato with arguments borrowed from Origen.[42] His episcopal persona, too, had developed much further. He presents himself as a fisherman like Peter, revelling in his ignorance, lowliness and 'plebeian condition' (133). The *consularis* had come a long way.

The exuberant performance of *De virginitate* was needed to head off a particular crisis. It illustrates the small scale of the community within which Ambrose was at this time still working. Only after 381 would the establishment of an imperial court at Milan attract to the city the brilliant Christian elite who supplied the bishop with his most notable friends (and adversaries). That Ambrose had succeeded in forging an identity for himself within this community is evident from his self-confessed notoriety as one who 'teaches virginity and persuades very many people' (*De virgt.* 25). The balance between such assertions of leadership and the diplomacy necessary to retain the confidence of his prickly and fissile community must have been delicate. We do not know whether conciliation was necessary after the confrontation that provoked *De virginitate*; a passage in the same speech, however, shows Ambrose seeking to make amends for another case where his ascetic zeal had caused offence. He had written another work immediately after *De virginibus*, this time

---

42. G. Madec, *Saint Ambroise et la philosophie* (1974), 41–45 (Plato), 121–124 (Origen).

exalting the life of continent widowhood. Just as his first book had been presented as the response to a request from distant admirers, so too *De viduis* incorporated advice that had been sought from the bishop by a particular widow in his congregation who was considering remarriage. But in urging the better course of celibacy Ambrose had gone too far, and made the unfortunate woman's dilemma an occasion to indulge his talent for plain speaking:

> You want to marry? Fine. A simple wish is no crime. I seek no explanations. So why make up an elaborate one? If you think your purpose is a decent one, just say so; if not, keep quiet. Don't shift the blame to God, or your relations, and say that you 'need protection'. I only wish you weren't in such 'need' of willpower! And don't say that you're doing it for the children's sake, when in fact you are robbing them of their mother. (*De viduis* 58)

The woman obviously protested at what was at best in poor taste, at worst a breach of confidence. When he published *De virginitate* soon afterwards, Ambrose deigned to apologize. Digressing somewhat from his theme, a contrast between the peace of Christ and the squabbles of the marketplace, he remarked: 'And so that the widow whom we mentioned in another book might know that I was speaking to give advice, not criticism, and that I was showing concern, not cruelty; by the grace of reconciliation, may she hear these words: "in the church the widow is justified, in the market she is cheated"' (*De virgt.* 46). One might wonder how much comfort this somewhat grudging retraction gave the widow, but it at least demonstrates Ambrose's need to respond to criticism.

The case again illustrates the small size of the bishop's audience, and the ever-present danger of his rhetoric rebounding against him. It shows, too, the impossible strains created by an attempt to establish an ascetic platform at the expense of his parishioners' own domestic interests. But the two could be kept apart. Ambrose seems to have succeeded in exercising his patronage of virginity without converting the Milanese en masse to the ascetic life. One of the most dramatic means of advertising his cause was through the spectacular ceremony of *velatio*, the initiation of the new virgin by the bishop into new profession. A contemporary source well evokes the heady atmosphere of such occasions, as the initiate moved forward through the candlelit church to her 'marriage' with Christ.[43] At Milan, these ceremonies continued despite the dearth

43. Nicetas Remes *De lapsu virginis* 19–20 (where the ceremony marks the climax of the Easter celebrations); cf. Amb. *De virg.* 3.1, on Marcellina's initiation at a crowded Saint Peter's.

of local recruits. As Ambrose exclaimed to his people in *De virginibus*, 'Virgins come here to be sanctified from Piacenza, they come from Bologna, they come from Mauretania that they might be veiled here. You see a wonderful thing. I preach here, and my persuasion takes effect elsewhere. If this is so, I ought to do my preaching elsewhere, so that I might persuade *you*' (*De virg.* 1.57).

Behind this engaging sophistry there are distinct signs of engineering. Why, after all, should postulants from Bologna, which already housed a thriving community of female ascetics, have wanted to travel a hundred miles for their consecration? The bishop of Milan was, by his own admission, not yet sufficiently famous to inspire pilgrimages. It seems, instead, that the candidates who arrived from Piacenza and Bologna represented raw material for Ambrose's ceremonies, and were supplied by his friends. The bishops of the two cities, Sabinus and Eusebius, emerge by their actions elsewhere as two of his firmest supporters; both played leading roles at Aquileia in 381, where Eusebius earned Palladius' derision as Ambrose's 'assessor', the clerk of his court.[44] Eusebius had also stood beside Ambrose when he faced his critics at Milan over his enthusiasm for asceticism;[45] it is attractive to identify him with Ambrose's correspondent of that name from Bologna, who received two letters written in an elaborately teasing style that betokens considerable intimacy, although it sets a number of puzzles for the historian.[46] The recipient of the letters had a family, two of whose members, a boy and a girl, were named for Ambrose; the latter, Ambrosia, was herself sent for consecration at Milan in 392.[47]

Sabinus was the deacon of Milan who conveyed the council of Rome's condemnation of Auxentius to Athanasius in Alexandria and visited Basil in Caesarea. It is likely that he was consecrated to his see

44. Pall. *Apol.* 117.
45. *De virgt.* 129: 'adest piscator ecclesiae Bononiensis'.
46. *Epp.* 26, 38 [54–55]; the identity was accepted by Palanque (*Saint Ambroise*, 470), against M. Ihm, *Studia Ambrosiana* (1890), 53, and most subsequent scholars. *PLRE* 1 is mistaken in making him the *PPO* of Italy in 395–396 (Eusebius 32, p. 307).
47. Eusebius' family is catalogued in riddling language in *Ep.* 38 [55].1: 'Faustinus uterque tibi redditus est, nobisque utrumque Ambrosium pignus resedit. Ipse habes quod primum in patre, et quod iucundissimum est in filio minore . . . nos, quod medium inter patrem et iuniorem filium'. This suggests that Eusebius had a son, Faustinus (the 'pater' who was restored to him; this Faustinus can be identified with the recipient of *Ep.* 8 [39]), with three children, Ambrosius, Ambrosia and (the youngest) Faustinus. *Ep.* 8 [39] shows that the elder Faustinus had a sister, married with children.

by Ambrose; he certainly remained in close contact with him, reading his works prior to publication to help eliminate any 'pleasantries of the forum' which the ex-advocate had inadvertently included.[48] The conclusion that these two loyal allies were forwarding their protégées to Milan to supply Ambrose with spiritual ammunition is almost inescapable.

The processions of girls arriving up the Via Aemilia to participate in Ambrose's ceremonies could hardly fail to enhance his prestige. Still more impressive was the production of candidates from the most remote corners of north Africa, 'from the furthest parts of Mauretania, its innermost recesses and outer reaches'.[49] The bishop invited his readers to contemplate this 'sweet fruit of chastity' ripening even in barbarian breasts. Even when 'families' are all in chains, he added, chastity cannot remain captive: 'grieving the injury of servitude, it avows the kingdom of heaven'. Various interpretations have been proposed for the situation thus described, but none convince. Neither Ambrose's phraseology nor the general context allow the girls to be seen as pilgrims attracted by the bishop's fame. The references to 'captivity' also make it impossible that they were refugees from religious persecution or barbarian attacks.[50] They were themselves barbarians, and must therefore be associated with the Moorish tribes rather than their victims among the Roman provincials.

These expressions—not to mention the 'iniuriam servitutis' at which the girls had wept—should make us think of the slaves who continued to serve the Christian empire and could be found in the bishop's own household.[51] The African virgins 'brought' to Milan might therefore be imagined among the slaves who were travelling with Ambrose's brother Satyrus when he was caught in a shipwreck off Sardinia;[52] perhaps they

48. *Ep.* 32 [48].3: 'pertracta omnia, sermones vellica; si in iis non forenses blanditiae et suasoria verba, sed fidei sinceritas est, et confessionis sobrietas'; cf. *Ep.* 37 [47].

49. *De virg.* 1.59: 'ex ultimis infra ultraque Mauretaniae partibus'.

50. Pilgrims: Palanque, *Saint Ambrose*, 45; F. Homes Dudden, *The Life and Times of Saint Ambrose* (1935), 148. Refugees from persecution by Nicomachus Flavianus: *PL* 16, 205. Displaced by warfare: Y.-M. Duval, 'L'influence des écrivains africains du IIIe siècle sur les écrivains chrétiens de l'Italie du nord dans la seconde moitié du IVe siècle', *AAAd* 5 (1974), 197n23b.

51. Ambrose's brother acted as 'censor servulorum' in the bishop's household (*De exc. frat.* 1.40) and was attended by slaves during his travels (44).

52. *De exc. frat.* 1.44, for the shipwreck and Satyrus' concern for the safety of his 'servuli'; the mention of cargo ('facultates') suggests that he was on the homeward leg back to Milan. The term *deductae*, used of the Mauretanian virgins by Ambrose, recurs at *De off.* 2.138: 'captivi deducti in commercio'.

had been recruited from the family's estate in Africa (which may have been located in Mauretania itself) and so escaped the chains that bound their *familiae*—here to be understood as slave establishments—by dedicating themselves to God and to the church of Milan.

A further step would be to see these girls precisely as captives: prisoners taken in war. The corners of Mauretania had experienced bitter conflicts in the previous few years, during the revolt led by the Moorish prince Firmus against Roman rule. After two years of hard struggle, Firmus committed suicide in 375 and his forces were crushed. The slave markets of the province will for some time afterwards have been crowded with captives, many of them Christians.[53] It is not impossible that the virgins who were brought to Milan were acquired from among these unfortunates.

This can only be speculation. In *De virginibus*, nevertheless, the girls were advertised to Ambrose's readers as barbarians from the furthest reaches of the empire; as such, they allowed the bishop to proclaim his commitment to asceticism without becoming too dangerously involved in the family strategies of his parishioners. At another level, the exotic and decorative fringe which they added to Ambrose's corps of attendant virgins reflects the showmanship that he brought to his church. One cannot but be reminded of the incessant scouring of the empire's frontiers conducted by men like Symmachus for prisoners or wild beasts to display to the admiring gaze of their audiences.

THE DEATH OF SATYRUS

Women dedicated to holiness provided a set of highly visible symbols for Christian Milan. Even their deaths were charged with significance. In the autumn of 378, as the empire reeled from the news of the calamitous defeat at Adrianople, several 'holy widows' of Milan died in close succession. Their lives had been taken, Ambrose averred, to spare their 'veteran' chastity the doubtful times that lay ahead.[54] This translation of a political crisis into sexual terms—which was presumably the predominant note sounded at their funerals—well foreshadows the

53. For Firmus' Donatist supporters, see W. H. C. Frend, *The Donatist Church* (1952), 73, 198–199. The revolt is described by John Matthews, *The Roman Empire of Ammianus* (1989), 367–376, who discusses the relic of the Holy Cross apparently owned by Firmus' father, Nubel (373, on *ILCV* 1822)—a fascinating sidelight on Mauretanian Christianity.

54. *De exc. frat.* 1.67.

'siege mentality' that would become a distinctive characteristic of Ambrose's church.[55]

During the same season, on September 18, the bishop buried his elder brother, Satyrus, who had succumbed to an illness after a journey to Africa.[56] The loss was keenly felt. Satyrus had abandoned his career upon his brother's consecration to help administer the Milanese see. In doing so he broke with his past as completely as had Ambrose, surrendering not only his hopes of advancement but also his economic autonomy. The two brothers had held their inherited property in common with their sister, a sensibly practical arrangement while they remained unmarried and required only an annual income to support their political (and Marcellina's ascetic) careers.[57] Ambrose's consecration and subsequent decision to give up his property to his church ought to have occasioned the division of the patrimony, presumably into three equal shares; but this did not happen. Marcellina relinquished her portion in exchange for the usufruct, which guaranteed her financial security in the event of Ambrose's premature death while reassuring the Milanese that she was no longer in a position to alienate the family assets for a worthwhile cause.[58] Satyrus' was the greater sacrifice. He refused to marry lest it divide the family, or to make a will (even upon his deathbed) in case his choice of legatees should reflect badly upon his brother.[59] In social terms, he had in effect annihilated himself.[60] He provided instead the domestic support that allowed Ambrose to devote his full attention to his public responsibilities—a strikingly unmanly role, recalling

55. Brown, *The Body and Society*, 348.

56. J.-C. Picard, *Le souvenir des évêques* (1988), 604–607, traces the date given in the *Martyrologium Hieronymianum* to a fourth-century Milanese liturgical calendar; for a different view, see A. Ambrosioni, 'Contributo alla storia della festa di S. Satiro in Milano', *Arch. Amb.* 23 (1972), at 73–77. Picard's date excludes the contexts proposed for Satyrus' death by Palanque (early 375: *Saint Ambroise*, 488–493) and Faller (Feb. 378: *CSEL* 73, proleg., 81*–88*); he places the event (without explanation) in 377, but Ambrose's tone far better suits the crisis of the following autumn.

57. For this type of property holding, the *frérèche*, see B. D. Shaw, 'The Family in Late Antiquity' *Past and Present* 115 (1987), at 25–26.

58. Paulin. *V. Amb.* 38.5: 'reservato usufructu germanae suae'. This arrangement presupposes that Marcellina had a claim upon the estates that Ambrose donated to the Milanese church—that is, that the donation was of the *entire* patrimony rather than the bishop's own portion. Ambrose and Satyrus still shared an 'indivisum patrimonium' at the latter's death: *De exec. frat.* 1.59.

59. *De exc. frat.* 1.59.

60. For the centrality of testation to the Roman sense of identity, see K. Hopkins, *Death and Renewal* (1983), 235–247.

that played by Chromatius' sisters at Aquileia a few years previously.[61]

Prayers, however, were not Satyrus' only contributions to his brother. His most important duties seem to have concerned the supervision of the family properties, the management of which was clearly little affected by their surrender to the church. It is not easy to gauge the scale of wealth that this patrimony represented, although the personal involvement of Satyrus in a series of voyages across the Mediterranean (one of them interrupted by a shipwreck off Sardinia) suggests strongly than an effort was being made to maximize the income from limited resources.[62] Although the family's possessions were scattered across several provinces, they consisted not of vast private fiefdoms, like those of the two Melanias or Paulinus of Nola, but of isolated estates precariously held. There seems to have been a property in Sicily;[63] but the only one certainly attested—and only because of the trouble it brought—was in Africa. A certain Prosper there sought to exploit the occasion of Ambrose's consecration so as not (in the latter's words) 'to give back what he had taken'.[64] The expression is somewhat opaque, and naturally presents the issue from the bishop's point of view, but it employs the language of litigation.[65] Had Prosper taken the initiative in one of the lawsuits that were a constant feature of property management and seized a piece of disputed land?[66] The church of Milan, he might have reasoned (or indeed argued in court), was not properly equipped to contest the case. If so, he reckoned without Ambrose and Satyrus, and perhaps

61. *De exc. frat.* 1.20: 'in quo domestica sollicitudo resideret, publica cura requiesceret'; cf. Jer. *Ep.* 7.6 (n. 36 above).

62. Symmachus seems only to have visited his African properties when his tenure of the proconsulate of Africa brought him within easy reach of them: J. F. Matthews, 'Symmachus and the *magister militum* Theodosius', *Historia* 20 (1971), 122–128. Satyrus' journeys (for the plural, see *De exc. frat.* 1.50: 'quoties post naufragium . . . maria transfretavit') recall rather that of Jerome's brother Paulinianus to Stridon, in 398, to sell off the family property (Jer. *Ep.* 66.14).

63. Inferred from *De exc. frat.* 1.17 and later evidence for estates on the island belonging to the Milanese church: Cassiod. *Var.* 2.29; Greg. Mag. *Regist.* 1.80; 11.6.

64. *De exc. frat.* 1.24: 'sacerdotii mei occasione redditurum se, quae abstulerat, non putabat'.

65. *Auferre* and *reddere* are conjoined in *CTh* 4.22.2 (381), on the seizure of property: 'ilico quidem possessio ei a quo ablata est reddatur'. The other laws under this heading are also relevant, especially those dealing with the problems of absentee landlords (4.22.1, 4).

66. Prosper has often been seen as a tenant or bailiff of Ambrose's estate (L. Ruggini, *Economia e società nell'"Italia Annonaria"* [1961], 85n224); the delicacy with which Satyrus treated him suggests instead a neighbouring landowner.

without the needs that drove them. The pressure put upon Ambrose's resources by his ambitious programme of church building was noted earlier; his accession to the priesthood will therefore have heightened rather than lessened his interest in his estates and the revenue that he expected of them.[67]

For several years the case dragged on, with Ambrose and Satyrus both trying to influence Prosper. Finally Satyrus, against his brother's advice that the affair was better left to intermediaries, decided to visit Prosper in person.[68] He duly achieved a settlement whereby the villain 'paid everything' but still showed gratitude for his creditor's 'moderation'.[69] That at least was how Ambrose presented the outcome to his people, who had a direct interest in it; the implied need to conciliate Prosper might suggest terms less dramatic than unconditional surrender. Satyrus then sailed to Italy, but he fell ill in Rome. Despite this, and the alarms that had already begun to make northern Italy seem dangerous (a highly placed acquaintance, as Ambrose could not resist mentioning, advised Satyrus personally against returning to Milan),[70] he nevertheless insisted upon travelling north. Prayers at the tomb of Saint Lawrence fortified him for the journey but secured him only the respite that allowed him to die in his brother's arms.[71]

Within the class to which Ambrose and Satyrus belonged, funerals had traditionally served to define the deceased and confirm his place within his community.[72] Nor had Christianity made any significant difference to the public rituals of death and mourning. The continuities of civic life are overwhelmingly apparent in another churchman's burial of a brother.

67. A further complication might have been the strains imposed by the recent war with Firmus, which had itself been provoked partly by fiscal exactions (Amm. Marc. 29.5.2–3; Zos. 4.16.3). Ambrose's estate is plausibly to be located in Mauretania, near Caesarea; Symmachus, who also owned property there, found occasion to recommend Satyrus to his brother Titianus (*Ep.* 1.63). Cf. Duval, 'L'influence des écrivains africains', 197.

68. *De exc. frat.* 1.26. Satyrus appears to have been absent from Milan, since Ambrose gave his advice by letter.

69. *De exc. frat.* 1.24.

70. *De exc. frat.* 1.32: 'cum a viro nobili revocareris Symmacho tuo parente, quod ardere bello Italia diceretur'.

71. *De exc. frat.* 1.17–19. Ambrose's remark that Satyrus was 'neglegens frigoris' on this final leg of his journey (1.50) has been used to date the episode to winter (refs. at n. 56 above); but the word makes better sense here in its medical acceptation, as a 'chill'.

72. J. M. C. Toynbee, *Death and Burial in the Roman World* (1971), 43–61.

Ten years before Satyrus' death, the presbyter Gregory of Nazianzus (son of the local bishop) had delivered a eulogy of his younger brother, the doctor and courtier Caesarius, which adheres firmly to the rules set out in the rhetorical handbooks: vivid set-pieces decorate a carefully controlled balance between praise and lamentation.[73] The performance has frequently been condemned as mechanical;[74] but this is to ignore the setting and social context of an occasion designed to bring the deceased back to life in the imagination of his fellow-citizens and to secure him a place in their memories by commemorating the attributes and honours they most prized.

Caesarius survives, a convincing and fully rounded representative of his class and culture. Satyrus, by contrast, remains curiously anonymous in the eulogy that Ambrose delivered at his funeral and published as the first book *De excessu fratris*.[75] There is no celebration of parentage or *patria*, no list of *honores*.[76] Not that Satyrus had lacked distinction. Ambrose notes in parentheses his oratorical skill as an advocate at the prefectural bar (*De exc. frat.* 1.49); the 'enthusiasm of the provincials' whom he governed testified to his justice (58). But these details (which suggest a career exactly parallel to his own) were incidental to the bishop, who concentrated upon his own relationship with his brother, recalling their intimacy and giving moving expression to his sense of bereavement.

The contrast with Gregory's speech has been explained by the greater depth of Ambrose's feelings for his brother, which caused him to give unrestrained vent to his love and grief.[77] But his speech is as highly structured and complex as Gregory's on Caesarius and must similarly be appreciated as a public performance. The difference lies in the setting: the funeral has been shifted from the forum to the church. Am-

---

73. Greg. Naz. *Or.* 7; discussed in J. Bernardi, *La prédication des pères cappadociens* (1968), 108–113.

74. Gregory's approach has often been compared unfavourably with Ambrose's: H. Savon, 'La première oraison funèbre de saint Ambroise', *REL* 58 (1980) 370–402, suspects in Gregory's expressions of grief that 'l'orateur sacrifie ici beaucoup moins au chagrin qu'aux bienséances et aux règles de l'*epitaphios*' (397).

75. The second book consists of the speech Ambrose delivered at the graveside a week after the funeral (cf. below, p. 77).

76. The difference in the biographical information supplied by the two eulogists is readily apparent in the entries in *PLRE* 1 for Satyrus and Caesarius (pp. 809; 171). For *patria* and *parentes* as the proper subject matter for a *laudatio*, see *De virg.* 1.20.

77. C. Favez, *La consolation latine chrétienne* (1937), 19, proclaims 'la sincérité de la douleur' and 'l'extraordinaire affection qu'Ambroise y exprime à chaque

brose's farewell to Satyrus is delivered as a sermon and incorporated into the liturgy; the biblical lesson of the day echoes throughout the text.[78] Ambrose therefore acts not only as a brother but also as bishop, presenting Satyrus to God as 'a brother's offering, a priest's sacrifice' (80). This was a far more potent part than Gregory had claimed for himself, and it necessarily transformed Satyrus' position. He became, in effect, an instrument of Ambrose's priesthood. Drained of all colour and individuality, Satyrus appears over and again as a complement to Ambrose himself, as his advisor, comforter and supporter (20). He becomes almost an inverse image of Ambrose, defining his episcopate by the responsibilities he had assumed for domestic discipline and debt collection, tasks too sordid for the clergy (41). In Satyrus we see only the bishop's shadow, who never took a step without him or disagreed over a single point (21); the two were even mistaken for one another, with various amusing consequences (38). The incidents are doubtless authentic, but the choice of perspective places Ambrose at the centre of the occasion, to the extent that he seemed to be burying part of himself (6).[79]

Within this framework, the external details of Satyrus' life became irrelevant. Only at the very moment of his death are we given a clear picture of him (19). Funeral speeches conventionally noted the timeliness of a man's departure,[80] but there are no obvious parallels for Ambrose's relentless recourse to the theme. It becomes the hinge upon which the various movements of the oration are articulated, recurring in particular at the close of both main sections of the formal lament. The refrain that Satyrus was 'happy in so opportune a passing' (31–33) introduces a graphic depiction of barbarian savagery (with the violation of virgins given special emphasis) and is resumed after a survey of his virtues (64).[81] There was no escape from the shadow of fear that lay over Milan in late 378: one important aspect of Satyrus' funeral was as an outlet for the people to express their own anxieties and sorrows.

But Ambrose announces, at the very opening of his speech, a greater

---

page pour son frère'; Savon's more sophisticated treatment—adducing the elegaic tradition—makes similar assumptions.

78. For this crucial point, see Y.-M. Duval, 'Formes profanes et formes bibliques dans les oraisons funèbres de saint Ambroise', *Entretiens Hardt* 23 (1977), 235–291, at 239–260, to which the following is much indebted.

79. 'Melior mei portio': cf. 80, 'haec mei . . . libamina'.

80. Favez, *La consolation*, 67–68.

81. Duval, while rejecting too precise a formal analysis of the speech ('Formes profanes et formes bibliques', 239–243), notes the significance of these junctures (244–246).

significance for the timing of his brother's death: it had been not only fortunate but also providential. In introducing the 'sacrificial offering' laid out on the bier as the instrument of the congregation's own salvation, moreover, Ambrose immediately directs attention away from his brother towards himself, and towards his ability to bear personally the sufferings of his whole people.

> I have always prayed that if there were any upheavals in store for the church or for myself, they should rather fall upon me and my household. Therefore, thanks be to God that in this time of universal dread, when because of barbarian invasions everything is a source of apprehension, I have settled the community's griefs by my own private loss, and the calamity which I feared for you all has been turned upon myself. And I pray that it should be hereby fully accomplished, that my grief should serve to ransom the people from their sorrows. Indeed I had no worldly possession, dearest brothers, more precious than such a brother, none more beloved, none dearer: but public matters take precedence over private concerns. My brother's own opinion, too, if anyone were to inquire into it, was that he would prefer to die for others than to live for himself. For that is why Christ died in the flesh for all of us, that we should learn to live not merely for ourselves. (1–2)

Satyrus is at once an exemplar of the Christian life and of Christian sacrifice, the instrument of Milan's deliverance.

The interplay adumbrated in this passage between public and private, family and city, is maintained throughout the speech. Satyrus had been the glory not only of his own family but of the whole *patria* (27); in death he became the common property of Milan, the city's talisman. 'You were taken from me', Ambrose consoled himself, 'that you might belong to everyone' (6). The bishop, too, had gained a new family. In the 'tears of the whole city, the prayers of all age groups and all social ranks', he saw the expression of almost a 'new form of family loyalty': 'nova quadam pietate'.[82] The tears of the *plebs sacra*, moreover, did not merely show their individual sorrow but amounted to the performance of a public service to ensure Satyrus' salvation: 'quoddam publicae officium et munus . . . gratiae' (28). Their contribution would provide the dead man with the connexions he needed to face the dread—and to the audience all too familiar—tribunal that awaited him (29).[83] This was a

82. Cf. 5, explicating the tears of the rich, old and young, and the 'lacrimae redemptrices' of the poor; the change from the second to the third person when speaking of the poor helps define Ambrose's audience.

83. The language of contemporary social relations informs this whole paragraph. Satyrus, having won the 'patrocinium' of the apostles through the tears

very different approach to the audience than Gregory's. Ambrose appealed neither to familiarity with the deceased and his background, nor to a holiday mood and anticipation of a rhetorical treat; his listeners were members of a church, performing a formal, collective act under his supervision.

If the congregation's supporting role was vital to the occasion, it did not overshadow the bishop's virtuosity. The rhythm of *De excessu fratris* is of a quite different order from other examples of its genre. It is pervaded by the vocabulary of mourning: *maeror, dolor, fletus, lacrima* and their derivatives occur no fewer than 149 times in the eighty short paragraphs of the work. Expressions of grief dominate the architecture: passages begin and close with confrontations between the speaker and his sorrow. 'Why do I weep?' (4); 'Where am I heading in my unmeasured grief?' (9); 'But the fault that we have committed with our tears is not serious' (10); 'My tears will therefore cease' (70, 72); 'My tears themselves are sweet' (74). The fond recollections of the brothers' relationship are charged with the same intensity, being presented throughout in physical terms of constant contact, embraces and kisses (8, 19, 23). A solemn, public kiss of farewell provides an entirely appropriate climax to the performance.

Much here is theatre. The speech has often been used as evidence for Ambrose's emotional nature;[84] such treatments fail, however, to recognize the skill with which these emotions are harnessed to support the bishop's statements about his own and his brother's importance for the community. The type of rhetoric outlined in the handbooks and employed with such fluency by Gregory assumes local roots and was therefore inappropriate for the commemoration of one newcomer to a city by another. The distinctive style of *De excessu fratris* therefore reflects the difference between Ambrose's situation and Gregory's: Satyrus' funeral served not so much to confirm the family's position in Milan as to establish it. His brother's tomb would anchor Ambrose in his adopted home: 'I have now begun not to be a stranger (*peregrinus*) here, where the better part of me lies' (6).

---

of 'tota civitas', arrives 'commendatus' for judgement before Christ and can therefore escape the tortures of death, 'divinae potestatis auctoritate'. The passage is set in its cultural context by Peter Brown, *The Cult of the Saints* (1981), 65–66.

84. Even Duval's exemplary treatment succumbs, presenting the oration as a 'véritable traitement homéopathique': 'Formes profanes et formes bibliques', 253–254.

The question of Ambrose's position within the Christian community at Milan informs the whole oration. Satyrus' funeral came only three months after Ambrose had confronted the opponents of his ascetic teachings with his *De virginitate,* and the issue of the bishop's leadership provides a theme to connect the two occasions. As his people listened, Ambrose debated with himself the same question of his responsibilities and competence as a teacher that had so exercised him when he wrote *De virginibus.* At one point, he pulled himself away from his lament with a sharp reminder to himself, put in the mouth of personified 'Scripture': 'Is this what you teach, is this how you instruct the people of God? Do you not know that the example you set puts others in danger?' (65). Earlier in the oration, he had recalled Paul's injunctions against mourning and asked his audience to excuse the poor example he was setting. He claims for himself a curious version of Pauline authority: unlike the apostle, he was not in himself a model for imitation, but set an example by his efforts to imitate him. 'We are not all suitable as teachers', he acknowledged, 'but we can all, let us hope, show an aptitude for learning' (9). His leadership could still only be moral rather than doctrinal; we might suspect that he remained reluctant to engage his enemies on the latter front. The one theological point raised in the oration—the full divinity of the incarnate Christ, an issue suggested by Jesus' tears—is left undeveloped.[85] Though much remained to be said on the subject, Ambrose explained, his present business was to provide consolation, not instruction (11–14).

The passage nevertheless reminds us that there were still important arguments to be won in Milan. To prevail in such debates, Ambrose needed to predispose his audience in his favour. This overriding need, rather than a uniquely intense fraternal affection, should explain the remarkable character of *De excessu fratris,* above all its extraordinary focus upon the speaker and his position. At one level, Satyrus' death was a godsend, giving Ambrose a privileged platform from which to address his people; he could thus assert a role for Satyrus—and for himself. If the message was audacious, there was nothing new in the method. Among the Roman elite, where the dead had always provided political ammunition for their kin, extravagant attentions to the departed often betoken a certain precariousness.

The need to establish his own credentials also explains another unusual feature of Ambrose's work. As published, it consists of two books,

85. The cautious, and strictly ecclesiological, polemic against the Luciferians (47) was perhaps a response to Ursinus' earlier activity at Milan.

the second being a speech delivered at the sepulchre one week after the funeral. The scene is still dominated by Satyrus, who again provides the occasion and the theme. But although Ambrose is ostensibly speaking to console himself, the audience is on this occasion treated to an unashamed parade of learning and linguistic dexterity. Cicero and the Bible are quarried with equal thoroughness to provide a series of vivid tableaux, ranging from the sexual undertones of pagan funerals to Lazarus' stumbling blindly from his tomb.[86] The theology, too, is secondhand, directed to targets comfortably uncontroversial. The beliefs of the 'poets and philosophers' on death are pilloried remorselessly, and the oration reaches its climax in an unravelling of the absurdities of metempsychosis, as Ambrose shakes his head sorrowfully at its exponents: 'I would prefer you to have a better opinion of your own worth, that you could believe yourselves destined to live, not among beasts, but in the company of angels' (De exc. frat. 2.131). A Christian audience could be gratified by so thorough a confirmation of their own superiority.[87] The effect was clearly encouraging for the bishop, who circulated a written version of both speeches under the somewhat misleading title of libri consolationis et resurrectionis.[88] The two complemented each other nicely in this published edition, the elaborate exegesis of the second sermon being 'sealed' by the intense personal stamp of the first. Thirty years later, when there was no longer any question as to Ambrose's authority as a teacher, the work remained in circulation as a doctrinal text, the opus de resurrectione.[89] By then, the tensions that had constrained Ambrose to circulate his teachings only upon the pretext of a private occasion had long since disappeared.

The De excessu fratris therefore offers important evidence for the techniques by which Ambrose established himself in Milan and suggests the difficulties he had to overcome. Above all, it shows him building a relationship with his people. Satyrus' funeral allows us to observe the moulding of the bishop's authority over his congregation, the basis for his successful defiance of the imperial government seven years later. In Ambrose's handling of the occasion we can glimpse the performing skills that were central to his success.

There was also a physical aspect to the performance. Satyrus was

86. De exc. frat. 2.12, 78.
87. The inference that Ambrose was preaching to a largely pagan audience (J. Mesot, Die Heidenbekehrung bei Ambrosius von Mailand [1958], 59) ignores the conventions of rhetoric.
88. Expl. Ps. 1 51.
89. Aug. De peccato originali 41.47.

buried in the *martyrium* of Victor, one of Milan's prized collection of imported martyrs; his sarcophagus was placed directly adjacent to the saint's.[90] Ambrose composed his epitaph, celebrating this intimacy in vivid language while ensuring recognition for his own part:[91]

> To Uranius Satyrus, his brother Ambrose
> Accorded the distinction of burial at the martyr's side.
> This the reward for his goodness, that the holy blood
> Should seep through and wash his remains, which lie beside.

The massive Basilica Ambrosiana that was eventually to overshadow Victor was perhaps already rising beside the chapel;[92] Satyrus served in death to stake the family's claim to this holy site. But in return, Ambrose surpassed even Gregory of Nazianzus in earning immortality for his brother. The anniversary of Satyrus' death was being celebrated by the Milanese church some twenty years later, and he emerged in due course as a full-fledged saint, whose cult has endured.[93]

90. The archaeology of the present chapel of San Vittore in Ciel d'Oro is discussed by A. Palestra, 'I cimiteri paleocristiani Milanesi', *Arch. Amb.* 28 (1975), at 25–26.

91. Uranio Satyro supremum frater honorem
   martyris ad laevam detulit Ambrosius.
   Haec meriti merces ut sacri sanguinis umor
   finitimas penetrans adluat excubias. (*ILCV* 2165)

92. Ambrose was engaged in constructing a church in 378; Satyrus chided him for his delays (*De exc. frat.* 1.20) when he returned from his last voyage. It seems more likely that Ambrose chose to bury Satyrus at a site he was already developing than that his interest in the area was awakened by the funeral. For the latter view, dating the commencement of Ambrose's basilica to c. 379, see R. Krautheimer, *Three Christian Capitals* (1983), 79; M. Mirabella Roberti, *Milano Romana* (1984), 120.

93. For the fourth-century commemoration, see above, n. 56. For the cult of Saint Satyrus established by Archbishop Anspertus in the ninth century, see Ambrosioni, 'Storia della festa di S. Satiro'.

CHAPTER THREE

AMBROSE AND GRATIAN

THE CHRISTIAN PRINCE

A year after Ambrose had buried his brother, he welcomed the twenty-year-old emperor Gratian, ruler of the west since his father Valentinian's premature death in 375, to Milan. The next four years would see Ambrose become, through his association with the emperor and his court, a figure of empire-wide importance. He is conventionally presented in a relationship with Gratian both intimate and influential, as his 'guide, philosopher and friend'.[1] Doubts have been raised over the initial scope of this influence, but Ambrose's eventual ascendancy over the emperor is still universally—and mistakenly—accepted.[2]

Only one source actually shows Gratian and Ambrose together. Sozomen describes how Ambrose interceded on behalf of a pagan senator under sentence of death: the bishop interrupted a private hunting exhi-

---

1. R. P. C. Hanson, *The Search for the Christian Doctrine of God* (1988), 795. A recent statement of the conventional view is R. Gryson, introduction to *Scolies Ariennes sur le concile d'Aquilée* (1980), 105–130; cf. A. Paredi, 'Ambrogio, Graziano, Teodosio', *AAAd* 22 (1982), 1:17–28.

2. The two most important critiques of Ambrose's initial influence are P. Nautin, 'Les premières relations d'Ambroise avec l'empereur Gratien', in *Ambroise de Milan*, ed. Y.-M. Duval (1974), 299–244, and G. Gottlieb, *Ambrosius von Mailand und Kaiser Gratian* (1973). Both nevertheless see the emperor succumbing quickly, in late 378 (Nautin, 244) or upon the receipt of *De fide* (Gottlieb, 44); cf. J. F. Matthews, *Western Aristocracies and Imperial Court* (1975), 187–188, where Ambrose has 'secured Gratian as a defender of the Catholic faith' by the end of 378 and thereafter enjoys his 'willing collusion'.

bition at the palace and carried his suit against the initial resistance of
'the emperor and his entourage'. The episode, which belongs to the last
year of the reign, shows Ambrose having to resort to uncomfortable
trickery to gain access to the emperor: even at this late date, intimacy
cannot be taken for granted.[3]

Evidence for the relationship derives almost entirely from Ambrose
himself. It amounts to a formidable mass of documentation: five books
de fide, 'on the faith', commissioned by the emperor and dedicated to
him as he set forth to war against the Goths; a warm exchange of letters;
three further books on the Holy Spirit, which emerged from this correspondence and were again addressed to Gratian; and generous acknowledgement of Ambrose's merits (and timely advice) in an imperial
rescript. Ambrose also pays several warm posthumous tributes to Gratian's piety and to their friendship.

The impressive solidity of all this is deceptive. Those honoured with
the opportunity to address the throne tended to flaunt—and thereby
exaggerate—their intimacy with the sovereign.[4] Routine imperial correspondence was littered with compliments and declarations of affection.
The false conclusion invariably drawn from this material—that Gratian
actually shifted from his father's nonsectarian pragmatism to an activist
commitment to the doctrines preached to him by Ambrose—is, moreover, dependent upon the false premise that he was a potential recruit
for the cause from the outset, as a zealous Nicene for whom Ambrose's
'Arian' enemies were anathema. Gratian never subscribed uncondition-
ally to any of the partisan labels bandied about by his churchmen; the
actions of his government were determined as much by the constraints
that operated upon the decision-making process as by his own initiatives
or Ambrose's influence. The many differences between Gratian's religious policies and his father's, and the shifts that occurred during his
own reign, are to be explained by changed political circumstances rather
than capitulation to Ambrose's dominating personality.

No regime in the Christian empire was less priest-ridden than that
of Valentinian I. The court of Trier, where Gratian grew to manhood,
presented a notoriously bleak face to visitors with its vehement displays
of imperial temper, harsh (and highly public) punishments, and pet
man-eating bears.[5] The clergy, too, appear to have been intimidated. No

3. Soz. HE 7.25.10–13.
4. T. D. Barnes, Constantine and Eusebius (1981), 265–267, discusses the fal-
sity of the impression given by Eusebius of Caesarea of his close relationship
with Constantine.
5. There is an excellent sketch of Valentinian's Trier in Matthews, Western
Aristocracies, 48–54.

Christian emperor ever spent so long in Gaul or achieved so much there as Valentinian, but he was remembered by its churchmen as being 'ungentle and proud'.[6] This ungentle pride consisted largely of a keen vigilance against clerical aggrandizement: an illicit appeal to the court by the Gallic bishop Chronopius incurred a fine (to be paid, appropriately, to the poor), and even the bishop of Rome was subjected to a public dressing-down.[7]

Valentinian was not entirely immune to clerical pressure. Martin of Tours successfully presented a petition at court shortly after his election (in 370/1). The account of the mission which circulated among his disciples nevertheless presents Valentinian, true to his image, refusing initially to see Martin and—when the saint finally obtained access through the power of prayer—'roaring' out a question at him. The forbidding front presented by the regime could not be penetrated without divine assistance: an angel led Martin past locked doors to Valentinian, who refused to budge from his throne until prodded by a minor miracle.[8] More prosaically, a churchman undeterred by the daunting facade of imperial power could hope to find allies at Valentinian's highly Christian courts. Doors might be opened, perhaps, by palace guards, like those entrusted with the arrest of the *notarius* Palladius in about 373, who left their prisoner unguarded to celebrate a festival at an all-night vigil, allowing him to escape them by suicide.[9]

Another devout Christian at the court was Jerome, a Pannonian like Valentinian (and Martin), whose career for a short time ran parallel to Ambrose's. After his studies at Rome, he apparently enrolled at the bar of the praetorian prefecture of Gaul at Trier, perhaps during the tenure of yet another Pannonian Christian, Viventius. For Jerome, who had received baptism before leaving Rome, service at court seems to have provided a useful preparation for a commitment to asceticism. He had access to theological literature, and nurtured his vocation with his companion Bonosus.[10] The quietness with which the two friends slipped away from Trier, so different from the fanfares attending the other great

6. Sulp. Sev. *Dial.* 2.5.6: 'inmitem ac superbum' (followed by a quite unfounded allegation of subservience to the influence of his Arian wife, Justina).

7. *CTh* 11.36.20 (July 369); 16.2.20 (July 370).

8. Sulp. Sev. *Dial.* 2.5.7–9: cf. Matthews, *The Roman Empire of Ammianus* (1989), 269.

9. Amm. Marc. 28.6.27.

10. For this stage of Jerome's career, see S. Rebenich, *Hieronymus und sein Kreis* (1992), 32–41, emphasizing the decisiveness of Jerome's decision to abandon his career and suggesting that the famous dream described in *Ep.* 22.30 belongs to its immediate aftermath. Jer. *Ep.* 5.2 mentions his transcription while at Trier of two works by Hilary.

'departures' of Jerome's career, suggests that their conversion aroused little controversy.

The church impinged remarkably little upon this highly Christian court. No longer did bishops gravitate towards Trier as they had in the reign of Constans. When Peter, Athanasius' successor in Alexandria, was expelled from his see, he sought refuge in Rome; the pope had also received an earlier delegation of eastern bishops, who eventually abandoned their plan to visit Valentinian in Gaul.[11] This reflects in part Valentinian's success in discouraging petitioners; but without the stimulus of direct involvement in wider affairs, the Gallic church also seems to have lost its political momentum. The bishops failed to sustain their sporadic resistance to imperially sponsored Arianism into the 360s. Their last contribution to the struggle was Hilary's council of Paris in 361; but even there the bishops appear to have done nothing more than accept the congratulations of the eastern homoiousians, conveyed by Hilary, upon the correctness of their beliefs. Like their compatriot M. Jourdain, perhaps, they were flattered to learn that they had been preaching orthodoxy all their lives, in which case Valentinian's success in maintaining a nonpartisan religious policy should be attributed not only to the strength of his own determination but also to the indifference of the local episcopate. The one document to illustrate the activities of the Gallic church under Valentinian, the proceedings of the council of Valence in 374, shows it to have been preoccupied with matters of discipline and protocol.[12]

For theological awareness and sophistication, after Hilary's death in 367 we have to look to the court itself and to the poetry of the rhetorician Ausonius. Ausonius' Christianity has received a welcome rehabilitation, and few now doubt the sincerity of his faith.[13] But the argument has been carried too far, to define his beliefs strictly in terms of Nicene orthodoxy. There were no priests to direct Ausonius' morning devotions in his private chapel; his allusions to doctrinal formulae in his prayer show familiarity with current concepts rather than a commitment to any particular creed and suggest a nonpartisan deployment of theological language to suit his own conceptions.[14] Ausonius also expresses the

11. Socrates *HE* 4.22 (Peter); 12 (Embassy of Eustathius). Cf. Soz. *HE* 6.19, 9.

12. A *discidium* is mentioned at the beginning of the council's synodal letter, without further elaboration (*CCL* 148, ed. C. Munier, p. 37); the canons published by the council are all disciplinary and of purely local scope.

13. See above all R. P. H. Green, *The Works of Ausonius* (1991), pp. xxvii–xxviii and in his commentary upon individual works.

14. Green claims Ausonius for the Nicenes on the strength of his prayer at *Ephemeris* 3 (*Works*, pp. 250–259); but the decisive phrase quoted from the Nicene

public self-confidence of the Christian laity of Valentinian's court in the poem he produced for an Easter celebration.[15] The clergy are absent even here, attention being focused instead upon the baptismal candidates and especially the 'everlasting reverence' maintained by Ausonius and his fellows in the congregation.

The doctrinal allusions with which the poem is studded seem almost deliberately teasing. The Son's relationship to the Father is characterized in immediate succession by the apparently homoean 'similar' and the much stronger 'equal'; Ausonius then introduces the vibrant phrase from the Nicene creed 'ex vero verum', but leaves his listeners to complete it for themselves: Was Christ true God from true God, or the true Son of the true Father?[16] But what must have struck the audience most was the closing prayer, with its brilliant application of trinitarian language to the political economy of the empire. Valentinian, like God the Father, is the *sator* of the two other Augusti, 'enfolding' both brother and son in his holy embrace. The assumptions implicit in the image are unmistakably 'Arian', the Father's supremacy underscored by the expression 'solus omnia habens' applied to Valentinian, which recalls Arius' own emphasis upon the exclusive qualities of the Father.[17]

One function of Ausonius' imperial trinity is to rationalize the

---

creed is left incomplete, and the creed of Rimini itself acknowledged Christ's generation 'before all ages' (cf. *Eph.* 3.9–11, 'anticipator mundi . . . generatus in illo/tempore cum tempus nondum fuit', and Green, *Works*, p. 252). The epithets used for Christ at 80–83, which avoid direct comparison with the Father, were also acceptable to homoeans: cf. n. 138 below for 'dominus et deus'.

15. J. L. Charlet, 'Théologie, politique et rhétorique', in *La poesia tardoantica* (1984), 259–287, presents a perhaps overpoliticized interpretation of *Versus Paschales*; Green, *Works*, pp. 269–273, errs in the opposite direction.

16. *Vers. Pasch.* 17–18: 'similemque paremque,/ex vero verum vivaque ab origine vivum'. Cf. Auxentius in Hilary *Contra Aux.* 14; for the scriptural basis of this reading, see Palladius *Apol.* 100. The required nouns are both supplied by *Vers. Pasch.* 16: 'tu natum, pater alme, tuum, verbumque deumque'. Note *Ephemeris* 3.82: 'filius ex vero verus'.

17. *Vers. Pasch.* 24–28. Green, *Works*, pp. 272–273, defends Ausonius' orthodoxy by minimizing the parallel, arguing that the 'twin Augusti' are Gratian and the infant Valentinian II. But Valentinian was not made an Augustus until after his father's death, and it would be highly presumptuous to claim the rank for him in the formal court setting implied by the poem. Green's reading of the imperial college's 'trina pietas' (*Vers. Pasch.* 29: 'their devotion to their three partners is threefold') is also forced. The poem perhaps belongs to before Valentinian II's birth in 371, removing any possible ambiguity.

anomalous and unprecedented promotion of Gratian to the rank of Augustus.[18] Valentinian went to considerable lengths to advertise his son's dynastic position and therefore to ensure continuity after his death;[19] but his plans were to a large extent thwarted by the circumstances of his premature death, by a stroke, in November 375 when Gratian was still only sixteen. More serious than the timing was the geography, for Valentinian had left his son behind at Trier when he set out for Illyricum for his campaign against the Sarmatians. A smooth transmission of power was therefore impossible: the unified power structure over which Valentinian had presided disintegrated in the ensuing confusion.

Valentinian's infant son was swiftly presented to the army, who hailed him as Valentinian II, a fellow-Augustus for his half-brother Gratian. The proclamation, ostensibly made in the latter's interest, to pre-empt a possible usurpation, was nothing less than a coup against the ministers currently entrenched around him. The original instigators, Equitius and the inevitable Petronius Probus, both had dangerous enemies at court; secret negotiations secured them the support of the ambitious general Merobaudes.[20] With a legitimate Augustus at their disposal and Valentinian's army at their back, the conspirators were able to dictate to Trier. The civilian officials who had been the chief instruments of Valentinian's 'terror', Maximinus, Leo, Simplicius and Doryphorianus, had all been eliminated within a year of the emperor's death, after a struggle in which Gratian's own part is unrecorded. But the most ominous feature of the outcome, and one which set a pattern for the future of the western empire, was the ascendancy of Merobaudes: with one of his two chief colleagues executed and the other eclipsed in the aftermath of the coup, and with a weakened civilian establishment, he enjoyed an unprecedented influence over the regime's strategy.[21] His stature was confirmed by his first consulship in 377.

18. The peculiarities of Gratian's position are well brought out by A. Pabst, *Divisio Regni* (1986), 94–97.

19. For Gratian's participation in the Solicinium campaign of 368, see Amm. Marc. 27.10.6; for other advertisements, see Symmachus *Or.* 3 (cf. Matthews, *Western Aristocracies*, 32–33) and *ILS* 771.

20. For the 'official version' of these events, see Amm. Marc. 30.10. Probus' involvement is noted by Rufinus *HE* 11.12, Equitius' by Aur. Vict. *Epit.* 45.10. Court antagonisms are reported at Amm. Marc. 29.6.3 (Equitius), 30.5.10 (Probus).

21. Sebastianus, cast as a potential usurper in 375 (Amm. Marc. 30.10.3) and subsequently transferred to the east (31.11.1), is presented as a victim of intrigue in Eunapius fr. 47 (44.3 Blockley). For the death of the *magister equitum* Theodosius, see A. Demandt, 'Der Tod des älteren Theodosius', *Historia* 18 (1969), 598–626.

Merobaudes' success in shaping Gratian's court to his satisfaction, however, led to the redundancy of the Augustus that he had himself created. Valentinian appears to have grown up in the palace of Trier, cared for by his brother but denied the equality in rank to which he was entitled.[22] His mother, the formidable Justina, was not present to press his interests; a likely reason is the presence among Gratian's advisors of the latter's own mother, Marina Severa, whom Justina had supplanted as Valentinian's wife.[23] With Gratian newly married and looking forward to heirs who would join his own line with that of Constantine, the boy's prospects must have appeared slight.[24] He was a mere shadow, dependent upon his brother's prowess and generosity even for the gilding of his statues.[25]

The last point we owe to Ausonius, who also offers a felicitous rationalization of Valentinian's place in the new scheme. Gratian had 'summoned' his half-brother to the purple, 'as though he were his son'; better still, he had co-opted him into the imperial college, like a priest of the old republic. Ammianus, whose account of Valentinian's accession shows the influence of a government version, uses exactly the same expression. The historian could only hint that Gratian had perhaps been excessively pious, 'gentle and dutiful as he was', in thus supervising his kinsman's upbringing.[26]

Ausonius could speak with authority. He emerged as the most spectacular beneficiary of the new regime, enjoying several years of dizzy eminence during which he disposed the prefectures and provinces of the west seemingly at will among his relatives and friends.[27] Gratian's affection for his former tutor was doubtless an important aspect of this

22. Gratian 'educated' Valentinian (Amm. Marc. 30.10.6), which should mean that he supervised his upbringing directly. The Gallic coinage consistently gives Valentinian the unbroken legend of a merely titular Augustus (J. W. C. Pearce, *The Roman Imperial Coinage* 9 [1953], 20–23, for Trier), while more distant mints present him as a ruling emperor either consistently (Rome: Pearce, 122–123) or intermittently (Aquileia: 96–97). The Illyrican mints reflect the Gallic model (Siscia: 148–149; Thessalonica: 178–179).

23. Amm. Marc. 28.1.57 shows Severa urging the execution of Doryphorianus. Justina's subsequent presence in Sirmium (Paulin. *V. Amb.* 11.1) implies that she had remained in Illyricum.

24. Gratian married Constantia, the teenage daughter of Constantius II, c. 374: Amm. Marc. 29.6.7.

25. Aus. *Epigr.* 5.

26. Aus. *Grat. Act.* 2.7; 10.48 ('in cooptando fratre'); Amm. Marc. 30.10.4 ('cooptandus in imperium'); 30.10.6 ('pietate nimia dilexit').

27. The 'Ascendancy of Ausonius' is analyzed by Matthews, *Western Aristocracies*, 56–87, and by H. Sivan, *Ausonius of Bordeaux* (1993), 119–141.

ascendancy, especially after the sudden disappearance of so many figures familiar from his father's reign. But the purge had also increased
Ausonius' political value as one of the few surviving representatives of
continuity;[28] his expertise also became indispensable in maintaining the
public tone of the new regime as Gratian's most creditable attainment,
his classical education, was pressed into service to define a new style of
government. Ausonius himself evokes the tone of Gratian's consistory
in the praise he lavishes upon the unprecedented care with which the
emperor's interventions were worded and the maturity of their delivery;
there were to be no more of the spectacular outbursts with which Valentinian had intimidated his court.[29] Just as Valentinian's closest associates had reflected (and contributed to) their master's lowering countenance, the most prominent of Gratian's courtiers were men who could
appreciate the new emperor's artistry and match the standards he set.
Siburius, who perhaps succeeded the brutal Leo as *magister officiorum*
and later attained the praetorian prefecture, cultivated an archaic literary style, while Ausonius's fellow-survivor Antonius won plaudits from
connoisseurs at Rome.[30]

But Ausonius was the ultimate guarantor of his pupil's cultural credentials. He also benefitted from the self-reinforcing character of the
new government's image, as his correspondence with Symmachus illustrates. The senatorial aristocracy of Rome embodied the cultural values
now espoused by the court: the elderly rhetor consolidated his position
by serving as their conduit to the sources of power, securing posts for
their protégés and indulgence for the misdemeanours of their friends
and thereby binding them to himself through debts of gratitude.[31]

Among those whom Symmachus recommended to Gratian's court
was Ponticianus, candid in thought and praiseworthy in manner of life.[32]
This paragon is plausibly identified with the senior government official

28. For the influence of Claudius Antonius, the only other minister known
to have survived in office from the previous reign, see Matthews, *Western Aristocracies*, 94.

29. Gratian's accomplishments are described at Aus. *Grat. Act.* 14.67, with
the illuminating afterthought at 15.68, 'nec patris tui gravior auctoritas'. There
is a vivid impression of Valentinian's temper at Amm. Marc. 29.3.2; cf. the
tongue-lashing of alleged cowards reported at 30.8.11.

30. Symm. *Ep.* 3.44 (Siburius); 1.89 for Antonius' 'loquendi phaleras' and
'senile quiddam planeque conveniens auribus patrum gravitate sensuum, ver-
borum proprietate'.

31. Symm. *Ep.* 1.30 (a plea for a courtier playing truant in Rome), 40 (to
retrieve the fortunes of a disgraced official), 43 (a *commendatio* for a lawyer).

32. *Ep.* 1.99 (to the *magister officiorum* Syagrius).

whom Augustine met in Milan some years later; his career thus fore-shadowed the latter's, leading from Africa to Rome (via a literary education) and then to the court. But Ponticianus also represents an aspect of life at Trier that had remained unchanged since Valentinian's day. He was a Christian, who lodged with three co-religionists (as Jerome had lodged with Bonosus a decade earlier). One day, as the four friends were walking in pairs through some gardens near the city walls, two of them came upon a cell used by some Christian ascetics and found inside a copy of the life of Antony. On reading it, they decided at once to abandon their careers and to imitate the Egyptian saint. Ponticianus and the fourth official congratulated them but could not bring themselves to join them and returned to the palace; the converts' fiancées demonstrated their support for the project by devoting themselves to a life of virginity.[33] The ground for such dramatic decisions had been prepared (like Jerome's) at the palace, with the emperor himself giving a lead. It was well known that he never took a decision without referring his purpose to God (one wonders whether this was a feature of the decision-making process in the consistory) or allowed a day to pass without 'adoring God', which perhaps implies daily attendance at a religious service.[34] All this represented the continuation of trends apparent under Valentinian, but the less forbidding face of Gratian's court emboldened Christian interest groups to present their claims directly. The suburban hermitage discovered by Ponticianus and his friends itself represents a significant development from Martin's extemporized demonstration of ascetic prowess. Ponticianus' *contubernales*, moreover, remained at Trier, unlike Jerome; the presence of these bureaucrat-monks on the emperor's doorstep blurred a distinction that had been kept clear in the previous regime.

Gratian failed to maintain the tight grip which Valentinian had kept upon the state. His reign saw aggrandizement at the government's expense by aristocrats and churchmen, and ultimately a military revolt. The emperor's inability to keep these interests in check was blamed by contemporaries on deficiencies in his character: he knew 'neither how to rule nor how to be ruled', and was manipulated by his advisors.[35] In their parting reflections upon their careers, Ponticianus' companions at Trier also deplored the capriciousness of a regime that left them to hope for nothing better than to become the prince's 'friends', a position that

33. Aug. *Conf.* 8.6.14–15.
34. Aus. *Grat. Act.* 10.43, 14.63.
35. Eun. fr. 57 (50 Blockley).

was still 'precarious and exposed to much danger'.[36] These conventional sentiments were perhaps brought into sharper focus by recollections of the bloody demise of Maximinus and his associates; the domination of the civil administration by a single family, and of the military by Merobaudes, adds a pervasive sense of fragility to the reign.

To be just, one should acknowledge the intrinsic difficulty of Gratian's position. The major constraint was geographical. The *comitatus*, stationed on the Rhine frontier for most of Valentinian's reign, had to a certain extent taken root there. The ascendancy of the Gallic notable Ausonius and Merobaudes, whose political interventions were all concerned directly with protecting the interests of the 'Gallic legions', was symptomatic. Gratian inherited the combination of strategic inflexibility and thralldom to special interests which threatened every Roman government, eloquently expressed in his two years of immobility in Gaul after his accession.[37] He was especially unfortunate, therefore, that the collapse of the lower Danube frontier forced him for much of his reign to operate far from Trier. He was as much a victim of the tensions that this new orientation set off as of his own inadequacies.

THE ILLYRICAN CHALLENGE

Ambrose's relations with Gratian were defined by a single event: the catastrophic battle of Adrianople in August 378, where the emperor's uncle Valens and the cream of the eastern army were destroyed by the Goths. Gratian had become involved in the war against the Gothic rebellion the previous year, when his plans to send an expeditionary force had been thwarted by Merobaudes, concerned as ever for the security of the Rhine. He was en route to the Balkans with his army in the summer of 378 when impatience and vainglory inspired his uncle to launch his fatal attack. Gratian could only withdraw to Sirmium for the autumn and winter as the invaders surged across the region. Illyricum and its

36. *Conf.* 8.6.15: 'et ibi quid non fragile plenumque periculis?'.

37. There is no evidence for the visit to Rome sometimes assigned to 376: the passage that T. D. Barnes adduces ('Constans and Gratian in Rome', *HSCP* [1975], at 328–30) from the *Breves enarrationes chronicae* refers to silver *stelai* erected to Gratian and his wife, which are clearly the basis of the inferred visit. The same source in the preceding chapter, on the basis of a similar deduction, claims a visit to Rome by Julian. Barnes notes (329) that Themistius *Or.* 13 does not prove an actual visit.

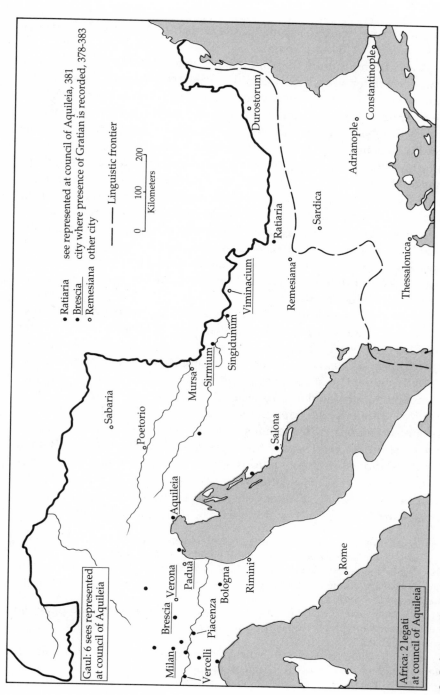

Legend (map):

- Ratiaria — see represented at council of Aquileia, 381
- Brescia — city where presence of Gratian is recorded, 378–383
- Remesiana — other city

—— Linguistic frontier

0   100   200
Kilometers

Gaul: 6 sees represented at council of Aquileia

Africa: 2 legati at council of Aquileia

Cities shown on map: Sabaria, Poetorio, Mursa, Sirmium, Singidunum, Viminacium, Ratiaria, Remesiana, Sardica, Durostorum, Adrianople, Constantinople, Thessalonica, Salona, Aquileia, Rome, Rimini, Bologna, Piacenza, Padua, Verona, Brescia, Vercelli, Milan

2. Italy and Illyricum.

eastern marches were to command the emperor's attention for much of the remainder of his short reign.

It was from Sirmium that Gratian first made contact with Ambrose, writing to ask for a profession of faith during the winter of 378–379. The same season saw momentous decisions being taken in the consistory, culminating in the elevation of the general Theodosius to the purple in January 379.[38] Otherwise, though, the business of government continued much as normal. The consuls for the coming year were designated and congratulated in the appropriate manner, their order of precedence duly established.[39] The sheer persistence of routine behavior is illustrated by the attempted crackdown upon absenteeism from the court, which was clearly aimed not at panic-stricken deserters but at the ingrained habit of wandering off at will to attend to private business; the periods of absence ranged from six months to four years.[40] And as always, petitions arrived from various quarters; even the governor of war-torn Thrace put in a successful bid for the use of imperial property in one of his province's cities.[41]

Among those seeking to secure benefits from the beleaguered government at Sirmium were rival Christian groups. The move from Trier had made the court more accessible; there might also have been hopes of exploiting its distractions after Adrianople to extract particular favours. Even the Donatists, against whom Gratian (following his father's example) had legislated in 376, secured a rescript that could justify their practices.[42] Meanwhile, Pope Damasus convened a council at Rome; the assembled bishops (who perhaps included Ambrose) wrote to Gratian to request further help against the supporters of Ursinus and the Roman Donatists and asked the emperor's approval for a new system of ecclesiastical jurisdiction. This latter request apparently sought to take advantage of the fact that Gratian was temporarily legislating for both the eastern and western halves of the empire. The emperor duly endorsed

38. I follow T. D. Barnes ('Religion and Society in the Age of Theodosius', in *Grace, Politics and Desire*, ed. H. A. Meynell [1990], at 162) in believing that Theodosius's accession was more probably thrust upon than inspired by Gratian. A military clique is persuasively identified behind the elevation by Sivan, *Ausonius of Bordeaux*, 121.

39. Aus. *Grat. Act.* 12.55–56; the emperor's deliberations concerning the most appropriate gift for his senior consul Ausonius are recorded at 11.53.

40. *CTh* 7.12.2.

41. *CTh* 10.2.1, accepting Mommsen's reading of Augusta Traiana and his identification of the city as Eski Zaghara (Beroea).

42. For the rescript, see p. 102 below; the law of 376 is *CTh* 16.5.6.

Rome's claim to hear the cases of deposed bishops in the western provinces—and of the metropolitans of the east.[43]

A more famous product of these same months was Gratian's 'law of toleration', assuring freedom of worship to all except Manichees, Photinians and Eunomians, and applauded by the fifth-century trio of ecclesiastical historians Socrates, Sozomen and Theodoret as the end of Valens' persecutions.[44] Modern scholars have often interpreted it instead as an anti-Nicene measure, a concession by Gratian to Arian pressure.[45] But this view is untenable: the law, as the sources state, concerned the east, and addressed the confusion caused by Valens' recall of the Nicene exiles shortly before his death. It is most easily seen as the response to an appeal by this latter group to regulate their position; but it did not offer them any particular privileges. Their freedom to organize their own communities did not affect the hierarchy of eastern bishops that had been established under Valens. These homoeans, who had never been outlawed in either half of the empire, remained secure, being if anything strengthened by the ban against the irritating Eunomians.[46] The relief with which the edict was received by the eastern Nicenes indicates the modesty of their expectations: there is nothing to suggest that Gratian's government was campaigning on their behalf.

No more did Gratian ask Ambrose for a statement of faith to equip himself for a catholic crusade. In Illyricum the emperor faced not only the Goths but also, as the flurry of ecclesiastical legislation shows, urgent reminders of his responsibility to maintain the peace of the church. It is against this background, and within the wider pattern of relations between rulers and bishops, that his request is best understood.

43. The appeal is preserved among Ambrose's letters (which implies, but does not prove, his participation in the council): *Ep. extra coll.* 7 (*CSEL* 82.3, pp. 191–197). *Coll. Avell.* 13, a rescript to the *vicarius* of Rome, gives Gratian's response. The council is discussed by Pietri, *Roma Christiana*, 741–748, but he fails to note the claim to hear appeals from eastern metropolitans. At *Coll. Avell.* 13.11–12 (answering *Ep. extra coll.* 7.9), cases involving bishops in the Italian and Gallic prefectures are contrasted with those 'in longinquioribus partibus', when metropolitans are to be heard at Rome.

44. Soc. *HE* 5.2.1; Soz. *HE* 7.1.3; Theod. *HE* 5.2.

45. Thus A. Piganiol, *L'empire chrétien*, 2d ed. (1972), 228–229; Meslin claims to detect a 'réveil' of Arianism as a consequence of the law (*Les Ariens d'Occident* [1967], 46n85), but the passage he adduces (Soz. *HE* 7.2) refers to eastern Macedonian groups.

46. For a recent confrontation between homoeans and Eunomians at Constantinople, see above, chap. 1, n. 21.

It was probably during the previous eighteen months, in 377/8, that Ambrose had made his first intervention in the ecclesiastical politics of Illyricum.[47] Our only source for the episode is a tantalizing notice in his biography:

> When he had gone to Sirmium to ordain Anemius as bishop, there was an attempt to drive him out of the church by the powerful queen Justina and a multitude who had gathered around her, so that they could proceed, in the same church but with the heretics in charge instead of Ambrose, with the ordination of an Arian. Ambrose, taking no notice of the disturbances created by a woman, had taken his place at the tribunal when one of the Arian virgins—more shameless than her companions—mounted the tribunal and grabbed his clothing, wanting to drag him to the women's section so that he could be beaten by them and driven from the church. (V. Amb. 11.1)

Ambrose reprimanded the importunate woman with a characteristic lecture on the dignity of their respective callings. The immediate effect remains unclear, but proceedings seem to have been postponed until the following day. The outcome was determined by the death overnight of his assailant, which struck 'no little fear' into his adversaries and allowed him to complete the ordination in peace.[48]

The involvement of a bishop of Milan in an election five hundred miles away was certainly irregular.[49] But a more important question than the strict legality of his intervention is its relation to the wider history of Illyrican Christianity. The conventional view presents it as a contribution to a wholesale, and largely unopposed, reconquest of the area for Nicene orthodoxy; stripped of this background it becomes a daring— and to its victims outrageous—raid against an entrenched ecclesiastical establishment.

The former position, which in its most developed form reduces Ursacius and Valens, the heroes of the previous generation, to colourful aberrations unrepresentative of their native region, rests upon weak foundations. It depends above all upon three documents relating to a 'council of Illyricum' which Theodoret of Cyrrhus included in his eccle-

47. Suggestions include 376 (Palanque, *Saint Ambroise*, 496); 376–377 (Pietri, *Roma Christiana*, 782; Meslin, *Les Ariens*, 45); 378 (Gryson, *Scolies Ariennes*, 107–108). A date as late as 380 is possible (Y.-M. Duval, 'Aquilée et Sirmium durant la crise Arienne', *AAAd* 26 [1982], 371n211), but the freedom of action allowed both Ambrose and Justina implies a point before the arrival of Gratian's court.

48. Paulin. *V. Amb.* 11.2.

49. See Gryson, *Scolies Ariennes*, 107, for the illegality of Ambrose's conduct.

siastical history of the mid-fifth century: two letters addressed to the bishops of Phrygia and Caria, one from the reigning emperors and the other from the bishops present at the synod, and the creed that the latter had produced.[50] Theodoret's text gives the emperors as Valentinian, Valens and Gratian, which produces a date of 367–375 and an implausible departure from the elder Valentinian's notorious reluctance to involve himself in doctrinal disputes. But by emending the order of the emperors to read Valens, Gratian and Valentinian [II]—the college of 375–378— scholars have posited a council in the immediate prelude to Adrianople, which has furthermore been located, on the basis of a later homoean reference to a 'blasphemy at Sirmium', in Sirmium itself.[51] On this view, Ambrose joined the Nicene bishops of Illyricum to exploit Gratian's four-day visit to the city in July 378 to install Anemius, to eliminate the surviving Arian prelates and to issue a declaration in support of their eastern colleagues.

But Theodoret's dossier cannot bear such a burden. One of the three texts is certainly foreign to any 'council of Illyricum': the creed is a Greek one which seems to have emanated from Antioch.[52] Nor does the imperial letter bear detailed examination. The emperors reel off a string of scriptural quotations and references without parallel in fourth-century imperial correspondence; there are more biblical citations here than in all Constantine's letters about Arius and his beliefs.[53] The emendation of Theodoret's imperial college to that of Valens, Gratian and Valentinian II moreover requires the attribution of the letter to Gratian alone, the other two names being included merely to satisfy convention; the doctrines proclaimed were anathema to Valens (and to the mother of the seven-year-old Valentinian II). But why should Gratian have expressed himself thus to the Phrygian episcopate? No other fourth-century emperor issued direct instructions like these to a colleague's subjects, which given the impossibility of enforcing them was sensible enough. The argument that Gratian exacted a doctrinal capitulation from his uncle as the price for his military support has no weight: it assumes an improbable com-

50. Theod. *HE* 4.8–9.

51. Gryson's presentation of this argument (*Scolies Ariennes,* 107–121) develops and refines the thesis of J. Zeiller, *Les origines chrétiennes dans les provinces danubiennes de l'empire romain* (1918), 308–343.

52. See the comments by L. Parmentier in his edition of Theodoret (*GCS* 19, p. lxxx = *GCS* 54, p. 366).

53. In the nine Constantinian letters collected by H.-G. Opitz, *Urkunden zur Geschichte des arianischen Streites* (1934–1935), only four citations are marked, against the ten discovered by Parmentier in this one letter.

mitment to Nicaea on Gratian's part, and an equally unrealistic freedom of communications between the two emperors in the hectic prelude to Adrianople.[54] The circumstances excluded any complex negotiations over the views to be preached to the Asian episcopate.

Theodoret, moreover, clearly has no idea of the historical import of these documents, introducing them only to demonstrate that Valentinian I was a true supporter of the Nicene cause and that Valens, as a willing cosignatory, was 'orthodox' at the start of his reign. It therefore seems safe to infer that he had no other evidence for the council apart from these texts, which had been buried in a Syrian archive for two generations. In this context, they pertain more to the history of the eastern church than to that of the Illyrican. The key to their origin lies in the third item, the letter from the Illyrican bishops urging their colleagues to implement the Nicene formula sponsored by the 'ruling power of the Romans'.[55] This in fact does little more than introduce one Elpidius, a presbyter who would help the Asian churches purge their ranks and restore orthodoxy to their teachings. That it was intended specifically as an instrument to enhance Elpidius' authority is suggested by the fourfold repetition of his name. The demonstrable inauthenticity of the creed and the highly dubious character of the imperial letter lend support to the further hypothesis that the whole dossier was manufactured to assist the presbyter in a campaign to influence the Asian churches.[56] Connexions in Illyricum were probably involved, but the council itself should be disregarded as a fiction that reflects the illusion of a wholeheartedly Nicene west shared by so many easterners during Valens' reign. There is no evidence that Elpidius' letters made the slightest impression upon the homoeans of Phrygia; they were quite possibly never used until the diligent Theodoret seized upon them two generations later to support his pet theories about the allegiances of Valentinian and Valens.[57]

54. Ammianus' attention to letters suggests their infrequency: he shows Gratian sending a dispatch to announce his victory over the Lentienses at 31.11.6 (cf. 31.12.1 for its arrival) and writing to urge Valens to await his arrival (31.12.4–5).

55. Theod. *HE* 4.9.1–9.

56. The fabrication is to be dated by the imperial letter to 367/75, probably towards the beginning of the period: Pope Damasus' termination of Liberius' tentative exchanges with the eastern homoiousians forced the easterners to resort to more dubious means of asserting their western connexions. A likely context is the aftermath of the anti-Nicene council of Caria c. 366: Soz. *HE* 6.12.4.

57. Socrates (*HE* 4.1) and Sozomen (*HE* 6.6) both make Valens heretical from the outset and Valentinian tolerant of Arianism.

Without Theodoret's council, the evidence for a Nicene revival in
Illyricum is modest indeed, consisting principally of two manifestos
from Italy which reflect the senders' wishful thinking rather than the
recipients' views. The propagandistic intentions behind one of these,
Damasus' synodal letter announcing the condemnation of Auxentius,
have already been discussed.[58] A decade earlier, a group of Italian bishops had written to those Illyrican colleagues 'who hold to the faith of
the fathers', perhaps encouraged by the common ground which Eusebius of Vercelli had recently discovered there even with such leaders as
Germinius of Sirmium.[59] But if so, they exaggerated the strength of the
reaction against Rimini. In a final flourish they declared that the condemnation of Ursacius and Valens and their companions had 'long since
been manifest': but the neighbours of these two arch-heretics would
watch them survive unscathed for a further decade, to die peacefully in
their sees.

Inside Illyricum the 'homoean consensus' endured. The complaints
of a harassed Nicene bishop show the persistence of 'Arian' assumptions among the people of a small town even at the very end of the
century;[60] but the best evidence comes, paradoxically, from a pair of texts
which seem to illustrate the crumbling of the authority of Ursacius and
Valens. When Germinius of Sirmium confronted his importunate parishioner Heraclianus in January 366, he firmly maintained that 'the Son
is not similar to the Father in every respect' ('non similis filius patri per
omnia');[61] but within a year there seems to have been a dramatic change
in his attitude. Challenged in December of that same year by Ursacius,
Valens and two other bishops to deny the rumour that he was now proclaiming similarity between Father and Son in all respects, he eventually
produced the explicit statement that Christ was indeed similar to the
Father in everything—'similis patri per omnia'.[62]

One point should be made clear: Germinius was not defecting to the
Nicenes or proclaiming the *homoousion*.[63] His only concern is to define

---

58. Above, p. 41.
59. Hil. *Coll. Antiar. Par.* B.iv.2.
60. Nicetas Remes. *De Spiritus Sancti potentia* 1; cf. *De ratione fidei* 3. For the
background, see A. E. Burns' useful introduction to his edition, *Niceta of Remesiana* (1905).
61. *Altercatio Heracliani* (*PLS* 1, 347).
62. Hil. *Coll. Antiar. Par.* B.vi.1.2 (*CSEL* 65, p. 161).
63. *Contra* Zeiller, *Les origines*, 304. Meslin, *Les Ariens*, 296–298, speaks
more judiciously of a limited 'rapprochement vers les Nicéens'; but even this is
overstated.

his beliefs in relation to those of Ursacius and Valens, and the difference that he asserts is far less significant than the common ground that remained. Germinius said nothing about the relative stature of Father and Son, and he failed to address the question of substance that was crucial to Nicene doctrines. His perspectives were narrower, as he shows when he chides Valens for his failure to remember exactly what had been agreed on during the negotiations with Constantius eight years earlier. They were old men now, these bishops who had wielded such influence, and were anxious to pass on their achievements to the next generation in an undiluted form. Rival groups of disciples had gathered around them. One of the grievances that set Valens and his friends at odds with Germinius was an unspecified indignity suffered by two bishops, Palladius of Ratiaria and Gaius, at the hands of Germinius' clergy. The situation was aggravated by the lack of routine contacts to alleviate tensions: nowhere in the two letters is it implied that Germinius actually met his critics, whose original concern about his doctrines was inspired by a 'rumour'.[64] The episode suggests the character of the Illyrican churches, isolated from one another by distance and habituated to independence;[65] there is no sign of a formal hierarchy to govern their mutual relations. But with this went a certain solidarity. The present conflict was purely domestic: Germinius was not excommunicated, and like his opponents he continued to look towards his colleagues in Illyricum for support and understanding, rather than beyond its borders.[66]

Germinius was not responsible for the inclusion of these two texts in a dossier compiled in Gaul, which is better explained as a leak. Government officials had sustained the controversy: a certain Vitalianus on the praetorian prefect's staff had informed Germinius of the eight bishops' concern, and he had sent his reply via an *officialis*, Cyriacus. But the prefect's *officium* included men of diverse doctrinal allegiance who were frequently required to visit Gaul for routine business with the imperial court. Hilary probably found this 'evidence' of Ursacius' and

---

64. *Coll. Antiar. Par.* B.v.1.2 ('quod rumor iactitat de te'); 2.2 ('querella pro iniuria a quibusdam clericis tuis Palladio et Gaio . . . facta': *CSEL* 65, pp. 159–60).

65. The geography of the controversy raises several other questions. Valens and Ursacius, for instance, were Germinius' nearest neighbours, Mursa and Singidunum both being less than 100 kilometres from Sirmium, yet they seem to have been dependent for information upon the much more distant Palladius and Gaius. Meslin places Gaius at Sabaria, 400 kilometres from Sirmium, the same distance as Palladius' Ratiaria but in the opposite direction (*Les Ariens*, 64–66).

66. It is worth noting in this context the scale of these exchanges, which involved a total of thirteen bishops; Zeiller, *Les origines*, 138–164, calculated a total of about two dozen sees in fourth-century Pannonia and Moesia Superior.

Valens' discomfiture at the hands of their old ally an irresistible epilogue to his documentary history of the enormities perpetrated by this pair; but its inclusion in this work argues a Nicene hunger for compromising material against their opponents rather than a crisis in the homoean camp.

In Illyricum, business went on as normal. As the generation of Ursacius and Valens died out, the churches were handed on to like-minded heirs; at Singidunum, Uracius was succeeded by his presbyter, Secundianus. The exception was Sirmium, which was stolen from them by Ambrose's intervention. The success of his coup can be explained in part by the quarrel between Germinius and his colleagues and the antipathy of his clergy towards visiting bishops. But it is also likely that Ambrose was able to exploit the connexions he had made in the city as advocate and assessor. The staff of the prefectural office at Sirmium have already been seen assisting in the conduct of ecclesiastical affairs; Ambrose's ability to arrive in time for the election might well reflect an initial notification of events through the express communications service available to his former colleagues, and he perhaps enjoyed some 'official' backing for his entry into the basilica. The most likely period for the episode— 377/8—allowed unusual scope for subordinates to usurp the prefectural authority, for Ausonius had succeeded in entrusting the government of the Illyrican provinces to his nonagenarian father.[67]

In Paulinus' biography, the episode serves principally to introduce the queen Justina and the 'countless schemes' that she subsequently hatched against Ambrose. Valentinian's mother had apparently remained in Illyricum when her son was taken into Gratian's care; the influence she obviously exercised over the Christian community in Sirmium suggests that she had devoted her retirement to pious works, like other imperial women in temporary eclipse.[68] It is plausible to imagine clergymen among her retinue helping to consolidate (or perhaps to shape) the homoean allegiances which would have a dramatic effect upon the events of the next decade and which will in turn have attracted sympathetic attention from the local episcopate.[69] The bishops' resentment at Anemius' installation would therefore be added to the personal humilia-

---

67. *PLRE* 1, Ausonius 5 (p. 139), tentatively dating the prefecture to late 377.

68. On Eudocia in Palestine and the semi-official character of her activities there, see E. D. Hunt, *Holy Land Pilgrimage in the Later Roman Empire* (1982), 221–248.

69. For a presbyter and deacon in Eudocia's entourage, see Hunt, *Holy Land Pilgrimage,* 237. It is not known when and how Justina's beliefs were shaped: homoean influence is unlikely from either her father, the Roman grandee Iustus (*PLRE* 1, p. 490), or her husbands, the usurper Magnentius and Valentinian.

tion Justina had suffered. Ambrose had made some powerful enemies in Illyricum, to whom Gratian's arrival in 378 promised an opportunity to seek revenge.

Gratian's instruction that Ambrose write 'something about the faith' has traditionally been regarded as a straightforward request from a zealously orthodox but theologically untutored youth, wary of the subtle heretics of Illyricum, to a bishop whose reputation was already established.[70] But each of these assumptions is at best questionable; and it has been convincingly argued that in presenting the commission in this manner, some two years later, Ambrose was deliberately obscuring the original circumstances.[71] He himself acknowledges, in the preface to the work, that he had *not* been asked to instruct the emperor: 'I would have preferred', he protests, 'to undertake the task of rallying you to the faith than that of arguing about the faith'.[72] Gratian's desire to 'hear' the bishop's 'faith' therefore amounted to a request to inspect his personal profession: Ambrose was being required neither to reinforce the emperor's beliefs nor demolish those of the homoean bishops, but to justify his *own* position.[73]

Gratian has been presented as a reluctant accomplice to these proceedings, cooperating with the homoean bishops only through political necessity.[74] But it was only later that these prelates were branded as heretics and potential traitors; in 378 the emperor had no reason to shun them. Indeed, in a sense he was coming home to them, for he had been born in the region at the moment of the homoean triumph of Rimini in 359. And had he not 'cherished the faith from the very cradle', attended by the (homoean) clergy of Sirmium or Cibalae?[75] He therefore had no cause to doubt the integrity of the men who warned him, in terms probably similar to those used by Hilary against Auxentius in 364, that the bishop of Milan's faith was suspect. Like his father, Gratian took steps

70. Palanque, *Saint Ambroise*, 50: 'Il nous prouve la réputation dont jouissait déjà l'évêque de Milan'; cf. Gryson, *Scolies Ariennes*, 114.

71. P. Nautin, 'Les premières relations'.

72. *De fide* 1.4: 'Mallem quidem cohortandi ad fidem subire officium quam de fide disceptandi'.

73. *De fide* 1.1: 'fidem meam audire voluisti'.

74. Nautin, 'Les premières relations', 239–240, suggests rather implausibly a danger that they might collaborate with the Gothic invaders.

75. *De fide* 1.2: 'ab ipsis incunabulis'. Gratian's birthplace is given as Sirmium in Aur. Vict. *Epit.* 47.1 but might better be assigned to the family home at Cibalae, in which case the nearest bishop was perhaps the arch-heretic Valens of Mursa!

to investigate these charges and wrote to ask Ambrose for a statement of his theological position.

While the motive for the attack on Ambrose lies in the outrage caused by his intervention at Sirmium, faith had not been the issue at the election of Anemius. As Hilary had discovered, moreover, heterodoxy was an extremely difficult charge to prove in the catholic climate of Valentinian's dynasty. One reason for preferring this approach to the more reliable (and entirely feasible) accusation of fomenting disturbance beyond the limits of his own territory must have been Ambrose's perceived vulnerability over doctrine, especially if—as is likely—reports of his difficulties at Milan and reluctance to engage in theological controversy there had reached Illyricum.[76] But a wider conflict also loomed, which provides the strategic background to the affair. Valens' death at Adrianople would inevitably cause profound changes within the eastern churches, which would in turn influence and be influenced by the relations of these churches with the west: the Nicene axis which Basil of Caesarea had so long sought had at last become a practical possibility. But much still depended upon the parties' success in presenting their case to the church at large and to the emperors, and here in particular the homoeans could hope to use Ambrose to their own advantage. Nicaea would be judged by its champions, and in the bishop of Milan they perhaps sensed that they had found a spokesman as potentially embarrassing to his party as the eccentric Marcellus of Ancyra had been forty years earlier.[77]

The plan failed because Ambrose had the political flair of an Athanasius to compensate for any theological vulnerability, and also because Gratian lacked the vigour of Constantius in his pursuit of ecclesiastical unity. Ambrose neglected to comply with the command, and the emperor failed to press him. Perhaps he was deflected by a graceful plea of *verecundia*, calculated to strike a chord in a prince whose own conspicuous modesty excited various responses.[78] Ambrose might also have expressed a preference to justify himself to the emperor in person; logistical considerations probably meant that the court's decision to return to Gaul via northern Italy was already known. This change in itiner-

76. See below, p. 122, for the appointment of Ambrose's opponent Iulianus Valens to the see of his native Poetovio in Pannonia in the later 370s.

77. For Marcellus, see Hanson, *The Search*, 217–235.

78. Such an excuse, which Ambrose used subsequently to Gratian (*Ep. extra coll.* 12 [1].1), might explain the remark at *De fide* 3.1: 'et verecundantem . . . ' Ausonius raves over Gratian at *Grat. Act.* 12.57: 'O felicem verecundiam tuam!'; Rufinus thought him 'plus verecundus quam reipublicae intererat' (*HE* 11.13).

ary, probably determined by the strategic importance of Aquileia (which commanded the Julian Alps, threatened by Gothic raiding parties after Adrianople), was to give Ambrose the chance to seize the initiative against his critics.[79]

Ambrose and Gratian first met in the summer of 379, when the emperor paid a fleeting visit to Milan en route from Aquileia to Trier.[80] The bishop was better able to make a favourable impression upon the emperor and his ministers on his own ground than through a text submitted for critical scrutiny. Well-placed mediators were also available, since after a decade's interlude Milan had in 376/7 again become the seat of a praetorian prefect.[81] Ambrose appears to have enjoyed good relations with Claudius Antonius, the prefect from 377 to 378, and with at least one member of his administration, the *advocatus* Manlius Theodorus; though his ties with Theodorus are only attested a decade later, they can plausibly be traced back to this earlier phase of Theodorus' career. Such contacts were investments: by 379 Theodorus had been promoted, and he returned to Milan in the emperor's entourage as his *magister memoriae*.

Ambrose's background and demeanour were also calculated to appeal to Gratian's other ministers. Auxentius' case in 364 had been entrusted to the *magister officiorum* and *quaestor;* in the summer of 379 these offices were probably held respectively by Syagrius, attested as Ambrose's close collaborator two years later, and Proculus Gregorius, a friend of Ausonius and Symmachus who would exercise his influence on behalf of Bishop Ithacius against his accusers in 383. Isolated scraps

79. Laws were issued from Aquileia on 2/5 July, and Milan on 31 July/3 August; the court had reached Trier by 14 September; evidence on O. Seeck, *Regesten der Kaisern und Päpste für die Jahre 311 bis 476 n.Chr.* (1919), 250–252. For Gothic incursions 'usque ad radices Alpium Iuliarum', see Amm. Marc. 31.16.7; cf. 21.12.21 for the strategic link with Aquileia.

80. The earlier dates often supplied for the first meeting, and hence for *De fide*, reflect an exaggerated view of the latter work's significance. Suggestions include a meeting in July 378 connected with the 'council of Sirmium' (Palanque, *Saint Ambroise*, 496–499, followed by Gryson, *Scolies Ariennes*, 110–113), a separate encounter in Sirmium in September 378 (Faller, *CSEL* 78, pp. 6–7), or one in Milan during the winter of 378/9 (Nautin, 'Les premières relations', 236–237). For the implausibility of these chronologies, see Gottlieb, *Ambrosius von Mailand*, 26–50.

81. No laws to Petronius Probus, who had ruled his vast 'central prefecture' from Sirmium, are attested after 375. Claudius Antonius is first recorded (as prefect of Italy and Africa) in November 377; he is plausibly identified with the recipient of Amb. *Ep.* 60 [90] at *PLRE* 1, p. 77.

of information about other officials reinforce this impression of a court at once pervasively Christian and extremely well bred.[82]

Ambrose obtained one important victory during Gratian's visit. The following year he acknowledged his debt to the emperor in a letter: 'You restored peace to my church; you stopped up the mouths (and if only the hearts as well!) of the heretics.'[83] These cryptic remarks are illuminated by a subsequent complaint by his opponent Palladius, who wondered aloud why Ambrose had asked for the emperor's 'indulgence', 'when by his command that you should not be found out in your impiety, no catholic teacher of truth may be heard speaking out against you by anyone?'[84] The blocked 'catholic' mouths were those of the homoean community in Milan, who had presumably sought to exploit the emperor's presence to state their own case against Ambrose and so reinforce the campaign of their Illyrican allies. But they had reckoned without Gratian's scrupulous refusal to prejudge the issue and his intolerance of schism, and their efforts backfired; Palladius' comment seems to imply that Ambrose used the emperor's endorsement to authorize suppression of his local enemies.[85] But Gratian's 'favour' to Ambrose did not release the bishop from his obligation. At a personal interview the emperor 'encouraged' him to produce the statement that his critics had demanded, and he exacted a promise to comply.[86]

However profound the eventual consequences of this meeting, its immediate significance should be kept in perspective. The court's presence in Milan was routine and transitory, and Ambrose had little time to make an impression. Gratian probably left without attending the bishop's Sunday service. The two laws that record his presence were issued on

82. E.g., Arborius (*PLRE* 1, pp. 97–98), *CSL* in 379 and later a friend of Martin of Tours; Catervius (*PLRE* 1, pp. 186–187), Arborius' successor in office, was buried at Tolentino in a Christian sarcophagus.

83. *Ep. extra coll.* 12 [1].2: 'Reddidisti enim mihi quietem ecclesiae perfidorum ora atque utinam et corda clausisti'.

84. Pall. *Apol.* 84: 'Cur preterea ab imperatore veniam postulas, cum ne tu impiaetatis arguaris eius precepto nullus catolicus doctor adversum te a quoquam audiatur?' This punctuation gives more satisfactory sense than Gryson's, for a new argument is introduced in the following clause. The connexion with Ambrose's remark was argued by Gottlieb, *Ambrosius von Mailand*, 42–44.

85. Hence perhaps the ironical question about 'venia' and also the rather cumbersome 'a quoquam': it was not just the emperor to whom the *doctores* were denied audience, but their legitimate constituency.

86. For the renewed order, see *De fide* 3.1: 'coram etiam ipse fueras adhortatus'.

31 July, a Wednesday, and 3 August, a Saturday; the court was perhaps already gone the following day.[87] One of these Milanese laws, which cancelled a rescript issued at Sirmium and banned all meetings of 'heretics' inside cities,[88] was long interpreted as a decisive volte-face by the emperor and proof of the spell cast over him by Ambrose, for the rescript was identified with the tolerance decree issued after Adrianople and the heretics with the Arians. But the foundations of this view were demolished by the demonstration that the law's targets (who are presented specifically as repeating the sacrament of baptism) were the African Donatists, and there is no need whatsoever to posit any involvement by Ambrose in this routine restatement of long-standing sanctions.[89]

Gratian duly hurried off towards Trier and his expectant consul Ausonius. Ambrose's position had not been greatly affected by the visit. It was probably already apparent that the emperor's presence would again be required on the Danube the following year, when the Illyrican bishops could resume their lobbying. Ambrose could take comfort in but a single aspect of the situation: the court would again travel via Milan, allowing him to stake his claim upon its attention as it moved to the war zone in the spring.

The bishop must have worked hard that winter. When Gratian returned to Milan in March 380 he was presented not with a simple profession of faith like Eusebius of Caesarea's justificatory creed to the council of Nicaea or the brief statement, accompanied by supporting documents, that Auxentius had presented to Valentinian, but with the two imposing volumes of *De fide*, which fill seventy-five pages in their oldest surviving manuscript.[90]

The contents are even more surprising than the length. Ambrose

87. The place of issue given for *CTh* 6.28.1 (4 August 379) is the chronologically impossible Trier. Seeck, *Regesten*, 109, proposed Tres Tabernae, a way station twenty-two miles southeast of Milan (*Itinerarium Burdigalense* 617 [*CCL* 175, p. 25]); this would represent a slight detour for Gratian, whose hectic itinerary towards Gaul is reported by Aus. *Grat. Act.* 18.82. See above, n. 79, for the court's arrival at Trier by mid-September.

88. *CTh* 16.5.5.

89. Gottlieb, *Ambrosius von Mailand*, 71–80.

90. Composition of *De fide* should be dated before, not after, Gratian's second visit to Milan in March 380, *pace* Gottlieb, *Ambrosius von Mailand*, 50: Ambrose implies only a single previous meeting at *De fide* 3.1. The traditional dating to summer/autumn 378 has no foundation: for the two passages adduced by Palanque (*Saint Ambroise*, 498: *De fide* 1.1, 2.142) see Gottlieb, 31–35, and below, n. 94.

did not write an apology; instead, interpreting Gratian's command as a commission to produce an 'official' statement of orthodoxy and refutation of the heretics, he presented himself as the emperor's spiritual spokesman for the forthcoming campaign against the Goths. The war was nothing less than a crusade in which Ambrose's *libellus* would be a decisive weapon. 'You prepare for victory, championing the faith, concerning which you requested from me a booklet' (*De fide* 1.3). The English cannot do justice to the remorselessness of the accumulated relative clauses: this is a splendid display of sophistry, misrepresentation on an heroic scale.[91]

After this remarkable opening flourish, Ambrose defiantly proclaims his Nicene faith and proceeds to deploy the standard repertoire of anti-Arian polemic in a manner which does his intellect little credit.[92] But there are some nice tactical touches. Having produced a grotesque caricature of Arianism, for instance, Ambrose 'sought' permission to address individuals, feigning momentary confusion: 'But which of them shall I choose, Eunomius or his teachers, Arius or Aetius?' He recovered quickly, reminding himself that they were 'several names, but a single heresy' (1.44). The Arians might be divided—'some follow Eunomius, or Aetius, others Palladius or Demophilus, or Auxentius or the inheritors of his perfidy, others again different masters'—but they were all ultimately of the same stock (1.45). The wholly unfounded assimilation of the homoeans (including the doyen of the Illyrican episcopate, Palladius) to the Eunomians did not stem from ignorance: as 'Eunomians', Palladius and his homoean colleagues would fall under the ban that Gratian had announced the previous year. It was a crude but effective means of putting his opponents on the defensive.

For all its excesses, Ambrose's style of presentation seems designed to appeal precisely to the literate Christianity with which Gratian's court was infused. Arianism became a hydra, 'which grows from its own wounds, and as often as it is beheaded gives forth new shoots; but, doomed to the fire, it will perish in flames'. Better still, it was like Scylla, with part of its body giving an appearance of Christianity; but unfortunately for those caught as they were swept past amid the wreckage of the faith, it was also girt about with monstrous beasts, and so 'tore them

91. Note, for instance, the wily transition from past to present tense, obscuring the long delay since the original commission: 'fidem meam audire voluisti'; 'fidem libello exprimi censuisti'; 'Petis a me fidei libellum' (1.1–2).

92. Hanson's survey of Ambrose's case (*The Search*, 669–675) amply justifies his introductory remark (at 669) that 'too often his arguments are, as rational discussion, beneath contempt'.

with the savage tooth of its foul teachings' (1.46).[93] The emperor was entreated to steer clear of its perilous cave.

The danger was not merely the product of Ambrose's rhetoric. He wrote *De fide* in the knowledge that Gratian was to spend the next season in Illyricum, at the very mouth of Scylla's cave. No effort is spared to prejudice the emperor against the influences that he might encounter there. Book 1 ends with a prayer that Gratian's ears might be 'cleansed' with divine wine and so be purged of any heretical dregs lurking there, and that he 'should not hold to alien and sacrilegious beliefs' but should prefer the faith even to his own *pignora* (1.134–136). Gratian, who remained childless, continued to treat young Valentinian II like a son; the diplomatic courtesies he was obliged to extend to the prince's mother Justina at Sirmium might allow her to extend her influence and promote her views.

At the conclusion of the second book, after another warning against clamorous Arians and their criticisms of his 'hasty and unpolished' work (2.129–135), Ambrose sets out his own political theology with the promise of military victory in return for doctrinal obedience. He first presents a chilling picture of the perils of heterodoxy. The Danubian provinces that had suffered most from the invasions constituted the heartland of heresy; the region was therefore fatally polluted, doomed to a cycle of crimes against religion and divine retaliation and making the adjacent lands innocent victims of their 'deadly neighbour' (2.139–140). But there was an alternative. Ambrose turns to God and invites him to look instead to Italy. Other standards were aloft there, not the legions' eagles but the name and worship of Christ. There was also a message for the emperor. Italy had been spared devastation because of its orthodoxy; the emperor too could find security by embracing an 'Italian' perspective. 'Here the mind of the emperor is not inconstant, but his faith is firm' (2.141–142). This gnomic utterance has been much misinterpreted. The contrast is not between Gratian and Valens (who was irrelevant to a comparison between Italy and the Danube, and had been dead for over a year)[94] but between Gratian's own firmness in Italy, where he was free

---

93. Court taste for mythological imagery is indicated by Augustine's reference to the Sirens in a work addressed to Theodorus, Gratian's *magister memoriae* (*De beata vita* 1.4), and Theodorus' own allusion, in his epitaph for his pious sister Daedalia, to her near-namesake Daedalus (*ILCV* 1700).

94. An assumed reference to Valens has been used to date *De fide* to 378, before the accession of the orthodox Theodosius (Palanque, *Saint Ambroise*, 57; Nautin, 'Les premières relations', 235). But other contemporaries failed to make

to exercise his devotion to Christ, and his vulnerability in Illyricum to the wiles of the heretics and the compromises that they forced upon him. The emperor's inconsistency is therefore accepted as a fact of life, but one which was contingent upon geography. There was a real issue at stake here, as the Gothic crisis forced the western court to seek a new centre of gravity. In exalting Italy over Illyricum and proclaiming it a source of spiritual and military stability, Ambrose was in effect tendering a bid for his own region.

This remarkable text cannot be understood in isolation from the circumstances of its publication. Gratian left Trier in the early spring of 380 and was in Milan by late April. Ambrose probably presented the book to him formally: if, as is possible, the emperor arrived in time for Easter, we might imagine a presentation ceremony held in association with the festival.[95] This would do much to reinforce the presumption of legitimacy which was Ambrose's most powerful weapon. De fide can therefore be regarded as an attempt to capitalize upon the emperor's fleeting presence to claim him for Italy and, by association, for a fully consubstantial Christ.

One wonders how the emperor reacted to this unexpected response to his request. He could hardly have ignored it; on the other hand, we should not imagine him devouring it in the palace library, then setting off to Illyricum firmly committed to Ambrose's views.[96] Need Gratian, in fact, even have read it through? Although he doubtless accepted the text with polite gratitude, it was intended not for his private meditations but in response to those who had questioned Ambrose's faith, hence as the basis for public discussion. Ambrose had devoted great skill and energy to ensuring that the discussion should be held upon his own terms and his own agenda, but the scale of this task was formidable; De fide, transported in the imperial archives to Sirmium, would there have to speak

---

the connexion between Valens' heresy and the defeat at Adrianople; Jerome, in the concluding entry to his Chronicle, misses a particularly inviting opportunity to do so. The point is first made by Rufinus HE 11.13, after the extinction of the house of Valentinian.

95. R. Gryson, 'Origine et composition des "Scolies Ariennes" du manuscrit Paris, B. N., Lat. 8907', RHT 14–15 (1985), 372, envisages the original De fide as a presentation copy, 'soigneusement calligraphié sur un luxueux parchemin'. In 380 Easter fell on 12 April; the codes put Gratian at Trier on 18 March and Milan on 24 April (Seeck, Regesten, 252–254).

96. Pace Gottlieb, who claims that Ambrose's prediction of victory won Gratian's affection 'in einem Augenblick': Ambrosius von Mailand, 44.

for itself. However sympathetic a hearing Ambrose might initially have obtained from friends and admirers at Gratian's court, he could not hope by the sheer effrontery of his counterattack to reduce his Illyrican critics to silence.

THE ADVENT OF THEODOSIUS

While Ambrose was finishing *De fide*, Gratian's colleague Theodosius proclaimed his own faith in an edict. His subjects were ordered to follow the religion taught by Damasus of Rome and Peter of Alexandria, to whose adherents alone the name 'catholic' was reserved. The 'demented and insane' remnant were branded as heretics. Although threatening these delinquents with nothing more concrete than 'divine vengeance', the law promises that this will be followed by imperial intervention.[97]

This dramatic declaration has been much discussed, and its exact purport is still debated.[98] But there is unanimity that it expresses the emperor's own long-held beliefs and reflects the characteristic doctrinal views of his native Spain. What little can be reconstructed of Theodosius' background, however, should encourage caution. His contact with the Spanish church appears to have been minimal. In 383 two petitioners judged it necessary to spell out to him the full details of a celebrated controversy that had occurred in Spain during his own boyhood; Theodosius appears to have accepted the justice of their highly tendentious (and certainly unofficial) version of events.[99] Ignorance is a better explanation for Theodosius' attitude than Luciferian sympathies. His piety is more plausibly rooted in Valentinian's court, where he served beside his

97. *CTh* 16.1.2: 'Cunctos populos' (27 February 380).

98. The basic discussion is still W. Ensslin, *Die Religionspolitik des Kaisers Theodosius d. Gr.* (1953), 16–27, arguing that the edict had the full force of law; cf. K. G. Holum, *Theodosian Empresses* (1982), 16–17. N. Q. King, *The Emperor Theodosius and the Establishment of Christianity* (1964), 28–29, presents it as an 'election manifesto and speech from the throne'; A. M. Ritter, *Das Konzil von Konstantinopel und sein Symbol* (1965), 28–31, as a nonbinding outline of policy.

99. The *libellus precum* (*Coll. Avell.* 2) appeals directly to Theodosius on the basis only of an assumed commitment to Nicaea (5) and rejection of Rimini (19), both of which could by 383 be inferred from his public statements. The availability of corroboration for the 'long and implausible' (Hanson, *The Search*, 337) account of Gregory of Elvira and Ossius (*Coll. Avell.* 2.32–47) is claimed from 'omnis . . . Hispania' (41); Theodosius in his reply (*Coll. Avell.* 2a) appears to have no more awareness of Gregory's case than of Heraclidas of Oxyrrhyncus'.

father (who insisted on baptism before his execution in 375/6) and won swift promotion.[100] It was in this milieu, too, that he found the close-knit circle of compatriots who accompanied him to the east: significantly, not a single Spanish clergyman is reported among them.[101] Theodosius arrived in the east a committed Christian, but there is no evidence that his piety or that of his associates had been harnessed in advance to the Nicene cause.[102]

Theodosius' edict was not the spontaneous fruit of a pious winter retreat. His court in Thessalonica fairly bustled with petitioners and lobbyists. The beginning of a reign was the best time (as Ammianus reminds us) for the unscrupulous to extract favours,[103] and Theodosius acquired a reputation for being ready to please.[104] Hence the hasty journey to the court of the *consularis Syriae* Carterius (himself an Italian appointed through the influence of Theodosius' prefect Neoterius), intent upon securing an official teaching post at Antioch for a protégé; his disastrous failure was attributed, significantly, to the effect of his abrasive behavior upon some of the emperor's influential friends.[105]

The conspicuous piety of Theodosius and his entourage inevitably attracted Christian petitioners too, as the aftermath of Valens' death had left many questions to be resolved between the churches of the eastern empire. The edict is best explained as the response to one such question,

100. Orosius *Hist. adv. paganos* 7.33.7.

101. For Theodosius' associates, see Matthews, *Western Aristocracies*, 107–113, 169–170 (with the remark that their piety cannot be associated 'with any particular religious movement in Spain itself'). The closest one comes to a clergyman is Dexter, son of the bishop of Barcelona (111): the fact that his father's claim to fame was a refutation of the Novatians (Jer. *De vir. ill.* 106) is an incidental reminder of the limited doctrinal interests and awareness of the Spanish clergy.

102. Theodosius' Spanish wife, Flaccilla, won acclaim at Constantinople for her 'disgust' at the Arians (Greg. Nyss. *Or. fun. Flacc.*, 489.4ff; cf. Soz. *HE* 7.6.3); but again we know nothing of her previous behaviour in Spain or of the development of her doctrinal attitudes.

103. Amm. Marc. 30.9.3. Possibly relevant are *CTh* 10.10.12–15 (issued from Thessalonica during 380), concerning the procurement of rescripts to secure vacant property; dubious claims were presumably being staked.

104. Zosimus describes the throngs approaching Theodosius 'on account of public and private needs, and going home after obtaining satisfaction' (4.25.1); cf. 4.27.1: Theodosius 'appeared affable to all who approached him'.

105. Lib. *Or.* 1.186: for Carterius' connexion with Neoterius, see A. F. Norman, 'Notes on Some Consulares of Syria', *BZ* 51 (1958), 75. At *Or.* 1.196 Libanius attributes the success of a later embassy, from the Antiochene *curia*, to support from the emperor's friends.

presumably from representatives of the same 'people of Constantinople' to whom it was addressed.[106] An open request for guidance from citizens genuinely puzzled by the different doctrines being touted in the capital is unlikely; the form of the pronouncement, with its unusual emphasis on the obligatory rather than the forbidden, suggests that it was intended as an endorsement of a specific group.[107] But this creates a considerable puzzle, for Theodosius' statement cannot have been particularly welcome to *any* of the capital's Christian leaders. Although anathema to the city's homoean bishop Demophilus, the views expressed offered little comfort to Gregory of Nazianzus, who had arrived in Constantinople the previous year to organize the Nicene community. Gregory's ally Meletius had gained singularly little encouragement from eight years of negotiations with the 'haughty' Damasus, and his own relationship with Peter of Alexandria was at best uneasy: having granted him recognition, the bishop was soon to sponsor an attempt to displace him.[108] Gregory fails to mention the edict even once in his voluminous writings from the period, which (besides giving a salutary warning against exaggerating its contemporary impact) indicates that his own party derived no advantage from it.[109]

Theodosius is more likely to have taken his advice from Thessalonica itself. The city's bishop Acholius enjoyed close connexions with Rome and (probably) with Alexandria.[110] But Acholius spoke for a distinct minority. Thessalonica was unusual among Greek-speaking cities for its staunchly Nicene background, but still more so for its close ties with the west and with Rome in particular. Theodosius was probably unaware of

106. Cf. *CTh* 10.18.2 (issued on 26 January, also to the people of Constantinople), on regulations for treasure trove. We might imagine anxious inquiries from those who had buried their valuables when the Goths appeared before the walls of the capital in 378.

107. All Theodosius' later anti-heretical laws begin by announcing their targets, either by name or in general terms: *CTh* 16.5.6–24. Cf. Gratian's anti-Donatist law of 379, *CTh* 16.5.5.

108. For Meletius and Damasus, see Pietri, *Roma Christiana*, 794–849. Gregory shows his exasperation at Peter's behaviour at *De vita sua* 847–864.

109. Against the alleged allusion to the edict in Greg. Naz. *Or.* 33.13, see the remarks of C. Moreschini in *SCh* 318 (1985), pp. 21–22.

110. The Ascholius, 'monk and presbyter', whose enthusiasm for Athanasius Basil applauds (*Ep.* 154) has been attractively but not conclusively identified as the future bishop of Thessalonica: see Y. Courtonne, *Saint Basile: Lettres*, tome II (1961), p. 97, n. 1. Acholius' 'frequent' journeys to Constantinople (Amb. *Ep.* 52 [16].2), although perhaps referring only to attendance at the council of 381, might imply contacts with like-minded Nicenes in the capital.

this. Strikingly unqualified to govern the east, never before having set foot there, he was acutely dependent upon local expertise. During the long months of his confinement in Thrace, he was therefore vulnerable to capture for a party cause. He was later to proclaim a more nuanced position in relation to the Trinity; his commitment to Nicaea itself, so strongly proclaimed at the beginning of his reign, seemed at one point to waver before the length of the task of demolishing the homoean church and the disruption that it caused.[111] One wonders whether, had he had a clearer idea of the nature and condition of the eastern churches at the outset, he would not have adopted a different approach. The military exigencies that confined Theodosius to Thessalonica and the battlefields of Thrace for the first twenty-two months of his reign would in this case assume an unexpected importance for the religious history of Europe.

Theodosius' protracted isolation in Thessalonica had a thoroughgoing effect upon the shape of his regime. Few emperors had come to power in a position of such dependence. Confined by the Goths to a city borrowed from his partner, Theodosius waged his inconclusive struggle with a motley—and again partly borrowed—army.[112] His generosity was therefore conditioned by an urgent need to establish himself, and his publicity was also driven by the need for self-assertion. In the circumstances, this was inevitably done at Gratian's expense. His demonstrable reliance upon the latter's military support limited his options; but a court panegyric celebrating Theodosius' accession had already in early 379 reduced Gratian to a mere messenger.[113] The new emperor's readiness to proclaim a doctrinal commitment, and the strident terms in which he did so, can plausibly be set against the same background.

Theodosius' concern to advertise his piety is further attested, and his relationship with Acholius confirmed, by the baptism he received from the bishop in the autumn of 380.[114] The serious illness which pre-

111. For the 'conference of sects' and the 'disturbances' that led Theodosius to convene it, see Soc. *HE* 5.10.1, Soz. *HE* 7.12.1.

112. Troops: Them. *Or.* 34.21, with D. Hoffmann, *Das spätrömische Bewegungsheer und die Notitia Dignitatum* (1969), 459–60. Eastern Illyricum: V. Grumel, 'L'Illyricum de la mort de Valentinian Ier (375) à la mort de Stilicon (408)', *REB* 9 (1951), 9–12.

113. Them. *Or.* 14, 182 c–d (with Pabst, *Divisio Regni*, 102). The ambivalence of Theodosius' position is best conveyed in Them. *Or.* 15, delivered in 381 before a campaign that would involve substantial western contingents (P. Heather, *Goths and Romans 332–489* [1991], 154–155), which shifts uneasily between Theodosius as 'ruler' and 'co-ruler' (see esp. 197d).

114. For the chronology, see Ensslin, *Die Religionspolitik*, 17–24.

ceded this has prompted many scholars to envisage a botched attempt
at the conventional deathbed baptism, wherein the emperor's unexpected recovery left him psychologically and institutionally a prisoner
of the church.[115] But however attractive to secular historians, the picture
is fundamentally mistaken: the records of other baptized emperors, like
Valentinian and Valens, demonstrate that a ruler did not *necessarily* sacrifice his freedom of action at the font. Theodosius' baptism was rather
another dramatization of his faith, serving to emphasize both the gravity
of his recent illness and the divine favour that lay behind his recovery.

A fifth-century source presents the emperor as anxiously catechizing
Acholius before receiving baptism, to ensure his orthodoxy.[116] Having
spent most of the preceding eighteen months in Thessalonica, the emperor cannot have needed to do this; but it is possible that the story
reflects a further dramatization of the emperor's faith, devised to allow
him to retain his authority even as an acolyte. The doctrines upon which
he quizzed the bishop, and so broadcast to the Christian public, were
naturally the latter's own. The partnership that developed between emperor and bishop was impressively ramified, Acholius supporting the
Gothic wars with prayers which reputedly repelled the enemy from
Macedonia and brought pestilence to their ranks.[117] The bishop's perceived influence with Theodosius can also be gauged by a letter written
from Damasus of Rome, delivered to Acholius by one Rusticus, a *silen-
tarius* on a mission from Gratian's court to the eastern government. Rusticus had received baptism at Rome (and obtained this introduction to
Acholius) in order to 'equip' himself for the task, a remarkable indication of how the character of Theodosius' government was viewed from
the west.[118]

The same letter of Damasus introduces yet another petitioner before
Theodosius' court at Thessalonica: the Egyptian Maximus, recently—
and controversially—proclaimed bishop of Constantinople.[119] Discussing the matter at greater length in another letter to Acholius and other
Macedonian bishops, who had apparently held a synod and produced a

115. The classic statement is by Otto Seeck, *Geschichte des Untergangs der
Antiken Welt* (1913), 5:137–138.

116. Soz. *HE* 7.4.

117. Amb. *Ep.* 51 [15].5–7.

118. Dam. *Ep.* 6 (*PL* 13, 369–370).

119. On Maximus, see J. Mossay, 'Note sur Héron-Maxime, écrivain ecclésiastique', *AB* 100 (1982), 229–236; there is a full treatment in the excellent but
unpublished thesis by E. R. Snee, 'Gregory Nazianzen's Constantinopolitan Career' (Ph.D. diss., University of Washington, 1981).

formal report, Damasus expressed outrage at the secret 'consecration' of the intruder and urged Acholius to help find another candidate properly qualified to enter communion with Rome.[120] Maximus remains an elusive figure, known to posterity only through the lurid accounts of his enemies, but the coup he launched against his benefactor Gregory of Nazianzus and his subsequent manoeuvres reflect the complex interplay between church and court, and between east and west. In presenting himself to Theodosius, Maximus could point to his own Nicene (and specifically Alexandrian) credentials; his failure was finally determined only by the united front presented by Damasus and Acholius, whose correspondence suggests that his rejection was less peremptory than the indignant Gregory claimed.[121] But Maximus had a further card to play. He is subsequently reported at Milan, where he presented the emperor Gratian with a book entitled *De fide*.[122]

We have already seen an embattled controversialist presenting his claims to Gratian in exactly the same terms. Without further evidence, it is impossible to determine whether Maximus was inspired by Ambrose's success, or whether the coincidence of title reflects the sheer number of petitions and manifestos masquerading as doctrinal addresses that an emperor could expect to receive. More significant is the fact that Maximus was able to make the appeal and receive the emperor's endorsement. The conventional view of Gratian and Theodosius as theological allies, working in tandem to secure the empire for Nicene orthodoxy, has no contemporary evidence to recommend it: only when Gratian was safely dead was he received within the Theodosian pantheon. Alive, they constituted alternative sources of patronage for churchmen who (as Maximus' appeal to Gratian and Damasus' concern over the see of Constantinople indicate) did not recognize political boundaries. Nor, whatever the claims later made on their behalf, were their attentions reserved exclusively for Nicenes. In the summer of 380, the ecclesiastical situation was still wide open.

Even if Theodosius' February edict was not deliberately intended to compete with Gratian's edict of tolerance, it announced the emperor's arrival as a force in ecclesiastical politics. But Gratian was unlikely to

120. Dam. *Ep.* 5; cf. Pietri, *Roma Christiana*, 787–788.
121. Gregory has Maximus ejected from court 'like a dog' at *De vita sua* 1001–1012. The account confirms the implication in Gregory's correspondence that he lacked connexions at Thessalonica: the most he could claim was that he was 'not yet the victim of slander' among Theodosius' entourage.
122. Jer. *De vir. ill.* 127.

relinquish lightly the responsibility that he had assumed towards the eastern episcopate in 378/9, and still less the supreme authority that he had thereby claimed. When he arrived at Sirmium in the summer of 380 to continue the struggle against the Goths, he announced a general council, to meet the following year at Aquileia in Italy. The site was logical: the city was convenient to both east and west, and its accessibility by sea was especially important while the situation in the Balkans continued to make overland communications difficult. But it also meant that the church would resolve its differences firmly under Gratian's auspices. The senior Augustus was moving to outbid Theodosius.

Since the council did not eventually meet in the form that was originally planned, the plans themselves can be reconstructed only in outline. But the eastern bishops were definitely invited: at the attenuated council eventually held at Aquileia in September 381, Palladius of Ratiaria launched immediately into a complaint against their absence, invoking Gratian's plans. Nor was any rebuttal produced to his unequivocal statement: 'The emperor himself told us that he had ordered the easterners to come'.[123] In describing this interview with Gratian, which is to be assigned to the same summer of 380, Palladius is at pains to stress the emperor's active involvement in instigating the council.[124] He summarized his conversation with the emperor in a letter read out to the council (but not recorded in the minutes), which prompted his enemies to press him for details: 'When the emperor was at Sirmium in person, did you thrust yourself upon his attention [to badger him into organizing the council], or did he himself compel you [to attend])?'[125] Palladius managed to avoid both the disreputable positions being imputed to him, while stressing the emperor's initiative in summoning the council and the terms upon which he himself had agreed to come: 'He (Gratian) said to me, "Go". I said, "Have the easterners been summoned?". He said, "They have been summoned"'.[126]

123. *Acta conc. Aquil.* 8; Ambrose could only reply by adducing the subsequent adjustments proposed by himself (cf. below, p. 124).

124. G. Gottlieb, 'Das Konzil von Aquileia', *AHC* 11 (1979), 293, assigns the interview to the immediate prelude of the council, arguing from the tone of the exchange that Palladius was seeking reassurance from a hostile emperor. This requires that Gratian told an outright lie; it also misses the point that Palladius' account is not a full report but a clarification made in the face of aggressive questioning.

125. *Acta conc. Aquil.* 10: 'Imperator cum praesens esset Sirmio, tu illum interpellasti an ipse te compulit?'.

126. *Acta conc. Aquil.* 10: 'Dixit mihi: "Vade", diximus, "Orientales conventi sunt?" Ait: "Conventi sunt"'. For this usage of *convenire* as 'summon', cf. Amb. *Ep.* 76 [20].2.

Gratian's council dovetailed neatly with the exchanges that he had been refereeing for the previous year. Palladius of Rataria himself supplies the connection: the only Illyrican to be named by Ambrose in *De fide* among the heretics 'to whom a response must be made', he had presumably presented the case against him during the emperor's previous visit to the Balkans.[127] The senior survivor of the generation of Ursacius and Valens, his record—as a presbyter since 335 and bishop since 346—carried considerable authority: few other churchmen ordained in the reign of Constantine were still alive.[128] Despite his disclaimer, it is likely that his interview with Gratian helped to shape the emperor's plans for the council.[129]

Palladius' influence might be suspected particularly in the council's proposed format. His dispute with Ambrose, the gravity of which had been brought home to the emperor by *De fide*, was now to be adjudicated by the assembled bishops of the Christian empire.[130] Gratian was thus spared the need to judge between two bishops both of whom he appears to have admired, but the greater beneficiary was Palladius. He was confident of his ability to prove Ambrose's incompetence before a qualified audience; better still, by personalizing the conflict in this way, he could hope to discredit Ambrose's Nicene doctrines together with their champion.

Palladius' confidence was grounded in *De fide*. The bishop of Milan had taken a considerable risk in presenting himself for scrutiny at Sirmium in the form of this lengthy and discursive polemic: whatever impression it might have made upon readers at the court, or even the emperor himself, it still had to fulfil its ostensible function of vindicating Ambrose's faith against his challengers. Gratian duly passed the book to Palladius, who immediately responded. He issued a pamphlet to correct

127. *De fide* 1.45–46. Gratian's march to Castra Martis in August 378 had brought him into the immediate vicinity of Ratiaria.

128. For Palladius' career, see Gryson, *Scolies Ariennes*, 81–83.

129. Ambrose appears to admit as much at *Gesta conc. Aquil., Ep.* 2 [= PL 16, Amb. *Ep.* 10].2: 'propter quos [sc. Palladius and a colleague] congregari concilium postulabant de extrema orbis parte Romani'. Gryson, *Scolies Ariennes*, 128–129, points out that the grammar of this convoluted clause does not actually assign the initiative to them, but I suspect that this reflects Ambrose's reluctance to acknowledge their authority. It is difficult to imagine who else the implied subjects could be.

130. The original terms of the council are summarized in Gratian's rescript *Ambigua* (*Acta conc. Aquil.* 3–4): 'Neque enim controversiae dubiae sententiae rectius poterant experiri quam si obortae altercationis interpretes ipsos constitutissemus antistites, ut vidilicet a quibus profiscuntur instituta doctrinae, ab isdem discordis eruditionis repugnantia solverentur'.

its libels (such as the accusation of Eunomianism) and publicize its shortcomings, which unfortunately survives only in an extract which the author chose to reproduce in a later work.[131] The format, with long citations from Ambrose followed by comments upon these, recalls some near-contemporary works by Palladius' fellow-Illyrican Jerome, as do the vigour and savagery of the contents and style.[132] The two surviving sections culminate in an excoriating dismissal of Ambrose's elaborate comparison between the diverse heretical sects and the mythological monsters, Scylla and the hydra. This parade of pagan literary learning was beyond the endurance of a man whose whole adult life had been spent in the service of the church.

> Cease, I beg you, this useless and superfluous recitation of clever trickery, but rather attend to the words of holiness which are necessary; desist from your monstrous comparisons, with which you have fitted out your long-winded address to show off your knowledge of literature; abandon the prodigies, the highly polished but vain recitation of which has caused the shipwreck of your faith, and recover at last an understanding of the truth from which a treacherous and unholy heresy has lured you. Search the divine Scriptures, which you have neglected, so that under their divine guidance you may avoid the Hell towards which you are heading on your own. (*Apol.* 87)

The magisterial tone, fully reflecting the elderly bishop's seniority, was in distinct and probably deliberate contrast to Ambrose's intemperate sallies.

Palladius had revealed his eagerness for a direct confrontation in the same passage. Scorning Ambrose for the emptiness of his challenges (presumably referring to his reliance on Gratian's authority to silence his Milanese opponents), he taunts him with his own assertion in *De fide* that he was ready to face the Arian leaders, himself included.

> An end, please, to this denigration of those to whom you promise to reply, but to whom you prefer to remain invisible, rich in your promises but stingy in repaying them. You are bold enough in your corner, but out in the open you become timid; you rage away in your hideout only to become shy in public, heated among your cronies but stiff and reserved in the company of rivals; you put your trust in words while showing no confidence in action. (*Apol.* 86)

131. This pamphlet, part of which forms the first section of Palladius' *Apology* (81–87), is presumably the work known to Vigilius of Thapsa as 'in refutatione dictorum eius [sc. Ambrosii] quaedam' (*Contra Arianos* 2.50: PL 62, 230) and refuted by him in another, lost, work. For the connexion between this section and the rest of the *Apology*, and for recent bibliography on the subject, see my 'The "Apology" of Palladius', *JThS*, n.s., 42 (1991), 34–58.

132. Jerome's *Contra Helvidium*, probably written in 383, uses exactly the same technique of quotation and comment.

Palladius' language bespeaks his confidence and suggests the enthusiasm with which he took up the emperor's plans for the council. Although neither the readership of this pamphlet nor the extent of its circulation are known, the massive 'second edition' of De fide that it provoked indicates how seriously Ambrose was forced to take its challenge.

But this was only one aspect of Palladius' response to De fide. His attack was not designed for the emperor's attention, or as a formal reply to the 'profession of faith' that Ambrose had produced. Whereas Ambrose had addressed his vituperation and polemic to Gratian, Palladius reserved his response for an ostensibly 'private' correspondence with his enemy and struck a note more appropriate for a churchman in his dealings with the emperor. He could look forward to settling accounts with Ambrose at the forthcoming council; the emperor was meanwhile brought into service to procure some additional ammunition. Evidence for Palladius' tactics comes in a letter to Ambrose from Gratian, probably written in the latter part of the emperor's stay in Illyricum in 380.[133] This document has invariably been used to illustrate Ambrose's overwhelming influence over the young prince and the intimacy of their relations; it has been taken as 'certain testimony' of the respect and esteem in which Gratian regarded him.[134] Such views reflect the effusive language of the airy 'invitation' to court with which the emperor begins: 'I think of you in your absence, and desire very much to be with you in the flesh as well as in my thoughts. Hasten to me then, holy priest of God' (1).[135] But it is a mistake to assume that a text of this nature necessarily reflects its author's feelings.[136] The letter, moreover, has traditionally been read exactly as Ambrose wished it to be read: it survives precisely because the bishop appended it as a preface to his De spiritu sancto, advertising

133. The *Epistola Gratiani* is edited by O. Faller, in *CSEL* 79 (1964), pp. 3–4; references in this and the following paragraph are to the letter. Palanque dated the letter to the early months of 380 (*Saint Ambroise*, 502; 'Un episode des rapports entre saint Ambroise et Gratien', *REA* 30 [1928], 291–301), leaving a gap of nearly two years after his date for De fide. The chronology presented here, following Gottlieb, *Ambrosius von Mailand*, 39–40, is derived from Ambrose's subsequent apology for having failed to come to Gratian during his 'return' (to Gaul, in autumn 380).

134. Palanque, *Saint Ambroise*, 67–68; Homes Dudden, *Saint Ambroise*, 192.

135. This 'summons', which is immediately forgotten, is clearly not the principal point of the letter: the main body demands the bishop's *tractatus*, not his presence.

136. Few would infer genuine affection from the almost identical phraseology used by Constantius II to Athanasius (quoted by the latter at *Hist. Ar.* 24); compare the closing formula, 'Divina te providentia multis annis conservet, pater dilectissime', with Gratian's 'Divinitas te servet per multos annos, parens'.

the book as the response to an imperial commission and bolstering its arguments with Gratian's imprimatur.[137]

The contents of Gratian's letter do not in any case reflect unconditional submission to Ambrose's teachings. The prince announces that he acknowledges Christ as 'my Lord and God', and adds that he would not impute to him 'the creature which I see in myself' (2). There is nothing here to which Palladius could not have agreed;[138] Gratian, if he had read Ambrose's work at all, had absorbed a singularly colourless version of his teachings. He wrote, moreover, to invite Ambrose to amplify the contents of his De fide. Why was such amplification necessary? We can dismiss the possibility that Gratian desired private instruction; more likely Palladius, besides circulating his reply to Ambrose's work, had suggested to the emperor that De fide had left some of the questions it raised unanswered. His larger purposes were well served by the request that the bishop of Milan should elaborate upon his brief remarks on the divinity of the Holy Spirit, proving 'by scriptural texts and arguments that he is God' (3);[139] for it was still deeply controversial whether such proof was possible, and even among those who accepted the consubstantial nature of the first two persons of the Trinity there were many who refused to take this further step.[140]

Ambrose waited until the court had left Illyricum and returned to Gaul, in the autumn of 380, before sending his reply.[141] His letter is a

137. Faller, CSEL 79, p. 5*, gives the textual tradition.

138. For Christ as 'dominus et deus noster', see Secundianus at Acta conc. Aquil. 65 (cf. Palladius Apol. 107). Arius himself insisted that Christ was not a creature 'like all the other creatures' (cf. Acta 41–43, for Arius' view that the Son was a 'creatura perfecta'), while Palladius deprecates the unscriptural term 'creatura' at Apol. 94. The expression 'aeternus', used of the Son by Gratian (Ep. Grat. 3), was also acceptable to Palladius on scriptural grounds (Apol. 102); his objection was to 'ingenito coaeternus' (82).

139. 'Augendo illic de sancto spiritu fidelem disputationem scripturis atque argumentis deum esse convince'. The question had been discussed somewhat breezily in De fide 1.8–11.

140. The creed of the council of Constantinople in 381 remained significantly silent concerning the Spirit's divinity (Hanson, The Search, 818–819). The difficulty of finding scriptural proof is nicely conveyed by Basil Adv. Eunomium 3.7 (adducing the 'silences of Scripture').

141. The codes show the emperor at Aquileia on 27 June and at Trier on 14 October (Seeck, Regesten, 254); between these dates must be inserted Gratian's visit to Sirmium, a summer campaign against the Goths (Cons. Const. s.a. 380: Chron. Min. 1, p. 243) and perhaps a settlement (below, chap. 4, n. 88). The return to Trier is the only occasion that can fit Ambrose's apology to Gratian, 'Reverthe . . . non occurri'; Palanque's argument (above, n. 133) for Gratian's

masterpiece, beautifully exploiting the conventions of correspondence to secure himself a favourable hearing.[142] Taking the emperor's invitation literally, he begins with an elaborate apology that plays upon the proven excuse of *verecundia* (1). He then proceeds to subject Gratian's letter to a detailed scrutiny, dwelling on its phraseology and calligraphy exactly as had Ausonius the previous year, in his thanksgiving for his consulship.[143] Often dismissed as empty flattery, this homage to the emperor's literary pretensions was the necessary preliminary to the close and subtle reading of his words.[144] Ambrose's emphasis upon his own services to the emperor (his prayers had helped ensure a safe journey back to Trier), and upon the benefits he had already received in return for his investment in the bishop, belong indeed to the traditional language of *amicitia*. But in quoting Gratian's bland pleasantries back at him, Ambrose also turned them to suit his own interests. In particular, Gratian's request for a statement of the case for the divinity of the Spirit was 'misinterpreted' to reflect the emperor's own beliefs: Ambrose rejoiced that divine inspiration had led the prince 'to a most fruitful claim for belief also in the eternal divinity of the Holy Spirit, . . . so that you should not impute to him the creature which you see in yourself' (8). This transfers to the Spirit a comment that Gratian had applied to the *Son*, and changes a truism acceptable (as we have seen) to Palladius into an explicit statement of support for Ambrose's own position. That careless readers of the emperor's letter—or better, those who have read it in conjunction with Ambrose's reply—have had no doubts about ascribing this position to Gratian is a tribute to Ambrose's skill as a publicist. By such techniques could emperors be captured.

Much ingenuity has been expended upon the reason for Gratian's request for 'the very same treatise you had given', which has seemed to imply that he required a fresh copy of *De fide*.[145] He has been seen passing his own copy to Theodosius for his colleague's edification, or return-

---

outward journey in early 380 juggles several laws to produce a tortuous itinerary (Trier-Aquileia-Milan-Aquileia-Sirmium) and forces the meaning of 'revertere' to apply it to the first leg.

142. *Ep. extra coll.* 12 [1]; text references in the following two paragraphs are to this letter.

143. Aus. *Act. Grat.* 9.43–10.50.

144. Palanque (*Saint Ambroise*, 70) regrets these 'flatteries adulatrices'; von Campenhausen (*Ambrosius von Mailand*, 44) sees the bishop lapsing into his former habits as an imperial functionary.

145. *Ep. Grat.* 3: 'Rogo te ut mihi des ipsum tractatum quem dederas'.

ing it to Ambrose so that the bishop could respond to Palladius' anno-
tations.[146] Both exaggerate the degree of Gratian's personal involvement.
The emperor simply wanted a complete text, and his phrasing suggests
a certain benign vagueness about the document at issue; Ambrose's reference to his 'two *libelli*' (7) pointedly specifies what he had written and
how it had been received. But he appears to have gone further. The verb
in 'misi duos libellos' is best read as a present perfect, signifying the
enclosure of the volumes with the letter.[147] The gift was both unsolicited
and—given the likelihood that Ambrose was already working on a further instalment of three volumes—curiously redundant.[148] The purpose
was to bring *De fide* once more physically to the emperor's attention and
to impress upon him the author's self-confidence. Ambrose's claim that
he 'will now fear no danger for the books, since they have been approved by Your Clemency' (7) is largely bravado but at the same time
reflects the ex-bureaucrat's awareness that controversies are not won by
quality of argument alone.

Gratian was probably unaware of the undercurrents of the struggle
being waged through him between Ambrose and Palladius. It was still
feasible for him to admire the sanctity of both men when in their respective company, and while deprecating their differences to reserve their
resolution for his forthcoming council. Ambrose's efforts to extract the
most positive message possible from Gratian's bland benevolence, while
beautifully illustrating the nuances of communications between ruler
and subject, reveal not a triumphant ascendancy over the emperor but
an anxious and uncertain struggle for recognition.

For the second year in succession, Ambrose was busy during the winter
of 380/1. He had written no fewer than six volumes by the spring: a

146. Theodosius: Faller, *CSEL* 79, p. 4; returned to Ambrose: Nautin, 'Les
premières relations', 243. H. Glaesener, 'L'empereur Gratien et saint Ambroise',
RHE 52 (1957), suggested somewhat desperately (474–475) that the copy originally presented had been produced in haste and was therefore difficult to read.
147. For this construction cf. Amb. *Ep. extra coll.* 1 [41].1 ('misi'); *Ep.* 37
[47].1 ('transmisi'); Hil. *Contra Aux.* 15 ('transmisi'). A historic perfect would
serve only to remind Gratian of the number of volumes originally 'sent' in 379
(to Sirmium, therefore, rather than the presentation suggested above, p. 105)
and sits awkwardly beside the subsequent 'interim'.
148. The phrasing of Gratian's request implies strongly that he was only
interested in the additional material, not the original *tractatus:* the 'augendo . . .
convince' clause is epexegetic, not conjunctive. It is unlikely that he reclaimed
the 'incomplete' original from Palladius.

remarkable but by no means unparalleled feat.[149] First there was the addition of three further volumes to *De fide*. Ambrose began with a statement regretting that the 'wicked minds' of certain troublemakers had made the sequel necessary; he then launched into a defence of his use of pagan literature which reveals Palladius as the principal mischief-maker.[150] But Ambrose chose not to engage in a point-by-point debate with his opponent. Perhaps he had only heard of Palladius' work at second hand. In any case, he refused to accept that any of the points he had raised in his first edition were subject to discussion, and to make this clear he reissued the first two volumes unchanged as part of the new five-volume edition. Preferring to take the offensive, he embarked upon a series of fresh attacks on positions attributed to the Arians. The material was again drawn from various polemical sources, chiefly Athanasius, but this time the bishop's organizing hand is less in evidence: in the last two books particularly, the bulk of the text seems to have been transcribed almost directly from his sermons.[151] Haste offers the most plausible explanation, as Ambrose strove to assemble as imposing a set of credentials as possible to present to the emperor. The same applies to his promised work on the Holy Spirit, which (as one critic noted with outrage) was largely culled from a treatise by Didymus, the blind scholar of Alexandria, but turned from good Greek into bad Latin and from a virile and compelling argument into something 'feeble and soft, sleek and pretty, decorated with prose that reeks of delicate perfumes'.[152] The criticisms are apt, yet they miss the point that Ambrose was not seeking to produce an instrument for scholars but a showpiece for his theological and cultural credentials that could also withstand critical scrutiny.[153]

Ambrose was writing to a deadline, for Gratian and the court were due at Milan in the spring. This was not to be another casual visit, in

149. Ambrose's energy palls beside the prodigious output of Augustine and Jerome; the spate of books produced by the latter in the later 380s is catalogued by J. N. D. Kelly in chaps. 14–16 of his *Jerome* (1975).

150. *De fide* 3.3, in particular, meets precisely Palladius' attack against the mythological references in the original: 'Et quia Hydraei nominis, et Scyllaei litoris comparationem induximus . . .'

151. 'Oral' features of *De fide* 3–5 are noted by Palanque, *Saint Ambroise*, 459–460.

152. Jerome *Interpretatio libri Didymi de spiritu sancto*, praef.: 'totum flaccidum, molle, nitidum atque formosum, et exquisitis hic inde odoribus pigmentatum'.

153. The unusual care taken over the prose rhythm of the work—'a very good *cursus mixtus*'—is suggestive of Ambrose's priorities: S. M. Oberhelman, *Rhetoric and Homiletics in Fourth-Century Christian Literature* (1991), 44–45.

transit to the battlefields of the Danube. A decision had been taken to implement a thoroughgoing reorientation of the imperial court and to install the emperor and his entourage in northern Italy. The basis for this move was doubtless strategic. Since Valentinian's reign, the Rhine frontier had remained secure, with the only serious Germanic incursion (by the Lentienses in 378) occurring in a region as accessible from Milan as from Trier; the situation in the Balkans, meanwhile, had required the emperor's constant attention. A permanent base in the Po valley, whose two chief cities, Milan and Aquileia, looked respectively north and east, offered a sensible alternative to the annual trek between Trier and Sirmium. The decision was also to have profound political consequences— among them, the vastly increased influence that Ambrose was to enjoy through sheer proximity to the government and access to its personnel. Ambrose was not the only beneficiary. Syagrius, the praetorian prefect of Italy, had a brief respite from his duties when he inaugurated the new year as consul, the first such celebration Milan had witnessed since 364. Among those invited to the festivities were the grandees of Rome;[154] the ancient capital was within relatively easy reach of Milan, and the 'accessibility that comes from proximity' encouraged a frequency of contact between the two cities, and a level of participation by senators in state affairs, that had been impossible while the court had remained at Trier.[155]

Typically, the sources give hardly an echo of the massive upheavals that must have marked the winter. Only such indications as the continuity between the coinage of the mints of Trier and Milan, which implies an extensive transfer of staff, give an impression of the scale of the relocation.[156] Gratian finally arrived in Milan in March 381, just in time for Easter.[157] He was greeted with the fruit of Ambrose's winter labours. Indeed, it is possible that the bishop presented the emperor with his *De spiritu sancto* as part of the season's festivities. The prologue envisages precisely the circumstances of Easter 381: invoking the masses of people whom Jesus had 'cleansed today' in Rome, Alexandria, Antioch and Constantinople through the bishops of those cities, Ambrose claims a

154. Symmachus, in mourning for his brother Titianus, sent his apologies: *Ep.* 1.101.

155. 'Viciniae facilitas': Symm. *Ep.* 1.102, again to Syagrius in Milan.

156. M. F. Hendy, 'Aspects of Coin Production and Fiscal Administration', *NC* 7.12 (1972), at 127, confirming a suggestion by Pearce, *Roman Imperial Coinage* 9, 72.

157. The codes show him at Trier on 27 February and at Milan on 29 March; Easter fell the previous day, 28 March. References in Seeck, *Regesten*, 256.

connexion between Constantinople's restoration to 'orthodoxy' and the subsequent submission, death and funeral of the Gothic leader Athanaric.[158] Then, in a movement that foreshadows a controversial sermon preached to another emperor, he turned to Gratian himself with some concrete examples of the Spirit's activity (1.19–26).[159] The surmise that this prologue formed the text of an actual Easter sermon (delivered, perhaps, in conjunction with a formal presentation of the whole work) once again suggests how a work that had been commissioned for one purpose, as a contribution to a debate between experts, could be presented quite differently as a royal command performance. In posing as the emperor's official exegete, Ambrose was again pretending to a more authoritative position than he actually held.

The principal example of the Holy Spirit's power which Ambrose quoted to Gratian illustrates all too clearly the pressures to which he remained exposed, even in his own city. The Spirit's hand was seen in a recent decision by the emperor, taken suddenly and without any advice, that a basilica should be 'restored' (1.20); Ambrose subsequently speaks of a *sequestratio* that had been revoked (1.21). The episode is mysterious. The topical impact obviously intended presupposes a recent event, which excludes the traditional association with Gratian's 'edict of tolerance' of 378.[160] But Ambrose's remarks do little to elucidate what had actually happened: his repetition of the technical term *sequestratio* and its variants four times in a single short paragraph (1.21) leaves the force of the word unclear, and an initial emphasis upon the emperor's responsibility is immediately contradicted.[161] If used in its formal sense, the term should imply litigation instituted against Ambrose's church to claim a basilica—by the homoeans, perhaps, to claim a church erected during Auxentius' tenure—and the building's seizure in the emperor's name (but in his absence) pending adjudication. Ambrose would in this case be celebrating Gratian's eventual decision in his favour, but the seriousness with which his enemies' claims had been treated would nevertheless be ominous.

---

158. *De spir. sancto* 1.17. Text references in the following discussion are to this work. For a comparable exploitation of Athanaric's arrival by an eastern propagandist, see Them. *Or.* 15, 190d.

159. Cf. *Ep. extra coll* 1 [41].26.

160. Cf. 1.19: 'proxime', and Gottlieb's discussion, *Ambrosius von Mailand*, 44–46.

161. Note the successive sentences at 1.21: 'basilicam sequestrasti ut fidem probares'; 'pietas tua . . . sic sequestravit, ut probaret'; 'patuit . . . omnibus et tuum non fuisse cum sequestrares'.

One possible instigator of such a suit is Iulianus Valens, who had acceded to the see of his native Poetovio after his previous skirmishes with Ambrose but had by autumn 381 been back in Milan for long enough to earn condemnation for 'gathering around himself men of his own stamp by illicit ordinations' and seeking 'to leave behind him, through certain abandoned wretches, a seedbed of his own impiety and wickedness'.[162] At about this time, too, young Valentinian's mother Justina arrived in Milan to begin her campaign against the bishop who had humiliated her at Sirmium, 'offering gifts and honours to excite the people against the holy man'.[163] Justina, often supposed to have arrived as a refugee from the Gothic invasion of 378,[164] is unlikely to have fled Sirmium while the western army was there to offer protection; but the political shifts that would inevitably accompany the relocation of the court promised opportunities to advance the claims of her son, now nine, who will naturally have followed his colleague and guardian (who still remained childless) to Italy.

But Justina's presence could have led to a less formal 'sequestration'. If she reached Milan during the winter of 380/1 with her faithful entourage from Pannonia, she might have invoked her authority as an Augusta to appropriate in the imperial name a church for her 'official' devotions, to relinquish it when Gratian himself arrived the following spring.[165] In this case, there would have been neither a formal seizure nor a revocation; Gratian himself would have taken no decision at all. The fourfold repetition of the term 'sequestration' would therefore serve to drive home a persuasive definition. It would not be the only occasion during his episcopal career that the ex-advocate resorted to misrepresentation.[166]

Certainty is impossible concerning either the exact nature of the challenge to Ambrose or the emperor's role in it; the incident neverthe-

162. *Ep. extra coll.* 4 [10].10.

163. Paulin, *V. Amb.* 12.

164. For this view (and as a consequence the dating of the sequestration to 378/9), see Palanque, *Saint Ambroise*, 60.

165. *CJ* 6.22.7 perhaps implies, *pace* Holum, *Theodosian Empresses*, 31, that Valentinian I had made Justina an Augusta. The argument in any case depends less upon formal titulature than upon the authority wielded over local officials by a queen mother. For imperial claims upon Milanese churches, see p. 175 below; for Justina's entourage, see Amb. *Ep.* 76 [20].12: 'quocumque femina ista processerit secum suos omnes coetus vehit'.

166. A play upon words for an alert audience might be suggested by the verb's occurrence, in a very different context, at the very beginning of *De spir. sancto*: '[Hierobaal] electionem sanctorum a purgamentis inanis paleae sequestraret' (1.1).

less suggests that Ambrose could still be exposed to embarrassment on his home ground. The bishop had meanwhile to prepare for his forthcoming confrontation with Palladius. The issue remained finely balanced. Ambrose's new publications were presumably greeted with applause from the literate Christians in Gratian's entourage but had still to meet the scrutiny of Palladius; only then would the massive confidence Ambrose had exuded in his writings be put to the test.

But the confrontation never took place, for Gratian's general council was sabotaged by his colleague. Theodosius' early advertisement of his faith had announced his intention to establish a close relationship with his 'own' eastern church. Although he had endorsed Gratian's plan for a single council in the west, he proceeded with his own schemes.[167] He had already, in 380, announced a meeting in Constantinople to determine the vexed question of the rightful bishop of that city.[168] This did not preclude a subsequent journey to the west. But Theodosius wanted to establish an exclusive claim upon his bishops; nor were the beneficiaries of his favour likely to oppose him.

After Acholius' Thessalonica, Theodosius was perhaps surprised by the complexity of Christian life in his capital. The day after his ceremonial entrance into the city in November 380, he interviewed the homoean bishop of ten years' standing, Demophilus, offering to guarantee his tenure in return for his subscription to the *homoousion*. The bishop refused and promptly reconvened his flock outside the city walls, where they continued to hold their assemblies for the following two decades.[169] Both had probably been bluffing at first, and they were perhaps equally taken aback by each other's obstinacy. But Theodosius' belief in the feasibility of orthodoxy was sustained, and his willingness to defy the majority bolstered, by the arrival in the capital of Meletius of Antioch, who had devoted the past two years to building an impressive coalition of Syrian and neighbouring bishops.[170] This was to be the basis of the

167. Gratian's assurance to Palladius that the eastern bishops had been summoned implies confidence in Theodosius' acquiescence in the planned council. Gryson's suggestion (*Scolies Ariennes*, 131) that both emperors changed their mind simultaneously was justly criticized by Y.-M. Duval in his review, *RHE* 76 (1981), 326.

168. The only item on the agenda mentioned by Damasus to Acholius (*Ep.* 5) is the appointment of a new bishop.

169. Soc. *HE* 5.7; Soz. *HE* 7.5.

170. Meletius' arrival: Greg. Naz. *De vita sua* 1514–1524. The culmination of his work in Syria, the council of Antioch in 379, is an elusive affair unreported

Theodosian 'state-church'; in January 381 the emperor issued his famous law *nullus locus*, which included Arians in a list of proscribed
sects, and sent invitations to some hundred and fifty bishops (predominately allies of Meletius) to Constantinople.[171] The need to appoint a
new bishop for the capital was but a pretext: the eastern church assembled to determine its own destiny, under the benevolent scrutiny of its
own Christian emperor.

THE COUNCIL OF AQUILEIA

Theodosius' unilateral decision to implement his own settlement of
the eastern church was acutely embarrassing for his colleague. The arrangements already made for summoning the eastern bishops to Aquileia, and the invitations that had presumably been issued to them, were
now redundant; the chosen representatives of the eastern episcopate
assembled at Constantinople in May 381 and conducted their business
(not without controversy) in the weeks that followed.[172] The scale of this
council and the consequent effect upon Gratian's planned meeting were
probably not immediately apparent in the west. There were, perhaps,
hopes that the easterners were using Constantinople merely as an assembly point and would proceed westwards after confirming the position of the bishop there. But eventually Gratian had to face the prospect
of cancelling his projected assembly and admitting publicly his defeat
by Theodosius.

It was Ambrose who rescued Gratian. The imperial rescript issued
in response to the changed circumstances (which survives as part of the
Acta of the council of Aquileia)[173] shows how the government explained
away the rebuff from the easterners. The original instructions are first
summarized: as was appropriate, bishops had been ordered to assemble

---

in the historians: G. Bardy, 'Le concile d'Antioche', *RB* 54 [1933], 196–213. The
153 participants implied by the documents sent to Rome (chiefly the letter *Confidimus quidem,* which Sabinus had delivered seven years earlier) strain credence:
some were probably created to 'shadow' established homoean prelates, to produce the 'new' episcopal generation of former soldiers, sailors and worse (Greg.
Naz. *De seipso et episcopis,* 154–175).

    171. *CTh* 16.5.6; Ritter, *Das Konzil,* 33–40.
    172. The council's proceedings are discussed by Ritter, *Das Konzil;* there is
a useful survey by Hanson, *The Search,* 805–820.
    173. *Acta conc. Aquil.* (hereafter *Acta*) 3–4.

to resolve a dispute between bishops. These arrangements, the rescript continues, were not now being changed, but a more effective way of implementing them had been proposed by Ambrose, who 'by his meritorious life and the favour of God has become famous as the bishop of Milan' (*Acta* 4). He had presented a *suggestio* to the effect that the main purpose of the council—the settlement of his three-year doctrinal dispute with his Illyrican opponents—could be achieved without recourse to a large assembly. Since 'the truth' was at issue between a few disputants only, they could save their colleagues the labour (and potential hazards) of involvement by establishing it among themselves: Ambrose and the bishops of the neighbouring cities of Italy were 'abundantly sufficient' to meet the claims being advanced by the opposition. The sophistry is concluded with conventional sentiments upon sparing elderly and sickly bishops the fatigue of a lengthy journey. The emperor's gratitude to Ambrose for this face-saving expedient was beyond doubt genuine. But he did not see that the revised council would deny Palladius the audience he needed to present his 'evidence' against Ambrose and thereby to expose both the bishop and the doctrines he so ineptly represented.

Palladius, moreover, remained unaware of the dramatic change of circumstances. His isolation can be attributed in part to the vigorous conflict the region experienced that year;[174] but he was also, perhaps, the victim of a conspiracy. Gratian's rescript was issued to Syagrius, the praetorian prefect of Italy, who was responsible for implementing its terms in Italy itself and conveying them to his colleagues and to the vicars under his jurisdiction. Palladius was later to allege a sinister connection between Syagrius and the original author of the proposal. He professed no surprise at the devices to which Ambrose had resorted at the council to engineer his deposition, 'since you were able, to the injury of religion itself, to annul the arrangements for a general council by a cunning suggestion, full of deceit, by which you both made a mockery of the priesthood by your trickery and laid waste the churches of God through human patronage, by the relentlessness and savagery of Syagrius'. A verse from Psalm 79 is then adduced to etymologize the prefect's name, to make him a 'wild boar' devastating a vineyard.[175] Palladius does not enlarge, but the accusation was probably connected with the prefect's responsibility for organizing his journey to Aquileia. He

---

174. Heather, *Goths and Romans*, 154–155.
175. Palladius *Apol.* (hereafter Pall.) 121: 'aper . . . ferus', translated from the Greek *sus* and *agrios*.

and his companion Secundianus arrived ignorant of the restrictions that had been imposed on the scope of the council and could reasonably complain of having received no official notification. Syagrius' role becomes the more significant in the light of the involvement of the staff of the prefectural *officium* in the previous exchanges between Germinius and his Illyrican colleagues. In the scattered Danubian sees, bishops seem to have depended upon these channels to conduct their correspondence and obtain information.

The assembly that Palladius and his partner found at Aquileia was discouraging indeed.[176] The core of the council consisted of ten Italian bishops, all loyal supporters of Ambrose; the empire was represented by two legates from Africa and two official delegations from Gaul, with a half-dozen other Gallic bishops, four Illyricans (including Anemius of Sirmium) and several others who defy identification.[177] This small and partisan gathering was a far cry indeed from the audience before which Palladius had hoped to demolish Ambrose. He could not, however, simply return home: withdrawal would have conceded too much to his opponents, allowing them to broadcast their own interpretation of it. Palladius, as his earlier actions had demonstrated, knew that it was essential to retain the initiative in controversy. He therefore participated in two preliminary meetings with the opposing party, after the first of which he wrote to challenge them formally to a public encounter. At a meeting in the basilica, he declared, he would prove to them that he was a Christian; more important, he would expose their subterfuges.[178] He thus hoped to put his own interpretation of the failure of the emperor's plans on the official record and to compel the present gathering to pre-

176. The council of Aquileia is discussed at length by Gryson in the introduction to his *Scolies Ariennes*, 121–143. Various aspects are considered in *Atti del Colloquio Internazionale sul Concilio di Aquileia del 381, AAAd* 21 (1981).

177. There are three separate lists of participants in the council. Twenty-four named bishops pronounce sentence against Palladius at *Acta* 54–64; *Acta* 1 lists thirty-two 'considentes'; the list of 'nomina episcoporum qui subscripserunt' which precedes this in the manuscript (Zelzer, *CSEL* 82.3, p. 325) adds five names and omits three. Iustus of Lyon and Constantius of Orange are identifed by Ambrose as 'legati Gallorum' at *Acta* 15; the council's *Ep.* 1 (Zelzer, p. 315: *PL* 16, Amb. *Ep.* 9) makes Constantius (with Proculus of Marseilles) the envoy of Viennensis and Narbonensis I and II.

178. The meetings were mentioned by the presbyter Evagrius at the council, 'ante quattuor dies et ante biduum' (*Acta* 11). Ambrose refers to Palladius' letter at *Ep. extra coll.* 4 [10].4 (a document also transmitted as *Gesta conc. Aquil.*, *Ep.* 2 [Zelzer, p. 316]), 'ante triduum provocassent'; this was presumably the same letter mentioned (and ordered to be read out) at *Acta* 10. Palladius returns to the subject at *Acta* 42: 'Mandavi ut sederetis ut arguerem vos: quare subrepistis imperatori?'.

pare (in the emperor's name) for the eventual implementation of those plans.

Palladius perhaps also relished what would probably be his first chance to meet Ambrose face to face. But if so he had underestimated his man, for Ambrose succeeded in turning the occasion into something very different from what he had proposed. When Palladius arrived with his colleague Secundianus at the appointed time, early in the morning of 3 September, he was ushered not into the basilica proper but into a small annex (Pall. 89), where his opponents were already seated in what seemed to be an arranged order, with minor clerics sitting among the bishops to give an exaggerated impression of the number present (Pall. 96). To Palladius' dismay, moreover, there were no laymen at all to witness the proceedings and guarantee their proper conduct.[179] Ambrose himself sat conspicuously beside the president of the council, Bishop Valerian of Aquileia, whose own chair was set apart to enhance his authority—a mark, claimed Palladius, of his opponents' aristocratic hauteur (Pall. 89).

The care with which Ambrose had made these preparations shows his determination to run the meeting according to his own devices. The official *Acta* of the council represent an aspect of this control, for the stenographers who recorded them were clerics of Ambrose's church.[180] This document is very curious. In form, it is utterly conventional: it begins with the date and location of the council and a list of the participants, and duly records the imperial rescript that gave the assembly its authority (*Acta* 1–3). But the transcript of the subsequent debate defies categorization. The various contributions were not, as often happened, reduced by an editor to their essentials of *relatio*, *sententiae* and acclamation;[181] nor again can they be explained as a judicial *cognitio*, since although he behaved much like a prosecuting magistrate, Ambrose concedes, at least formally, his opponents' equality in status to himself.[182] Nor, perhaps, did the record ever exist in a complete form: all manu-

179. This question reemerged at the very end of the council (*Acta* 51–52); Palladius mentioned it at the start of his *Apology*, but the mutilated state of the text makes it impossible to determine the exact context (Pall. 91).

180. Ambrose's *notarii* were the subject of repeated protests by Palladius: *Acta* 34, 43, 46–47, 51; Pall. 97.

181. This was the format used for the *Acta* of Serdica: H. Hess, *The Canons of the Council of Sardica, A.D. 343* (1958), 24–41.

182. H. J. Sieben, *Die Konzilsidee der alten Kirchen* (1979), 482–492, compares the procedure with a 'Kaiserlicher Kognitionsprozess', but acknowledges (at 486) the significance of Ambrose's offer to debate the issue with Palladius at *Acta* 5, 'Unde vis adstrue'. Sieben accepts too easily Ambrose's right to act as presiding magistrate in the case.

scripts derive from a fifth-century copy that breaks off abruptly, for no apparent reason, in the middle of the interrogation of Secundianus.[183] The decision thus to 'publish' these minutes, which must have been taken by Ambrose and his allies, is the more puzzling in that the arguments they record more than once show the bishop of Milan at a disadvantage.

One might suspect that the *Acta* were not meant to be read too closely. In other words, like *De fide* and *De spiritu sancto*, this is a text that was produced less for its contents than for its appearance and manner of presentation. As the physical embodiment of Ambrose's council, it 'normalized' proceedings whose irregularities might well have caused concern, and so gave an authoritative stamp to the condemnation of Palladius and Secundianus. That these verdicts were in fact deeply controversial (and therefore required Ambrose to be at his most assertive) is confirmed by a very different account of the council, which has survived in the margins of the fifth-century manuscript of the *Acta*. The *Apology* of Palladius amounts almost to the alternative *Acta* of Aquileia.[184] These two very different texts can in fact be seen as competing exercises in the presentation of the affair. The battle rumbled on well into the next century: nearly sixty years later, in the margins of the same manuscript that preserves Palladius' comments, his admirer Maximinus subjected Ambrose's performance to withering scrutiny in his own commentary on the *Acta*.[185]

Palladius is our only source for the first skirmishes in what was to be a long morning.[186] Ambrose seems to have seized the initiative immediately by confronting Palladius with a letter that Arius had written to his bishop, Alexander, in about 320, and by asking him to join the others present in denouncing the contents (Pall. 90). This was hardly the type of discussion that Palladius had wanted or anticipated; he was required to respond to a strange text that did not reflect his own beliefs without

183. This text, *Par. Lat.* 8907, is highly corrupt but lavishly produced; the conclusion in mid-folio is therefore unlikely to be the result of scribal impatience or interruption. The end is marked with an *amen*; see Zelzer, *CSEL* 82.3, p. 368 (and cf. her remarks in the Prolegomena, pp. clvi–clxx).

184. Gryson offers a full discussion of the text and its problems in the introduction to his edition: *Scolies Ariennes*, 83–100. See also my 'The "Apology" of Palladius', with further bibliography.

185. Maximinus' remarks (which include the *Epistula Auxentii*) constitute sections 1–80 of the scholia: see Gryson, *Scolies Ariennes*, 63–79.

186. Proceedings lasted from dawn to the 'seventh hour', the early afternoon: Amb. *Ep. extra coll.* 4 [10].5.

even, it seems, being given a copy to which he could refer. He therefore protested that he had come to Aquileia not to discuss an irrelevant text but to participate in a disputation about the faith (Pall. 91). He declared himself eager, nevertheless, to make the best of the situation: although the present assembly could not claim the name or authority of a general council, he was willing to participate in a preliminary discussion that could help establish the terms of reference for the future council. It was perhaps in this context (or else in mild deprecation of Ambrose's abrupt introduction of the letter of Arius) that he made a conciliatory remark which his enemies would quote back at him later in the day: 'We come as Christians to Christians' (*Acta* 12). However, his account of these opening exchanges (despite an unfortunate lacuna at an important point) shows him at pains also to present his own agenda. First he registered a protest against one of the more reckless charges Ambrose had included in *De fide*, that he and his fellows were responsible for the Goths' success in devastating the Danubian provinces (Pall. 91). Palladius' ultimate objective, the public demolition of the doctrines presented in *De fide*, would have to be reserved for its proper audience, but it served his purposes to focus discussion upon Ambrose's work from the outset. In conjunction with this came the demand that the present meeting should be less restricted: unfortunately, Palladius' request for lay observers, and the exchanges this provoked, can only be glimpsed in a tantalizing fragment of a mutilated passage (Pall. 91–92).

But Ambrose proved inexorable, and the discussion returned to Arius' letter. It is difficult to catch the tone of the debate at this point. Ambrose seems to have worked his way through the letter, which consisted of a long series of attributes of the deity (eternal, good, wise, true) that Arius had applied to the Father alone, and after reading each term he fired off questions about Palladius' opinion.[187] With nothing particular at stake, Palladius seems to have been relatively patient in the face of this approach, and concerning one clause at least—where the Son was described as a creature—he agreed, on scriptural grounds, that the term was inappropriate (Pall. 94).[188] Having won this admission, Ambrose at

187. Palladius does not describe this phase of the proceedings in detail; the subject matter of the discussion can nevertheless be inferred from his remarks elsewhere (cf. below, p. 132).

188. This admission was later exploited by Ambrose, in the formal session of the council: 'Ante horam citra actam cum legeretur quia Arrius dixit creaturam Christum negasti' (*Acta* 43). Note that this phrase occurs at the very end of Arius' letter; for the text, see Opitz, *Urkunden zur Geschichte des arianischen Streites*, no. 6 (p. 12).

once asked Palladius to confirm it by signing a statement condemning Arius. Palladius suspected a trap: by subscribing to an official document he would implicitly recognize the council's status, undermining his claims of its invalidity and prejudicing the work of the general council for which he still hoped (Pall. 95). He therefore demurred, suggesting that more constructive use be made of the common ground thus established by settling an agenda for the future council (Pall. 96).

Palladius was correct in his assessment of Ambrose's motives in pressing for a signature, but he had underestimated his opponent's resourcefulness. Although Ambrose had spent several hours softening Palladius up for the demand for his signature, he responded immediately to the failure of this tactic by implementing an alternative strategy. He summoned forward his *notarii* and declared that the preliminaries were concluded and formal business would now commence (Pall. 97). The transition has been generally accepted as a natural one, an impression reinforced by the official *Acta*, which begin at this point.[189] But the impression is misleading. No public business had been reserved for the session of 3 September, and Palladius' analysis of Ambrose's abrupt declaration—'your stealthy conspiracy was now brought out into the open as a public act of brigandage' (Pall. 97)—rings true. Ambrose, however, had prepared this second plan (which carried the risk of taking actions in the emperor's name which had not received his prior approval) just as thoroughly as he had his original gambit. When Palladius and Secundianus, outraged at this manipulation of the meeting, attempted to leave, they were physically restrained and were intimidated with expressions of open hostility (Pall. 97).

Scrupulous in his adherence to the proper forms, Ambrose ordered the rescript from which he derived his authority to be read (*Acta* 2–4). There was no attempt to recall the emperor's original command, although its terms still remained valid.[190] Then Ambrose began again with Arius' letter. The repetition in this second phase of the council of exactly the same questions that had already been asked at considerable length must have lent the proceedings a somewhat artificial air. The conditions

189. Gryson, *Scolies Ariennes*, 137–138, fails to mark the dubious legitimacy of this shift to a process 'en bonne et due forme'.

190. This was expressly stated in Gratian's rescript: 'Nec sane nunc aliter iubemus ac iussimus non invertentes praecepti tenorem' (*Acta* 4); the original summons probably made the equal status of the disputants clearer than did the rescript, which implies a direct contest by the clause 'a quibus proficscuntur instituta doctrinae, ab isdem discordis eruditionis repugnantia solverentur' (3), but obscures the point with its glowing testimonial to Ambrose.

offered by Ambrose to Palladius were equally unrealistic. Repeating the first term of the letter—the Father was *solus sempiternus,* alone in being everlasting—he asked him either to condemn this statement or to justify it, reminding him that the Scriptures were available for reference (*Acta* 5). The passage of argument that followed was completely at cross-purposes. Faced with the insistent demand that he state his views upon Arius' claim, Palladius simply refused to acknowledge the authority of his inquisitor and jury, and appealed to Gratian's original plans for the council and the terms upon which he had agreed to appear for the present occasion. It was at this point that his own letter was read out to the assembly, although the stenographers failed to record its contents.[191] No trace of a competing agenda survives in the *Acta.* They also, inevitably, conceal a feature that Palladius claims to have been prominent in this part of the proceedings: silence.[192] Ambrose was forced to concede a sort of defeat before Palladius' patience. Without extracting a single comment from him on the point at issue, he declared his failure to condemn Arius' position tantamount to accepting it and went through the formality of inviting the senior bishops in turn for their opinions (*Acta* 15–16).

Had Palladius persisted in maintaining his silence, it would probably have been difficult for the council to have pronounced against him, or at least to have persuaded uncommitted observers of the validity of their sentence. But as the *Acta* continue, we see the bishop of Ratiaria gradually being drawn into the argument; it is this process that makes the document so compelling to read. Palladius may have been driven to respond by a reluctance to leave the initiative entirely to his opponents or by a feeling that their control over the proceedings was so complete as to leave him nothing to lose. But it is also possible that he detected vulnerability behind Ambrose's bravado. Although the secretaries whom Ambrose had produced with such a flourish were obviously not neutral, Palladius could have calculated that they were unlikely to achieve a successful falsification of their minutes, or for that matter, given their junior rank, to dare to attempt one. Despite the odds against him, it was therefore worth trying to knock his opponent off his poise and stamp his own authority upon the record. His first essays were tentative: when Ambrose produced the next term, *solus verus,* Palladius responded with a

191. The letter must have been read after Ambrose's command, 'Legatur epistula Palladii', and Palladius' response, 'Legatur plane' (*Acta* 11); the questions then put to Palladius ('Imperator cum praesens esset . . .') must bear directly upon the contents. For the likely thrust of the letter, see above, p. 112.

192. Pall. 99, referring to this exchange over the term *sempiternus:* 'Prout etiam diu silentium habitum est'.

combination of scriptural citations and silence (*Acta* 17–21).[193] The result was as inconclusive as before, but a trace of uneasiness might be detected in Ambrose's outburst (of very dubious propriety or legality), 'You do not have the freedom to make a statement' (*Acta* 21).

Palladius reserved his first serious attempt at a counterattack for the next term Arius had applied to the Father, *solus immortalis*. He again began with a scriptural quotation, to show that this was a mere truism. But he then asked a question that seems only indirectly connected with the subject, whether the name Christ was human or divine (*Acta* 22). The reply was handled not by Ambrose but by his friend Eusebius of Bologna, whose conduct at the council was to earn him the scornful label of Ambrose's 'assessor' (Pall. 117). Palladius' *Apology* also supplies a plausible reason for this particular intervention. A large section of the tract is devoted to a discussion of each of the points Ambrose had proposed, and under *solus immortalis* he records an exchange with the bishop of Milan precisely over the status of the name of Christ. The question was a trap, since there was ample scriptural evidence for the name's divine connotations: it was Christ who died, and this offered implicit support for Arius' assertion. Ambrose did not handle the situation particularly well, hesitating before giving an answer that Palladius was able to turn to his own ends (Pall. 107).[194] This exchange does not appear in the *Acta:* barring excision, the most likely explanation is that it had occurred during the previous, informal discussion. We should not forget that everything that occurred in the council proper had been rehearsed at length in the preliminaries, allowing both parties to familiarize themselves with the terrain on which the final combat was played out. Palladius had therefore sensed a weakness, which he could hope might lead Ambrose into exactly the self-exposure that he had long anticipated. But while Eusebius fielded the awkward theological points for him, Ambrose retrieved the situation by diversionary tactics: he invoked his chorus of anathematizing bishops, insisted that discussion be confined to the particular question of Arius' opinions, and then moved abruptly to the next clause (*Acta* 23–26).

A pattern became established in the subsequent exchanges. To each

193. Cf. Pall. 100, where Palladius describes his interventions at this point as intended 'non quo disputationi locus daretur, sed ut tua qua ipsum filium conplice patrem solum verum adseris Deum retunderetur blasfemia'.

194. 'Cumque ad hoc obiectum tibi fuisset an Cristi adpellationem humanam crederes, tu aliquamdiu cunctatus tandem respondisti, "et humanam et divinam"'. The exchange is well discussed by Hanson, *The Search*, 109–110, with the comment that 'Palladius here trapped Ambrose nicely'.

of the propositions presented by Ambrose, Palladius provided answers strictly confined to scriptural terms and refused to discuss the wider implications.[195] At length, however, he attempted to seize the initiative himself, interrupting his interrogators to ask them directly whether they accepted that 'the Father is greater' (*Acta* 33). It was again Eusebius who responded to this, Ambrose showing himself reluctant to depart from his prepared script (*Acta* 35). Just when Palladius had succeeded in drawing out his opponents, however, he made a fatal blunder. Confronting Ambrose with one of the decisive proof texts on this subject, 'I go to the Father because the Father is greater than me', he misquoted the gospel passage—or rather, he cited a conflation of two passages that was current in Greek, but apparently not Latin, theological discourse.[196] The difference was minor and did not affect the sense (Palladius' version was 'he who sent me is greater than me'), but Ambrose pounced at once: 'Today we can prove that the divine Scriptures are being falsified by you' (*Acta* 36).

Palladius' slip had cost him much more than the initiative: it touched the heart of the issue between the two men, their respective competence to teach and interpret the Bible. Ambrose was therefore able to cite it triumphantly to Gratian.[197] Palladius betrays the gravity of his mistake by the pains he takes in the *Apology* to explain his citation as a deliberate amalgam of the two passages, 'a compendium of the faith, not a blasphemous profession' (108). It was shortly after this unfortunate incident, and the chorus of 'anathema' that ensued, that Palladius, provoked by the comment by Sabinus of Piacenza (another of Ambrose's long-standing associates) that Arius' blasphemies were 'much less than those of Palladius' (*Acta* 38), again tried to leave the room. Once more, however, he was detained by force.

The fight was still by no means over, and Palladius was able to produce further awkward questions for his tormentors.[198] But his remarks were increasingly concerned with practical or procedural points: the accuracy of the minutes being taken, the competence of his 'judges', the absence of the easterners, and the need for neutral lay observers. He

195. Thus proceeded the discussions over 'solus sapiens' (*Acta* 27), 'solus bonus' (28–30), 'solus potens' (30–32), and 'omnium iudicem' (33).

196. See Hanson, *The Search*, 836, citing parallels from Eusebius of Caesarea and Eunomius. The two texts are John 14:28 and 11:42.

197. *Ep. extra coll.* 4 [10].6–7.

198. Note particularly the exchange over the status of the incarnate Christ at *Acta* 40–41: Eusebius again intervenes on Ambrose's behalf, and the discussion is ended with an abrupt transition to another term.

could be forgiven a renewed sense of nervous outrage at this stage; only now, perhaps, did he realize that his opponents were planning to use the present discussion as the basis for pronouncing sentence upon him. Our own familiarity with the outcome of the council should not blind us to the audacity of the course upon which Ambrose now embarked. He adopted his most formal manner to give the magistrate's *pronuntiatio*, and glossed the terms of Gratian's rescript to establish the meeting's authority to give a verdict upon Palladius (*Acta* 52–53). After a unanimous shout of assent from the assembled bishops, he asked them in turn for their *sententiae*, again in the style of a secular process. After Valerian had given the first of these responses (which grind on for five pages of the printed text: *Acta* 54–64), Palladius uttered his final judgement on the proceedings: 'Coepistis ludere, ludite', 'You have begun your game, play on!' (*Acta* 54).

Secundianus, who had hitherto remained silent, was then made to stand before the assembly. The refusal of a seat to the aged prelate signalled the abandonment of any pretence of a discussion between colleagues.[199] So did Ambrose's brusque command, during the ensuing proceedings, that the defendant 'be silent'; to reinforce the 'judge's' authority, his words were echoed by his faithful 'assessor' Eusebius (Pall. 117). But it appears from the surviving portion of the *Acta* (which break off soon after the interrogation begins) that this failed to intimidate Secundianus, who replied vigorously to Ambrose's peremptory questions and matched them with his own. One interchange, recorded by Palladius, shows him quite at his ease with a distinctly stiff Ambrose. The debate had moved to the notorious text Proverbs 8:22, 'the Lord created me', which the homoeans referred to the Son and therefore justified his designation as a created being.[200] When Secundianus asked teasingly whether he wished this awkward passage to be condemned, Ambrose replied abruptly that he did not 'wish' what he 'knew' to be the case. He was nevertheless drawn into a clarification, and his insistence that the passage referred to the incarnation could well have led him into difficulties (Pall. 110). Although the proceedings ended with the formality of a sentence against Secundianus, there was no tame surrender to the inevitable.

199. Pall. 117: 'inpar stans iudicaretur'.
200. For the role of this passage in contemporary debates, see M. Simonetti, *Studi sull'Arianesimo* (1968), 9–87 ('Sull'interpretazione patristica di *Proverbi* 8, 22'). An impression of its centrality can be obtained from a glance at the *index locorum* of Hanson's book; the thirty-five entries for this text represent more than double the total for its nearest rival.

The outcome was never in doubt, but we should not therefore ignore the details of the proceedings. Only through these can we appreciate what each side had hoped to achieve, and the difficulties that they
faced. The overt pressure was naturally upon the two homoean bishops,
isolated in a hostile environment (their only companion seems to have
been one Attalus, a presbyter who makes a brief and somewhat puzzling
appearance in the *Acta*)[201] and assailed by the choruses of anathema orchestrated by Ambrose and by the insults of his clerics, whose jeers at
the venerable Palladius are recorded by their victim (Pall. 116).[202] The
self-control that Palladius and Secundianus maintained is in these circumstances admirable—the more so when it is remembered that they
had arrived at Aquileia with an agenda of their own. There was naturally
little point in confronting Ambrose before his friends with the written
evidence of his own ignorance and incoherence that a severe critic could
discover in *De fide* and subsequent works, and indeed it seems that Palladius and Secundianus failed to bring their carefully compiled dossier
to the meeting on 3 September. The frustration must have been considerable. At times, perhaps, they regretted not having taken the risk of a
direct challenge even against the odds facing them. The longest continu-
ous exchange in the *Acta* comes at the very end, where Secundianus,
having apparently taken the measure of Ambrose, attempted to change
the course of the discussion: 'I have answered as I should, by making a
profession. We have your exposition: we will bring it, let it be read out'
(*Acta* 74).[203] In other words, rather than continuing to exchange extemporized 'professions', Secundianus wanted to deploy the written
evidence which he possessed of Ambrose's beliefs. His opponent refused to entertain the idea, and responded brusquely: 'You should have
brought it today. But you are only trying to wriggle free. Ask me for a
profession [of faith]; and I ask you for a profession: Is the Son of God
truly God?' (ibid.). Nor had Palladius succeeded in resisting temptation.
Towards the conclusion of his hearing, Ambrose had asked him to jus-

201. *Acta* 44–45. Attalus is described in the council's subsequent letter to
Gratian (*Ep. extra coll.* 4 [10].9) as a 'pupil' of Iulianus Valens, condemned for his
praevaricatio in retracting an earlier subscription to the Nicene creed. He is perhaps to be associated with Valens' Italian *seminarium* (10).

202. Ambrose's deacons and lectors allegedly mocked Palladius' 'canitiem
execrandam et senectutem . . . abominabilem', to their bishop's visible satisfaction. For the obedient shouts of Ambrose's colleagues, see Pall. 99: 'cum tu cla-
mares et conspiratio omnis tumultuose in modum voluptatis perstreperet'.

203. 'Habemus vestram expositionem, afferemus, legatur': the manuscript
reading 'afferimus' (Zelzer, p. 367) requires emendation in the light of Ambrose's
reply, 'hodie afferre debueras'.

tify an accusation of impiety that he had earlier made against him. Palladius replied: 'We will bring your exposition. When we have brought it, then a disputation will be held' (*Acta* 50).[204] On this occasion, Ambrose made no reply except to demand yet again that Palladius condemn the 'impiety of Arius'. These small incidents are important; above all, they suggest how different the council might have been if the homoeans had been able to force Ambrose onto the defensive.[205]

That Ambrose made the final verdict appear so inevitable should, conversely, be taken as a tribute to his management skills. The various occasions where his touch momentarily failed him are useful indications of the difficulty of the task he had set himself, and help put his overall success in retaining control in its proper perspective. Such aspects as the anathemas obediently produced by his colleagues, for instance, should not be taken for granted. It was no mean achievement to harness a diverse body of bishops (a species notoriously jealous of their individual authority) to any coordinated activity, and the *Acta* duly show some apparent deviations from the planned script. An unsolicited (and barely coherent) outburst by Anemius, who will be remembered as Ambrose's nominee at Sirmium, seems to have been intended to establish his own equivalence in rank to the representatives of Gaul and Africa (*Acta* 16); many questions of precedence had doubtless had to be worked out carefully in advance. Ambrose also relied on the complaisance of the elderly Valerian, nominal president of the council, and his restraint from exercising initiative from the chair. One intervention by Valerian suggests the wisdom of this policy (but also shows that it could not be enforced): he 'explained' Palladius' truculence by volunteering the information that he had been ordained by Photinians, a baseless charge quite unhelpful to the prosecution and studiously ignored by Ambrose (*Acta* 49). There were even some crossed purposes with Eusebius, the most reliable of Ambrose's henchmen, when he tried to bring Secundianus into a discussion that Ambrose had reserved for Palladius alone (*Acta* 28). Small incidents like this help convey the scale of Ambrose's achievement. The faithful support given by Eusebius and Sabinus was indispensable; on several occasions, as we have seen, their interventions served to steer discussion back upon its proper course. But above all, it was Ambrose who had devised the plan of restricting debate to the dis-

204. 'Expositionem vestram afferemus'. Zelzer mistakenly emends the possessive to 'nostram', and in spite of the required sequence of tense she preserves the present 'afferimus' (p. 356).

205. I discuss this *expositio*, proposing an identification with a section of Ambrose's *De fide*, in 'The "Apology" of Palladius', at 46–52.

cussion of Arius' letter, whose terms he had mastered in advance, and who kept doggedly to this prepared text.[206] If this in part bears out Palladius' belief that he would be able to overwhelm Ambrose in an open contest, it demonstrates beyond question the tactical skills of the bishop of Milan. The 'brigandage' against Palladius at Aquileia was therefore a piece of pure opportunism, the ruthlessness and audacity of which cannot but command a certain admiration.

THE AFTERMATH OF AQUILEIA

The verdict against Palladius and Secundianus by itself meant little; in the previous generation, Ursacius and Valens (not to mention Auxentius of Milan) had survived several such decisions. The council therefore sent a delegation to enlist support from the emperor Gratian, who was probably still campaigning in the Balkans. Their letter begins with an elaborate salute, thanking the emperors for organizing the council and for their consideration to the bishops in ensuring that 'none who wished to attend should be absent, and none who did not wish to attend should be compelled' (*Ep. extra coll.* 4 [10].1).[207] The lengthy development of this theme (2–3) confirms that Gratian had not anticipated the use Ambrose had made of his mandate; some tact was needed to explain to the emperor the transactions that had just been completed in his name.[208]

The ostensible purpose of the embassy was to obtain imperial support to expel the deposed bishops from their sees and to help the envoys appoint replacements who would have to be imposed, it can be inferred, upon reluctant congregations (8). Considerable art was therefore employed to establish the fact, which must have come as a surprise to Gratian, that the venerable Palladius and his colleague were Arians. The bishops repeat the heresiarch's name eight times in three short paragraphs (4–6), ramming the point home by enclosing a document for the

---

206. Palladius' exasperated outburst sums it up: 'Tuis responsis confutatus, cum iam nihil aliud ad sciscitationem cerneres superesse, siquidem non ulla sit in te scientia scripturarum qua posses premeditata vel ab aliis suggesta amplius quaerere, rursus veluti ad unicum imperite infidelitatis suffugium, ad epistolam redeundum duxisti' (Pall. 109).

207. The letter (concerning the transmission of which cf. above, n. 178) was addressed to the three emperors in accordance with convention, but the contents make it clear that it was intended for Gratian. References in this and the following paragraph are to this letter.

208. This point is well made by Palanque, *Saint Ambroise*, 97–98.

emperor's attention ('so that Your Clemency might shudder at it as we did'): the letter of Arius which Ambrose had used, against Palladius' bitter protests, as the test of orthodoxy. Nor is Palladius' 'falsification' of the Scriptures forgotten (6).

The bishops then turn to some dangers closer to home, a useful reminder of the insecure platform from which their confident utterances were made. Iulianus Valens, who remained at large in Milan itself and was 'contaminating' the flourishing cities of Italy, received particular attention (9–10). After the dramatic charges levelled against him, including the 'betrayal' of his own city of Poetovio to the Goths, the council's request that he be sent back there seems remarkably modest: it probably reflects not only the exaggeration of his alleged treachery but the overriding desire of the Italian bishops to be rid of him. Ambrose's Illyrican allies had their own problems, and help was requested against the Photinians at Anemius' Sirmium (12).[209]

The outcome of these requests is unknown; but they succeeded in establishing a formal link with the court, and so inaugurated a sequence of letters to Gratian and Theodosius which represents by far the most sustained set of negotiations between a western council and the imperial government since Rimini. In these letters, moreover, the bishops at Aquileia, their numbers swollen by at most a handful of newcomers,[210] transform themselves into the collective embodiment ('brought together into one') of the western church, their mission to defend 'the whole body of the church scattered all over the world'. The delegates from Africa and Gaul, whose initial role was purely supplementary, likewise assent in their provinces' name to petitions that cannot possibly have been anticipated in their mandate.[211]

Much here was improvised, as the council sought to create an agenda to justify its expanding pretensions. The process had already begun, somewhat inauspiciously, even before the arrival of Palladius. Ambrose and his friends had secured authorization from Damasus to

209. The Photinians, with their impeccable anti-Arian credentials, presumably provided strong competition for Anemius after the death of Germinius (who had displaced Photinus in 351); Gratian's 'edict of tolerance' of 378 had retained sanctions against them. Photinus himself seems to have died in c. 376: see Zeiller, *Les origines*, 262–270.

210. The discrepancies between the various attendance lists (above, n. 177) probably reflect the addition of late arrivals.

211. 'Conducti in unum': *Ep. extra coll.* 6 [12].2; 'totum corpus ecclesiae': *Ep. extra coll.* 5 [11].2. Legates: *Ep. extra coll.* 6 [12].6 ('et Africanae et Gallicanae ecclesiae per legatos obsecrant'); the letter to their sponsors (*Gesta conc. Aquil.*, *Ep.* 1 [9]) mentions only the condemnation of Palladius and Secundianus (cf. *Ep. extra coll.* 4 [10].3 for their 'adtestationes evidentes' against Arianism).

hear the case of Bishop Leontius of Salona, but when they voted to depose him he departed for Rome, where he was received into communion by the pope; he reappeared at Aquileia at the time of Palladius' own hearing, 'broadcasting the news to the ears of the public' and demanding reinstatement.[212] But the breakdown in communications between Rome and Aquileia had evidently been repaired by the time of the council's second petition to the court, an attempt to frustrate a *relatio* from the urban prefect which apparently suggested a pardon for Damasus' old rival Ursinus (*Ep. extra coll.* 5 [11]). The letter's contents imply that the council now had access to official channels of communication; the phrasing, which plays much upon the concept of *verecundia* that Ambrose had exploited in his previous dealings with Gratian (5), demonstrates a certain expertise at handling these channels.

Much more ambitious in scope was the council's next letter (*Ep. extra coll.* 6 [12]), copies of which were sent—as the contents clearly show—to Theodosius as well as Gratian. The bishops applaud the ejection of heretics from their churches in both parts of the empire but contrast the 'unbroken and single communion of the faithful' stretching from Thrace to the western ocean with the dissensions and discord that divided the orthodox churches of the east (3–4). Of particular concern was the pressure being exerted upon the faithful in both Antioch and Alexandria, the followers of bishops Paulinus and Timothy, by certain 'catholics' whose faith had wavered during the troubles of the previous reigns. There is a clear allusion here to Meletius, leader of the principal Nicene community in Antioch but long shunned because of his homoean antecedents by westerners, who had committed themselves to his rival Paulinus.[213] Having been prevented by an 'enemy invasion' from sending a delegation to organize a settlement at Antioch themselves, the bishops remind the emperors of their earlier prayer that the 'agreed procedure' be followed in the event of the death of either Meletius or Paulinus, with the survivor assuming control of both communities (5). They request

212. Pall. *Apol.* 125. The language is difficult: the emphatic use of the second person ('audistis', 'a vobis') suggests an original verdict by the council itself, but Leontius' 'arrival' at Aquileia ('illo advenisset') implies a separate occasion. I suspect that Palladius' wording reflects his own point of view: Leontius 'arrived' rather than 'returned' to make his appeal because this was the only stage Palladius had himself witnessed ('tempore conspirationis vestrae apud Aquileiam', i.e., 3 September). Cf. R. Gryson, *Le prêtre selon saint Ambroise* (1968), 188.

213. For the tangled negotiations between Damasus of Rome and the churches of Antioch, see especially Pietri, *Roma Christiana*, 791–849; there is no evidence of how Damasus responded to the overture from Meletius' council of Antioch in 379.

a further council, at Alexandria, where a definitive agreement can be reached over which bishops to accept into communion (5–6).

Most modern readers have been too dismayed by the letter's presumption to attempt to follow its logic.[214] Others have been baffled by its silence concerning the council of Constantinople, held earlier the same year, and especially by the nonsense that the death of Meletius at the same council apparently makes of the elaborately phrased allusion to the situation in Antioch.[215] But the argument has been constructed with considerable care, linking a general concern over intercommunion with the particular case of Antioch. The bishops are at pains to establish the legitimacy of their interest in the latter, citing their receipt of letters from both parties in the eastern disputes, 'and especially from those who were at variance in the Antiochene church' (4). Paulinus' faction was represented by the presbyter Evagrius;[216] we might surmise that Meletius, schooled by his long travails never to reject an overture from the west, had responded to Gratian's original announcement of the council with a conciliatory note that was construed as an invitation to intervene. Considerable ingenuity is expended to forestall objections to this fragile claim. The bishops' failure to announce it earlier is masked by the professed 'belief' that their wishes over the succession had been made known to the emperors, while the 'tumults' of the Gothic war excused their failure to intervene themselves. The abrupt shift to the proposed council of Alexandria is intended to demonstrate restraint: instead of exercising their own right to impose a settlement, they suggested that the eastern bishops themselves should decide, 'by extensive discussions', which of their number are eligible for western communion. Alexandria was the natural site, as the one see with which the west maintained 'indissoluble ties' of communion; Theodosius himself had designated it a touchstone of orthodoxy.[217]

The letter is largely exploratory. Ambrose (clearly the principal au-

214. Pietri calls it 'une véritable provocation' (*Roma Christiana*, 862); cf. Homes Dudden's remark: 'It must be admitted that in his dealings with the eastern church Ambrose failed to exhibit his usual statesmanlike sagacity' (*Saint Ambrose*, 216).

215. This prompted Palanque to redate the council from September to May, despite *Acta* 1 ('III Nonas Septembres'): *Saint Ambroise*, 504–506, followed by Pietri, *Roma Christiana*, 862n2. The manuscript date was convincingly defended by J. Zeiller, 'La date du concile d'Aquilée', *Studi Bizantini e Neoellenici* 5 (1939), 327–332.

216. Pall. *Apol.* 96. Gryson's hesitations concerning Evagrius' identity (*Scolies Ariennes*, 131) seem overcautious.

217. *CTh* 16.1.2; recently confirmed in *CTh* 16.1.3 (30 July 381).

thor) was evidently anxious not to offend Theodosius, devising the council of Alexandria as a more palatable alternative—to be conducted under the emperor's own auspices—to the council of Aquileia's enforcement of its legitimate interests at Antioch. He even left room for manoeuvre over Paulinus by wrapping his case in hypothetical terms. At the same time, the principal purpose of the letter was to impress Gratian: having reaped such profit from the collapse of the emperor's original plan, Ambrose was now proposing to implement a version of it himself. The council of Alexandria would be at most an adjunct to Aquileia, to complete its work and reassure its members; by convening it Theodosius would be conferring belated recognition upon the authority of Gratian's council.

Ambrose's sole leverage over Theodosius, as is clear from the letter, was the council of Aquileia's right to enforce the 'agreement' between Meletius and Paulinus concerning the Antiochene succession. But here the bishop had placed too much confidence in Evagrius, a source whom Palladius had singled out among the 'conspirators' at Aquileia as especially 'experienced in faction' and who would use these skills, honed at Valentinian's court, to prolong the Antiochene schism after Paulinus' death.[218] He served his cause with equal verve at Aquileia, for the agreement was a pure fiction.[219] Nor, in all probability, did Ambrose appreciate how closely the issue affected Theodosius, whose fragile coalition of bishops risked losing its cohesion with the death of Meletius. Much had been invested in a smooth succession: but the installation of Meletius' presbyter and confidant Flavianus, despite being held in conjunction with Meletius' spectacular (and imperially sponsored) funeral, had provoked widespread local opposition.[220] Theodosius could not afford any ill-informed interference from Paulinus' western supporters and replied with a pointed rebuke for their partisanship and ambition.[221]

By the time this reply reached Italy, the council had already dispersed. Ambrose nevertheless responded, addressing Theodosius on behalf of 'the other bishops of Italy' (*Ep. extra coll.* 9 [13]). Still more remarkable than this arrogation of authority is the change in the bishop's tone. Abandoning the evasiveness of the previous letter, he roundly

218. 'In factionibus usitatior': Pall. *Apol.* 96. For Evagrius' consecration, in 388/9, see Theodoret *HE* 5.23.2–4.

219. F. Cavallera, *Le schisme d'Antioche* (1905), 232–243.

220. Soz. *HE* 7.10.5–11.1.1; Soc. *HE* 5.9.

221. This can be inferred from Ambrose's subsequent letter, *Ep. extra coll.* 9 [13].6: 'nec quaedam nos angit de domestico studio et ambitione'.

proclaimed the authority of the council of Aquileia, 'prescribed for the bishops of the whole world', against the one hundred and fifty bishops at Constantinople 'who avoided the general council' (4). He nevertheless constructs his argument as carefully as before, discovering a flaw in the settlement of the eastern church which Theodosius had presumably announced. He could do no more than protest at the 'imposition' of Flavianus, managing to restate the essence of his original objection without reference to the phantom 'pact' (2); but this had been conducted through the 'agreement and advice' of Nectarius, Theodosius' nominee to the see of Constantinople, whose own status was subject to question (3). There was already a prior claimant—not Gregory of Nazianzus, the impropriety of whose position had already exercised the bishops at Aquileia (4)—but the Egyptian Maximus, whose travels from Constantinople had finally brought him, via Thessalonica, Egypt and Gratian's court in Italy, to the council of Aquileia. Ambrose, justifying Maximus' appeal to the west by reference to the precedents of Athanasius and Peter, deplored the easterners' failure either to allow him a hearing themselves or to await a verdict from the west before electing Nectarius. The situation, made yet more intolerable by the alleged rejection of Nectarius by his consecrators (5), therefore demanded either the restoration of Maximus to his see or discussion at a council to be held at Rome (6).

The abrupt announcement of this Roman council 'of ourselves and the eastern bishops', and its brisk (and somewhat specious) justification by reference to Acholius' role at the council of Constantinople (7), is very different from the cautious and respectful plea for a council at Alexandria. But this time Ambrose did not have to plead, for the council had already been authorized. He saves his most telling stroke until last, informing Theodosius that he was writing 'at the admonition of the most blessed prince, the brother of Your Piety' (8). The remark, to be understood in connexion with the invitations to this Roman council which Gratian issued to the eastern episcopate, announces a collaboration that is the key to the whole letter. It appears that Ambrose's previous letter had impressed Gratian and his advisors more than Theodosius, suggesting the bishop as an effective champion for the west's claims. The council of Rome was therefore devised to succeed where Aquileia had failed, reuniting the churches in a single communion under the aegis of the western emperor, and this letter shows Ambrose fulfilling his charge to produce an agenda that would compel Theodosius' acquiescence. The trenchancy and authority with which he handles his brief therefore reflects a significant change in his position. The bishop had taken silk.[222]

Unfortunately, Ambrose had again been misled. The allegations against Nectarius were quite without foundation, while the letters of communion which Maximus had brought from Alexandria had long since been repudiated and Maximus himself abjured by the entire eastern episcopate. Damasus of Rome had been party to Maximus' exposure a full year earlier;[223] Ambrose's failure to consult the host of his prospective council suggests the haste with which he had concocted it. There was also, perhaps, a certain reluctance to scrutinize too closely the credentials of a bishop endorsed by Gratian on the strength of a book about the faith. Whatever his reason, by his mistake Ambrose lost whatever hope there might have been of prodding Theodosius towards cooperation.

Ambrose showed impressive dexterity in adversity. When the inevitable counterblast from Theodosius arrived, taking him to task for spreading rumours and dismissing his claims as presumptuous, importunate and unreasonable, he was still able to find an answer (*Ep. extra coll.* 8 [14]).[224] Maximus is discreetly ignored; but Theodosius had apparently rested his case against the need for a further council upon the elimination of the Arian problem, which offered Ambrose a handle. He drew the emperor's attention to a heresy that had never been discussed at a general council and whose advocates had escaped direct confutation: Apollinarism, which accepted the *homoousion* but denied a human mind (*nous*) to the incarnate Christ (4).[225] It was a nice point,

---

222. *Contra* Palanque, who interpreted the letter as a *refusal* by Gratian to involve himself: 'il se décharge de tout responsabilité en invitant Ambroise à écrire lui-même à Théodose' (*Saint Ambroise*, 99). This forces the sense impossibly and ignores the evidence for the imperial summons (below, n. 233; cf. Palanque, 103n142).

223. Dam. *Epp.* 5–6 (*PL* 13, 365–370).

224. 'Silemus . . . ne serere fabulas et alloquia cassa videamur' (2); 'non deferrimus praeiudicum'; 'neque . . . aestimandum convicium fuit' (6); 'non fuisse irrationabile postulatum' (7).

225. Although *Theodosius* is usually presented as introducing the issue of Apollinarism as an accusation against Ambrose (Pietri, *Roma Christiana*, 864; Palanque, *Saint Ambroise*, 101), this ignores not only the tactical background to the correspondence but also the grammar of Ambrose's letter, which (at 4) contrasts 'hi', whom Theodosius had mentioned (the 'Ariani' are the most likely candidates, having appeared in the previous sentence), with 'illi', the Apollinarists, a fresh topic.

for despite the condemnation of these doctrines at Constantinople, Timothy of Beirut, one of their most notable advocates, had appeared on the council's list of signatories.[226] Ambrose was therefore on solid ground when he solemnly quoted Theodosius' own letter upon the need for decisive condemnations, with both parties present: 'It was for that reason that we requested a council of bishops' (5).[227] At a stroke, Ambrose had revised the entire agenda of the council of Rome. He had even discovered a recent precedent, an otherwise unknown appeal by a presbyter of Constantinople for a 'synod of easterners and westerners' to be held in Achaea (6); a general council had therefore been desired 'by the easterners also', and Rome was at present safer than Illyricum (7).

This must be seen largely as a cosmetic exercise, for Ambrose's council was beyond rescue. An impressive array of westerners, including Britto of Trier and Acholius of Thessalonica, duly joined the veterans of Aquileia at Rome in the summer of 382;[228] but the only eastern representatives were the fellow-travellers Paulinus of Antioch and the heresiologist Epiphanius of Salamis, bringing in their train Jerome to begin his short but spectacular career 'at the court of Damasus'.[229] From the main body of the episcopate came only a calculated snub. Even the amiable Theodoret detected sarcasm in the message conveyed by their token delegation of three bishops (escorted by court officials), which thanked the westerners for this belated interest in eastern affairs and regretted their inability to attend.[230] The choicest barb is their explanation that although they had received Gratian's invitations they had been unaware that the council would convene at *Rome*; they had assumed from 'the letters sent by Your Honours after the synod in Aquileia to the emperor Theodosius' that there would be a meeting in Constantinople, and had prepared accordingly. The reference can only be to Ambrose's two post-conciliar letters, neither of which states unequivocally that the

226. Apollinarism is condemned in the council's first canon; for Timothy's subscription, see C. H. Turner, *EOMIA* 2, p. 438 (no. 18). See also the discussion by J. N. D. Kelly, *Early Christian Creeds*, 3d ed. (1972), 333–337.

227. For previous western denunciations of the Apollinarists (after the disastrous start when Damasus received them into communion), see Pietri, *Roma Christiana*, 812–832; cf. 841–842 for the endorsement at Rome of an appeal against Timothy of Beirut in 377/8.

228. Pietri, *Roma Christiana*, 866–871.

229. Kelly, *Jerome*, 80–82; Rebenich, *Hieronymus und sein Kreis*, 141–144.

230. Theod. *HE* 5.9.1–18; his comments are at 5.8.11. The *aulici* are reported by Pope Boniface, *Ep.* 15.6.

council will take place in Rome; the inference that by a safe, maritime location he meant Constantinople is therefore legitimate, if perverse.[231] Lacking 'the wings of a dove' they were stranded, but sought to satisfy the westerners with a brief statement that included a condemnation of Apollinarism.[232] They then reviewed the Nicene regulations for episcopal elections, concluding with a glowing account of the 'canonical' appointments of Nectarius and Flavianus. The bishops at Rome could only produce an ineffectual repudiation of Flavianus and affirm their support for Paulinus, while also elaborating their own refutation of the teachings of Apollinaris.

Modern scholars tend to judge Ambrose's *Ostpolitik* by its results, and therefore deem it an unqualified failure. But our perspectives are too commanding. It is salutary to recall that without the letter fortuitously preserved by Theodoret we would probably judge the council, despite everything, a successful assertion of western authority. Sozomen reports only Gratian's dispatch of the invitations to the easterners, while Jerome recalls serenely how 'imperial letters had brought the bishops of east and west to Rome on account of certain dissensions in the church', as if the whole project had gone according to plan.[233] We need not doubt that Gratian, on campaign in the Balkans, was presented with an equally positive version.[234] Ambrose's horizons, too, were much narrower than his ostensible goal of restoring universal ties of communion would suggest. The churches of east and west had little actual contact with each other and little mutual interest; their paths had already diverged, the inevitable result of geography, language and above all the rival sources of imperial patronage which sustained them. Throughout these exchanges, Ambrose was more concerned with the western court than the eastern church, and in these terms he must be credited with a remarkable success. We need only compare the nervous tactfulness of the first letter from the council of Aquileia with the verve and confidence

231. Theod. *HE* 5.9.9.

232. Theod. *HE* 5.9.10–13: copies of the doctrinal statements produced at Antioch in 379 and Constantinople in 381 were attached to edify the western bishops.

233. Soz. *HE* 7.11; Jer. *Ep.* 108.6. Pope Boniface later presented the eastern delegation submitting meekly to Roman authority: *Ep.* 15.6.

234. Gratian's visit to Viminacium (Seeck, *Regesten*, 258) requires a journey of nine hundred kilometres in a fortnight, implying a serious crisis, but might belong to 381. The emperor's presence in Illyricum is nevertheless likely on general grounds: see Heather, *Goths and Romans*, 171.

of his statements to Theodosius in the name of the Italian episcopate to appreciate his achievement. What mattered most, perhaps, was his gift for having the last word, which quite obscures the catalogue of blunders these letters contain. Their publication shortly after his death by the faithful Paulinus is eloquent testimony to Ambrose's success: Paulinus can have had no idea of the ammunition he was providing for the bishop's future critics.[235]

The churches of east and west were therefore polarized around their respective emperors. In both cases, however, relations between the emperor and his ecclesiastical allies remained highly unstable. Theodosius was persuaded by the disturbances his pro-Nicene campaign had provoked to summon the 'conference of the sects' to Constantinople in 383, to the great alarm of his Nicene protégés.[236] In the west, the bishops had not secured any commitments from Gratian at Aquileia, and their reiteration in three successive letters of their expectation that Palladius and Secundianus would soon be unseated is ominous.[237]

Palladius indeed could still hope to prevail. The *Apologia* which he produced in the aftermath of Aquileia, although conventionally interpreted as the empty defiance of a lost cause, was a serious attempt to reverse the council's verdict.[238] Palladius intended his challenge to Ambrose—that they should examine each others' published works at an extended hearing in the *curia* of Rome, the audience to include not only pagan senators but also Jewish scholars (*Apol.* 139)—to be taken up, but not directly by Ambrose, his ostensible addressee. His real target audience, to whom he looked for an 'imperial command' that would publicize the rival treatises, was at the court, and his argument was shaped accordingly. The charge of 'deceiving' the emperor, which had discomfited Ambrose at Aquileia, was dropped;[239] Palladius, who must by now

235. All these letters belong to the first group of *epistulae extra collectionem*; Zelzer, *CSEL* 82.3, pp. lxxxv–lxxxvi, identifies Paulinus as the editor. We might surmise that Paulinus (who fails to mention the council in the *Vita*) saw them as further evidence of Ambrose's 'sollicitudo omnium ecclesiarum, interveniendi etiam magna adsiduitas et constantia' (*V. Amb.* 38.3).

236. For this council, see Soc. *HE* 5.10; Soz. *HE* 7.12.

237. *Ep. extra coll.* 4 [10].8: Palladius and Secundianus are to be kept forcibly from their churches, 'ut in damnatorum locum . . . sancti subrogentur sacerdotes'; 5 [11].1: 'effectum concilii decretis putamus minime defuturum'; 6 [12].3: 'quibus tamen nunc post concilii sententiam . . . opinamur ilico consulendum'.

238. I discuss the political context of the *Apologia* in 'The "Apology" of Palladius', 72–76; for the date, see Gryson, *Scolies Ariennes*, 96.

239. *Acta* 6, 8, 10, 42. Ambrose evades the question on each occasion.

have understood the reasons for the collapse of Gratian's conciliar strategies, knew better than to burden his readers with analysis of their past
failures.[240] He concentrated solely upon the two basic arguments on
which his appeal for a rematch ultimately rested: that Aquileia had not
been a genuine council, and that the doctrinal case against Ambrose had
still to be answered.

Hence the curious format of the *Apologia*, which begins with a
lengthy extract from *Contra Ambrosium*, which Palladius had published
two years earlier.[241] In a presentational device that exactly matches Ambrose's own unrevised 'second edition' of *De fide*, Palladius was showing
that his original arguments against that book still stood. A quotation
from *De fide* also provided a starting-point for the present onslaught.
Ambrose had said that *all* the Arian leaders, 'Palladius or Demophilus,
and Auxentius . . . had to be answered' (*Apol.* 83 [*De fide* 1.45]): the
absence of these other bishops from Aquileia meant that Ambrose had
failed to meet his own prescribed terms (*Apol.* 88). It was a somewhat
sophistical point;[242] but then Palladius was pleading a case, and tortuous
subtlety of argument was as fundamental to forensic rhetoric as the invective he heaped so liberally upon Ambrose. Nor does Palladius ever
lose sight of his two central themes. His analysis of the preliminary exchanges (89–96) is designed simply to make the point that 'it was not a
council';[243] both phases of the discussion of Arius' letter are treated together, in order to bring out more clearly the 'blasphemous' Sabellianism implicit in Ambrose's interpretations (97–111).[244] The verdicts pronounced by Ambrose (112–121) prompted some wry reflections upon
the bishop of Milan's episcopate but served chiefly to introduce a technical point: it was 'as clear as daylight' that an adversarial hearing—the
form Gratian had specifically announced—could not be adjudged by

240. Palladius' sole political target, the prefect Syagrius (*Apol.* 121), was
probably safely dead. See *PLRE* 1, p. 863, for the likelihood that he 'died in office
before 382 April 2'.

241. For this earlier work, see above, p. 113; for the relationship of this
extract to the rest of the *Apologia*, see my 'The "Apology" of Palladius', 36–39.

242. Note also that Palladius discreetly ignores Eunomius and Aetius, the
other heretics challenged by Ambrose, and mischievously applies Ambrose's allusion to his predecessor at Milan to Auxentius bishop of Durostorum (cf. *Apol.*
140). The rest of the eastern episcopate is also smuggled into the package
('adunato suo consortio': *Apol.* 88).

243. *Apol.* 89: 'concilium non esset' (cf. 91: 'non esset concilium'). The word
'concilium' occurs ten times in these seven sections.

244. The charge of Sabellianism is made at *Apol.* 99; cf. 98, 101, for
'blasphemy'.

one of the parties.[245] Even the apparent digression against the 'arrogance' of Damasus (122–127) helps reinforce the point that Ambrose was not a judge, nor his 'conspiracy' a council;[246] it also leads neatly to the climax of the case, the systematic demolition of a 'blasphemy at Sirmium' (128–138), which is to be identified with Ambrose's own published teachings.[247]

Palladius' final challenge, which again reasserted his confidence that to crush Ambrose he needed only to meet him under properly regulated conditions, came to nothing—yet another initiative which foundered upon the inertia of the regime. But Gratian remained willing to listen. He continued to grant access to Ambrose's homoean critics and even to convey their arguments to the bishop, who published his response to one such sally as a postscript, addressed directly to the emperor, to his treatise *De incarnationis dominicae sacramento*.[248] Ambrose explained how he had quashed an earlier claim that the 'generate' Son could be equal to the Father who had generated him, with his statement that generation was a function of nature rather than power. His enemies had now turned the question around with a 'damnable tergiversation': 'How *can* the generate and the ingenerate be of a single nature and substance?' (79). The first of these points had been raised by Palladius;[249] it is tempting to imagine the elderly bishop continuing his relentless scrutiny of Ambrose's every utterance. But even if the challenge came from elsewhere, the passage shows clearly that Gratian, far from maintaining an unconditional Nicene allegiance, continued even after the council of Aquileia to respond to questions of doctrine.

245. *Apol.* 114: 'quod inter disceptantes cognitio non e diverso altercantis, sed arbitrii auditoris iudicium flagitet'. Gratian's rescript referred to the case as an *altercatio* (*Acta* 3); Ambrose had acknowledged an 'officium . . . de fide disceptandi' (*De fide* 1.4).

246. *Apol.* 122. There are three separate arguments: by reading out Damasus' letters himself, Ambrose had forfeited his claim to the authority of a judge (*Apol.* 122); in Damasus' absence the session lacked conciliar status (*Apol.* 123–124); and the bishops' apparent complaisance in the pope's rehabilitation of Leontius rendered all their verdicts unsafe (*Apol.* 125–126).

247. I argue that Palladius' target here was *De fide*, against the conventional identification of the 'blasphemy' with the creed of a Nicene council of Sirmium, in 'The "Apology" of Palladius', 46–52.

248. *De inc. dom. sacr.* 79–116; 80 for 'per te mihi propositae quaestioni'. For the date and circumstances, see the introduction to Faller's edition, *CSEL* 79 (1964), pp. 44*–48*.

249. *Apol.* 111: Palladius seizes upon a careless remark in *De fide* (1.1.8–9) to claim that Ambrose himself acknowledged that the son was 'genitum principali potestate', 'ut in generando non naturam sed potestatem probes parentis'.

The circumstances in which *De incarnationis dominicae sacramento* was produced also show the limits of Ambrose's ascendancy. Paulinus records an interruption to the bishop's preaching from two *cubicularii*, attendants of the emperor's bedchamber, who put a question concerning the incarnation and arranged to hear his reply the following day at the Portian Basilica. The two men, typical of the biographer's heretics, were 'full of swollen pride' and went for a carriage ride instead of keeping their appointment (only to suffer, Paulinus shuddered to relate, a fatal traffic accident). Ambrose therefore extemporized an appropriate introduction to the text he had prepared, and delivered it to the audience that had gathered.[250] Whatever the factual basis of this salutary tale, with the court's arrival he had clearly acquired critics as well as admirers and was subject to direct pressure in his own church. Ambrose had indeed found favour with Gratian as a theologian, as is nicely illustrated in a recently published exegetical essay sent to the emperor in response to his 'repeated inquiry'.[251] But his was not the only Christian voice to which Gratian gave ear, and he never succeeded in enlisting the emperor definitively for his cause.

THE FALL OF GRATIAN

The struggle between Ambrose and Palladius took place at the same time that other battles were being fought out in the shadow of Gratian's court, between churchmen competing to tap the emperor's indiscriminate benevolence. During precisely this period, a clash between a controversial Spanish ascetic and the conservative-minded church establishment of the region, for example, was spilling over into the court at Milan.[252] Priscillian and his followers had been investigated by a Spanish council in 380, but without a decisive result; Priscillian himself was then consecrated bishop of Avila and, having collected damaging material against his principal opponent, Hydatius of Emerita, prepared to hale him in turn before a council. At this point Hydatius resorted to the imperial authorities: he warned the government in Milan (and Ambrose) about his 'Manichee' enemies. His language was well calculated to pro-

250. Paulin. *V. Amb.* 18.
251. L. Machielsen, 'Fragments patristiques non-identifiés du manuscrit Vatican palimpseste 577', *SE* 12 (1961), at 537–539.
252. The fullest account of Priscillian's dealings with the Spanish church and Gratian's government is by H. Chadwick, *Priscillian of Avila* (1976), 8–42; cf. Matthews, *Western Aristocracies*, 160–165.

duce the desired response, and a rescript was duly delivered which ordered the expulsion of these 'pseudo-bishops'.[253] Hydatius applied himself with great enthusiasm to its enforcement, provoking his victims to
appeal to the government. They wrote to announce their willingness to
face a secular tribunal, challenging Hydatius to make good his accusation of Manicheism. But they received only belatedly the bland reply
from the *quaestor* at Milan that their appeal was 'just'.[254]

Priscillian and his friends therefore decided to present their case in
person, travelling first to Rome in the hope of securing a purely ecclesiastical resolution of the affair. When Damasus refused to grant them an
audience, they proceeded to Milan and found Ambrose equally obdurate. But other channels were available. Through the support of the *magister officiorum* Macedonius, they obtained a rescript cancelling the previous one and restoring them to their churches.[255] Returning to their
sees, they exacted their revenge upon their persecutors with help from
the provincial governor. Hydatius disappears from the picture, but his
accomplice Ithacius was arraigned as a 'disturber of the churches' and
fled to Gaul to escape trial. From there another round of the contest
began. Ithacius persuaded the praetorian prefect Gregorius at Trier of
the justice of his cause, which the prefect in turn argued in a *relatio* to
the emperor. But Macedonius (inspired, enemies claimed, by Priscillian's bribes) had the case transferred from the prefect's jurisdiction to the
vicarius of Spain; Ithacius was to be conveyed there by *officiales* sent to
Trier from Milan, but he frustrated the plan by going into hiding.

In the end, the affair showed up the impotence of Gratian's government; throughout its course, moreover, it illustrates the vagaries of the
process by which the government made its decisions. The emperor was
confronted in succession with at least three versions of the affair, all of
them entirely plausible: Hydatius', mediated through Ambrose; Priscillian's, through Macedonius; and Ithacius', through the prefect's report.
Gratian could hardly be expected to make a rational choice between
these versions, but he was probably unaware of the problem, each measure being submitted for his consideration separately and as a prepack-
aged *suggestio*. No emperor was able to escape this difficulty, but Gra-

253. Sulp. Sev. *Chron.* 2.47.6.

254. Prisc. *Tract.* 2.15. Although Chadwick (*Priscillian of Avila*, 40) associates
the *quaestor*'s message with Priscillian's visit to Milan, the context strongly suggests an exchange of letters.

255. Sulp. Sev. *Chron.* 2.48–49. For these events, see A. R. Birley, 'Magnus
Maximus and the Persecution of Heresy', *Bulletin of the John Rylands Library* 66
(1982–83), at 19–24.

tian's court seemed unusually susceptible to the twin evils of inadequate central direction and interference from special interests. The government's handling of the Priscillianist affair provoked a bitter indictment from Sulpicius Severus a generation later: 'Everything was for sale there, through the greed and might of a few men'.[256]

A similar context of court intrigue might be suggested for yet another exercise of imperial authority during the same period, the removal of the altar of Victory from the senate house in Rome.[257] This measure, introduced in late 382 as part of a package that withdrew funding for the traditional cults of the capital, was not devised by Ambrose;[258] we should look instead to the Christian careerists in Gratian's entourage, and particularly to the increasing numbers who arrived to assume office from Rome. The measure is most plausibly seen as an extension of the sporadic anti-pagan initiatives taken by Roman Christians, conveyed to Milan by the increased traffic between senate and court.[259] Gratian would have been asked simply to advertise the pious spirit of the age (and incidentally reap a windfall for the treasury) by eliminating an insignificant anomaly; Theodosius' previous repudiation of the pontificate might also have been presented as an object for emulation. The emperor, who had never visited Rome, will not have anticipated the outcry that the initiative provoked from traditionalist senators.[260] More significantly, he never heard the opposition case: when a delegation arrived at Milan to protest to the emperor (bringing with them Gratian's pontifical robes to remind him of his responsibilities), they found their way blocked by 'wicked men' and failed to obtain an audience.[261] Ambrose

256. *Chron.* 2.49.3: 'omnia ibi venalia erant, per libidinem ac potentiam paucorum'.

257. A. Chastagnol, *Le préfecture urbaine à Rome sous le bas-empire* (1960), 157–159, wrongly interpreted this famous episode as the culmination of a 'creeping barrage' organized by Gratian; the best discussion of the strikingly patchy sources is still A. Cameron, 'Gratian's Repudiation of the Pontifical Robe', *JRS* 58 (1968), 96–102.

258. His explicit denial to Eugenius in *Ep. extra coll.* 10 [57].2 ('non fuisse me auctorem cum tollerentur') is to be believed, despite Palanque's recourse to 'l'hypothèse invincible de l'influence d'Ambroise' (*Saint Ambroise*, 119).

259. The overlap is nicely illustrated by the apparently concurrent tenure of the urban and praetorian prefectures by the Christian aristocrat Valerius Severus in the spring of 382 (*PLRE* 1, p. 837).

260. Against the alleged visit of 376, cf. n. 37 above.

261. Symm. *Rel.* 3.1, 'denegata est ab improbis audientia', and especially 20, 'tegite factum quod senatui displicuisse nescivit. Siquidem constat exclusam legationem, ne ad eum iudicium publicum perveniret'. For the robe, see Cameron, 'Gratian's Repudiation'.

had reached the emperor first, presenting a *libellus* forwarded to him by Damasus and signed by 'countless' senators, who asserted that they had not authorized the protest and threatened to cease attending the senate if the measures were revoked.[262] This petition had probably been drummed up by Damasus from the 'backwoodsmen' who had earned their senatorial rank through service with the emperor and normally took little interest in the *curia*'s business; it successfully gave the required impression, and kept the emperor ignorant of the strength of opposition to his measure. Ambrose's role in this affair, which he seems to have carried out with complete success, was purely obstructive.

Like the Priscillianist case, the affair reveals the limited reach of Gratian's government. Both issues also reveal Ambrose involved in politics at the highest level but unable to impose himself consistently. The intercession reported by Sozomen, which was mentioned at the beginning of this chapter, illustrates his difficulties. The condemned man's pagan allegiance and his declaration that Gratian was 'unworthy of his father' imply a connection with the anti-pagan laws, the elder Valentinian having carefully left the Roman cults undisturbed; the bishop's struggle to obtain a hearing is more significant than his eventual success.[263] It was not enough, moreover, to cultivate the emperor alone. Another case, described by Paulinus, involves Ambrose submitting a plea for clemency to the *magister officiorum*, the same Macedonius whose support for Priscillian has just been described. When the bishop arrived at the minister's *praetorium* to make his appeal, he found the doors shut in his face, by Macedonius' express command, and was unable even to secure an interview.[264] Power at Gratian's court was distributed across a complex network of interlocking (and often conflicting) interests; the circumstances did not allow the bishop to exercise any consistent influence over the government.

But within a year of the removal of the altar of Victory, and before Macedonius could secure a decisive victory for Priscillian, Gratian had been toppled by a military revolt led by the commander of the British army, Magnus Maximus. Many contemporaries believed that Gratian had brought the coup upon himself. Some pagans saw it as retribution from the gods whom the emperor had spurned; even those sympathetic to the general tenor of the regime deplored the rampant greed of the emperor's friends, and the excessive licence which his modest good na-

262. *Ep.* 72 [17].10.
263. Soz. *HE* 7.25.10–13; Palanque, *Saint Ambroise*, 113–115.
264. Paulin. *V. Amb.* 37.

ture allowed them.[265] A specific piece of advice from these overmighty friends was widely believed to have had a direct bearing upon the emperor's fall. He had been persuaded to show conspicuous favours to a body of Alans who had been recruited at great expense, showering them with gifts and even dressing in their costume; the 'hatred' that this engendered among the rest of the army, it was alleged, had sealed Gratian's fate.[266]

This personalized explanation is typical of ancient historiography. The modern historian might point instead to certain structural features of Gratian's reign, above all the massive effect that the redeployment of the army to northern Italy must have had. Under Valentinian, the stabilization of the Rhine frontier had created a nexus of powerful interests, centred around the many recruits from the Rhineland whose families and other local connexions anchored the main field army there. The gravitational pull of the region was shown in the use made by Merobaudes of a pretended threat to the Rhine frontier after Valentinian I's death; it was confirmed in 377 when the same Merobaudes, the consistent advocate of the 'Rhine interest', quietly frustrated Gratian's plans for a Balkan campaign.[267] The departure of the court for Italy, however sensible strategically, can only have disrupted this pattern of relations. Although too much should perhaps not be read into a moralizing tale about stereotyped 'barbarians', the controversy over the regiment of Alans might be related to this situation as a government attempt to consolidate its new Danubian orientation by creating a new elite without any ties to Gaul. The advisors who urged Gratian to consort with these exotic warriors would therefore appear in a more creditable light. On the other hand, the army's hostility would prove, after all, well founded: the new recruits represented a direct threat to their own position.

The pervasive influence attributed by the sources to the emperor's advisors need not be blamed solely upon Gratian's ineffectual good nature or inattention to the business of government. In Italy, as we have seen, the court was faced with influences far more complex and powerful than those which could be brought to bear on Trier.[268] The aristocrats of Rome had a pernicious ability to annex the machinery of government

265. The pagan view is reflected by Zosimus at 4.36.5; note also the judgements of Ammianus (31.10.18–19) and the Christian Rufinus (HE 11.13).

266. Zosimus 4.35.2; Aur. Vict. Epit. 47.6.

267. Amm. Marc. 30.10.3; 31.7.4.

268. This is a recurring theme of Matthews' Western Aristocracies, well brought out in a review article by P. Wormald, 'The Decline of the Western Empire', JRS 66 (1976), 217–226.

to serve their own ends; their generally accepted claim to embody Roman traditions and values allowed an easy confusion between their own political and economic interests and those of the empire as a whole. We cannot determine exactly how far the government was in thrall to these interests after 381, but the increased volume of Symmachus' contacts with the court (his correspondence burgeons throughout the 380s) suggests a trend. This 'colonization' of the government helps explain why the emperor was perceived to be at the mercy of his advisors. The church, too, profited from the move to Italy to claim—through Ambrose—a higher profile in the court's religious life and a place for its business on the imperial agenda. But imperial authority, once made broadly available, could be usurped by factions: by Priscillian and his enemies, or by militant Christians in the Roman senate. Amid the clamour of these competing interests, it is not surprising that Gratian was pulled in various directions, nor that he attracted resentment from the victims of the policies to which he lent his name.

No emperor was ever fully in control of his empire; but Gratian, fatally, was *seen* to have lost his grip. The weaknesses described above would not have sufficed to persuade Maximus to risk rebellion had they not been thrown into sharp relief by the insouciant disloyalty of his colleague. Theodosius' declaration of ecclesiastical independence was only part of a general consolidation of his own autonomy in the east, which culminated in the proclamation of his five-year-old son Arcadius as Augustus on 19 January 383. Gratian, who was not consulted and never recognized the promotion on his coinage, was powerless to interfere with his partner's dynastic projects. Maximus, a fellow-Spaniard who claimed a family connexion, may well have hoped for approval from the ambitious emperor of the east.[269]

The coup was effected cleanly. Maximus crossed the Channel in the summer of 383, while Gratian was engaged against the Alamanni in Rhaetia, and established himself near Paris. The emperor broke off his campaign and marched north, but when he hesitated to commence battle the troops deserted wholesale to the usurper. Behind their treachery can be detected the hand of Merobaudes, loyal to the same strategic principles that had informed his previous actions.[270] With a minimum of bloodshed, an imperial presence was restored to the Rhine frontier. Gra-

269. For Gratian's coinage, see Pearce, *Roman Imperial Coinage* 9, xix–xxi, 72. For Maximus and Theodosius, see Pacatus *Paneg.* 24.1 ('et adfinitate et favore iactanti'), 31.1.

270. B. S. Rogers, 'Merobaudes and Maximus in Gaul', *Historia* 30 (1981), 82–105, esp. 100–103.

tian fled. Abandoned by all but a handful of his followers and spurned by his Gallic subjects, he was trapped and then killed (against orders, it was later claimed) by one of Maximus' subordinates.

Contemporary reactions to Gratian's death are muted, his squandered talents attracting more comment than the crime of his murder, and pathos predominating over outrage. For Jerome in 395 he had become one of a series of emperors reduced to helplessness, 'betrayed by his own army, refused admission to the cities he approached, a plaything for his enemy'.[271] Only Ambrose exhibits any real vehemence. In his commentary on Psalm 62 he introduces the emperor abandoned and alone, much as did Jerome; but Gratian swiftly becomes a Christ-like symbol of betrayed innocence, with Maximus at once his Judas and Pilate. In *Apologia David*—written at about the same time—the murder, a blow against the Lord's Anointed, becomes the source of the calamities that immediately beset the empire.[272]

But Gratian's most arresting appearances in Ambrose are in juxtaposition to his two colleagues. The bishop imagined him, a decade after his death, welcoming Valentinian II to heaven. A Jonathan to his brother's improbable Saul, he evoked from Ambrose an echo of David's cry, 'How dear he was to me!', and supplied him with a new catalogue of imperial virtues: 'faithful to the Lord, pious and gentle, pure-hearted and chaste'.[273] Three years later, he reappeared to embrace the dead Theodosius: the two emperors walked together in Ambrose's imagination, sharing memories of their acts of clemency on earth.[274] But already in 384 the bishop was taxing Valentinian with his half-brother's memory, and the legacy of his 'pious virtue'; in 390 he would use the 'dear name' of Gratian to ingratiate himself with Theodosius.[275] Gratian became in Ambrose's hands both a stick and a carrot, setting a standard for his successors and providing them with a mark of recognition.

Gratian played this role more effectively, and yielded more easily to Ambrose's proprietary claims, in death than he had alive. But if these

271. Jer. *Ep.* 60.15; cf. Amm. Marc. 31.10.18.
272. *Expl. Ps. 61* 17; 24–25; *Apol. Dav.* 27. The latter was written shortly after 388: P. Hadot in *SCh* 239 (1977), 33–37 (the arguments at 37–43 for the exact date of spring 390 are ingenious but fragile). The psalm commentary also follows Maximus' defeat, despite Palanque (*Saint Ambroise*, 518–519): 'vindicta paululum comperendinata est' (*Expl. Ps. 61* 26) is a past perfect.
273. *De ob. Val.* 74, 79.
274. *De ob. Theod.* 52.
275. *Ep.* 72 [17].15; *Ep. extra coll.* 11 [51].17.

texts exaggerate the personal intimacy of the two men, they attest the importance of their relationship for Ambrose. For by 383 the bishop's position was very different from when he had first met the emperor, and it had changed dramatically in the two years since the installation of the court at Milan. His opportunities and responsibilities as bishop of an imperial capital not only determined the course of his entanglements with the Illyrican bishops and with Theodosius but also broadened his horizons in every other direction. His physical proximity to the emperor encouraged Hydatius and Priscillian to put their arguments to him from Spain, and Damasus to forward the counterpetition concerning the pagan subsidies from Rome. Milan's new importance, meanwhile, brought him into contact with an increasing number of secular officials.

The best index of Ambrose's changed status is another obituary, written during the winter of 382/3, for Acholius of Thessalonica. Ambrose sent his condolences to his clergy and people and to the bishops of Macedonia, who had evidently written to him to report their loss and inform him of their selection of a successor. While this in itself indicates Ambrose's stature, in his reply to the bishops he claims a more direct link with the Macedonian church: their solicitude was unnecessary, for he had already known of Acholius' death. 'You ask who told me this, when your letters had not yet arrived?' Since the seas had been closed for winter and the roads blocked by barbarians, his readers are invited to suppose that the spirit of Acholius himself must have brought him the news.[276] Despite having met Acholius only once, Ambrose was therefore qualified to write his definitive obituary; moreover, he claimed the meeting as a 'special' bond with the dead bishop, distinct from the many he shared 'in common' with the people and clergy of Thessalonica and the local episcopate. Ambrose takes pains to remind his readers that the privileged information at his disposal went beyond anything they had themselves supplied, even when congratulating them on their choice of a successor. 'This is not the first time I have heard of his merits and goodness; I did not learn of them in your letter, but I did recognize them in what you wrote'.[277]

Ambrose also replied to a note from the new bishop Anysius. 'I have long since had a hold upon you, although this is the first time I am reading you; I have you known by your merits, although I have not yet

276. *Ep.* 51 [15].2. See the discussion by R. Lizzi, *Vescovi e strutture ecclesiastiche nella città tardoantica* (1989), 20–25.

277. *Ep.* 51 [15].2.9; cf. 10 for 'illud . . . speciale'. Ambrose uses a similar device at *De obit. Val.* 23.

seen you with my eyes'.[278] Ambrose reproduces the same formulae with which devout contemporaries conjured up 'instant friendships' with like-minded strangers, but here his resolutely physical language goes further than usual.[279] In this letter he in effect claims Anysius for himself, as the heir to an Acholius whom he had himself defined. The authority stamped so confidently upon both these letters directly reflects Ambrose's access to information, which was in turn a by-product of Milan's role as an imperial capital; lines of communication in the fourth century led no longer to Rome, but to wherever the emperor happened to be. The significance of Gratian's reign for Ambrose was the establishment of the court at Milan; the significance of the emperor's fall was the threat that the centre of gravity would shift back to the Rhine. Ambrose's anxiety to avoid this would shape his behaviour for the next five years, involving him in unexpected, and paradoxical, allegiances.

278. *Ep.* 52 [16].1.
279. Cf. Peter Brown, *Augustine of Hippo* (1967), 160–161, for the tone of Paulinus of Nola's correspondence.

• CHAPTER FOUR •

PERSECUTION

THE NEW REGIME

Gratian had left his young brother, with the apparatus of his civil administration, at Milan. There are distinct echoes of 375 in the negotiations that ensued between Maximus, who controlled (as had Merobaudes) both a dead emperor's army and his corpse, and the surviving Augustus, who was again stranded five hundred miles away, surrounded by apprehensive beneficiaries of the previous regime. But Maximus was immeasurably stronger than Merobaudes, and Valentinian, having been kept firmly in the background at Gratian's court, had nothing to bargain with except his legitimacy. The logical outcome was that he should travel to Trier as he had eight years before, but to perform a rather different role. By joining Maximus' court he would lend plausibility to the usurper's protestations of loyalty to the house of Valentinian; his presence would meanwhile confirm a verdict of misadventure upon Gratian's death, as the regrettable consequence of the emperor's own foolishness.

But, surprisingly, there was no seamless transition to the new ruler, as champions emerged to defend Valentinian's rights and protect him from absorption into the court of Trier. Gratian's entourage suffered casualties: the *magister officiorum* Macedonius, who had opposed Ambrose during the Priscillianist affair, was thwarted in a bid for asylum during the commotion that followed the emperor's death; he was fending off prosecution at Rome (with considerable success) a year later.[1] But like his predecessor, Leo, Macedonius was a politically ephemeral figure, who became vulnerable at the death of the imperial patron on whose behalf he had made himself unpopular. Such men could do little for Valentinian in 383. What 'saved' the prince (or ensured that he played out his largely decorative role in Milan rather than Trier) was the active support of members of the senatorial aristocracy, who needed to maintain a court in Italy in order to consolidate the foothold in government they had established under Gratian. This applied equally to pagan senators, whose (not implausible) interpretation of Gratian's 'disestablishment' of their cults as ill-considered and ill-informed assent to unscrupulous advisors underscored the need to keep the imperial ear open to their own wiser counsels.[2] As if to announce the interplay between Milanese court and Roman aristocracy that was to be so notable a feature of the following four years, the ubiquitous Petronius Probus appeared in Milan, at the very moment of Gratian's death, to begin a record fourth term as praetorian prefect.[3]

The Milanese court could not survive solely on the strength of the illustrious names of Probus and his immediate successors in office, Nonius Atticus Maximus and Vettius Agorius Praetextatus.[4] Since Maximus had eliminated Gratian by securing the defection *en bloc* of the western army, there can have been no 'loyalist' forces except isolated units not involved in the ill-fated Gallic campaign. But despite the steep tilt of the military balance in Maximus' favour, one of Gratian's generals emerged to lead the resistance. The Frankish officer Bauto, who had led an expedition to the Balkans several years earlier, became the mainstay of Valentinian II's government, dominating the consistory even on matters unrelated to military affairs and assuming (albeit by default) the only nonimperial consulship awarded under the regime; such was his prominence that Maximus accused him, somewhat ironically in the light of his

1. Paulin. *V. Amb.* 37; the episode is more plausibly located to Milan than Gaul. For Macedonius' subsequent escapades, see Symm. *Rel.* 36.

2. Symm. *Rel.* 3.20.

3. Probus' office is attested by two laws, both of whose manuscript dates are problematic: plausible emendations are from 19 January 383 to 19 August (six days before Gratian's death), and from 26 October 384 to the same date in 383. See *PLRE* 1, p. 739.

4. *PLRE* 1, Maximus 34 (pp. 586–587), and p. 262 below for his connexion with Ambrose; the evidence for the distinguished career of Praetextatus is presented at *PLRE* 1, pp. 722–724.

own plans, of seeking a kingdom for himself in Valentinian's name.[5] The sources do not say what forces were initially available to Bauto; a plausible guess (but no more than that) would make him a *comes per Illyricum* under Gratian, the commander of units unaffected by the gravitational pull of the Rhine.[6] If Bauto had been involved in implementing Gratian's redeployment towards the Danube, this would have set him apart from his compatriot Merobaudes, the consistent advocate of the Rhine interest. The hypothesis has its attractions, helping to explain the general's commitment to a cause that must have looked forlorn indeed in 383 and providing a context for his ability to organize at short notice a force of Alans (the tribe that had brought so much unpopularity upon Gratian) and Huns in its defence. The Gothic troops who later formed an important pillar of Valentinian's military establishment might also be associated with Bauto's Illyrican and Balkan connexions.[7]

But these resources could not be mobilized immediately, and Maximus would soon learn of any initiative against him.[8] Dissimulation was therefore necessary: hope was held out to the usurper that Valentinian would come meekly to Trier and submit himself to his tutelage. The instrument of this deception was Ambrose himself, at first sight perhaps the least expected member of the coalition that formed around Valentinian, for Ambrose's support for the new regime was not (as has conventionally been assumed) the automatic consequence of his intimacy with Gratian and abhorrence of the emperor's murderers. The relationship between Gratian and Ambrose cannot by itself explain the bishop's readiness to travel to Trier to tell lies on Valentinian's behalf. For although the prince himself, apparently nurtured in the same atmosphere of enthusiastic piety as his brother, was perfectly acceptable,[9] Ambrose

5. Ambrose quotes the usurper at *Ep.* 30 [24].4, '"ille Bauto, qui sibi regnum sub specie pueri vindicare voluit"', and stresses Bauto's participation in a religious controversy (*Ep. extra coll.* 10 [57].3). Bauto replaced Praetextatus, consul designate for 385, after the latter's sudden death in December 384.

6. Bauto was *magister militum* in autumn 384 (*Ep. extra coll.* 10 [57].3), a promotion as likely to have been won under Valentinian as Gratian. He had led a Balkan campaign in 381: Zosimus 4.33.1 (for the date, see P. Heather, *Goths and Romans 332–489* [1991], 155).

7. Huns and Alans: below, n. 27; Goths: below, p. 182.

8. Maximus' brother Marcellinus, at Milan in autumn 383 (Amb. *Ep.* 30 [24].9), is possibly to be identified with the (*vicarius?*) Marcellinus who received *CTh* 9.27.5 (4 April 383).

9. Amb. *De ob. Val.* 15–18 convincingly presents a Christian prince painfully conscious of his duty to set an example to his court: when teased for inter-

cannot have welcomed the prospect of his mother, Justina, his own formidable and long-standing rival, gaining the opportunity to promote her
cherished homoean cause. Maximus, on the other hand, seems to have
trumpeted from the outset of his reign his devotion to the 'catholic faith'
of Nicaea.[10] Ambrose's allegiance is a striking illustration of his priorities. Like the pagan senators of Rome, he was less concerned with the
regime's ideological complexion than with retaining his access to the machinery of government. The court's presence in northern Italy promised
him ample opportunity, under normal circumstances, to obstruct the
implementation of uncongenial policies.

Pressure might also have been applied to recruit Ambrose to Valentinian's party. The bishop's highly public expressions of devotion to Gratian had implied a commitment, and a demand that he make good these
protestations perhaps explains his remark, made many years later, that
Valentinian had been 'placed in his arms' by Justina. This suggests a
dramatic gesture contrived by the queen, physically entrusting her son
to the bishop's protection.[11] Ambrose could not easily have refused. One
of his favorite biblical refrains, with which he regularly taxed his parishioners, was the injunction to protect the widow and the *pupillus*, and
here Justina's son was being denied his inheritance by the usurper.[12] The
power of such appeals should not be underestimated: twenty years later,
in Constantinople, John Chrysostom reluctantly yielded before the same
combination of a tearful Augusta and a helpless imperial child.[13]

Ambrose arrived at Trier in the late autumn of 383 to buy time for
the loyalists in Milan. There are precedents for clerical involvement in
diplomacy, but none at this level, and none that involved outright

---

rupting his official duties to take his meals at the early hour usual for children,
he hosted banquets at which he ostentatiously refused to eat anything. He naturally attended Ambrose's church: see below, p. 167.

10. Maximus announced his 'catholic' faith and abhorrence of Arianism in
386 (*Coll. Avell.* 39); his statement that he ascended 'ad imperium ab ipso statim
salutari fonte' (*Coll. Avell.* 40.1) might imply the incorporation of baptism into
his formal accession ceremony.

11. *De ob. Val.* 28: 'ego Iustinae maternis traditum manibus amplexus sum'.
The explicit mention of Justina, the only time Ambrose ever names her, might
suggest an actual incident.

12. The texts which Ambrose quoted at Maximus (*Ep.* 30 [24].5), Isaiah 1:17
and Psalm 67:6, are conjoined frequently in his works: *De vid.* 13; *De virgt.* 12;
Exp. ps. 118 20.47.

13. Soc. *HE* 6.11 (Eudoxia and Theodosius II).

fraud.[14] The only evidence for this episode is a letter written somewhat later by Ambrose himself, and so doubly distorted, but the main outlines seem clear enough. To the bishop's deferential but vague appeal for 'peace' Maximus, who of course desired precisely this, replied in the same precise terms that his *comes* Victor, who had crossed paths with Ambrose en route, was delivering at Milan: Valentinian should come to him 'like a son to his father'.[15] Ambrose, having come to Trier specifically to avert this, therefore introduced a red herring to prolong the negotiations without specifically conceding the issue. It would be unfair, he protested, to make a boy and his widowed mother travel across the Alps in the harsh conditions of winter; it was surely inconceivable, he added, that the boy should embark upon such a journey *without* his mother.[16] The remark implies that Justina had not featured in Maximus' original plans for Valentinian, and the usurper can be forgiven for thinking that Ambrose was negotiating exact conditions. He may have sympathized with the bishop's apparent desire to see the queen removed from Milan. Ambrose's subsequent protest against the accusation of duplicity—'it is certain that we could not have agreed on terms [for Valentinian's journey to Trier], for that was not in my mandate'[17]—therefore dissembles his own failure to clarify the scope of his mandate. Maximus certainly believed that he was close to a deal; when his own envoy Victor returned from Milan with a less encouraging (but still inconclusive)[18] message, he dispatched Ambrose back there, presumably to implement the terms of the more accommodating 'agreement' they had just struck. But by this time troops had been mobilized to defend the passes of the Alps, and as he returned Ambrose crossed paths with another legation from Milan bringing a final declaration of 'independence.'[19] The usurper

14. Ammianus records presbyters sent to negotiate with the Romans by Fritigern (31.12.8: few modern scholars are as sceptical of their good faith as was Valens) and by the Moorish rebel Firmus (29.5.15).

15. *Ep.* 30 [24].7. Ambrose's acknowledgement of the usurper's supremacy ('tunc ut inferiori pacem petebam': *Ep.* 30 [24].3) suggests that he accepted this claim to 'paternity'.

16. *Ep.* 30 [24].7: 'sine matre autem tanto itineri dubiis rebus committeretur?'.

17. *Ep.* 30 [24].7: 'spondere nos id non potuisse certum est, quod non mandatum erat'.

18. Ambrose's remark, 'negatum ei, quod postulabat' (*Ep.* 30 [24].7, referring to Victor's embassy to Milan), must exaggerate the finality of this refusal, for a further embassy was later dispatched from Milan to repeat the message.

19. *Ep.* 30 [24].7. Ambrose crossed paths with this group at Valence, about three-quarters of the distance between Trier and Milan; their departure from

learned too late that he would have to fight to impose his will upon Milan, and the onset of winter prevented him from exploiting his military superiority to press for an immediate conclusion.

Ambrose's embassy was of decisive importance. Maximus' failure to absorb or eliminate the last vestige of the house of Valentinian fatally marred the surgery that had excised Gratian from the body politic, and left a highly visible scar. War seemed likely as the new year opened: Maximus, who retained a secure military predominance, threatened to achieve by force what had been denied him by Ambrose's equivocations.[20] But Valentinian's supporters, having had time to establish themselves as a credible government, now made a tidy solution impossible. Their advertisement of the prince's claims had a decisive effect, above all, on the position adopted by Theodosius, to whom Maximus' background had probably recommended him as an attractive alternative to Gratian. Although there is not the slightest evidence of any active complicity by Theodosius in Maximus' rebellion, he had little cause to bestir himself, other things being equal, to avenge his senior colleague.[21] With the consolidation of Valentinian's government in Milan, however, other things were no longer equal. The prince's supporters betook themselves to Theodosius, presenting him with an appeal to 'avenge the monarch slain in his youth, and to save the only survivor of the dynasty'.[22] Such a plea, with influential voices behind it, could not easily be ignored.

Valentinian's claims upon Theodosius could be reinforced, more-

---

Milan will have coincided with the garrisoning of the Alpine passes, mentioned in the same sentence.

20. D. Vera, 'I rapporti fra Magno Massimo, Teodosio e Valentiniano II nel 383–384', *Athenaeum*, n.s., 53 (1975), 267–301, discusses the evidence for political and military activity in detail; the following account accepts the main outlines of his interpretation.

21. Reaction to earlier, implausible theories that Theodosius was involved in the usurpation has been too extreme: neither J. F. Matthews' attribution to Theodosius of 'honest loyalty to the dynasty that had made him emperor' (*Western Aristocracies and Imperial Court* [1975], 176) nor H. R. Baldus' inference from his coinage of a bid to save Gratian ('Theodosius der Grosse und die Revolte des Magnus Maximus', *Chiron* 14 [1984], 175–192) seems to me convincing. Vera, 'I rapporti', 277–282, argues persuasively from Zosimus 4.37 that Theodosius recognized Maximus in the immediate aftermath of the usurpation.

22. Themistius *Or.* 18, 220d, reproducing the appeal for a domestic audience. Maximus' complaint (Amb. *Ep.* 30 [24].10), 'quod se ad Theodosium imperatorem potius contulerint, qui sunt cum Valentiniano imperatore', may well have been aimed specifically at the appeal, which betrayed the spirit and perhaps also the letter of his agreement with Ambrose.

over, by considerations of *Realpolitik.* The empire's centre of political gravity remained located firmly in the west, which had been bequeathed secure frontiers and an efficient, well-disciplined army by Valentinian I; the east, meanwhile, was still suffering the consequences of the destruction of its army at Adrianople and faced renewed Persian claims upon Armenia. However congenial a colleague he obtained in the west, Theodosius was doomed to permanent subordination while the elder Valentinian's inheritance remained intact. Hence the appeal of young Valentinian's invitation that he, and not Maximus, act as his 'father': he would at once put a weakened Italian court in his debt and see the west divided against itself. The attractions of Spanish family connexions and Nicene religious solidarity dimmed before this prospect. Military forces were duly mustered at Constantinople in 384, and a probably bemused public was informed that this was a mere continuation of their emperor's previous policy.[23] In the event, no actual intervention was required; an arrangement was reached which, although its terms remain problematical, seems to have satisfied the minimum conditions of the two western parties. Maximus gave up his demand that Valentinian come to his court and received in return the formal recognition that he required.[24] The two western courts spent the next three years glowering at each other across the Alps. Without striking a blow, Theodosius had become the empire's supreme arbiter of power.

The equilibrium produced by Theodosius' recognition of Valentinian could never be other than unstable. The very survival of the Milanese court denied Maximus lasting security, for it offered a perpetual reminder of the bloodstained origins of his regime. This fragility was embodied vividly in the limbo to which Gratian's corpse was consigned: the usurper was reluctant to inter him himself and unwilling to concede a propaganda victory by surrendering him to Milan. The body remained unburied several years later; its ultimate fate is unknown.[25] The in-

23. So I interpret Themistius' laboured discussion of Theodosius' 'first expedition', which can only refer to his negotiations with Maximus the *previous* year (383); the defensive tone does not therefore imply criticism of the failure of an 'expedition' to achieve concrete results (Matthews, *Western Aristocracies,* 178; Vera, 'I rapporti', 292–295), for no campaign had actually taken place. Themistius was instead trying to explain his master's previous dealings with Maximus in the light of his newly discovered concern for Valentinian.

24. Vera, 'I rapporti', 295–297, discusses the problems presented by the evidence for this settlement. Matthews (*Western Aristocracies,* 176n2, 179) denies any recognition of Maximus by Theodosius until 386.

25. The recovery of Gratian's body was the ostensible purpose of a second embassy to Maximus by Ambrose (the occasion of his *Ep.* 30 [24]), most plausibly

stability is reflected also in the strategic paralysis that seized the west. Pincer movements against the troublesome Alamannic tribes from the Rhine and Danube frontiers, essayed by both Constantius and Valentinian I, were now out of the question;[26] independent incursions into barbarian territory by either government, on the other hand, were bound to provoke suspicion.[27] Valentinian's regime, an artificial entity dependent upon external support, had its own problems. A severe food shortage struck peninsular Italy in 383, and a further crisis affected Rome the following year, prompting emergency measures from the urban prefect that bear the stamp of panic.[28] These problems might reasonably be associated with an overall structural weakness. Significantly, it was to the government of Constantinople that the citizens of Rome looked in 384.[29]

But the frailty of Valentinian's government did not necessarily displease the partners in the coalition that sustained it. Their loyalism was determined above all by the opportunities for pressing their own interests which proximity to the government afforded; hence that government's ineffectiveness might have been part of its appeal. Two converging studies of a vicious Christian diatribe against an unnamed 'prefect', the *Carmen contra paganos*, have persuasively identified its target as the distinguished senator Praetextatus, praetorian prefect in 384 and consul designate at his death that December.[30] Neither the poet's gloating over the prefect's lingering death nor his derision at his antics can conceal his alarm at the glare of publicity in which he had been able to flaunt his idolatry: the people of Rome had 'seen' him lead processions at the Me-

dated to 386. Amb. *De ob. Val.* 79 is not evidence that Gratian was eventually buried in Milan.

26. For these campaigns, see Amm. Marc. 16.11.3; 28.5.8.

27. An expedition launched under Valentinian's auspices against the Alamannic Iuthungi, either in late 383 or 384, brought a complaint from Maximus that Bauto had sent 'Alans and Huns against him' (Amb. *Ep.* 30 [24].8). Despite Ambrose's protestations, the raid was probably intended as at once a demonstration of force and a diversion on Maximus' flank.

28. These two crises are discussed by J.-R. Palanque, 'Famines à Rome à la fin du IVe siècle', *REA* 33 (1931) 346–356; see also L. Cracco Ruggini, 'Fame laborasse Italiam', in *L'Italia settentrionale nell'età antica* (1976), 83–98. For the expulsion of *peregrini* from Rome in 384, see p. 273 below.

29. Symm. *Rel.* 9.7.

30. L. Cracco Ruggini, 'Il paganesimo romano tra religione e politica (384–394 d.C.)', *MAL* 8.23.1 (1979), 3–141; F. Dolbeau, 'Damase, le *Carmen Contra Paganos* et Hériger de Lobbes', *REAug* 27 (1981), 38–43. The poem is now to be read in D. R. Shackleton-Bailey's edition, *Anthologia Latina* 1.1 (1982), pp. 17–23.

galensian festival, with distinguished senators in attendance.[31] Such was
the freedom of action enjoyed by the power brokers behind Valentinian's throne.

But in the pursuit of their diverse interests members of the coalition
occasionally collided. This happened when Symmachus, assuming the
urban prefecture in the summer of 384, sought to capitalize upon Praetextatus' initiatives by securing a formal revocation of the package of
anti-pagan measures which Gratian had introduced two years earlier
and which Ambrose had defended against a previous protest. Symmachus obtained a mandate from the senate to send an official *relatio* on
the subject and produced a judicious and eloquent plea for reversion to
'the religious condition that long benefitted the state'.[32] This third *relatio*,
while fully deserving its reputation as Symmachus' stylistic masterpiece,
also shows great tactical astuteness. By presenting the central issue as
tolerance and expressly refusing to challenge the Christians or to question their supremacy (he offered prayers, he said, not a battle), Symmachus hoped that the petition would remain nonpartisan, a sensible
remedy for a bitterly held grievance. He won some success, even finding
Christians at the Milanese court willing to speak in his support.[33]

The bishop of Milan, however, took a very different view. When
Ambrose heard of the petition he forestalled it with a memorandum
of his own to the emperor.[34] Dire implications are discovered in Symmachus' deceptively reasonable request. Valentinian will appear to be
sponsoring paganism himself (3); the sacrificial smoke from the restored
altar will cause nothing less than a renewed 'persecution' of the Christian senators who choke upon it (9). Detailed arguments follow: the petition is void because it did not command authentic support from the
senate (10–11); the case should be referred to Theodosius, 'whom you

31. *Carm.* 103–109. The poet's particular attention to the festivals of Magna
Mater (cf. 65, 77) might suggest that Praetextatus had sponsored these in March/
April 384, before leaving to take office in Milan (where he is first attested on
21 May).

32. *Rel.* 3.3. This celebrated incident is discussed by Matthews, *Western Aristocracies*, 203–211; there is a full commentary in R. Klein's edition of the documents, *Der Streit um den Victoriaaltar* (1972).

33. As was acknowledged by Ambrose: 'Quod si aliqui nomine Christiani
tale aliquid decernendum putant . . .' (*Ep.* 72 [17].8).

34. *Ep.* 72 [17]: references in the text of this paragraph are to this letter.
Symmachus' petition appears to have taken the church by surprise: explaining
why there was no counterpetition from Damasus this time, Ambrose can only
say that 'omnes conveniremus episcopi, nisi incredibile hoc et repentinum ad
aures pervenisset hominum' (10).

have been accustomed to consult over almost all matters of importance' (12); Ambrose should be given a copy of the *relatio* himself, to allow him to prepare a detailed refutation (13). His objections are becoming ever more elaborate, strangling the bill with time-consuming technicalities, when suddenly he announces that the church will not tolerate an adverse decision. Valentinian will meet an uncomfortable reception on his next visit to the cathedral: 'you will find no bishop, or else one who will resist you' (13). The ominous rebuke that Ambrose imagines from this 'bishop' (14) is vigorously seconded by Gratian and Valentinian I (15–16); he then returns to the level of practical politics with a brusque, matter-of-fact conclusion: 'Now that you realize that the passage of such a decree would constitute an injury, first to God and then to your father and brother, I request that you do what will help secure your safety before God' (17).

Ambrose's later, somewhat complacent remark that Valentinian 'heard' his *suggestio* and acted on the consistory's approval can only mean that the emperor accepted this central plea that he 'neither promulgate nor subscribe to' the legislation Symmachus was proposing. His own reply to the *relatio*, which has created the impression of a reasoned 'debate' over the issue, was a purely academic exercise.[35] But if Ambrose did not triumph by force of reason, nor were his threats the key to his success. His efficiency in anticipating the government's intentions and decisiveness in acting upon his information were both important factors; but Ambrose relied above all upon the favour the government owed him. He spells his position out plainly, almost crudely, at the start of the key passage in which he moved from minutiae to menace: 'And so, mindful of the legation recently entrusted to me . . .' (12).[36] The manner in which Ambrose had chosen to call in the debt that had been incurred at Trier would rankle, and eventually rebound against him, but this resounding assertion of his right to intervene in a *causa religionis* strikingly demonstrates the rewards that his support for Valentinian had yielded.

Nor should Symmachus' defeat and his evident unhappiness in the

35. Ambrose's summary of the affair to Eugenius (*Ep. extra coll.* 10 [57].3) adduces only the arguments which he advanced in *Ep.* 72; there is no basis for the widespread assumption that his *Ep.* 73 [18] ever appeared on the consistory's agenda.

36. 'Memor legationis proxime mandatae mihi'. The expression is often referred mistakenly to Ambrose's intervention with Gratian in 382 (Zelzer, *CSEL* 82.3, p. 17), but this had consisted only of forwarding a 'libellus' (*Ep.* 72 [17].10); compare the references at *Epp.* 76 [20].23 ('legationis'), 30 [24].1 ('superioris legationis'), and *De ob. Val.* 28 ('legatus').

latter part of his prefecture suggest senatorial disenchantment with the regime. His peers continued to thrive: one 'very powerful senator' had bound so large a clientele to himself through favours and threats that financial officials despaired of checking his depredations; only an up-start African lawyer briefly resisted.[37] More legitimate opportunities at-tended the widening of the senate's diplomatic horizons beyond Milan, to Constantinople. In the same effusive letter in which he thanks Theo-dosius for his help in the supply crisis of 384, Symmachus reports the senate's erection of a statue in honour of the emperor's father.[38] The gesture sums up Italy's relationship to the eastern court. Theodosius' predominance was exercised not in formal, institutional terms—for no machinery existed to allow the administration of a distant court by re-mote control[39]—but through a series of relationships with the governing elite of Italy. Nor were these relationships focused exclusively on Theo-dosius. Symmachus, for instance, was gratified to receive belated con-sular gifts from Theodosius' Frankish *magister militum*, Richomer; he consolidated the connexion with a letter conveyed to Constantinople by the rhetorician Eugenius, whose profession was likely to commend him to Richomer.[40] The fragmentation of political authority in the west cre-ated opportunities for members of the eastern government (many of them, like Richomer, themselves of western extraction) to extend the range of their patronage. Eugenius' subsequent promotion to a *western* court office, on Richomer's recommendation, is symptomatic.

Some members of Theodosius' entourage sought direct advantages from the west. Such was Neoterius, praetorian prefect at Milan in 385, whose tenure is conventionally interpreted on the basis of his previous term as Theodosius' prefect (380/1) as an instrument of Theodosius'

37. Aug. *Conf.* 6.10.16, describing Alypius' term as assessor to the *comes largitionum Italicarum*. It might be noted that Alypius failed to secure any subse-quent appointment in Italy: see J. J. O'Donnell, *Augustine: Confessions* (1992), 3:37.

38. *Rel.* 9. For full discussion (not all of it apposite), see D. Vera, 'Le statue del senato di Roma in onore di Flavio Teodosio e l'equilibrio dei potere imperiali in età Teodosiana', *Athenaeum*, n.s., 57 (1979), 381–403.

39. Ambrose's claim that Valentinian routinely consulted Theodosius (*Ep.* 72 [17].12) is plainly polemical: had this procedure been operative, his interven-tion against Symmachus would have been unnecessary. He was perhaps exploit-ing the single precedent of the original appeal to Theodosius for help against Maximus.

40. Symm. *Epp.* 3.59, 61. Richomer's appreciation of oratory: Libanius *Or.* 1.216–220. Despite Symmachus' own interpretation of the belated gifts, I am inclined to see them as exploratory: prompted perhaps by Symmachus' recent prominence as urban prefect?

'protectorate'.[41] But Neoterius' six-month term, the only appointment at Milan that can conceivably be traced to Theodosius, is insufficient evidence for the eastern emperor's (intrinsically unlikely) ability to confer such posts; nor would it reflect well on his ability to supervise policy-making. The one government initiative that can plausibly be dated to Neoterius' tenure—the first round in the great struggle between Valentinian and Ambrose—is unlikely to have been to Theodosius' taste.[42] Neoterius is therefore to be seen as a carpetbagger, exploiting the opportunities available at the western court (and perhaps his connexions with the Roman aristocracy)[43] to advance his own interests. To the same category belongs the general Promotus, who obtained a post in Africa in about 385 which brought him into contact with Symmachus; a friendship with Bauto was probably established during the same period.[44] These appointments, revealed casually and fleetingly in the sources, hardly suggest a government with a clear sense of direction.

There survives one particularly vivid impression of Valentinian's Milan. The court seems to have lacked many of the instruments traditionally employed to sustain and project the appropriate images of imperial authority. One effect of Maximus' usurpation was to sever the links between the schools of Gaul and the Valentinianic dynasty; in 384, Milan encountered difficulties in recruiting a rhetorician. In the absence (itself noteworthy) of any locally available talent, the selection was delegated to Symmachus, then urban prefect of Rome. The post duly went to a little-known provincial named Augustine, who had spent but a single year in Rome (much of it in his sickbed) struggling, with limited success, to establish a teaching career.[45] He did not even have the backing of powerful connexions, as the Manichean patrons who recommended him to Symmachus will not have belonged to the latter's milieu.[46] Augustine's résumé looks singularly lacklustre beside that of the poet Claudian, who when he made the same journey northwards a de-

41. Matthews, *Western Aristocracies*, 179.

42. Neoterius is attested in office for the period 1 February–26 July 385: the first confrontation with Ambrose occurred the same year, and before the latter date, since the court spent the last five months of the year in Aquileia.

43. See Symm. *Ep.* 5.46, for Neoterius' Roman origins.

44. Symm. *Ep.* 3.76; Promotus later raised Bauto's orphaned daughter Eudoxia with his own children: Zosimus 5.3.2. No strategic implications can be discovered in the appointment.

45. *Conf.* 5.13.23. The post was with the *civitas* of Milan ('ut illi civitati rhetoricae magister provideretur'), so did not bring Augustine the same automatic proximity to the court as Ausonius had enjoyed at Trier.

46. For Augustine's Manichean friends at Rome, see S. N. C. Lieu, *Manichaeism in the Later Roman Empire and Medieval China* (1985), 137–138.

cade later, to a court that was in some respects as makeshift as Valentinian's, had already secured a certain fame (and the patronage of the powerful Anicii) by his verse panegyric for the consulate of Petronius Probus' two sons.[47] Rhetorical posts at Valentinian's capital seem, then, to have generated comparatively little competition. Augustine, moreover, found his job far less satisfactory than would Claudian and has left a bitter record of his disillusionment and discomfort at the lies he had to tell, praising the valiant deeds of a child-emperor before an audience who knew the truth.[48] The difference between the two men is not to be explained only in terms of their relative integrity. Soon after arriving in Milan, Claudian established a relationship with the power behind his emperor's throne which was to endure for the remainder of his career and guarantee him fame and prosperity. Valentinian's court lacked a single focus of this sort, and Augustine's afternoons were consigned to an arduous and frustrating search for reliable patrons.[49] His difficulties well reflect the shifting, elusive balance of power at Milan. It is perhaps not surprising that he was increasingly drawn to, and eventually captured by, one of the city's few solid and reliable institutions: the church of Bishop Ambrose.

THE FIRST ROUND

Valentinian II, poised uneasily between the scarcely disguised hostility of one 'colleague' and the overbearing protectiveness of another, depended upon an ill-assorted coalition held together more by self-interest than by dynastic loyalty or mutual cohesion.[50] His supporters nevertheless recognized the danger of disruptive collisions: hence Symmachus' deprecation in his third *relatio* of any intention to challenge the church's interests. Against this background, the campaign against Ambrose and his church upon which Valentinian's government embarked in 385/6 is little short of astonishing. A long and bruising confrontation between emperor and bishop escalated from a formal request for the cession of a basilica to arrests and an armed blockade, with alleged attempts to kidnap or even assassinate the bishop. And the whole

47. This phase of Claudian's career, 'from panegyrist to propagandist', is discussed by A. Cameron, *Claudian* (1970), 30–45.
48. *Conf.* 6.6.9: 'cum pararem recitare imperatori laudes, quibus plura mentirer, et mentienti faverentur ab scientibus'.
49. *Conf.* 6.11.18.
50. Note the intimations of difficulties between a senator and general in Symm. *Ep.* 4.15, to Bauto.

struggle was for nothing: it merely displayed to the world the impotence of the Milanese government and prompted the solicitous intervention of its enemies at Trier.

The sources offer an explanation for this apparent exercise in self-destruction. It was the emperor's mother, Justina, according to Augustine, who 'persecuted' the bishop and unleashed her *rabies feminea* against him; Paulinus fails even to mention Valentinian in his account of Justina's *furor* and the *dementia* of her hirelings, a presentation echoed by Rufinus and the Greek historians Sozomen and Socrates.[51] This version originated with Ambrose himself, who painted Justina—'that woman' to his sister—in the lurid colours of a Jezebel.[52] The Old Testament scene that Ambrose describes being reenacted in Milan has influenced all subsequent interpretations of this episode. Deceived by feminine counsel, the king reached out greedily for the modest vineyard of another Nabuth, and his whimsical obsession with a subject's ancestral 'inheritance' again threatened to end in bloodshed.[53]

But the 'persecution' Ambrose so powerfully evokes cannot easily be squared with the political realities of Valentinian's Milan. Even had Justina been willing to risk the internal stability and external security of her son's empire to pursue her feud with Ambrose, and had she enjoyed Valentinian's unconditional submissiveness, such recklessness would never have been tolerated by the other parties who held important stakes in Valentinian's regime and to whom the limits to the emperor's actual power were an open secret. Even if not actively committed to Ambrose's church, these men had a clear interest in preserving stability. Yet all branches of the government—executive, legislative and military—were to become embroiled in a confrontation that brought Milan to the brink of a bloodbath. Justina and a cadre of fanatical co-religionists could not have achieved this by covert manipulation, or Valentinian by imperial fiat. For the queen's 'madness' to have yielded such results, the infection must have spread much further than Ambrose would have us believe; or else, perhaps, the bishop's diagnosis needs revision.

That convenient abbreviation, the 'court', embraces diverse individuals, groups and interests; a complex interplay of personalities and procedures was involved in the formulation and implementation of any particular measure. Valentinian himself, thirteen in 385, had had little

---

51. Aug. *Conf.* 9.7.15; Paulin. *V. Amb.* 13.1; Ruf. *HE* 11.15–16; Soc. *HE* 5.11; Soz. *HE* 7.13.

52. *Ep.* 76 [20].12 ('femina ista'); 18 ('"etiam Heliam Iezabel cruente persecuta est"'). The latter designation is taken up by Gaudentius, *Praef. ad Benivolum* 5; cf. Ruf. *HE* 11.15.

53. *Sermo contra Aux.* 17.

opportunity during his nine years in the purple to exercise the vast powers formally invested in him, but he cannot be dismissed as a mere ci-
pher. The struggle with Ambrose clearly meant much to him personally,
and we should neither doubt the authenticity of his desire to worship
God in what he believed was the appropriate manner, nor underesti-
mate his resentment at the thralldom he felt the bishop was imposing
upon him. He was prepared to vent his anger upon his generals and
seriously disconcerted Ambrose with a private message sent on his own
initiative.[54] Such strokes were no doubt infrequent, but Valentinian at
least participated in all decisions made by the government, and it was to
him that ministers reported.[55]

By contrast, Ambrose's long-standing enemy Justina operated at
some distance from the formal machinery of decision-making. Whatever
her personal influence over her son, she was not in a position consistently to supervise the actions taken in his name.[56] She had her friends
in the palace, the 'multitude of Arians who stood with Justina', and
could offer gifts or the promise of office to attach men to herself. But the
number of posts in the queen's gift must have been limited, and bribery
cannot by itself explain very much. Various specific favours could perhaps be bought, but not the full-scale deployment of the government's
resources against Ambrose.[57] Those of Gratian's courtiers who had upheld the homoean cause against the bishop, moreover, probably acted
in partnership with the queen (or independently, along parallel lines)
rather than under her leadership. As for the homoean clergymen who
almost certainly played an important part in formulating the campaign
against Ambrose, we have no information whatever about their relationship either to Justina or to the government.[58]

But Justina's creatures and allies all operated in subordinate capaci-
ties; it was the palatine ministers and the generals who would deploy

54. *Ep.* 76 [20].22.

55. E.g., *Ep.* 76 [20].2: 'intimaturum se imperatori diceret', of the praetorian
prefect.

56. Ambrose's failure to name Justina in his formal letter to Valentinian,
Ep. 75 [21], illustrates both the selectiveness of his presentation and her 'unofficial' status. Significantly, Maximus in 386 identified Bauto, rather than Justina,
as the power behind the throne (at Amb. *Ep.* 30 [24].4).

57. Friends: Paulin. *V. Amb.* 15.1. The one recorded attempt at bribery,
to induce the *magister memoriae* Benivolus to withdraw his opposition to pro-
homoean legislation, failed: Ruf. *HE* 11.16.

58. Auxentius, Ambrose's principal homoean opponent, is never once juxtaposed with Justina in our documents: for the selectiveness of these sources,
cf. p. 185 below.

soldiers in the streets of Milan and order the arrest of the bishop's supporters. Eusignius, the praetorian prefect at the height of the crisis in 386, did not owe his office to loyalty to an Arian queen; he belongs, rather, to the class who had originally put her son in power. Proconsul of Africa (a post reserved almost exclusively for the more blue-blooded members of the Roman senate) in 383, Eusignius inhabited the world of Symmachus, with whom he maintained a sometimes strained acquaintance.[59] When he went in person to Ambrose's church to present an ultimatum to the intractable bishop, we may be sure that he was not the reluctant lackey of a petulant adolescent and his crazed mother. It remains to be seen, then, why men like Eusignius allowed, and even participated in, a campaign that caused so much disruption to the delicate balance of Valentinian's empire.

The first episode in the conflict shows the need for a more sophisticated explanation than the machinations of a fanatical clique. In the first half of 385 an incident occurred which the bishop recalled the following year as evidence of his fortitude in the face of the authorities. He had been summoned to the palace, where 'a debate took place before the consistory in the presence of the senior ministers [*primates*]', during which he claims to have been confronted with the emperor's peremptory desire to 'snatch away' a basilica from him.[60] But the formal setting in which the demand was made, and the presence of the chief officers of state to second it, suggest that this powerfully charged terminology is misleading. The invitation to attend the consistory, an honour rarely granted to churchmen in the fourth century, shows the emperor's advisors to be following a strictly legitimist approach.[61]

Ambrose has succeeded in drawing for posterity a firm distinction between emperor and church, which lends plausibility to his designation of any imperial intervention in ecclesiastical affairs as an invasion. Familiarity, however, has dulled the stridency of this cry. The boundaries that the bishop conjures so starkly for us were blurred in both the political assumptions and the religious practice of the age. Christian emperors enjoyed considerable freedom of action and could select from a number of vehicles available for the expression of their piety; the various

---

59. On Eusignius, see *PLRE* 1, pp. 309–310. He clashed with Symmachus over the boundary of a Sicilian estate: Symm. *Ep.* 4.71.

60. *Sermo contra Aux.* 29.

61. The important point that Ambrose never sought to challenge the emperor's demand on *legal* grounds during the struggle was well made by A. Lenox-Conyngham, 'Juristic and Religious Aspects of the Basilica Conflict of A.D. 386', *SP* 18 (1985), 1:55–58.

'catholic' churches that received their blessing in the fourth century were still too narrow to contain them. Nor did they expect their bishops to cramp them. It is worth considering, therefore, the effect of Ambrose's remark the previous autumn that he might resist Valentinian in church or embarrass him by refusing to celebrate mass in his presence.[62] The threat, highly offensive to Valentinian, might also have concentrated minds among those concerned to maintain a steady projection of his imperial image. It was vitally important that the emperor's devotions be conducted in a stable environment, as Valentinian had few other outlets, apart from his Christianity, to display his prowess. In his declarations that his subjects should remain free from workaday distractions on Sundays and his proclamations of amnesty for all but the most serious crimes at Easter, we catch a reflection of the public tone of his regime;[63] it anticipates nicely the intense piety displayed to their subjects by the boy-emperors Arcadius and Honorius a decade later. Concern to maintain this tone might have made Valentinian's ministers receptive to the claims of the homoean clerics attached to the palace, whose commitment to the dynasty was unconditional and who at the very least offered a counterweight to the overweening bishop.

Ambrose's summons to the palace should therefore be associated with a decision that the emperor would celebrate a particular festival (the obvious candidate being Easter, Valentinian's 'annual ceremony of prayer', which in 385 fell on 13 April)[64] elsewhere than the bishop's cathedral, with homoean clerics presiding. Ambrose's protest that this constituted an invasion suggests that the court was demanding for this purpose one of the churches regularly used by the bishop's own congregation. Perhaps this was so; still, Ambrose's notion of a simple clash between 'emperor' and 'church', with the former seeking to expropriate the latter's property, misrepresents the issue.

The disputed basilica was probably the Portiana, a building located outside the walls of Milan.[65] The government's choice of this particular

62. *Ep.* 72 [17].13.

63. Sunday observance: *CTh* 8.8.3 (November 386); Easter amnesties: *CTh* 9.38.7 (384); 9.38.8 (385). The style of Valentinian's government (and, incidentally, its orientation towards Rome) is nicely conveyed by his summons of—and studious coolness towards—an actress whose charms had reputedly been 'ruining the noble youths of Rome': *De. ob. Val.* 17.

64. *CTh* 9.38.7: 'Religio anniversariae obsecrationis . . .'

65. When the conflict was resumed the following year, the court initially changed its tactics and demanded the cathedral itself: '*nec iam* Portiana hoc est

church cannot convincingly be explained by obedience to Theodosius' law of 381 banning all intramural assemblies by heretics, for neither the emperor nor a group working under his patronage would conceivably have accepted the label of 'heretic', or by the discretion afforded by an obscure and remote site.[66] A very different background is suggested by the Portian Basilica's only other appearance on the historical record, as the place nominated by Gratian's two *cubicularii* for their debate with Ambrose upon the incarnation.[67]

The debate had been proposed by the two courtiers themselves, who interrupted Ambrose's preaching (presumably in his cathedral) to make their challenge. This raises the question in what sense the basilica was Ambrose's own. Little is known about a fourth-century bishop's control over the churches in his city, especially as it concerned the grey area between the clear-cut poles of the cathedral and other centrally administered churches, on the one hand, and the private oratories incorporated into domestic dwellings, on the other.[68] Distinctions between different types of building were probably often blurred, and especially so in an imperial capital, where an emperor required a setting appropriate for the expression of his own Christian identity. The term 'palace church', often applied to the buildings used for imperial devotions, is not a particularly happy one, suggesting as it does a homogeneity barely detectable in structures that range from modest chapels to cathedrals. Imperial ceremonial was too versatile and flexible to be captured in a single designation or architectural form.[69] But it is nevertheless clear that an emperor, who was attended by a permanent corps of clergymen as well as the prelates found invariably in the court's train, had a claim upon certain church buildings in his capital cities. The local bishops were not excluded from these, but they appeared there by invitation and

---

extramurana basilica petebatur' (*Ep.* 76 [20].1; the issue subsequently focused on the Portian Basilica, *Ep.* 76 [20].3, 4). Cf. A. Lenox-Conyngham, 'The Topography of the Basilica Conflict of A.D. 385/6 in Milan', *Historia* 31 (1982), at 357; Palanque, *Saint Ambroise*, 144, considers the identification 'fort possible'.

66. For this argument, e.g., Lenox-Conyngham, 'The Topography', 357, following O. Seeck, *Geschichte des Untergangs der antiken Welt* (1913), 5:201.

67. Paulin. *V. Amb.* 18.1.

68. Ambrose offered mass at the house of a *clarissima* at Rome: Paulin. *V. Amb.* 10.1; For Gregory of Nazianzus' church at Constantinople, the Anastasia, as a private audience-chamber, see J. Bernardi, 'Nouvelles perspectives sur la famille de Grégoire de Nazianze', *VC* 38 (1984), 352–359, at 354–356.

69. Evidence for the range of types involved is collected by G. de Angelis D'Ossat, *Studi Ravennati* (1962), 4–71.

subject to specific restraints. Macedonius of Constantinople was expelled from his see after angering Constantius II (and a large part of his congregation) by his unauthorized interference in the internal arrangements of the Apostoleion, the imperial church *par excellence*.[70] In this context, the court's interest in the Portian Basilica and their persistence in the conflict with Ambrose becomes clearer.

The Portian Basilica is so called only by Ambrose and Paulinus and never appears thereafter in the records of the church of Milan. But it is possible that the bishop's designation is a partisan one and that the church also went by another name.[71] Its palatine associations suggest one of the surviving structures of late antique Milan oddly absent from the fourth-century record: the present church of San Lorenzo.[72] The case for the identification rests only upon circumstantial arguments and must for all its attractions remain inconclusive.[73] San Lorenzo nevertheless deserves a brief examination, if only to convey some of the physical features relevant to the issue in 385. This elegant and sophisticated church, 'the most beautiful in Milan', is constructed with a lavishness and solidity strikingly different from the herringbone brickwork of Ambrose's own churches.[74] Its location just beyond the southwestern gate

70. Soc. *HE* 2.38.33–40; 42.1. Socrates' attempt to relate the issue to doctrinal controversy is unconvincing; cf. G. Dagron, *Naissance d'une capitale* (1974), 404–405.

71. Note the rival names given to the church held by the followers of the antipope Ursinus in 366: to them it was sanctified as the 'basilica Liberii' (*Coll. Avell.* 1.6), while the authorities knew it as simply the 'basilica Sicinini' (Amm. Marc. 27.3.13; cf. Ruf. *HE* 11.10. Soc. *HE* 4.29 claims specifically that the 'palace of Sikinine' was 'not a church'). The Ursinians, conversely, referred to the church of Saint Lawrence where Damasus was acclaimed simply as 'basilica in Lucinis': *Coll. Avell.* 1.5.

72. The hypothesis that San Lorenzo is of fourth-century date, an imperial foundation and identical with the Portian Basilica, was presented by A. Calderini, G. Chierici and C. Cecchelli in *La basilica di san Lorenzo maggiore in Milano* (1951); for subsequent refinements, see D. Kinney, 'The Evidence for the Dating of San Lorenzo in Milan', *JSAH* 31 (1972), 92–107, and R. Krautheimer, *Three Christian Capitals* (1983), 81–89.

73. The identification is automatically excluded if San Lorenzo is assigned to a later date: c. 390 was proposed by S. Lewis, 'San Lorenzo Revisited', *JSAH* 32 (1973), 197–222 (resting on dubious assumptions concerning the political background of Theodosius' presence in Milan), and the early fifth century by M. Mirabella Roberti, *Milano Romana* (1984), 137–156, and by E. Cattaneo, in *La basilica di san Lorenzo in Milano*, ed. G. A. dell'Acqua (1985), at 18–20.

74. Quotation from Krautheimer, *Three Christian Capitals*, 83; for construction techniques, see W. Kleinbauer, 'Toward a Dating of San Lorenzo in Milan', *Arte Lombarda* 13 (1968), 1–22 (although his arguments on dating are invalid).

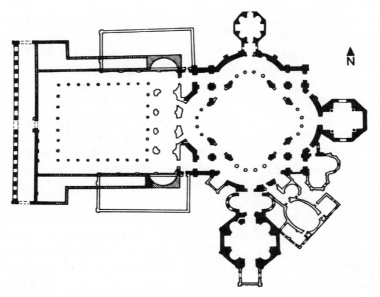

3a. San Lorenzo, plan. Reproduced by kind permission of
Professor R. Krautheimer.

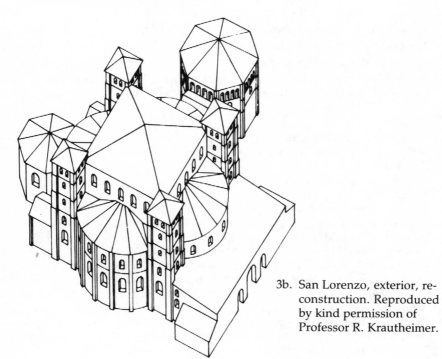

3b. San Lorenzo, exterior, reconstruction. Reproduced
by kind permission of
Professor R. Krautheimer.

of the city puts it near the probable site of the palace complex (which continues to elude the archaeologist's spade).[75] But the feature most strongly suggestive of imperial patronage is the reuse in its foundations of materials from Milan's amphitheatre (the largest in northern Italy), which appears to have been demolished specifically for this purpose. Indeed, one of the two chapels attached to the central circular hall may have been designed as an imperial mausoleum.[76] If so, the most likely author of the original project is Constantine's youngest son, Constans, who was awarded Italy and Illyricum in the settlement of 337 and might well have commissioned facilities to match the grandiose churches at his brothers' disposal in the 'established' Christian capitals of Constantinople and Trier. But Constans removed to Gaul and fell there to an usurper. Constantius avenged but did not rehabilitate him; although he may well have supervised completion of his brother's planned mausoleum, he immediately consigned Constans himself to convenient oblivion.[77] But the palatine associations would have remained, and Ambrose's claim to exclusive rights over a vacant imperial mausoleum would be tendentious indeed.

Unlike the other churches that dotted the peripheries of Milan, San Lorenzo neither marked the site of a particularly venerated grave nor, apparently, contained any imported relics. The site had in fact been reclaimed from a marsh (hence the need for the massive slabs from the amphitheatre for its foundations) and seems to have served previously as a rubbish tip.[78] There is no record of when the association with Saint Lawrence developed, but it perhaps originated with the miraculous re-

75. The puzzle of the palace of late Roman Milan is well expounded by N. Duval, 'Les palais impériaux de Milan et Aquilée: réalité et mythe', *AAAd* 4 (1973), at 152–55.

76. D. Kinney, '"Capella Regina": S. Aquilino in Milan', *Marsyas* 15 (1970–71), 13–35.

77. Kinney's proposal ('"Capella Regina"', 34–35) that the mausoleum was designed for Valentinian I is unconvincing. The group who acclaimed Valentinian II in 375 would not have missed the opportunity to assert their legitimacy with an imperial funeral had the site been available (Valentinian I's corpse was sent immediately to Constantinople, where it waited seven years for burial). Cf. Krautheimer, *Three Christian Capitals*, 90–91), although his convoluted hypothesis of a mausoleum for Gratian (built before he had ever set foot in Milan) doubling as an 'Arian cathedral' is untenable. Athanasius in 358 accused Constantius of 'pretending to build a tomb' for Constans (*Hist. Ar.* 69); Constans' anniversaries are ominously absent from the calendar of 354: M. R. Salzman, *On Roman Time* (1990), 141–142.

78. Kinney, 'The Evidence for the Dating', 101.

pair of a chalice that a careless deacon had broken in the church; Lawrence, the natural object of a deacon's prayers, might have established his patronage over the church by the miracle.[79] Before this, however, there was little to recommend the complex to the attention of the Milanese faithful who conducted their pious tours of the graves around the city, and it had no obvious part to play in the cycle of festivals linking the other suburban churches to the cathedral. It is not clear, therefore, how often the bishop and his people would have had cause to assemble there.

The specific identification of the Portian Basilica with San Lorenzo, although attractive, must remain hypothetical. The hypothesis nevertheless serves to illustrate the sort of claim the emperor could have made on a church, and the areas of Christian activity that lay beyond the bishop's control. These are further indicated by the access to church buildings that the homoeans at court already enjoyed. Rufinus shows Justina herself rousing her supporters against Ambrose by 'chattering in the churches'.[80] It is possible, therefore, that the court's planned 'seizure' of a 'basilica of the church' was nothing more than the intention to use a church that they already considered their own.

Ambrose now was in a much stronger position than when he had acquiesced, four years previously, in the temporary 'sequestration' of a basilica. The claim upon the court arising from his mission to Maximus, which he had exploited the previous year, would continue to stand him in good stead,[81] and by successfully calling Valentinian's faith 'into account' against Symmachus, he had staked a powerful claim to be the emperor's sole interlocutor before God.

The court, whose agreement that Valentinian should attend an Arian service was clearly intended to undermine this alarming claim, failed to anticipate the lengths to which Ambrose would go to defend it. The summons to the consistory shows them attempting instead to avert any possible conflict by making clear their intentions and meeting whatever objections the bishop might advance: the honour of the invitation (which was probably Ambrose's first) was intended at once to reassure

79. Greg. Tur. *De gloria martyrum* 45. The association with Lawrence evidently predated the construction of the chapel of San Sisto in c. 500; perhaps it can be related to the adoption of the church as a site for episcopal burials (from c. 450: J.-C. Picard, *Le souvenir des évêques* [1988] 58–66).

80. Ruf. *HE* 2.15: 'garrire in ecclesiis'.

81. Above, p. 167. Ambrose would return to the point each time he addressed Valentinian in the subsequent conflict: *Ep.* 76 [20].23, *Ep.* 75 [21].20.

and to disarm him.[82] It also, more subtly, implicated Ambrose in their designs. Although he had an opportunity to register his dissent at the consistory, he also incurred a responsibility to abide by whatever consensus was reached there. But the court had underestimated Ambrose's resourcefulness. The interview was interrupted: 'When the people learned that I had gone to the palace, they headed there in such a surge that their force was irresistible; when the *comes militaris* and his forces set out to disperse the crowd, they all offered themselves for death in the cause of their faith in Christ' (*Sermo contra Aux.* 29). Recalling the incident a year later, Ambrose did not explain how the populace had 'learnt' of his appointment at the palace. It nevertheless seems highly likely that the bishop had himself had a hand in organizing these reinforcements for his case, which clearly took the court by surprise and upset their delicate plans. As the situation threatened to run out of control, they turned helplessly to Ambrose, who seized the opportunity to impose his own terms upon the situation. Emerging from the palace, he calmed his people with a solemn pledge that 'nobody would invade any basilica of the church'. The court could do nothing about this travesty of their proposal.

This episode, so tantalizingly alluded to in the *Sermo contra Auxentium*, allows the first view of Ambrose's people in action. In the escalating crisis of the following year they would provide the bishop with a powerful if volatile weapon, exhibiting a forcefulness that could not have been anticipated from Ambrose's initial hesitant attempts to unite his flock around himself. The gradual process of mobilization must have been largely invisible; hence the impact of the people's appearance in the streets, eloquently attested by the consistory's immediate capitulation. At one level, the incident illustrated the weakness of Valentinian's government before any well-organized lobbying; at another, it announced Ambrose as a force to be reckoned with. It is therefore difficult to share his surprise that, despite his good offices to the government in suppressing a potential riot, his people's behaviour was counted against him. *Invidia*—he repeated the word three times in recalling the episode, as if to emphasize its injustice—was the inevitable concomitant of power.[83]

82. Cf. John Matthews' remark, in another context (but also involving Ambrose), that the protocol of the consistory could function 'as a mode of defence against over-insistent subjects': *The Roman Empire of Ammianus* (1989), 268.

83. There is a pained protest at *Sermo contra Aux.* 29–30: 'Et cum pro beneficio meum sit officium postulatum, tamen quod populus ad palatium venisset mihi invidia commota est'.

THE EASTER CRISIS OF 386

The government's campaign against Ambrose was renewed, on a much enlarged scale, the following year. After spending the latter part of 385 at Aquileia, perhaps to supervise military operations on the Danube, the court returned to Milan in the winter and immediately, on 23 January 386, issued a law that solemnly affirmed the freedom of assembly of those who followed the faith as laid down at Constantius' councils of Rimini and Constantinople.[84] Any 'turbulent' opposition from those who considered that such freedom belonged exclusively to themselves (a thrust clearly aimed at Ambrose) would be treated as treason and a capital offence; surreptitious appeals against the enactment would also be punished.[85]

The last clause of the law recognizes the vulnerability of the legislative machinery to sabotage. Court officials had access to the imperial rubber stamp: it was evidently feared that attempts to cancel the law would receive expert assistance from such quarters. Even during the drafting stage, the *magister memoriae* Benivolus had resigned rather than contaminate himself with heresy, while his subordinates, the corps of *memoriales*, were felt to have a particular affinity with Ambrose's church.[86] The law's promulgation in the face of such opposition demands explanation. Neither the teenage emperor's whims nor his mother's machinations suffice, since the measure must have enjoyed support from Valentinian's ministers. Nor is a desire to curb Ambrose's pretensions in itself adequate. The pragmatists of the court must have been persuaded that the law was not only reasonable but enforceable.

The previous year's capitulation had been prompted by the inability

84. *CTh* 16.1.4: 'Damus copiam colligendi . . .'. The law probably owes its survival in the code, a stroke of remarkable good fortune for the historian, to the compilers' confusion of Constantius' council of Constantinople with Theodosius' 'orthodox' council of 381.

85. The relevant clauses run: 'scituris his, qui sibi tantum existimant colligendi copiam contributam, quod si turbulentum quippiam . . . faciendum esse temptaverint, ut seditionis auctores pacisque turbatae ecclesiae, etiam maiestatis capite ac sanguine sint supplicia luituri, manente nihilo minus eos supplicio, qui contra hanc dispositionem nostram obreptive aut clanculo supplicare temptaverint'.

86. Benivolus: Gaudentius *Praef. ad Benivolum* 5; Ruf. *HE* 11.16; Soz. *HE* 7.13.5. The *memoriales* were singled out when restrictions were imposed by the government during Easter week: *Ep.* 76 [20].7.

of an anonymous *comes militaris* to cope with Ambrose's people. The
military would clearly have a decisive say in any renewed campaign; and
there are important signs that it was presented specifically to appeal to
their interests. During the subsequent contest Ambrose would make
great play of the identity of many of his 'Arian' opponents as 'barbarians', Goths serving in Valentinian's army. The point recurs in a remark
to Marcellina, a homily to his congregation, and even a tirade addressed
directly to a delegation of Gothic officers.[87] The power of anti-barbarian
prejudice had been demonstrated by Gratian's experience with his regiment of Alans; but Valentinian's Goths, like his brother's Alans, are to
be explained not as an imperial whim but as the result of a military
reorientation from the Rhine towards the Danube. Valentinian, moreover, had even less choice than his brother. Building up his forces almost
from scratch and without access to the traditional western recruiting
grounds of the Rhineland, he was compelled to look to the Danube ba-
sin. A plentiful reservoir of potential recruits was available among the
peoples uprooted by the Hunnic incursions of the 370s, their military
skills honed by conflict with the empire. Goths, whether recruited indi-
vidually or settled with their families and serving as *foederati*, formed a
vital component of Valentinian's army.[88]

Most of these Goths, it seems, were Arian. The Tervingi whom
Valens admitted to Thrace in 376 had thereupon adopted homoean
beliefs.[89] Some of them, after the peace with Theodosius in 382, were
perhaps attracted westward to Milan by prospects of pay and pro-

---

87. *Ep.* 76 [20].12: 'quibus ut olim plaustra sedes erat, ita nunc plaus-
trum ecclesia est'; 16 (from a sermon): 'videtis quanta subito moveantur: Gothi
arma gentiles . . .'; 9: 'Aderant Gothi tribuni, adoriebar eos dicens: "prop-
terea vos possessio Romana suscepit ut perturbationis publicae vos praebeatis
ministros?"'.

88. The Goths rebuked by Ambrose (*Ep.* 76 [20].16) should, as *tribuni*, have
belonged to the regular army; the reference to 'waggons' (12) suggests settlers.
For the distinction between these two categories, see J. H. W. G. Liebeschuetz,
Barbarians and Bishops (1990), 32–47. Zosimus 4.34 states that in c. 380 Gratian
'conceded' that a body of Goths under their leaders Alatheus and Saphrax
should 'take' (*katechein*) Pannonia and Upper Moesia. Despite the cogent objections of Heather, *Goths and Romans*, 334–336, I remain inclined to accept the
traditional interpretation that this refers to a settlement similar to that organized
in Thrace by Theodosius in 382 (and therefore a likely source for Valentinian's
foederati); for possible archaeological corroboration, see R. MacMullen, *Corruption and the Decline of Rome* (1988), 203.

89. P. J. Heather, 'The Crossing of the Danube and the Gothic Conversion',
GRBS 27 (1986), 289–318.

motion in Valentinian's service. The beleaguered prince was presumably willing to offer generous terms. But these Goths constituted only part of their people, and Gothic Christianity extended much further; the efforts of the 'apostle' Ulfila, during the reign of Constantius II, had given it a pronounced homoean tendency.[90] Although his direct personal impact was limited, his short-lived mission on Gothic soil failing to penetrate the social elite, Ulfila trained a body of clerical disciples who became the natural vehicles for the Christianization of the Goths on Roman soil and determined its doctrinal direction. The Nicenes were slow to develop a rival missionary enterprise. Ambrose seems to have made no efforts to 'convert' the Milanese Goths: he scornfully consigned them to a 'waggon' for their church, at the margins of religious life in the city.[91]

By contrast, there was a disciple of Ulfila at Milan in 386. Auxentius of Durostorum, a Roman citizen entrusted as a boy to Ulfila's care, had been passionately attached to his master and had attended his funeral at Constantinople in 383; the subsequent cancellation of the 'Conference of the Sects', the reason for the octogenarian Ulfila's journey to the capital, confirmed his equally passionate contempt for the Nicenes.[92] His move to Milan was likely spurred by the bleak prospects in Theodosius' empire, especially after Ulfila's death and the abandonment of the council of 383, and the attractions at Milan of Justina's patronage and homoean parishioners, both Roman and Gothic; he may also, perhaps, have wished to confront Ambrose. Palladius had named Auxentius be-

90. On Ulfila, see P. J. Heather and J. F. Matthews, *The Goths in the Fourth Century* (1991), 133–153.

91. John Chrysostom took a more positive approach in Constantinople: Liebeschuetz, *Barbarians and Bishops*, 169–170.

92. The identity between Auxentius of Durostorum—known only from his own *Epistula de vita Ulfilae* (henceforth *Ep. Aux.*), incorporated into the same collection of scholia that includes Palladius' 'Apology' (sections 42–63 in Gryson's *SCh* edition), and one reference in Palladius (*Apol.* 140)—and Ambrose's opponent has been doubted, on insufficient grounds, by R. Gryson, *Scolies Ariennes*, 58–59, and G. Nauroy ('Le fouet et le miel', *RecAug* 23 (1988), at 11n24). The question turns upon Ambrose's claim that his enemy had changed his name from Mercurinus to Auxentius for tactical reasons: 'quia hic fuerat Auxentius episcopus Arrianus, ad decipiendam plebem quam tenuerat ille se vocaret Auxentium' (*Sermo contra Aux.* 22). Ambrose seems here to flaunt the polemically valuable 'discovery' of Auxentius' original name, but his own explanation for the change is unconvincing; the pagan-sounding Mercurinus was probably dropped when Auxentius went to live with Ulfila as a boy (*Ep. Aux.* 55).

side Demophilius of Constantinople as a future challenger to the bishop of Milan after Aquileia.[93] The more favourable climate of Valentinian's court at last offered hope of bringing the bishop of Ratiaria's campaign to a successful conclusion.

Auxentius is the key to the struggle that followed. There is no reason to doubt Ambrose's claim that he was the author of the January law;[94] through it, moreover, he was bringing together a formidable coalition. He offered Valentinian a credible alternative to Ambrose; important elements at court would be impressed by his concern for the morale of the hitherto marginalized Goths, in seeking to include them within his projects. The homoean community at Milan, above all, had been brought directly within the scope of imperial legislation.[95] This marks a considerable difference from the previous year, when (to judge from Ambrose's brief account) the issue had turned solely on the *emperor's* use of a basilica, with the homoeans at best incidental beneficiaries. We should not doubt that Auxentius had an agenda of his own which only partly overlapped with the court's.

But the main thrust of Auxentius' law, and the reason for its acceptance by the court, was that it promised to avert a repetition of the previous year's fiasco. It did not innovate: the 'freedom of assembly' that the emperor so emphatically granted to the homoeans was not a right created ex novo but an existing one confirmed and clarified.[96] Adherents of the creed of Rimini did not need statutory protection. They were not Arians, so were immune from Theodosius' recent legislation; no west-

93. Pall. 140 (the last sentence of his *Apology*): 'scito tam Palladium ⟨quam⟩ Auxentium inter ceteros consortes . . . ubicumque examen haberi placuerit . . . glorioso ac salutari certamini non defuturos'. Theological similarities between Palladius and Auxentius are noted by Gryson, *Scolies Ariennes*, 173–200 (cf. Hanson, *The Search*, 105–106).

94. *Sermo contra Aux.* 23–25 ('cruentas leges ore dictans, manu scribens'); the arguments of G. Gottlieb, 'Der Mailänder Kirchenstreit von 385/386', *MH* 42 (1985), 52–54, that this refers to a separate *lex de fide* are unconvincing and take Ambrose's rhetoric too literally.

95. The character of this homoean congregation is discussed by H. O. Maier, 'Private Space as the Social Context of Arianism in Ambrose's Milan', *JThS*, n.s., 45 (1994).

96. Without the preamble to clarify the context, the phrasing—'Damus copiam colligendi', 'conveniendi . . . patescat arbitrium'—is no more precise than in other contemporary legislation. The law nevertheless fails—unlike, e.g., *CTh* 16.5.5—to annul any previous measures. For similar phraseology used to clarify an existing law, see *CTh* 4.6.6, 'Damus patrum arbitrio', reiterating the provisions of 4.6.4.

ern assembly had yet matched the scale and authority of the signatures collected by Constantius at Rimini. Nor was de facto toleration an issue. The homoean seedbed left at Milan by Iulianus Valens had probably germinated undisturbed. Moreover, Auxentius, whose name carried a certain magic for the people of Milan, preached regularly beyond the narrow confines of his sect—even to pagans.[97] He also attracted some whose ambitions Ambrose had thwarted, and even baptized members of his flock.[98]

We receive only occasional glimpses of this homoean church-in-waiting at Milan. Ambrose's version has prevailed; above all, three documents collected in the tenth book of his correspondence provide the necessary basis of any reconstruction. The formidable problems of interpretation presented by these texts run far deeper than their polemical distortions. Each belongs to a different genre. *Epistula* 75 (21 in the Maurist collection) replies formally to an imperial *mandatum*; the *Sermo contra Auxentium* (*Ep.* 75a) is a speech to Ambrose's faithful in the manner of Cicero's Catilinarians; in *Ep.* 76 (20) the bishop reports a series of tense confrontations to his sister in a vivid, spare style. Each illuminates one aspect of the conflict with the concentrated glare of a searchlight beam, but they are played deliberately upon the enemy's weaknesses and allow no overall view of the battlefield.

The most fundamental difficulty concerns chronology. In what order should we read these texts? The 'published' order, organized by category of recipient, is of no help.[99] Internal evidence provides two fixed points: the letter to Valentinian and the *Sermo* both follow the law of January 386, and the events described in *Ep.* 76 occurred in the immediate prelude to an Easter festival. Around these, various permutations have found eloquent advocates. But the range of possibilities has been

97. Ambrose explicitly attests such services at *Sermo contra Aux.* 25; he interprets Auxentius' name as a ploy 'to deceive the people' (22) and taunts him for failing to convert a pagan audience: 'cui tractanti cotidie non crediderunt' (26). This last passage might conceivably refer to a military congregation.

98. *De off.* 1.72 recalls a sedulous friend whose application to join the clergy Ambrose had nevertheless rejected because of his 'indecorous deportment': 'Arianae infestationis tempore, fidem deseruit.' Baptized converts: *Sermo contra Aux.* 37 (cf. n. 160).

99. M. Zelzer, in her splendid edition of these letters (*CSEL* 82.3), asserts that their arrangement in the book, 'ab ipso Ambrosio compositum', is chronological (Proleg., p. xxxiv); but this is not true for the book as a whole, which presents 'ecclesiastical' business first (*Epp.* 70–71), then 'imperial' (*Epp.* 72–75), and finally two letters to Marcellina.

significantly reduced by the demonstration that the Holy Week in question in *Ep.* 76 was in 386, and that *Ep.* 75 was produced in the immediate
aftermath of the *Sermo*.[100] The question whether the *Sermo* was preached
before or after the drama of Easter 386 is still debated. I adopt the latter
sequence, which has won widespread acceptance;[101] it should nevertheless be noted that the reverse order has been followed in the most
substantial recent discussion of the question.[102] While both chronological schemes depend more upon overall plausibility and coherence than
upon demonstrable connexions, this latter view exaggerates the immediate impact of the law's promulgation in attributing to it a psychological
effect which encouraged the court to take the immediate (and curiously
inconsequential) initiative of proposing a debate.[103]

For religious life at Milan continued unchanged after 23 January.
Ambrose and his congregation assembled in the cathedral; the emperor
conducted his devotions with his preferred clerics inside the structures
associated with the palace; the homoeans continued their assemblies.
Only at Easter, when the emperor put his piety on display before his
subjects for the most important celebration of the Christian year, would
the consequences be felt. Ambrose would not find it easy this time to
obstruct the emperor's declared wishes. A repetition of the previous ambush had been forestalled: any disturbance would be traced to the
bishop and punished accordingly. We must not for a moment forget the
peril to which Ambrose exposed himself during the ensuing struggle:
not of martyrdom, a glory he courted enthusiastically, but of public ac-

100. The brilliant study by J. H. van Haeringen, 'De Valentiniano II et Ambrosio', *Mnemosyne* 3.5 (1937), 152–158, 28–33, 229–240, supersedes all earlier—and invalidates much later—work.

101. This chronology was argued by van Haeringen and is supported by
the important recent contributions of Lenox-Conyngham, 'The Topography',
and Gottlieb, 'Der Mailänder Kirchenstreit'.

102. Nauroy, 'Le fouet et le miel': an exemplary study of the interrelation-
ships between the relevant documents, to which the following is at several
points indebted.

103. Nauroy adduces a psychological advantage supposedly gained through
the law ('Le fouet et le miel', 14, 40), while accepting the 'illogisme de ce débat
qui rend caduc ou superfétatoire la loi' (15). His detailed chronological arguments (28–41) are devoted to the demonstration, already accomplished by van
Haeringen, that the *Sermo contra Auxentium* does not belong to Easter week; he
then simply assumes that the speech preceded Easter, dismissing the alternative
without argument as 'invraisemblable' (34n103). The assumption that only the
holding of an Easter service was involved puts too narrowly ecclesiastical a focus
on the struggle, in which Valentinian and his friends had invested considerable
political capital.

ceptance of the interpretation, set out in the law, that his resistance was the work of 'an author of sedition and a disturber of the peace of the church'. No wonder, therefore, that his sister Marcellina, her nerves perhaps heightened by the rigours of Lent, was agitated by dark dreams as the season of joy approached.[104]

On 27 March, two days before Palm Sunday (for which an imperial procession was perhaps planned), the 'mass of disturbances' was set in motion. A high-ranking delegation of *viri illustres* from the consistory (another indication of the level at which Valentinian's initiatives had won approval) visited Ambrose with a request for the use of the Basilica Nova, the lavish cathedral at the centre of Milan (1–2). Although this can plausibly be seen as an opening bid, the court's confidence in demanding the bishop's own church is striking: having precluded a repeat of the previous year's disturbance, they evidently felt able to give absolute priority to the emperor's needs. The requirement that Ambrose not only hand over the basilica but ensure that 'the people did not create any disturbance' clearly invokes the sanctions of the law: he would have to answer himself, it is implied, for any such disturbance. But Ambrose's reply, that 'a temple of God cannot be handed over by a priest', introduced an entirely different concept. *Traditio* carried powerful resonances among Christians.[105] Although the court will not have seen the issue in these terms at all, and had good grounds to question their relevance, Ambrose discovered here the justification he needed for his resistance. His relentless exploitation of the slogan in the following days helped him establish an initiative against his opponents. It has also succeeded in misleading posterity about the issue at stake in the conflict.

The court seems to have underestimated Ambrose's capacity to defy them within the limits of the law. By replying at cross-purposes to this initial delegation, he kept negotiations alive, avoiding the clear choice they were trying to impose between surrender and open defiance. A more significant aspect of the bishop's tactical astuteness emerged the following day. 'There was an acclamation in the church' (3): Ambrose had presumably reported the court's request and invited a response from the congregation. He then put this expression of support to immediate use. The praetorian prefect Eusignius arrived in the church to

104. *Ep.* 76 [20].1. Text references in the rest of this section are to this letter.
105. The heavy emotive charge dated back to the persecutions; W. H. C. Frend, *The Donatist Church* (1952), 10–11, well characterizes this, by comparison with wartime 'collaboration'.

present a new demand (probably drafted by the consistory after the previous day's stalemate), designed to accommodate the bishop's prerogatives. The demand for the Basilica Nova was dropped; instead, the bishop's people were asked to leave the Portian Basilica free for the emperor's use. But Ambrose's chorus was now on song: their response, 'shouted back' at the prefect, was a firm refusal.[106] They appear to have echoed the bishop's reference to *traditio*, despite the complete inapplicability of this concept to a building that was as much the emperor's as theirs. The prefect, no doubt bewildered at this turn of events—but unable to fault the bishop, who had not provided his congregation with any *immediate* cue[107]—retreated to report this rebuff to the emperor. Things were not proceeding according to plan; on his own terrain, Ambrose was an awkward opponent.

Ambrose was again at his church the following day, Palm Sunday, to conduct the service. After dismissing the catechumens, he retired to instruct the baptismal candidates in the adjacent baptistery. There he received important news: *decani* had been sent from the palace to the Portian Basilica to decorate it with the hangings that were an indispensable part of imperial ceremonial, a clear indication of the court's intention to proceed with their own service.[108] There was a further item. 'Part of the people' were heading for the church: a group from Ambrose's congregation were planning to forestall the emperor by occupying the basilica themselves (4). The initiative of the people, without direct leadership from either the bishop (whose remark that he 'remained at his post and began to conduct the Eucharist' amounts to an alibi) or his clergy, took the court by surprise. The plan had been to use any breach of the January law as an occasion to punish Ambrose; but the bishop could disavow involvement in his followers' enthusiasm. The game was delicate and dangerous. On their way to the Portian Basilica the party, encountering the Arian presbyter Castulus, could not resist the temptation to set about him. Ambrose recognized the gravity of this clear breach of both public order and the right to assemble guaranteed to the homoeans under the January law. On learning of the incident—he was kept informed with remarkable efficiency—he sent some presbyters and

106. For the legitimacy conferred by such shouts, see C. Roueché, 'Acclamations in the Later Roman Empire', *JRS* 74 (1984), 181–199.

107. The acclamation that preceded the prefect's arrival might nevertheless be suspected to have served as a warm-up for the congregation.

108. Nauroy, 'Le fouet et le miel', 77–79, discusses the much-debated question of the significance of these hangings and concludes firmly that they were decorative rather than tokens of sequestration.

deacons to rescue the unfortunate Castulus and presumably to restore discipline to the zealous people; he also wept 'bitter tears' as he proceeded with his much-interrupted mass, praying that any blood split as a consequence of the brawl should be his own (5).

The bishop's prayer that the *populus* be spared was granted and the crowd duly reached their destination. Their sit-in at the Portian Basilica added a new dimension to the conflict. Forcible ejection of the squatters promised to be a messy business, and bloodshed in church was the sort of publicity that Valentinian could least afford. They were therefore, for the moment, ignored, nor was any action taken against Ambrose himself. Until conclusive evidence was available of the bishop's personal involvement in a crime, the government lacked the confidence (and probably the will, considering the bishop's parishioners in the consistory) to move decisively. The response to the affray was instead to impose a swingeing fine, two hundred pounds of gold, upon 'the whole *corpus negotiatorum*', and to imprison some of its members pending payment. The victims, who represented an organization concerned with the provisioning of the capital, clearly included devoted supporters of Ambrose ('They answered', he continues, 'that they would give as much again, or double that, if it were required, provided that they could keep their faith' [6]), but the punishment is unlikely to have been an arbitrary blow against the bishop's allies. The government otherwise observed a scrupulous respect for legality, and had to do so to retain public credit and its own internal unity. Probably a significant number of Castulus' assailants were from the rank-and-file of the *corpus*, whose senior members could be held responsible (as a parallel case illustrates) for their subordinates' embroilment in ecclesiastical partisanship.[109] If the ultimate purpose was to isolate Ambrose by exerting pressure on his supporters, it seems to have succeeded: the fine was apparently paid and the imprisoned *negotiatores* perhaps released.[110] The court also sought to secure discipline within its own ranks by an order that all palace staff

---

109. *CTh* 16.4.5 (September 404, concerning the disturbances over the expulsion of John Chrysostom): *nummularii* and other *corpora* were held responsible for their members: 'ut unumquodque corpus pro his, qui de suo numero conventus celebrare inlicitos detegentur, ad quinquaginta pondo auri solutionem multae nomine adstringatur'. These corporate penalties are stated to be more severe than the fines of three pounds of gold levied upon individual slaveowners for each of their slaves thus involved: if a similar scale was applied at Milan, we should imagine a maximum of about sixty men involved in the brawl.

110. The government later refunded the fine (*Ep.* 76 [20].26); there is no mention of any prisoners needing release.

refrain from attending Ambrose's church lest they become involved in insurrection.[111] Equally pressing, one suspects, was the need to prevent the passing of information to the bishop, whose actions thus far had presupposed accurate knowledge of the court's intentions. Negotiations meanwhile continued. The *honorati*, the retired bureaucrats who feature so prominently in the churches of Italy,[112] were instructed 'under the direst threats' to procure the 'surrender' of the (Portian) basilica (7). Ambrose's extension of the scope of *traditio* to cover the termination of an 'unofficial' occupation is characteristically audacious. He also perhaps misrepresents the nature of the interview. The *honorati* were qualified by background and experience to understand the government's perspective; threats were probably tempered with blandishments.[113] Every possible means was being tried to make Ambrose see reason.

But the bishop remained impervious, perhaps conscious of a position of increased strength as his followers became more firmly entrenched in the Portian Basilica. Easter, meanwhile, was drawing nearer. It was therefore in obdurate mood that Ambrose received on Tuesday (31 March) a further delegation, this time drawn from the military and including *comites* and *tribuni*. He dismissed their demand for *traditio*; nor was their attempt to invoke the letter of the law any more successful. Against the emperor's legitimate rights to the Portian Basilica Ambrose invented a higher category of property, the 'divine', which was not susceptible to ordinary laws. He obfuscated his arguments with traditional forensic techniques, offering an inappropriate alternative (the surrender of his own property) and protesting emotionally his willingness to suffer imprisonment or death (8).[114] He retained the initiative throughout the

111. There is again a parallel from the Chrysostom conflict, *CTh* 16.4.4 (January 404): 'cuncta officia moneantur a tumultuosis se conventiculis abstinere', with loss of rank and confiscation of property the penalty for disobedience. I interpret Ambrose's expression 'temperare a processu iubeantur' as prohibiting church attendance rather than all movement whatsoever.

112. The *honorati* of Aquileia were sought by Palladius as adjudicators at the council held there in 381 (*Acta* 51); an impressive example of the type is Ambrose's supporter Benivolus in retirement at Brescia: 'sicut honoratorum nostrae urbis, ita enim dominicae plebis dignissimum caput' (Gaud. *Praef. ad Beniv.* 2). Cf. C. Pietri's remarks on the 'petite société d'aristocrates palatins', in 'Une aristocracie provinciale et la mission chrétienne', *AAAd* 22 (1982), 1:117–120; Matthews, *Western Aristocracies*, 183–186.

113. See Paulin. *V. Amb.* 45.2 for a deputation organized by Stilicho: 'convocatis ad se nobilissimis viris illius civitatis, . . . partim interminatus est illis, partim blando sermone persuaderet'.

114. On the status of these arguments, see the important comments by Lenox-Conyngham, 'Juristic and Religious Aspects'.

interview. The officers warned him of the intention to deploy troops to restore order at the Portian Basilica,[115] but this evoked (besides a shudder of horror, a prayer that he should not outlive 'the funeral of our great city and of all Italy', and a further offer of his own life) a pointed rebuke directed specifically at the Gothic tribunes among the delegation, the 'accomplices in this public disturbance' (9). Inside his own church, the bishop could stand the logic of the situation upon its head. A final demand, that he 'restrain his people', was equally ineffective; having pointed out that his responsibility was to refrain from fomenting unrest among them (a responsibility in which he could not be shown to have failed), Ambrose claimed that only God could calm their excitement. His counteroffer, that if they thought him an *incentor*, a firebrand, they should punish him accordingly and banish him to whatever desolate spot they wished, was made in the confidence that it would not be accepted. After the departure of the envoys, Ambrose spent the rest of the day in the Old Basilica;[116] he then returned to sleep at his house, 'so that if anyone wished to arrest me, he should find me ready' (10).

The next morning, Wednesday, the government made good its threat: troops were sent to blockade the Portian Basilica (11).[117] There were shrewd reasons behind their orders to allow people to enter freely but not to leave.[118] If the bishop organized relief or reinforcements for his partisans, he would implicate himself in the occupation; if not, the

115. Despite the tense that Ambrose uses ('horrebam quippe animo cum armatos ad basilicam ecclesiae occupandam *missos* cognoscerem') it is clear that the court had not yet deployed troops, who first appeared in the streets the following morning (*Ep.* 76 [20].11). For the chronology of this phase, see Nauroy, 'Le fouet et le miel', 44–45.

116. On this church, see Lenox-Conyngham, 'The Topography', 356–358; cf. Nauroy, 'Le fouet et le miel', 45–46, for the likelihood that the basilica was adjacent to the Basilica Nova, although the suggestion that it was actually the cathedral is unconvincing. Ambrose's use of this building was probably connected to the Holy Week liturgy; it is also possible that he kept the Basilica Nova clear to advertise his compliance with the government's demand of the previous week (it had become evident on Palm Sunday that the government would not attempt to occupy it themselves) and so 'prove' his obedience.

117. 'Ante lucem ubi pedem limine extuli, circumfuso milite occupatur basilica': for construal of this difficult sentence, see Lenox-Conyngham, 'The Topography', 358–359; Nauroy, 'Le fouet et le miel', 48–51.

118. For these orders, see Paulin. *V. Amb.* 13.1–2 (to be assigned to this occasion and not the 'long siege', a much more relaxed affair during which even a blind man was permitted to walk out of the front doors of the church), who attributes it to divine agency rather than government tactics, 'ut adversis scutis ecclesiae fores servarent nec egredi dimitterent, sed ingredi ecclesiam plebem catholicam minime prohiberent'.

leaderless crowd in the basilica could be expected to falter and eventually to surrender to the troops guarding the exits. The court could therefore ignore Ambrose's taunt that even with this military support the Arians still did not dare show themselves (12): only after the basilica had been cleared would the court's celebration commence, without fear of interruption or disorder. The bishop meanwhile led a service at the Old Basilica, learning by his congregation's groans of the siege at the Portian Basilica; he then heard that a further crowd had assembled in the New Basilica and wanted a *lector* to read to them.

Ambrose's serenity in the face of all this must have been impressive. Its basis soon became apparent, when his service was again interrupted. Some of the soldiers who had been posted at the Portian Basilica had come into the city and now entered the bishop's church. An understandable panic ensued among the women, until the soldiers—of barbarian origin, but loyal Nicenes[119]—declared that they had come 'not for battle, but for prayer'. This triggered off a series of acclamations urging that the united body should set off for the Portian Basilica, which were reinforced by news that the people there were demanding Ambrose's presence (13). The bishop showed a statesmanlike reluctance to force a confrontation; only incidentally did he let slip that these spectacular desertions had not been entirely spontaneous, since he had announced that the troops would otherwise be excluded from communion.[120] Valentinian's army, stationed in Milan for the better part of three years and billeted among the townspeople who formed the bishop's congregation, was vulnerable to such pressure. The Goths were unusual in maintaining a distinct identity; for most soldiers, local influence was subtle, persistent and difficult to resist.[121] By exploiting this hold, Ambrose once

119. Ambrose calls them *gentes* (20–21); the casual sneers at the Goths in the same sermon (16, 20) imply that they were non-Gothic, but not (as Nauroy claims, 'Le fouet et le miel', 55n157) that the Goths were an insignificant minority in Valentinian's army.

120. 'Praecepissem ut abstinerentur a communionis consortio' (13). This was probably done the previous day, after the deployment was announced; it explains the message conveyed by a group of soldiers to the emperor on Wednesday that they would follow him if they saw him join the 'catholics' but would otherwise cross over to Ambrose's congregation: 'se ad eum coetum quem Ambrosius cogeret transituros' (11).

121. The complexities of the relationships between soldiers and their hosts are sketched by R. MacMullen, *Soldier and Civilian in the Later Roman Empire* (1963), esp. 96–97. There is a wonderfully vivid picture of a soldier conforming out of self-interest to the Christian practices of his pious landlady in a Syriac tale set in Edessa in 395: *Euphemia and the Goth*, ed. F. C. Burkitt (1913), chap. 13 (and cf. chaps. 41–45 for the bishop's role).

again blunted the court's initiative. Even if (as is likely) the numbers who actually deserted were small, the psychological impact must have done much to offset the effect of the deployment at the Portian Basilica.

Ambrose capitalized on the arrival of these reinforcements by improvising a sermon, quoted at length in his letter to Marcellina. The Book of Job, the morning's text, had come to life: Ambrose saw Job in each of his people, in their patience and courage. They had expressed these qualities, needless to say, through an acclamation addressed to the emperor, striking the appropriate tone of resilient passivity: 'We ask you, Augustus; we do not fight, nor do we fear, but we ask you' (14). Two of the temptations of Job had been inflicted upon Ambrose himself through his parishioners, who represented both his endangered 'wealth' and his 'good sons', for whom he daily repeated the required sacrifice; but now they were caught up in the ruinous business—Ambrose repeated his strikingly inappropriate phrase of the previous day—of 'public perturbation'. The only torment left for the bishop was the physical pain and torture that he earnestly desired (15).

The whisperings of Job's wife urging him to rail against God led Ambrose via the present troubles ('see how much is instantly set in motion: Goths, arms, pagans; fines on merchants, punishment of the righteous' [16]) to the congenial theme of the temptress. Eve had led Adam from the mandate of heaven, leaving him naked but for the wretched fig leaf of his 'law' (17). Other women had pushed their menfolk into persecution: Jezebel against Elijah, and Herodias against the Baptist. Disclaiming any comparison with these exalted victims, Ambrose imperiously quotes John against the emperor's 'adulterous' desire for a basilica: 'It is not right that you shall have her'.[122] In doing so he slips easily into language that must by now have been familiar to his audience. 'Hand over the basilica': to the emperor's demand there could be but one answer.[123] God's property belonged to God, and Caesar's to Caesar; palaces were the emperor's sphere, churches the bishop's (18–19). At this point, news arrived—a further interruption in this momentous service—that the hangings in the Portian Basilica had been taken down, signalling the provisional abandonment of the planned celebration there.[124] The Nicene soldiers, whose desertion had almost certainly prompted this reversal, duly provided Ambrose with the theme for the triumphant per-

122. Cf. above, p. 63, for another polemical application of this text.
123. That this is a rhetorical question worked into the sermon, rather than an actual conversation that interrupted it (as presented in Zelzer's text), is demonstrated by Nauroy, 'Le fouet et le miel', 58.
124. The palace staff must have been able to enter the occupied basilica to do this: a valuable indication that the level of tension should not be exaggerated.

oration. He reminded the congregation of their fearful chanting, that morning, of Psalm 79 with its sombre refrain of the *gentes* 'coming into' the Lord's inheritance (20): the 'nations' had come to occupy the basilica and surround it with arms, but had truly 'come into the Lord's inheritance' by joining the congregation as 'co-heirs of God'. In the transformation of foes into defenders and apparent adversaries into allies, Ambrose naturally saw the direct intervention of Jesus, who had made his people safe: 'You have removed my sackcloth and clothed me with joy' (21).

Amid this jubilation, Ambrose fails to report in its proper place in the narrative an event of the utmost significance. When the removal of the *vela* was announced, he sent some presbyters to attend the party occupying the Portian Basilica.[125] This represented exactly the 'official' sanction for the occupation that his enemies had been awaiting from the start. Ambrose had at last declared his hand. Perhaps he thought victory secure, and that the removal of the hangings meant a final surrender to the combination of popular protest and the soldiers' earnest pleas, especially since he knew that the latter had been conveyed to the emperor through (and seconded by) entreaties from the *comites* (22).[126] But he had been premature. A *notarius* arrived from the emperor asking Ambrose to explain the dispatch of his presbyters to the Portian Basilica: 'If you are a usurper, I wish to know it, that I may consider how to prepare myself against you'. Ambrose's blustering reply cannot conceal his embarrassment. The repetition of *tyrannus* and its variants eight times in a single paragraph (23) shows how important it was to suppress its application to his own behaviour. Valentinian's military backers would not continue to support a plan that now threatened to produce only mutiny and massacre, but still less would they tolerate open treason from Ambrose. Without any real force to sustain it, the regime could not afford such insults to the imperial mystique.

On the heels of this sobering interview came an alarming report that the hangings in the Portian Basilica, which had been taken down but not removed, had been damaged, apparently 'torn by children who were playing' (24). Whatever the cause, this was desecration, a direct attack

125. We are only informed of this two chapters later (chap. 22), when Valentinian himself wrote to protest against it.

126. 'Haec ego dicebam miratus imperatorem studio militum, obsecratione comitum, precatu populi posse mitescere'. The counts' *obsecratio* might perhaps be identified with the angry exchange between Valentinian and his generals described at chap. 27; either or both might be associated with the plea presented on Wednesday morning.

on Valentinian's person: an immense symbolic importance attached to the purple cloth in which the emperor's every public appearance was enfolded, and awful consequences attended even unsubstantiated or entirely innocent transgressions.[127] Firm grounds had at last been established for treating the occupation of the Portian Basilica both as Ambrose's direct responsibility and as *maiestas;* reprisals in the name of the imperial dignity were likely to command popular support. There must have been intense discussion in the consistory over the next twelve hours on whether to mete out the appropriate punishment or to accept the excuse of a harmless juvenile prank. Meanwhile the troops (only a minority of whom had deserted to Ambrose) remained at their posts outside the Portian Basilica;[128] inside the city, the bishop and his people spent the whole day 'in sorrow'. That night the bishop judged the presence of the troops too threatening for him to return home. The prospect of arrest, which he had welcomed the previous day, had now become dangerously real. But he turned his confinement to good use, spending the night in the Old Basilica 'reciting psalms with the brethren' (24). We infer from another source that this was the occasion when he first divided the congregation into two antiphonal choirs: this brilliant improvisation, which was to be developed further during a later, more prolonged vigil, must have done much to restore the recently punctured morale of his congregation.[129]

There was another striking change of mood the next day, Thursday. From the day's prescribed text, the Book of Jonah, Ambrose derived a powerful if opaque prophecy: 'The sinners will be brought to repentance'. His audience, following his meaning, responded by expressing the 'hope' that it would be so, and by the end of the sermon he had duly transformed the sinners from Jonah's endangered Ninevites to the Milanese cabal responsible for the 'destruction which had been prepared for the city'. This danger, proclaimed Ambrose in an impressive conclusion, 'had been removed' (25). Not for the first time that week, his timing was

127. For some examples, see Amm. Marc. 14.9.7; 16.8.4, 8.

128. Nauroy, ('Le fouet et le miel', 65) claims that *all* the troops at the Portian Basilica had deserted, and that Ambrose's subsequent references to troops 'guarding' and 'withdrawing from' a basilica (*Ep.* 76 [20].24, 26) are to the Old Basilica; but there is no hint of this in the text.

129. The most likely interpretation of Augustine's report (*Conf.* 9.7.15) that Easter 387 was 'annus . . . aut non multo amplius' after the introduction of this style of singing is that Ambrose's choirs had first performed to nonpartisans like himself at the *previous* Easter service; as a nonparticipant he would not have distinguished clearly between the two 'sieges', or between the first use of the choirs and their subsequent development.

perfect (which encourages suspicions that he was being informed of the course of the consistory's deliberations):[130] news immediately arrived of the withdrawal of the soldiers from their blockade of the Portian Basilica and the repayment of the fines exacted from the *negotiatores*. While the congregation applauded joyfully, soldiers burst into the church to announce the glad tidings and rushed to the altar to make their sign of peace with the traditional kiss (26).

The exuberance of the celebration should not obscure the narrow margin—and provisional nature—of Ambrose's victory. In deciding against a final confrontation, the court had chosen the lesser of two evils. Ambrose had not answered the homoeans' case, and the damaging labels attracted by his behaviour threatened to stick: *tyrannus* and even harsher names were voiced abroad. The *praepositus sacri cubiculi*, the eunuch Calligonus, sent a forthright message: 'You show contempt for Valentinian while I live? I will have your head!' This was not merely a courtier's spite. Ambrose could expect repercussions. The prayer with which he closed his letter to Marcellina, that his enemies' weapons be directed at his own head rather than at his church (28), had at the time of writing a fair chance of being fulfilled.

AGAINST AUXENTIUS

Ambrose's account of Holy Week stops short of Easter itself. But the threat from Calligonus with which he concludes his letter to Marcellina suggests that the exhilaration of Maundy Thursday soon evaporated. The court's 'surrender' had resolved little. Valentinian had neither made any formal concessions to Ambrose's church nor been ushered into its fold: despite his soldiers' pleas, he is unlikely in the extreme to have appeared at the cathedral for Easter Sunday. Perhaps he had already left Milan. A fortnight later a law was published from Aquileia: the departure, evidently organized with considerable haste, might plausibly have been effected in the two days between the abandonment of the siege and Easter.[131] This would remove the troops from Ambrose's subversive

130. Cf. his knowledge of Valentinian's bitter retort (in which the echo of his own watchword of *traditio* was perhaps deliberate) to the *comites* who passed on the soldiers' request that he attend Ambrose's church: '"Si vobis iusserit Ambrosius vinctum me tradetis"' (27). For a possible context, see n. 126.

131. *CTh* 13.5.17 (20 April: Easter fell on 5 April). The constitution is addressed in the rubric to Principius, who held office in August–December 385; I

influence and cheat the bishop of the prime fruit of victory. Constantine himself had equipped the mobile court with the accessories and personnel that would have enabled Valentinian to improvise an Easter service on the road.[132] Such a celebration, if somewhat austere, would at least have allowed the emperor the freedom of worship which Ambrose had sought to deny him.

Although the hypothesis of a homoean Easter service for Valentinian and his court cannot be pressed in the absence of supporting evidence, it serves to delineate the limits of Ambrose's victory. His achievement in thwarting the emperor's plan was fundamentally negative. Valentinian had eluded him; the *comites* had not delivered up their ruler in chains. Their final veto on the Holy Week campaign, moreover, had been prompted by fears of mutiny or bloodshed rather than commitment to the bishop's cause, which must from their perspective have seemed dangerously divisive. Ambrose could not afford to provoke them further. He took care to send a more appropriate signal when the court returned to Milan:[133] flaunting his piety and vulnerability, he passed unescorted before the palace 'every day' on visits to his parishioners or to the martyrs' graves in the western suburbs.[134]

Valentinian and his friends, who returned to Milan determined to avenge the discomfiture of Holy Week, faced the converse problem of being unable to act without the support of their backers, who would not tolerate the risks of military or direct political action. A strategy was therefore devised which could command their assent. Ambrose was not to be attacked on his own ground but brought before the consistory so that its members could inspect the 'tyrant' for themselves. The plans are difficult to reconstruct in detail, since they are known only through the

---

follow Seeck, *Regesten,* 270, in retaining the manuscript date. It took Theodosius and his court less than eighteen days to travel from Aquileia to Milan in 388: Seeck, 275.

132. Soc. *HE* 1.11. The 'presbyter of the palace' recorded at Constantinople by Palladius of Helenopolis (*Dial.* 20) is a rare but significant attestation of the permanent retinue of imperial chaplains.

133. The codes provide no information upon the court's movements between mid-April (*CTh* 13.5.17) and early June. A return to Milan in mid-May seems most likely, to allow several weeks for the exchanges described in this section before Ambrose's discovery of the martyrs on 17 June.

134. *Sermo contra Aux.* 15 (cf. *Ep.* 75 [21].18). Visits to the 'martyrs' were perhaps connected with the construction of the Basilica Ambrosiana at the tomb of Victor; the *Martyrologium Hieronymianum* also records the commemoration of Victor's anniversary on 8 May.

protests Ambrose lodged against them and the derision he heaped upon them for his people's benefit. But they revolved around a debate 'on the faith', *de fide*, between Ambrose and Auxentius, the homoean bishop in attendance upon Valentinian, which would be held in the presence of the consistory before a panel of (perhaps ten) *iudices* selected by the two combatants, and supervised by the emperor himself.[135] Described in these terms, the arrangements appear somewhat curious and seem to bear out Ambrose's criticisms of illogicality, superfluity, and dissimulation of their ultimate purpose.

But Ambrose's presentation is partial. His insistence upon the impropriety of laymen 'judging' bishops obscures the nature of the *iudicium* involved, but the hearing cannot have been intended (as he at one point implies) to produce a sentence of deposition against the defeated contestant. It was to be neither a trial nor (an interpretation frequently adopted, but again resting on a polemical digression by Ambrose) an attempt to ratify the terms of the January law.[136] The circumstances recall instead the hearing held at Milan some twenty years earlier, when the elder Auxentius faced his importunate challenger Hilary. The latter, it will be remembered, had addressed his accusation to the emperor, who had convened a hearing to test his claims. His son seems now to have been following the same procedure. An *interpellatio* from Auxentius against Ambrose can easily be envisaged: one likely claim would be that the bishop was denying him his right, specifically guaranteed by Valentinian's law (and sanctioned, besides, by what seems an unbroken tradition in the west of freedom of worship for homoeans), of practising his faith.[137] It would be no easy matter for Ambrose to justify his opposition to Auxentius' ministry by 'proving' him a heretic, for Valentinian's

---

135. Ambrose summarizes the arrangements in *Ep.* 75 [21].1, to Valentinian: a tribune had ordered him to choose his *iudices,* as Auxentius had his, and added 'quod in consistorio esset futura certatio arbitro pietatis iudicio tuae'; at *Sermo contra Aux.* 26 Auxentius is said perhaps to have chosen 'four or five' judges. The theme of *de fide* is implied by Ambrose's constant reference to the subject: *Ep.* 75 [21].2, 4, 5, 15, 17.

136. Thus, most recently, Nauroy, 'Le fouet et le miel', 14–15. But the January law did not (despite *Ep.* 75 [21].9–12) forbid criticism or discussion of its terms, only 'turbulent' resistance or 'clandestine' attempts at repeal. Gottlieb ('Der Mailänder Kirchenstreit', 49–54) recognizes this and supposes a *second* law to have been at issue in the debate. It seems far more likely, however, that Ambrose was confusing matters with a quibble.

137. Ambrose implies at *Sermo contra Aux.* 29 that Auxentius had taken the initiative in requesting the debate before Valentinian ('De imperatore vult commovere invidiam . . .'); he shifts to an indefinite plural to describe his opponents in the same chapter.

court would no more be moved by a simple abjuration of the council of Rimini than had his father's. A further element in the challenge was perhaps a citation from Ambrose himself. In *De fide* the bishop had attributed a string of monstrosities to the Arians and then reeled off the names of 'those who must be answered': Palladius, Demophilus and Auxentius. Palladius had failed at the council of Aquileia to extract this promised reply; Auxentius may well have hoped, in the more sympathetic climate of Valentinian's Milan, to hold Ambrose to his word.[138]

There is another sense in which Auxentius can be seen as Palladius' heir. The bishop of Ratiaria had always maintained that, given fair conditions, he could expose the doctrinal confusion and exegetical incompetence behind Ambrose's bluster. His final attempt to secure such conditions had been to suggest a debate before the senate of Rome; Valentinian's conspicuously blue-blooded consistory was an equally august forum.[139] The consistory was not, it must again be stressed, in any sense dominated by a homoean clique. The most significant members were those whose intervention had cut short the emperor's campaign at Easter, and it was for their benefit that the debate was being organized, to prove to them the wantonness of Ambrose's claim to exclusive control over religious activities in Milan. Such, indeed, was Auxentius' confidence that he seems to have included at least one pagan among his nominated *iudices* (whose function is never made clear in Ambrose's diatribe but probably involved the adjudication of a specific question of fact advertised in the terms of the debate).[140] It is tempting to see reflected in this choice Auxentius' target group of court magnates (besides senators like Praetextatus, at least one pagan held high military office under Valentinian),[141] who even without any ideological commitment to him could be expected to recognize not only the expediency but also the justice of his case.

Ambrose responded dramatically to this subtle and careful approach, retreating to his church in the company of his congregation.[142] There was

138. *De fide* 1.44–46.

139. Besides the prefect Eusignius, Valentinian's entourage included the *comes rei privatae* Gorgonius, a 'brother' of Symmachus who spent his leisure on his estate in Picenum (*PLRE* 1, p. 399; Symm. *Ep.* 1.39).

140. *Sermo contra Aux.* 26. These 'cognitores' (cf. *Ep.* 75 [21].1, 'iudices') seem equivalent to the ten bishops who attended Hilary's debate with Auxentius in 364: cf. above, p. 26.

141. Viz. Rumorides: Amb. *Ep. extra coll.* 19 [57].3.

142. The ancient sources do not identify this church. Modern scholars tend to assume the Portian Basilica on the basis of Paulin. *V. Amb.* 13.1–2 (e.g.,

more to this than a repetition of a proven tactic: the bishop was manoeuvring for position; he was as determined to continue the struggle
on his own terrain as were his enemies to transfer it to theirs. He needed
to present the studied reasonableness of Valentinian's proposals as a
cover for the renewal of persecution by other means. The presence of
soldiers outside the church, signalled by the metallic clash of their arms,
allowed him to re-create the siege mentality he had so effectively conjured up in the days before Easter. Ambrose and his people took shelter
from this convenient 'blockade', and there ensued a stalemate of several
days before the court resumed negotiations with the bishop.

This delay on the government's side was probably caused by surprise: Ambrose had again wrong-footed them with his presentation of
the issue. Their confusion stemmed from their not seeing what was happening as a siege at all. Any attentive reader of Ambrose's account will
have to agree: attackers and defenders alike appear woefully incompetent in the roles attributed to them. A door on the lefthand side of the
basilica, thought by the bishop's supporters to have been safely closed
and barricaded, was discovered wide open; but although it had remained so for 'many nights', the soldiers who were searching for a
means of access to the church failed to find it. Still more striking is the
casual departure from the building of a blind man, leaving the 'double
doors' at the entrance to the church likewise wide open.[143] The troops
evidently had no interest in either forcing their way into the basilica or
preventing Ambrose's people from leaving it. We might instead imagine
a few pickets posted to monitor events and prevent the mobilization of
a crowd like those which had marched to the Portian Basilica at Easter
or to the palace the previous year. The bishop seized upon their presence to declare himself under siege, and so found an excuse for disobey-
ing the emperor's summons.

This second siege was invented by Ambrose. The bishop deserves
credit for sustaining his people's sense of danger and their commitment
in the face of their oppressors' inactivity. Liturgical innovation helped
him maintain momentum. His division of the congregation into antiphonal choirs for singing psalms, during the night of Wednesday of Holy

---

Lenox-Conyngham, 'The Topography', 363), but this passage is better associated
with the Easter siege, which—because the threat of violence was more real—
will have made a more significant impression upon contemporaries. Ambrose is
more likely to have based himself in a church where he and his people felt comfortable, the Basilica Nova or Vetus.

143. *Sermo contra Aux.* 10.

Week, had already created a sense of increased participation in the liturgy.[144] But if the themes of persecution and endurance recurrent in the Psalms lent themselves well to the present situation, still more apposite were the hymns that Ambrose composed by himself and which he now taught to his choirs.[145] Through these hymns, the people were able to broadcast their belief in the Trinity and so emphasized that their defiance represented doctrinal commitment rather than political insurrection. Most of the hymns were designed to mark specific points in the daily round (dawn, early morning and evening, respectively, for the three Ambrosian hymns known to Augustine),[146] providing a framework for the long days during which the *pia plebs* 'stood guard'.[147] A round-the-clock liturgy was thus improvised, each day and night being punctuated by services and song. Ambrose in this way imposed his own logic upon the protracted imprisonment in the church. The hymns, as his opponents realized, were part of the great 'deception' whereby the bishop sustained the illusion of siege and persecution.[148]

It is not known for how long Ambrose was permitted to weave his spells undisturbed. Several days, at the least, elapsed before the emperor moved to implement his own plans.[149] Dalmatius, a *tribunus et*

144. Like so many of Ambrose's innovations, the practice was current in the east. Theodoret *HE* 2.24.8–9 attributes its invention to Flavian and Diodorus at Antioch in the 350s; both its popularity and the controversy it engendered are reported by Basil (*Ep.* 207).

145. The sequence suggested here is hypothetical, but I believe logical. Neither Augustine (*Conf.* 9.7.15) nor Paulinus (*V. Amb.* 13.3) distinguishes between the introduction of hymns and of choral psalms, but neither was an eyewitness. On Ambrose's compositions, see the edition and commentary supervised by J. Fontaine, *Ambroise de Milan: Hymnes* (1992); Fontaine's introduction (at 16–102) discusses the historical and literary context.

146. 'Aeterne rerum conditor', 'Iam surgit hora tertia' and 'Deus creator omnium': attested at *Retract.* 1.21, *De natura et gratia* 74 and *De beata vita* 4.35/ *Conf.* 9.12.32. It is perhaps significant that the last two cases show lines from Ambrose's evening hymn occurring to Monica and Augustine during the evening.

147. *Conf.* 9.7.15.

148. *Sermo contra Aux.* 34: 'Hymnorum quoque meorum carminibus deceptum populum ferunt'.

149. 'Many nights' had passed by the time the *Sermo contra Auxentium* was delivered (7: 'tot noctibus'; cf. 10, 'per plurimas noctes'). During the interim Ambrose was apparently ordered to surrender church plate (alluded to at 5), perhaps following a claim by Auxentius to a share in the church's property. It is also possible that the aim was to take an inventory of the treasure, to make a formal attack against Ambrose for dispersing it (p. 55); this was a charge used against Chrysostom (Photius *Bibl.* 59.18a.4; cf. Pall. *Dial.* 13 for the investigation).

notarius, arrived at the basilica with a formal demand that Ambrose nominate his judges according to instructions, as Auxentius had already done. To prevent further evasion, Valentinian seems to have declared expressly that failure to comply would be treated as *contumacia,* wilful disobedience, and punished accordingly.[150] The message also included the offer of a compromise. If Ambrose could not bring himself to face Auxentius, he was free to leave Milan and 'go where he pleased', accompanied by his loyal followers (if they so desired).[151] Valentinian was determined this time to retain the initiative. Ignoring the bishop's posturing, he reduced the issue to a straightforward command that left his opponent no room for manoeuvre. Jury selection was far less suitable for translation into the emotive language on which Ambrose relied than had been the *traditio* of a basilica. Refusal to cooperate would therefore expose the bishop as a contumacious mischief-maker and justify to the world (and in particular to the men of influence at the Milanese court) Valentinian's actions against him.

Conversely, Ambrose needed to prove his innocence of *contumacia* by demonstrating that he was merely the instrument of his people's will. It was a tall order, for his mobilization of popular support involved risks. By casting himself in exactly the demagogic role that his opponents had designed for him, he had placed himself at the mercy of his followers' unpredictable behaviour. Repetition of the indiscipline exhibited during Easter week in the mauling of Castulus and the tearing of the hangings was this time likely to prove fatal. Even more dangerous than overexcitement was boredom: the government's failure to press their 'siege' would inevitably erode the spirit of defiance which the bishop had artificially induced.[152]

The limits to Ambrose's hold over his people became apparent by their alarmed response to Dalmatius' delivery of Valentinian's ultimatum and their fear that the bishop would accept the offer to withdraw.[153] To reassure them, he had to affirm in the most vehement terms his determination never to abandon his church: he would endure even if dragged

---

150. See *Ep.* 75 [21].1 for the instructions; the elaborate defence against *contumacia* in 2–3 strongly suggests that this was part of the emperor's message.

151. *Ep.* 75 [21].18; *Sermo contra Aux.* 1 shows that this offer was part of the official *mandatum.*

152. According to Augustine (*Conf.* 9.7.15), the hymns and psalm-singing were introduced precisely 'ne populus maeroris taedio contabesceret'.

153. Ambrose recalls their reaction at *Sermo contra Aux.* 1; it is unnecessary to assume with van Haeringen ('De Valentiniano II et Ambrosio', 29–32) that he seriously considered accepting the offer.

away by physical force, and was ready to suffer 'the priest's usual fate' if Valentinian behaved 'as royal power generally does'.[154] The emperor was probably well satisfied with Dalmatius' report of this inflammatory response; obdurate reiteration of the slogans of Easter could only alienate Ambrose's possible supporters at court. But the bishop still had to make his formal reply, and when he presented his proposals to his people shortly afterwards, he was able to guide their responses more effectively. The sense of defiance and solidarity that he had nurtured among his people, through song and prayer during the long days and nights when they had been barricaded in the church, was given resounding expression. The Christians of Milan had found their political voice.

The framework within which Ambrose elicited his people's voice was, characteristically, liturgical. It was during a mass held soon after Dalmatius' visit that he delivered a sermon which ranks among the masterpieces of antique political rhetoric: the *Sermo contra Auxentium*.[155] The speech, which must have been largely improvised, began with a reassurance to his troubled audience: he would never 'desert' them (*Sermo contra Aux.* 2). Having thus rejected one of Valentinian's alternatives, Ambrose considered the other: 'If only I could be sure that the church would not be handed over to the heretics!' (3). Without elaborating upon this pregnant exclamation, a reprise of the *traditio* theme irrelevant to the present situation (since Auxentius was not contesting Ambrose for control of his cathedral)[156] but calculated to revive memories of Easter, Ambrose moved swiftly to reasons for rejecting the proposed debate: a bishop should do his fighting in church rather than at the palace; in the consistory, Christ belonged in the judge's seat, not in the dock. Only

154. This oral reply, which was later followed by the written one of *Ep.* 75, is summarized at *Sermo contra Aux.* 1.

155. Text references are to this speech. There is a fine study of the rhetorical structure by M. Testard, 'Observations sur la rhétorique d'une harangue au peuple dans le *Sermo Contra Auxentium* de saint Ambroise', *REL* 63 (1985), 193–209.

156. Despite *Sermo contra Aux.* 17–18, the possession of particular churches was not the central issue between Ambrose and Auxentius, who was already conducting regular services in Milan (above, n. 97). The decisive proof is Ambrose's silence concerning the issue, the hinge of his arguments during Holy Week, in his letter to Valentinian (below, p. 207). The exclamation at *Ep.* 75 [21].19 ('utinam . . . Arrianis ecclesia minime traderetur') matches *Sermo contra Aux.* 3 in exploiting the ambiguity of *ecclesia* as building and institution; cf. *Ep.* 75 [21].6.

after establishing the harshness and corruption of the court did Ambrose suggest to his people that he should indeed go, to save them from the dangers ('the clangour of arms, with which the church is surrounded') that threatened them. The imagery of Easter was reintroduced: assuming once more the identity of Job, Ambrose welcomed the prospect of experiencing at last the ultimate temptation of physical suffering (4). He recalled the propriety and humility of his demeanour towards the emperor in what had perhaps been their most recent exchange (his refusal to surrender church plate), as if to emphasize the injustice of these prospective torments; only then did he appeal to his audience for permission to go forth and suffer in Christ's cause and for them to be his 'spectators' (5–6). The contest with Auxentius had been transformed into something very different from what Valentinian had envisaged: the confrontation between martyr and persecutor.

In the space of a few paragraphs, Ambrose had reversed the issue and was now arguing that he *should* set out to obtain his martyr's crown. The actual setting drifted out of focus as one of the day's gospel texts was adduced to prove resistance to a divine ordinance both wrong and futile (8–9). A series of examples, progressively more elevated and remote from the present circumstances, illustrated the point. From incidents in the current 'siege' (10), Ambrose moved to how Elijah and Peter, sustained by the prayers of their followers, had survived persecution by kings (11–12) and to the encounter between Peter and Christ at the gates of Rome, which fortified the apostle for his martyrdom (13). He had reached Jesus himself, and the security which Christ had enjoyed until the time appointed for his arrest (14), when he returned abruptly to the present and to his own case: like Jesus, he too had walked safely under the very noses of his enemies. With the issue pitched at this level, the emperor's offer—'Depart from the city and go where you will'—was simply bathetic. Having dismissed such 'luxury', Ambrose (perhaps eager to skate over the implication that the torments upon which he had earlier dwelt did not actually feature in the emperor's plans) returned to the dark threats and rumours that beset him. Among them were the harsh measures being bandied about by Auxentius ('who calls himself a bishop'); only now, two-fifths of the way through the speech and in the dubious company of assassins and death sentences, does Ambrose introduce his adversary (15).

Auxentius had filled the whole world with lamentation and tears, composing with his own hand instructions for the expulsion of catholic priests, or their death if they resisted, and for the proscription of any *curiales* who obstructed the implementation of his commands. We can hardly hope to recognize the emperor's *mandatum* beneath Ambrose's rhetoric, which seems to merge it with the January law into a single monstrous instrument of destruction directed by Auxentius, 'a sword that flies through all the cities' (16).[157] Still less relevant to the present issue was his next assertion that Auxentius, 'his mouth bloody and his hands stained with gore', was claiming a basilica from him.[158] In both cases, Ambrose's discourse was governed not by the immediate situation but by the day's readings. The psalm from the current service—'God said to the sinner, "What right have you to recite my laws?"'—had answered Auxentius' legislative initiatives. The Old Testament reading had inevitably revived the alarms of Easter week, with the story of honest Nabuth dying in defence of his rightful inheritance against an unstable ruler and the demonic queen who dominated him (17). The 'basilica' of Easter is beautifully elided into the wider 'church' which was now at issue, as Ambrose brushes aside the charge of *contumacia* with a return to his favourite theme of *traditio* and a rousing appeal to the 'inheritance' of the Milanese church (18).

There follows another brilliant transition, from Jezebel and her hapless son back to the present villain. 'And to whom shall I surrender?' asked Ambrose, and for an answer he had only to look again at the gospel text he had discussed earlier. He recognized in Auxentius' complaints against him the Jews' resentment at the acclaim for Jesus on his entry into Jerusalem (19), and in his political machinations and designs against the people's innocent faith the work of the moneychangers and sellers of doves who were expelled from the Temple (20). Auxentius' own 'exclusion' from Christ's temple was justified by a liberal dose of innuendo drawn from the rich tradition of forensic calumny (22).[159] His own planned 'cleansing of the temple' was reduced to a grotesque parody of Christ's; by expelling the pious with instruments of iron—sword and axe—he defined himself conclusively as Jeremiah's Judah, his sin inscribed upon his breast by a pen of iron and a point of adamant (23).

Only now did Ambrose introduce the main plank of Auxentius' ini-

157. Gottlieb interpreted this and other passages to imply a sweeping *lex de fide*, introduced after Easter to impose the creed of Rimini upon Valentinian's subjects ('Der Mailänder Kirchenstreit', 39–40, 51–54). It seems more likely that Ambrose is here, as elsewhere, applying a *reductio ad absurdum* to the terms of the January law.

158. See above, n. 156.

159. For a useful discussion of another (exactly contemporary) application of this tradition, see R. L. Wilcken, *John Chrysostom and the Jews* (1983), esp. 94–127 ('Fourth-century preaching and the rhetoric of abuse').

tiative. 'Does this man, full of blood and gore, dare to make mention to me of "discussion"?' In these terms the proposal was absurd, but Ambrose continued to exploit the day's readings to argue his case. Paul's maxim, 'Since man is not justified by the works of law . . .', demonstrated decisively that the enactment of 23 January, upon which Auxentius' challenge was ultimately founded, could count for nothing beside 'faith' (24). The same text allowed Ambrose to launch into a brief discussion of Christ's divinity (25), before interrupting himself to remind the people that Auxentius wished to debate this question not in their presence but before a handful of pagan adjudicators, the thought of whose participation immediately prompted a volley of scriptural citations (26–28). Ambrose then rapidly covers a series of miscellaneous charges, notably the *invidia* aroused by his behaviour the previous year (29–31) and the accusations of witchcraft against his sponsorship of choral hymn singing (34), before drawing himself up for his stately conclusion: 'It seems, therefore, that a satisfactory response has been made to their points'; this entitled him to make the intriguing countercharge that Auxentius was rebaptizing converts to his cause (37).[160]

As has long been recognized, this speech cannot be understood without reference to the audience's participation.[161] The sudden shifts of direction, occasionally amounting to a complete reversal, reflect the punctuation of their roars of approval or protest, while the staccato bursts in the final paragraphs seem to represent items offered up for popular ratification. But if the whole occasion was organized as a question-and-answer session, it took a special form. The central question concerned the emperor's *mandatum*, and although Ambrose distorted it almost beyond recognition, he was careful to recommend to his people that they allow him to comply. The answer was a resounding no: by manoeuvring his people into refusing his requests, Ambrose had made himself their prisoner. Besieged twice over (indeed, three times over: a group of bishops, fortuitously at hand, also denied him permission either to partici-

160. The rite, interpreted by M. Meslin (*Les Ariens d'Occident* [1967], 388–90) as a standard 'Arian' practice and a sign of the sect's growing extremism, was more probably intended to advertise Auxentius' success in persuading baptized members of the Milanese church to defect. Rebaptism was still widely practiced: in 385 some Spanish bishops were contemplating rebaptizing Arians: Siricius *Ep.* 1 (*PL* 13, 1131). Augustine's remark (*De haer.* 46) that he knew that the Arians rebaptized Catholics, but not how they dealt with converts from other sects ('Rebaptizari ab his catholicos novimus; utrum et non catholicos nescio'), was probably based upon the memory of Auxentius' activities.

161. This was perhaps the most important contribution of van Haeringen's to the understanding of this text: 'De Valentiniano II et Ambrosio', 29–32.

pate in the debate or to leave the church),[162] he was no longer free to obey Valentinian.

Ambrose's formal reply to the emperor's *mandatum*, written in the aftermath of this service, amply demonstrates the talent lost in him to the Roman bar.[163] From the doubt implied in the very first sentence whether Valentinian had really authorized Dalmatius' mission, the letter is a masterpiece of obfuscation. Ambrose first deprecated the emperor's plan to chair the proposed debate, citing as precedent a rescript of Valentinian I (2); the authority of the emperor's father, which had previously served Ambrose well in the altar of Victory affair, was invoked not only against the charge of *contumacia* (3) but also in implicit assent to the bishop's own slogan: 'in a *causa fidei*, when has a layman ever sat in judgement over a bishop?' (4–5).[164] The terms of the debate offered further material. The official silence over the identity of Auxentius' *iudices*, mentioned already in the first paragraph of the letter, raised doubts: if there really were any, they should come to the basilica, a more appropriate venue than the consistory, 'since the issue concerns the bishop of our church' (6). Ambrose's claim to the see was made in emphatic if perhaps misleading terms (7);[165] meanwhile, the challenger's status was subjected to a quibble, 'for I do not *know* that he is a bishop, nor do I know where he is from' (8).

Ambrose then moved from these delaying tactics to question the legality of the arrangements. A clause in Valentinian's January law had explicitly forbidden any attempts to overturn it, but one possible outcome of the debate, the defeat of Auxentius, would amount to precisely such a reversal. The emperor was therefore urged to respect his own enactments or else to rescind completely a law that he had already in part withdrawn (9–10). Ambrose protested also against the impossible position of his own appointed *iudices*, who could hardly be expected to stand alone before the emperor and tell him, 'I do not approve of your law' (11). If Valentinian truly wished questions of doctrine to be explored, he should entrust the matter to his bishops without circumscribing them by legislation. 'Remove your law, therefore, if you wish there to be a contest' (15–16).

162. *Ep.* 75 [21].13, 17–18. This was probably an informal gathering rather than a synod: Nauroy, 'Le fouet et le miel', 16n48.

163. *Ep.* 75 [21]. References in the text in the following paragraphs are to this letter.

164. Cf. Ambrose's reaction to Palladius' demand for lay adjudicators in 381 (*Acta conc. Aquil.* 52).

165. Cf. above, p. 47.

But these arguments, Ambrose at last revealed, were purely academic. He would indeed have come to the consistory to present his case in person, notwithstanding his misgivings, 'if the bishops and people had permitted me; but they say that discussions about the faith should be held in church before the people' (17). Issued from the security of captivity, his refusal could not incur the charge of *contumacia*. Ambrose's helplessness was sufficiently convincing to the court to deny his enemies any purchase against him, and Valentinian's initiative evaporated once more.

The resulting standoff left both sides in exposed—and ultimately untenable—positions. Ambrose's protestations made it difficult for Valentinian to justify his continued campaign against him to the Milanese populace or his own government; persistence would suggest petulance or undue maternal influence and lend credence to the bishop's cries of persecution. There was also pressure from abroad. A letter from Maximus had arrived after Easter remarking on how effectively the present 'disturbance and convulsion of the church' would play into his own hands—if he were Valentinian's enemy. Asserting instead his 'close and sedulous concern' for the prince, Maximus lectured him upon the greatness of God and the inviolability of doctrines 'developed and confirmed through so many ages', citing in support of his argument (like Ambrose) the successes vouchsafed to Valentinian's orthodox father and the recent destruction of Mursa, a former bastion of Arianism.[166] Stalemate could only bring further and more insistent advice from this quarter.

Ambrose, meanwhile, was in an equally delicate position. The January law remained in force, and Auxentius' claims had not been withdrawn. But without any manifestation of the predicted persecution, he could not hope to prolong the imprisonment that he had so brilliantly devised. And as tension slackened, resistance to the emperor's proposals would become less justifiable to political circles in Milan. Both bishop and emperor looked ultimately to this same constituency, the 'court' in its broader sense, and both had the same problem of presentation in relation to it: neither had yet succeeded in raising his cause above the level of faction. In these circumstances, any definitive victory was impossible. As the year moved into summer and a fresh crisis erupted on the Danube to encourage a closing of ranks,[167] both sides must have feared that time was running out.

166. *Coll. Avell.* 39.
167. *CTh* 1.32.5 (29 July) reports that procurators of mines in Macedonia, Dacia and Upper Moesia had abandoned their posts because of *hostilis metus*.

THE MARTYRS

Not long after Valentinian's abortive initiative, the bishop emerged from his fortress to advertise his commitment to unity. The occasion was the completion in early June of a church in the western suburbs of Milan, which must have received its finishing touches even while the crisis of 385/6 was raging. This large and lavishly decorated basilica was Ambrose's personal stake in the Hortus Philippi, the most venerable part of Christian Milan; it had also been designed to annex the adjacent chapel of the martyr Victor, where the bishop's brother Satyrus was buried.[168] But the function of the new church—already popularly called the Ambrosian—differed strikingly from contemporary episcopal bequests like Damasus' church (dedicated to Saint Lawrence) at Rome, which preserved the pope's name and library for posterity.[169] Ambrose's basilica was to remain more directly his own: he intended to be buried beneath the altar.[170] At one level, this represented a challenge to his enemies. Even if they killed him, the *martyrium* now ready for him would provide a focus for his people's continued loyalty. Ambrose's expectations of violent death, so frequently expressed at this time, form the background to his proposal; they also perhaps obscure its radicalism.[171] No previous bishop is known deliberately to have arrogated to himself so liturgically potent a resting place. The burial of Meletius of Antioch in the sarcophagus of the martyr Babylas, the nearest parallel, did not challenge that saint's preeminence;[172] moreover, it was organized by Meletius' controversial successor Flavianus, whose advertisement of his predecessor's merits helped establish his own legitimacy. Ambrose's advance publicity

168. For the Basilica Ambrosiana, see F. Reggiori, *La basilica Ambrosiana* (1941); G. Bovini, *Antichità cristiane di Milano* (1970) 220–250; Mirabella Roberti, *Milano Romana*, 120–124. Decoration with scriptural scenes can be inferred from the explanatory *tituli* to these (*PLS* 1, 587: for discussion, S. Merkle, 'Die ambrosianische Tituli', *RQA* 10 [1896], 185–222). On the Hortus Philippi, see M. Cagiano d'Azevedo, 'Lo "hortus Philippi" di Mediolanum', *Atti del IX congresso internazionale di archeologia cristiana* (1978), 2:133–140.

169. See C. Pietri, *Roma Christiana* (1976), 464–467.

170. *Ep.* 77 [22].13: 'dignum est enim ut ibi requiescat sacerdos ubi offerre consuevit'.

171. Ambrose had presumably intended originally to be buried beside Satyrus: cf. *De exc. frat.* 1.78.

172. G. Downey, *A History of Antioch* (1961), 415; for the burial as part of a systematic campaign (initiated by Meletius himself) to 'capture' Babylas from the homoeans who had introduced the cult to Antioch, see H.-C. Brennecke, *Studien zur Geschichte der Homöer* (1988), 154–155.

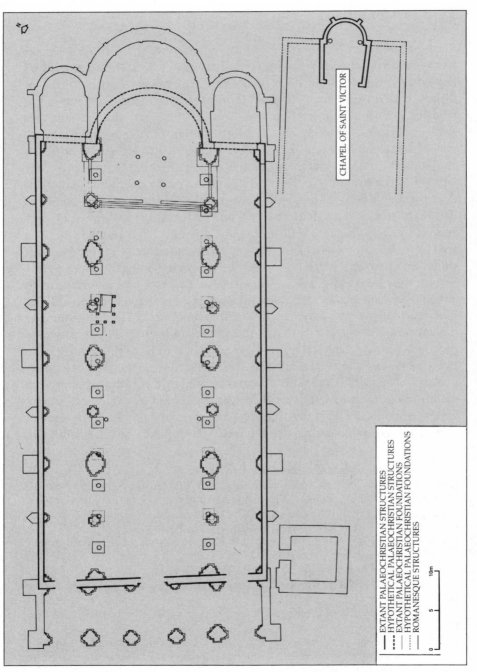

CHAPEL OF SAINT VICTOR

—— EXTANT PALAEOCHRISTIAN STRUCTURES
- - - HYPOTHETICAL PALAEOCHRISTIAN STRUCTURES
······ EXTANT PALAEOCHRISTIAN FOUNDATIONS
········ HYPOTHETICAL PALAEOCHRISTIAN FOUNDATIONS
—— ROMANESQUE STRUCTURES

0   5   10m

4. Basilica Ambrosiana, plan. Reproduced by kind permission of Professor M. Mirabella Roberti.

for his own funeral arrangements, while no less political, was far more explosive.

The dedication of the basilica gave Ambrose a valuable opportunity to rally his supporters. But when the proceedings had already been completed, events took a remarkable turn. An appeal came from the congregation: 'Dedicate the church as you did the Basilica in Romana'.[173] The original centrepiece of this latter church, a recent construction by the bishop designed to honour the apostles, was a collection of imported relics. Their deposition must have made an impressive spectacle, but it is not obvious why the Basilica Ambrosiana, which already boasted one martyr in the adjacent chapel and was promised the bishop himself for its own altar, should have required similar enhancement. Perhaps the demand was spontaneous, perhaps there had been a subtle prompt; but few in the audience can have anticipated the bishop's response. Rather than resorting to another *translatio* from a city better endowed with a Christian pedigree than his own 'sterile' Milan, Ambrose vowed to equip his new church as requested, 'if I can discover the remains of some martyrs'. He felt a 'rush of presentiment' immediately upon making this commitment (1); the whole city must have experienced something of a shock wave, as friends and foes alike braced themselves to see how the bishop would fulfill his self-imposed task.

Ambrose's handling of the expectations he had generated was masterly. On 17 June, perhaps the morning after the original announcement,[174] he led the way to one of the most prominent monuments in the Hortus Philippi, the *memoria* of the martyrs Nabor and Felix. With a boldness that dismayed even his clerics, he ordered digging to commence in front of the chancel rails, an area at once sanctified through proximity to the martyrs and profaned by the daily trampling of the faithful.[175] When 'appropriate signs' appeared, Ambrose brought forward some victims of demonic possession who were awaiting exorcism. As the remains of the two bodies emerged, one of the possessed women

---

173. *Ep.* 77 [22].1; all text references in this section are to this letter. For discussion, see E. Dassmann, 'Ambrosius und die Märtyrer', *JAC* 18 (1975), 49–68 (esp. 52–57); J. Doignon, 'Perspectives ambrosiennes', *REAug* 2 (1956), 313–334; V. Zangara, 'L'*inventio* dei martiri Gervasio e Protasio', *Augustinianum* 21 (1981), 119–133.

174. Aug. *Conf.* 9.7.16 mentions a dream ('per visum') that perhaps reinforced Ambrose's original presentiment.

175. Paulin. *V. Amb.* 14.1: the spot was where 'ambularent omnes qui vellent ad cancellos pervenire quibus sanctorum Naboris et Felicis martyrum ab iniuria sepulcra defendebantur'.

suffered a seizure and threw herself down beside the newly revealed grave. The demon seems to have implored the skeletons to show mercy, addressing them by name as Gervasius and Protasius;[176] the bishop and his party stood impassively by, offering no cues. The authenticity and identity of the remains were thus established, and confirmation was provided by certain old men who recalled hearing the names and reading them upon the stones that had once commemorated the martyrs.[177] The skeletons ('of extraordinary size') were unearthed and arranged in proper order and, as evening fell, were taken to the nearby Basilica Faustae.[178] The crowd drawn by the spectacle celebrated a vigil through the night, punctuated by exorcisms that demonstrated the martyrs' powers.

More was to come. The following day (18 June), the relics were set upon litters and carried in procession to Ambrose's new basilica (2), accompanied by the singing of psalms. Crowds of the sick and afflicted of Milan struggled to touch the martyrs or to gain access to their healing powers by holding strips of cloth up against them. People could be seen shrugging off their illnesses, and reports circulated of miraculous cures. In Milan, it seemed, the age of the apostles had returned (9). Such at least was the bishop's view when, flanked by the martyrs, he addressed his people at the Basilica Ambrosiana (3–13). The sermon nevertheless reads as if it were aimed as much at the court as at his own partisans. The martyrs had been obtained, he stressed, for the whole city: 'they are to benefit everyone and do harm to nobody'. They could also serve to defuse the *invidia* that Ambrose acknowledged had been created by his mobilization of his community against the palace. The martyrs would include the latter under their protection; let them come, therefore, and inspect Ambrose's new bodyguards (10). Gervasius and Protasius were 'legitimate' weapons who provided him, for the first time since the January law, with a positive platform from which to institute negotiations.

There was still, however, a significant element of bluff in this pre-

176. Ambrose does not say this specifically, but it seems clear that the martyrs' names were revealed by such means; cf. P. Courcelle, *Recherches sur les "Confessions" de saint Augustin* (1968), 146. Augustine speaks of demons addressing Gervasius and Protasius (and Ambrose) 'expresso nomine' at *De cura pro mortuis gerenda* 17.

177. *Ep.* 77 [22].12: 'Nunc senes repentunt se aliquando audisse horum martyrum nomina titulumque legisse'. This testimony must have been used to confirm rather than establish the martyrs' names (*pace* Zangara, 'L'inventio', 128–129): an inquiry among the spectators for recollections of 'lost' martyrs once venerated at the site would have been too suggestive of collusion.

178. Tentatively identified with the oratory later known as San Vitale by Bovini, *Antichità cristiane*, 134–135.

sentation. Ambrose had organized the spectacle of the *inventio* with consummate skill, and the festivities had generated a momentum of their own. But he needed to put a seal upon the episode as quickly as possible. Quite apart from the illegality of unauthorized translations of relics, affirmed in a recent law,[179] the credentials of Ambrose's martyrs might not have stood prolonged or critical scrutiny. The criteria by which they had been identified, demonic protests and old men's reminiscences, were hardly rigorous, and their miracles had been wrought only upon the bishop's own dependents. Ambrose therefore needed to preempt any counterattack. In his sermon, he expressed his desire to see Gervasius and Protasius safely interred in their new home that same day; this would at least represent a formal confirmation by the community of the martyrs' status. But the people failed to appreciate the need for haste. Ambrose had succeeded only too well in imparting a rhythm of slow, majestic ceremony to his project, and the congregation, anxious perhaps to secure the largest crowd possible, demanded that the final installation be deferred until the following Sunday. Unable to afford so long a delay, the bishop negotiated the compromise of postponement for a single day (14).

Those who had remained in attendance upon the bishop since the excavation the previous morning were thus able to summon family and friends for the historic occasion. But even this shortened delay proved Ambrose's fears justified. The 'multitude of Arians inside the palace' began immediately to voice their suspicions, attributing the demonic testimony that had first identified the martyrs to the histrionics of paid accomplices.[180] One attempt to discredit these partisan demons is recorded by Paulinus as having had fatal consequences for the 'victim' (a member of the palace staff), who was accidentally drowned in a bath during an unsuccessful attempt to restore him to his senses.[181]

The criticisms seem nevertheless to have hit home. When Gervasius and Protasius were installed the following day, amid further exorcisms and before an audience drawn from all ranks of Milanese society, Ambrose produced his rebuttal (15–23).[182] Against the charges of fabrication

179. *CTh* 9.17.7 (issued by Theodosius, 26 February 386).

180. Paulin. *V. Amb.* 15.1, with the important information that the demons had confessed themselves tormented by Ambrose as well as by the martyrs.

181. *V. Amb.* 16.1–2, treating the case as homicide; Meslin more plausibly explains it as a failed application of 'le remède de la douche froide': *Les Ariens d'Occident*, 55.

182. Ambrose's notably polemical Hymn 11 was possibly composed overnight for performance at the same service: for its topicality, see Y.-M. Duval in *Ambroise de Milan: Hymnes*, at 487–490.

he appealed to the evidence of the audience's own senses: they could hear for themselves the voices of demons and could see the relief and joy of those freed by the martyrs from demonic possession or physical illness. One particularly spectacular beneficiary of the relics' power was Severus, a former butcher who had been blind for many years and now lived off the church's charity. He had touched the martyrs' bier with his handkerchief; when he then applied it to his eyes, his sight was immediately restored. The case, the ex-advocate maintained, was watertight, with respectable witnesses available to authenticate Severus' credentials (17).[183] But there was no need for a formal hearing. The Arian sceptics had merely shown themselves as bad as—indeed, worse than—the Jews who had insisted upon examining the background of the blind man cured by Jesus (18).

The *invidia* of Ambrose's opponents, a stiff-necked and jealous minority, is the central theme of his sermon. If this ill-feeling was directed against himself, he insisted, it was misplaced: he was only the martyrs' impresario and neither took any credit for nor sought to derive any personal benefit from their works (19). But if they resented Gervasius and Protasius, they only exposed their own true heretical nature. The martyrs had made their doctrinal position abundantly clear: the demons routed by them had confirmed that salvation depended upon belief in the full divinity of all three persons of the Trinity, particularly the Holy Spirit (20–21). Here was dramatic 'proof' that the teachings of Nicaea represented the authentic tradition of the church of the persecutions; in their *invidia* against the martyrs the Arians admitted that their own beliefs were innovations. Ambrose's claim to represent an overwhelming majority against a jealous clique was borne out by the crowds that the event had drawn; neutrals or even sceptics from the political classes of Milan cannot but have been impressed by the force of their numbers.[184]

---

183. These witnesses were those 'quorum ante sustentabatur obsequiis', the pious (and at least modestly well-off) donors from whose charity he had subsisted. Severus was clearly a spectacular advertisement for Ambrose's case: he dominates Augustine's account of the *inventio* (*Conf.* 9.7.16; cf. Paulin. *V. Amb.* 14.2) and afterwards remained in the Basilica Ambrosiana to provide living proof of the martyrs' powers (Paulin. *V. Amb.* 14.2: 'nunc usque').

184. We might perhaps imagine Augustine at the scene: he seems not to have witnessed the *inventio* itself or seen the skeletons during the *translatio* (he claims the bodies as 'incorrupta' at *Conf.* 9.7.16), but later described himself as a 'testis' of the event (Aug. *Sermo* 286.5.4). Participation in this final installation would explain the apparent discrepancy, although Courcelle (*Recherches*, 150) denies it any particular significance; O'Donnell (*Augustine: Confessions*, 3:112), judiciously reserves judgement.

Nor, once drawn onto the bishop's own territory by the ceremony, could they easily ignore his logic. Ambrose's theme of unity was in any case well chosen to appeal to those anxious to restore concord to Milan. The occasion was as much a timely exhibition of the bishop's commitment to this cause as a triumphant display of his faction's strength.[185] Therein lies the explanation for its success in 'crushing the frenzy of persecution'.

Ambrose's letter ends abruptly with the close of his sermon, and leaves us ignorant of how his victory was confirmed. Some sort of public gesture probably marked the conclusion of the persecution.[186] A formal legislative measure is unlikely: the January law, whose promised tolerance for the homoeans had been incidental to the main issue throughout, did not need repeal. But perhaps Valentinian was persuaded to take Ambrose's hint and came to pay his respects to the new martyrs. A gesture of goodwill would have spared him the need to make an explicit surrender to the bishop or to join his congregation.

Justina and her friends—and Valentinian himself—remained unpersuaded.[187] Their case, unheard at the time, merits brief consideration, not least because of its mishandling by rationalist advocates who have approved the queen's 'derision' at 'the theatrical representations which were exhibited by the contrivance, and at the expense, of the bishop'.[188] In these terms, the charge fails to convince. It requires an Ambrose both improbably villainous and anachronistically enlightened, for the metaphor upon which it depends is flawed. The fourth-century cult of the martyrs was not a pantomime staged for the vulgar but a channeling of powerful energies too intractable for the bishop to have controlled at will, and too pervasive for him to have thought to try.[189] Moreover, this

185. Historians tend to focus exclusively upon the latter: 'Ambrose, now sure of his position, turned triumphantly to the offensive' (Matthews, *Western Aristocracies*, 190).

186. Several sources note a definite conclusion to the episode: Aug. *Conf.* 9.7.16 (quoted at the end of the last paragraph); Paulin. *V. Amb.* 15.1; Paul. Nol. *Carm.* 19.328.

187. Augustine states explicitly that her mind was 'ad credendi sanitatem non applicatus' (*Conf.* 9.7.16); Theodoret (*HE* 5.15) presents Valentinian as still 'Arian' in 387.

188. Edward Gibbon, *The Decline and Fall of the Roman Empire*, ed. J. B. Bury (1909), 3:169; cf. Seeck, *Geschichte des Untergangs der antiken Welt* (1913), 5:207 (on Ambrose's 'Mirakelmaschine'); Meslin, *Les Ariens d'Occident*, 53–55.

189. For a beautiful evocation, see Peter Brown, *The Cult of the Saints* (1981), 1–49; 37 for the electrical analogy.

approach invariably calls forth a defence in terms of Ambrose's character.[190] Both sides thus trivialize and evade the central issue, for if the bishop had not crept out beforehand to make any 'secret preparations', neither was he the passive instrument of external forces. Ambrose took certain initiatives which raised important questions; and Justina joins Palladius and Auxentius on the list of those who wanted, but failed, to interrogate the bishop on points of detail.

The idea of looking underground for martyrs, as so often with the bishop's innovations, was at the time gaining currency elsewhere.[191] His timing was as masterly as when he had introduced his hymns; but the key question concerns his choice of place. Digging in a graveyard, he was likely to find something, eventually; and the site he chose was both oddly unsuitable for his ostensible purpose and singularly likely to yield results. Sixty years earlier, it had had a cult superimposed upon it: Nabor and Felix were imports, introduced from Lodi by Ambrose's predecessor Maternus.[192] Acquired precisely in order to supply Milan's deficiency of sanctified remains, they would hardly have been used to suppress an existing cult; but their *memoria* may well have been built in a spot with particular associations for the city's Christian community. Gervasius and Protasius are best explained, perhaps, as innocent casualties of Maternus' development. Ambrose might have been informed of a seam of burials beneath the church of Nabor and Felix (there were perhaps clerics with more exact memories than the old men and their vague recollections of *tituli*) or have made the inference for himself, but his instincts probably played a greater part than any calculation. Ambrose's boldest strokes were fortified, he claimed, by divine inspiration, and his claims were vindicated to others and to himself by his success.[193]

These considerations allow us to take due measure of Ambrose's achievement. The outstanding feature of the episode is his supremely confident management of events. Ambrose had launched upon a course

190. A. M. H. Jones, *Later Roman Empire* (1964), 959 ('it is difficult to attribute a deliberate hoax . . . to a man of Ambrose's character'); H. Delehaye, *Les origines du culte des martyres*, 2d ed. (1933), 93 (protesting 'la droiture et l'élévation du caractère de S. Ambroise'). The question continues to distract: J. Fontaine criticized Brown's brilliant image of Ambrose the 'impresario' for implying 'une vaste mis en scène' (*AB* 100 [1982], 17–41).

191. Besides the eastern precedents, there had been many 'discoveries' at Rome during Damasus' recent overhaul of the catacombs: *Lib. Pont.* 39; Dam. *Epig.* 27, 49, 80, Cf. Pietri, *Roma Christiana*, 529–546.

192. J.-C. Picard, *Le souvenir des évêques* (1988), 38–41. The tradition is reflected in an Ambrosian hymn: see the discussion by G. Nauroy in *Ambroise de Milan: Hymnes*, 445–453.

193. For two striking examples, see *Epp. extra coll.* 1 [41].28; 11 [51].14.

of action during which he could never hope to predict exactly what would happen next; in doing so he had drawn to himself the attention of the whole city, from the feverish excitement of the spiritually and physically sick to the intent scrutiny of his enemies, while the uncommitted looked on with dispassionate curiosity. But he rode the storm he had created with majestic aplomb, providing a commentary for all the extraordinary events that occurred and making the necessary adjustments when the situation seemed to be slipping from his grasp. Words like 'calculation' and 'manipulation' are much too cold: for all the statuesque calm of his demeanour, Ambrose was holding a wolf by the ears. If he can be suspected of having made his own luck, he had still had to brave many imponderables. The bishop had gambled, and won.

With victory came also the opportunity for vengeance. Valentinian and Justina were powerless to protect their most vehement partisans. The loyal eunuch Calligonus was executed upon evidence brought by a courtesan;[194] the outspoken courtier Euthymius was bundled into exile in the very carriage he had himself planned to use for the abduction of the bishop, whose solicitude and gift of provisions can have given him little comfort.[195] Public declarations of concord, although they cannot have concealed these symptoms of instability, were in the circumstances essential to restore the regime's credit. Having done so much to upset the original equilibrium at Milan, Ambrose had to play his part in advertising the renewal of harmony. His second mission to Trier, in the second half of 386, can be seen as an attempt to do precisely this.[196] He presented Maximus with a rescript from Valentinian, which perhaps replied to the usurper's earlier 'advice' against religious persecution, and with the request that Gratian's body be released at last for burial in Milan. But above all, the embassy marked a definitive and highly symbolic end to the hostilities between Valentinian and Ambrose: the bishop was reliving the episode that had originally bound him to the emperor's service.

The course of Ambrose's embassy to Maximus nevertheless shows

194. The punishment was mentioned by Ambrose in 388 (*De Ioseph* 34) and by Augustine (*Contra Iulianum Pelagianum* 6.14.41). It therefore probably occurred before the latter's departure from Milan in early summer 387.

195. Paulin. *V. Amb.* 12.3–4. If Paulinus is correct in dating the banishment to exactly one year after the planned kidnapping, it belongs in May–June 387 (cf. *Sermo contra Aux.* 15, for the 'carrum').

196. The date depends upon a synchronization with the execution of Priscillian: some scholars have put it as early as 384. See, in favour of 386, H. Chadwick, *Priscillian of Avila* (1976), 137; also Palanque, *Saint Ambroise*, 168–175; 516–518.

the political damage wreaked by the conflict and by the exposure of the contradictions riddling Valentinian's regime. To avoid awkward questions about his ruler's ecclesiastical policies (and his own views upon them), Ambrose sought a private interview with Maximus; but the usurper, who had no reason to spare him any embarrassment, compelled him to appear in the consistory.[197] With no room for manoeuvre, Ambrose embarked upon a remarkable exchange of recriminations (later repeated to Valentinian with a warning, well founded, that Maximus was preparing for war) which nicely suggests the diplomatic bankruptcy of the Milanese government: truculence was now the only public stance which its representatives could convincingly adopt. If Ambrose's contributions to the slanging-match showed characteristic vigour, they did nothing to promote the normalization of relations with the court at Trier upon which Valentinian's long-term security depended.

Valentinian's government never recovered from the shock dealt it by the clash with Ambrose. The emperor assumed the consulate for 387, marking the occasion with lavish benefactions and generous pardons; the regime's supporters gathered to lend their weight to the festivities.[198] But the demonstration of strength was unconvincing. The presence at Milan during this same period of 386/7 of Timasius, one of Theodosius' leading generals, was perhaps intended to shore up the government; but the acknowledged influence of this newcomer only confirms the established order's weakness.[199] Another index of waning confidence in the Milanese court was a series of defections among men previously lured there by hopes of wealth and preferment. The city's public rhetor resigned abruptly at the end of the autumn vacation of 386, giving his employers little time to find another 'vendor of words' for the forthcoming term. His friend Alypius had meanwhile withdrawn his own legal expertise from the market; another African, the *agens in rebus* Evodius, joined them when they left Milan altogether the following spring.[200] Each had his own reason for leaving, but cumulatively such cases perhaps contributed to an impression of a sinking ship being quietly abandoned.

197. Ambrose gives his report of this embassy in *Ep.* 30 [24]; the discussion concerned principally the conduct of his first mission, in 383.

198. Symm. *Epp.* 3.52 (to Eutropius); 3.63 (to Richomer, reporting his summons 'cum multis amplissimae curiae proceribus').

199. Symm. *Epp.* 3.72–73, entrusting to Timasius' care two cases which he also commended to the *PPO* Eusignius (*Epp.* 4.73, 67). Unlike the previous visitors Neoterius and Promotus, Timasius appears to have held no office at Milan.

200. Aug. *Conf.* 9.5.13 (Augustine's resignation); 9.6.14 (Alypius: at 8.6.13 he had still been 'expectans quibus iterum consilia venderet'); 9.8.17 (Evodius).

In 387 a further deterioration of the situation on the Danube prompted Valentinian to seek 'a more secure peace' with Maximus and to request reinforcements from him.[201] One cannot but wonder, in this connexion, whether the morale and discipline of Valentinian's army ever recovered from the near-mutiny of Easter 386. The message was not lost upon Maximus. He effected an apparently bloodless invasion of Italy during the summer, Valentinian and his entourage taking flight to Thessalonica.[202]

201. Zosimus 4.42.3–5.
202. Zosimus 4.42.6–7; cf. Soc. *HE* 5.11.11–12, for the presence of Probus among those who escaped with Valentinian.

CHAPTER FIVE

AMBROSE'S PEOPLE, I: MASTER OF CEREMONIES

CONSTRUCTING A COMMUNITY

It was appropriate that Augustine, Alypius and Evodius all left the service of the state for baptism in Ambrose's church. The events of 386 had proved the church a stronger fortress than the palace, and the times remained uncertain. But to infer from these defections a polarization in Milan between church and state would be mistaken. The collisions of 385/6 had not involved two clearly defined organizations but rival groups each seeking to assert its claim to a distinct identity. The present chapter will explore further the interdependence that bound Ambrose's church to the government at Milan, despite the persuasive definitions with which the rhetoric of the basilica conflict abounds. The distinctively Christian character of public life at Milan made for a thoroughgoing overlap between religion and politics: many faces from the consistory must have appeared each Sunday in the bishop's basilica.

Nor, as has often been assumed, was the essence of the conflict with Valentinian a deep-rooted antagonism between the local population and a 'foreign' court. In imperial Milan, such distinctions hardly applied. The three converts mentioned above were all Africans, from the same obscure *municipium* of Thagaste; the bishop's only identifiable follower during the anxious vigil of the siege was Augustine's mother, Monica. A robust widow of curial stock and independent means, already in her mid-fifties when she arrived at the capital, Monica retained all the characteristics of her small-town Christian upbringing during her few years in Italy.[1] Nor was Benivolus, the most senior of Ambrose's known supporters against Justina, a citizen of Milan. His home was Brescia, where he reappears the following decade in affluent and pious retirement, and where he had learnt his Christianity from the notably uncompromising Filastrius.[2] Brescia is only seventy miles from Milan, but the narrow horizons imposed by the discomforts of travel and local particularism meant that it was exposed only intermittently to the capital's direct influence.[3] Ambrose enjoyed a remarkable success in naturalizing these foreigners.

The Milanese congregation included men like Ponticianus, another *agens in rebus* of African extraction who (unlike his colleague and compatriot Evodius) had apparently reconciled baptism with a successful court career.[4] Other pious careerists settled at Milan after retirement. The former *tribunus et notarius* Nicentius owned an estate at Altinum near Aquileia but evidently preferred to remain with his comrades from the court and his friend the bishop; despite the pain of his gout, he continued to attend church.[5] Manlius Theodorus, too, retired from politics towards the end of Gratian's reign to pursue his philosophical interests in a well-appointed villa in the Milanese suburbs. He was perhaps a native of the city; but his connexions were with the court, and his panegyrist failed to exploit any local roots when he assumed the consulate in Milan in 399.[6] With him in the capital was his sister Daedalia, a consecrated virgin whose conspicuous burial-place adjacent to the twin graves of Victor and Satyrus suggests a similar prominence in life.[7]

The high profile of such people in Ambrose's church reflects an im-

1. There is a splendid portrait of Monica in Peter Brown, *Augustine of Hippo* (1967), 28–34.

2. See Gaudentius *Praefatio ad Benivolum* 2 (written after c. 395) for Benivolus' leadership of the city's *honorati* and *dominica plebs;* 4 for Filastrius.

3. The *Itinerarium Burdigalense* shows five stages between the two cities; a visit by the bishop of one to the other was an event to be remembered (below, p. 276).

4. Ponticianus' baptism is implied by *Conf.* 8.6.14: 'fidelis'. Augustine's account of his devotions—'saepe prosternebatur in ecclesia crebris et diuturnis orationibus'—is perhaps based on autopsy at the cathedral of Milan.

5. Amb. *Ep.* 56 [5].8; Paulin. *V. Amb.* 44.

6. Claudian's reference (*Pan. Mallio Theodoro* 124–125) to Theodorus' 'penates' in 'Ligurum moenibus' is to a long-established home, but not necessarily to his birthplace.

7. For the location of Daedalia's tomb, see *ILCV* 1700; for her epitaph, composed by Theodorus, see P. Courcelle, 'Quelques symboles funéraires du néoplatonisme latin', *REA* 46 (1944), 65–73.

portant aspect of Milanese society. The *curiales*, who in other capitals (particularly Antioch in Syria, where they had centuries of civic tradition to sustain them) fought a stiff rearguard action in defence of their political identity and economic interests against the periodic irruptions of the court,[8] remain almost invisible in Ambrose's Milan. The likelihood that the *corpus negotiatorum*, which paid so heavily for its loyalty to the bishop at Easter 386, overlapped significantly with the *curia* only confirms the point. Although the functions of the *corpus* remain obscure, they were probably related to the supply problems created by the court's presence in the city.[9] In other words, the identity of the Milanese *curia* was subsumed beneath its imperial function. This contrasts not only with Antioch but also with Constantinople, whose senatorial class developed within two generations a collective identity and a network of political, economic and ecclesiastical interests.[10] In Milan, Ambrose had no Olympias to sustain him with her wealth and influence; he was by the same token spared the encouragement that a Castricia or Marsa could give to an already hostile empress.

Only one *civis* of Milan can be identified with certainty among Ambrose's congregation: the *grammaticus* Verecundus, who lent Augustine his rural estate at Cassiciacum.[11] Although his wife had been baptized, Verecundus could not bring himself to make the same decisive commitment, apparently because of the tenacious grip of his sexual needs.[12] But in telling us this, Augustine betrays the influence that he himself exerted. Sexual renunciation was never a central, or indeed an explicit, part of Ambrose's call to baptism.[13] It was a preoccupation that Augus-

---

8. For the complex vicissitudes of the Antiochene *curia* in the fourth century, see especially J. H. W. G. Liebeschuetz, *Antioch* (1972). Note, at 126–132, the paradoxical contrast between its vigour in confronting Gallus and Julian and the closer supervision imposed upon it by officials in the 380s, when there was no imperial presence in the city.

9. See, above all, L. Ruggini, *Economia e società nell' "Italia Annonaria"* (1961), 106ff. M. Mirabella Roberti, *Milano Romana* (1984), 75–77, describes the city's vast *horrea*, with two parallel magazines, each 23 × 68 metres (i.e., each slightly larger than the Basilica Ambrosiana). If this complex, as seems plausible, is connected with the activities of the *corpus*, it offers a striking impression of the scale upon which the organization operated.

10. G. Dagron, *Naissance d'une capitale* (1974), 147–190; 'La formation d'une classe senatoriale'.

11. Aug. *Conf.* 8.6.13 ('Mediolanensi . . . civi').

12. Aug. *Conf.* 9.3.5.

13. Peter Brown, *The Body and Society* (1988), 350–351, sees Verecundus' attitude as an independent response to the tone of Ambrose's preaching, but the

tine had brought with him to Milan and that conditioned his understanding of the bishop's preaching. He transmitted this concern to his
friend Verecundus, persuading him to reject any Christian initiation that
did not involve the most austere self-denial. Strangers thus acted as Ambrose's interlocutors with the citizens of Milan—a remarkable illustration of local effacement before, and deference towards, the glittering
talents of the court.[14]

Geography helped place Milan more firmly in the shadow of the
court than other capital cities of the late empire. Each of them was a
palimpsest, with the uniform structures of imperial pomp and government apparatus overlaying a municipal organization with its own local
history and character. The complex idiosyncrasies of Antioch and Constantinople have already been briefly noted; other places were able by
their very remoteness to absorb and naturalize their visitors. At Trier,
for example, the tombstone of a Syrian who had been co-opted into the
curia proclaims his allegiance to his adopted home as a 'Belgic Rome'.[15]
But Milan, crucially, was too close to the original Rome to be anything
but a pole of comparison with it.[16] The city had its own history and a
long-standing prosperity founded upon its strategic location and rich
hinterland.[17] As a capital, however, it was the conduit through which
one set of outsiders, the senatorial aristocracy of Rome, brought its influence to bear upon another, the imperial court; various 'Milanese' interests were caught up in and subsumed by this dominant relationship.
One effect was to make Milan, from an emperor's point of view, an unusually governable capital, with none of the social and cultural com-

---

wife was apparently able to reconcile baptism with conjugal relations. The question of continence is significantly absent from Ambrose's specifically baptismal
works, *De sacramentis* and *De mysteriis*; the fragments from his lost *De sacramento
regenerationis vel de philosophia*, adduced by J. J. O'Donnell (*Augustine: Confessions*
[1992], xxxviii–xxxix, nn58–59), are known only in selective quotations by Augustine and are therefore inconclusive.

14. Verecundus also depended upon his African friends professionally: the
overqualified Nebridius agreed to act as his assistant when 'he was greatly in
need' (*Conf.* 9.6.13).

15. Cited by E. Wightman, *Roman Trier and the Treviri* (1970), 62; her discussion of the character of fourth-century Trier, at 62–67, suggests many illuminating parallels and contrasts with Milan.

16. Thus Ausonius *Ordo nob. urb.* 7.11: a hymn to Milan is concluded with
praise for the city's success at holding its own in the shadow of Rome: 'nec iuncta
premit vicinia Romae'.

17. P. Garnsey, 'Economy and Society of Mediolanum under the Principate', *PBSR* 44 (1976), 13–27.

plexities that so baffled Julian at Antioch. It had provided a pliable stage for Maximian, Constantine, Constans, Constantius II, Valentinian I and Gratian to act out their imperial roles; it would later extend the same welcome it had given the usurper Magnentius to Maximus and Eugenius. This record of docility (and the civic passivity which must in large part explain it) should be taken into account when assessing the shock that the resistance to Valentinian II must have generated, and in measuring Ambrose's achievement in bringing this resistance to a successful conclusion.

Ambrose's church effectively created an identity for Christian Milan, bringing together the city's diverse social groups. Members of the court, and those brought to Milan in its train, were the most dynamic element in this compound, and Ambrose's decisive achievement was to channel their aggressive piety into official ecclesiastical institutions. Various advantages accrued: the attendance of the mighty at the cathedral compelled Augustine's initially reluctant attention, while recruits like Daedalia, 'distinguished of birth and richly endowed in worldly goods', boosted the prestige of Ambrose's corps of consecrated virgins.[18]

Daedalia's tombstone also proclaims her the 'mother of the needy'. The pensioners of the church—'the blind and the lame, the feeble and the elderly'[19]—were another important segment of Christian Milan and were Ambrose's most visible and obdurate supporters during his confrontation with Valentinian. He mentions, and does not deny, the charge that their devotion had been nurtured by financial assistance. The methods by which charity was managed at Milan might add a particular edge to the accusation. The wealthy elite gave their alms to the destitute and crippled who haunted the basilicas not as individuals (as at Rome)[20] but through the mediation of the church. Daedalia exercised her 'motherhood of the poor' as a consecrated virgin under the bishop's discipline, and even Monica's modest offerings to the poor were given at mass.[21] Ambrose's control over the process of almsgiving allowed him

18. The point would need modification if the family was native to Milan (cf. n. 6); but the wealth that distinguished Daedalia is likely to have been accumulated through her brother's career under Gratian. 'Humble' origins are plausibly surmised for the family at *PLRE* 1, pp. 901–902.

19. *Sermo contra Aux.* 33.

20. For Pammachius' charitable exhibitionism at Saint Peter's, see Jerome *Ep.* 48.4; cf. *Ep.* 22.32 for a matron's almsgiving at the same site.

21. *Conf.* 6.2.2: Monica was persuaded 'ut et quod posset daret egentibus et sic communicatio dominici corporis illic celebraretur', her alms thus being linked to the Eucharist.

boldly to identify the particular benefactors of his miraculously cured parishioner Severus, the men 'by whose services he had previously been supported'.[22] Here again, the bishop's confident supervision lends an appearance of coherence to the congregation.

But the cohesion of Ambrose's church is not reducible to material terms or individual social relationships. The church was an idea, whose power rested ultimately in the force with which it was impressed upon people's minds. And it was here especially that the Christians of Milan commanded the services of a virtuoso. One of the most potent spells the bishop wove around his community was the congregational singing of psalms and hymns, which endured long after the emergency of 386 had ended to become a trademark of Milanese Christianity.[23] Its principal value was to unify the congregation: singing helped concentrate their attention and drown out background noise (an interesting sidelight on conditions during the liturgy); in more elevated terms, it produced a *symphonia* from the *plebis concordia*—an 'uproar in unison' of young and old, rich and poor.[24] This symphony reached across the barriers of class, generating a sense of solidarity which, the bishop believed, quelled anti-social habits and distracted men from their propensity to avarice.[25] By joining their voices in song, the people of God could transcend the dizzy social chasms which in real life separated them; the church's choir could accommodate even the emperor, without feeling the 'haughtiness of his power'.[26]

In a sense, Ambrose's opponents were right: this effect was a trick, an illusion. The solidarity conjured up through song operated only within the walls of the church and neither changed the actual structures of society nor healed its divisions. But even this fleeting appearance of community offered comfort to the many uprooted Christians of Milan, whether nomadic careerists who had left their homes to follow the court or victims of the manifold injustices of the age.[27] In the former category belongs Augustine, who has left striking testimony to the power of the

22. *Ep.* 77 [22].17.

23. References are usefully collected in J. McKinnon, *Music in Early Christian Literature* (1987), 125–134; for an appreciation of Ambrose's role as 'théoricien et maître de la poésie liturgique', see J. Fontaine, *Naissance de la poésie dans l'occident chrétien* (1981), 127–141.

24. Attention: *Exp. Ps. 118* 7.25; noise: *Explan. Ps. 1* 9; unity: *Hex.* 3.23, *Exp. Evang. sec. Luc.* 7.237–238.

25. *Exp. Ps. 118* 7.29; cf. *Explan. Ps. 1* 9.

26. *Explan. Ps. 1* 9: 'sine potestatis supercilio'.

27. The court's presence was of course itself the cause of considerable local disruption: see the sensitive discussion by Ruggini, *Economia e società*, 84–111.

spell cast by the choirs of Milan. At his baptism, he later confessed, he was 'keenly moved by the sweet singing of Your church. Those voices flowed into my ears, truth seeped into my heart, and feelings of devotion welled up; tears ran down, and it was well with me that they did' (*Conf.* 9.16.14). It was no small achievement to overwhelm in this way the tough-minded rhetor, whose professional expertise (and past experience with the Manichees) heightened an innate alertness to the tricks by which the emotions could be manipulated. In retrospect, even when his own experience as presbyter and bishop had taught him how easily delight in the melody could distract people from the contents of hymns or psalms, Augustine continued to justify the practice by reference to the tears 'which I shed at the singing of the church in the first beginnings of the recovery of my faith'. He gave his approval hesitantly, for it flew in the face of his austere instincts, and he left open the possibility of retraction.[28] Perhaps the spell wore off and, in the more authentically face-to-face society of Hippo, Augustine began to forget the importance of such illusions; but Ambrose's magic must have been potent indeed, thus to have muddied the thoughts of the most lucid mind of the age.

BEYOND THE WALLS

No less remarkable, and no less artificial, than the community Ambrose created inside his cathedral was the new Christian Milan he built outside it. His most enduring contribution to Milan was a series of towering basilicas standing outside the city walls, among the graves of the Christian dead. These areas, crowded and confused after centuries of piecemeal, essentially private development, were traditionally the setting for a style of worship whose intimacy and volatility discouraged participation (and precluded domination) by the ecclesiastical establishment.[29] Ambrose's interventions therefore merit close attention.

The building that the bishop designed for his own burial, the Basilica Ambrosiana, was set among the most celebrated of Milan's Christian graves, those of the city's small clutch of martyrs and the eminent faithful who had succeeded in obtaining nearby plots. Ambrose's church, however, was much more than a contribution to the existing pattern. Dwarfing the surrounding monuments, it provided a new focus for the

28. *Conf.* 10.33.49.
29. The character of the cemetery areas is sketched by Peter Brown, *The Cult of the Saints* (1981), 31–35.

untidy sprawl of the Hortus Philippi. There were casualties. Saint Victor's grave was first absorbed into the bishop's project, then overshadowed by those of Ambrose's 'own' martyrs; their discovery also occasioned the plunder of the shrine of Nabor and Felix, the most distinguished of Milan's saints. The bishop's initiatives in effect realigned the religious topography of the whole area. No less overbearing in scale are two basilicas whose fourth-century shells survived, intact but unnoticed, until they were revealed by repairs and restoration after World War II: San Nazaro (Ambrose's Basilica Apostolorum or Basilica in Romana) to the southeast of the city and San Simpliciano to the north.[30] What little is known of their physical setting does not suggest that either was an organic growth. Ambrose's basilicas did not emerge from Christian Milan but were imposed upon it to reshape the city in an image devised by the bishop.

Three great churches surrounded Milan.[31] The sheer scale of Ambrose's work has prompted suggestions of a grand design. But the thesis of a pastoral programme to serve the capital's expanding suburbs fails to appreciate the functional difference between the central cathedral, the place for regular worship, and these cemetery basilicas.[32] The idea of a deliberate duplication of the vast churches that encircled Rome, while placing due emphasis upon their function as *martyria*, can have no more than incidental relevance given the vastly different patterns of development between the two places.[33] To attribute so unitary a conception to a programme that developed over two decades is neither realistic nor just to the flexibility Ambrose showed in adapting his buildings to suit changed circumstances. The Basilica Ambrosiana, for example, was

30. A useful survey of these discoveries is M. Mirabella Roberti, 'Contributi della ricerca archeologica all'architettura ambrosiana milanese', in *Ambrosius Episcopus*, ed. G. Lazzati (1976), 1:335–362.

31. The case for identifying the lost medieval church of San Dionigi as another Ambrosian basilica, marking the fourth point of the compass in the east, is presented by E. Cattaneo, 'San Dionigi: Basilica paleocristiana?', *Arch. Amb.* 27 (1974), 68–84. The identification remains highly speculative.

32. E. Villa, 'Come risolse Sant'Ambrogio il problema delle chiese alla periferia di Milano', *Ambrosius* 32 (1956), 22–45.

33. R. Krautheimer, *Three Christian Capitals* (1983), 79; although differing on this and several other points of detail, this section is deeply indebted to Krautheimer's chapter on Milan (69–92). Also valuable is E. A. Arslan, 'Urbanistica di Milano Romana', *ANRW* II 12.1 (1982), 179–210, whose interpretation of Ambrose's programme as an attempt to heal the architectural 'bipolarity' caused by the court's presence in the city is nevertheless too abstract to explain the bishop's actual constructions.

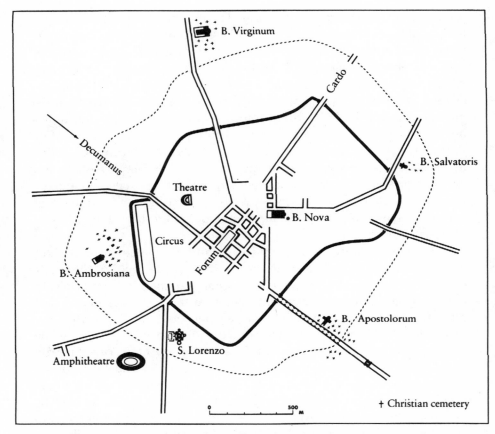

5. Milan and its churches, c. 400. Reproduced by kind permission of Professor R. Krautheimer. *Note:* There is no reliable evidence that S. Dionigi, the Basilica Salvatoris, was of fourth-century date.

probably his first initiative, taken under political pressure and financial strain, and with the objective of establishing him physically within Milan's Christian heritage.[34] The church was no doubt designed as a *coemeterium*, to adorn Victor's adjacent grave, with Ambrose envisaging eventual burial with Satyrus in the place of honour beside the martyr. In 386 the bishop's announcement of his plans for interment beneath the basilica's main altar—a dramatic decision that reflects the intensity of the struggle with Valentinian—suddenly shifted the focus of the site. But this personality cult was exclusively for partisan consumption. With the installation of Milan's new *patroni* Gervasius and Protasius under the altar, the church was transformed into a point of reference for the whole city.

The harmony symbolized by Gervasius and Protasius had a particular appeal to the court. Ambrose's drastic realignment of his city's physical and spiritual structures might be related more generally to the presence in Milan of so many powerful transients, none of them nurtured in local traditions. A direct connexion can be inferred in the case of a church the bishop completed before the Basilica Ambrosiana, although it was probably started rather later, in the early 380s: the Basilica Apostolorum.[35] The church shares the Ambrosiana's characteristic features: the tall, dignified profile and the herringbone brickwork interspersed for the sake of economy with wide mortar beds. But the design is far more exciting, transforming the single-nave basilica into a cross by the addition of two lateral arms at its midpoint.[36] No western precedents exist for this plan, which seems to belong instead to a tradition inspired by Constantine's Apostoleion and revived in the eastern Mediterranean from the late 370s, most notably with the new church of Saint Babylas at Antioch. In his architecture as well as his sermons, it seems, Ambrose was striving to keep his people abreast of current fashions in the more sophisticated east. Also relevant, perhaps, was the rivalry between Gratian and Theodosius, which was central to the politics of the early 380s and which must have seemed likely, given the youthfulness of both emperors, to set the tone for the rest of the century. Theodosius had the advantage of possessing the magnificent stage of Constantinople, built to show off the imperial power to best advantage. Gratian, notwithstand-

34. For the context, cf. p. 55 above.

35. On this church, see especially E. Villa, 'La basilica ambrosiana degli Apostoli', in *Quaderni di Ambrosius*, supplement to *Ambrosius* 39 (1963), 15–74.

36. S. Lewis, 'The Latin Iconography of the Single-Naved Cruciform Basilica Apostolorum in Milan', *Art Bulletin* 51 (1969), 205–219; 'Function and Symbolic Form in the Basilica Apostolorum at Milan', *JSAH* 28 (1969), 83–98.

ing all the 'wonderful things' available at Milan, could not easily compete.[37] Ambrose's church should perhaps be regarded as a contribution
to the cause: Milan's new Apostoleion can be seen as not merely an imitation of its Constantinopolitan model but also a challenge to it.

The basilica was dedicated at some point before June 386, with a
memorable service at which the installation of relics seems to have made
a particular impression.[38] The identity of these saints has naturally excited curiosity. An entry in the *Martyrologium Hieronymianum* has supplied, for many modern scholars, an answer to the question and an exact
date for the dedication. A celebration is recorded on 9 May to mark the
ingressus into the Basilica Apostolorum of relics of saints John, Andrew
and Thomas.[39] The eastern provenance of these martyrs, and particularly the imperial associations of Andrew, resident since 357 in the
Apostoleion, has suggested that they were gifts from Theodosius. But
perhaps the evidence of the *Martyrologium* has been seized upon too
eagerly. The May entry refers only to an *ingressus in basilicam*, without
associating it (as is the case in an otherwise similar entry concerning
Aquileia)[40] with a *dedicatio*. Moreover, another entry concerning Milan,
for 27 November, commemorates John and Andrew, together with Luke
(Andrew's companion in the Apostoleion) and the Chalcedonian martyr
Euphemia.[41] This occasion has plausibly been envisaged as the original
arrival of the relics at Milan; but it seems somewhat odd that a collection
of relics sent to inaugurate Ambrose's new basilica should have entered
the city five months earlier, with sufficient pomp to earn the occasion a
place in the Milanese church's liturgical calendar. There is no reason,
however, to suppose that deposition in Ambrose's basilica, far less the
place of honour at its dedication, was the specific intention behind the
dispatch of the relics. Other occasions for their arrival present themselves. Twice in the decade after the basilica's construction, an eastern

37. The 'mira omnia' catalogued by Gratian's tutor Ausonius at *Ord. nob.
urb.* 7 included those characteristic vehicles of imperial self-presentation, the
'populique voluptas/circus et inclusi moles cuneata theatri' (4–5).

38. A secure *terminus ante quem* is given by the people's demand (probably
on 16 June 386) that Ambrose dedicate his new basilica 'sicut in Romana': *Ep.* 75
[22].1. The same passage is evidence of the impact of this earlier dedication.

39. *AASS* Nov. 2.2, p. 241: 'Mediolani de ingressu reliquiarum apostolorum
Iohannis, Andreae et Thomae in basilicam ad portam Romanam'.

40. For 3 September (*AASS* Nov. 2.2, p. 485): 'in Aquileia dedicatio basilicae et ingressio reliquiarum sanctorum Andreae Apostoli, Lucae, Iohannis,
Eufemiae'.

41. *AASS* Nov. 2.2, p. 623. Note that these are the same saints honoured at
Aquileia on 3 September: see previous note.

court marched to northern Italy: the relics may well have arrived in their train, expressions of Theodosius' piety and the divine support for his cause. The time that elapsed between their arrival in Milan and the eventual installation of John and Andrew (with the addition of Thomas, who presumably arrived separately) in Ambrose's church suggests that the gift was an act of choice by these powerful visitors.[42]

The medieval tradition of the Milanese church provides an alternative identification for the original relics which seems particularly appropriate for a 'basilica in Romana': the Roman apostles Peter and Paul.[43] This version, although not traceable to any ancient source, is corroborated by archaeological evidence. A decorated silver reliquary casket was unearthed from under the basilica's altar by Charles Borromeo in 1578, the antiquity of which has been established by the decipherment of some graffiti written in a late Roman cursive hand.[44] On the lid is represented Christ, flanked by two figures whose iconographical details make their identification as Peter and Paul irresistible. When the casket was opened, moreover, it was discovered to contain (to the likely disappointment of Borromeo and his entourage) mere pieces of fabric: the relics seem therefore to have been cloth strips, an early example of the *brandea* that would become the characteristic Roman form.[45] The gift of Peter and

42. An *ingressio* on 27 November suits either of Theodosius' campaigns, in 388 and 394, although the latter is excluded if the Milanese relics belong with the batch deposited in Aquileia in September; the May *depositio* was not necessarily in the year immediately after the *ingressio*. Paulinus relates the *depositio* of Nazarius at the basilica (28 July 395: below, p. 363) to a recent installation of apostolic relics: 'ubi pridie sanctorum apostolorum reliquiae summa omnium devotione depositae fuerant' (*V. Amb.* 33.3: this reading is to be preferred to the emendation 'pridem'). Paulinus, whose comment suggests autopsy, is not attested at Milan before 394.

43. For reflections of this tradition in the nomenclature of the basilica, see J.-C. Picard, *Le souvenir des évêques* (1988), 52n111; further arguments are advanced by Y.-M. Duval, 'Aquilée et la Palestine entre 370 et 430', *AAAd* 12 (1977), at 305–309. It is not necessary to accept the fully developed (and ideologically loaded) version of the medieval Milanese historian Landulfus Senior, who has the 'Roman' Simplicianus acting as intermediary.

44. P. L. Zovatto, 'L'urnetta argentea di S. Ambrogio nell'ambito della rinascenza teodosiana', *Critica d'Arte* 13–14 (1956), 2–14. The graffito is discussed by E. Villa, 'Un autografo di Sant'Ambrogio', *Ambrosius* 30 (1954), 65–68.

45. A. Palestra, 'La prima visita pastorale della basilica di S. Nazaro compiuta da S. Carlo Borromeo', in *La basilica degli Apostoli e Nazaro martire nel culto e nell'arte* (1969), 81–95. Although there are no explicit references to *brandea* before the sixth century, relics of the apostles like those brought to Constantinople by Theodosius' courtier Rufinus in 391 were presumably of this type. Cf. E. Villa,

Paul can be associated with the energetic propagation of their cult in Damasan Rome;[46] the two apostles were similarly promoted in Ambrose's Milan, with an official celebration of their feast day as early as 378 and (perhaps) a hymn composed by the bishop.[47] From a Milanese point of view, these martyrs were also particularly suitable for the objective of matching Constantinople's Apostoleion. Through Ambrose's church, the western capital could pull rank on its upstart counterpart on the Bosporus, which boasted only Peter's less famous brother and Paul's obedient disciple.

There was naturally more to Ambrose's new church than its architectural innovations and imported relics. But there is a curious puzzle concerning the practical function of the Basilica Apostolorum. Unlike the Ambrosiana, the church was not designed in relation to a Christian burial site (although there was at least one such site in the vicinity); the tombs immediately surrounding it seem to be largely pagan.[48] The location was determined by other reasons entirely than those of religious topography. Ambrose's church was built directly beside, and at right angles to, the Via Romana, which ran southeastwards from the city. This was the main ceremonial entrance to Milan, with a colonnade running beside it for some six hundred metres beyond the gates and culminating in a triumphal arch.[49] The atrium of Ambrose's church will have abutted this street, its entrance either incorporated into the colonnade or interrupting it. The basilica was therefore linked directly to the capital's ceremonial activities and can be interpreted as an attempt to add a specifically Christian dimension to the *adventus* ceremony. This again suits the circumstances of Gratian's relocation of his court to Italy: Ambrose was constructing a place within Christian Milan for the newly arrived imperial entourage.

A further service provided by the basilica, again for the benefit of the court, was as a burial ground for the elite. Hemicycles built into both

---

'Il culto agli Apostoli', *Ambrosius* 33 (1957), at 257–258; Duval, 'Aquilée et la Palestine', 306n188.

46. C. Pietri, 'Concordia Apostolorum et Renovatio Urbis', *MEFR* 73 (1961), at 297–305; J. M. Huskinson, *Concordia Apostolorum* (1982), 77–91.

47. Feast: *De virgt.* 124; Y.-M. Duval has recently surveyed the evidence for Ambrosian authorship of the hymn 'Apostolorum passio' and argued for 'une prudente réserve' (*Ambroise de Milan: Hymnes,* ed. J. Fontaine [1992], 520).

48. For tomb fragments incorporated into the masonry of the new church, and the lack of any nearby Christian burial dated before 401, see Lewis, 'Function and Symbolic Form', 92. Cf. below, p. 363, for the grave of Celsus.

49. Cf. above, p. 47.

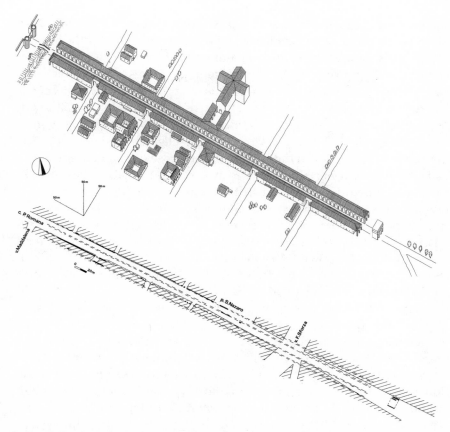

6. Basilica Apostolorum and Via Porticata, reconstruction. Reproduced by kind permission of Silvana Editoriale.

walls of each lateral arm offered a privileged resting place within easy reach of the relics. One beneficiary who nicely illustrates both the geographical range and the cultural attainments of the court was the Egyptian doctor Dioscurus, whose epitaph commemorates in both Greek and Latin his 'voice sweeter than honey'. It is tempting to imagine Dioscurus among Ambrose's choir; a further attractive step is to identify him with Augustine's correspondent of that name.[50] The accommodation of individuals like this, of diverse background and religious temperament, was the key to the cohesion and discipline of Ambrose's church. Manlia Daedalia, whose own burial in another of Ambrose's basilicas has already been mentioned, is significant in this context also, as the owner of a private collection of relics that was deposited in the Basilica Apostolorum; another of Borromeo's discoveries in the church was a small reliquary inscribed with her name.[51] Disruptive consequences could attend the acquisition by powerful individuals of their own collections of relics—'the privatization of the holy', as it has aptly been termed.[52] Nothing is known of the negotiations involved in the 'renationalization' of Daedalia's relics, but their installation in the Basilica Apostolorum suggests another dimension to the building's function as a means by which the court elite was integrated physically within Ambrose's Milan.

The Basilica Apostolorum thus performed several different functions simultaneously. But like the Basilica Ambrosiana (and unlike the Roman cemetery basilicas), it was intended primarily for the celebration of the Eucharist.[53] The design and internal arrangements (the altar seems to have been situated originally at the centre of the church) appear curiously unsuitable for this purpose; with its supplementary roles of *martyrium* and burial hall, and the symbolic weight with which its cruciform design was charged, the building seems overloaded. When used as a Eucharistic hall, the arms and chancel became redundant, a problem that probably helped prompt a major rearrangement of the interior a decade after the dedication. In 395, as we shall see, Ambrose discovered another martyr near the church and translated him to the basilica, installing him (and relocating the main altar) in the conven-

50. E. Farrario, 'Una antica iscrizione scoperta a Milano nella basilica degli Apostoli', *Epigraphica* 10 (1948), 62–68; M. David, 'Appunti per lo studio della pavimentazione tardoantica della basilica dei SS. Apostoli', *Sibrium* 15 (1980–81), 177–194.

51. E. Villa, 'Il culto agli Apostoli', at 263.

52. See Brown, *The Cult of the Saints,* 34, for the expression and the influence conferred upon a woman at Carthage by her relics.

53. This point is well made by Lewis, 'Function and Symbolic Form', 94–96.

tional position in the apse. The times had changed: the governments of Honorius and Arcadius were even more sharply at odds than Gratian and Theodosius, but their hostility found quite different expression. At one level, the installation of Nazarius is therefore a response to the obsolescence of Ambrose's original design. The bishop's dexterity is apparent in the poem inscribed for display within his remodelled church, fragments of which were discovered during the postwar restoration. Ignoring the apostles, Ambrose painstakingly argues the relevance of the cruciform design (now functionally redundant) to his new martyr, both as a symbol of his 'victory' and because 'he whose palm was once a cross now has a cross as his resting place'.[54] However farfetched, the bishop's erudite explication of the puzzle, like the solutions to the 'riddles' of Scripture which his sermons proposed, can be assumed to have appealed to the taste of his congregation.[55]

At about the same time as the Basilica Apostolorum was being transformed into the church of San Nazaro, yet another church was under construction to the north of the city. The precise date and circumstances of the founding of San Simpliciano are unknown: Ambrose's involvement and an original title of 'Basilica Virginum' are supplied only by later tradition. But the distinctive profile and the pattern of the brickwork reveal the bishop's hand. Architecturally the church is perhaps the best balanced of the three, retaining the cruciform design of the Basilica Apostolorum but reducing the lateral arms to little more than the conventional transept.[56] No clues survive to the function for which it was originally intended (there seems again to have been no particular sanctity attached to the site), but it duly received martyrs of its own. Only months after Ambrose's death in 397, a Christian mission launched by the late bishop's disciple Vigilius of Trent in the Alpine Val di Non produced three 'martyrs'; they were conveyed to Milan and installed with great ceremony in a chapel attached to the church. As we will see, the

54. *ILCV* 1800: 'crux cui palma fuit crux etiam sinus est' (10). Paulinus nevertheless claims that Nazarius had been decapitated (*V. Amb.* 32.3).

55. A similar context might be suggested for Ambrose's verses on the 'octagon of baptism', inscribed in the baptistery attached to the Basilica Nova (*ILCV* 1841). The poem has been cited as evidence that Ambrose himself was responsible for the construction of the baptistery (M. Mirabella Roberti, *Milano Romana* [1984], 115); but it is difficult to believe that the baptistery was not part of the original design of the basilica. Ambrose's poem is better seen as an attempt to claim the baptistery for himself and thus to override its 'Arian' connotations.

56. The fullest description is by E. A. Arslan, 'Osservazioni preliminari sulla chiesa di San Simpliciano in Milano', *Arch. St. Lom.*, n.s., 10 (1947), 5–32; see also G. Bovini, *Antichità cristiane di Milano* (1970), 256–281.

arrival of their cult in Milan was a 'political' event organized to enhance the position of the Milanese see. It seems appropriate to attribute to Ambrose the architectural setting for this continuation of his work.

The bishop's buildings dominated the fringes of Christian Milan, landmarks that made the contours of the city's sacred hinterland readily intelligible. At the same time, they created a controlled environment within which Ambrose could regulate the activities of the faithful and, above all, accommodate the piety of the heterogeneous and transient court. The confidence his behaviour exudes is a measure of his achievement. He did not panic, like many of his colleagues, before individualistic expressions of lay piety. The African lawyer Alypius, after a long winter retreat in a rural villa in which he had developed an idiosyncratic intellectualist approach to Christianity and sought to subdue his body by walking barefoot across the frozen Italian soil, returned to Milan for baptism at the bishop's hands. Similar practices among upper-class laymen a few years earlier had prompted cries of heresy from certain Spanish bishops.[57]

Ambrose's confidence shows itself in his prohibitions as well as his tolerance. Another African, Augustine's mother, Monica, came up against these on a justly famous occasion. Arriving at a cemetery to honour the memorials to the sainted dead with gifts of cake, bread and wine, as had been her custom at home, she found her way blocked by a janitor who informed her that the bishop had forbidden such practices.[58] Ambrose's reason for the prohibition—that this custom of *refrigerium* was a pagan contamination of the church, nothing but a disguised version of the feast of the dead, the Parentalia—is now known to have quite misrepresented a tradition with perfectly respectable Christian antecedents.[59] A measure of the contentiousness of the claim can be found in the vehemence with which two of the bishop's disciples, Gaudentius in Brescia and Augustine in Hippo, expostulated to assert it.[60] Unlike them, however, Ambrose seems not to have engaged in controversy over the issue.[61] He put his trust not in words but in deeds, posting men around the cemeteries to enforce his interpretation. Monica's experience

57. Aug. *Conf.* 9.6.14. Cf. H. Chadwick, *Priscillian of Avila* (1976), 17–20.
58. Aug. *Conf.* 6.2.2.
59. Brown, *The Cult of the Saints*, 26–30, with bibliography at 140.
60. Gaud. *Tract.* 4.14: 'Parentalia; Parentalia, inquam, unde idolatriae malum extulit caput erroris'; cf. Aug. *Ep.* 29.
61. The one reference to graveside celebrations in his works, *De Helia* 62, is parenthetical.

shows the suburban cities of the dead, so often a source of deviance and dissent, being tamed by the church establishment.

Meanwhile, inside the towering basilicas of the suburbs, a constant routine of services was conducted by the bishop and his ministers, linking these peripheral areas directly to the centre. This 'colonization' of the suburbs also appears in another aspect of extramural Christianity at Milan. Outside the city walls was a monastery, as Augustine discovered two years after his arrival.[62] Monks, untainted by the *saeculum* and resistant to authority, could (like the relics of saints) present dangerous competition to the clerical establishment. The urban ascetics of Constantinople helped wreck the career of John Chrysostom.[63] Bishops of other cities, Antioch, Alexandria and Caesarea, conducted careful diplomacy with the holy men of their hinterlands; these men were powerful supporters but resisted any imposition of episcopal authority or patronage. At Milan, on the other hand, the monks were domesticated. They lived under the supervision of a presbyter, 'an excellent and most learned man' who at the same time imposed a strict discipline on the bishop's behalf.[64] Their low profile allowed them to go unnoticed even by a man with as wide-ranging a curiosity as Augustine. At the same time, they served the church as models of piety and obedience: by visiting them Augustine learned to admire the orderliness of their lives, remote from ordinary life. The style of monasticism he inspected, like the new practices his mother adopted in the cemeteries, was licensed by the bishop. Nowhere, perhaps, was Christian life supervised as comprehensively— and effectively—as in Ambrose's Milan.

ERUDITE SUAVITY

Ambrose's most direct point of contact with his people was through his weekly sermons in the Basilica Nova, during which sceptical connoisseurs and ardent believers alike would 'hang on his lips'.[65] Such responses present a considerable challenge to the modern imagination. We have only the dense and elliptical treatises into which he repackaged his sermons for publication; such excitement as these texts have stirred

62. *Conf.* 8.6.15 ('et erat monasterium . . . extra urbis moenia).

63. See, most recently, Liebeschuetz, *Barbarians and Bishops* (1990), 210–214.

64. Aug. *De moribus ecclesiae* 1.70: 'vir optimus et doctissimus'. On discipline, cf. p. 253 below.

65. Aug. *Conf.* 5.13.23, 'verbis eius suspendebar'; 6.1.1, 'in ora Ambrosii suspendi' (of Monica).

has concerned their remarkable range of Greek sources, which modern scholars are far better able to appreciate than the Monicas and Augustines of Ambrose's original audience.[66] It is nevertheless from these treatises that we must attempt to reconstruct the tone of his sermons. Through them alone can we hope to appreciate Ambrose's impact upon his listeners: 'to develop the ears of his late Roman audience'.[67]

The mainspring of Ambrose's preaching should therefore be sought in the dense and intricate chains of scriptural citations which alone hold together the sprawling 'collages' of his exegetical writings.[68] The bishop's constant recourse to biblical quotation and paraphrase suggests what was truly distinctive about his pastoral style. For Ambrose reproduced in his sermons the texture and rhythm of the Bible itself: his preaching was nothing less than an exercise in scriptural mimesis. His actual exegesis, in comparison, was of secondary importance. He deployed his scholarship—his extensive adaptations from other authors and scatterings of textual variants, Hebrew etymologies and quotations in Greek—almost impressionistically, to suggest the range and depth of possible meanings rather than to explicate them systematically.[69] Important consequences follow for the character of relations between Ambrose the preacher and his audience.

66. The fountainhead of modern scholarship on this topic is P. Courcelle, *Recherches sur les "Confessions" de saint Augustin*, 2d ed. (1968), 93–138; for Ambrose's approach to his sources, see especially H. Savon, *Saint Ambroise devant l'exégèse de Philon le Juif* (1977), and G. Madec, *Saint Ambroise et la philosophie* (1974).

67. Brown, *The Body and Society*, 363. Much work on the relationship between Ambrose's treatises and their homiletic core is vitiated by excessive use of his two baptismal works, the stenographic transcript *De sacramentis* and the highly polished *De mysteriis*, as a control: post-baptismal instruction was given in very different circumstances from the formal weekly sermon. There is much suggestive statistical information, not always convincingly interpreted, in S. M. Oberhelman, *Rhetoric and Homiletics in Fourth-Century Christian Literature* (1991), 21–62; cf. 101–109 on the catechetical texts.

68. G. Nauroy, 'L'Ecriture dans la pastorale d'Ambroise de Milan', in *La monde latin antique et la Bible*, ed. J. Fontaine and C. Pietri (1985), 371–408. The whole of the present section is heavily indebted to this paper. For Ambrose's exegetical method, see also L. F. Pizzolato, 'La Sacra Scrittura fondamento del metodo esegetico di sant'Ambrogio', in *Ambrosius Episcopus* (1976), 1:393–426, with bibliography.

69. Nauroy, 'L'Ecriture', 404, superseding earlier arguments that these elements reflect redaction for publication. Nauroy applies his method with brilliant success in two case studies: 'La méthode de composition d'Ambroise de Milan et la structure du *De Iacob et beata vita*', in *Ambroise de Milan*, ed. Y.-M. Duval (1974), 115–153; 'La structure du *De Isaac vel de anima*', *REL* 63 (1985), 210–236.

Ambrose's learned ruminations are quite unlike the sermons of any contemporary bishop. That they lack the conversational intimacy that Augustine cultivated in his basilica at Hippo (a fifth the size of the Basilica Nova) is perhaps unsurprising; more significant is the difference from the thrust and clarity of the homilies that John Chrysostom delivered in the great cathedral of Constantinople.[70] Absent, above all, from Ambrose's meditations is the sense of a concrete message needing to be driven home: his Biblical *catenae* are rarely subordinated to an organizing theme. This in turn implies a distinctive pastoral approach. As with his building programme, gradual and piecemeal evolution is more likely than a systematic grand strategy.[71] His initial self-projection as a model student of Scripture (from which the studied meditations of his maturity seem a logical development) also recalls the assertive defensiveness of the Basilica Ambrosiana as it was originally conceived.[72] But the particular attention thus focused, from the outset, upon the person of the bishop must also have conditioned responses to his scriptural idiom. With Ambrose, the preacher becomes identified with his text.

An important dimension of Ambrose's persona was the character—at once highly visible and oddly indeterminate—of the learning he paraded in his sermons. Visitors were allowed free access while he refreshed himself, after his arduous receptions, by reading. Elsewhere in the Roman world this would lead naturally to exposition of the obscurities contained in the text or discussion of the questions raised; but Ambrose preferred to meditate in silence rather than to share his knowledge in a study group, and while he read 'his voice and his tongue were still'. Spectators were left to ponder his reasons.[73] But the blurring of the boundary usually apparent between the exegete and his subject matter can only have added to the potency of Ambrose's synthesis of Scripture

70. On Augustine's preaching, see F. van der Meer, *Augustine the Bishop* (1961), 412–452; cf. Liebeschuetz, *Barbarians and Bishops*, 171–188, for John. Comparison between (for example) *De Joseph* and Chromatius *Sermo* 24 suggests the difference between Ambrose's exegetical approach and that of his neighbours: the topic deserves systematic research.

71. Nauroy ('L'Ecriture', 378–382) correctly stresses that the sermons were addressed to ordinary Christians (against earlier assumptions of an audience of intellectuals); but his suggestion of a programme designed to inculcate a comprehensive 'biblical culture' is implausible, given the circumstances of delivery (for which see R. MacMullen, 'The Preacher's Audience [A.D. 350–400]', *JThS*, n.s., 40 [1989], 503–511).

72. See above, p. 76 (and cf. Nauroy, 'L'Ecriture', 401, for developments in Ambrose's style); on the buildings, p. 229.

73. *Conf.* 6.3.3.

and scholarship. This is the key, perhaps, to the vision, vouchsafed to an Arian critic in Ambrose's audience, of an angel whispering into the bishop's ear.[74] When Ambrose preached, he sounded 'like the Bible'.[75]

Hardly less dramatic was Ambrose's impact upon another long-standing enemy of 'the catholic faith'—Augustine, whose decision to resume, after a lapse of ten years, his status as a catechumen was taken within a matter of months of his arrival at Milan and appears to have been a direct response to the bishop's preaching.[76] But it has proved difficult to establish any precise intellectual debts. Ambrose's style did not lend itself to systematic instruction: he ranged across the Old Testament, unraveling one mystery after another through application of a figurative interpretation, an exhilarating fizzing of paradoxes which conjured up the possibility that sense could be made of the whole. This hope, which encouraged Augustine to approach the Bible in a new spirit, seems to have been the bishop's most important contribution at this stage.[77] Augustine's response to him as a 'learned champion' therefore recalls the conversion of the disputatious Arian: both were captivated by a persona rather than a specific argument.

Augustine's intellectual progress at Milan hinges primarily upon his encounter with the heady currents of Neoplatonism. As he describes it, this unfolds entirely outside Ambrose's cathedral, among a disparate collection of pagans, laymen and clerics united only by the 'books of the Platonists'. In De beata vita we meet the retired courtier Manlius Theodorus, the enthusiastic devotee of these texts; in the Confessions, the 'swollen-headed somebody' who introduced Augustine to them, and Ambrose's presbyter Simplicianus, with whom he discussed them (and who described his own dealings with Plotinus' translator). Augustine's

74. Paulin. V. Amb. 17.

75. Nauroy, 'L'Ecriture', 404.

76. J. J. O'Meara, The Young Augustine (1954), 121, rightly stresses the significance of this step, misinterpreted by Courcelle (Recherches, 90); J. F. Matthews' suggestion (Western Aristocracies and Imperial Court (1975), 215) that Augustine was perhaps only 'falling in with the habits of the court' is unduly cynical.

77. Conf. 5.14.24 ('uno et altero et saepius aenigmate soluto . . . reprehendebam desperationem meam'); De util. cred. 8.20 ('me commoverant nonnullae disputationes Mediolanensis episcopi ut non sine spe aliqua de ipso vetere Testamento multa quaerere cuperem'). Augustine's new insights into the nature of evil and divine incorporeality, adduced by O'Meara in this context (The Young Augustine, 120–121), belong to a later stage of his development. This is of course to summarize dogmatically a relationship 'whose eddies may escape the historian' (Brown, Augustine, 87); for a fuller account, and a different interpretation, see A. Pincherle, 'Ambrogio ed Agostino', Augustinianum 14 (1974), 385–407.

painstaking collation of the contents of these precious books with the authoritative truths he had now accepted in the Bible, however, has been made with hindsight to appear unduly circuitous, for the required composite of Plotinus and Scripture has been discovered ready-made in certain sermons preached by Ambrose.[78] The significance of this discovery continues to excite controversy, but the most telling aspect in the present context is Augustine's apparent failure, even in retrospect, to notice the bishop's Neoplatonist citations.[79] It had probably never occurred to him to look. Ambrose was defined in his imagination as the 'man of God' and his preaching as the 'sober drunkenness' of God's wine. The phrase, taken from an Ambrosian hymn (and ultimately, unknown to Augustine, from the Alexandrian Philo), is an eloquent tribute to the bishop's success both in controlling his image and in making his sources his own.[80]

Ambrose did not lead Augustine to Plotinus; but the reverse may in some sense be true.[81] Ambrose's initial recourse to Greek sources was a response to his situation after assuming office; his hasty adaptation of Didymus for *De spiritu sancto* was also made under pressure. The likelihood that his cluster of Neoplatonic sermons begins from the mid-380s invites the suggestion that the appearance of this material upon his reading list reflects the presence in Milan, in the train of the imperial court, of precisely the likes of Theodorus—and Augustine. These Platonist courtiers, although not hostile to the bishop like their homoean colleagues, nevertheless presented an implicit challenge to the reputation for learning which he had so assiduously cultivated. The impenetrability of Ambrose's Platonism even to modern research is a measure of his success in rising to this challenge. His appropriation of Plotinian vocabulary fully confirmed his intellectual credentials, while his subordination of these philosophical concepts to his scriptural idiom encouraged Christian Platonists to regard him as a point of reference rather than a debating partner.[82] Ambrose's Neoplatonic sermons might there-

78. Courcelle, *Recherches*, 106–138, 336–344; for a judicious survey of subsequent discussion and the present state of the question, see Madec, *Saint Ambroise et la philosophie*, 60–71.

79. This cardinal point was made by J. J. O'Meara, 'Augustine and Neo-Platonism', *RecAug* 1 (1958), at 100.

80. *Conf.* 5.13.23: cf. O'Donnell, *Augustine: Confessions*, 2:320–321.

81. Cf. Courcelle, *Recherches*, 138n2.

82. The Platonists' view of Ambrose is well conveyed by Augustine's two references to 'sacerdos noster' in *De beata vita* of 386, addressed to Theodorus: his *sermones* covered the same questions as Theodorus' (4), while a line from one of his hymns was an unanswerable 'awakening to the faith' (35).

fore show his preaching being adapted, like his buildings, to accommodate the imperial court.

Manlius Theodorus and his friends would, on this interpretation,
have detected no subtle signals either in the bishop's use of their prized
texts or in the contempt for philosophy expressed even in direct borrow-
ings from Neoplatonic sources, like the sneer at 'Platonic banqueters'
with which Ambrose laces an extensive paraphrase of Plotinus.[83] Nor
would their less sophisticated fellow-parishioners have thought to apply
Ambrose's strictures to the philosophical amateurs of Milan. Responses
were conditioned by an environment in which the tomb of Theodorus'
sister (inscribed with its Neoplatonic epitaph) could stand beside Ambrose's brother's. Besides, the bishop's despised philosophers, like his
Jews, were understood to belong by definition to an alien world outside
the basilica.[84] Ambrose used these figures to point contrasts with his
own 'people of God' assembled within the church; his invective did not
single out individual members of his congregation but defined them
collectively.

The temptation to exaggerate the intellectual aspect of Augustine's
response to Ambrose should likewise be resisted. How far the two men
remained from a meeting of minds is clear from the sole attested exchange of letters between them. After the final crisis of conversion (precipitated not by pastoral attention but by a social call from an African
fellow-courtier) Augustine had departed for a long retreat at the rural
estate of Cassiciacum.[85] Although this was conceived as a preparation
for baptism, he had not consulted Ambrose concerning his agenda; only
towards the end of the holidays did he write to tell the bishop of all that
had happened and to ask what he should read to make himself ready
for the sacrament. He received the bare instruction to read Isaiah, which
he abandoned after finding the first part unintelligible.[86] But Augustine,
significantly, did not express disappointment. He did not expect a dialogue with Ambrose, who was understood to operate at a different level
of discourse. We catch something of this in the bishop's sole 'contribution' to the discussions at Cassiciacum: three words from his evening

83. *De bono mortis* 21: for discussion, see Madec, *Saint Ambroise et la philosophie*, 69–71.

84. For the Jews in Ambrose's preaching, see p. 303 below; they are juxtaposed with philosophers at *Expos. Evang. sec. Luc.* 5.70.

85. For Augustine at Cassiciacum, see Brown, *Augustine*, 115–127.

86. *Conf.* 9.5.13. Augustine's gloss on Ambrose's choice of book ('credo
quod prae ceteris evangelii vocationisque gentium sit praenuntiator apertior')
shows that he had been left to make this inference for himself.

hymn, delivered in a sudden (and not particularly apposite) outburst from Monica, brought a long afternoon of philosophical discussion to an abrupt but satisfactory close, grounding it in orthodoxy.[87] Ambrose was an oracle, expected not to participate in arguments but to finish them.[88]

It is on this level, too, that we can best appreciate the effect of his preaching and the peculiarly austere charm that delighted Augustine— and compelled his reluctant attention—when he first came to listen.[89] The *suavitas* that informed the rhythms of Ambrose's sermons (and like-wise his hymns) is far more elusive for the modern reader than his eru-dition, which can be confirmed through indices and concordances; but it is perhaps more fundamental to the spell his preaching cast over his audience.[90]

A rather different aspect of the relation between the speaker and his audience can be approached through another—much more straightfor-ward—exchange of letters between Ambrose and a correspondent on a rural estate. The Romulus who received two letters from the bishop can be identified as Pisidius Romulus, *consularis* of Aemilia-Liguria in 385/6.[91] In the best aristocratic tradition of amateur scholarship, Romulus had posed certain problematical texts to test the bishop's exegetical vir-tuosity. One was an obscure curse from the book of Deuteronomy: 'I shall make the sky bronze, and the earth iron' (Deut. 28:23). Ambrose expressed surprise that Romulus' present situation, with the 'pretti-ness of the countryside and the fertility around you', had not already suggested the answer to him: drought and famine. His interpretation hinges upon the ingenious conceit (taken, without acknowledgement, from Philo) that from the 'iron earth' of scarcity would issue the iron

87. *De beata vita* 35: 'Fove precantes Trinitas'.
88. *Conf.* 6.3.4: Ambrose as an *oraculum*. Cf. Aug. *Ep.* 54.2.3, where a re-mark by Ambrose is treated 'tamquam eam caelesti oraculo acceperim'.
89. 'Et delectabar suavitate sermonis': *Conf.* 5.13.23. The ensuing compari-son with a Manichean guru—'quamquam eruditioris, minus tamen hilarescentis atque mulcentis quam Fausti erat'—makes the initial characterization almost paradoxical, 'mulcens' and 'suavis' being near-synonyms.
90. Augustine uses 'suavis' of Ambrose's hymns at *Conf.* 9.6.14. Poetic ele-ments have often been noted in Ambrose's prose: see Nauroy, 'L'Ecriture', 404, for 'les sondages suggestifs du poète' in his exegesis, and especially J. Fontaine, 'Prose et poésie: L'interférence des genres et styles dans la création littéraire d'Ambroise de Milan', in *Ambrosius Episcopus* (1976), 1:124–170.
91. *PLRE* 1, pp. 771–772; cf. Matthews, *Western Aristocracies*, 193–195. If Romulus' visit to the countryside is dated to his term of office, it might represent a prudent retreat from the current disturbances.

weapons of civil war, as the famine victims competed for the few supplies available. The brutality of this interpretation is strikingly at odds
with the learned tone, complete with Virgilian echo.[92]

Romulus more probably took his cue from the tone than from the
contents. In the other letter, Ambrose sets the correspondence in a thoroughly bland context. Exactly like Symmachus, he announces his purpose as the cultivation of *officia* and the reinforcement of his ties with
Romulus.[93] This second letter was also in response to a scriptural puzzle.
Why, asked Romulus in relation to the episode of the Golden Calf in
Exodus, did Moses order each of the Levites to murder his 'nearest'?
Ambrose has seemed to bring the slaughter uncomfortably close to
contemporary reality;[94] but the thrust of his argument is towards the
deeper spiritual meaning. The Levites, those 'whose portion is God', are
viewed as those who have given themselves up completely to His service, 'killing' their flesh. Their 'nearest' was therefore the body ('for
what is so near as is the body to the soul?'); and, to complete the correspondence, the sword that each of them was ordered to 'place upon his
side' was the Word of God.[95] With this bravura line of reasoning (also
plagiarized from Philo)[96] Ambrose translated the whole bloody episode
into the Christian sage's achievement, like the traditional philosopher's,
of mastering his passions. In these letters, he does not so much exhibit
the disturbing intransigence of his outlook as skilfully translate the bleak
world of the Old Testament into a familiar classical idiom. These exegetical exercises involved him in a pleasurable excursion into 'liberalis
scientia'.

Ambrose's comfortable relationship with Romulus illustrates his
close association with government personnel; but it also bears upon
the congregation's understanding of his pronouncements. Ambrose
assumed that rural life would suggest images of fertility and plenty
to Romulus. The landscape had traditionally fulfilled this function for
the members of the leisured class whose villas dotted the countryside;
in Ambrose's preaching, however, the countryside was also presented
as the scene of far less innocent activities. Burning with avarice, the

92. *Ep.* 44 [68]; cf. Philo *De praemiis et poenis* 132. The tone of Ambrose's
invocation of 'species . . . agri et praesens fertilitas' recalls certàin remarks by
Symmachus (*Ep.* 1.58, 8.44).

93. *Ep.* 48 [66].1.

94. Matthews, *Western Aristocracies*, 193–194.

95. *Ep.* 48 [66].8–10.

96. Cf. Philo *De ebrietate* 69–71.

wealthy *possessor* sought to absorb the modest plots of his humbler neighbours and so drove them from their ancestral fields: 'The peasants in a body are leaving their lands. The poor man migrates, with his family of little children; behind him follows his wife, weeping bitterly, as though she were attending her husband to the tomb' (*De Nabuthe* 1). Ambrose's memorable portraits of the types who perpetrated these crimes—restless and insatiable, arrogant but nervous—have evoked admiring comment. The bishop has been seen as a champion of the poor against the excesses of the wealthy, and as an important brake upon the acquisitive urges of the rich speculators who capitalized on the court's arrival in Milan.[97]

To believe so is to assume that Ambrose set out to address himself to specific contemporary injustices, and that his audience would have understood his words in this sense. But there is little to suggest that even his set-piece invectives against avarice would have been seen as attacks upon particular targets.[98] There was an important difference in this respect between Ambrose and John Chrysostom, whose audiences in Constantinople thrilled to see his eyes fasten upon individuals as he raged against the luxury and greed of the elite. But because John avoided social relations with the wealthy Christians of the capital, his words and gestures during church services—his only direct point of contact with these eminent parishioners—were interpreted as direct threats.[99] Ambrose's words belonged within the context of the wide and sophisticated network of contacts evoked in the correspondence with

97. A recent example is V. R. Vasey, *The Social Ideas in the Works of Saint Ambrose* (1982); a precise target for Ambrose's invective is discovered in the 'gretta nobilità locale' of Milan by L. Cracco Ruggini, 'Ambrogio di fronte alla compagine sociale del suo tempo', in *Ambrosius Episcopus* (1976), 1:230–265, at 242–245.

98. The three treatises *De Nabuthe*, *Del Elia* and *De Tobia*, respectively against avarice, drunkenness and usury, are perhaps deceptively direct and accessible. 'All three help a reader to understand how Ambrose came by his great reputation as a preacher; his other works tend to leave the reader skeptical as to his oratorical powers' (Vasey, *The Social Ideas*, 24); but his contemporary audience is more likely to have recognized them as variations upon his characteristic scriptural themes.

99. Liebeschuetz, *Barbarians and Bishops*, 171–178, discusses John's preaching at Constantinople; for the crucial evidence of 'Martyrius', F. van Ommeslaeghe, 'Jean Chrysostome et le peuple de Constantinople', *AB* 99 (1981), 329–349. John owed his brilliant success with a similar style of preaching at Antioch (characterized by Brown, *The Body and Society*, 307–317) to his audience's familiarity with their home-grown 'star'.

Romulus. Romulus might indeed have been untainted by the vices of his peers; but the cultural assumptions implicit in Ambrose's remarks on the character of rural life betray his own background as a *possessor*.[100] Such associations will also inevitably have influenced his audience's perceptions of the bishop. Just as responses to his attacks on philosophy will have been conditioned by awareness of his connexions with Theodorus, his listeners will have weighed his harangues upon greed and insatiability against his long-standing friendship with that prime example of boundless appetites (and the attendant nervous disorders), Sextus Petronius Probus.[101]

Ambrose's works do not give any conclusive evidence for either the social conditions prevailing in Milan or his own ideological position. The keen but completely misguided debate on whether Ambrose embraced communism (echoes of which still reverberate in some quarters)[102] was generated by the assumption that Ambrose's writings offer a clear window upon his own beliefs; much recent work on social history depends on the similar assumption that his observations accurately reflect the state of contemporary Italy. In both cases, the translucence of the medium in which Ambrose was working and the political character of his preaching have been exaggerated. The background to his diatribes might better be compared to his excursions into Neoplatonism. Crucial passages claim firsthand experience; but the claims, it turns out, were lifted from his Greek sources.[103] One such passage in the tract against usury (*De Tobia*) does seem to be original, but it is highly unlikely that Ambrose actually shamed a creditor who had refused to allow burial of an indebted client, by granting him possession of the corpse. This grotesque scene looks very much like a satirical display piece (which might, incidentally, have offered a reassuring standard of comparison for the many members of the congregation currently lending money at interest)

100. Ambrose's pleasantries can be contrasted with Augustine's bitter onslaught against the exploitation of a rural labour force by another Romulus (*Ep.* 247: not the same man, despite *PLRE* 1, p. 772).

101. For the endurance of the connexion, see Paulin. *V. Amb.* 21 (the cure by Ambrose of a favourite slave of Probus).

102. Vasey, *The Social Ideas*, 126–136, attempts to assist those perplexed by the 'strong communistic or socialist savor' of certain passages in Ambrose.

103. Thus the 'Vidi ego' of *De Nabuthe* 21 (Basil *Hom. in illud dictum Evangelii sec. Luc.*, '*Destruam horrea mea*', 4) and *De Tobia* 29 (Basil *Hom.* 2 *in Ps.* 14, 4); Ruggini's argument that the circumstantial details contributed by Ambrose prove his 'direct experience' of identical events (*Economia e società*, 95n252, 195) carries little conviction.

designed to allow the bishop to indulge in some extravagant word play.[104]

Ambrose's protests against the excesses of the wealthy owe more to patient reading than to close observation of his congregation's behaviour. Hence even what seem to be direct challenges lose their immediacy. The bishop excoriated the 'habits of the rich', especially their involuntary fasting when frustrated acquisitiveness left them wretched and unable to touch their food: 'At such times you may see them gathering at the church, dutiful, meek and assiduous—but only so that they might obtain a result from their crime' (*De Nabuthe* 44). This seems an invitation to the congregation to examine the pallid faces of the Christian aristocrats assembled in their midst; but the modern reader risks seizing too eagerly upon it. Ambrose did not linger: this particular passage was his cue to appropriate the prophetic voice of Elijah to rebuke King Ahab, but he did not intend to evoke the crimes of Valentinian II. Only on very rare occasions were his references concrete. The biblical tone that so thoroughly infused his public performances prepared listeners for 'mysteries', not detailed accusations of wrongdoing. Ambrose's whole style and presentation ensured that any glass he held up to his society was bound to be riddling and dark.

The bishop's perceived relationship with his society also conditioned the interpretation given to his words. It was because John Chrysostom stood outside normal patterns of social intercourse that his statements so alarmed the citizenry of Constantinople and were subject to misrepresentation by his enemies;[105] Augustine, on the other hand, has sometimes disappointed his readers by the depth of his immersion in the patterns of small-town life in Hippo and his acceptance of so many of the inequities of that society.[106] Ambrose differs from them both. His denunciations of the crimes of the mighty were as heady and uncompromising as John's, and insisted upon standards of justice and political behaviour that had disappeared with the golden age. But his audience

104. *De Tob.* 36–37: 'Quoties vidi . . .' Note the jingle of 'funus' and 'faenus', 'mors and 'sors'; also the punning upon the two senses of 'nexus' and 'caput'.

105. Soc. *HE* 6.15, for John's enemies giving distorted reports of his preaching to the authorities.

106. A contrast drawn upon this basis between Augustine and Ambrose was effectively demolished by Peter Brown, who dismissed the latter's apparent radicalism as 'a textbook dictum unrefined by experience' (*Religion and Society in the Age of Saint Augustine* [1972], at 333–334).

would know better than to take these literally. Ambrose, in this respect more like Augustine than John, was firmly anchored in his city, and familiarity gave his people a key to understanding his words; if his sermons are more complex and more difficult to decode than Augustine's, this is largely because an imperial capital afforded a more sophisticated audience than a Numidian municipality. The aggressive Italian gentry and energetic courtiers who thronged the basilica of Milan would not have thought to recognize themselves in the monsters of avarice which their bishop presented to them, nor would they have seen their own investments in property around the capital as the 'eviction' of the weak from their ancestral plots and the 'defrauding' of widows and orphans.

One source, however, does present Ambrose's harangues against greed as direct 'interventions' with individuals. According to the Milanese deacon, his biographer Paulinus, 'He groaned intensely when he saw avarice, the root of all evils, which can be lessened neither by plenty nor by lack, increasing more and more among men and especially among those who were in positions of power, so that his task of intervening with them was very grievous, because everything was being torn apart for money' (V. Amb. 41.1). To judge from the catalogue of clarissimi and other luminaries who fill his pages, Paulinus was somewhat dazzled by the elevated circles in which Ambrose moved.[107] His own ingenuousness perhaps lends a certain weight to his picture of the bishop's forthrightness with the mighty, but as the passage continues, he begins to speak in his own person in a manner which suggests that his own later experience had coloured his memories. The profound horror of mammon which Paulinus expresses must have ill suited him for his own post as defensor et procurator of the African estates of the Milanese church;[108] the chicanery to which his work exposed him, moreover, was perhaps exacerbated during the years of his tenure by the exodus of Roman aristocrats to their African estates after Alaric's sack, for not all will have come to liquidate their assets for pious purposes.[109] To Paulinus, disadvantaged in his dealings with these experienced and masterful neighbours, Ambrose's diatribes against avarice may well have acquired a

107. At V. Amb. 30.2 he reports a conversation about Ambrose between the general Arbogast and some Frankish 'kings', overheard by an acquaintance of his—a wine waiter, possibly a slave.

108. Praedestinatus 88 (PL 53, 617); see A. Paredi, 'Paulinus of Milan', SE 14 (1963), 206–230, at 208–209.

109. The impact made by the Roman refugees in various fields is discussed by Brown, Augustine, 340–341; Matthews, Western Aristocracies, 300: Courcelle, Histoire littéraire des grands invasions germaniques, 3d ed. (1964), 56–67.

resonance and a prophetic force. The Italian disease diagnosed by the bishop was spreading: 'This state of affairs first inflicted every evil upon Italy; subsequently everything is turning to the bad'.

Ambrose's words seem to have had a similar effect upon Paulinus as upon Augustine: they were an oracle upon which he meditated and which he interpreted in the light of his own experience. But few members of the bishop's audience can have taken his denunciations as literally as did Paulinus. The only tone that Augustine recalled from his regular attendance at Ambrose's sermons, over the better part of two years, was suave erudition: the rhetor was at that time 'gasping' for wealth and was engaged in the assiduous pursuit of the inheritance, if not of a widow or orphan, then certainly of an heiress.[110]

In Milan, Augustine saw the society around him in symbolic terms. A drunken beggar, for instance, inspired thoughts on the absurdity of conventional notions of happiness.[111] This was entirely in keeping with the spirit of Ambrose's church. The poor were indeed present there, but only—as the 'images of Christ'—to serve the bishop as a powerful visual aid.[112] Ambrose should not be encumbered with anachronistic concerns for social change. The fortunes of individuals might be subject to sudden and dramatic alteration, but the categories of wealth and poverty remained immutable. Nor can Ambrose's insistence upon the moral neutrality of the two states conceal his own enduring affinity for the outlook associated with the rich. His assumptions are bleakly illustrated in a casual remark that evidence upon a medical question from an 'experienced and wealthy' midwife deserved particular credence, because 'neither poverty nor ignorance cast doubt upon her trustworthiness'.[113]

The conventions of rhetoric within which Ambrose operated bound him, in any case, to this wealthy, educated elite.[114] He was far less concerned to condemn the excesses perpetrated by individual members of this class than to create a sense of coherence between them and the rest of the Christian community by elaborating what their shared allegiance to the church actually meant. The rigid boundaries around the community of the faithful which were conjured up in Ambrose's sermons thus served to define that community and to offer an appropriate identity to its members. Walls—according to story that circulated in Ambrose's

110. *Conf.* 6.6.9: 'inhiabam honoribus, lucris, coniugio'.
111. *Conf.* 6.6.9.
112. *Exp. Ps. 118* 10.26: 'imagines Christi'.
113. *Ep.* 56 [5].8.
114. The constraints under which a preacher operated are trenchantly delineated by MacMullen, 'The Preacher's Audience'.

Milan—'made Christians';[115] when they stood within the walls of Ambrose's cathedral, Theodorus was not an idle philosopher nor Petronius Probus a rapacious oppressor. The *plebs Dei* was in essence a rhetorical construct, sustained as much by Ambrose's preaching as by hymns and choral singing. The achievement should not be regarded lightly. Milan's social tensions—the *invidia* of the poor against the *fastidium* of the rich[116]—were probably exacerbated by the city's rootlessness, its dependence upon the wealth that came from the temporary presence of a mobile court and the courtiers, careerists and litigants who arrived in its train. These people were accommodated in the city through the church, which they in turn enhanced by their presence, supporting its dependents with their alms. The relationship, masterminded by the bishop, generated a potent illusion of solidarity within Christian Milan and lent a comforting appearance of solidity to the fundamentally improvised structures of the capital.

For all their clarity, the boundaries Ambrose drew around his people did not under normal circumstances appear exclusive. A stranger arriving in Milan could expect a welcome 'in the proper episcopal manner', with no awkward questions asked about his own beliefs.[117] Because of this, the scope of the territory that Ambrose had staked out for himself within the capital was concealed. So extensive were the ties between church and government, so obvious their mutual dependence, that a lasting symbiosis could have been assumed. There was a rude awakening in 385/6. The conflict was not between the native population of the capital and 'foreigners'; that distinction is meaningless in cosmopolitan Milan. While Ambrose capitalized upon (and doubtless exaggerated) the importance of the unmistakably alien Goths to his opponents, his real achievement was to have naturalized so many of the city's *other* temporary residents. Monica, the stubborn African widow who had come to Milan to promote her son's court career, was prepared after only a year in the city to die with her bishop for a cause whose intricacies she is unlikely to have understood. 'Converts' like Monica enabled Ambrose, at the moment of crisis, to mobilize a church against Valentinian, and the government was unable to respond. Ambrose describes a series of

---

115. *Conf.* 8.2.4 (Simplicianus' account of the conversion of Victorinus).

116. *Explan. Ps. 48* 5.

117. Thus the sceptical Manichee Augustine in 384. Note also the false assumptions, Photinian and Apollinarist respectively, that Augustine and Alypius continued to make about the nature of 'catholic' Christology, apparently while they attended Ambrose's services (*Conf.* 7.19.25); they seem to have been left to discover their mistakes for themselves.

isolated messengers bringing their increasingly petulant demands to the imposing assembly in his basilica, only to retreat in confusion. The account, however stylized, underlines that there was, at the decisive moment, no state to match Ambrose's church. The church was an essentially theatrical production; but the government could not compete even on these terms. Their own ceremonies were aborted, and in the Portian Basilica the trappings of state were reduced literally to tatters. Meanwhile, choirs whose members should have been the emperor's natural allies were singing psalms of defiance. There could be no more vivid a symbol of the triumph in Ambrose's Milan of *ecclesia* over *imperium*.

CHAPTER SIX

AMBROSE'S PEOPLE, II: FRIENDS AND INFLUENCE

NEGOTIA: AMBROSE ON DUTY

The boundaries between Ambrose's church and the state were not overrigid. The bishop's success in outfacing Valentinian owed much to his extensive connexions with government institutions and personnel. Ambrose relied on various relationships to secure his political purchase. He enjoyed close contacts with court society in Milan and numbered even the pagan Symmachus among his Roman acquaintances. No less sedulous or wide-ranging were his dealings with his episcopal colleagues in northern Italy. Each of these relationships merits close attention.

The sources, notoriously, care little for the routines of social relations. We are offered a glimpse of the bishop surrounded by 'crowds of men pursuing their affairs' and assisting them in their pursuit, only because these preoccupations prevented him from providing spiritual direction to a parishioner who had become disenchanted with such *negotia*.[1] Ambrose's biographer, too, notes the bishop's business activities only in passing. The *notarius* Theodulus (a member, like Paulinus, of the church's corps of secretaries) was rebuked by Ambrose for laughing at one of his colleagues who had tripped and fallen. This happened, Pau-

---

1. *Conf.* 6.3.3: Augustine was kept from Ambrose by the 'catervis negotiosorum hominum, quorum infirmitatibus serviebat'.

linus casually remarks, when the bishop 'was heading for the palace and we were following, in accordance with our duties';[2] the implication is that such visits were regular occurrences.

The retinue that attended the bishop on these visits shows that he operated not as an individual but as the head of an organization. Ambrose's attention to the outward appearance of his followers is reflected in his treatment of a clergyman whose 'insolent gait' offended him; another candidate for the priesthood was rejected simply because of his undignified deportment.[3] Nothing was allowed to spoil the solemnity of the church's public face. Ambrose also imposed a strict discipline upon his clergy, suppressing any untoward exhibitions of individualism. Gerontius, a deacon skilled at languages, rhetoric and medicine, was given a year's penance when he began to claim private religious experiences; when he decided that his talents would be less inhibited elsewhere and obtained the see of Nicomedia, Ambrose did everything in his power to wreck his career.[4] Equally remorseless was the harrying of Sarmatio and Barbatio, two monks who had rebelled against the disciplines of the monastery at Milan.[5] But these men were exceptions. Ambrose created at Milan a loyal and efficient corps of subordinates, moulded in his own image. There is bitter testimony to this from Palladius, who inveighed against the rough handling he received at Aquileia from Ambrose's subalterns, 'men trained by you after your own character'.[6] Few bishops managed so much, and Ambrose's achievement is the more impressive given the circumstances in which he had assumed office.[7] The respectful and orderly retinue that attended Ambrose at the palace and elsewhere allowed him to meet the grandees with whom he dealt on equal terms. It was as such a figure, fully engaged in the society of his city, that

2. *V. Amb.* 35: 'cum ad palatium pergeret eumque pro loco officii nostri sequeremur'.

3. *De officiis* 1.72: above, p. 55. Note also the concern for outward appearances reflected at 1.246: the 'minister altaris' should be *seen* to be 'arrayed with the appropriate virtues'.

4. Soz. *HE* 8.6.3–8. Ambrose wrote to Nectarius urging him to eject Gerontius, but was thwarted (significantly) by the latter's influence with the court of Constantinople. No action was taken until Chrysostom's accession, after Ambrose's death in 397.

5. *Ep. extra coll.* 14 [63].7–9; *Explan. Ps.* 36 49.

6. *Apol.* 116: 'et lectorum et ministrorum a vobis pro moribus vestris institutorum . . . impiaetas'.

7. Contrast the fate of Chrysostom, another energetic 'outsider' who tried to remould his clerical establishment: J. H. W. G. Liebeschuetz, *Barbarians and Bishops* (1990), 208–216.

Augustine first saw him. 'I thought him a successful man, in the terms
by which the world judges, since such powerful figures showed such
respect to him'.[8]

But Ambrose was more than just another potentate. He was celibate,
a self-imposed burden that Augustine thought strange and hard. There
was a paradoxical contrast between his asceticism and his public face,
which is best expressed by setting his reputation for self-mortification,
as a man 'of much abstinence, and many vigils and toils, whose body
was wasted by daily fasts',[9] against the 'relic of the dalmatics', the pair
of gorgeous robes preserved by the church of Milan and traditionally
claimed for Ambrose.[10] One of them, a silk damask decorated with
scenes from a lion hunt, reflects exactly the sort of senatorial fashion
Ammianus deplored. Few other bishops can have cut so grand a figure.[11] Ambrose was therefore equally at home in the *saeculum* and in his
basilica. This surefootedness made him a vital asset to a generation that
was exploring a territory still unmapped, where clerics struggled to find
their bearings in the glitter of the Christian empire and the pious officials of an increasingly Christianized government tried to reconcile their
duties with the precepts of the faith. In the confusion, Ambrose presented himself as a serene and readily accessible guide to the perplexed.

A magistrate named Studius, for example, could approach him for
advice on the morality of capital punishment.[12] The question was of
immediate relevance, since the taint of bloodshed bore heavily upon
contemporary Christians: a decree from the bishop of Rome declared
roundly that those officials 'who had exercised the world's justice mani-
festly cannot be free from sin'.[13] Ambrose's message, which demonstrates a close familiarity with the practicalities of law enforcement, was
much more reassuring.[14] A Christian judge still enforced Roman laws,

8. *Conf.* 6.3.3: 'felicem quendam hominem secundum saeculum opinabar,
quem sic tantae potestates honorarent'.

9. Paulin. *V. Amb.* 38.1.

10. The claim has recently received impressive corroboration; see H. Granger
Taylor, 'The Two Dalmatics of Saint Ambrose', *Bulletin de Liaison, Centre International d'Etude des Textiles Anciens* 57–58 (1983), 127–173.

11. Amm. Marc. 14.6.9; note Augustine's remark, *Sermo* 356.13, that an expensive silk robe would suit neither his profession nor his principles.

12. *Ep.* 50 [25].

13. [Siricius] *Ep. ad Gallos episcopos* (10).13.

14. Ambrose (*Ep.* 50 [25].3) deprecates the tactic of avoiding bloodshed by
leaving criminal cases untried (cf. p. 45: for the crucial reading 'innocentes', see
the edition of M. Zelzer, *CSEL* 82.2 [1990], at p. 57).

and though his faith should incline him towards mercy, it also justified the punishment of the wicked; he was 'God's avenger against those who do evil'.[15]

This endorsement, besides protecting Studius against harassment from his more rigorous co-religionists during (and after) his term of office, revealed an affinity between the apparently incongruous values of church and government. Difficulties could arise at many levels. Another magistrate who sought Ambrose's help was Polybius, a former proconsul of Africa who required an introduction to the eminent Gallic bishops Phoebadius and Delphinus. But Polybius apparently rejected the bishop's original effort, addressed jointly to the two prelates, and insisted upon a separate letter to each. Ambrose complied, but at the same time produced the letter that actually survives in the correspondence: again addressed to Phoebadius and Delphinus together, it argues the propriety of the original format by adducing the precedent of Paul's correspondence.[16] The episode illustrates Ambrose's role as a go-between for state and church; but the real significance of the missive (and especially of its publication) was to assert a distinctively Christian variant upon the niceties familiar to Polybius and his class. In dealing with the *saeculum*, the church did not have to abandon its own biblical idiom. Ambrose uses his improvised excuse for an apparent *faux pas* as a signpost marking out a Christian approach to the complexities of social intercourse.

The best-known of Ambrose's writings can also be construed as a signpost, a more complex exercise designed at once to make the church intelligible to the *saeculum* and to annex the latter's traditional territory. *De officiis* was ostensibly addressed to his ecclesiastical 'sons', the presbyters and deacons of the Milanese church; but as has often been noted, its scope reaches far beyond the *presbyterium*.[17] Most readers (of this as of any other contemporary book) will have been leisured sophisticates able to appreciate the virtuosity of the bishop's variations upon his Ci-

---

15. *Ep.* 50 [25].1: 'Dei vindex . . . in eos qui male agunt'.
16. *Ep.* 47 [87], quoting (inappropriately) the Epistle to Philemon.
17. A unitary work, with the clerical dedicatees an essentially literary device, is argued by W. Steidle, 'Beobachtung zu des Ambrosius Schrift *De officiis*', *VChr* 38 (1984), 18–66; 'Beobachtung zum Gedankengang im 2. Buch von Ambrosius, *De officiis*', *VChr* 39 (1985), 280–298. Cf. K. Zelzer, 'Zur Beurteilung der Cicero-Imitatio bei Ambrosius', *WS*, n.f., 11 (1977), 168–191. The views of M. Testard, for a composite actually intended for the use of the clergy, are summarized conveniently in his introduction to his edition of *De officiis: Saint Ambroise: Les devoirs*, tome I (1984), 21–39.

ceronian theme.[18] To such readers the claims the bishop implicitly made for his clergy will have been striking and unexpected: the self-mastery upon which he constantly insisted, the traditional achievement of the philosopher and more recently the province of his Christian counterpart, the holy man, is unlikely to have been associated in the conventional mind with the routine tasks performed by the 'servant of the altar'. The book therefore proclaimed an elevated (if demanding) image for the clergy to live up to, but its contemporary impact was probably more ideological than practical. Although Augustine refers to De officiis as 'books full of useful instructions', he cites them only for their title, to justify the use of the 'secular' word officiosus in a Christian context; the passage suggests that like many recognized classics, the work was more referred to than read.[19] But here again, what impressed Augustine was Ambrose's self-confidence in appropriating for the church a concept that had seemed irremediably tainted by its secular connotations. Ambrose, he said, was 'not afraid': the bishop was able to deal so successfully with the world precisely because he did not fear it.

Ambrose also gave concrete advice. Augustine all his life treasured the Milanese bishop's institutum—he must finally have plucked up the courage to ask Ambrose how to cope with society's demands—and awarded it the same status as the injunctions of Saint Paul. The concise package of instructions, like the teachings of a desert father,[20] offers clear rules for negotiating the minefield of social relations. "[A man of God] should never seek a wife for anyone, nor should he supply a reference for anyone wishing to secure a government post, nor should he accept an invitation to dine in his own home city' (Possidius V. Aug. 27.4). The three headings—weddings, jobs and dinners—nicely cover the problems awaiting the gently born western ascetic, more reluctant than his Coptic counterpart in Egypt to make an absolute break with the familiar warmth of civic life when he renounced the world. Ambrose's rules provided such men a way to advertise their dissociation from society without enduring annihilation.

18. Possible readers are noted below, at pp. 272 and 277. The many literary studies of this work rarely tackle the question of how contemporaries might have approached it or what use they might have made of it.

19. Aug. Ep. 82.21, failing to cite Ambrose's own (admittedly tenuous) argument for the term's biblical basis at De off. 1.25. There is no other allusion to the work until Cassiodorus.

20. The passage is presented in this context by P. Rousseau, Ascetics, Authority and the Church (1978), 145.

Closer inspection of the three headings recorded by Possidius will clarify the point. Ambrose knew (as Chrysostom, to his cost, did not) the importance of the business that was conducted at table.[21] But various temptations and dangers presented themselves on such occasions, and a committed ascetic was bound to be a difficult guest. Ambrose's rule looks like a tactful response to this situation: while exerting himself to the utmost to fulfil his episcopal duties of *hospitalitas,* he made it plain that he did not expect his hospitality to be reciprocated in Milan. Several sources attest to his success in establishing the episcopal residence at the centre of the capital's social life. Sulpicius Severus shows him playing host to consuls, and Arbogast, a pagan Frankish general, boasted of the dinners that they had shared.[22] At the bishop's table these men could expect to meet transients like the proconsul Polybius, en route from Africa to Gaul, ambitious *peregrini* freshly arrived from Rome, like the new rhetor Augustine, who came to call upon the bishop, as well as more permanent fixtures like the chorus of *viri militares* whose devotion to Ambrose remained unshakeable even after his death.[23]

Ambrose participated fully in the exchanges necessary to maintain his social position without compromising his sacerdotal obligations. Moreover, when travelling abroad he did not let his fastidiousness interfere with the need to establish and consolidate contacts with his social peers: his rules applied only inside Milan. At Rome he accepted an invitation from a woman of senatorial rank, and he lodged at Florence with Decentius, a *vir clarissimus.*[24] An apparently absolute rule thus proves in practice to allow considerable flexibility.

Marriages were another central preoccupation of the wellborn and ambitious. Sickly aristocrats, according to one sardonic commentator, travelled from Rome to Spoleto for the jollifications of a wedding feast and to receive the gifts of gold customarily on offer.[25] The actual ceremonies were but the culmination of a long process that absorbed the energies and diplomatic skills of the elite. Symmachus, their represen-

21. For John's antisocial attitude and its results, see Liebeschuetz, *Barbarians and Bishops,* 215–216.

22. Sulp. Sev. *Dial.* 1.25.6; Paulin. *V. Amb.* 30.1. Note also Jer. *Ep.* 52.11 to Nepotianus (who had served at the Milanese court) on the 'shameful spectacle' of consul's lictors outside an episcopal residence and on provincial governors dining with ascetics.

23. They are recorded at a 'convivium' with the Milanese clergy by Paulinus (*V. Amb.* 54.1).

24. Paulin. *V. Amb.* 10.1; 28.1. No source shows Ambrose receiving hospitality from his episcopal colleagues.

25. Amm. Marc. 14.6.24.

tative in this as in so much else, recommended hopeful young men to prospective fathers-in-law and canvassed support for their suits.[26] Ambrose, the patron of virgins and passionate advocate of the celibate life, could hardly involve himself in activity of this sort. His injunction, as relayed by Augustine, explicitly renounces matrimonial politics. Closer inspection, however, suggests that the bishop had not abandoned the field but had merely moved the goalposts. A rider to his precept states that a bishop should reserve his intervention in negotiations until the final stage, when he could offer (at the couple's request) his 'confirmation' and blessing for the match.[27] Not the least valuable of the services provided by the church of Milan to its clients was a sophisticated marriage ceremony, quite as impressive as the traditional one.[28] It is therefore not surprising, despite Ambrose's renunciation of any involvement in the process, to find the church assuming an important place in the marriages of Milan's Christian society and to see the city's marital dramas being played out in the bishop's own territory.

A certain Sisinnius had disowned a son who had plunged into marriage without his permission. Ambrose promoted reconciliation energetically, asking the angry father to contact his son and negotiating separately with the errant couple; he had encouraged the bride, he tells Sisinnius, to make a difficult winter journey to 'hibernate in your parental affections'.[29] He does not say how the case had come to his attention, but his protestations on the young couple's behalf suggest that the church had been involved in ratifying their union. The benevolent protection of Ambrose's church is implicit in the plans for another match, albeit one that proved abortive. While Augustine was busy furthering his professional career, his mother sought to establish him socially by a suitable match and duly discovered an heiress (one surmises a network of pious contacts developed through her indefatigable devotions). The project was invested in an atmosphere of holiness, Monica apparently negotiating with the prospective in-laws that Augustine should mark his marriage by receiving baptism.[30] Only two years later he would be baptized into a lifetime of sexual continence, dedicated to God's service;

26. *Epp.* 6.3; 7.120; 9.7, 43, 49. The importance of the wedding itself as a social occasion is illustrated at *Ep.* 6.35.

27. Poss. *V. Aug.* 27.5: 'petitum interesse debere sacerdotem, ut vel eorum iam pacta vel placita firmarentur vel benedicerentur'.

28. On the development of a Christian marriage service during this period, see J. Gaudemet, *L'église dans l'empire romain* (1958), 515–539; 536 for Ambrose.

29. *Ep.* 35 [83].10.

30. *Conf.* 6.13.23: 'iam promittebatur maxime matre dante operam, quo me iam coniugatum baptismatus salutaris ablueret'.

but Augustine the courtier had seen Ambrose's church more as the means to establish his social position than as a route to otherworldly renunciation.

The attitudes that led the great men of the state to bring their matrimonial plans to Ambrose's door are well illustrated by a further thwarted plan. Paternus, holder of a high court office, sought the bishop's help in securing a rescript from the emperor to allow him (in contravention of a recent law) to unite his son to a granddaughter.[31] The authority of Ambrose's view of this case was acknowledged even by Paternus' 'own' bishop;[32] but Paternus had misjudged his man, for he received an uncompromising refusal, which seems to have missed a subtle exegetical point adduced to support niece-marriage.[33] The incident, besides indicating the sort of expectations his more eminent parishioners might have of him, shows Ambrose at the very centre of the Milanese court's matchmaking. There had even been a letter from Cynegius, the son on whose behalf Paternus had been making his plans, encouraging the bishop to resist.[34] Few cases can have been as controversial as this one; it suggests, however, that circumstances spared Ambrose the need to 'seek a bride for anyone'. His place in such transactions was guaranteed.

Ambrose also made a policy of refusing to recommend candidates for the imperial service. His stated reason sounds eminently practical: unsatisfactory performance by his protégés might rebound against him.[35] But this cannot have been the whole story, since that prolific referee Symmachus seems neither to have taken responsibility nor in-

31. *Ep.* 58 [60]. Theodosius' prohibition of marriages within the fourth degree, mentioned by Augustine (*Civ. Dei* 15.16.2), was reaffirmed in 396 (*CTh* 3.12.3); Symmachus also attempted to win an exemption (*Ep.* 9.133: discussed by S. Roda in his commentary, *Commento storico* [1981], at 298–301).

32. *Ep.* 58 [60].3. It is interesting that as mobile as a figure as Paternus, a (probable) Spaniard who held office in Africa and Italy, should have remained in contact with one particular church in this way.

33. *Ep.* 58 [60].9 makes a puzzling reference to the case of Abraham and Sarah, 'ut aliquis uxorem suam sororem diceret', probably in response to a point made by Paternus. I owe to Adam Kamesar the suggestion that this perhaps exploited a Jewish Aggadah making Sarah Abraham's niece; see G. Vermes, *Scripture and Tradition in Judaism* (1961), 75–76. The Aggadah was apparently accepted by some Syrian Christians (cf. Theodoret *Ep.* VIII); one thinks of the various contacts made in this area by the likes of Achantia, wife of Paternus' relative Cynegius.

34. *Ep.* 59 [84]. For the possibility that the marriage went ahead regardless, see Matthews, *Western Aristocracies*, 143–144.

35. Poss. *V. Aug.* 27.5: 'ne militiae commendatus ac male agens, eius culpa suffragatori tribueretur'.

curred blame for those who failed to live up to his enthusiastic praises. The system of *commendatio* was all-important for the maintenance of the imperial bureaucracy; the power brokers who kept it working must therefore have received allowance for their occasional misjudgements. Moreover, these *commendationes*, playing as they did a central part in the exchange of favours which upper-class *amicitia* required, cannot lightly have been renounced. Other churchmen seem to have felt no compunction in using their influence to further the careers of relatives and friends; several such testimonials survive from Basil of Caesarea, at times disconcerting his admirers.[36] Ambrose's output, by contrast, is all of a piece and maintains a proper distance from the demands of the *saeculum*.

But like other aspects of the 'spiritual' character Ambrose exhibits so well, this reticence cannot be taken at face value. Remote from the centres of power, Basil needed to address his old acquaintances and fellow-students in fairly direct terms. Distance precluded subtlety: by contrast, few of Symmachus' letters, written within the much cosier network of relations linking Rome with Milan, actually recommended a particular person for a specific post. Many of his letters, indeed, claim not to be *commendationes* at all.[37] At Milan, Ambrose was at the very heart of this network. He could therefore eschew the troublesome business of recommendation, exercising his influence (and providing those who danced attendance upon him with their opportunities for advancement) less formally, at occasions like the banquets that attracted the elite of court society. The third prohibition can therefore be compared to the other two; they all advertised the bishop's disengagement from the *saeculum* without diminishing his influence with the world or hindering the performance of the duties by which that influence was sustained and enhanced. The clarity of these rules is therefore deceptive, suggesting a boundary that Ambrose was able in practice to cross at will.

Those in search of professional advancement were not the only beneficiaries of Ambrose's connexions. One Titianus had been making plans for his granddaughter; presumably, like Paternus, he was organizing a dynastic marriage for the girl. But her father, Titianus' son-in-law, was opposed to the project, and he enjoyed the powerful support of the

---

36. See B. Treucker, 'A Note on Basil's Letters of Recommendation', in *Basil of Caesarea*, ed. P. J. Fedwick (1981) 1:405–410.

37. A few examples from many: *Epp.* 1.63 (below, n. 47), 67; 3.66, 77; 4.6; 5.66.

magister officiorum Rufinus, who was with Theodosius in Milan during the years 388–391. Even after the court's return to the east in the spring of 391, Rufinus' influence continued to prevail. In 392, however, Ambrose wrote to Titianus to announce that he had won an 'innocent victory': Rufinus had just been promoted to the prefecture of the east and would thenceforth relinquish both his official involvement in the case and (as Ambrose assured Titianus) his ability to exert unofficial pressure.[38] The announcement clearly came as news to Titianus, which suggests that Ambrose enjoyed privileged access to information on appointments. His confident statement that Rufinus had been neutralized by his appointment also bespeaks Ambrose's political expertise: as a 'friend' of Rufinus, he could disentangle the complex power structure that linked Milan to Constantinople in 392.[39] The letter's chief significance, however, is to illustrate how Ambrose managed his cases. Titianus' difficulties must have begun at least a year earlier, when Rufinus was in Milan, but Ambrose did not forget his client's problem during the long stalemate that ensued. The present letter responded directly to the news of Rufinus' promotion, not to any further appeal from Titianus; Ambrose must have kept his files very well organized. The actual advice to Titianus was to seize the opportunity and complete his projected settlement. Ambrose's businesslike attitude was not the least of his qualities as a patron.

Amicitia imposed various obligations, among them the performance of commissions at second hand, on behalf of the friends of friends. A letter to his Bolognese friend Eusebius shows Ambrose engaged in such a cause.[40] After some unspecified misconduct in business related to the Roman harbour of Portus, a prefectural *apparitor* under Eusebius' patronage had come before the praetorian prefect in Milan and faced the confiscation of his property. Eusebius therefore wrote to Ambrose, who takes up the story in his reply: 'As soon as I received your letter, I saw the prefect and put in a plea for the accused; the prefect immediately granted forgiveness and ordered the letter which he had issued about the confiscation of his goods to be countermanded' (*Ep.* 26 [54].1). The elaborate puns that follow do not dissemble the *apparitor*'s guilt. He had been lucky, mused the bishop: without so well-connected a *gubernator*

38. *Ep.* 45 [52]. This note is discussed by H. L. Levy, *Claudian's In Rufinum* (1971), 253–255, and M. Clauss, *Der Magister Officiorum* (1980), 81–82; both infer wrongly that Theodosius' return to the west was imminent.

39. *Ep.* 45 [52].1: 'gaudeo vel illo, ut amico'.

40. *Ep.* 26 [54]. I am inclined to identify the recipient with the bishop of Bologna: cf. above, p. 66.

(and the prompt delivery of the latter's message) he would have been left 'naked' before the due processes of law. The breezy cheerfulness of this note reveals the man of affairs in Ambrose, the bishop who inspired a slightly resentful admiration for his handling of *negotia:* he appears as poised and comfortable in the Milanese *praetorium* as in his own basilica.

Another frontier that Ambrose bestrode was between the Milanese court and the Roman aristocracy. For senators looking north to further their careers and private interests, the bishop—as a professed Roman permanently entrenched in Milan—was a sound investment. We are given only brief impressions of the axis between the two cities and Ambrose's part in it.[41] A short note replying to a greeting from one Atticus, plausibly to be identified with Nonius Atticus Maximus, 'pillar of the city' and briefly praetorian prefect at Milan in 384, merely offers congratulations upon Atticus' choice of Priscus, an old friend of the bishop's, to deliver his salutation.[42] But the importance of such 'accredited' postmen to conduct the often delicate business transacted between the two cities, and the easy overlap between the personnel of church and *saeculum,* is indicated by the reappearance of Priscus at Milan with a message from Pope Siricius.[43]

Nor was it only old friends who delivered the bishop's mail; outsiders, too, could hope to earn credit by such services. A case in point is Antiochus, the *vir clarissimus* who brought a letter to Ambrose from Alypius, a Roman grandee from the Anician clan,[44] who reappears in the correspondence of Symmachus as an 'opportunist politician' from the east seeking advancement in Theodosius' train.[45] The senator's business with the bishop was no mere exchange of politenesses, for the note delivered by Antiochus had apparently crossed with two letters from Ambrose to Alypius.[46] Even this brief glimpse of the exchange reveals the

41. For some illuminating glimpses of traffic between Ambrose in Milan and Petronius Probus' Roman mansion, see Paulin. *V. Amb.* 21, 25. Note also *ILCV* 419, from the turbulent year 386: a Roman youth dying in Milan and brought home for burial.

42. *Ep.* 42 [88]; see *PLRE* 1, Maximus 34 (pp. 586–587).

43. *Ep.* 41 [86]. The juxtaposition of the two letters in Ambrose's collection is to be noted.

44. *Ep.* 61 [89].

45. Symm. *Ep.* 8.41; for the identification (and description), see J. F. Matthews, 'Gallic Supporters of Theodosius I', *Latomus* 30 (1971), 1080–1081.

46. The exchange gains added resonance from the vicissitudes of Alypius' dealings with the court: he survived a brief 'purge' in his youth to become urban prefect in 391, apparently as a supporter of Theodosius, and subsequently emerged from another cloud under Eugenius to win further favours from the Theodosian dynasty: references in *PLRE* 1, Alypius 13 (p. 49).

bishop much more thoroughly immersed in political society than could ever be guessed from the dour prohibitions he passed on to ascetically inclined admirers.

AMICITIA: AMBROSE AND SYMMACHUS

The best documented and most intriguing of Ambrose's senatorial connexions at Rome is his pagan adversary in the altar of Victory contest. Eight letters from Symmachus to the bishop, barely distinguishable in style and contents from the rest of his voluminous correspondence, reveal a paradoxical friendship between the two men which has long exercised the interest of scholars. But although bishop and senator have seen regular service as symbols of their society's capacity for *concordia*, the basis of their relationship has never been fully explained.

The widespread belief that a blood tie linked these two members of the *gens Aurelia* (to which belonged also their mutual acquaintance Aurelius Augustinus and, thanks to the edict of Caracalla, countless others) rests upon two elusive references: Ambrose's mention of some advice given to his brother Satyrus by 'the noble Symmachus, your parent', and Symmachus' commendation of a Satyrus, 'our common brother', to his own brother Titianus.[47] Neither passage is conclusive. The concordance yields nearly two pages of 'brothers' for Symmachus, some of whom he admits were quite unknown to him;[48] the equally generous scope of *parens* is indicated by the controversy over the identity of the Symmachus invoked by Ambrose.[49] But Symmachus' note to Titianus is itself a powerful argument against kinship, since he would hardly have needed to commend a real cousin in such terms to his brother.[50] His brusqueness

47. *De exc. frat.* 1.32 (cf. above, p. 71); Symm. *Ep.* 1.63. The case for a family connexion has been presented in detail by T. D. Barnes, 'Augustine, Symmachus and Ambrose', in *Augustine: From Rhetor to Theologian*, ed. J. McWilliam (1992), 7–13.

48. A good example is Sperchius, enthusiastically praised at *Ep.* 5.66.5–6.

49. Palanque (*Saint Ambroise*, 489–490) and S. Mazzarino (*Storia sociale del vescovo Ambrogio* [1989], 13 and 77n152) identify him as Avianius Symmachus, the urban prefect of 364/5, *PLRE* 1 (p. 867), as Avianius' better-known son, the orator and epistolographer. Barnes' claim ('Augustine, Symmachus and Ambrose', 8) that Ambrose's use of 'tuus' here implies actual kinship is unconvincing: if anything, his exclusion of himself from the relationship suggests the opposite.

50. Symmachus' asseveration that he was *not* commending Satyrus fits a conventional pattern: a similar formula is used at *Ep.* 2.9 on the strength of the bearer's 'Roman' origins.

betokens not intimacy but another situation: the Ambrosii, insecure and vulnerable as they tried to reorganize their African estates, were seeking support from the more established landed families in the area. The 'paternal' advice given by Symmachus confirms the relative status of the two families during these anxious years for Ambrose, when Symmachus' patronage reflected sufficiently well upon him to be worth broadcasting to the congregation.

The links between senator and bishop cannot be explained in terms of family solidarity. Nor should we see them simply as a reflection of the common ground shared by two aristocrats. Appeal is often made on this count to the altar of Victory debate and the 'great formal courtesy' with which it was conducted: Ambrose and Symmachus are presented as men able to speak the same sort of language, despite differences of opinion. But as we have seen, there was never a debate upon the subject at all. Symmachus' *relatio* was short-circuited in the imperial consistory, and Ambrose's detailed rebuttal of the urban prefect's arguments was compiled *after* the question had been settled. The issue has been transmitted to posterity in a framework devised by Ambrose, which was designed specifically to create the illusion that he defeated Symmachus upon the latter's own terms. The success of this version is shown by Ambrose's own appeal to it against an attempt to reopen the question in 393, and by Prudentius' use of the dossier prepared by the bishop for his versification of the episode in 402.[51] But Ambrose had addressed his famous 'reply' to Symmachus to precisely the likes of Prudentius; the two protagonists in the supposed debate had in fact never confronted one another at all.

Similar problems attend the use of Symmachus' letters to the bishop as evidence for the unproblematic persistence of amicable relations between them for twenty-five years.[52] No personal warmth can be discov-

---

51. 393: p. 345, below. The purely literary character of Prudentius' work was argued by A. Cameron, *Claudian* (1970), 240–241; for a likely context for its composition, see J. Harries, 'Prudentius and Theodosius', *Latomus* 43 (1984), 69–84. Further evidence of Ambrose's success in distorting the question is Paulinus' wretchedly inaccurate summary (*V. Amb.* 26): note his comment that *Ep.* 73 [18] was so effective 'ut contra nihil umquam auderet Symmachus vir eloquentissimus respondere'.

52. This approach informs the discussion by M. Forlin Patrucco and S. Roda, 'Le lettere di Simmaco ad Ambrogio', in *Ambrosius Episcopus*, ed. G. Lazzati (1976), 2:284–297. Scepticism was expressed by J. Matthews, 'Symmachus and His Enemies', in *Colloque genevois sur Symmaque*, ed. F. Paschoud (1986), 163–175; the present discussion aims principally to elaborate his brief remarks at 173–174.

ered in these documents, which exhibit several peculiarities to set them apart from other groups in the senator's published correspondence. Each of the eight letters (enough to treat the set as a reasonable sample)[53] is devoted to an item of business, with none of the salutations, apologies for not writing or recriminations for silence that leaven the petitions to other public men. The letters themselves are strikingly austere, without the effusive compliments or entreaties for a prompt reply with which other correspondents are besieged; nor does Ambrose receive any news of Symmachus' health or an inquiry concerning his own, despite being as confirmed a valetudinarian as the senator. Without any polite attentions to link the individual letters, the series assumes a staccato rhythm: each letter is isolated, triggered (it seems) by the appeal of a third party or the exigencies of a particular situation.

None of Symmachus' other correspondents receives such brusque treatment. Of nine notes addressed to Julianus Rusticus, for example, two acknowledge the receipt of letters, two more present respectively an apology and an excuse for belated replies, and one expresses thanks for Julianus' solicitude after the death of Symmachus' brother. The six letters received by Proculus Gregorius include bantering admiration for his classically correct prose style and good-natured complaints about his prolonged silences, matched by an elegant rebuttal of Gregorius' criticism of Symmachus' own taciturnity.[54] Nor can Ambrose be classified with Symmachus' more distant 'business associates'. Although eight of the nine letters addressed to Paternus (the same man who had unsuccessfully solicited Ambrose's support for his dynastic schemes) are commendations, requests for help or acknowledgements of services rendered, they nevertheless touch regularly upon personal matters. They also articulate with perfect clarity the mutual benefits in the relationship between the two men: Paternus' successive posts as proconsul of Africa and *comes sacrarum largitionum* enabled him to do favours for Symmachus, who promised in return to organize expressions of gratitude from the senate and people of Rome.[55]

The matters referred by Symmachus to Ambrose do not have the same translucence. To understand what brought the two men together

53. The number is slightly above average for book 3, whose twelve correspondents receive a total of ninety-one letters.

54. Julianus: *Epp.* 3.1–9 (only one letter in this group, *Ep.* 3.3, is a *commendatio*); Gregorius: *Epp.* 3.17–22.

55. *Epp.* 5.58–66; note especially the assurance in *Ep.* 5.65 that the 'gratia' of Paternus' 'beneficium' will reach 'et ad senatum . . . et ad populum'. On Paternus, cf. p. 259 above.

and sustained their relationship, we must turn again to the political and
social nexus that bound Rome and Milan. The parvenu capital looked
south to Rome for talent and to borrow the lustre of its cultural credentials; the senatorial aristocracy in turn needed its outlets at the court of
Milan. Their shared involvement in this Rome-Milan axis brought Ambrose and Symmachus together. Despite the difference in the services
that each provided to the careerists who moved between the two cities,
there were inevitably overlaps between their customers: the rhetorician,
newly arrived in Milan through a recommendation from Symmachus,
who presented himself at the bishop's residence is a celebrated instance
of what must have been a common experience. The 'friendship' between
Ambrose and Symmachus was formed through such cases. Neither man
need have sought it; both were victims of their friends and clients, busy
men whose own horizons were not circumscribed by religious allegiances and who would not expect their requests to be refused upon
such grounds. One such was the *vir clarissimus* Dysarius, an eminent
doctor who asked Symmachus to smooth the path to Milan for a homonymous relative by providing an introduction to Ambrose's *patrocinium*. Symmachus duly wrote to aver his willingness to serve his friend,
expressing satisfaction at gaining the opportunity to cultivate Ambrose
'by presenting a salutation'[56]—a fine sentiment, but hardly convincing
when one considers the scores of men who arrived north with Symmachus' blessing but without any message for the bishop.[57]

Both Symmachus and Ambrose had their reputations enhanced by
their ability to answer such requests; but they did not always relish doing so. In this group of letters, indeed, alert readers have discovered
various barbs beneath the bland surface of Symmachus' prose.[58] Tensions were inevitable within a relationship imposed upon both parties
by their social and political situation, and generous scope for conflict
was allowed by the formal rules of *amicitia*. The case of Dysarius, despite
its complexity (with four people involved, A asking B to recommend C
to D), was perhaps unusually straightforward: the sponsor's profession
alone would have recommended him to Ambrose, who can elsewhere
be found in earnest consultation with the *archiatri* of Milan on abstruse

56. *Ep.* 3.37. Dysarius the doctor reappears as a character in Macrobius'
Saturnalia: N. Marinone, 'Il medico Disario in Simmaco e Macrobio', *Maia,* n.s.,
25 (1973), 344–345.

57. Note especially book 2 of the correspondence: at least 25 men are supplied with letters of introduction to Flavianus during his tenure of the praetorian
prefecture at Milan in 390–394. It is perhaps significant that none of the letters
to Ambrose is dated to this period.

58. See especially Matthews, 'Symmachus and His Enemies'.

questions of gynaecology.[59] Other cases ran less smoothly. The bishop furnished two visitors to Rome, Dorotheus and Septimius, with an introduction to Symmachus. But the single note Ambrose had given them prompted Symmachus to express surprise and dismay that Dorotheus had not been accorded any individual credit; Symmachus offered to vouch for him himself, to encourage the bishop to be more forthcoming.[60] This exposure of Ambrose's inability to handle the basic formulae of polite society can only be seen as disingenuous.[61] Perhaps poor Dorotheus had to return to Milan to deliver this letter himself; the episode can in any case have done little for Ambrose's reputation as an effective referee. He appears much less authoritative here than with his ecclesiastical colleagues: unlike the bishops of Gaul, Symmachus would not allow Ambrose to make up the rules of social intercourse as he went along.

This letter therefore shows Symmachus enjoying an advantage over Ambrose; but he in turn needed the bishop. The other six letters in the correspondence all show him trying to engage Ambrose's services where they were most effective, to protect men from the sanctions of the law. Symmachus no doubt found it distasteful to appeal to the church but was nevertheless driven into Ambrose's arms at the behest of clients who recognized the scope of the church's influence. He writes, for instance, on behalf of one Eusebius, a young man condemned in the criminal courts, to secure Ambrose's help towards obtaining an imperial pardon. Symmachus makes it clear that the initiative was not his own: it was Eusebius, he informs Ambrose, who had desired this recourse to 'proven sources of patronage' and had wanted 'the prospects for his petition to be placed in your care'.[62] But the letter also illustrates Ambrose's vulnerability to pressure. There is no suggestion of Eusebius' innocence; the best colour that could be put upon his offence was as a young man's mistake. The bishop was nevertheless expected to lend his support. As we have seen, he intervened quite casually with the praetorian prefect to save the crooked friend of a friend; here, perhaps, we can glimpse a less congenial aspect of his duty to secure mercy.

Not all the requests for the bishop's intervention were as straight-

---

59. *Ep.* 58 [5].8.

60. *Ep.* 3.32. The two were perhaps young men visiting Rome to complete their education: for Symmachus' patronage of such cases, cf. *Ep.* 4.20 (congratulating a courtier upon his student son's eloquence); 5.74 (reporting to a government minister upon two students under consideration for court appointments).

61. Note that Symmachus himself was prepared to write joint commendations: thus *Epp.* 5.40, 74.

62. *Ep.* 3.35: 'deferri in tuam curam spem petitionis optavit'.

forward as Eusebius'. Sallustius, the urban prefect in 386, 'desired assistance' from Ambrose in a matter which, although it seems to have involved litigation, was too complex or sensitive to be committed to paper.[63] The case, one suspects, was one where the Roman aristocracy's internal wranglings had spilled over into the Milanese court. Symmachus reminded Ambrose of a previous commitment to Sallustius, expressed in many 'spontaneous' favours, and urged him to continue the good work. The bishop seems to have balked at the task, for he soon received a second letter reminding him of his assurance that Sallustius had 'long since been accepted' into his care.[64] Behind the soothing tone—Symmachus protested himself certain that Ambrose, 'a man whose memory is firm', did not need reminding of his responsibilities—there lurks a threat. Speedy production by Ambrose of the desired *beneficium* would ensure that Symmachus had 'no further need to act'; further procrastination would presumably provoke further, stronger admonitions. Ambrose was expected to fulfil his commissions, and his performance was closely monitored.

Ambrose was committed to Sallustius by an explicit declaration of favour which Symmachus was able to quote back at him. The routine politenesses of public life will have demanded from the bishop many such declarations, generating responsibilities and debts that could later be called to account. Magnillus, one of three brothers in whose careers Symmachus took a particular interest, had served a term in Milan as *consularis* of Aemilia and Liguria. During this time he had made Ambrose's acquaintance and won his 'affection'. A further term of provincial office proved less happy for Magnillus: his conduct as *vicarius* of Africa from 391 to 393 was subjected to an inquiry which prevented his return to Rome. Ambrose's 'religious intervention' was therefore solicited to remedy his plight.[65] One aspect of the problem was probably political: Magnillus' position during Eugenius' usurpation, as a subordinate of Flavianus who continued to traffic with Rome while claiming to uphold Theodosius' interests, was not without ambiguity. In any case, a remark elsewhere in Symmachus' correspondence reveals that the case was closely fought, the satisfactory outcome eventually hinging

63. *Ep.* 3.30. The statement (in *Ep.* 3.31) that Sallustius was 'laborans' suggests that his difficulties were legal; cf. *Epp.* 7.89; 4.51. It is not necessary to assume, with J.-P. Callu, *Symmaque: Lettres*, tome II (1982), p. 41, that this matter preceded Sallustius' prefecture.

64. *Ep.* 3.31: 'Itero postulatum pro Sallustio amico meo et, ut ipse adseverasti, a te quoque in curam dudum recepto'.

65. *Ep.* 3.34: 'Nosti optimi viri maturitatem . . .'

upon a sympathetic judge and the favourable testimony of character witnesses.[66]

Ambrose's liability to such service, implicit in Symmachus' request, was more than merely an occupational hazard. For in his case the constraints of *amicitia* reinforced the standard charitable obligations of a bishop; and he remained always under scrutiny from Rome.[67]

Yet another aspect of the proximity of Rome to Milan is displayed in the remaining letter in the selection. Symmachus invites Ambrose to withdraw from the involvement he was rumoured to be planning in a lawsuit between Caecilianus, *praefectus annonae* at Rome and a connexion of Symmachus, and one Pirata.[68] The 'invitation' was forcefully put. Symmachus argued the unfairness of acting against a man 'absent [from Milan] in the fulfilment of his public duties' and reminded the bishop of the adequacy of the apparatus of secular justice. 'There are laws, there are courts, there are magistrates to which a plaintiff can take recourse without harming your conscience'. This makes it clear that the intervention Symmachus was deprecating was not an intercession with the secular authorities, as he had sought in the other cases, but the transference of the suit to the bishop's own jurisdiction. The *episcopalis audientia* remains, it must be admitted, a deeply puzzling institution, whose workings are barely illuminated by the various—and mutually inconsistent— imperial pronouncements upon the subject preserved in the codes.[69] The ill-defined scope of a bishop's judicial activity left much to the inclinations (and stature) of the individual prelate. Some, while diligent in fulfilling their responsibility to settle their flock's disputes, made no secret of their irritation at having to do so.[70] Not so Ambrose: although he was kept busy by the crowds of men pressing their *negotia* upon him, he

66. *Ep.* 9.122.

67. For another possible aspect of this scrutiny see below, p. 362, discussing Symmachus' appeal on behalf of a second disgraced official from Eugenius' regime (*Ep.* 3.33).

68. *Ep.* 3.36; for detailed discussion, see P. Bruggisser, 'Orator disertissimus', *Hermes* 115 (1987), 106–115.

69. W. Selb convincingly argues that the incoherence of this legislation reflects the clergy's relative indifference towards their right to exercise civil jurisdiction: 'Episcopalis Audientia von der Zeit Konstantins bis zur Nov. XXXV Valentinians III', ZRG 84 (1967), 167–217. See also W. Waldstein, 'Zur Stellung der Episcopalis Audientia im spätrömischen Prozess', in *Festschrift für Max Kaser*, ed. D. Medicus and H. H. Seiler (1976), 533–566.

70. Aug. *Exp. Ps. 118* 24 berates those who 'instant urgent precantur tumuluantur extorquent'. Cf. Selb, 'Episcopalis Audientia', 214–217.

gave no sign of discomfort at the burden.[71] The former barrister and judge was, we should presume, perfectly at home in the episcopal court.

A distinctive feature of Ambrose's judicial work was his easy relationship with the secular system, which is nicely illustrated by his letter to one Marcellus, a priest or bishop, probably of curial rank.[72] When Marcellus had attempted to transfer some property to his widowed sister on condition that it should revert upon her death to his church, his brother Laetus had contested the arrangement and brought the case before the prefect's court in Milan. There followed the delays and expenses characteristic of fourth-century litigation, as matters ground on in the expensive hands of the advocates of the prefectural bar; when the time allotted by the court was finally exhausted, the case was transferred to Ambrose. The bishop insisted in his letter to Marcellus (whose apparent ignorance of this development suggests that the principals took little part in the proceedings) that the lawyers had been determined to ensure that the prefect should not decide the business of a *sacerdos*. This assertion totally misrepresented what was clearly a last resort. The expedient was, however, uncontroversial. Permission seems to have been granted automatically to the two teams of lawyers ('Christiani viri': it is no surprise that they, like so many members of the Milanese establishment, should have belonged to Ambrose's congregation) to request the bishop's services as *cognitor*.[73] His acceptance was carefully qualified: he would agree only to help arrange a settlement, not to pronounce a definite verdict for either party. Details were then thrashed out with the *togati*, legal niceties clearly taking second place to practical considerations like the efficient cultivation of the estate and the payment of the taxes upon it. Laetus' claim to the property was accepted, but he agreed to pay the sister a fixed income from the revenue. Ambrose's easy cooperation with the lawyers reminds us of his barrister's past, which is also betrayed in the passage of the letter that commends the solution to Marcellus as a 'victory': 'You have all triumphed, but nobody more completely or more gloriously than yourself'.[74] A difficult brief, requiring Ambrose to report nothing less than the total collapse of Marcellus' original plan, is here handled with considerable aplomb.

71. Aug. *Conf.* 6.1.3.
72. *Ep.* 24 [82]. The case is analyzed by F. Martroye, 'Une sentence arbitrale de saint Ambroise', *RD* 4.8 (1929), 300–311; Marcellus' background is discussed by F. D. Gilliard, 'Senatorial Bishops in the Fourth Century', *HTR* 77 (1984), at 167–168.
73. *Ep.* 24 [82].2–3.
74. *Ep.* 24 [82].9.

It was Ambrose's readiness to intervene in such cases that disturbed Caecilianus. His situation, however, was very different from that of Marcellus and Laetus. On that occasion Ambrose had deliberately refused to deploy his full authority; here Pirata ('or his procurator': Symmachus' remark again suggests the extent to which litigation was conducted indirectly, through subordinates) was expecting the bishop to exploit the power, granted by Constantine, to transfer a suit to his own court if only one of the parties so requested and with no appeal against the episcopal verdict.[75] But Ambrose's impartiality was subject to doubt. Caecilianus had heard 'from a reliable source' that Pirata hoped for the bishop's favour. So it was not, perhaps, merely their wish to exploit the corruption of the secular courts that drove Symmachus and Caecilianus to ward off the bishop;[76] from their point of view, the justice dealt out by the ecclesiastical court must have seemed equally corroded.

Symmachus' confidence in addressing the bishop—'I said that you were not in the habit of undertaking financial cases'[77]—deserves consideration. The case between Marcellus and Laetus, after all, was a wrangle over property which fell into the category of *pecuniariae actiones;* the bishop's reference in his letter to Marcellus of the special problems when one party was a cleric suggests that he usually dealt with cases between laymen.[78] But corroboration of Symmachus' description of Ambrose's 'usual practice' is available, and from a surprising source. *De officiis* allows one exemption from the clergyman's primary responsibility to provide justice: 'It is permitted for you to remain silent in a matter which involves money'.[79] In a later passage, concerning the odium that could arise from involvement in inheritance disputes, this 'permission' is presented more strongly: 'And so it is not for the priest to intervene in a financial case'.[80] The publicity Ambrose gave to his tenets on the proper mode of clerical behaviour—which we have identified as a central aspect of his ideological achievement—seems here to have rebounded against

---

75. *Sirm.* 1 (333). This case is valuable evidence that unilateral appeals to a bishop's jurisdiction were still possible in the late fourth century, despite Jones ('it cannot possibly have outlasted Julian': *LRE*, 418) and Selb (the law was possibly spurious and was in any case quickly forgotten: 'Episcopalis Audientia', 215). The law is likely to have remained a dead letter except for the few bishops sufficiently confident to invoke it.

76. For this view, see Forlin Patrucco and Roda, 'Le lettere', at 289.

77. *Ep.* 3.33: 'Negavi solere te recipere in tuam curam pecuniarias actiones'.

78. *Ep.* 24 [82].3 (on suspicions of 'necessitudinis sacerdotalis gratia'); cf. 5 (on the 'persona sacerdotis').

79. *De off.* 2.125: 'in negotio dumtaxat pecuniario'.

80. *De off.* 3.59: 'in causis pecuniariis'.

him. He had imposed theoretical limits upon his own activity, which Symmachus was able to exploit to circumscribe his actual behaviour.

But how did Symmachus acquire such ammunition? It is unconventional, to say the least, to imagine him reading *De officiis*. Although pagan and Christian authors drew upon the same literary traditions, there is little evidence of interest on either side in the other's use of this common stock.[81] Yet Symmachus' own efforts to ignore the distinctive features of Christianity in his published works themselves betray acute consciousness of the new religion's intrusive presence.[82] If Symmachus and his literary friends were to notice one book among the formidable output of their Christian contemporaries, moreover, it would surely have been this attempt to usurp and supersede one of 'their' classics. Indeed, *De officiis* seems written so that only those with a mental concordance to (or their own copy of) Cicero's original could properly appreciate it. These cultured circles were as much the target audience as were the clerics to whom it was dedicated, and the relatively small literary world of Rome bridged the religious divide. Perhaps Symmachus, who was presented to posterity as the keeper of Cicero's shrine,[83] was invited by his peers to offer an opinion upon this somewhat presumptuous reworking of the deity's masterpiece and took the opportunity to store up a few telling quotations for use against the author.[84]

So direct a connexion between Symmachus and *De officiis* is not required by the argument; the reference to Ambrose's 'usual practice' could have been supplied by a third party. The existence of an interest at least upon this level gains plausibility from a passage in *De officiis* that had in effect booby-trapped the book against any readers sympathetic to Symmachus. A lengthy digression (which strains the Ciceronian framework to the limit)[85] dwells upon the iniquity of expelling *peregrini*, in an extended contrast between the responses of two recent prefects of Rome to corn shortages. Catastrophe had been averted by the first, a 'saintly old man' who organized a collection of gold among the senators to se-

---

81. See, in general, the discussion by Alan Cameron, 'Paganism and Literature in Late Fourth Century Rome', in *Entretiens Hardt* 23 (1977), 1–30.

82. When occasion demanded, Symmachus seems to have been capable of quoting Ambrose back at himself: see below, p. 362.

83. Macrobius *Saturnalia* 2.3.1: 'aedituus'.

84. K. Zelzer, 'Zur Beurteilung der Cicero-Imitatio bei Ambrosius', argues (at 190) that Ambrose wrote *De officiis* with pagan readers in mind.

85. *De off.* 3.45–52; all derived from an afterthought in Cicero's *De off.* 3.47 on the contrast between apparent expediency and humanitarian duty: 'male etiam qui peregrinos urbibus uti prohibent eosque exterminent'.

cure provisions for the populace. The second, however, overreacted to a temporary shortage and ordered a general expulsion of nonresidents from Rome. Ambrose's silence concerning the identity of this latter prefect is not to be interpreted as charitable tact.[86] No contemporary could miss the reference to the most dismal episode in Symmachus' unhappy term of office. The whole section is gratuitous, designed solely to point the contrast between the two men: there was considerable irony, and not a little malice, in this presentation of Symmachus as a Ciceronian *exemplum*.

Ambrose's rhetoric is not designed to illuminate the actual situation. His central point, however, was that Symmachus' action was not only cruel but absurd. During the delay in the arrival of the grain fleet, supplies could easily have been brought from the Italians, but it was these people whose 'sons' were being expelled. These men were moreover *corporati*, engaged under official licence in the provisioning of the city. The contradiction here gave Ambrose his material; his comments were no doubt originally issued at the time (so soon after the altar of Victory affair, the opportunity to attack Symmachus was perhaps especially welcome), but he still revelled in the paradox when *De officiis* was written some five years later:

> There is nothing more shameful than this, to exclude someone as an alien and to make demands of him as though he were your own. Why do you eject a man who feeds himself from his own store? Why do you eject a man who feeds *you*? Do you keep your slave but thrust out your 'father'? Do you accept his corn but refuse him your affection? Do you extort from him your sustenance and offer no gratitude in repayment? (*De off.* 3.49)

The contradiction attacked here has been given a still sharper focus by the brilliant hypothesis, advanced thirty years ago, which identified the *corpus* to which these Italians belonged with the same *corpus negotiatorum* whose members suffered in 386 for their allegiance to Ambrose.[87] This organization, according to the theory, was engaged in selling the agricultural surplus of northern Italy on the open market at Rome. Such important businessmen are not, to be sure, immediately recognizable in the hapless refugees whose plight the bishop painted so vividly;[88] the

86. For this interpretation, see J.-R. Palanque, 'Famines à Rome à la fin du IVe siècle', *REA* 33 (1931), at 349–351.

87. L. Ruggini, *Economia e società nell' "Italia Annonaria"* (1961), 112–146.

88. This weakness in Ruggini's theory, noted by A. Chastagnol (*JRS* 53 [1963], 212), was central to the critique by E. Faure, 'Saint Ambroise et l'expul-

rhetorician's artistry can plausibly be blamed for this, conflating as it does the specific case of the Italian *corporati* (the illogicality of whose expulsion provides the main plank of the attack) with the more general misery inflicted upon the mass of the evicted, the marginal figures who lived precariously off the wealth of Rome. The displaced poor of the Campagna and the perennially unpopular *pantapolae* had no doubt been the intended targets of Symmachus' reluctant decree.[89] For once, however, the machinery of the Roman bureaucracy seems to have worked *too* efficiently. All foreigners who did not enjoy the direct patronage of the capital's elite were vulnerable, even the gently born and socially privileged.[90] We might imagine the agents of the Milanese *corpus* being caught up in this zealous activity and arriving disconsolate in Milan to receive their bishop's outraged sympathy. Their inclusion among Symmachus' 'victims' had probably, therefore, been accidental; but it gave the bishop a handle which the expulsion as planned (a measure welcome to the Roman populace and whose intended targets had no spokesmen to articulate a response) would not have done.[91]

The preceding section of *De officiis*, moreover, provides conclusive evidence against Ambrose's credibility as a witness. He examines the profits reaped by farmers during corn shortages and briskly demolishes their justifications.[92] Such men, the bishop argued, behave not only antisocially but against nature itself, praying for bad harvests and weeping over rich ones; their vaunted 'industry' amounts to no more than cunning, fraud and downright robbery. These are splendid sentiments, and enthusiastically taken up by those who see Ambrose as a campaigner for social justice;[93] but the sequel gives pause. The *peregrini* selling their

---

sion des pérégrins de Rome', in *Etudes . . . dédiées à Gabriel le Bras* (1965), 1:523–540; Faure's own identification of the *corpus* with the *navicularii* of Rome is nevertheless unconvincing.

89. Symmachus' evident distress over the measure, expressed in *Ep.* 2.7, shows that he considered it an unavoidable last resort.

90. For the immunity of three thousand dancing-girls but not (it seems) an independent-minded historian, see Amm. Marc. 14.6.19.

91. J. Durliat, in a recent discussion of the passage (*De la ville antique à la ville byzantine* [1990], 518–522), concludes that its contradictions render it historically worthless: 'Ambroise mêle tout'. But his own interpretation, as a generalized exhortation to aristocratic generosity, misses the *ad hominem* edge. For the popular appeal of expulsion decrees, see Amm. Marc. 28.4.32.

92. *De off.* 3.37–44.

93. Thus V. R. Vasey, *The Social Ideas in the Works of Saint Ambrose* (1982), at 163.

corn during the shortage of 384 must have been enjoying exactly such a windfall. In striking juxtaposition to each other, these passages illustrate not Ambrose's concern to give a balanced picture[94] but a fundamental imbalance in his outlook. Unsparing in his denunciations of sin and immorality, he was nevertheless prepared to defend his friends and clients to the hilt.[95] His inability to see crime except as an attribute of his enemies, or as an abstract vice, is perhaps one of his most 'Roman' characteristics.

Equally typical of Ambrose's background was the maintenance of 'amicable' relations with Symmachus long after this unhappy affair. But *amicitia* should not be confused with friendship. Many scholars have been beguiled by the blandness of Symmachus' letters. Even those alert to the barbs contained there have interpreted the partnership in a positive light, to show how men of goodwill (or hard heads) could transcend the rhetoric of religious conflict and do business with one another.[96] But this fails to reach the mainspring of the relationship. Symmachus would doubtless have preferred to have forwarded his clients to more congenial associates in Milan, and Ambrose to have obeyed his own precept that considerations of *religio* should override all else. But neither could afford to live up to his ideals.

The relationship between Symmachus and Ambrose was the fruit of necessity, imposed upon them in their common struggle to perform the favours and services upon which their reputations rested and from which they derived their political influence. Which of them gained the most benefit from it? The impression given in the letters, that Symmachus exercised the initiative as the senior partner, provides a welcome corrective to Ambrose's packaging of the altar of Victory affair to suggest the orator's vapidity and obsolescence. And although it has had less effect upon posterity, Symmachus' inclusion of Ambrose in his collection as just another 'contact', sandwiched between the amiable Marinianus and the eloquent Hilarius, can be regarded as a presentational exercise of a similar sort. It is appropriate, however, that neither Ambrose nor Symmachus finally succeeds in pinning the other down: we can leave this strange pair of bedfellows manoeuvring still for position, within the elaborate rules prescribed by *amicitia*.

94. As Ruggini implies: 'quasi per contraposizione' (*Economia e società*, 116).
95. Compare Ammianus' description of Petronius Probus, quoted at p. 50 above.
96. Cf. Matthews, *Western Aristocracies*, 191: Ambrose represented to Symmachus 'a court contact and potential patron, like any other influential figure connected with the government'.

CONCERTATIO: AMBROSE AND THE BISHOPS

'Friends' like Symmachus, no matter what tensions the relationship involved, shed great lustre upon Ambrose: the honour he was seen to receive from such powerful figures made him seem a fortunate man. But scarcely less visible or impressive than these attentions were those paid him by his episcopal colleagues. At Milan, the faithful could see bishops visiting from neighbouring sees in conference with their pastor and could occasionally hear them perform under his benevolent eye.[97] These visits reflected a much wider range of contacts that Ambrose cultivated with the Italian bishops. Chromatius of Aquileia, Vigilius of Trent and Gaudentius of Brescia—in their own right a remarkable efflorescence of talent—are united by their regard for Ambrose, to whom they clearly looked as a leader and an inspiration.[98]

Ambrose was already working in close conjunction with other Italian bishops during the first uncertain years of his episcopate. His early difficulties might indeed have prompted interest in Milan's vast ecclesiastical hinterland; for Ambrose's ascendancy over the Italian churches, which spilled far beyond the borders of Aemilia-Liguria to Florence and Aquileia, was not inevitable. He did not enjoy any institutionalized authority over the region, which offers little evidence for any unifying ecclesiastical structures.[99] The works of Zeno of Verona, whose career overlapped with Ambrose's, show scant concern with the world beyond his city; the bishop was fully preoccupied by the struggle to establish

97. Augustine remembered Filastrius of Brescia with Ambrose at Milan: *Ep.* 222. Ambrose invited Filastrius' successor to deliver a sermon at a feast of Peter and Paul: Gaudentius *Tract.* 20.1.

98. The careers of these bishops have been set in their historical context in R. Lizzi's excellent *Vescovi e strutture ecclestiastiche nella città tardoantica* (1989), a constant point of reference in what follows; cf. Lizzi, 'Ambrose's Contemporaries and the Christianization of Northern Italy', *JRS* 80 (1990), 156–173. Also useful is C. Truzzi, *Zeno, Gaudenzio, Cromazio* (1985).

99. The question of Milan's 'metropolitan' status in the fourth century has been much discussed: G. Menis, 'Le giurisdizioni metropolitiche di Aquileia e di Milano nell'antichità', *AAAd* 4 (1973), 271–294, argues (at 284–289) from Milan's status as a provincial capital; I follow E. Cattaneo, 'Il governo ecclesiastico nel IV secolo nell'Italia settentrionale', *AAAd* 22 (1982), 2:175–187, attributing Ambrose's dominance solely to the force of his character. Ambrose's failure even once to invoke any formal authority (even in sixty pages of printed text, attempting a controversial intervention at Vercelli: *Ep. extra coll.* 14 [63]) is in telling contrast with Basil of Caesarea's manner of exercising metropolitan authority.

the claims of Christianity within Verona itself.[100] Ambrose's close connexions with his colleagues represent a new development in the ecclesiastical history of northern Italy.

The principal evidence is Ambrose's correspondence. His letters to
his colleagues are primarily expositions of biblical puzzles, written in
highly scriptural language; but this no more elevates the relationships
concerned to a purely spiritual level (or deserves dismissal as pious mys-
tification) than does Symmachus' invocation of a *religio amicitiae* in his
exchanges with his fellow-senators.[101] Moreover, just as Symmachus' *religio* was sufficiently catholic to embrace at least two Christian bishops,
Ambrose addressed certain pious laymen much as he did churchmen,
to the considerable confusion of later readers.[102] This assimilation of
clerical correspondents to aristocratic friends implicitly elevated them to
the social and cultural level of the latter.[103] From his letters, as from *De
officiis*, Ambrose's colleagues could learn to comport themselves like
leaders (and to cultivate the social self-image necessary to sustain the
performance) and so to assert themselves within their competitive and
introverted communities.[104] For even if Ambrose's background was less
eminent than has generally been supposed, in education and experience
he nevertheless enjoyed a dizzy advantage over the modest respectability of the Italian clergy.[105] He could therefore play an equivalent role
for them as he did for the *saeculum:* once again he mediates between two
worlds, the authoritative interpreter of one to the other.

The contours of the two sets of relations follow a similar pattern.
Ambrose's position in Milanese society was sustained by Roman connexions; but even more important for his ecclesiastical standing were his
links with the Christian Rome. The church of Rome loomed even larger

100. Zeno's sermons seem often to assume a contrast between a small
Christian audience and the sinful, hostile majority of their fellow-citizens:
cf. Lizzi, 'Ambrose's Contemporaries,' 163–164. For the local context, see C.
Truzzi, 'La liturgia di Verona al tempo di San Zeno', *StP* 27 (1980) 539–564.

101. Matthews, *Western Aristocracies*, 5–9, sketches the complexities of
Symmachus' 'religion of friendship' with notable sensitivity.

102. The *consularis* Romulus was identified by the Maurists as a rural clergyman (*PL* 16, 1227D); a bishop of Verona is transformed into a praetorian prefect by *PLRE* 1 (p. 863, Syagrius 3). Cf. chap. 2, n. 46 on Eusebius of Bologna.
For Symmachus' bishops, see *Epp.* 1.64; 7.56.

103. Lizzi, *Vescovi e strutture*, 15–28.

104. Lizzi, *Vescovi e strutture*, 28–36; cf. F. E. Consolino, *Ascesi e mondanità
nella Gallia tardoantica* (1979), 23–37.

105. Lizzi, *Vescovi e strutture*, 17.

at Milan than did its aristocracy. The gravitational pull exerted by the new capital brought even as reluctant a traveller as Symmachus several times up the Via Aemilia; no pope felt obliged to follow this course during Ambrose's episcopate. Ambrose himself, on the other hand, paid several visits to his 'native land' on specifically ecclesiastical business; the greetings conveyed to Pope Siricius by his friend Priscus match those which the same man delivered to the senator Atticus, and their pleasantries are very different from his usual scriptural tone.[106] To an enemy he seemed no more than a lackey of the bishop of Rome, fawning upon him in the ignoble guise of a client.[107]

Such criticism in a sense reflects a truism. Northern Italy was still a frontier zone of Christianity, with a handful of bishoprics scattered across a huge area.[108] These sees retained their individual customs and practices, and had no tradition of—or provision for—coordination or concerted action. Their only common denominator was Rome, whose preeminence can hardly be overstated. The western churches still lacked (outside Africa) the regional coherence and administrative structures that the east was developing through its metropolitans. Even where such titles were recognized, they were liable to be ignored by appeal to Rome, whose wide-ranging claims to jurisdiction had been sanctioned by the western episcopate at Sardica in 343 and were emphatically confirmed by Gratian in 378. Whereas Gaul and Spain were each compelled by distance and encouraged by provincial solidarities to develop a certain regional identity, moreover, Italy lay directly in Rome's shadow. Rome had given the churches of northern Italy their lead: the council of Milan in 355 was convened as a result of papal initiative, and its ill-starred resistance to the emperor was led by a Roman appointee.[109] It

106. *Ep.* 41 [86]: cf. above, p. 262. Another papal emissary, the presbyter Syrus, is likewise the sole subject of *Ep.* 46 [85] to Siricius; the encomium is couched in scriptural language appropriate to Syrus' vocation.

107. Palladius *Apol.* 123: Damasus' pretensions were sustained by 'familiarium et clientulorum adsensione', from Ambrose and the Italian bishops.

108. Only ten sees are attested in Aemilia-Liguria before Ambrose's episcopate: Milan, Bergamo, Bologna, Brescia, Tortona, Modena, Parma, Pavia, Piacenza and Vercelli. For the (in several cases inconclusive) evidence, see F. Lanzoni, *Le diocesi d'Italia* (1927), 2:767–820, 1071–1056, with a summary at 1059–1060. The sees of Como and Lodi were probably created by Ambrose; also perhaps those of Ivrea and Novara (Lanzoni, 2:1059–1060; cf. below, n. 138).

109. The same ingredients of imperial influence (in this case from Constans) and papal authority can be traced in the (admittedly highly obscure) proceedings of the previous council of Milan, in 345: the outcome was a letter of submis-

was towards Rome, moreover, that Auxentius' opponents had looked in the decades after the council. A fair proportion of the region's bishops had meanwhile followed the lead of this Cappadocian stranger. Their complaisance illustrates the extent to which northern Italy remained, at the outset of Ambrose's episcopate, an ecclesiastical vacuum.

Ambrose, of course, filled the vacuum. There was nothing overtly anti-Roman in the identity he was to create for the northern Italian church.[110] Far from it: the bishop's attention to the apostles Peter and Paul fully accorded with contemporary papal propaganda; in public pronouncements he reiterated Peter's importance as the *primatus fidei* and Rome's as a guarantor of communion.[111] No wonder, therefore, that the Roman establishment regarded him as one of their own: he was 'noster Ambrosius' to Jerome (at that time presenting himself as a spokesman for the church of Rome) in 384.[112]

If Ambrose appeared from the Lateran no more than an able subordinate, the Milanese knew better: ultimately, the bishop belonged to them.[113] He absorbed the traditions of his adoptive church and defended the peculiarly Milanese tradition of washing the feet of the newly baptized against any imposition of a Roman standard.[114] Even practices apparently at odds with his ascetic rigorism enjoyed the bishop's wholehearted support, as Monica learned to her surprise when she demanded, through her son, an explanation for the lack of a Saturday fast at Milan.[115] Ambrose replied by asserting the primacy of local tradition, adducing his own different behaviour at Rome and at Milan. This appeal to the two aspects of his ecclesiastical dual nationality managed both to equate the parvenu church of Milan with the mother-city of western Christianity, and to construct Milan's ecclesiastical identity explicitly by reference to Rome.

---

sion from Valens and Ursacius to Pope Julius (Hil. *Coll. antiar. Par.* B.ii.6). See the discussion in Hanson, *The Search*, 312–313.

110. Ambrose's attitude towards the Roman church has been much discussed, often in the light of anachronistic ecclesiological issues. The best survey of the question is by R. Gryson, *Le prêtre selon saint Ambroise* (1968), 164–218.

111. *De inc. dom. sacr.* 32; cf. *De exc. frat.* 1.47 on communion.

112. Jer. *Ep.* 22.22.

113. 'Coepi enim iam hic non esse peregrinus': *De exc. frat.* 1.6.

114. *De sacr.* 3.5. Note the concluding remark: 'In omnibus cupio sequi ecclesiam Romanam; sed tamen et nos homines sensum habemus; ideo quod alibi rectius servatur et nos rectius custodimus'.

115. Aug. *Ep.* 54.

Ambrose's special relationship with Rome is also a key to his authority over his Italian colleagues, which was not derived from a formal institutional position. He acted instead as a point of contact between Saint Peter's city and its northern satellites.[116] His role as Rome's spokesman had not yet been fully refined at Aquileia, where he earned Palladius' derision for 'playing the servant' by reading out three letters from Damasus; much had changed when, upon receipt of a letter from Siricius eleven years later, he mobilized the Italian episcopate to confirm the pope's condemnation of the Jovinianists.[117] This response went far beyond the echo: the Milanese council adduced biblical texts and a recent law to justify the pope's stance, proclaiming the especial validity of the 'creed of the apostles, which the church of Rome forever protects and conserves'. The episode illustrates both Ambrose's usefulness to Rome and his instinctive identification with and appropriation of its authority. He was at a sufficiently safe distance from the city to prevent the self-aggrandizement that this involved from producing tension.[118] There were nevertheless ominous implications for Rome in a bishop's casual remark that Ambrose spoke 'as if he were the successor of the apostle Peter'.[119] By the end of his career the churches of Italy no longer had to look beyond the Apennines for authority.

But the best illustration of the nuances of Ambrose's relationship with Rome, and its bearing upon his position in Italy, is the letter he wrote in late 386 to the bishops of Aemilia concerning the following Easter, when the date produced by the authoritative Alexandrian cycle would fall outside the limits traditionally recognized at Rome.[120] Am-

116. For the participation of other bishops in the Milanese feast of Peter and Paul, cf. n. 97 and chap. 2, n. 45. It is also possible that the Basilicae Apostolorum at Lodi (Amb. *Ep.* 5 [4].1) and Como (Lizzi, *Vescove e strutture*, 57n179) were designed to share the relics which Ambrose had received from Rome: cf. E. Villa, 'Il culto agli Apostoli nell'Italia settentriole alla fine del sec. IV', *Ambrosius* 33 (1957), at 249–250. The question is complicated by the subsequent arrival of eastern apostolic relics, which occasioned the construction of churches at Aquileia and Brescia.

117. Aquileia: Pall. *Apol.* 122. The synodal of the council of 393 is published as *Ep. extra coll.* 15 [42]; for discussion, see Palanque, *Saint Ambroise*, 260–263, and Pietri, *Roma Christiana*, 901–905.

118. But note Palladius' attempt to expose the contradiction latent in the relationship: below, p. 282.

119. Gaudentius *Tract.* 16.9.

120. *Ep. extra coll.* 13 [23]. For full discussion, see M. Zelzer, 'Zum Osterfestbrief des hl. Ambrosius', *WS* 91, n.f. 12 (1978), 187–204; the suggestion (203) that Ambrose wrote at Theodosius' behest is implausible.

brose nevertheless defends the former calculation, explaining its method
at length with arguments taken (without acknowledgement) from a recent work by Theophilus of Alexandria. Though the letter is evidently
neither a binding instruction nor a response to a plea for advice (a further indication of Ambrose's lack of formal metropolitan status), it implicitly asserts the same status as the 'festal letters' of the Alexandrian
popes. At the same time, however, Ambrose is careful to justify himself
by reference to Rome. His studiously vague explanation, that he had
had to write on the subject because 'several bishops of the Roman
church have written to ask my opinion', perhaps implies informal suggestions that he use his access to Greek sources to produce a treatise.
Recourse to this 'commission' to assert his authority over the local episcopate—and perhaps to set the liturgical calendar of northern Italy at
variance with that of Rome[121]—can be explained by the circumstances.
In the months that followed the Easter crisis of 386, the bishop needed
to consolidate his ties with his colleagues and advertise their purely ecclesiastical basis.

The Italian bishops served Ambrose well. He had first invoked their authority after Aquileia in 381; their shadowy presence would subsequently be cited to Valentinian and Theodosius to justify impertinence
and outright defiance.[122] Ambrose was no mere turbulent priest, setting
himself single-handed against the court, but represented a powerful if
loosely defined 'church of Italy'.

Through Ambrose's correspondence, we can see this organization
function upon two distinct levels. In concrete terms, the sheer thoroughness with which he maintained contact with his colleagues ensured
Ambrose an important role in their own mutual dealings. One letter
shows him accepting a gift of truffles from Felix of Como with elegant
thanks (and a probably irresistible pun) and preparing to forward the
gift in part to other friends.[123] The process recalls exactly the conventions
of aristocratic relations observed elsewhere in the empire.[124] The same

121. The traditional Roman computation put Easter on 21 March in 387; the
Alexandrian calculation used by Ambrose placed it on 25 April.

122. For the sequel to Aquileia, see p. 141. Appeals to unspecified 'episcopi'
recur at *Epp.* 72 [17].10, 13 (the altar of Victory); 75 [21].17 (the confrontation of
386); 74 [40].29 (Callinicum). Cf. the 'synod' cited at *Ep. extra coll.* 11 [51].6
(Thessalonica).

123. *Ep.* 43 [3]. 'Tuber' means both truffle and ulcer.

124. Cf. Ausonius *Ep.* 24 to Paulinus (thanking him for a gift of fish sauce);
note also Basil of Caesarea's exchange with Antipater, the *praeses* of Cappadocia,
Epp. 186–187.

Felix also received a salutation upon the anniversary of his consecration, which conveyed greetings from a third bishop, Bassianus of Lodi.[125] Both cases place Ambrose at the centre of a network of communications: from Milan, letters of instruction, exhortation and advice radiated outwards to the churches of Trent, Verona, Claterna, Piacenza and Vercelli.

These texts also present what might be called the ideological aspect of Ambrose's relationship with his peers. The letter on the date of Easter shows him employing, as a substitute for the formal powers of a metropolitan, the same expertise as a learned exegete that he displayed to his parishioners. One of his colleagues, indeed, saw Ambrose exactly as did Monica, as a teacher from whose mouth streamed 'the rivers of living water'.[126] Ambrose's learning was a key aspect of his authority. The *insignia institutionis* which a newly consecrated bishop, Vigilius of Trent, obtained from Ambrose consisted of a letter devoted largely to a disquisition, illustrated by reference to the story of Samson, upon the dangers of mixed marriages.[127] Constantius, another recent appointee, was sent an elaborate meditation upon the theme of the labourer being worthy of his hire, and Felix of Como received as his anniversary 'present' a short treatise on the Holy of Holies.[128]

These exegetical essays generally take a concrete issue as their starting-point. They are nevertheless unlikely to have had any directly practical application as either specific advice for dealing with problems peculiar to these sees or material for a hesitant novice's sermons. Vigilius, for instance, most probably did not learn anything he did not already know about Trent from Ambrose's letter, nor will he have been able easily to incorporate the highly stylized and idiosyncratic discussion of Samson into his own preaching. A more significant function of these letters was symbolic: to accredit their recipients as followers of Ambrose. Admission into the circle of churchmen who conducted their communications in this rarefied way, and whom Ambrose would commemorate in his publications, was a privilege.[129] The bishop of Milan

---

125. *Ep.* 5 [4].

126. Gaudentius *Tract.* 16.9; cf. Aug. *Conf.* 6.1.1.

127. *Ep.* 62 [19]. For a possible connexion between 'insignia institutionis' and contemporary administrative practise, see R. Lizzi, 'Codicilli imperiali e *insignia* episcopali', *RIL* 122 (1988), 3–13.

128. *Epp.* 36 [2]; 5 [4].

129. For Ambrose's announcement of his plan to publish his letters, see *Ep.* 32 [48].7 (to Sabinus): 'Haec tecum prolusimus quae in libris nostrarum epistolarum referam, si placet, atque in numerum reponam, ut tuo commendentur nomine'.

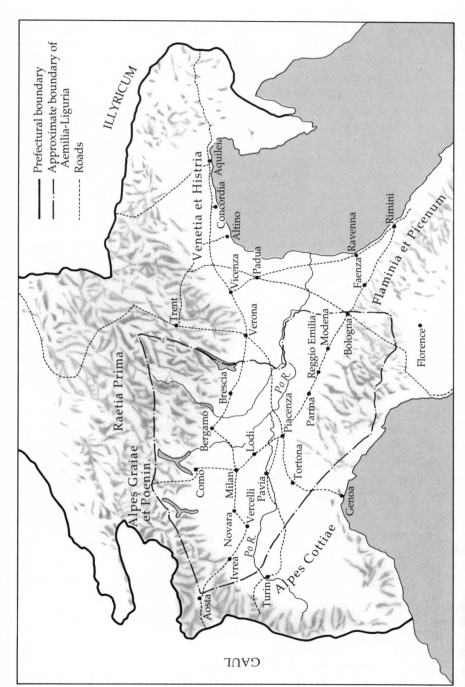

ILLYRICUM

Prefectural boundary
Approximate boundary of
Aemilia-Liguria
Roads

Venetia et Histria

Aquileia
Concordia
Altino
Vicenza Padua
Verona

Flaminia et Picenum

Rimini
Ravenna
Faenza

Bologna
Florence

Trent

Reggio Emilia
Modena
Parma

Raetia Prima

Brescia
Po R.
Piacenza

Bergamo
Lodi
Tortona

Como
Milan
Pavia
Genoa

Alpes Graiae
et Poenin.

Novara
Vercelli
Po R.
Ivrea

Alpes Cottiae

Turin

Aosta

GAUL

7. Northern Italy.

thus helped to mould a new elite within the Italian church, with himself at their head.

The function of these letters might also be compared to that of the relics Ambrose distributed in quantities quite unprecedented in the west and over an extraordinary geographical range. Within a generation Gervasius and Protasius were celebrated not only throughout Italy but as far away as Rouen, Bordeaux and Hippo, through what can only be described as a marketing strategy.[130] The 'blood' recovered when the martyrs were excavated was bottled for export while the skeletons remained intact at Milan; as if to establish their credentials, these capsules appear to have been distributed in conjunction with parcels made up from the apostolic relics that had arrived at Milan from the east.[131] Ambrose had discovered his martyrs, as he had developed his learning, amid tensions within his own city. In both cases, the repackaging of these domestic weapons for export suggests a rare capacity for adaptation; it also suggests, yet again, that his prestige abroad was just as improvised as had been his authority within Milan itself.

An Ambrosian tone was exported to the Italian churches also through such appointments as those of the Milanese deacon Felix to the bishopric of Bologna and the *notarius* Theodulus to Modena, both mentioned in passing by Paulinus.[132] These men had imbibed the bishop's teachings at first hand, and had learnt by observation the patterns of behaviour that were packaged for wider circulation in *De officiis*, such as the 'gressus probabilis', the manner of deportment which conveyed 'an air of authority, a weight of seriousness and a mark of tranquillity' without any appearance of effort or contrivance.[133] They thus were the natural leaders for the next generation of the Italian church. Milan's developing

130. Victricius *De laude sanct.* 6; Marquise de Maillé, *Recherches sur les origines de Bordeaux chrétien* (1959), 28–38; Aug. *Sermo* 286; Paul. Nol. *Ep.* 32.10, 17; Gaudentius *Tract.* 17.12.

131. Blood: Gaudentius *Tract.* 17.12; cf. Amb. *Ep.* 77 [22].2, 12, 23. The quantity distributed evidently puzzled later generations; an explanation is retailed by Gregory of Tours, *De gloria martyrum* 46. Apostles: Luke, Andrew and Thomas (cf. p. 230) are mentioned by Paulinus and Gaudentius, Andrew and Thomas by Victricius; all three also mention John the Baptist, while the Evangelist's relics are reported at Milan: a confusion is likely.

132. Paulin. *V. Amb.* 46.1; 35.1.

133. *De off.* 1.75.

position as an avenue of promotion must have had helped recruitment
to the clergy there.[134] What effect this had elsewhere in the region,
however—whether the talent of other churches was skimmed off by
Milan, or the appointment of Milan-trained bishops was felt as an intrusion by communities accustomed to comfortable introversion—cannot
be determined.

One happy intervention by Ambrose ensured the succession of Gaudentius to the see of Brescia in the mid-390s.[135] Gaudentius was a product of the Brescian church, having been nurtured under the somewhat
eccentric influence of Bishop Filastrius; he subsequently expanded his
horizons and was touring the holy sites of the east when the latter died.
Ambrose in effect blackmailed him into abandoning the pursuit of personal piety by organizing an oath from the Christians of Brescia that
they would accept none but him as their bishop. This heavy-handed
approach worked: at his consecration, an evidently reconciled Gaudentius modestly invited the bishop of Milan to set an authoritative seal
upon the proceedings.[136]

Ambrose intervened controversially in another election at about the
same time, in Vercelli.[137] Against his own preferred candidate, Honoratus, an ascetic with Milanese associations, was ranged a local preference
for a wealthy leader and the influence of two refugees from Ambrose's
monastery in Milan. The obscurity into which Eusebius' see had fallen
during the long tenure of Limenius (who had supported Ambrose at the
council of Aquileia but is never once mentioned in his surviving writings) might conceivably have been attributed to Milanese aggrandizement and thus have galvanized the opposition. There is no telling; nor
does the evidence permit a direct connexion to be drawn between Honoratus' eventual appointment and the almost simultaneous dismember-
ment of the vast see, which saw bishoprics carved out at Novara, Ivrea,
Aosta and Turin.[138] In at least one of these cases, the credit for installing

134. The Milanese clergy included an African (Paulin. *V. Amb.* 54.1); Paulinus of Nola was 'invited' to join (*Ep.* 3.4). Few bishops can have had enough
clerical candidates to insist upon satisfactory gait (*De off.* 1.72) or clerical continence, a point well made by Peter Brown, *The Body and Society* (1988), 357.

135. For Gaudentius' consecration, see Lizzi, *Vescovi e strutture*, 97–109.

136. Gaud. *Tract.* 16.9.

137. Ambrose's intervention culminated in the massive *Ep. extra coll.* 14 [63];
for discussion and bibliography, see Lizzi, *Vescovi e strutture*, 46–50.

138. The late but circumstantial *Vita Gaudentii* attributes the nomination of
the first bishop of Novara to Ambrose: see Lanzoni, *Le diocesi d'Italia*, 2:1032–

the first bishop goes to Ambrose: Milan thus displaced Vercelli, the traditional guardian of these communities. In the circumstances, a certain resentment would be understandable.

Although such lines of thought soon falter through lack of evidence, they remind us of the narrow limitations of our material. Any reader can see that the choruses of approbation that hailed Ambrose's onslaughts at the council of Aquileia were orchestrated; so too was the appearance for consecration at Milan of virgins from across northern Italy. The impression of an Italy enthusiastically and spontaneously united behind the energetic prelate of Milan cannot be taken on trust. Even Ambrose's friends must sometimes have suffered under the pressures generated by his leadership. A bishop of Pavia, for instance, was once faced with a demand that he surrender a sum of money entrusted to him by a widow, apparently to meet a debt she had subsequently incurred. Against the perfectly legitimate claim, backed by the authority of the *magister officiorum* (who made an *agens in rebus* available to enforce it) and an imperial rescript, the sympathetic clergy and even the widow's powerful friends were helpless. But the bishop, having 'shared his counsels' with Ambrose, embarked upon an extraordinary campaign of defiance: he physically prevented the removal of the sum from the *conclavia* where he had stored it until the deadlock was broken by the return of the deposit intact to the widow.[139] We are not told whether the creditor had meanwhile dropped his case; if not, of course, this 'solution' will not have helped the woman greatly. But even so, the bishop's heroics are noteworthy. One cannot but wonder whether he would have embarked upon such a course had he not first received advice from Ambrose.

The advice Ambrose made so widely available could serve not only to sustain his brother bishops but also to subvert them. After conducting a routine disciplinary case within his community, Syagrius of Verona was understandably aggrieved to learn that Ambrose had not only heard an appeal (without any obvious authority to have done so) but also reversed the original verdict. A complaint to Ambrose was met, however,

---

1034. Cf. F. Savio, *Gli antichi vescovi d'Italia: Il Piemonte* (1898), 6–8, attributing the foundation of sees not only at Ivrea but also at Turin, Aosta, Alba, Asti, and Acqui to the period 395/7 and 'la mano di S. Ambrogio'. Novara and Ivrea were subordinate to the church of Vercelli in the 350s: see Eusebius Verc. *Ep.* 2 (*CCL* 9, p. 104).

139. *De off.* 2.150–151. Ambrose's references to 'praeceptis imperialibus' and 'imperator' exclude Palanque's suggestion (*Saint Ambroise*, 526) that this was an arbitrary exaction during Maximus' occupation of Italy.

by a long account of the facts of the case as Ambrose had interpreted them, followed by a second letter restating, through exegesis of an Old Testament episode, the basis of this judgement.[140] The issue had involved the explosive compound of property and asceticism; doubts had been cast upon the chastity of a consecrated virgin named Indicia by a brother-in-law whose principal concern seems to have been to bring her under his own control.[141] Syagrius' approach to this potentially ugly matter had been to avoid a formal process, but Ambrose instituted a full hearing at Milan. His method, as he describes it, appears scrupulous and fair; but Syagrius might reasonably have entertained doubts about his motives for intervention, and even about his impartiality. Indicia, it emerged, was a family friend who had lived for a time with his sister Marcellina in Rome.[142] That there is no other record of contact between Ambrose and Syagrius (who was absent from the bishop's councils at Aquileia and Milan) is not necessarily significant, given the lacunae in the sources, but the episode should alert us to possible strains within Ambrose's society of Italian bishops.

There are indications that Ambrose's hold over his region was incomplete. Casual references in three documents reveal a rogue bishop, Urbanus, still active in Parma in 381.[143] There is nothing in Ambrose's writings to suggest his existence. The vociferous support given to Ambrose by such allies as Eusebius, Sabinus, Chromatius and Vigilius (and their appearance in his published correspondence) therefore need not imply that their enthusiasm for him was universally shared. Disgruntled survivors from Auxentius' era or shy provincial bishops like those, 'their eyes fixed upon the ground', who so impressed Ammianus perhaps kept themselves apart from the Ambrosian establishment:[144] perhaps the Italian church had been hijacked by a well-organized and articulate minority. The episcopal records contain many gaps. It is not known who held the sees of Rimini, Ravenna or Padua during Ambrose's episcopate; nor is there any evidence that important cities like Cremona, Mantua

---

140. *Epp.* 56–57 [5–6]; the opening words of the first letter give the gist of Syagrius' protest: 'Prospiciendum esse ne de nostro obloquantur iudicio carissimi nostri Veronenses, propriis texuisti litteris'.

141. The case is discussed by F. Martroye, 'L'affaire "Indicia"', in *Mélanges P. Fournier* (1929), 503–510; cf. V. Busek, 'Der Prozess der Indicia' *ZRG* (Kan. Abt.) 29 (1940), 447–461.

142. *Ep.* 56 [5].21.

143. *Ep. extra coll.* 7.5 (from the Roman council of 378); *Coll. Avell.* 13.6; Pall. *Apol.* 125. Cf. Gryson, *Le prêtre selon saint Ambroise*, 174–176.

144. Amm. Marc. 27.13.15.

and Reggio even *had* bishops before the fifth century. The argument from silence cannot be pressed, for the only fourth-century evidence for bishoprics in such cities as Como, Genoa and Lodi comes from Ambrose himself, either directly in his writings or through the attendance list of his council at Aquileia. Hints emerge of various forces resistant to the pull of Milan. To the landlords of Vercelli we might add the Illyrican Arians of Forum Cornelii, who posed enough of a threat at a forthcoming episcopal election there for Ambrose to ask one of his protégés to intervene.[145]

No direct challenge to Ambrose ever emerged from within the Italian church. It fell to a pair of Illyricans to present the case against the style of leadership exercised by the bishop of Milan. His aristocratic demeanour, which rubbed off on his associates, appalled Palladius of Ratiaria, who deplored their 'distinctive brand of arrogance', which was reflected even in the seating arrangements of the council of Aquileia.[146] Palladius assailed Ambrose for introducing into religious debate the interrogation techniques of the law courts, 'in order that you could extract an answer which had, with good reason, been denied you in private discussion, by inflicting the terror which a magistrate commands, as though you held public authority' (*Apol.* 97). But Palladius' *Apology* did much more than rage at Ambrose's manners. Palladius concluded with a challenge aimed at both Ambrose's claim to exegetical prowess and his association with the church of Rome, the twin pillars of his ecclesiastical position. Ambrose was invited, if he had any 'confidence in his faith', to an exhaustive debate, stretching for thirty or forty days, which would be based upon the 'authority of all the Scriptures'. The discussion was to take place at Rome: 'for Italy', Ambrose was reminded, 'is as much your province as it is Damasus', and Rome as much your mother-city as his'.[147] Palladius had spotted the mutually satisfactory ambivalence in the bishop of Milan's relations with the pope, recognizing that while his adulation of Damasus fed the pope's pretensions as a 'prince of the episcopate', it coexisted with a readiness to ignore his authority.[148] By bringing the two men together, he could hope to reveal the contradiction.

145. *Ep.* 35 [2].28. These Illyricans are less likely to have been 'refugees' from the Gothic invasions (Palanque, *Saint Ambroise*, 501) than clergymen associated with Iulianus Valens: the previous consequences of their perfidy, to which Constantius is advised to draw attention, are probably conciliar condemnations.

146. *Apol.* 89: 'pro vestro speciali fastu altissimo'.

147. *Apol.* 139: 'certe tam tibi quam Damasso provincia est Italia, genetrix Roma'.

148. *Apol.* 124: 'adrogantia . . . Damasi'; 'per vestram conibentiam ut princeps episcopatus excuset'. Palladius then discusses (125–126) the council of

Palladius never had a chance to expose Ambrose as the impostor he believed him to be. Nor did another famous adversary. The tributes that Jerome had initially accorded Ambrose for his orthodoxy and his promotion of virginity soon turned sour. After his abrupt departure from Rome in 385, he subjected various of the bishop's works to critical scrutiny, discovering evidence of both fraud and incompetence in the use of Greek theologians. He never explains this reversal of attitude, but a connexion between Ambrose (either as participant or, more likely, as impassive object of an appeal for aid) and the 'senate of Pharisees' who drove him from Rome has plausibly been suggested.[149] Perhaps Jerome had by then already begun to voice an opinion of Ambrose's exegetical abilities and integrity. When a copy of Didymus' treatise on the Holy Spirit came into his hands in 384, he immediately conceived the idea of a translation into Latin, dedicating the project to Damasus.[150] The debt Ambrose's recent *De spiritu sancto* had owed to this work will soon have become apparent, and Jerome was certainly tactless enough to have blurted out his findings. He unleashed his venom shortly afterwards from Bethlehem, deriding Ambrose as an 'ugly crow, decked out in another's feathers'.[151] Some years later, Jerome's companions Paula and Eustochium complained to him of the verbal tricks and intellectual somnolence of Ambrose's commentary upon Luke, which they had apparently just received from their Roman friends (a nice example of how widely the bishop's works were distributed), and asked for a translation of Origen's original homilies on the subject. The task was congenial: in his preface, Jerome again presented Ambrose as an ugly, ill-omened crow, 'resplendent with bright hues stolen from other birds'.[152] Other shafts directed against Ambrose's professional competence and episcopal manner can be detected throughout Jerome's work.[153]

Aquileia's refusal to acknowledge Damasus' rehabilitation of Leontius of Salona, whom they had condemned: logic should compel them, he suggested, either to admit their 'human error' and reverse their previous verdict, or to excommunicate Damasus.

149. A. Paredi, 'S. Gerolamo e S. Ambrogio', *ST* 235 (1964; *Mélanges Eugène Tisserant* 5), 183–198.

150. Jer. *Ep.* 36.1.

151. See L. Doutreleau, 'Le prologue de Jérôme au *De spiritu sancto* de Didyme', in *Alexandrina: Mélanges Mondesert* (1987), 297–311.

152. Jerome's prologue to his version of Origen's homilies on Luke is well discussed by F. Fournier in his introduction to the *Sources Chrétiennes* edition (*SCh* 87, 1962), at pp. 70–74.

153. Catalogued by Paredi, 'S. Gerolamo e S. Ambrogio'; note also the attack in the prologue to the commentary on Ephesians against writers of books

But Jerome, like Palladius before him, failed to secure a platform
from which he could challenge Ambrose directly; he displays an un-
characteristic reluctance even to mention the bishop by name.[154] Ambrose's chorus of friends, who had shouted Palladius down so efficiently
at Aquileia, would not be distracted by such murmurs. Neither the cries
of his colleagues, however, nor the acclamations raised on his behalf by
the faithful in 386 constituted the basis of a secure ascendancy. With
such backing, Ambrose had made himself heard throughout Milan and
across Italy. But he needed, in the last resort, an audience prepared to
listen. The courts of Gratian and Valentinian were to an extent captive:
dependent upon Milan, they came to rely upon the services the bishop
provided. But the geopolitical configurations of the empire were liable
to abrupt shifts, and the invasion of Maximus in 387 created a new situation. Much more disruptive, however, was the triumphant arrival the
following year of another emperor. By 388 Theodosius had become
firmly rooted in Constantinople. Having no compelling need to listen to
Ambrose, he would present the most serious challenge that the bishop
ever faced.

---

with titles like *De avaritia*, *De fide* and *De virginitate*, mixing selected scriptural
quotations with 'eloquentia saecularis' and applying 'pompatica sermo' to com-
monplaces. A reference to Ambrose is argued by W. Dunphy, 'On the Date of
St. Ambrose's *De Tobia*', SE 27 (1984), 27–36.

154. The same obliqueness applies also to Jerome's notorious entry for Ambrose at *De vir. ill.* 124: 'Ambrosius Mediolanensis episcopus, usque in praesen-
tiam diem scribit, de quo quia superest, meum iudicium subtraham, ne in alte-
rutram partem, aut adulatio in me reprehendatur aut veritas'.

CHAPTER SEVEN

AMBROSE AND THEODOSIUS

THE SETTING

The relationship between Ambrose and Theodosius was soon transformed into myth. The two men had within a generation of their deaths already been frozen into the postures that would for centuries inspire emulation from tough-minded clerics and pious rulers, and feed the imaginations of scholars and artists alike—the bishop standing before his church, sternly charging Theodosius with the responsibility for a massacre of innocent civilians, his own subjects; the proud and hot-tempered prince coming (eventually) to acknowledge guilt and submitting with humility to the penance ordained by the church.[1] Although this encounter at the church door has long been recognized as a pious fiction devised to illustrate the proper attitude of a Christian monarch to the church, it continues to exercise its spell even upon contemporary scholarship. Ambrose and Theodosius remain individuals, two masterful men locked in a battle of wills.

Psychology frequently underpins modern interpretations, providing the heavy symbolism of the fifth-century portraits with a naturalistic gloss. Ambrose has been credited with a profound impact upon Theodosius, effecting the emperor's conversion to 'genuine' Christianity. A

---

1. Sozomen *HE* 7.25.1–7; Theodoret *HE* 5.17–18. For this account and its subsequent development, see R. Schieffer, 'Von Mailand nach Canossa', *Deutsches Archiv für Erforschung des Mittelalters* 28 (1972), 333–370.

less sympathetic version attributes to Theodosius a superstitious piety that left him particularly susceptible to the bishop's hectoring.[2] The relationship has remained direct and personal even for those who have minimized its political significance.[3] Impressive documentation seems to support such interpretations. A verbatim transcript of a sermon shows Ambrose 'rampant in his cathedral', bringing pressure to bear upon a clearly reluctant emperor; a personal letter from the bishop announces to Theodosius his 'excommunication', its tone firm but sensitive, its manner discreet; at a memorial service for Theodosius, finally, Ambrose gave a moving expression of his 'love' for the emperor. These texts suggest the vicissitudes of a genuine relationship between two individuals, which cuts through the bland courtesies in which the friendship of Symmachus is swathed.

But it is dangerous indeed to read these documents (all of them produced by Ambrose himself) as a reliable guide to the relationship as a whole or as a direct presentation of the bishop's feelings towards Theodosius. Sermons loaded with biblical language and delivered in a liturgical context, a formal letter (no less formal for being confidential) to the sovereign: these texts reveal Ambrose the bishop, not the man, addressing himself to Theodosius' imperial persona. Moreover, both men were constrained by the organizations that they represented, the eastern court and the Italian church. Rather than illustrating the growth of a friendship based upon mutual affection and respect, the documents that present Ambrose's dealings with the emperor reveal a process of negotiation between these institutions. The eventual alliance between Theodosian court and Ambrosian church, around which so many myths have been fabricated, was a strange affair, consummated only after a series of false starts and misunderstandings. If personalities played their part in creating both the initial awkwardness and the final resolution, political factors were much more important.

The process that eventually brought Ambrose and Theodosius together was set in motion in the summer of 387, with the flight of Valentinian and his entourage before the onset of Maximus. The fugitives established themselves on the eastern marches of Valentinian's territory

2. For the former view, see J. R. Palanque, *Saint Ambroise et l'empire romain* (1933), 245–250; for Theodosius' 'vulnerability', see A. H. M. Jones, *The Later Roman Empire* (1964), 165–169.

3. There has been a recent tendency to treat Theodosius's penance as a private, 'pastoral' matter: thus R. Gryson, *Le prêtre selon saint Ambroise* (1968), 277–290, followed by A. Lippold, *Theodosius der Grosse und seine Zeit*, 2d ed. (1980), 170.

at Thessalonica, a city whose strategic value had made it an important pawn in the relations between east and west. Theodosius now hastened there for what was probably his first meeting with his colleague, an encounter of which we possess two very different accounts. The ecclesiastical sources show Theodosius lecturing the hapless prince upon the connexion between his present plight and his heretical inclinations, and extracting from him a humble acknowledgement of past error and a commitment to orthodoxy for the future. In Zosimus the eastern emperor falls victim to the charms of Valentinian's sister Galla, presented to good effect by an artful mother.[4] Both tales, implausible in themselves, should reflect aspects of the publicity produced by the emperors at Thessalonica: politic advertisement of religious solidarity, in the circumstances necessarily on Theodosius' terms, and a matrimonial alliance to commit the east to war on behalf of the house of Valentinian. Theodosius might otherwise have found it difficult to muster support for an expensive and hazardous conflict with Maximus and the army which, as he was doubtless reminded, had served the elder Valentinian so well.[5] His determination to face this powerful enemy, curious in view of his previous indifference to (and subsequent treatment of) the younger Valentinian, probably owed more to anxious calculation than to loyalty: with Italy and the upper Danube added to his territory, Maximus had become the strongest member of the imperial college. Opportunism might also have sharpened Theodosius' zeal for Valentinian's cause. Also present in Thessalonica were key members of Valentinian's military and civil establishments, Arbogast and Petronius Probus, who would eventually attach themselves to Theodosius; any promises of support made by these men will have helped induce Theodosius to face the hazards of war.

In the event, the campaign was short and in its final stages relatively bloodless. Maximus' Alpine defences were outflanked, and he was handed over to his enemies by his own troops for summary execution on 28 July (or perhaps August), 388.[6] Theodosius has secured for himself the credit for this triumph, which is often forgotten to have been a joint venture. Valentinian contributed part of Theodosius' expeditionary force in the Balkans, himself commanding a naval expedition that diverted much of the usurper's strength and secured at least one victory, in Sic-

4. Theod. *HE* 5.15.1; Zosimus 4.44.2.
5. These considerations are well set out by K. G. Holum, *Theodosian Empresses* (1982), 45–46. Richomer, Theodosius' *magister militum*, had served as *comes domesticorum* under Gratian.
6. J. F. Matthews, *Western Aristocracies and Imperial Court* (1975), 224–225.

ily.[7] The prince was easily of age, at seventeen, to lay plausible claim to military renown (irrespective of his formal rights, as Augustus, to a share in the glory);[8] his colleague's monopoly of the laurels of war therefore raises certain questions. The tendentiousness of what became the official version, the rescue by Theodosius of a helpless youth and a generous restoration to his throne, might in any case have occasioned suspicions.[9] These are given substance by the chance survival (in a source from Gaul, which remained beyond Theodosius' direct reach) of an alternative presentation, wherein Valentinian is shown recovering his own kingdom.[10] The discrepancy, small in itself, underlines a point of cardinal importance: any analysis of western politics during this period must recognize the wholesale contamination of the tradition by Theodosian propaganda.

Theodosius' bid to take over the west was a hostile one, for it involved displacing its rightful ruler. Scholars have missed the full implications of this by assuming that the bid was uncontested and that Theodosius automatically took power in 388.[11] The idea rests not only upon an uncritical acceptance of distorted material but also upon some questionable assumptions concerning the exercise of power. Valentinian's sovereignty had remained unimpaired during the flight to Thessalonica, a city in his own territory, and he returned the undisputed ruler of the lands that he had claimed since 383: the full inheritance of Gratian. The presence in his realm of another Augustus, even one loaded with the plaudits of triumph and attended by a victorious army, did not diminish his rights. Any exercise of his own imperial prerogatives in the west by Theodosius (the hearing of petitions, for example, or the enactment of laws) reflected only the collegiate status of the Augusti. They appeared

7. One of the four leaders of Theodosius' army was Arbogast, who had succeeded Bauto to the command of the western forces (Zos. 4.53.1). The naval expedition is described at Zos. 4.45.4–46.1; for Sicily, see Amb. *Ep.* 73 [40].22–23.

8. Gratian was nineteen when he won his victory over the Lentienses in 378; at Constantinople, Theodosius had shared the honours in his recent triumph over the Greuthungi with the nine-year-old Arcadius (*Cons. Const.* s.a. 386: *Chron. Min.* 1, p. 244).

9. Thus Rufinus *HE* 11.17; Aug. *Civ. Dei* 5.26; cf. Zos. 4.47.2, with the curious comment that this restoration seemed appropriate 'in relation to his benefactors', presumably referring to the house of Valentinian: is this an attempt by a hostile tradition to rationalize Theodosius' apparent generosity?

10. Sulp. Sev. *V. Mart.* 20.9.

11. Thus Matthews, *Western Aristocracies*, 225 (on Theodosius and 'his newly regained provinces'); A. Pabst, *Divisio Regni* (1986), 105.

in public as equals, with formal precedence belonging to Valentinian as the senior Augustus. Any assertion by Theodosius of his own supremacy required the manipulation of ceremonies designed to express an ideology of fraternal solidarity.[12]

What, then, of the 'realities' of power? Only a few laws directed to western officials survive for the period from the autumn of 388 to the following spring; the appointment by Theodosius of officials like the praetorian prefect Trifolius does not amount to the exercise of 'government'.[13] And however great the immediate impression made in the west by Theodosius, it must have been recognized that he would not be a permanent fixture there. Valentinian's administration, although disrupted and dislocated by its recent traumas, could be expected to consolidate its position;[14] but until then, westerners had a choice between two separate (although in practice often overlapping) courts to which to bring their petitions or appeals. The two parallel series of gold coins issued during this period provide the most vivid surviving evidence of this dualism. Their mint marks, with the Greek letter theta identifying Theodosius' issues, indicate nicely the anomalousness of the latter's position.[15] It was he, not Valentinian, who was the outsider. His problem was therefore a considerable one: in order to establish the ascendancy he desired in the west, he had to align it towards himself and thus away from its 'natural' axis.

Theodosius therefore had to win over the oligarchy that had created Valentinian and sustained him until 387. Roman aristocrats and Frankish generals had supported the Italian court in order to pursue their own interests; they had not sought a strong ruler in 383 and therefore had no reason to discard Valentinian now, after his 'failure' against Maximus. Far from it: the prince could with charity be considered to have redeemed himself by his participation in the reconquest, and the long life that stretched ahead of him promised stability and continuity as his

12. One promotional device available to Theodosius was the reception (alone, as far as we can tell) of embassies from eastern cities bearing victory crowns: P. Petit, *Libanius et la vie municipale* (1955), 418–419, gives evidence for such legations from Antioch and Emesa.

13. Trifolius received his first law during Theodosius' march west, at Stobi in June 388; he had previously held office under the same emperor in Constantinople. Cf. *PLRE* 1, p. 923.

14. We should note such continuities in the personnel of 'western' government as Messianus, proconsul of Africa in 385–386, who reappears with Valentinian at Trier, in 389: *PLRE* 1, p. 600.

15. M. F. Hendy, 'Aspects of Coin Production and Fiscal Administration', *NC* 7.12 (1972), at 138–139.

friends and mentors consolidated their positions around him. Against this, Theodosius could offer few long-term benefits except to those individuals upon whom he conferred his 'friendship'. His very successes indicate the ambiguity of his task. He managed, for instance, to secure the loyalty of Valentinian's senior general, Arbogast (who had inherited Bauto's command), while ruthlessly stripping the western army of its best units.[16] Among the Roman senate, too, the advantages that certain persons seem to have derived from Theodosius' friendship were won at the expense of their peers.[17]

The Italian church, with Ambrose its chief representative, had formed the third element in the alliance behind Valentinian. The bishop of Milan had perhaps more cause than anyone to offer the prince a warm welcome home. Valentinian's public repudiation at Thessalonica of his flirtation with heterodoxy settled the religious question definitively in his favour; the death of Justina soon afterwards sealed the issue forever.[18] The bishop, officially vindicated, was free to promote his version of past quarrels.

Although the peculiarities of Ambrose's literary output make any association between a given work and a particular historical context hazardous, certain passages seem to reflect precisely this situation. De Ioseph, which has been plausibly dated to the autumn or winter of 388, celebrates among other things the belated punishment of the eunuch Calligonus, who had upheld Valentinian's rights against Ambrose so vehemently in 386. Calligonus, safely disgraced, could be presented as one of the villains of 386 who had 'fraudulently worked upon the king's feelings'.[19] The emperor, on the other hand, had become an innocent victim

16. For Arbogast's succession, see Zos. 4.53.1; his loyalty to Theodosius rather than Valentinian is shown most clearly in his reaction to the latter's attempt to remove him from office (Zos. 4.53.2–3). The defection might owe something to the influence of his uncle, Theodosius' general Richomer (for the relationship, see Zos. 4.54.1). The transfer of western units to the eastern army is noted by Zos. 4.47.2 and analyzed by D. Hoffmann, Das spätrömische Bewegungsheer und die Notitia Dignitatum (1969), 469–519, esp. 476–487.

17. Note Symmachus' frustration in 389 at a rescript from Theodosius awarding a suit to Probus, overturning an original verdict in his own favour: Ep. 2.30 ('Iustitiam perdidi').

18. Rufinus (HE 12.17) and Sozomen (HE 7.14.7) have Justina dying during the war with Maximus; in Zosimus (4.47.2) she survives to assist her son in the immediate aftermath. For her posthumous demonization, see esp. Paulin. V. Amb. 20.1–3.

19. De Ios. 34–36: for the date, see Palanque, Saint Ambroise, 522.

of such machinations. Ambrose was not always so respectful, or so subtle: a passage from his commentary on Luke recalls Nabuth, one of his alter egos from 386, 'standing up to the king's desire', 'feeling no terror at the royal threats'.[20] Nabuth's vineyard, however, had now become a port, 'the harbour of faith', towards which sailors were hastening to return, kissing their native shores and giving thanks at their release from *error*. Both meanings of this word—a straying from home and from truth—were particularly appropriate for Valentinian and his entourage, restored to Italy and to orthodoxy. The whole passage, which sees the country lying secure beneath the protective shield of the apostles and martyrs, can be read as a celebration of this felicitous restoration.[21] Ambrose's gloating over past victories, if indeed somewhat ungracious, was incidental to the rejoicing.

Theodosius, meanwhile, remained absent from the bishop's effusions. It is most unlikely that this was accidental, for the arrival of the eastern court in Milan in the autumn of 388 threatened to disrupt the pattern of ecclesiastical activity that Ambrose had created at Milan. The monopoly he had established over Christian life there was very different from the situation obtaining at Constantinople, where the great men of the court indulged their own pious tastes without necessarily consulting the local bishop. At least two of Theodosius' companions in Milan, Rufinus and Promotus, left well-documented traces of their initiatives in the eastern capital.[22] Still less was the emperor shackled by any episcopally imposed restraints. At the Conference of Sects in 383, the ecclesiastical establishment of Constantinople had merely reacted to a series of imperial initiatives, the issue being eventually resolved by the prayerful deliberations of the emperor himself.[23]

When this formidable and confident array of pious laymen arrived at Milan, the bishop lacked lines of communication, like those he had

20. *Expos. Evang. sec. Luc.* 9.23–33; citations from 33. For the date, see Palanque, *Saint Ambroise*, 533–534.

21. Palanque unaccountably sees this passage as a 'panegyric to Theodosius' and claims that *De Ioseph* ignores Valentinian's claims to sovereignity (*Saint Ambroise*, 199–200); this quite reverses the logical sense of Ambrose's words.

22. For Rufinus, see Matthews, *Western Aristocracies*, 134–136; a group of Gothic monks were settled on Promotus' property in 404 (Joh. Chrys. *Ep.* 207). Note also the prominent role played by the wives of members of the 'Theodosian establishment' (including the widows of Timasius and Promotus and of another *magister militum*, Saturninus) in the controversy concerning Chrysostom: J. H. W. G. Liebeschuetz, *Barbarians and Bishops* (1990), 217–227.

23. Soc. *HE* 5.10; Soz. *HE* 7.12.

developed with the courts of Gratian and Valentinian, to smooth out the inevitable difficulties. An incident described by Sozomen, which must be one of the first encounters between Ambrose and Theodosius, exposes the difference between their assumptions concerning the emperor's place in the church and their failure to communicate across the gap. At the time for communion, Theodosius attempted to join the presbyters at the altar to receive the sacrament, only to be ordered back to his place among the faithful by Ambrose.[24] The occasion must have caused considerable embarrassment to both parties: the proper, dignified rhythm of both ecclesiastical and imperial ceremonial was broken, before a crowd of doubtless mortified observers. Such failures of stage management were rare in public life, and still more so in the well-ordered routines of the church of Milan. Theodosius, for all his devotion and orthodoxy, could not but be an uncomfortable proposition for Ambrose's church.

CALLINICUM

A far more serious misunderstanding soon set Ambrose at odds with the eastern emperor. While the bishop was visiting Aquileia, either in the immediate aftermath of Maximus' defeat or during the subsequent months, news arrived from the east of an affray in the city of Callinicum on the Euphrates: a Christian gang, led by the local bishop, had plundered and destroyed a synagogue.[25] The report came from the *comes orientis*, under whose jurisdiction the city fell;[26] his reference of the case to an emperor fifteen hundred miles from his own headquarters in Antioch (itself a hundred and fifty miles from Callinicum) represents an extreme case of the tendency, deplored in so many imperial pronounce-

24. Soz. *HE* 7.25.9.
25. *Ep.* 74 [40].6; *Ep. extra coll.* 1 [41].1. The latter passage (Ambrose sent a letter, 'Aquileiae posito') perhaps implies that Theodosius was already in Milan (he arrived in October 388; the inference is made by Paulinus at *V. Amb.* 22.1); Ambrose's visit to Aquileia has been associated with the episcopal consecration of Chromatius, whose predecessor, Valerian, died on 26 November (Palanque, *Saint Ambroise*, 523–524).
26. This 'comes orientis militarium partium' (*Ep.* 74 [40].6) has been seen as a military commander (Matthews, *Western Aristocracies*, 232n6), but Ambrose was either confused by the titulature of the *comes orientis* or was stressing his military responsibilities (cf. Libanius *Or.* 19.36) in order to emphasize certain implications of Theodosius' response.

ments, to pass the responsibility for controversial decisions upwards to a higher authority.[27]

Theodosius was evidently unimpressed. He brusquely rebuked the *comes* for bothering him with a matter of routine discipline, ordering him to punish the criminals and arrange compensation for the victims; the bishop of Callinicum himself was to bear the cost of rebuilding the synagogue.[28] Christians, it would be shown, had to remain within the law. But when Ambrose learned (we are not told how) of the *relatio* and the emperor's answer, he could not suppress his dismay. Moreover, he discovered a point that Theodosius had perhaps overlooked. The special attention reserved for the bishop of Callinicum involved a double danger: if he paid the proposed penalty, the bishop would betray his faith, since taking responsibility for the construction of a synagogue was a clear (if technical) breach of a Christian's duty to abhor Jewish rites.[29] Theodosius was probably more impressed, however, by the alternative envisaged by Ambrose: the bishop might refuse to comply with the order and unrepentantly claim full responsibility for the arson, saddling *comes* and emperor with a potential martyr.[30] To emphasize his point, Ambrose sought to take the ultimate responsibility upon himself, claiming that *he* had given the original orders to the mob at Callinicum in order to remove all places 'where Christ is denied' from the face of the earth. There were excuses—albeit somewhat obscure—for his own inactivity in Italy.[31] The emperor was perhaps surprised at the vehemence and melodramatic presentation of this argument, but could not gainsay its force. A second order to the *comes* was hastily drafted (without, how-

27. The *comes* appointed in early 388 was strongly Christian (Lib. *Or.* 1.255); if, as is likely, the same man was still in office, he might have appealed to Theodosius rather than the court at Constantinople in the hope of receiving authorization of leniency. The matter would have been given short shrift from the new prefect at Constantinople, the upright pagan Eutolmius Tatianus (whose predecessor, the zealous Christian Cynegius, had arguably sown the wind reaped at Callinicum: cf. Matthews, *Western Aristocracies,* 140–142).

28. *Ep.* 74 [40].18 (a 'cognitio' to be held; the 'sublata donaria' to be traced). For the bishop's punishment, see *Ep.* 74 [40].6: 'Iussisti vindicari in ceteros, synagogam ab ipso aedificari episcopo'.

29. *Ep.* 74 [40].7: 'aut praevaricari cogatur . . .'. Theodosius' own law of 384 (*CTh* 3.1.5) had threatened punishment to any Jew who involved even a lapsed Christian in his religion ('Iudaicis sacramentis adtaminet').

30. *Ep.* 74 [40].7: '. . . aut subire martyrium'.

31. *Ep.* 74 [40].8. It is difficult to infer the physical destruction of any Italian synagogues, even from natural causes, from Ambrose's bluster: 'Si obiciatur mihi cur hic non incenderim, divino iam cremari coepit iudicio, meum cessavit opus. Et si verum quaeritur ideo segnior fui, quia non putabam hoc vindicandum'.

ever, Ambrose's receiving official notification) which cancelled the fine imposed upon the bishop of Callinicum.[32]

This success emboldened Ambrose to make the much more ambitious demand that the whole case be dropped. When several initial approaches yielded no result, the bishop composed a letter to the emperor, which he later published as part of his collected correspondence (*Ep.* 74 [Maurist ed. 40]).[33] Any pride he felt in the contents or style has not been shared by readers of the present age. The document has appeared to expose Ambrose, to the dismay of his admirers, as both bully and bigot: the 'unbalanced zeal' of his intervention seems 'as regrettable as it is (in a man of his character and antecedents) surprising'.[34] But the letter is much more complex, and much less expressive of Ambrose's flaws of character, than such judgements imply. Ambrose's most recent editor has revealed several alterations to the original in the published version of the letter, and one fundamental change: the 'original' survives as an appendage to a different letter, among the miscellaneous *Epistulae extra collectionem* released after Ambrose's death.[35] The whole letter, moreover, is composed with painstaking care. Even the *exordium*, a collage of the bishop's favourite rhetorical *topoi* concerning the appropriate relationship between a priest and emperor, develops these specifically to suit his present case. In his demand for the same *libertas* that 'good' emperors like Theodosius allowed their subordinates, and for the same right as they to offer a *suggestio* (2–4), we can glimpse an outsider's view of the tight-knit Theodosian establishment, resentful of the easy access to the emperor that its members enjoyed.

Ambrose's arguments are elaborately organized and require close attention. A careless reader might not realize that his opening salvo, an eloquent and persuasive appeal on behalf of the bishop of Callinicum (6–8), was redundant, for that issue had already been resolved by Ambrose's earlier intervention. He included it in his letter to help establish the framework for his present bid, which sought to argue that by sparing the bishop the revised order had simply transferred the same impossible dilemma to the *comes*. By complying, he too would become a 'praevari-

32. *Ep.* 74 [40].9: 'Rogavi enim clementiam tuam [with the appeal that has just been described] et licet ipse hoc revocatum [the specific penalty for the bishop] adhuc non legerim, revocatum tamen constituamus'.

33. References in the text will henceforth be to this letter.

34. F. Homes Dudden, *The Life and Times of Saint Ambrose* (1935), 379. Jones is blunter: Ambrose was 'exceptional in his bigotry' (*Later Roman Empire*, 949).

35. M. Zelzer, *CSEL* 82.3 (1982), pp. xx–xxiii; cf. below, p. 308, for the revised ending.

cator' (9); but since he was unlikely to disobey the emperor's instructions, which had been Ambrose's key card in the bishop's case, there is only a brief and vague allusion to the possibility (30).

Very much the ex-barrister, Ambrose disguised the inapplicability of his parallel by introducing and developing several lines of argument only loosely related to his major theme. He discovered precedents for his case in the emperor's clemency to rioters at Constantinople (13) and Antioch (32), and in the unpunished destruction of Christian basilicas by Jews in Julian's reign (15, 21). He perhaps drew upon his own judicial experience to paint the likely course of the investigations, with the Jews exaggerating their claims and the Christians menaced with torture, imprisonment and death (19). Ambrose had also come to recognize the areas to which emperors were particularly sensitive, and we might well discern a trick learnt in 386 in the suggestion that the *comes'* Christian soldiers might refuse to obey their orders (9, 18).

All this, it must be said, does not add up to a convincing argument. So contrived is Ambrose's case that he conflates Callinicum with an entirely separate incident. Halfway through his letter, he abruptly introduces another recent fracas in Syria which had required the emperor's attention, the destruction by some monks of a gnostic chapel (16). This episode, which has mistakenly been assumed to have been part of the rioting at Callinicum, can be located from Ambrose's reference to the festival of the Maccabees to the immediate hinterland of Antioch.[36] Ambrose was simply trying to bring home to Theodosius the sheer scale of the Christian militancy that he was attempting to suppress and the number of potential martyrs confronting him (17).[37] Not that the Syrian monks, whose activities excited considerable dismay in government circles, served the bishop's purpose particularly well: the transition back to Callinicum, via a garbled allusion to a persecuting governor from Julian's reign, is therefore distinctly awkward (17–18).[38] Ambrose seems to

36. The festival of the Maccabees (held on 1 August) is discussed by E. Bikerman, 'Les Maccabées de Malalas', *Byzantion* 21 (1951), 73–83; his conclusion that it was introduced in about 380 nicely undermines Ambrose's contention that the monks were acting 'ex consuetudine usuque veteri'. The inference of a single affray at Callinicum (cf. Palanque, *Saint Ambroise*, 205; Matthews, *Western Aristocracies*, 232) was first made by Paulinus, *V. Amb.* 22.1.

37. Ambrose subsequently makes only a passing reference to the incident, at 26; he was probably surprised when Theodosius subsequently made an issue of it.

38. In the original letter (*Ep. extra coll.* 1a.17) Ambrose confuses the victim with the judge (*PLRE* 1, p. 180: Capitolinus 2); the name is omitted from the published version.

have worked the incident into his argument for no better reason than that he happened to know of it. The ineptness of his overall case similarly reflects how little information he had about either the actual situation in the east or the best way to approach Theodosius.

The contrast here with the altar of Victory affair, when Ambrose had been able to anticipate many of Symmachus' arguments, procure a copy of the *relatio* and monitor the course of the decisive debate in the consistory, brings out the bishop's lack of access to Theodosius' court. Only an urgent need to open a channel of communications can explain his remarkable persistence with an unpromising brief so little related to his own interests. His real purpose becomes apparent at the end of the letter, when he carefully introduces an entirely different grievance which he 'wished to be brought to the attention' of Theodosius: presbyters and deacons were being 'dragged from their holy office after thirty—nay, innumerable!—years of service, and assigned to municipal responsibilities' (29). For the first time in a generation there was an emperor in Italy to whom the city councils might profitably appeal, and the local churches were understandably nervous.[39] It fell to Ambrose (probably under pressure from his episcopal colleagues)[40] to make representations on their behalf. The burnt synagogue of Callinicum was essentially a pretext. By asserting the episcopate's right to be consulted in a *causa religionis* (27), Ambrose was intending above all to put such cases on Theodosius' immediate agenda.

It is not surprising, under these circumstances, that Ambrose failed. His individual arguments vary greatly in cogency and relevance; probably more confusing to his readers was his tendency, steadily more marked in the latter half of the letter, to abandon his pragmatic tone and laboured sophistry for the scriptural rhetoric of his preaching, which reduced everything to a single, simple question: 'Will you give the Jews this triumph over the church of God?' (20). The force of such language should not be dismissed, the assumptions behind it having been implicit

39. Ambrose's 'thirty years' might hark back to the activity in Italy of Valentinian I, whose concern for the *curiae* is expressed in *CTh* 12.1.59–62, 16.2.17. But episcopal alarm was more probably prompted by an isolated case than by the application of a consistent policy: Theodosius might have upheld the rights of a council in a context like that presented by Pacatus, *Paneg.* 37.

40. An inference from the twice-repeated exclamation (at *Ep.* 74 [40].29) 'Quomodo hoc excusabo apud episcopos?', and the statement that they were 'complaining' and 'writing' about the situation. Chromatius' consecration (above, n. 25) would offer an occasion for these 'querelae' to be put directly to Ambrose.

in imperial rhetoric since Constantine; but the Christian emperors had consistently refused to translate their rhetoric into reality and had never before been challenged to do so.[41] Nor was the consistory accustomed to being accosted by a prophet.[42] Yet it was with the voice of Nathan that Ambrose delivered his appeal to Theodosius. 'The youngest of his brethren', like David, he had been chosen king by divine will and granted victory against the odds by God's direct intervention. How then could he answer Christ's complaint: 'I made you triumph over your enemies, and do you now grant my enemies a triumph over my people?' (22). Having further pointed the contrast between Theodosius and Maximus (23), Ambrose proceeded to explain: having been given so much, Theodosius ought to 'love' the more. The cryptic allusion to Luke's account of Simon the Pharisee is elaborated by the identification of the prostitute with the church, who had entered the house to 'eject the Jew, and keep Christ for herself'. It was therefore inconceivable that the synagogue should now debar the church from the home of Christ—and this 'at the home of Christ's servant, that is, from the breast of faith' (24).

On this Ambrose rested his case; but his logic made no concessions to the busy ministers for whose agenda his letter was intended. The consistory therefore seems, in pardonable exasperation, to have ignored it. No further change of instructions was sent to the *comes*, no common ground was established between Ambrose and the court of Theodosius. The bishop's intervention had apparently failed entirely.

But Ambrose had not staked everything upon the letter alone. He knew when he wrote it that he could soon expect to see the emperor at church; the passage he quoted from Luke seems to have been chosen specifically to anticipate the reading at the forthcoming service. Modes of argument that probably made little sense in the emperor's consistory would acquire a more impressive resonance in Ambrose's church, where the congregation had long been fed upon the contrast between the 'unbelieving, ungentle and sacrilegious woman' of the synagogue and the

41. See R. M. Wilken, *John Chrysostom and the Jews* (1983), 50–52, for the venomous tone and limited scope of fourth-century legislation. His argument that Theodosius abandoned Constantine's abusiveness ignores the language of 'contamination' in *CTh* 3.1.5.

42. A. Honoré has recently suggested ('The Making of the Theodosian Code', *ZRG* 103 [1986], at 211–215) that the pagan senator Nichomachus Flavianus had already been appointed Theodosius' *quaestor*, and so joined the consistory, in the autumn of 388.

spotless virgin of the church.[43] There is no evidence that the bishop's disquisitions upon such topics were complicated by actual contact with or even consciousness of the local Jewish community; 'his' Jews were drawn from Scripture to help point his favourite contrast between letter and spirit, their narrow literalism providing a foil for the fertility of the Christian vision.[44] They had performed this role in both the sermons ascribed earlier to this period: in the discussion of Luke's parable of the vineyard, the Jews are identified as the tenants who killed their master's son; more imaginative is *De Ioseph*, where they appear in succession as wild beasts, a dry well and a people deprived of 'spiritual cement'.[45] This was the note which Ambrose had begun to sound at the end of his letter: the emperor was being prepared for a wholesale translation of the issue into the bishop's favourite spiritual language.

In thus setting the stage for the appearance of Theodosius and his entourage at church, Ambrose was seeking neither confrontation nor an opportunity to 'humiliate the secular power'.[46] What he required from the emperor was still basically recognition, a sign of willingness to accept the local terms of reference during his stay in Italy. He seems, however, to have misjudged Theodosius' intentions and underestimated the scope of his ambitions. Theodosius, on the other hand, seems not to have anticipated any resumption of the Callinicum question by the bishop; this is apparent from his very appearance at the basilica, which perhaps transmitted a misleading signal of encouragement to Ambrose.

The course of the service that followed only emphasized this lack of

43. The synagogue, 'incredula inmitis sacrilega', is set against the 'virgo sine ruga' at *Exh. virg.* 67; any number of parallel contrasts can be discovered in Ambrose's works.

44. Typical images: *De par.* 66; *Explan. Ps. 1* 41; *Explan. Ps. 35* 20; *Expos. Ps. 118* 21.12; *Expos. Evang. sec Luc.* 7.96–108, 160. A 'dialogue' has sometimes been assumed beneath this rhetoric: H. Savon, *Saint Ambroise devant l'exégèse de Philon le juif* (1977), 99, 117, surmised contacts with Jewish leaders from Ambrose's use of Philo; L. Cracco Ruggini, 'Ambrogio e le opposizioni anticattoliche', *Augustinianum* 14 (1974), 409–449, postulated good relations between Ambrose and the Jews of Milan, interrupted only when the Jews allied themselves with Arians and pagans, and then with Maximus, in the 380s. Neither convinces.

45. *Exp. Evang. sec. Luc.* 9.23–33; *De Ios.* 15–17.

46. This is the interpretation followed by most scholars: Palanque, *Saint Ambroise*, 219; A. Piganiol, *L'empire chrétien*, 2d ed. (1972), 283; F. Kolb, 'Der Bussakt von Mailand', in *Geschichte und Gegenwart*, ed. H. Boockmann, K. Jürgensen, G. Stolttenberg (1980), 46–47.

-mutual understanding. Thanks to the survival of a transcript of Ambrose's sermon, the episode is bathed in an unusually clear light—artificial, of course, having been arranged by Ambrose himself, who included the text of his sermon (complete with stage directions at a crucial point) in a letter to his sister (*Ep. extra coll.* 1 [Maurist ed. 41]).[47] But this itself indicates the thoroughness with which he prepared his renewed appeal to the emperor. Such care is also evident in the organization of his sermon, which embraced two of the texts read at the service, beginning with a single phrase, 'Take up your rod of almond wood', derived from the Old Testament reading (Jeremiah 1:11). The rod was associated by the bishop, in his characteristic style, with the staff of Aaron, conflating prophetic *auctoritas* with priestly authority. A priest's role was therefore to offer 'useful' advice, not merely what was calculated to please (*Ep. extra coll.* 1.2). The argument is dense but thorough: like Jeremiah's almond, the prophet/priest's advice is bitter and hard on the surface but fruitful inside (3).[48] The rod itself was likewise only part of the process of correction, for spiritual consolation would follow punishment. A similar scheme is applied to the apostle's injunction to 'correct, rebuke, encourage', which also matched two harsh things with one gentle one. The harshness was meanwhile justified as a remedy against excessive sweetness, which tempered the sickness of *adulatio* with the salutary bitterness of *correctio* (4).

Ambrose seems here to be at great pains to defuse in advance any offence that his remarks might cause. He then prepared his audience for an unusually concentrated and complex discussion by the repetition, in full, of the gospel reading about the anointing of Jesus at the house of Simon the Pharisee (*Ep. extra coll.* 1.5; Luke 7:36–50). Theodosius, remembering the letter, would be expected to take particular note. But Ambrose began in general terms, invoking the vast scope of divine generosity to convey the implications of the term *fenerator*, moneylender, which had appeared in the gospel passage (6–7). All humans, he reminded his audience, remain indebted; the burden of sinfulness had not been abolished by Christ but transferred to his account (8). The scale of these debts massively outweighed all those incurred between men. But we should not, urged Ambrose, take the benevolence of our creditor for

47. This was, moreover, accompanied by a copy of the earlier letter to Theodosius (*Ep. extra coll.* 1.1: 'quam simul misi'). References in the text are to the letter to Marcellina.

48. The figure is taken, somewhat ironically in the context, from Philo: *Vita Moys.* 2.178–183.

granted: the parable of the unmerciful servant conclusively proved the need to forgive others their debts, and those to whom most is given— the first direct echo of the letter—are obliged to forgive the most (9).

Ambrose moves cautiously at first. The mutual forgiveness that animated the church, and inspired uncomprehending admiration from Jewish onlookers (10), reflected its identity as Christ's body, which he anatomizes into its conventional members, meritorious hands and alms- giving belly. Less expected—and hardly convincing—was the identifi- cation of the feet of Christ with certain lowly commoners, who would be 'washed' by those who forgave them their sins and 'set them free' (11). Ambrose minimizes the awkwardness with two favourite tactics, an irrelevant exclamation ('And if only I were worthy to be Christ's sandal!') and a shift of emphasis: the theme of foot-washing provided ample material to assert the moral superiority of Christian over Jew. The synagogue, typified by Simon the Pharisee, had no water to wash Christ's feet (12), no hair to wipe them (13); it could offer no kiss (14–15), except perhaps that of the traitor Judas (16), nor any oil to anoint his feet. The ingenious proof of this last point was the Jews' notorious stiff- neckedness, a sign of their inability to lubricate even themselves (19); their failure to recognize the dove sent out by Noah furthermore indi- cated that they lacked even the olive (21). The synagogue, barren and bankrupt, could not possibly compete with the spiritual resources of the church.

This argument reveals the vandals of Syria in a new light: presented in their turn as Christ's feet, wrongdoers who nevertheless deserved indulgence (23), they were offered to the emperor as the means to estab- lish his Christian credentials. Ambrose once again assumes the guise of Nathan to lay these credentials before Theodosius, in a passage that closely echoes his letter (25). But the emphasis had changed: criticism is almost outweighed by a long and detailed review of the divine sanction to the emperor's legitimacy. The bishop's final appeal, moreover, offered Theodosius a role in the church that was anything but subordinate:

> Show, then, your love for Christ's body, that is, the church; pour water upon his feet, plant kisses on them, so that you might not only forgive those who have been taken in sin but also, by granting your peace, offer them harmony and tranquillity. Put perfume upon his feet, that the whole house in which Christ rests might be full of your ointment, and all who sit with him may delight in your fragrance. For such is the man who honours the wretched, over whose forgiveness the angels rejoice as much as they do 'over one sinner who repents'; the apostles are glad, the prophets are pleased. . . . Therefore, since all men are necessary,

protect the whole body of Lord Jesus, that he might watch over your kingdom also with his heavenly regard. (26)

With this final flourish, Ambrose invited Theodosius to show his solidarity with his fellow-Christians. Rather than attempting to dictate to the emperor, he had prepared the ground for a mutually beneficial ceremony. Theodosius, by granting mercy to the avowed 'sinners' of the east (which would not, under these terms, set a precedent to legitimize future attacks on synagogues), would receive the acclaim of the expectant Christians of Milan, and Ambrose would gain the recognition he required.

But the emperor balked at playing David to the bishop's Nathan. At the end of the sermon he exchanged some remarks with Ambrose, puncturing the bishop's soaring homily with brutal common sense. The rights of church against synagogue, he suggested, had been adequately guaranteed by the withdrawal of the original penalty against the bishop of Callinicum; moreover, nothing in Ambrose's sermon had exculpated the monks who had attacked the Valentinians. A vehement interjection by the *magister militum* Timasius reinforced the latter point (27). Unable in the circumstances to argue his case in detail, Ambrose had to exploit instead his own control of the ceremony and the emperor's desire to avoid public embarrassment. He stood his ground, looming above the seated emperor, until after a pause—and a further brief exchange— Theodosius finally agreed to abandon the whole matter (28). Although this has often been called a humiliation, it is unlikely to have appeared so to the spectators, who had merely seen the emperor grant, after due consideration, the bishop's fulsome plea for mercy.[49] The unusual setting and dramatic climax to the intercession served only to give greater publicity to Theodosius' gesture of benevolence.

Although appearances were preserved, however, the nature of the

49. Ambrose, crucially, does not indicate whether the conversation was a shouting match in the hearing of the congregation or an exchange of urgent whispers between the imperial party and the bishop. Much depends on whether the emperor interrupted the service to address Ambrose when he 'descended' to the altar after the sermon ('ubi descendi ait mihi': 27) or the bishop himself initiated the conversation by 'descending' from the apse to where Theodosius was seated. In the latter case, which was assumed by Paulinus (*V. Amb.* 23.2: 'descendenti de exhedra') and which I consider far more probable, Ambrose's behavior will have been that of a suppliant, and his frank exchange with the emperor and Timasius 'private' (although ears were no doubt being strained); he then simply returned to the altar ('ad altare accessi': 28) to continue the service.

final exchange leaves no doubt that something had gone badly wrong
with the exhibition of the emperor's mercy. Theodosius' reluctance to
respond to the bishop's cues is especially puzzling when he stood to
gain so much from public endorsement of his position in Italy. But it
was precisely this point that appears to have created the difficulty, for
Ambrose failed to appreciate the sort of confirmation that Theodosius
required. The words of 'Nathan' bear a second reading. Theodosius/
David was indeed a king chosen by God; but he ruled only the *eastern*
part of the empire, as the successor of Valens (25). During the campaign
against Maximus, therefore, the Lord had led Theodosius into a strange
land where he had subsisted off 'other men's food'; Theodosius could
not be presented more clearly as an outsider in Italy. So far does this
characterization go that his retirement to his native Spain after his father's death becomes a period of 'exile', 'in foreign lands' (24). Such language betokens a thoroughgoing misunderstanding: for all the skill he
lavished upon his appeal to the emperor, and the care to offer him a
positive image as the defender of his fellow-Christians, Ambrose had
completely missed Theodosius' most pressing concern.

The loser in this unhappy affair was Ambrose. Theodosius had been
forced to concede clemency in a case he felt deserved exemplary punishment; but such concessions were an occupational hazard of the imperial
office. As compensation, moreover, he could enjoy the gratitude and
admiration which he had no doubt inspired among the Christians of
Milan. The bishop, however, had failed entirely to win the emperor's
sympathy. Therefore in presenting the episode to his contemporaries
(and to posterity), Ambrose had to put an appropriate colour upon it.
The letter to Marcellina is carefully constructed to show the bishop's
conversation with Theodosius as one where he himself had exerted all
the pressure: he 'would not have gone up to the altar' (to continue the
service) unless Theodosius 'had made a full promise' to revoke the *cognitio* (28). Perhaps not; but his resolve had not been tested.

Equally jarring are Ambrose's claim to have felt a particular intima-
tion of the divine presence at the Eucharist and his concluding remark
that 'all thus fell out according to plan'. But these features are editorial.
Having failed to achieve the agreement he had desired, it might be suspected, Ambrose was forced to present the occasion as a victory won
at the emperor's expense. In its final form this involved an important
change to the text of his earlier letter to Theodosius. Added to the end
of the published version was a warning that set the whole episode in a
new light, showing Ambrose acting to a preconceived plan and with
scant regard for the imperial dignity: 'I have acted as respectfully as has

been possible, so that you might pay heed to me in the palace—lest, if it should prove necessary, you should be forced to pay heed to me in church'.[50] Such bravado perhaps reassured Ambrose's constituents that their bishop's behaviour had after all been to some purpose and had achieved a result; yet it only confirmed the unsuitability of the Italian church as a vehicle for the emperor's propaganda campaign. This of course continued; Theodosius' ability to do without Ambrose's services offers an index of the bishop's relative lack of political importance. The emperor turned instead to the real foundation of Valentinian's power: the senatorial aristocracy of Rome.

In the spring of 389, Valentinian II departed for Gaul to expunge the last traces of Maximus' regime and rally the Gauls to the legitimate order by resuming his father's career as the guardian of the Rhine frontier.[51] But the young prince's authority was circumscribed from the outset. Arbogast had already arrived with the troops the previous autumn to eliminate Maximus' fellow-Augustus, his young son Victor, and to restore the breached frontier; he was now 'urging the emperor' to authorize him to launch a campaign across the Rhine into Frankish territory.[52] The emperor in question, we can infer from Arbogast's later behaviour, was Theodosius.

Valentinian's relations with his civilian staff were more complex. His first praetorian prefect in Gaul, one Constantianus, is a mysterious figure who is usually, but without much evidence, regarded as a creature of Theodosius.[53] Constantianus was soon replaced by the same Neoterius who had served as Valentinian's prefect in Italy in 385 (and, before

---

50. *Ep.* 74 [40].33: cf. Zelzer, *CSEL* 82.3, p. xxii. The expression was perhaps intended to echo Ambrose's challenge to Valentinian II in 384, also published in book 10 of the correspondence (*Ep.* 72 [17].13). For the date of publication (after Theodosius' death), see Zelzer, pp. xxiii–xxiv.

51. For the particular importance of imperial *praesentia* to the Gauls, see E. Wightman, *Gallia Belgica* (1985), 211–219; cf. R. Van Dam, *Leadership and Community in Late Antique Gaul* (1985), 9–36.

52. Sulpicius Alexander, qtd. Greg. Tur. *HF* 2.9.

53. For the identification with a previous vicar of Pontica, see *PLRE* 1, p. 222 (Constantianus 2), and Matthews, *Western Aristocracies*, 226 (a 'known supporter' of Theodosius). But the only fourth-century eastern vicar known to have held *any* praetorian prefecture was Constantine's friend Ablabius. No *vicarius Ponticae* is recorded in any subsequent office, and the two whose origins are known (Philagrius and Aristaenetus) were native to the diocese. We might envisage instead a relative of Valentinian: the name appears in Justina's family (*PLRE* 1, Constantianus 1).

that, Theodosius' in the east in 380/1). The scope of Neoterius' career proves him more prepared to travel to obtain office than were most contemporaries; by the same token, he was uncommitted to any particular regime.[54] Valentinian no doubt retained the services of some who had attended him in Milan and Thessalonica and owed him a more personal loyalty;[55] but there was a steady infiltration of Arbogast's protégés into the civil *officia*.[56] Despite the brave pomp of his *adventus* ceremonies at Lyons and Trier,[57] the prince was poorly equipped to assert his authority.

While Valentinian struggled to establish himself in Gaul, Theodosius was capturing Rome. He celebrated a solemn arrival into the city on 13 July 389 and stayed until the end of August, a period that coincided exactly, and probably by design, with the previous year's campaign against Maximus. Theodosius was exploiting to the full his one claim upon the gratitude of the west.[58] His purpose was to establish himself and his dynasty (represented by his young son Honorius, following discreetly in his train) as the focus of political authority, an ambition that found its perfect echo in the panegyric delivered by the Gallic rhetor Pacatus in the senate house to emperor, court and senate.[59] Not the least of Pacatus' accomplishments (which earned him a proconsulate soon afterwards) was his elimination of the senior Augustus from the contemporary scene. In his version, the war had involved only Theodosius and Maximus, the latter provoking hostilities by encroaching upon Theodosius' territory (30.1–2). Valentinian is explicitly mentioned only in connexion with Theodosius' accession, a 'small boy' (11.5) under Theodosius' 'guardianship' (3.5). The possibility is allowed that he would

54. Much earlier in his career, in 365, Neoterius had travelled from Gaul to Africa to secure the province for Valentinian I (Amm. Marc. 26.5.14). Note that he had received a consulate from Theodosius in Milan a few months before arriving at Valentinian's court: cf. below, p. 312.

55. One Armonius is mentioned as a loyal member of Valentinian's council at Joh. Ant. fr. 187 (= Blockley, Eunapius fr. 58.2). Personal adherents of Valentinian are also implied by Ambrose at *De ob. Val.* 27, *Ep. extra coll.* 10 [57].12.

56. Thus Sulpicius Alexander (Greg. Tur. *HF* 2.9).

57. Note the reproduction for the ceremony at Trier of the coin types used by Valentinian I: J. W. C. Pearce, *The Roman Imperial Coinage* 9 (1951), at p. 30 (no. 88).

58. The visit is a likely occasion for the inauguration of the annual commemoration of the usurper's defeat, still celebrated in the sixth century: Procopius *Bell. Vand.* 1.4.16. The chronicles report the dates of Theodosius' arrival and departure (*Cons. Const.* s.a. 389: *Chron. Min.* 1, p. 245; Marcell. com. s.a. 389: *Chron. Min.* 2, p. 62), perhaps reflecting the publicity surrounding the visit.

59. The speech (to which citations in the text refer) has been translated, with a useful introduction and commentary, by C. E. V. Nixon, *Pacatus: Panegyric to the Emperor Theodosius* (1987).

'one day' prove himself valorous, but meanwhile the responsibility for Pannonia, Illyricum and even Gaul rested with Theodosius (11.4). Theodosius even secured, somewhat implausibly, an equal share in Valentinian's kinship with Gratian, and thus in the latter's inheritance: Gratian had been concerned lest the 'royal robe' he was to pass on to his 'brothers' should be defiled by the usurper (42.3). But wherever possible, Valentinian was forgotten altogether. Theodosius' sons are the future *imperatores* (16.5); 'everybody knows' that the empire will remain forever in the hands of Theodosius and these sons (45.3). There was no place for Valentinian beside these 'twin guarantees of the state'.

Pacatus expunges Valentinian from both the past and the future. The sympathetic audience needed to appreciate such a presentation had, by the final phase of Theodosius' visit, been secured.[60] The panegyric celebrates the successful achievement of the visit's principal objective: the 'conversion' of the Roman senate. Theodosius needed the support of the great Italian families to establish the claims of his dynasty, and he clearly found such men easier to deal with than Ambrose's church. His methods were sung by Pacatus: 'Friendship, a term once used of private citizens, you not only summoned to the palace, but you clothed it in purple, wreathed it in gold and installed it upon the throne' (16.2). Theodosius, *amicitia* incarnate, won the senate with wholesale bribery. Lamenting that he could not find a court appointment for everyone, the emperor guaranteed at least consolation prizes for the disappointed: a friendly word, a dinner or a kiss (20.1–2).

Among the beneficiaries was Symmachus, whose letters well illustrate Theodosius' courtship of the aristocracy. Symmachus began with the disadvantage of a compromising panegyric upon Maximus to his name, but secured rehabilitation as he realigned himself towards Theodosius. In the autumn of 388 he had helped organize an embassy to the two emperors concerning the current grain shortage.[61] Symmachus had here recognized Valentinian and Theodosius as exercising power conjointly, but he soon learned the advantages of displaying a more precise allegiance. Theodosius had shown his diplomatic skills by persuading him of his goodwill even while judging an appeal against him, in favour of Valentinian's senior surviving patron, Petronius Probus;[62] his friend Flavianus meanwhile fed him stories of the emperor's generosity.[63] During the visit to Rome various acquaintances from the court nudged him

60. See Nixon, *Pacatus: Panegyric*, p. 9, for the date.
61. *Ep.* 2.52.2; cf. Amb. *De Ios.* 38–39.
62. *Ep.* 2.30.2.
63. *Ep.* 2.22.1: 'beneficia domini nostri Theodosii frequenter enumeras et urgueri merita tua magnis praemiis adseveras'. Cf. *Ep.* 2.23.

back into political life.[64] When a further corn shortage was averted in 389 by the procurement of extra supplies from Macedonia (an area that remained, as far as can be ascertained, formally under Valentinian's jurisdiction), Theodosius alone received the credit; Symmachus asked Richomer to report to the 'lord of the world' the happy accomplishment of his benefaction.[65] It was Theodosius himself who subsequently invited Symmachus to Milan, to attend the consular celebrations for 390;[66] Symmachus declined, but wrote enthusiastically to the new consul, Neoterius, of the 'emperor of divine good faith' who had conferred the honour.[67] Theodosius' partner Valentinian, who had assumed the consulate at Trier as Neoterius' colleague (in celebration of the fifteenth year of his reign), was forgotten. Theodosius had upstaged him, reorienting his former friends towards himself at Milan.

Theodosius needed such attentions from Symmachus and his friends, to whose allegiance he had no constitutional claims; there was nothing to prevent them from looking beyond Milan to Trier for the arbitration of their disputes and the furtherance of their careers. But Theodosius dazzled them with his generosity. Symmachus seems to have ignored the Gallic court; the only (singularly tactless) request he presented there was that Valentinian should confirm the reappointment of Alexander, a *tribunus et notarius* who had deserted him in 387.[68] Such exemplary conduct helped earn him the consulate for 391. The appointment was of course made formally by the imperial college,[69] but the pretence could be dropped among friends. Symmachus invited Manlius Theodorus to share his rejoicing at the 'sacred and divine judgement' of Theodosius, while encouraging Flavianus with the prospect that the emperor's 'customary regard for his friends' would soon produce similar results for himself.[70]

It was during this honeymoon between emperor and senate that the third round of the altar of Victory contest was fought. This obscure epi-

---

64. Correspondence emerging from the visit was conducted with Rufinus, Stilicho (both of whom Symmachus apparently met for the first time in 389), Timasius and Promotus (who had been in Italy previously), as well as with his long-standing acquaintance Richomer.

65. *Ep.* 3.55; cf. *Ep.* 3.82 to Rufinus, where the effusive praises of the 'venerabilis pater patriae' are precisely aimed: 'Scio haec in aures eius esse ventura'.

66. *Ep.* 3.85 (to Rufinus), seeking 'veniam de augustissimo principe imperati mihi itineris'; cf. *Ep.* 5.34 to Hephaestion.

67. *Ep.* 5.38.

68. *Ep.* 5.39 (to Neoterius).

69. *Ep.* 9.149.

70. *Epp.* 5.13; 2.62.

sode is recorded only in a single paragraph of a later letter from Ambrose to the usurper Eugenius, and there elliptically: a 'legation of the senate' had made a request (but not unanimously) 'of this nature', a phrase that refers back to the preceding account of Symmachus' petition in 384.[71] The embassy must have followed Theodosius' return to Milan in autumn 389, after his success at Rome had freed him from any need to deal gently with the bishop. The present incident looks like an attempt by Ambrose to force himself upon the emperor's attention; but his reminder of the political implications of the Christian faith succeeded only in trespassing upon the sensitive area of Theodosius' relationship with the aristocracy of Rome.

It is not known exactly what the embassy asked, since their initiative was aborted when Ambrose presented an *insinuatio* to the emperor. It is usually assumed that they sought an official reversal of Gratian's 'disestablishment' of 382, but so blunt a proposal is unlikely. Even had Theodosius been persuaded to countenance the idea, the most optimistic senator cannot have hoped for the necessary consensus from a consistory that included men of the stamp of Rufinus (whose souvenirs from the recent visit to Rome included relics of the apostles Peter and Paul), Timasius and Promotus. A more limited petition is more plausible: perhaps Theodosius was invited (like Constantius in 357) to fill the vacancies that natural wastage had created in the priestly colleges of Rome since 382.[72] Although no longer *pontifex maximus*, the emperor remained the obvious source of authority for such appointments, and Theodosius had shown in Rome that he found the exercise of patronage congenial.

What Ambrose was interrupting, on such a view, was not an attempt formally to reverse Gratian's earlier enactments but a cosy, mutually advantageous arrangement between Theodosius and his senatorial friends. The emperor might legitimately have regarded such favours as innocuous; once advertised as a *causa religionis*, however, the measure became untenable. In the Christian empire, favours to pagans were no more defensible than were favours to Jews, but the bishop will not have received any more gratitude from the emperor for his zeal in point-

---

71. *Ep. extra coll.* 10 [57].4: 'intimata senatus legatione huiusmodi, licet non totus poposcerit'.

72. Praetextatus (d. December 384) and Alfenius Ceionius Iulianus (*PLRE* 1, pp. 474–475; d. September 385) were respectively *augur, xvvir sacris faciundis* and *pontifex Vestae*; and *viivir epulonum, xvvir s.f.* and *pontifex maior* (to give only their 'Roman' priesthoods). Appointments to the colleges had traditionally been made by the emperor, as *pontifex maximus*; for Constantius, see Symm. *Rel.* 3.7.

ing this out than he had for his defence of the synagogue-wreckers at Callinicum.

Ambrose seems particularly concerned in his account of his intervention to gloss over the emperor's response. This reflects the purpose of the letter to Eugenius, to justify his strong stand against the latter's purported concessions to the pagans of Rome. After reporting Theodosius' assent to his intervention, he therefore added a curious clause to the effect that he had kept his distance from the emperor for several days, but without incurring his wrath.[73] This withdrawal has been variously interpreted—by adjustments to the punctuation or the text—as having *preceded* the emperor's final assent or as marking, uncontroversially, the conclusion of their business.[74] But it is far more likely that Ambrose was here exerting himself to paper over the one gaping hole in his argument to Eugenius: Theodosius had been so angry at his intrusion into a matter which did not concern him (or rather, at his annexation of a deal between the emperor and his friends to the agenda of the church) that he banned him from court. By 393, of course, Ambrose had been rehabilitated and could therefore hope to dismiss this period of disgrace as irrelevant: 'Theodosius accepted my plea. Granted, there were a few days when I did not approach him, but this was not because he bore me any resentment. For I was acting not to further my own interests but for the good of the emperor and of my own soul; "I spoke in the presence of the king, and was not put to shame"'.[75] Few churchmen of the age sounded the psalmist's brave note as effectively as Ambrose; but the sonorous capstone to his argument cannot disguise its flimsiness.

Ambrose's intrusion, moreover, provoked countermeasures. Informal contacts at court, the most likely source of his information concerning the senate's initiative, had become available as former associates of Valentinian—and of Ambrose himself—attached themselves to Theo-

---

73. *Ep. extra coll.* 10 [57].4: 'insinuationi meae assensionem detulit et sic aliquibus ad ipsum non accessi diebus nec moleste tulit, quia non pro meis commodis faciebam . . .' (text and punctuation as in Zelzer, *CSEL* 82.3, p. 207).

74. The former view is reflected by the Maurist editors, who inserted 'tandem' before 'assensionem' (*PL* 16, 1176A: accepted by many scholars, including Palanque, *Saint Ambroise*, 222 n 125); the latter is implied by R. Klein's punctuation (*Der Streit um den Victoriaaltar* [1972], at p. 164), placing a full stop after 'diebus'. This makes more elegant Latin than in Zelzer's edition, but the sense (that Ambrose did not visit Theodosius because their transactions had been completed) seems impossibly bathetic.

75. With the punctuation: 'assensionem detulit. Et sic aliquibus ad ipsum non accessi diebus, nec moleste tulit . . .'

dosius' establishment.[76] The emperor now sought to deny Ambrose any further opportunity to speak out, by depriving him of his 'natural right' of hearing: heavy punishments were announced for anyone henceforth caught leaking information concerning the consistory's business.[77] This must have inhibited the bishop's conversations with the pious careerists who came to present their compliments. He had to prevent himself from overhearing any compromising information they accidentally let slip; 'or I can listen with my ears open but my mouth blocked, unable to speak about what I have heard for fear of putting into danger those who come under suspicion of having passed on the information'. The whole tortured sentence reflects the author's embarrassment: this was perhaps the lowest point of Ambrose's career.

THESSALONICA

Within months of this apparently decisive break, a dramatic change of fortune forced Theodosius into the arms of Ambrose's church. In the summer of 390 the troops stationed in the Balkan city of Thessalonica were unleashed upon the civilian population: 'for three hours the city was given over to the sword, and very many innocent people were slain'. The massacre was evidently a mistake, and it dealt a potentially catastrophic blow to the reputation for competence and clemency that Theodosius had cultivated. But the details remain veiled in obscurity. The only descriptions occur in ecclesiastical sources (or in works derived from these), which present it within a highly personalized framework. A fit of anger, fuelled by demons in some versions, by evil counsellors in others, provoked the emperor to order the slaughter; eventually his feelings of remorse, carefully worked upon by Ambrose, triumphed over his pride and led him to enroll within the church's order of penitents.[78] It has proved difficult to produce a historically plausible account from these materials. A recent survey of the evidence has reached the

76. A possible example is Romulus, Valentinian's *consularis Aemiliae* in 385; he reappears as Theodosius' *comes sacrarum largitionum* in Constantinople in 392, having presumably joined his court at Milan (*PLRE* 1, p. 772).

77. *Ep. extra coll.* 11 [51].2–3.

78. The sources for the massacre and penitence are Ruf. *HE* 11.18; Paulin. *V. Amb.* 24; Aug. *Civ. Dei* 5.26; Soz. *HE* 7.25; Theod. *HE* 5.17–18. The fullest recent account is Kolb, 'Der Bussakt von Mailand'; cf. P. R. L. Brown, *Power and Persuasion in Late Antiquity* (1992), 109–113; Schieffer, 'Von Mailand nach Canossa'.

pessimistic conclusion that either the event was a 'surd', an irruption of imperial temper which upset the normal balance of Theodosius' mind, or else the 'evidence as it stands and as it is ordinarily represented does not basically represent what really happened'.[79]

The latter thesis is far the more convincing. Moreover, the remarkable opacity of the evidence as it stands is highly significant: this transformation of a political event into an object lesson in moral theology is not to be taken for granted as a 'natural' historiographical process. It seems, furthermore, to have been quite thoroughgoing. The otherwise useful counterpoint to the church's effusions over Theodosius provided by the fragments of the pagan sophist Eunapius, and the somewhat erratic incorporation of his work into the sixth-century *Historia nova* of Zosimus, fail us here. To argue from the silence of this pair, although for obvious reasons hazardous, is legitimate in this instance because Zosimus, following Eunapius, offers a full account of events occurring in the environs of Thessalonica during this period, yet there is not a word concerning this glaring blot on Theodosius' record.[80] The historical tradition concerning the massacre represents a triumph for Theodosius, who is absolved before posterity from criticism over the slaughter.

The surviving sources do not provide us with the raw materials for a reconstruction of the event itself but reflect, at one remove, a particular mode of presentation. Acceptance of their terms therefore leads inescapably to the impasse that has frustrated so many historians. We must begin instead with the decision-making machinery of Roman government, for it was not simply an unmediated outburst of imperial rage that brought blood to the streets of Thessalonica. Due attention to the processes through which the emperor's anger was channelled will suggest a more complex and confused pattern of causation; the confusion will, in turn, offer an explanation for the astonishing sequel to the carnage.

Details of the event itself have been all but blotted out in the sources by lurid accounts of bloodletting, but part of the background can be sketched in. Our most circumstantial account, in Sozomen, conveys an atmosphere of tension between the citizens of Thessalonica and the troops stationed there. The city was not accustomed to the role of garrison town. When it had last done such service, during Theodosius' makeshift efforts against the Goths in 379/80, the new emperor's presence had alleviated the burden for the inhabitants. Ten years later, it was

79. C. W. R. Larson, 'Theodosius and the Thessalonian Massacre Revisited—Yet Again', *SP* 10 (1970), 297–301.

80. Zosimus 4.50, the conclusion of his Thessalonican narrative, echoes Eunapius fr. 58 (fr. 55 Blockley).

again a Gothic threat that occasioned the quartering of troops under Butheric, 'the commander of the forces in Illyricum', far from their usual bases.[81] Zosimus records a rebellion in Macedonia during the preparations for the war against Maximus, among the federates whom Theodosius had summoned to his aid.[82] An immediate punitive operation was successful, although Zosimus' claim that it 'destroyed most of them' probably reflects the optimistic language of a victory dispatch; the survivors continued to operate from the 'marshes of Macedonia' for three years until Theodosius returned from the west to exterminate them a second time.[83] The rising gains a further dimension from a tantalizingly imprecise aside by the poet Claudian which suggests that it be identified with Alaric's first rebellion against the empire.[84] Butheric and his troops were left with the frustrating task of containing these marauders, whose raiding tactics and remote bases assured them security, while the populace of Thessalonica had both to maintain these troops and to endure the damage inflicted by the Goths.

Against this background, Sozomen's account of the antecedents to the crisis is entirely plausible. A celebrated charioteer insulted Butheric's honour by making sexual advances to one of his attendants and was arrested and thrown into prison. There followed a riot, during which the general was killed.[85] The gravity of Butheric's murder must not be underestimated. The death of a *magister equitum* at the hands of a mob in Constantinople in 342 had brought the emperor Constantius rushing to the scene, to punish the populace by curtailing their privileges.[86] The murder of a single Gothic soldier, again at Constantinople, had only a few years earlier prompted Theodosius to immediate action.[87] But the crisis at Thessalonica was aggravated by the emperor's inability to supervise a response in person; the long miles between Macedonia and the Po valley can only have distorted his perception of what had happened

81. For Butheric's name and title, see Soz. *HE* 7.25.3; *PLRE* 1, p. 166, makes him a *magister militum per Illyricum*. The Illyrican forces seem usually to have been deployed upon the middle Danube: Vetranio was based at Mursa in 350, Lucillianus at Sirmium in 361 and Equitius in the same area in 374.

82. Zos. 4.45.3.

83. Zos. 4.48–49.

84. Claud. *De VI cons. Hon.* 105–109 (written in 404); in favour of the identification, see P. J. Heather, *Goths and Romans 332–489* (1991), 184–186.

85. Soz. *HE* 7.25.3.

86. On the murder of Hermogenes by supporters of Bishop Paul, see Soc. *HE* 2.12–13. Cf. G. Dagron, *Naissance d'une capitale* (1974), 430–435.

87. Lib. *Or.* 20.14. The whole civic community was punished, with bread rations being halted for 'half a day'; this perhaps means that one of the regular distributions was cancelled.

and what the situation required. We cannot know exactly what messages were passed through the imperial postal system during the weeks of uncertainty that followed; but the outcome was clearly unexpected and shocked the empire. When the news was reported to a synod of bishops then in session, 'there was nobody who did not groan'.[88]

Something, it is clear, had gone badly wrong with the implementation of the emperor's justice. Despite the gravity of the crime, Theodosius failed spectacularly to win any applause for his vindication of public discipline. What had happened? It is impossible that the emperor had simply miscalculated, cold-bloodedly ordering the massacre without anticipating the outraged response. Panegyrists were available to condition the public to react appropriately to deliberate initiatives. The sources stress, instead, the *lack* of due deliberation before the massacre, showing Theodosius decreeing this excessively cruel penalty in the heat of anger.

Although the picture of a Spanish emperor succumbing to his temper has seemed credible enough, we should be wary. Anger was a conventional, even a necessary, attribute for a late antique monarch. Valentinian I had amply demonstrated how effectively imperial ferocity could inhibit subjects from presuming too much upon his benevolence; Ammianus was displaying the anachronism typical of a Roman historian when he maintained that 'the ruler of an empire should shun all extremes like a precipice'.[89] But these outbursts were not allowed to interfere with the proper conduct of affairs. An elaborate system of valves regulated the furnace of an emperor's temper: the 'malicious' courtiers who fanned the flames and the prudent men who cooled them were different parts of the same system. Those (including Ambrose)[90] who have seized upon the pernicious influence of the courtiers to explain the massacre at Thessalonica are mistaken, for the time that elapsed before orders were issued proves that the usual safeguards were in place. Even Ambrose, a *persona non grata*, could claim to have had several distinct opportunities to present the case for clemency.[91]

The usual 'system' of imperial decision-making and enforcement

88. Amb. *Ep. extra coll.* 11 [51].6.

89. Amm. Marc. 30.8.2. For the rules governing fourth-century anger, see Brown, *Power and Persuasion*, 48–61.

90. *Ep. extra coll.* 11 [51].4: 'Utinam . . . nullus accendat'. Ambrose had previously attributed Valentinian II's antipathy towards himself to the emperor's advisors: 'habet a quibus exasperatur' (*Ep.* 76 [20].27).

91. *Ep. extra coll.* 11 [51].6: 'immo quod ante atrocissimum fore dixi, cum toties rogarem'. The point is well made by Kolb, 'Der Bussakt von Mailand', 49.

was therefore operative over Thessalonica, but somehow it malfunctioned. To diagnose the failure, we can compare an almost contemporary case where Theodosius won universal acclaim for his exercise of justice following an outbreak of urban disorder. In the great Syrian metropolis of Antioch in 387, the city council had led a public appeal against a new tax to the representatives of imperial authority.[92] The protest degenerated into a riot, involving not only extensive damage to property but specific acts of treason: the images of the imperial family were defaced and the emperor's statues torn down. The affront to the emperor was at least as serious as the murder at Thessalonica. The imminent war with Maximus, whose own images had recently been paraded through the east, made for a highly sensitive political context, while Theodosius' relations with Antioch were complicated by his own failure, even after a decade in power, to have visited the city.[93] But lines of communication were nevertheless open. Bishop Flavianus hastened to Constantinople to explain the circumstances and plead for mercy; two senior courtiers meanwhile arrived in Antioch, to judge the suspects of higher rank and supervise the implementation of appropriate punishments. Justice was seen to be done, and those who were spared were effusive in their gratitude and praise to the emperor.

Although the tribunals at Antioch were thorough in their pursuit of the guilty, the citizens escaped the reprisals they had originally feared. Initially, rumours had spread that troops would be set loose upon the city to kill and plunder at will: crowds of refugees soon blocked the roads from the city.[94] Thessalonica has often been regarded as the unlucky victim of the same weapon of last resort which Antioch had been spared, but this is to miss the differences between the two cases. Above all, there are no signs that the reprisals feared at Antioch were judged inappropriate. In his (retrospective) appeal against so drastic a measure, Libanius was reduced to sophistries which seem remarkably feeble against the claims of equity or humanity that might have been advanced.[95] The

92. For the 'Riot of the Statues', see Brown, *Power and Persuasion*, 104–108, with bibliography.

93. Zos. 4.37.3 reports images displayed in Alexandria by Cynegius; for acclamations there in favour of the usurper, see Lib. *Or.* 19.4. The palace at Antioch had been empty since the departure of Valens in 378, the longest such vacancy since its construction under Diocletian.

94. Lib. *Or.* 19.39; 20.5; 23.12.

95. At *Or.* 19.40–42 Libanius protests against the unfairness of including in such reprisals women and citizens who had been sick or absent from Antioch at the time of the outrage; the arguments are no different in principle from those which he subsequently employs against the imposition of a fine (at 43–44).

orator appears to accept the city's collective responsibility for the original outrage, which had involved (at least by association) its official representatives, the *curia* and *honorati*. However horrific, collective reprisals
against the whole population would therefore have been intelligible, a
brutal counterpart to the city's loss of civic status and the closure of its
institutions. By contrast, the killings at Thessalonica are universally presented as irrational and illogical, and the victims as innocent.

Comparison with Antioch makes it clear that the scene of the massacre cannot have been, as the ecclesiastical historian Rufinus claimed,
the circus at Thessalonica, or the occasion an invitation extended to the
populace to assemble there to watch a chariot race.[96] The setting is
widely accepted among modern scholars, perhaps for its dramatic visual
quality; but in the tense atmosphere after Butheric's death, while the
people waited anxiously for any news or rumour from the court, the
announcement that the emperor had ordered a special fixture at the hip-
podrome would have struck a very odd note indeed.[97] For such an ambush to succeed, moreover, total secrecy was necessary; but even Ambrose (as we have seen) could claim to have spoken out against the
emperor's project. A message from him (or anyone else party to the plot)
to a friend in Thessalonica would have foiled the plan. Rufinus has probably transposed Theodosius' vengeance to the scene of the original
crime. Sozomen places the riot that led to Butheric's death at a time
'when some magnificent games were about to be held'. The charioteer
whom the general had arrested was demanded 'as being necessary for
the contest': the demand, we can plausibly imagine, took the form of an
acclamation from the imprisoned star's fans immediately before the start
of the scheduled races. In that case, responsibility for Butheric's murder could have been attributed with some precision. The fatal riot had
not been led, as at Antioch, by the city's representatives, but by a faction: the fans of whichever colour the absent charioteer was due to race
under.[98]

96. Ruf. *HE* 11.18: 'ad ludos circenses invitari populum eique ex improviso
circumfundi milites . . . iubet'.

97. A vivid impression of the atmosphere can be obtained from the famous
homilies *De statuis*, preached by the presbyter John Chrysostom to the apprehensive Christians of Antioch as they awaited news; note esp. *Hom.* 2.1–2; *Hom.*
3; *Hom.* 6.2–3. At *Hom.* 17 John mentions the emperor's order that the hippo-
drome be closed.

98. Amphilochius of Iconium lamented (*Iambi ad Seleucum* 172–178) the disastrous consequences of circus riots in 'destroying once-famous cities'; this passage, which has been plausibly associated with Thessalonica (cf. R. Browning,
CR, n.s., 21 [1971], 138), offers support for the argument that the *origin* of the
crisis involved bloodshed in the circus.

If that was so, the universal horror at the indiscriminate nature of the retaliation becomes intelligible; but the emperor's decision to inflict such a punishment becomes still more bizarre. We might hesitate, however, before accepting the unanimous view of the sources that what actually happened at Thessalonica was in exact compliance with the emperor's orders. Imperial instructions were susceptible to misinterpretation or distortion;[99] since there was neither precedent nor logical basis for Theodosius to order a massacre, this may well have happened in the present case also. Sozomen offers an important hint with his remark that the soldiers had been ordered to execute a 'stated number'.[100] How was this total calculated? Rather than an arbitrary quota assigned to each soldier or unit, we might suppose that there was a more precise list; and (to apply this to the hypothesis advanced above) Ammianus makes it clear that a charioteer's fans were recognizable to the authorities.[101] But Sozomen's account also shows organization breaking down, as a merchant tried unsuccessfully to offer himself in place of his sons and a slave substituted himself for his master.[102] The money that changed hands in these transactions robbed the emperor's vengeance of its grim but impersonal majesty. What is worse, the wrong people were seen to suffer. The sources seem less shocked by the number of casualties than by the fate of the innocent, mown down beside the guilty 'like corn at harvest time'.[103]

Further comparison with Antioch suggests how the situation might have run out of control. The procedures set in motion after the riot of the statues were complex and impressive. The *comes orientis* was at hand to deal with the less significant criminals, while the suspects of higher rank were set aside for judgement by the two senior officials dispatched from Constantinople, whose previous connexions with the city's elite gave their justice a human face; the soldiers accompanying them, as outsiders, were terrifying but disciplined automata who could be relied upon to execute their commands.[104] What proved disastrous at Thessa-

99. Cf. the events that led to the destruction, shortly after Thessalonica, of the Serapeum in Alexandria: see below, p. 332.

100. Soz. *HE* 7.25.4: '*rheton . . . arithmon*'.

101. The fans of the arrested charioteer Philoromus in Rome were given short shrift by the prefect Leontius: Amm. Marc. 15.7.2.

102. Soz. *HE* 7.25.6–7.

103. Theod. *HE* 5.17.3; cf. Paulin. *V. Amb.* 24.1, 'plurimi interempti innocentes'.

104. The process is fully described by G. Downey, *A History of Antioch* (1961), 426–433; the brutal intimacy characteristic of Roman justice is well illustrated by the treatment meted out to the red-haired Peter Valvomeres at Rome (Amm. Marc. 15.7.3–5).

lonica was the use of Butheric's own subordinates and soldiers to avenge him, without any apparent participation by the civil authorities.[105] The garrison's intimacy with the city was bound to affect its performance. The hunt for designated criminals collapsed into a wholesale settling of accounts, with profit probably (to judge from the bargains reported by Sozomen) the chief consideration of the underpaid soldiers. One gang, with cool calculation, waited at the docks to arrest unsuspecting visitors as they disembarked.[106] Their efficiency reflects two years of familiarity with the city and the location of its wealth and is perhaps the real key to the reaction that the episode provoked. By its awful demonstration of strength at Thessalonica the army, which by its constant presence in the cities had come to replace the domestic slave population as the enemy within, had briefly made the collective nightmare of the respectable classes come true.

The sufferings of wealthy visitors naturally ensured widespread publicity for the massacre. Meanwhile, Theodosius could neither defend nor disown it: unable to impose discipline upon the faraway troops, he was compelled by the much-proclaimed myth of imperial omnipotence to accept the ultimate responsibility. The best face he could put upon the situation was of a hasty order countermanded too late.[107] He there-fore solemnly took steps to prevent a recurrence, with a famous law issued from Verona in mid-August.[108] A procedure was established for crimes 'where, in accordance with our examination of the case, we have ordered a rather severe punishment, contrary to our usual practice, against certain individuals': sentence would be deferred for a period

105. A *vicarius Macedoniae* and *consularis Macedoniae* were both based at Thessalonica, the former nominally equivalent in rank to the *comes orientis;* neither is mentioned in the sources.

106. Soz. *HE* 7.25.4.

107. This excuse was already current in 390: Ambrose quotes it back at Theodosius (*Ep. extra coll.* 11 [51].6), describing the massacre as something 'quod ipse sero revocando grave factum putasti'.

108. *CTh* 9.40.13. The code, notoriously, dates the law to 382; but the con-ventional emendation to 390 stands, despite the vigorous arguments of R. M. Errington, 'The Praetorian Prefectures of Virius Nicomachus Flavianus', *Historia* 41 (1992), 439–461. The testimony of Rufinus (*HE* 11.18), published before the code's publication, is decisive. Errington's suggestion of a garbled oral tradition (at 455) is unconvincing; Rufinus probably followed an informant particularly interested in imperial legislation (cf. *HE* 11.16). The silence of the Milanese sources, emphasized by Errington at 454, simply reflects the irrelevance of the law to their interpretation of events. Nor is the error in the code 'unique' (Er-rington, 454n71): cf. *CTh* 15.5.2, *CJ* 8.36.3. For Errington's proposed redating of Flavianus' prefecture, see below, n. 175.

of thirty days. But this rationalization was still inadequate. The law endeavoured only to correct excessive speed in implementing punishments: undue haste, it was implied, had been the error involved at Thessalonica. But Theodosius, who had perhaps underestimated the extent of the outrage, would not be able to dispel it until he had acknowledged its underlying cause: the innocence of the victims.

The solution was provided by Ambrose, who turned the catastrophe into a public relations triumph for the emperor. To the admiration of his Christian subjects, Theodosius was seen to humble himself before the discipline of the church; he took his place in the *ordo poenitentium* at Milan, among the sinners who gathered at the basilica to demonstrate their repentance to God, and tearfully solicited the prayers of the faithful.[109] This dramatic gesture, once seen as a formal capitulation of empire to church in anticipation of Canossa, has more recently been interpreted in more modest terms as a victory for Theodosius' conscience over his pride.[110] But this psychological approach mistakes the nature of a penance that was not an act of lonely soul-searching but an exhibition enacted before the Christian community of Milan. Theodosius, so much of whose work as emperor consisted of making carefully stylized public appearances, cannot but have been aware of these spectators. If any perspective upon the affair is to be privileged, it is theirs: we must therefore ask how they would have regarded the spectacle of their Augustus abasing himself before them.

The idea that the issue was fundamentally a private or pastoral one owes much to a remarkable letter from Ambrose to Theodosius that prepared the emperor for his penance, setting out a moral and ideological framework to justify and rationalize it.[111] When the emperor, who had been away on apparently routine business,[112] returned to Milan, the bishop was not there to greet him. The official explanation for his absence was a serious bout of illness, but Theodosius learnt from the letter

109. For the penitential rite at Milan, see R. Gryson, *Le prêtre selon saint Ambroise* (1968), 275–290.

110. N. Q. King, *The Emperor Theodosius and the Establishment of Christianity* (1961), 69: 'In his humility and repentance we may see Theodosius' greatest achievement'.

111. *Ep. extra coll.* 11 [51]; references in the text are to this letter.

112. Theodosius' visit to Verona in August and September, attested in the codes, was probably made either to supervise dealings with the Alamanni (cf. Gratian's presence in Verona in June 383: Soc. *HE* 5.11.2) or to escape the summer humidity of the central Po valley. Neither Gratian (apart for his first visit, in transit, in 379) nor Valentinian II is recorded at Milan during these two months.

that this was merely an excuse: Ambrose, pressed by his horrified colleagues and alarmed by ominous dreams, had removed himself to avoid
having to celebrate the Eucharist with the bloodstained emperor. He had
preferred, he wrote, to set out his position 'secretly' for the emperor's
'reflection', rather than provoke him by a public confrontation (5). That
the letter is at least partly in his own hand specifically designates the
contents as confidential (14). This has encouraged historians to treat it
with particular respect, as a rare example of 'direct' communication in
an age that set so much store by formality and literary pretension. But
Ambrose's approach was no less formal for being private. Even the confidentiality is misleading: though it allowed Theodosius a certain room
for manoeuvre, no reply can possibly have been given to the letter before its terms had been subjected to keen debate among the emperor's
counsellors.

Attention should be paid to the letter's terms. Much indeed is conventional: the opening protestation of long-standing *amicitia* and recol-
lection of past *beneficia* (1) would not be out of place in a Symmachan
epistle. Ambrose is careful in setting out his case. The emperor's *impetus
naturae* ('a forcefulness in your nature') is acknowledged as the reason
for this circumspection; all would be so much better, the bishop reflected, if Theodosius were allowed to deal with this failing himself, to
control himself and conquer his inclinations by his piety (4). The connexion with the events at Thessalonica is unstated but clear. To the
theme of imperial irascibility, adumbrated in the recent law, was added
the attractive idea that the damage had been done not by the emperor's
temper itself but by the various influences that acted upon it. Though
hardly a point to commend itself to Theodosius' entourage (or to help
the historian unravel the actual causes of the massacre), reallocation of
responsibility was to be taken further as the story of Thessalonica developed.[113] But what must have most arrested Theodosius was the inference Ambrose drew from the present situation. What was required, he
claimed, was reconciliation (6); the emperor's casual extermination of the
people of Thessalonica was a 'sin' that needed atonement. Theodosius
was a man and, as such, had been exposed to temptation. His piety had
earned him the envy of the devil himself, and the emperor now had to
conquer the evil one (11).

113. Theodoret *HE* 5.18.3. Ambrose became more explicit in 395 (*De obitu
Theodosii* 34: 'peccatum suum, quod fraude aliorum obrepserat'), when one of
Theodosius' advisors was readily identifiable, from a Milanese perspective, as a
villain. But Ambrose is far less likely to have had Rufinus in mind in 390 than
Timasius, who was, ironically, probably in the congregation to hear *De obitu
Theodosii* in 395.

'I advise, I request, I plead, I entreat': Ambrose claimed to be using such language from sorrow, because Theodosius 'did not grieve at the death of so many innocent people' (12). This must be disingenuous. Had the emperor not been unhappy at the highly publicized massacre, Ambrose's letter would have been futile (and subsequent events unintelligible). The bishop's tone reflects not the stoniness of Theodosius' heart but the intrinsic delicacy of the appeal. No precedents existed for the reconciliation Ambrose was proposing; more important, his own standing was doubtful. The shadow of Callinicum lies heavily over the present letter. But the *sacerdotii auctoritas* which Ambrose had then invoked was now explicitly withheld; rather than being peremptorily urged to listen, Theodosius was asked, more gently, 'not to be impatient' (7).[114] After the previous contretemps, the bishop made it quite clear that he was not seeking to 'confound' the sinner (11). Perhaps, indeed, the most impressive aspect of Ambrose to emerge from this letter is his ability to learn from his mistakes. His previous failure to recognize Theodosius' most pressing concern, by presenting him as only an eastern ruler, was also rectified. Theodosius was addressed as 'the father of Gratian' (17): his youngest son's name advertised a western orientation which the bishop duly picked up.[115] He went further: in piety he 'preferred' Theodosius 'to many emperors, found only one to equal him' (13). The one, of course, was Gratian; Theodosius had definitively supplanted Valentinian in Ambrose's affection.[116]

For all the improvement in technique, the type of relationship that the bishop sought to establish with Theodosius had not changed. The emperor was once more offered David—'king, prophet, ancestor of Christ according to the flesh' (7)—as his model, while the bishop resumed his prophetic garb. So closely does the parallel run that Ambrose even muddles a direct biblical reference, substituting his previous persona, Nathan, for Gad (8).[117] But Nathan had almost reversed his approach to the sinner. Instead of elevating the repair of a synagogue to a triumph handed to the Lord's enemies, he now reduced the awful bloodshed of Thessalonica to the mundane routines of wrongdoing: 'for

114. 'Noli ergo impatienter ferre, imperator, si dicatur tibi . . .'; cf. *Ep.* 74 [40].1, 'Itaque peto ut patienter sermonem meum audias; nam si indignus sum qui a te audiar, indignus sum qui pro te offeram'.

115. This Gratian is argued to have been an actual son of Theodosius and Galla, rather than the Augustus of 367–383, by S. Rebenich: 'Gratian, a Son of Theodosius, and the Birth of Galla Placidia', *Historia* 34 (1985), 372–385.

116. For Valentinian's claim to piety, see above, p. 174; Ambrose had in 384 held up Gratian's 'titulos piae virtutis' to him for emulation: *Ep.* 72 [17].15.

117. The reference is 2 Samuel 24.

it is not surprising that a man should sin, although it is reprehensible if he does not acknowledge that he has done wrong, and fails to humble himself before God' (9).

The status of this document has been much misunderstood, with too precise a meaning attached to Ambrose's statement, 'I dare not offer the sacrifice, if you wish to participate' (13). This does not announce a general excommunication for Theodosius. Only Ambrose was involved, he alone having learnt (through a dream) that to offer the Eucharist in the emperor's presence was 'not permissible' (14). He had not told the dream to his colleagues, who in turn had failed at their synod to translate their own outrage at the emperor's crime into any formal, collective response; only 'the communion of Ambrose' had been deemed relevant (6). But even this seems to have gone unannounced, for Ambrose's letter implies that the emperor was unaware of any previous sanctions against himself. Theodosius had meanwhile been at Verona for at least a month after news of the massacre reached Italy, without his rights to the sacrament being challenged. He had no reason to fear a formal ban from the Italian churches.

The letter's confidentiality suggests instead the opposite. Theodosius was being offered the initiative: if he responded to the terms presented by Ambrose and professed his penitence with the appropriate tears, he would be granted reconciliation with God. And if not? Then 'forgive what I do, inasmuch as I am putting God first' (17). This is not to be taken as a threat to confront Theodosius. Ambrose was showing his 'preference' for God by absenting himself from Milan; all the emperor had to forgive, therefore, was his failure to attend the *adventus* ceremony. Like Symmachus when he declined his invitation to the consular ceremonies at the start of the same year, Ambrose was punctilious in his excuses for missing a formal court occasion. At one level, therefore, the letter belonged to a familiar category of deferential apology; Theodosius could have read it as such and ignored it.

Eventually, of course, the emperor responded positively. But the circumstances in which the letter was delivered, and the negotiations that followed, remain completely obscure. Paulinus' dialogue, where the emperor at first demurs and cites the precedent of David to justify monarchical misdemeanours, simply dramatizes the terms of Ambrose's letter.[118] Theodosius cannot have been so poorly versed in Scripture not to see the flaws in this defence, even without Ambrose's explicit reminder that David *had* atoned for his crimes (7–10). Theodosius' reasons for wariness at Ambrose's approach—he too must have recalled the bish-

118. *V. Amb.* 24.2.

op's earlier initiatives—did not include a breezy unconcern for the blood-bath that had been perpetrated in his name. The emperor had every reason to welcome the diagnosis of the calamity as the effect of sin, for as such it could be redeemed. But dare he trust the bishop and submit to the discipline of penance that had been recommended? How, above all, would his Christian subjects react to the sight of him among the professed sinners of the capital? We cannot know how he reached his decision to take the risk, but the discipline that Ambrose could be seen to exercise over his congregation was probably a factor: Theodosius' humiliation would be a controlled one, and its course predictable. There was even a blueprint for the process in Ambrose's recent booklet *De poenitentia*, which like the letter to Theodosius stresses the positive aspects of public penance by making the sinner the focus for the people's prayers and tears.[119] Excommunication was thus conceived not as a rejection by the church but as an opportunity to achieve a deeper integration within it.

All went smoothly. Theodosius played his part perfectly, making a profound impression upon his Christian subjects: 'He acknowledged his crime; tearfully professing his responsibility, he performed public penance in full view of the whole church, and completed the time appointed for this patiently, and without any of the haughtiness typical of kings' (Ruf. *HE* 12.18). Rufinus' account abbreviates much. There must have been careful preparations to alert the Christians of Milan and condition their response, which likely included a formal *correptio* where the bishop rebuked the emperor for his sin and imposed the penalty.[120] Various questions of protocol had to be settled: one wonders, for instance, what negotiations preceded the decision that Theodosius should put aside the imperial robes, the outward aspect of Rufinus' *regale fastidium*.[121] As for the *tempus adscriptum*, there is no worthwhile evidence for the length of

119. *De poen.* 1.80: 'velut enim operibus quibusdam totius populi purgatur, et plebis lacrimis abluitur, qui orationibus et fletibus plebis redimitur a peccato, et in homine mundatur interiore'; cf. 1.90; 2.54–57. For composition shortly before 390, see Palanque, *Saint Ambroise*, 527–529. The relation between Theodosius' penance and the *Apologia David* is unclear: see the discussion by P. Hadot, *SCh* 239 (1977), 33–43.

120. It is possible that such an occasion was the basis for Paulinus' account of the exchange between emperor and bishop (*V. Amb.* 24.2); even, perhaps, of the story in Sozomen of the encounter at the church door. But Paulinus' account can be explained as an inference from Ambrose's letter, and Sozomen's as a conflation of the incident with the story of Babylas of Antioch and the emperor Philip, as elaborated by John Chrysostom. Cf. Schieffer, 'Von Mailand nach Canossa', 339–342.

121. Amb. *De ob. Theod.* 34: 'stravit omne quo utebatur insigne regium'.

time the emperor had to maintain his humble posture. The fifth-century fantasy of Theodoret, where the emperor languishes in his palace for eight months after Ambrose has turned him away at the church doors, until finally at the approach of Christmas he begs and receives forgiveness, has enjoyed undeserved credence as a chronological peg: the details are inventions, and the penance itself compressed to a single moment. For want of any information to the contrary, we might suppose that Theodosius' penitence followed the usual pattern and was formally ended in April 391, at the ceremony held annually on Maundy Thursday.[122]

Theodosius' patient humility bore triumphant fruit. Not only was he formally forgiven his sin, but he wiped the stain of Thessalonica from his political record. No source records the massacre in isolation; it is everywhere set in the context supplied by the emperor's penance. Even the mighty, after all, were susceptible to the malice of demons; Theodosius had succumbed, but saved himself by his exemplary *humilitas*. The victims of Thessalonica became examples not of the cruelty (or inefficiency) of an absolute ruler, but of the power of the evil one. Ambrose, meanwhile, had amply justified the trust placed in him. The earliest accounts of the episode do not mention him at all; the emperor retains the full spotlight, with only the anonymous 'bishops of Italy' to urge him to repent.[123] This presentation betokens considerable restraint from Ambrose, who could easily have anticipated those later historians who have trumpeted his role as the activator of Theodosius' conscience. But no personal conflict was allowed to interfere with the cosmic struggle between good and evil, whose shadow obscures the all too human tensions that had originally caused the catastrophe at Thessalonica.

No alternative version survives. Theodosius' anger and humility were imprinted definitively upon the record, finding their way even into the 'neutral' secular tradition.[124] But this theological explanation for the catastrophe also silenced the ideological opposition; the whole episode

122. The occasion is marked by Ambrose at *Ep.* 76 [20].27. Brown's suggestion (*Power and Persuasion*, 112) of a single gesture of repentance compresses events unduly.

123. Thus Rufinus and Augustine: the latter's dependence upon the former is argued by Y.-M. Duval, 'L'éloge de Théodose dans la *Cité de Dieu'*, *RecAug* 4 (1966), 135–179.

124. Particularly remarkable against the background of Thessalonica is the domestication of Theodosius' temper in Aur. Vict. *Epit.* 48.13: 'Irasci sane rebus indignis, sed flecti cito; unde modica dilatione emolliebantur aliquando severa praecepta'.

is absent from Zosimus (and, by implication, from Eunapius as well). Bafflement would provide one explanation. Criticism of Christianity in the pagan tradition was traditionally presented obliquely: to discuss the upstart religion directly and in its own terms would have conceded too much to it. An artful reductionism was therefore employed, translating churches into places of asylum and bishops into demagogues or other equally recognizable types of public figure.[125] The only irreducibly Christian ceremony mentioned in the whole of Zosimus' work is the baptism of Constantine, famously presented (after Eunapius) as an expedient offered to the emperor to rid him of the bad conscience with which his purge of his family had saddled him.[126] By the later fourth century, baptism—as the most widely available and easily accessible of the sacraments—was susceptible to such an interpretation, but this was because to outsiders the process appeared painless and superficial. Theodosius' penance took him deep into new territory which even ordinary Christians blushed to enter. Pagan critics, *a fortiori*, could not pursue him there.[127]

Theodosius did not, of course, do his penance to escape censure from the tradition represented by Zosimus; nor is the emphasis upon publicity in the present interpretation intended to reduce it to an exercise in cynical manipulation. The dichotomy between public and private, political and pastoral, inherent in many modern accounts is inherently false. We are in constant danger of underestimating how closely the emperors identified themselves with their public faces, and conversely how much of themselves they put into their performances. We can no more pry the two apart here than in Constantius' exhibitions of rigid immobility or Valentinian I's of violent rage.[128] By kneeling in Ambrose's church, Theodosius added a new role to the imperial repertoire which gave full expression to the deep religiosity and abiding sense of human frailty that (we need not doubt) he shared with his Christian contemporaries. The unusually dramatic and innovative character of the

125. Thus Zos. 4.40, 5.18.1 (church as asylum); 5.23 (Chrysostom as demagogue). The criteria employed by Ammianus are not dissimilar.

126. 2.29.3–4. On this passage, and the Christian refutations, see F. Paschoud, 'Zosime 2,29 et la version païenne de la conversion de Constantin', *Historia* 20 (1971), 334–353.

127. Amb. *De ob. Theod.* 34: 'privati erubescunt'. The only pagan critic who seems to have noted the tactical possibilities of penance was Julian, exceptional for both his knowledge of the religion of the 'Galileans' and his eagerness to discuss it: *Caesares*, 336B.

128. The complexities of imperial role-play are well discussed by J. F. Matthews, *The Roman Empire of Ammianus* (1989), 231–252.

part involved a certain unpredictability and risk, attesting to the crisis
that persuaded Theodosius (and his advisors) to accept it; it also betokens the expertise and sensitivity of the man responsible for the staging. The penitence of Theodosius reveals Ambrose as the supreme impresario of the Christian empire.

Whatever the motives, the emperor's decision to seek readmission
to Ambrose's flock changed the face of politics at Milan. Theodosius was
promoted to the company of the saints,[129] and Ambrose had at last won
honour as a prophet. The immediate effect was to reduce the consequences of Thessalonica to manageable proportions. But the partnership
established between bishop and emperor would continue to evolve,
with eventual ramifications that neither could have anticipated.

THE END OF VALENTINIAN

Theodosius' tearful submission in Ambrose's church, and the forgiveness of his sin pronounced by the bishop, heralded the inauguration
of a special relationship: never before had a ruler placed himself so completely in a churchman's hands. But Ambrose did not thereby secure a
personal ascendancy over Theodosius. The mistaken interpretation of
the emperor's penance as a crisis of conscience has led many scholars to
exaggerate its impact and to imagine Ambrose guiding the emperor in
the aftermath to ever more unequivocal expressions of faith.[130] But it is
highly unlikely that the two men ever had the opportunity to develop
an authentically personal relationship. Ambrose was neither Theodosius' confessor (no reliably attested spiritual director can be discovered
in the fourth-century sources) nor his semi-permanent ecclesiastical advisor, as Ossius had been under Constantine, or Ursacius and Valens
for parts of Constantius' reign.[131] There is no evidence that Ambrose saw

129. This was accomplished finally in *De obitu Theodosii*; but note the promise in *Ep. extra coll.* 11 [51].16, that Theodosius' castigation 'tibi erit commune
cum sanctis'.

130. See especially Palanque, *Saint Ambroise*, 250–252 (cf. Seeck, *Geschichte
des Untergangs*, 5:232). W. Ensslin, while rejecting the idea that Ambrose exercised 'absolute power' over a 'perfectly obedient' emperor, has him 'taken into
his trust' (*Die Religionspolitik des Kaisers Theodosius d. Gr.* [1953], 75); Lippold,
Theodosius der Grosse, 170, denies that Theodosius 'let himself be ruled by Ambrose' but fails convincingly to redefine the relationship.

131. The nearest equivalent to a confessor is perhaps the Arian presbyter
who allegedly suborned Constantine and Constantius II (Ruf. *HE* 10.11), a sig-

the emperor with any frequency or that they ever met alone. The good-will that the bishop had won by his services after Thessalonica made him a favoured lobbyist, not a power behind the throne.

One particular enactment has often been cited as evidence for Ambrose's influence on imperial policy. A famous law, issued from Milan on 24 February 391, instructed the prefect of Rome that 'nobody shall pollute themselves with sacrifices, nobody shall slaughter an innocent beast as an offering, nobody shall enter shrines or wander through temples and do reverence to images shaped with human workmanship'.[132] An association with Ambrose has seemed irresistible: having received absolution at Christmas 390, the emperor is seen marking his 'conversion' with an overt repudiation of his pagan friends at Rome. But on closer reading, the law seems unable to bear such weight. Its provisions addressed certain types of provincial governor who, 'either on tour or in a city', exploited their official position to enter temples and, in defiance of previous legislation, hold formal ceremonies there. The targets appear to have been the governors of the suburbicarian provinces, men recruited almost exclusively from the senatorial families of Rome and otherwise conspicuous for maintaining traditional patterns of civic munificence and local patronage.[133] The clear and narrow definition of the measure's scope invites comparison with other similarly phrased enactments, specific measures to respond to a petition or the laying of information. *Delatio*, a report that these pagan activities were actually taking place, offers the best explanation for the present law;[134] nor is

---

nificantly junior figure. For Ossius' fourteen-year stint with Constantine's highly mobile court, see V. C. de Clerq, *Ossius of Cordova* (1954).

132. *CTh* 16.10.10: 'Nemo se hostiis polluat, nemo insontem victimam caedat, nemo delubra adeat, templum perlustret et mortali opere formata simulacra suspiciat'.

133. The law (uniquely) prescribes different penalties for *consulares* (6 lbs. of gold), *correctores* and *praesides* (4 lbs. each); all three grades occur in suburbicarian Italy, while the only other western *corrector* governed the insignificant province of Savia. The *iudex* for whom the much heftier fine of 15 lbs. was established is probably, to judge from the severity of the penalty, the prefect of Rome himself. For the distinctive features of these magistracies, see B. Ward-Perkins, *From Classical Antiquity to the Middle Ages* (1984), 20–26.

134. The prescription for equivalent fines upon the governor's *officium*, 'si non et obstiterit iudici et confestim publica adtestatione rettulerit', not only indicates the formal, public character of the activities concerned but also suggests a likely source for the original complaint: disgruntled Christian *officiales* had perhaps not anticipated having to bear so heavy a responsibility for suppressing their governors' pagan practices.

there any reason to identify the informant as Ambrose, who had never previously betrayed the slightest interest in residual activities in the temples.[135]

The persisting belief in Ambrose's responsibility for the law reflects an exaggerated idea of its importance, as a final proscription of paganism in the west.[136] But the contents of the enactment do not live up to the fiery rhetoric of the prescript, which itself adds nothing new. It simply reiterates the long-standing government concern to abolish sacrifice; the 'prohibition' from entering temples is no more than a typically rhetorical elaboration on this theme.[137] There is therefore no indication that the law embodied a comprehensive programme, and it seems neither to have hastened the slow death of paganism at Rome nor dampened Symmachus' enjoyment of his consular year.[138] Nor again does the dispatch, four months later, of a similar command concerning the Egyptian temples to the *praesentalis Augustalis* and the *comes Aegyptii* provide evidence for a concerted attack by Theodosius against Rome and Alexandria, the last great bastions of paganism.[139] The dramatic assault on Alexandrian paganism was a local initiative, taken after another imperial command had been turned to ends that cannot have been intended; the reissue of the 'Roman' law might also have been solicited by interested parties at Alexandria. For the emperor all that was involved was the casual rubber-stamping of a measure already possessing, in theory, universal validity. Once posted at Alexandria, however, it offered legitimacy to those who intended an unusually literal application of imperial

135. Ambrose's only concern during the altar of Victory 'debate' had been over sacrifices 'in templo victoriarum' (*Ep.* 72 [18].31); his failure to mention the present measure in his later letter to Eugenius is important evidence against both his own involvement and the law's contemporary significance.

136. Thus Palanque, *Saint Ambroise*, 251; Piganiol, *L'empire chrétien*, 285, calls it 'une sentence de mort'.

137. *CTh* 16.10.4 ('claudi protinus templa'), 16.10.7 (against anyone who 'templum . . . putaverit adeundum'), both in explicit connexion with sacrifice; cf. 16.10.6, specifying the death penalty for those 'quos operam sacrificiis dare vel colere simulacra constiterit'.

138. For the law's failure to make an imprint on the archaeological record, see Pietri, *Roma Christiana*, 437–438.

139. *CTh* 16.10.11, interpreted in this sense by F. Thélamon, *Païens et chrétiennes au IVème siècle* (1981), at 254. For the relationship between the laws, see J. Gaudemet, 'La condamnation des practiques païennes en 391', in *Epektasis: Mélanges Daniélou* (1972), 597–602, whose conclusions are not incompatible with the present argument. For events at Alexandria, see Ruf. *HE* 11.22; Soc. *HE* 5.16; Soz. *HE* 7.15. The fullest discussion is Thélamon's.

rhetoric.[140] Such were the perils of the information gap that separated an all-powerful emperor from his subjects and left his imprecise thunderings to be interpreted by men who frequently had agendas of their own.

The law concerning the Egyptian temples was issued from Aquileia. Theodosius was marching home, having made profitable use of the two years that he had spent in Italy after Valentinian's departure for his thankless watch on the Rhine. By the spring of 391, Theodosius had aligned to himself most of the key players in western political life. If Ambrose's eventual adhesion had been largely fortuitous, the aristocrats of Rome had been won (as we have seen) by a judicious courtship. Nicomachus Flavianus, an embodiment of their best traditions, had been appointed praetorian prefect by Theodosius during the summer of 390 and continued to hold office in his interest. That Flavianus' tenure was also in the interests of his own class is indicated by the stream of letters he received while in office from Symmachus, seeking consideration for aspirants to office or anxious litigants.[141] Flavianus seems to have been left very much to his own devices after Theodosius' departure. The codes record one law reaching Milan from Vicenza and one from Concordia while Theodosius was still in Italy, and thereafter silence.[142] This is no doubt partly the accident of survival—the western prefectures are far less well represented than the eastern in the codes—but contrasts suggestively with the preceding two years. The most likely explanation is that Theodosius' practice of legislating for Italy, defensible enough while he was there in person, lapsed when he left. Fantasies like an Italian protectorate carved out by a farsighted Theodosius for the future benefit of Honorius (and watched over meanwhile by trusted friends like Ambrose) must be discarded.[143] Theodosius, who aimed only to prevent Valentinian from exercising his legitimate rights in Italy, deliberately created a political vacuum there, seeking to bind those who prof-

140. Brown, *Power and Persuasion,* 113–115: 'Once again, Theodosius allowed local events to outstrip him'.

141. Examples include *Ep.* 2.9 (introducing 'de septem montibus virum'); 2.42 (inquiring after the progress of an advocate at Flavianus' bar); 2.33 (a reminder of the procedures appropriate for a trial involving senators); 2.41 (a plea for an ex-governor due to appear before Flavianus' court). All these letters belong to the period 390–394: cf. below, n. 175.

142. Seeck, *Regesten,* 278.

143. The thesis is presented in various forms by von Campenhausen, *Ambrosius von Mailand,* 244; V. Grumel, 'L'Illyricum de la mort de Valentinian Ier', *REB* 9 (1951), at 19–21; and A. Pabst, *Divisio Regni,* 345–346.

ited from this situation to himself by self-interest. The resulting political paralysis allowed such anomalies as the interference in a projected Milanese marriage by a *magister officiorum* from Constantinople, a thousand miles away.[144]

From Ambrose's point of view, the departure of Theodosius was a mixed blessing. His authority as the 'friend' of the emperor and his ministers was enhanced in the prevailing uncertainty, as his handling of the Titianus affair illustrates. But it was difficult to extract specific favours at long range. A case in point, which delimits the extent of Ambrose's hold over Theodosius after the penance, concerned the continuing dispute over the bishopric at Antioch. In 381 Ambrose had refused to recognize the accession of Flavianus after the death of Meletius, pressing instead the claims of the latter's saintly but intractable rival Paulinus. Paulinus' death in (probably) 388 solved nothing, for on his deathbed he consecrated as his successor Jerome's wealthy and well-connected friend Evagrius. Perhaps Evagrius' accession prompted Ambrose to reopen the Antiochene question with Theodosius; a council was duly decreed, to be held in Capua during the winter of 391/2.

But Ambrose was not the only bishop with a claim upon Theodosius' benevolence. Flavianus had, arguably, succeeded in preventing a massacre at Antioch in 387 by his tears, and by bending to these Theodosius had earned as much credit as he did by his own weeping in Ambrose's church after Thessalonica. The bishop of Antioch simply ignored the imperial summons to the council of Capua, which did not convene until Theodosius was back in Constantinople and therefore within reach of his influence.[145] To Ambrose's dismay, Flavianus obtained his own imperial rescript, which excused him from the council and so protected him from accusations of contumacy. When Ambrose's subsequent attempt to entrust the matter to the bishop of Alexandria foundered for similar reasons, he displayed the bad grace of a man beaten at his own game: 'Again our brother Flavianus has taken recourse to the assistance provided by petitions and the suffrage of imperial rescripts. In vain therefore the labour of so many priests has been wasted, and we must turn again to the judgements of the *saeculum* and to rescripts' (*Ep.* 70 [56].3). But even these renewed efforts were in vain: Flavianus remained undisturbed, and after his protégé, John Chrysostom, was promoted to Constantinople in 397, the west was no longer able to resist his claims.

---

144. Viz. Rufinus against Titianus, above, p. 260.

145. Palanque, *Saint Ambroise*, 255–259. Cf. F. Cavallera, *Le schisme d'Antioche* (1905), 283–287; Pietri, *Roma Christiana*, 1278–1281.

In 398, the year after Ambrose's death, Flavianus was admitted at last to the communion of the western church.[146]

The incident suggests that Ambrose's power—his ability to get things done—receded after Theodosius' departure. What, meanwhile, of Valentinian? Theodosius' elaborate plan to strand him on the margins of the empire until his own sons were assured predominance flew in the face of the fact that Italy remained, in the last resort, part of Valentinian's inheritance.[147] Whatever obligations had been discovered to confine him to Gaul could not keep him there indefinitely. It was therefore in an atmosphere of increasing tension that the *magister militum* Arbogast sought to restrain him, in a grim game of brinkmanship that was eventually fatal to them both.[148] For although Arbogast succeeded in confining Valentinian physically within Gaul, Theodosius' strategy was bound eventually to fail: it was simply impossible to control the west (let alone in despite of its legitimate ruler) by remote control from Constantinople. Valentinian was meanwhile able to assert himself at least indirectly. His ostentatious piety, for instance, recommended him to the Gallic bishops, on whose behalf he unsuccessfully invited Ambrose to mediate a settlement to Priscillian's unhappy legacy, the Felician schism.[149] Temptation presented itself to Valentinian, through a delegation of senators from Rome who sought (yet again) to reopen the question of pagan privileges.[150] Although obscure, the venture shows nicely how Theodosius' hold over those who had hailed him in the Roman senate had diminished in his absence: these same men were now offering Valentinian an opportunity to outbid his partner. His piety nevertheless prevailed over the political considerations argued by his counsellors.

External forces precipitated the inevitable crisis. Theodosius' measures bear direct responsibility: by tying Valentinian to the army in Gaul, he had effectively demilitarized Italy. During the early spring of 392, barbarian raiders were reported in the Alps, causing alarm at Milan—

146. Pietri, *Roma Christiana*, 1285–1288.

147. This is acknowledged by Ambrose, at *De ob. Val.* 22: 'suum regnum' (cf. *De ob. Val.* 7, 'de Valentiniani partibus').

148. Zos. 4.53; Sulpicius Alexander, in Greg. Tur. *HF* 2.9.

149. *De ob. Val.* 25: Valentinian's final invitation to Ambrose was explicitly *not* to a synod of Gallic bishops, 'propter quorum frequentes dissensiones crebro me excusaveram' (cf. *Ep. extra coll.* 11 [51].6, a synod in Milan in 390 'propter adventum Gallorum episcoporum'); the context implies that these excuses had been made to Valentinian.

150. *Ep. extra coll.* 10 [57].5 ('legatio a senatu intra Gallias missa'); cf. *De ob. Val.* 52. The embassy to Valentinian described at *De ob. Val.* 19–20 (albeit barely recognizable among the misrepresentations) is that of 384.

and also some uncertainty. The nearest available forces were Valentinian's, but Theodosius was unlikely to look kindly upon an explicit invitation to his fellow-Augustus to establish himself in Italy. The prefect Flavianus, who knew Theodosius' mind better than anyone, declined to involve himself in an appeal to Vienne. Instead, the mission was delegated to Ambrose, who after some initial reluctance agreed to go to Valentinian and 'secure the peace of Italy'.[151]

The subsequent round of formalities illustrates beautifully the tactical uses of court protocol. The emperor seized upon the invitation even before it was delivered, issuing orders as soon as the projected embassy was reported for way stations to be set up across the Alps and staff dispatched to make ready the palace at Milan. Ambrose, perhaps taking fright at the limelight cast upon his mission, immediately tried to excuse himself on the grounds that the emperor's arrival was so clearly imminent.[152] To no avail: a rescript arrived from Vienne demanding his appearance in person to offer a formal pledge to Arbogast and thus to accept responsibility for the venture.[153] The prince (who had been brought up in a hard school) showed his political cunning by adding the request that Ambrose baptize him. No bishop, least of all Ambrose, was likely to refuse such an invitation. After some further delays, he therefore set out for Vienne.

The bishop delayed too long, for he was still only halfway across the Alps when news reached him that Valentinian had been found dead. Suicide is the only plausible verdict for a death that benefitted nobody,[154]

151. *De ob. Val.* 24: 'Iam promiseram me profecturum, respondens vel honoratis petentibus vel praefecto ut tranquillitati Italiae consuleretur'.

152. *De ob. Val.* 24: 'ecce postridie litterae de instruendis mansionibus, invectio ornamentorum regalium, aliaque eiusmodi quae ingressurum iter imperatorem significarent'. That this was specifically in response to news of Ambrose's projected mission ('postridie' therefore not being meant literally) is clear from the foregoing: 'Quin etiam cum rumor quidam ad Viennensem pertulisset urbem, quod invitandi eius ad Italiam gratia eo pergerem; quam gaudebat, quam gratulabatur me sibi optato fore' (*De ob. Val.* 23).

153. *De ob. Val.* 25. Ambrose's expression ('vadem fidei tuae habere me apud comitem tuum velles') is unlikely to mean that he was required as a 'mediator' between Valentinian and Arbogast (Palanque, *Saint Ambroise*, 268; cf. T. A. Kelly in his commentary on *De ob. Val.*, at 266–267); the wording at 27 suggests a specific matter for which he was required to stand surety.

154. See B. Croke, 'Arbogast and the Death of Valentinian II', *Historia* 25 (1976), 235–244. The counterarguments of P. Grattarola, 'La morte dell'imperatore Valentiniano II', *RIL* 113 (1979), 359–370, depend upon an overliteral interpretation of Ambrose's rhetoric.

least of all Arbogast, who despite the suspicions raised by his well-publicized clashes with Valentinian made no political capital from his death. Instead he waited helplessly for Theodosius to take control of the situation, but his patron had neither the means to assert himself constructively from Constantinople nor the imagination to comprehend the west except as a potential threat to himself.

Among the false friends discomfited by Valentinian's sudden death (possibly the most effective political stroke of the unhappy prince's whole career) was Ambrose, whose failure to arrive when expected had coincided with, perhaps even provoked, the prince's final despair. In the convoluted self-exculpation which he addressed to the prince's corpse, he tried to make the best of the uncomfortable truth that 'everybody pronounced my absence to have been the cause of your death'.[155] Equally uncomfortable was the fact that the mission to Vienne had breached the invisible barrier between Italy and Gaul. Ambrose admitted in a letter to Theodosius that the prince's desire to receive baptism from him personally was 'irrational', there being so many venerable prelates available in Gaul; but he explained it as a token of the prince's love for him, for which he cannily held Theodosius himself responsible. He continued in the same vein: 'I hold you, my lord, to be the judge of my feelings and the interpreter of my thoughts':[156] there must have been much anxious mind-reading between Vienne, Italy and Constantinople as Theodosius' allies measured their own complicity in Valentinian's fate against his and against each others'.

Embarrassment suffuses much of Ambrose's letter to Theodosius, his first in the months since Valentinian's death. He had received a note from the emperor which had 'burst into' the silence in which he had been 'hiding', chiding him perhaps for his failure to express his grief over the tragedy. A remark to this effect would explain Ambrose's exploitation of the word *dolor* and its cognates in the letter, and especially his grateful acknowledgement of Theodosius' 'testimony to my sorrow'.[157] The long-range politics of the fourth century were conducted by just such cautious responses to imperial hints: we can therefore appreciate Theodosius' difficulty in obtaining concrete information about what was happening in the west.

155. *De ob. Val.* 28.
156. *Ep.* 25 [53].3: 'Te, imperator, arbitrum teneo affectus mei, te mentis mei interpretem'. Cf. 2, for Valentinian's devotion to Ambrose 'a te infusum'.
157. 'Testimonium meo dolori': *Ep.* 25 [53].3 (also 'hunc non doleam?'). After the opening, 'Silentium meum rupit sermo clementiae tuae' (1), the main body begins with the emphatic 'Doleo enim, fateor, dolore acerbo' (2).

Theodosius' letter to Ambrose had accompanied a rescript that answered what had probably been his only 'official' communication from Milan, a request for guidance concerning the disposal of Valentinian's body. Arbogast had sensibly rid himself of the corpse, dispatching Valentinian on his planned journey to Milan for the authorities there to decide whether to honour him as an assassinated emperor, damn him for conspiracy against Theodosius or write him off perfunctorily as a suicide. Theodosius' rescript duly authorized burial with imperial honours but, by failing to give a verdict on the cause of death, consigned the affair to political limbo: the house of Valentinian was to be disposed of with as little controversy as possible. As if to symbolize the indifference felt towards Valentinian, not even a coffin had been prepared for him; but here at least Ambrose could prove his worth. His tone changes entirely as he reports the discovery of a porphyry *labrum*, 'most suitable for this purpose' insofar as it resembled the tomb (on the outskirts of Milan, a short walk from the Basilica Ambrosiana) of the tetrarch Maximian.[158] Some 'very precious' slabs of porphyry had also been found to cover the royal remains. The result, makeshift but impressive, perfectly illustrates the bishop's talent for improvisation.

Enclosed in this secondhand splendour, Valentinian was displayed to the Christians of Milan for a final commemoration.[159] Any irony in the delivery of the *consolatio* in a church which the emperor had once demanded for himself, and which he can but rarely have graced with his presence, was drowned in the sorrow that Ambrose evoked: 'Over what should I weep first?' he began, urging his people to offer their tears as 'payment' to Valentinian for his fatal bid to come to their aid (*De obitu Val.* 2). His principal point of reference, however, was not the contemporary situation but the Book of Lamentations (3–8): Valentinian dissolved into the liturgical rhythms of the funeral service itself, his political identity quite obscured by the biblical prism through which the bishop held him up for view.

Spectators were invited to see in the corpse the 'young lover, radiant and ruddy' (58) of the Song of Songs (which replaced Lamentations as the bishop's principal hermeneutical tool), stamped with the image of Christ. The effusion of images that follows seems wildly inappropriate for the ruler of an empire: his belly was 'a casket of ivory' (as the reposi-

158. *Ep.* 25 [53].4; on Maximian's tomb, see M. Mirabella Roberti, *Milano Romana* (1984), 96–100.

159. Text references are to *De obitu Valentiniani*; the speech is well discussed by Y.-M. Duval, 'Formes profanes et formes bibliques dans les oraisons funèbres de saint Ambroise', *Entretiens Hardt* 23 (1977), at 260–274.

tory of scriptural knowledge: 59) and the joints of his thighs 'like collars' (meaning that he had retained his grace after victory in war: 68); his navel, 'a round bowl, filled with mixed wine', represented his soul, manufactured by God and equipped with the virtues (69). The descriptions dazzle, while Valentinian himself lies safely hidden beneath the purple surface.

In many respects the treatment accorded Valentinian resembles that given many years before to Satyrus. The wave of collective sorrow overwhelms, while actual details of Valentinian, his conduct as an emperor and the circumstances of his last days arise only occasionally to point a moral or generate a biblical parallel. The only visual focus, apart from Valentinian himself, is provided by his pious sisters, Grata and Iusta. The emperor lived on through the physical imprint he had made upon the two girls: 'he would kiss his sisters on the hand, on the head' (36); 'he loaded your heads not with jewels but with kisses; rather than cover your hands with badges of royalty, he brushed them with his imperial lips' (38); 'let him clasp you with a brother's kiss, let him be there always in your eyes and in your kisses, in your conversations and in your thoughts' (41). The princesses replace the successor around whom imperial funerals usually revolved, clinging to their brother's tomb, making of it their 'royal palace' (42). [160]

Valentinian had meanwhile moved into a distinctly unpalatial environment. Towards the end of the speech Gratian appears, to welcome him to heaven in the language of the Song of Songs: '"Come", he said, "my brother, let us go out into the fields, let us rest in the hills; let us rise at dawn and enter the vineyards"' (72). Gratian's impeccable reputation was a guarantee for his half-brother's credit, good both in heaven and (we may suppose) among those of the faithful puzzled at the honours being given to their former persecutor, who had died unbaptized and a presumed suicide.

But the climax was reserved for Valentinian's principal guarantor, and the true centrepiece of the oration: Ambrose himself. The bishop had exhibited at the outset his own grief as an example for his people; the whole speech is punctuated by his sighs, his laments and his personal recollections of the deceased, including a lengthy apology for his own part in the emperor's last days (23–27). Ambrose dominates the closing passages, coupling Valentinian definitively with Gratian in his final intercessions; 'both of them blessed, if my prayers have any force'

160. Compare the role of Marcellina at *De exc. frat.* 1.33, 76; but contrast Honorius in *De obitu Theodosii* (below, p. 357).

(78). He makes of himself the focus of both their lives. Gratian, 'all too sweet to me', had died with the bishop's name on his lips, while Valentinian had pinned all his last hopes on him, looking to him 'not only as a father but as a redeemer and liberator' (80). In presenting the situation in these terms the bishop was assuming a heavy responsibility: he might, it is implied, have saved the prince. But Ambrose was able to bear the weight. His speech, for all the lamentation, is hugely self-confident; the might-have-beens with which it concludes suggest not anguish but a melancholy regret. If only Ambrose had known Valentinian's wishes earlier, if only the prince had sent word secretly before it was too late—such ifs captured the tragedy of the youth's untimely end.

De obitu Valentiniani has rightly been acclaimed as a tour de force.[161] The miserable and politically explosive circumstances of Valentinian's death are almost lost in the surge of helpless pity that Ambrose evoked. The allusions to conflict between Valentinian and his comes (25, 27) could be taken as an invitation to associate the latter with the 'enemies and persecutors' mentioned elsewhere (34); but the point is never driven home, and remains susceptible to a generalized interpretation. So too with an apparent reference to the factional struggle inside the palace at Vienne, which concludes with the claim that Valentinian 'offered himself up for all' and 'died to save all those whom he loved' (35). The principal effect of such statements is to present Valentinian to the Milanese (like Satyrus before him) as a Christ-like victim surrounded by a mysterious haze of the divine.

Against this is the initial suggestion, no less striking for being dismissed in an indignant rhetorical question, that Valentinian's proposed expedition to Italy was a 'crime' (2). Arbogast's professed anxiety about the activities of the emperor's entourage is also noted (27). But the listener is never allowed to linger over such details, and is led carefully away from controversial specifics: 'I speak only of the suddenness of his death, not of its nature; for I use the language not of accusation but of grief' (33). Ambrose's bravura makes the circumstances of Valentinian's death irrelevant: if he assures him a place in heaven, he does so ultimately upon his own personal guarantee rather than the prince's merit.

Ambrose allowed a wider audience to appreciate the finesse with which he had eased Valentinian into Gratian's embrace without pointing an accusatory finger at Vienne. The redaction of De obitu into its present form for publication must have followed its delivery almost immediately, for subsequent events were soon to render the bishop's studious even-

---

161. 'A masterly performance': N. H. Baynes, JRS 34 (1944), 140.

handedness obsolete.[162] An eager readership can be assumed, especially at Constantinople, combing the text for clues to the situation in the west and nodding their approval at the discretion with which the bishop had concluded the earthly affairs of the house of Valentinian.

But the modern reader, scanning the document with similar care, perhaps misses an important point. Valentinian's funeral cannot be reduced to Ambrose's text: the bishop, having unleashed the full force of his organizational and rhetorical powers on the prince's behalf, could not then return the genie to the bottle. He had quite surpassed the paltry materials available to him—a miserably unsuccessful prince and a homemade approximation to the proper imperial accoutrements—to provide a farewell truly worthy of an emperor. What signals did this splendid occasion give out? From Vienne, Arbogast might well have regarded the honour being done to Valentinian with anxiety. A close reading of the subtle equivocations in the text would not have comforted him. The failure to declare Valentinian a suicide left little middle ground before Arbogast became a murderer. In other words, the nuances of *De obitu Valentiniani* were perhaps irrelevant. Both Theodosius and Arbogast had, since the prince's death, been waiting upon events. Ambrose's capacity to conjure a spectacle from limited resources had transformed the prince's modest funeral into an event of consequence. Within weeks, a new emperor had been proclaimed at Vienne:[163] Ambrose should take some incidental credit for this, and for nudging the empire towards a further round of civil war.

THE LAST VICTORY

The accession of Eugenius was not a deliberate challenge to Theodosius. The new Augustus immediately dispatched an embassy led by

---

162. The tone of the preface added for publication (*De ob. Val.* 1: 'Etsi incrementum doloris sit, id quod doleas scribere') implies the immediate aftermath of the funeral; the repetition of the term *dolor* five times in the paragraph recalls the letter to Theodosius (n. 157, above).

163. Eugenius was proclaimed on 22 August 392; since Valentinian, who had died on 15 May, had been at Milan for 'two months' before the funeral (*De ob. Val.* 49), the latter event cannot easily be put before the end of July (cf. *Ep.* 25 [53].5, 'vix . . . superiorem aestatem transegimus'). There is no reason to put the funeral *after* the proclamation, despite von Campenhausen, *Ambrosius von Mailand*, 248 n 5 (followed by Palanque, *Saint Ambroise*, 272, 544): the 'horum amore' of *De ob. Val.* 39 refers to Gratian and Valentinian.

the Athenian rhetor Rufinus to give assurances of goodwill and seek friendship, and a delegation of Gallic bishops was also sent to swear to Arbogast's innocence.[164] The sophistication of this diplomatic offensive reflects Eugenius' contacts at the eastern court, which had probably counted high among his qualifications for his new post. The former rhetorician had been recommended to Arbogast by the latter's uncle Richomer, now Theodosius' senior marshal, whom he had met while travelling between Rome and Constantinople during the sensitive period of the mid-380s.[165]

But it needed more than a Eugenius to bridge the gap now dividing east and west. It must have been abundantly clear at Vienne (and at Milan, for that matter) that Theodosius' emasculation of Valentinian had been a disaster, condemning the west to confusion and conspiracy: the westerners needed an imperial *praesentia*, fully empowered to defend them from the barbarians and to answer their petitions. But Theodosius could not accept even so unthreatening a figurehead as Eugenius. After his long struggle for supremacy within the imperial college, he would brook no rival. Perhaps he was conscious of failing health and anxious to bequeath an undivided empire to his sons; or else he simply failed to recognize the lesson of the previous few years, that one part of the empire could not reliably be governed from the other. His decision to reject Eugenius was not, however, taken lightly. Weeks, even months, of calculation and discussion seem to have elapsed before the verdict was announced: Valentinian had been murdered and his throne usurped. Only then did Theodosius take account of Galla's tears and pronounce himself ready to exact vengeance for his brother-in-law.[166]

While Theodosius pondered, Arbogast and Eugenius consolidated their position. During the autumn they demonstrated to the Germans that the empire's domestic turmoil had not impaired its strength by a campaign beyond the Rhine, which obtained them large numbers of Frankish and Alamannic recruits.[167] It was probably during this expedi-

164. Rufinus: Zos. 4.55.4; 'nonnulli sacerdotum': Ruf. *HE* 11.31. It is not impossible, as F. Paschoud suggests in his edition of Zosimus (*Zosime: Histoire nouvelle*, tome II.2 [1979], p. 459, n. 205), that these were two elements of the same embassy.

165. Symm. *Epp.* 3.60–61; for the commendation to Arbogast, see Zos. 4.54.1. The regime is discussed by J. Szidat, 'Die Ursupation des Eugenius', *Historia* 28 (1979), 487–508.

166. Zos. 4.55.4 describes Theodosius' equivocal answer to Rufinus; cf. 4.55.1, for Galla's tears. The break must have been made public by early 393, when the east refused to recognize Eugenius' consulate and the west Honorius' accession as Augustus (23 January).

167. Sulpicius Alexander, in Greg. Tur. *HF* 2.9.

tion that Arbogast impressed some Frankish chieftains at a dinner party by mentioning his friendship with Ambrose.[168] Eugenius, too, had enjoyed friendly relations with Ambrose, but when he tried to reaffirm these by writing to him, the bishop at first refused to reply.[169] A prudent desire to avoid a premature commitment is the most likely explanation for this tactic (the same, it will be recalled, that he had employed when first saluted fifteen years earlier by Gratian), and Ambrose was soon enough writing to plead consideration for men worried about their prospects under the new regime.[170] If Ambrose had to be pushed by these petitioners into establishing contact with Eugenius, other churchmen, like the Gallic bishops who travelled to Constantinople on his behalf, were more forthcoming. Two separate parties of Roman senators also approached the new Augustus, seeking once again the restoration (in some form) of the city's pagan cults.[171] The emperor, however, was too astute to make any immediate commitments: it was enough to establish contact and offer vague assurances of goodwill.

The ultimate vanity of Theodosius' scheme to realign Italy towards himself is shown by the speed with which the new regime won over Italian opinion. All that was required was an open hand. Some prisoners from the Frankish campaign were dispatched to the Roman arena, to entertain the populace and lend distinction to the senators whose games they graced; the plan went slightly awry when a contingent of Saxons disgraced themselves by outwitting their guards and committing mass suicide.[172] Direct largesse was more reliable. The rebuffed pagan senators, for instance, were consoled with generous *ad hominem* grants.[173] Such munificence smoothed Eugenius' path across the Alps; the emperor and his entourage appear to have met no opposition when they established their headquarters in Milan in the spring of 393.[174]

Nicomachus Flavianus, who four years earlier had professed himself

168. Paulin. *V. Amb.* 30.

169. *Ep. extra coll.* 10 [57].11: 'in primordiis imperii tui scribenti non rescripsi' (cf., for their previous contacts, 'cui privato detulerim corde intimo').

170. *Ep. extra coll.* 10 [57].12: 'ubi causa emersit officii mei, pro his qui sollicitudinem sui gerebant, et scripsi et rogavi'. These men are perhaps the same endangered supporters of Valentinian II mentioned at *De ob. Val.* 35.

171. *Ep. extra coll.* 10 [57].6: 'petierunt legati ut templis redderes . . . iterum alteri postulaverunt'.

172. Symm. *Ep.* 2.46: the prisoners were the 'munificentiam principis' and had been intended for display in the games to celebrate the quaestorship of Symmachus' son (autumn 393).

173. *Ep. extra coll.* 10 [57].6: '[viris] bene meritis de te donaveris'.

174. The 'invasion' can be reconstructed only from Italian epigraphical sources, which from mid-April recognize Eugenius' consulate.

overwhelmed with the great rewards he had received from Theodosius, welcomed Eugenius to Milan. He thus secured appointment to a further term as prefect, with a transition so smooth as to be imperceptible except on the bureaucratic records.[175] One need not, to explain this striking betrayal of his benefactor, surmise revulsion at the increasingly emphatic Christianity of Theodosius' public style;[176] considerations of *Realpolitik* suffice. None of the alternatives to collaboration—defiance of the usurper, flight to the east, or withdrawal from public life—can have held much attraction for a man whose connexions with Theodosius had been based upon mutual self-interest, whose political attachments were to Rome and its aristocracy and who, we can assume, had come to relish the exercise of power. A choice had to be made, and in the last resort Eugenius could offer Flavianus more than could Theodosius. Benevolent *praesentia* prevailed over indulgence from afar.

Ambrose, on the other hand, absented himself from the new emperor's entry into Milan. His withdrawal can be seen as an attempt to retain a certain freedom of manoeuvre. Unlike Flavianus, he was under no formal obligation to identify explicitly with one emperor or the other, but uncomfortable commitments would be incurred by the inevitable public encounters with the new regime at Milan. How could he avoid welcoming Eugenius to church, or Arbogast to dinner? He therefore repeated another tactic from his repertoire and found a pretext to withdraw, informing the emperor of his decision by letter.[177]

Ambrose did not shun Eugenius, as Paulinus claimed and many since have believed, because the emperor had capitulated to pressure and restored pagan cult.[178] This interpretation, which derives from Am-

---

175. Flavianus is *praef. praet. iterum* on the two inscriptions that record his career (*ILS* 2947–2948); hence the argument, most recently presented by Errington, 'The Praetorian Prefectures', for an earlier prefecture in 382. But for Flavianus to have held the 'pinnacle of all honours' (Amm. Marc. 21.16.2) before the quaestorship (securely dated to 388/9) involves a far more violent departure from the conventional pattern of promotions than Errington implies (at 447); the most convincing reconstruction of the evidence remains A. Honoré and J. F. Matthews, 'Some Writings of the Pagan Champion Nicomachus Flavianus', in *Xenia* 23 (1989), 9–48.

176. Thus Matthews, *Western Aristocracies*, 237–238.

177. *Ep. extra coll.* 10 [57]; subsequent text citations will refer to this letter.

178. Paulin. *V. Amb.* 26.3: 'aram Victoriae et sumptus caerimoniarum . . . oblitus fidei suae concessit'. Paulinus' only source is Ambrose's letter: his sole independent detail, the final, successful 'petition' from Flavianus and Arbogast (the two villains of his subsequent account: *V. Amb.* 31.2), is simply an inference to explain Eugenius' apparent volte-face.

brose himself, is perhaps the most audacious of all the misrepresentations the bishop perpetrated during his career. 'Fear of the Lord was the
reason for my withdrawal', he announced at the beginning of his letter
to Eugenius; 'my custom is never to put more weight upon the favour
of any man than upon that of Christ' (1). In order to explain this porten-
tous statement to the presumably puzzled (and sincerely Christian) emperor, Ambrose embarked upon a careful recapitulation of the events of
the previous decade: 'Symmachus, that most eminent gentleman, sent a
dispatch when he was prefect of the city to the younger Valentinian of
blessed memory, asking that what had been taken away from the temples should be restored' (2). Historians have been so grateful for the
blow-by-blow account of the altar of Victory dispute which is thus introduced that they have failed to see its complete irrelevance to what
follows:

> When Your Clemency assumed the reins of empire, it was learnt that
> these things had afterwards been granted to men who, eminent though
> they are in the state, are of the pagan persuasion. Indeed it might
> perhaps be said, my Lord Emperor, that you did not yourself restore
> anything to the temples but merely gave gifts to men who had de-
> served well of you; but you know that for fear of the Lord we must act
> constantly. (6)

Ambrose describes the two unsuccessful embassies sent to Eugenius
and then the emperor's grants to the petitioners. Exploiting to the full
the imprecision of the neuter plural and the gerundive, he associates
these gifts with the revenues originally demanded.[179] Too many readers
have followed Paulinus in inferring that they were actually identical and
that Eugenius had cunningly 'privatized' the state cults by allocating
their funds to individuals.[180] But the cults were the public expressions of
the relationship between the Roman people and their gods, conducted
by magistrates and supervised by priests organized upon a collegiate

179. The 'illa' in the passage cited refers back to the distant 'templis quae
sublata fuerant' (2), by implication the 'sumptus sacrificiorum' mentioned there;
the content of the donation is left unstated in the sentence that follows the
quoted passage ('postea ipsis qui petierunt donandum putasti': 6).
  180. Paulinus' reference to 'sumptus', like the mention of the altar of Victory, shows that he has taken Ambrose's hint and read the letter to Eugenius in
the light of the previous controversy (see *Ep.* 72 [17].3 for 'sacrificiorum . . .
sumptum; cf. *V. Amb.* 26.1). Funds for ceremonies are presumed to be at issue
by F. Paschoud, *Roma Aeterna* (1968), 77, 81; Matthews, *Western Aristocracies*,
240–241, J. J. O'Donnell, 'The Career of Virius Nicomachus Flavianus', *Phoenix*
32 (1978), 137, 139; and M. R. Salzman, *On Roman Time* (1990), 234.

basis. Covert *ad hominem* grants, as has long been recognized, were meaningless in this context, and Eugenius' initiative has been derided accordingly.[181] But the transactions described by Ambrose were far less devious.

Ambrose's letter, despite the references to 'what had been taken away from the temples', actually argues that *any* gift from the emperor to these pagan nobles was unacceptable, since 'whatever they do will be yours' (8).[182] The emperor's gifts were of themselves innocent; if a connexion is to be conjectured with the previous dispute, they are most plausibly to be identified with the estates belonging to the priestly colleges, which had been a subsidiary and somewhat obscure issue between Ambrose and Symmachus in 384. These lands, which naturally had no intrinsic link with the temples or their cult, were now at the emperor's disposal; it would have been an appropriate and unexceptionable gesture to divide what survived of them after previous disbursements among the disappointed ambassadors from Rome.[183]

We should not, therefore, be misled by the noble, solemn words that the bishop addressed to Eugenius: 'Although the power of an emperor may be great, nevertheless reflect, your majesty, how great God is; he sees "the hearts of all men", he examines their inner consciences, he knows "all things before they happen", he knows the innermost secrets of your heart' (7). Rather than encouraging such self-examination, the letter probably prompted a reaction of suspicious bemusement. Ambrose evidently realized that the logic of his position was vulnerable. He ex-

181. The cardinal point of the need for *public* funding was raised by J. F. Matthews, 'Symmachus and the Oriental Cults', *JRS* 63 (1973), 175–176. Eugenius' alleged subsidies receive their most scathing dismissal from O'Donnell, 'The Career of Flavianus', 139, as 'money which he tried to "launder" by channelling through private hands', 'a half-hearted attempt to buy support'.

182. The same point is made in the elaborate biblical parallel at 9–10, doubly confusing for its reference to a 'rex' and to 'sumptus' for a sacrifice. Neither is relevant, since Ambrose compares Eugenius only to the 'patres' who chose the envoys: 'non gentilibus dederunt pecunias sed viris fidelibus'.

183. Symm. *Rel.* 3.13 ('agros . . . fiscus retentat'); Amb. *Ep.* 73 [18].16 ('sublata sunt praedia'): discussed with bibliography by D. Vera, *Commento storico alle "Relationes" di Quinto Aurelio Simmaco* (1981), 45–47, but with the emphasis upon the long-term effects of Gratian's ban on bequeathing property to the priesthoods rather than the more immediate resentment of Symmachus and his friends concerning these estates, which they had long administered (*Ep.* 1.68, on the 'saltus Vaganensis'). A law of Honorius (*CTh* 16.10.20, 415) guarantees security of tenure for any such properties which 'ad singulas quasque personas vel praedecentium principum largitas vel nostra maiestas voluit pervenire'.

erted himself to explain his own previous approaches to Eugenius (inspired, he asserted vaguely, by a 'just fear': 12) and his signal failure to rally other churchmen to his interpretation of the emperor's gifts (11).[184] But Ambrose did not expect a reply.[185] The letter was designed only to allow him to make his withdrawal from Milan impressively; he was counting on Eugenius' having more urgent concerns than to tax him with his inconsistency.

No less contrived than Ambrose's withdrawal into 'exile' was the manner in which he presented his absence from Milan. He could not, in the spring of 393, convincingly claim to be fleeing an apostate or persecuting regime; nor was it prudent to set himself explicitly at odds with a ruler who might yet become a permanent fixture in the west. Instead, his absence was billed as a provincial tour. He describes in some detail the events at Bologna, the first recorded destination, in a sermon given shortly afterwards at Florence.[186] The account recalls with striking fidelity an earlier crisis of Ambrose's career. The bishop of Bologna had learned in a dream that two Christian martyrs, Agricola and Vitalis, lay buried anonymously and forgotten in the local Jewish cemetery; Ambrose joined him in searching for the remains and exhuming them.[187] It was a 'triumph' for the Christians, who after a search among the Jewish graves—'as if picking out a rose among thorns' (7)—dug up not only the human remains of the martyrs but also shards of wood and nails, which (according to the excavators) provided evidence for crucifixion (9). The Jews who had gathered to watch were treated to a powerful demonstration of the Christian message. As he gathered the nails, Ambrose imagined that the martyr was shouting to them: 'Reach out your hands and put them into my side; do not be unbelieving, but have faith' (9).

Despite the aggressive tone of these words, modern scholars have in general treated the episode as an example of peaceful interaction, even cooperation, between the two communities.[188] But this is to read a

184. 'Etsi solus restiti'; the implication must be that Ambrose was unable to confront Eugenius with a general condemnation from the Italian episcopate.

185. Perhaps the most significant feature of the letter is that it does not ask Eugenius to do anything, not even to revoke his gifts; contrast Ep. 74 [40].31 ('dictari iube aliam'); Ep. extra coll. 11 [51].11–12 ('tollas hoc peccatum').

186. Exhortatio virginitatis 2–8. Text citations refer to the speech.

187. Paulin. V. Amb. 29.1.

188. L. Cracco Ruggini, 'Ambrogio e le opposizioni anticattoliche', Augustinianum 14 (1974), 409–449, at 441.

figurative description as reportage. Ambrose presents the Jewish spectators and Christian excavators capping each others' verses of the Song
of Songs, for all the world like the choirs that he had trained in Milan:

> We were surrounded by Jews as the holy relics were carried away. The
> people of the church were there, cheering and rejoicing. The Jews said,
> 'Flowers have appeared on the land', when they saw the martyrs. The
> Christians said, 'The time for cutting is here. Now the reaper receives
> his wages. Others have sown, and we reap the harvest of the martyrs'.
> The Jews, hearing the cheering voices of the church, again said to one
> another, 'The dove's call has been heard in our land'. (8)

The ingenuity of the references suggests strongly that, as so often
with Ambrose, the scriptural framework has been imposed as an explanatory device. The bishop had produced several previous exercises
in the interpretation of this same biblical passage.[189] So too with his subsequent claim about the Jews' 'knowledge' of the martyrs (8), which
exploits the same verse of Psalm 18 that had inspired his preaching on
the two successive days of the *depositio* of Gervasius and Protasius.[190]
Biblical resonances took priority over accurate reporting. There is in
fact nothing to indicate that the Jews had 'known' of the martyrs concealed in their cemetery, and little reason otherwise for confidence in
Ambrose's identification.[191] The operation was not so much a peaceful
transfer from one community to another of items whose preciousness
was recognized by both as it was a sacrilegious commando raid. What
actually happened in the graveyard was therefore probably less ceremonious than Ambrose's account suggests. The Christians trampled the
burial ground of the Jews, ransacked a particular section of it and carried
off their spoils.

The aggression was carefully controlled, with no burnt synagogue
to provoke a response from the Milanese government. The Jews could

189. Other essays are *Exp. Evang. sec. Luc.* 3.27; *De interp. Iob et David* 2.3;
Exp. Ps. 118 6.24; *De Isaac* 35.
190. *Ep.* 77 [22].6–8, 15.
191. Ambrose's claim that the Jews had 'honoured' the martyrs and competed for nearby tombs (*Exh. virg.* 7) means no more than that they had sought
burial in their own cemetery. There are no secure parallels for Christian martyrs
being buried by Jews; the case of Hermes, Aggaeus and Caius (*AASS*, 4 January:
cf. M. Simon, *Verus Israel* [ET 1986], 459 n 99) was probably a doublet for this one
(it is located in 'Bononia in Oriente'), and that of Vincent and Orantius (*AASS*,
22 January; also cited by Simon) involved the gift of a private burial plot from a
Jew to a Christian bishop.

only watch the plundering helplessly, victims of an assault that almost seems designed to allow the Christians a morale-boosting victory at their expense. Suspicions are encouraged by parallels with the bishop's previous *inventio:* the Jews serve to point the same well-rehearsed scriptural moral as had the Arians in 386. They were, by comparison, incidental victims; but this time Ambrose was unable to take on his enemies at the imperial court directly.

Explicitly manipulative language is as inappropriate on this occasion as it was in 386 (or over the penance of Theodosius in 390), and for the same reasons. The original initiative, moreover, came not from Ambrose but from the bishop of Bologna, who was vouchsafed the news of the hidden martyrs in a dream.[192] At one level the episode is therefore yet another example of how Ambrose's activity in Milan set a pattern for the surrounding region; there had also long been more specific links between Ambrose and Bologna. Eusebius, his loyal 'assessor' at the council of Aquileia, was perhaps still governing the see; a man of that name had been applauded the previous spring for supplying a virgin, Ambrosia, for consecration to virginity at Milan.[193] Although direct collusion can be excluded, the lines of communication between Ambrose and his hosts at Bologna were well established.

The archaeologically improbable notion that Christian martyrs were buried in a Jewish cemetery also makes sense when one considers the shadow cast by Milan over its hinterland. After the spectacular discoveries of 386, other cities conscious of their lack of a Christian pedigree might well have brooded over the treasures that perhaps lay hidden in their peripheries. In the absence of an area like the Hortus Philippi, rich in traditional associations, speculation is likely to have fastened upon the burial ground of the Jews, who enjoyed so special a place in Christian history and the Christian consciousness. Ambrose's contribution, then, would have been to translate inchoate thoughts into direct action, and to provide the commentary that made this action intelligible and

192. Paulin. *V. Amb.* 29.1: 'sancti martyres sacerdoti ipsius ecclesiae revelassent'.

193. The occasion was marked by *De institutione virginis,* dedicated in the manuscripts 'ad Eusebium'. For the family, see above, p. 66. There are certain difficulties about relating this speech to the other evidence: the preface seems to be addressed to Ambrosia's *father,* while Eusebius is more likely to have been the grandfather. Possibly the preface to the father (Eusebius' son Faustinus) belongs to a different version from that dedicated to Eusebius himself; there is no critical edition of the speech to allow the question to be resolved satisfactorily.

lent it an aura of triumph. He thus exhibited once again his expertise (to borrow a particularly felicitous image) as the great 'electrician' of the cult of saints.[194] But it is difficult to believe that the circuitry was installed, either on this occasion or in 386 (or indeed when Ambrose discovered yet another martyr in 395) for routine domestic purposes. Agricola and Vitalis were employed to illuminate the whole of northern Italy with their message of Christian fortitude and triumph.

When Ambrose left Bologna, he took with him the 'supplementary relics' found with the martyrs' remains, the nails and the wood, as his *apophoreta*, souvenirs of the triumphal banquet. After a visit to Faenza he was invited by the Florentine church to perform the consecration ceremony for a basilica recently erected by Juliana, a wealthy widow.[195] The service involved a double celebration, for Juliana's daughter was at the same time initiated into a life of dedicated virginity, and the bulk of Ambrose's sermon rehearses the themes he had sounded since the very outset of his career, most recently when he had consecrated Ambrosia in Milan the previous spring. It was a spectacular occasion, the 'great rejoicing and exultation' of the congregation matched by the protests of demons in torment.[196] But the most remarkable aspect of Ambrose's speech is its apparent normality. There is little to distinguish it from the bishop's previous address on the same subject at Ambrosia's consecration, delivered before his own people; only the slightest hint betrays that the speaker was now cut off from his home city and faced the prospect of a further indefinite term in 'exile'.[197] The studied pretence that business was continuing as usual suggests again the sheer irrelevance of Ambrose's proud words to Eugenius. Far from signalling a dignified protest at the emperor's implicit apostasy, the bishop sought to conceal from the world his shunning the emperor's face.

Meanwhile, the church of Milan had been left leaderless. A letter from Ambrose to his clergy, plausibly to be assigned to this period, implies that morale suffered and priests were tempted to abandon their profession.[198] The retreat of the Milanese church from the public arena,

194. Peter Brown, *The Cult of the Saints* (1981), 37.

195. 'Apophoreta': *Exh. virg.* 1; Juliana: *Exh. virg.* 10; Ambrose's route: Paulin. *V. Amb.* 27.1.

196. Paulin. *V. Amb.* 29.2.

197. The remarks on the 'saeculi incommoda' (*Exh. virg.* 91) are strikingly generalized: 'Hic quidem luctamur, sed alibi coronamur. Non de me tantum, sed de omnibus hominibus communiter sum locutus'.

198. *Ep.* 17 [81]; for the date, see Palanque, *Saint Ambroise*, 548.

where it had been so vigorously engaged for the previous decade, had in turn an effect upon the character of Eugenius' government: the church played no part in its public life. Ambrose's slur that the emperor had capitulated to the pagans of Rome thus had the effect (no doubt unintended) of a self-fulfilling prophecy, as his cause was taken up by other publicists. Flavianus, inspecting the entrails of animal sacrifices during a visit to Rome, declared that Eugenius' victory was 'certain'.[199] The emperor had not solicited such endorsements, nor did his regime offer an umbrella for anything as comprehensive as a pagan revival.[200] Flavianus was simply taking advantage, with typical aristocratic bravura, of a period of uncertainty. The point would be strengthened rather than weakened with acceptance of the traditional identification of Flavianus as the target of the *Carmen contra paganos*, for the author of that elusive diatribe treats the shocking and ridiculous ceremonies conducted by his anonymous prefect as characteristic senatorial follies rather than the restoration of outlawed practices.[201] The *Carmen*, for all its gloating, describes a Rome where paganism is still endemic.

Any impression of paganism created by the new regime did not reflect so much the prominence of Flavianus and Arbogast (who merely match pairings like Praetextatus and Rumorides under Valentinian II) as the absence of any countervailing Christian spokesmen.[202] Nor, we can safely assume, did the clergy of Milan challenge the new order, as Paulinus claimed, by 'spitting back' the emperor's gifts at him and refusing him the right of attending their services.[203] This merely develops a point

---

199. Ruf. *HE* 11.33.

200. Modern scholarship has drastically reduced the scope of the 'pagan revival', as described by H. Bloch in *The Conflict between Paganism and Christianity in the Fourth Century*, ed. A. Momigliano (1963), 193–218 (cf. *HTR* 38 [1945], 199–244); the minimalist position is trenchantly stated by J. J. O'Donnell, 'The Demise of Paganism', *Traditio* 35 (1979), 43–88, and 'The Career of Flavianus'.

201. The sole mention of a resumption of discontinued cults refers explicitly to the populace, not the 'proceres' who are the author's main preoccupation (*Carmen* 33, as emended in the most recent edition: 'ad sac⟨r⟩a confugeret populus, quae non habet olim?'). I find Praetextatus a more convincing candidate as the prefect, despite the massive restatement of the case for Flavianus by L. Musso, 'Il *praefectus* del *carmen contra paganos*', *ArchClass* 31 (1979), 185–240.

202. Arbogast's patronage appears also to have been available to Christians: see *Praedestinatus* 86, on dealings between a dissident sect at Rome and the court.

203. Paulin. *V. Amb.* 31.2: 'munera imperatoris . . . ab ecclesia respuebantur nec orandi illi cum ecclesia societas tribuebatur'.

made in Ambrose's letter to Eugenius; perhaps, too, the clergy of Milan had in retrospect interpreted to their own credit the emperor's failure to attend the cathedral after the bishop's disappearance.[204] Furthermore, Paulinus' notice explains a threat made by Arbogast and Flavianus upon their departure from Milan to face Theodosius: when they returned victorious, they said, the great basilica in the centre of the city would be used as a stable, and the clergy enlisted in the army.[205] This looks less like a declaration of war against an intransigent church than a joke at the expense of an impotent one.[206] The cathedral now seemed a bulky irrelevance within the political topography of Milan, and Ambrose's redundant 'soldiers of God' appeared ripe for redeployment.

The outright paganism with which Eugenius' government has been tainted is a hostile travesty, whose origins can be traced back to the propaganda of Theodosius. The eastern emperor made an even less plausible avenger for Valentinian than he had been for Gratian; the death of Galla, together with a stillborn child, robbed him of his last direct link with the murdered prince.[207] To mobilize the east for yet another civil war, Theodosius therefore announced a crusade against the apostates and unbelievers who had usurped the western throne. The prophecies of the hermit John of Lycopolis were pitted against Flavianus' Etruscan haruspices;[208] Christ rode to war to unseat Jupiter. The two finally confronted one another at the Alps, where the latter's statues stood ready to hurl thunderbolts at the enemy.[209] More effective were the human soldiers of Eugenius, who emerged from the first day's fighting at the river Frigidus with a clear advantage.[210] But the desperate cry with which the eastern emperor rallied his troops—'Where is the God of Theodosius?'—was answered by the timely defection of a portion of Eugenius'

204. Amb. *Ep. extra coll.* 10 [57].8 ('Quomodo offeres dona tua Christo? . . . Quomodo Christi sacerdotes tua munera dispensabunt?'). Paulinus, if he was recruited in Florence in 393 as certain passages in the *Vita* suggest, was probably greeted on his arrival at Milan with stories of heroic confrontation.

205. Paulin. *V. Amb.* 31.2.

206. Cf. *V. Amb.* 30, for a lighthearted comment at a dinner party being transmitted through Paulinus (and a Christian servant of Arbogast) into the mythology of the Milanese church.

207. For the political importance of the family tie, see Holum, *Theodosian Empresses*, 46–47.

208. John: Ruf. *HE* 11.32; Soz. *HE* 7.22.8.

209. Aug. *Civ. Dei* 5.26. It is possible that these 'simulacra Iovis' overlooking the road into Italy were innocent landmarks surviving from an earlier age.

210. For the sources for the battle and the various problems they present, see Paschoud, *Zosime: Histoire nouvelle*, tome II.2, appendix C, at pp. 474–500.

forces and by a miraculous wind which blew into his enemies' faces, turning their own javelins against them and lending irresistible force to those of the Theodosians. Victory was complete: Eugenius was led in chains to Theodosius and hustled off to execution, while Arbogast and Flavianus cheated a like fate by suicide. Theodosius had become, at last, the undisputed master of the empire.

Ambrose had hastened back to Milan as soon as Eugenius and his forces had set out for the front, arriving (a month before the battle of the Frigidus) in early August.[211] Repairs were no doubt necessary to the morale of clergy and congregation, and there were contingency plans to be made in case Theodosius' invasion were repelled and Arbogast and Flavianus attended their emperor back to Milan in triumph. After weeks of what must have been anxious waiting, a bulletin arrived from Theodosius, addressed personally to Ambrose, announcing his victory and instructing the bishop to offer a mass of thanksgiving (4). This was not only a mark of honour: without Theodosius' letter it is impossible to tell how much he knew, and what he thought, of Ambrose's actions during the previous year. The bishop's reply, however, suggests that the emperor had expressed some dissatisfaction. 'You have judged . . . that I was absent for quite a long time from the city of Milan', began Ambrose; he skilfully evaded the charge of dereliction of duty by playing upon his return to his city, proof of his confidence that 'the succour of heaven would attend Your Piety' (1).[212] He had left Milan, he emphasized, only to avoid contact with a man who had 'polluted himself with sacrilege' (2). Such sophistry is unlikely to have impressed Theodosius, who could cite Ambrose himself on a bishop's duty to confront sacrilege directly.[213]

But Ambrose could offer Theodosius services more valuable than martyrdom. In the same letter that fends off the emperor's criticisms, he continues by describing at length the procedure he had devised to celebrate his triumph: 'I brought the letter of Your Piety with me to the altar, I put it on top of the altar, I held it in my hands as I offered the sacrifice,

211. *Ep. extra coll.* 2 [61].2 ('Reverti itaque circiter Kalendas Augustas'); the Frigidus was fought on 5–6 September. Text references are to this letter.

212. Ambrose's letter (especially the remark quoted in the previous note, which continues 'ex illo resedi hic ac me clementiae tuae augusti apices repperunt') implies that Theodosius was ignorant of his return and had ordered the *cubicularius* to search Italy for him.

213. *Ep.* 74 [40].1. Ambrose was intervening over Callinicum to ensure 'ne quid sit quod ascribendum mihi etiam de sacrilegii periculo'.

so that your faith should speak through my voice, and the words written by an Augustus should perform the function of a priestly offering' (5). There was no precedent for this incorporation of imperial victory in the Eucharist.[214] Great self-confidence was required on the bishop's part to apply something as theologically ambiguous as success in a bloody civil war to the liturgy, but it provided a dramatic illustration of the divine sanction behind Theodosius' triumph. The glossy package thus produced for a potentially awkward message can only have impressed the emperor.

The reception of Theodosius' dispatch restored Ambrose's church to the centre of political life in the capital. Among the audience at the thanksgiving service were numerous servants of Eugenius' regime, who had sought asylum at the church when they heard the news of defeat.[215] These men presented a political problem to Theodosius, who could afford neither to display excessive severity nor to appear to offer clemency too casually; his perfunctory forgiveness of Maximus' court had evidently failed to bind the beneficiaries to himself. Ambrose supplied the necessary drama. In his initial letter to Theodosius, he had already asked him to gratify the church by giving absolution to the 'sinners'; the deacon Felix then conveyed a further note (prompted, Ambrose says, by pity at the suppliants' tears) which appealed to the emperor's sense of clemency and piety while recognizing that 'it is a large favour that we are asking'.[216] The guilty were kept in suspense: a *tribunus et notarius* arrived from Theodosius to supervise them, while Ambrose set off for Aquileia to plead for them in person.[217] Forgiveness was duly obtained—'easily', adds Paulinus, rather missing the point in his concern to magnify his hero. The emperor did obeisance to Ambrose, professing that he had been 'saved' by the bishop's merits and prayers. The Eugenian court, it was thus demonstrated, had needed an exceptional patron to outweigh their crimes; the mercy afforded them was an almost incidental part of Theodosius' show of reverence to the bishop. The emperor had found an appropriate means of making a necessary compromise, and Ambrose had ensured the gratitude of a number of functionaries who would continue to serve at Milan. Six years after their fumbled negotiations over Callinicum, Theodosius and Ambrose could now offer their public a highly polished double act.

214. See the discussion by M. McCormick, *Eternal Victory* (1986), 107–109.
215. *Ep. extra coll.* 3 [62].3: 'qui ad matrem pietatis tuae ecclesiam petentes misericordiam confugerunt'.
216. *Epp. extra coll.* 2 [61].7; 3 [62].3–4: 'grande est quod petimus'.
217. Paulin. *V. Amb.* 31.1.

Ambrose then hurried back to Milan, anticipating the emperor by a single day.[218] It was a welcome whose staging needed an unusual degree of tact. The Milanese citizenry, having greeted so many 'triumphant' emperors in the past decade, doubtless had their responses pat; but the victorious eastern troops were accompanied to the city by the remnants of Arbogast's army, now assigned to Theodosius' trusted marshal Stilicho. The Frigidus was probably refought many times that winter in the taverns and regimental messes of Milan, for Arbogast's officers could be expected to resist the 'official version', which made their general a treacherous murderer and a reckless instigator of civil war.[219] This delicate situation helps explain the muted tone of Theodosius' victory celebrations, one of prayerful regret rather than triumphalism. In recognition of the blood he had spilt, the emperor refrained from communion after his arrival in Milan, pressing Ambrose's church into service a second time as the vehicle for reconciliation with his western subjects.[220]

To complicate matters further, Theodosius was dying. Even while he was being portrayed for a Roman audience as aglow with healthy perspiration, slightly breathless after his martial exertions but ready for further campaigns across desert or steppe, he was critically ill with dropsy. A dark, rainswept winter at Milan can only have aggravated his condition.[221] Theodosius just had time to improvise a 'succession' by welcoming his ten-year-old son, Honorius (with his younger half-sister, Galla Placidia), who had made a hasty journey from Constantinople. The church again played its part, the emperor 'greeting' his children there and 'entrusting' them to the bishop's care. Theodosius marked the occasion by ending his own self-imposed abstinence from communion, advertising Honorius as the harbinger of peace and normality.[222]

218. *V. Amb.* 32.1.

219. Antagonism between the two armies has convincingly been inferred from Claud. *De bello Gild.* 293–301: A. Cameron, *Claudian* (1970), 162–165.

220. *De ob. Theod.* 34.

221. See Claud. *In cons. Olybr. et Prob.* 112–135 for the idealized picture. Theodosius' illness precludes the journey to Rome described at Zosimus 4.59 and defended by A. Cameron, 'Theodosius the Great and the Regency of Stilicho', *HSCP* 73 (1969), at 248–264; see F. Paschoud, *Cinq études sur Zosime* (1975), 100–183. 'Iuges pluviae . . . et ultra solitum caligo tenebrosior': Amb. *De ob. Theod.* 1.

222. Paulin. *V. Amb.* 32.1; cf. Amb. *De ob. Theod.* 34. The sources are divided over whether Theodosius summoned Honorius before or after he fell ill: the former is argued by Cameron, 'Theodosius the Great', 267–274, but the prince's nonparticipation in the campaign might suggest that no long-term plans had been made.

Soon afterwards, in mid-January, the focus of imperial ceremony switched to the circus, where a cycle of dynastic anniversaries was due to be celebrated.[223] Theodosius made his final public appearance at the preliminary games on 17 January 395. He failed to reappear for the afternoon session, sending Honorius in his place; that evening he died, not yet (it seems) fifty years old.[224]

The earthquakes that had presaged the passing of Theodosius also heralded a new phase of political instability. No sooner was the emperor dead than Stilicho, the new commander of the western army (and despite his Vandal ancestry a connexion of the imperial house, by marriage with Theodosius' niece Serena), made a striking announcement: on his deathbed Theodosius had appointed him guardian over not only Honorius but also his elder brother, Arcadius.[225] There was no legal basis for a regency over the eighteen-year-old Arcadius, and the circumstances in which it was allegedly conferred were highly suspicious; but not the least explosive aspect of Stilicho's claim was the makeshift character of the court over which he presided. The civilian officials that Theodosius had brought from the east, a skeleton cadre insufficient even to continue the routine business of government during the campaign, were now assigned to ministries staffed by dispassionate survivors of Valentinian's and Eugenius' reigns (and in some cases perhaps Maximus' too). Hopeful adventurers from the western provinces converged upon Milan, avid for office and honours.[226] This aggregation, supported by a twice-defeated army, did not amount to a convincing power base.

Constantinople was the natural centre of political gravity in the post-

223. The anniversary of the accessions of Theodosius and Arcadius fell on 19 January; Honorius' was 23 January. Socrates (*HE* 5.26) refers to victory games: this is probably a mistaken inference, but if true the postponement of victory celebrations would be another illustration of Theodosius' unusually muted response to his triumph.

224. Soc. *HE* 5.26. For his age (60 in Socrates), see Aur. Vict. *Epit.* 48.19, 'annum agens quinquagesimum'.

225. See Cameron, *Claudian*, 38–45, for the audacity of the claim.

226. For the 'Theodosian' background of Honorius' principal courtiers, see Matthews, *Western Aristocracies*, 258–262, and p. 365 below. Likely veterans of Eugenius' regime include Macrobius Longinianus ('long service' in the *memoriales*: Matthews, *Western Aristocracies*, 260; but *PLRE* 2, p. 686, interprets the evidence differently) and the Paulus commended by Symmachus in 398/9 after long service ('iamdiu') in the *aerarium* (*Ep.* 4.37); cf. Honorius' *quaestor* Felix (below, chap. 8, n.2), and perhaps the poet Prudentius. Symmachus' correspondence reveals three Gallic brothers all presenting themselves at Milan in 395, two of them apparently obtaining office.

Theodosian world. The dynastic establishment, a long-serving group tested by service to the regime, had been functioning smoothly around Arcadius since Theodosius' departure the previous year.[227] Their credentials as the embodiment of dynastic continuity and the advisors of the senior Augustus were impeccable; but the continuing absence of Theodosius' army at Milan exposed them, after the revolt of the Goths in Thrace in the immediate aftermath of the emperor's death, to an acute security crisis.[228] The threat to Constantinople, and the divisions it created within the eastern court, did much to lend momentary plausibility to Stilicho's preposterous claim.

Stilicho depended much on wasting assets. The officers of Theodosius' army were not subject to his authority and could not be restrained indefinitely from leading their men home.[229] Moreover, Theodosius' remains were due to be dispatched to the place long prepared for them in Constantine's mausoleum. But first Stilicho put this potent dynastic symbol to good use, appointing Ambrose—as his first service to the new order in Milan—to offer a final farewell to the emperor. A commemoration service was organized at the Sunday Eucharist forty days after Theodosius' death, allowing the emperor to make a last appearance before the congregation who had witnessed his penance four years previously.[230] But it was more than a routine domestic ceremony. Representatives of the two armies crowded into the church to hear the bishop and witness what was in effect the formal inauguration of the new regime.[231] Stilicho took a conspicuous position at the front of the congregation, while Honorius was granted the exceptional privilege of a place beside Ambrose at the altar.[232]

227. For this 'Arcadian establishment', see Liebeschuetz, *Barbarians and Bishops*, 132–145. The codes give no laws of Theodosius after his departure from Thrace in 394, in contrast to the campaign against Maximus; Arcadius *did* issue a series of laws, although there are none from him in 388–391. We can therefore infer that Theodosius left the formal apparatus of government in Constantinople.

228. Liebeschuetz, *Barbarians and Bishops*, 57–58; Heather, *Goths and Romans*, 199–201.

229. Timasius had been Stilicho's superior during the campaign against Eugenius (Zos. 4.57.2); he will have remained in charge of the eastern contingent when Stilicho was assigned the western command (Zos. 4.59.1).

230. See *De ob. Theod.* 3 for the occasion.

231. *De ob. Theod.* 7–8 explicitly addresses Theodosius' troops; the recurring emphasis on the late emperor's readiness to pardon defeated enemies (5, 12–14, 16–17) suggests their presence.

232. At *De ob. Theod.* 5 Stilicho is referred to indirectly as 'praesenti parenti', implying that he was easily visible to the audience; *De ob. Theod.* 3 for Honorius

The sermon that Ambrose preached to this assembly brilliantly exploits the setting, conjuring an illusion of continuity between Theodosius and the young prince.[233] He dutifully pairs Honorius with Arcadius, making them the joint objects of the army's loyalty and God's concern—and, almost as an afterthought, of the 'parental' supervision of Stilicho. Everything had been handed by Theodosius to his sons: empire, power, and titles. There would therefore be no change of policy under the new regime, with *indulgentia* continuing to be the order of the day (5). Theodosius' soldiers were rallied to the young emperor standing before them by an elaborate rhetorical appeal. Honorius' age, Ambrose urged, was no impediment. In a complex equation, which teased out new meanings from the clichés of imperial propaganda, he argued that the army's faith supplemented the emperor's years, just as the emperor's faith (as had been proved by Theodosius at the Frigidus) lent courage to the army (6–8).[234] The same message was then rephrased more simply, that the debt incurred to Theodosius on the battlefield should be paid to his sons (11). It seems clear that Honorius' claims upon Theodosius' army could not be taken for granted.

Few of his soldiers can have recognized the Theodosius that Ambrose introduced to justify his obligation. The one martial exploit of this 'pious emperor, forgiving emperor, faithful emperor' (12) was to leap from his horse in the midst of battle and ask the whereabouts of his God (7). But Ambrose was giving a sermon, not a *laudatio*, and sought scriptural resonances rather than exact recollections. The texts read earlier in the service supplied the framework within which Theodosius was defined; in the central passage of the oration, particularly, he is subsumed completely into the language of Psalm 115, which the congregation had just sung. 'I have loved': put into the emperor's mouth, the expression is repeated again and again—twenty-two times in six short paragraphs—to describe the emperor's dealings with God and among men (17–22). Theodosius almost becomes the psalmist himself, to play in death the Davidic role that Ambrose had tried to create for him in their previous encounters.

But the relationship is drained of all its previous tension. Ambrose,

---

('assistente sacris altaribus'). Ambrose had denied Theodosius access to the altar: see above, p. 298.

233. Text citations henceforth are to the *De ob. Theod.*; the speech is discussed by Duval, 'Formes profanes et formes bibliques', at 274–291.

234. For the allusion to the coin legend *VIRTUS EXERCITUS* in this passage, see S. MacCormack, *Art and Ceremony in Late Antiquity* (1981), 336 n 250.

who had twice threatened to cease his intercessions with God on the emperor's behalf, now attended him with his prayers to 'the holy mountain of the Lord'. The speech reaches a climax with a powerful and sustained flight of imaginative rhetoric describing the emperor's ascent into heaven (37–40).[235] Awaiting him there were members of his family and his predecessor, Constantine, whose appearance prompted Ambrose to launch an extensive digression (which perhaps reflects information recently acquired from Theodosius' entourage) upon his mother, Helena, and her discovery of the true Cross (41–51).[236]

At the centre of this celestial welcome committee stands Gratian, who receives Theodosius with a pomp very different from the discreet attentions he had bestowed two and a half years earlier upon Valentinian:

> 'Kings will walk in Your light'. The princes Gratian and Theodosius will walk, indeed, in front of all the others, shielded now not with the arms of their soldiers but by their own merits, and clad not in robes of purple but in the clothes of glory. Here on earth they delighted greatly in showing mercy to men; how much more will they soothe themselves in heaven, recounting the many they spared and recalling their piety? (52)

The image is much at variance with actual relations between Gratian and Theodosius. But Ambrose was not concerned with historical accuracy. Theodosius' appearance beside Gratian, the last wholly respectable ruler of the western provinces, anchored his dynasty in the west.

Still stronger than Gratian's embrace was that of Ambrose himself. 'I loved the man': the bishop echoed the psalmist's words to describe his own feelings for Theodosius (33). He loved him for his compassion and humility, and for his preference (as evinced by his readiness to perform penance) for rebuke over adulation (34). It was towards himself, moreover, that the emperor's last words had apparently been directed (35).[237] But this is no more a straightforward, spontaneous reflection of Ambrose's sentiments than was his lament for the wretched Valentinian. Compared to his lachrymose effusions over the latter, the treatment given to Theodosius is almost cool; the oration proceeds in a markedly more controlled manner than its predecessors. This tells us nothing about the bishop's affections, which are irrelevant to De obitu Theodosii. Rather than setting a personal seal upon an intimate friendship with

235. See MacCormack, Art and Ceremony, 148–150, for detailed discussion.
236. For this passage in the context of the developing legend of the Cross, see E. D. Hunt, Holy Land Pilgrimage in the Later Roman Empire, A.D. 312–460 (1982), 41–42; also S. Borgehammar, How the Holy Cross Was Found (1991), 60–66.
237. This touching detail must be set beside the similar claim made about both Gratian and Valentinian: above, p. 340.

Theodosius, the speech seeks to define the emperor for a public that had seen him operate in a variety of roles. The bishop's approach here was anything but disinterested. In death, Theodosius was definitively captured for Ambrose's church, where he has remained imprisoned, historiographically, ever since.

Ambrose finally claimed his ascendancy over Theodosius by outliving him, and because the new regime needed his help to advertise its claims. For Ambrose's version of Theodosius also served the interests of the emperor's younger son. The east had expected Theodosius to return 'escorted by the army of Gaul and resting upon the strength of the whole world' (56). The 'mightier and more glorious Theodosius, attended by a band of angels and a throng of saints' whom they eventually got was a shadow; the army that followed the corpse back to Constantinople (and thereupon demonstrated how effectively it had absorbed Ambrose's message of 'loyalty' by tearing to pieces Stilicho's rival, Rufinus) was denied any infusion of western reinforcements.[238] That this has not generally been seen as the bad faith that it was should be credited in part to Ambrose, who helped lend to the partnership of Honorius and Stilicho—an arrangement at once opportunist and frail—the ideological substance of the Theodosian inheritance.

238. See Zosimus 5.4.2 for an eastern view of the poor quality of the forces returned by Stilicho in 395; the passage is discussed by F. Paschoud, *Zosime: Histoire nouvelle*, tome III.1 (1986), pp. 82–84.

CHAPTER EIGHT

SANCTITY

DEATH

Ambrose's farewell to Theodosius commanded the attention of the whole empire. His version of the emperor was soon being echoed by a bishop of Constantinople and parodied by an artful westerner.[1] *De obitu Theodosii* was also scrutinized by men with more practical purposes. Those like Symmachus, lobbying strenuously in the aftermath of Eugenius' fall on behalf of less prudent friends, needed clues to the likely character of Honorius' regime in order to obtain leverage over it. Symmachus put a lifetime of diplomatic experience to work assembling a posse of likely sympathizers to assist the younger Flavianus, doubly compromised by his own tenure of the urban prefecture and his father's treachery.[2]

The demand that Flavianus repay the salary that his father had received from Eugenius was of particular concern to Symmachus. A similar punishment had been imposed upon another friend, one Marcianus. Marcianus' office under Eugenius is not recorded, but it is unlikely to have been the proconsulate of Africa, which has often been assumed

---

1. For John Chrysostom's use of *De obitu Theodosii*, see S. G. MacCormack, *Art and Ceremony in Late Antiquity* (1981), 336 n 249; for possible allusions in the *Historia Augusta*, see A. M. Honoré, 'Scriptor Historiae Augustae', *JRS* 77 (1987), 164–165.

2. *Epp.* 4.19, 51; 5.47; to the Gallic brothers Protadius and Florentinus and the *quaestor* Felix (a possible survivor from Eugenius' reign: *PLRE* 2, p. 459).

from his appearance in the *Carmen contra paganos* as a man 'lost' to Christianity by being made a proconsul.[3] Despite the prestige that their republican office carried, proconsuls were small beer on the wider political stage; it would hardly have been worth dunning Marcianus for the modest stipend that the largely ceremonial post presumably carried. Nor should Marcianus, who is attested as a *vicarius* in March 384, have needed to renounce his faith a full decade later to secure a post which he could have claimed on seniority and which the tenure of Ambrose's correspondent Paternus in 393 proves to have been reserved neither for supporters of the usurper nor for pagans.[4] The proconsulate, like the *Carmen*, belongs rather to the *saeculum Praetextati* and can be fitted either before or (more likely) immediately after the vicariate.[5] But it should occasion no surprise that Marcianus, whose well-publicized renunciation of his Christianity must have commended him to Flavianus, re-emerged during the usurpation. His punishment implies that he had held, like Flavianus, a senior court office; we might therefore imagine him among the frightened suppliants who took refuge in Ambrose's church after the catastrophe at the Frigidus.

It was to Ambrose that Symmachus turned to save Marcianus from 'injustice', sending two letters in close succession. The bishop's recruitment for the defence of this notable apostate is somewhat curious, but a precise calculation might be discerned behind Symmachus' second appeal. He protested that Marcianus' honest poverty had left him unable to repay his *pretia annonarum*; but there were precedents, he added, of penalties which 'the imperial clemency has now relaxed, in the cases of many office-holders of the same period'.[6] This echoes a declaration that had occupied a prominent place in *De obitu*. 'There is nothing finer', the bishop had pronounced, 'than the fact that the promised relaxation of exacting payments, which applies to a huge number of people, has been

---

3. *Carmen contra paganos* 56: 'perdere Marcianum sibi proconsul ut esset'. The evidence for Marcianus' career is set out in *PLRE* 1, pp. 555–556, where the proconsulate is assigned to 393/4.

4. Note also that the laws addressed to Paternus and his successor Flaccianus were issued from Constantinople: it is not certain that Eugenius made any appointments in Africa.

5. Eusignius is last attested as *proconsul Africae* in June 383; the next known governor, Messianus, is first attested in September 385. Marcianus' vicariate, which coincided with Praetextatus' prefecture, would have allowed him to commend himself to the latter.

6. *Ep.* 3.33: 'quae iam multis eiusdem temporis iudicibus imperialis clementia relaxavit'. Symmachus refers to his earlier petition in the first sentence of this letter.

made Theodosius' legacy after his death: an inheritance of indul-
gences'.[7] The grandiloquence betrays how little in terms of positive
benefits the new regime could actually offer;[8] but it represented a commitment. Symmachus pounced, and Ambrose cannot have found it easy
to disown a cause he had so unequivocally endorsed. The situation fits
the relationship between the two men; it also suggests a parallel with
the year 383, as powerful forces manoeuvred discreetly around a boy-
emperor to advance their own interests.

As if to recall the era of Valentinian, there was even a martyr discovered in Milan in 395. The bishop unearthed the body of the martyr Nazarius in a privately owned garden in the suburbs of the city. The circumstances of his passion remained a mystery, but the miraculous state
of the body's preservation, the copious blood and the severed head provided sufficient evidence of his authenticity.[9] Ambrose showed the same
mastery of the situation as he had in 386. When Nazarius' body had
been exhumed and placed on a litter, the bishop went with his attendants to pray at the tomb of the martyr Celsus, which stood in the same
garden. Not only had such plots remained in private hands, but in
his twenty years as bishop Ambrose had never before been to pray at
Celsus' graveside.[10] There were thus definite limits to his control over
the Christian suburbs of Milan. But his entourage saw profound significance in these belated attentions to Celsus, 'for it was a sign that a martyr had been found, if the bishop went to pray at a place where he had
never before been'. Ambrose's own actions and gestures by now suf-

7. *De ob. Theod.* 5: 'Nihil, inquam, speciosius et in morte servatum est, quam
quod—inmane quantis—promissa annonarum exigendarum relaxatio, dum mo-
ratur, facta est successio eius indulgentiarum hereditas'.

8. 'Annona' should be understood here as referring, like Ambrose's usage
at *Ep.* 30 [24].4, to salaries rather than taxes (as interpreted by L. Ruggini, *Economia e societa nell' "Italia Annonaria"* [1961], 57 n 132): the salaried servants of the
state in the oration's original audience will hardly have appreciated the pay cut
that a tax reduction would have implied for them.

9. Paulin. *V. Amb.* 32.2–33.4 is our only source; the *Martyrologium Hieronymianum* (*AASS* Nov. 2.2, pp. 400–401) gives the date for the *inventio* as 28 July.

10. The common assumption that Ambrose discovered *two* martyrs on this
occasion, Nazarius and Celsus (Palanque, *Saint Ambroise*, 313; Homes Dudden,
Saint Ambroise, 318–319), depends upon a misunderstanding of the (admittedly
confusing) account in Paulinus. The episode at Celsus' grave is a parenthesis,
after which the expression 'translato . . . corpore martyris' (33.3) marks a resumption from 33.1, 'Quo levato corpore martyris'. There is an important difference of tense between the references to the newly discovered Nazarius (32.2:
'erat . . . positum'; cf. 14.1, 29.1) and to Celsus in his recognized grave, 'positus
est' (33.1).

ficed to define the event and to validate his *inventio*. Nazarius was transplanted to the apse of the Basilica Apostolorum, giving the church a new (and more logical) configuration. The occasion also reaffirmed the church's original association with the court, for Stilicho's wife, Serena, provided the martyr with an appropriate setting by adorning the building with Libyan marble. Moreover, the benefaction had a precise political focus, for it was intended to secure the safe return from the battlefield of her husband and to confirm the couple's claims over both emperors.[11] One can readily imagine the Milanese court assembled around their new martyr to pray for the safety of their principal champion and the realization of his ambitions.

But marble was not the only commodity the court procured from Libya, nor was Ambrose's church the only place where the new regime displayed itself. Honorius assumed the consulate for 396 at Milan, marking the occasion with games that featured leopards.[12] While the Christians of Milan sat with their irreligious fellow-citizens at the festivities, the praetorian prefect Eusebius mounted a raid upon Ambrose's church, using soldiers supplied by Stilicho. The objective was to remove one Cresconius, an acknowledged criminal who had sought asylum from the authorities at the church's altar. The soldiers brushed aside the attempts of Ambrose and his clerics to protect their suppliant and dragged Cresconius off to where the games were being held. The episode again recalls the clash of a decade earlier, not least in the fact that the officers leading the raid were Arians. This time, however, there was no crowd of followers to defend the church against heretical invasion, and the bishop could only lie weeping in front of the altar. His tears nevertheless had their effect. When the soldiers arrived at the games to report the success of their mission, the leopards broke loose from the arena and bounded towards the very place where 'those who were triumphing over the church' were sitting, mauling them badly. Stilicho subsequently apologized to the bishop, diplomatically spending several days 'making amends to him'. This was merely a gesture. Cresconius was duly tried and sent into exile; the church was left to find what consolation it could from the relative leniency of the sentence.

Another episode involving Stilicho illustrates the character of rela-

11. *ILCV* 1801. The expression 'pius Ambrosius' is a compliment, not evidence that the bishop was already dead; the language of the first four lines implies that the donation was contemporaneous with the translation. The 'germanis . . . suis pignoribus propriis' whom Serena prayed she might 'enjoy' must be Honorius and Arcadius, her adoptive brothers (and 'wards').

12. Paulin. *V. Amb.* 34 ('Libycarum ferarum . . . munus').

tions between Ambrose and the government. A favourite slave of the general's had been possessed by a demon. After being cured, he remained in the Basilica Ambrosiana among the colourful crowd of the church's dependents, sick and sane alike, who spent their lives gathered there.[13] From the basilica this resourceful person commenced a traffic in forged letters of appointment to the imperial service.[14] These transactions offer an illuminating sidelight upon the range of activities conducted in Ambrose's great cemetery basilicas and indicate that ambitious courtiers might have had other motives than prayer for visiting them.[15] The crime was eventually discovered, apparently when the credentials of the new 'tribunes' were challenged. These men were arrested but then released upon Ambrose's intercession; the slave himself, because Stilicho was reluctant to punish him, was left to the bishop's mercy and was duly apprehended trying to escape from the basilica. Brought before Ambrose, who with a few words unleashed an impure spirit upon him, the slave was convulsed in torment; a crowd of spectators looked on with understandable fear and wonderment.

This remarkable blurring of the boundaries between government and church, with commissions distributed from Ambrose's basilica and felons consigned to the bishop for punishment, reflected the composition of Honorius' court. Eusebius, the aggressive prefect mentioned earlier, was an exception; his predecessor Dexter, the son of a bishop, was 'given over to faith in Christ'.[16] After Eusebius, in January 397, Ambrose's long-standing parishioner Manlius Theodorus was tempted from his philosophical studies by a second prefecture.[17] Another old friend, Pisidius Romulus, was back in the west during the same years and received further promotion from the Milanese court.[18] Honorius' *comes sa-*

13. Severus, the blind butcher healed in 386, was still at the basilica when Paulinus wrote his biography: *V. Amb.* 14.2.

14. *V. Amb.* 43.

15. For oath-taking (presumably to confirm a business deal) in the same basilica, see Aug. *Ep.* 78.3.

16. *PLRE* 1, p. 251. We can only speculate what Dexter had made of Jerome's caustic entry for Ambrose in *De viris illustribus*, which had been dedicated to him.

17. Theodosius' resumed career and its culmination in the consulship for 399 is celebrated in Claud. *Pan. Mallio Theodoro*; the ambition to which the philosopher thus succumbed has plausibly been seen as a reason for Augustine's partial recantation at *Retract.* 1.2, 'quamvis docto et Christiano viro, plus tribui quam deberem'.

18. Romulus was prefect of Rome c. 406; since he had held office at Constantinople in 392, he presumably returned with Theodosius in 394.

crarum largitionum, Paternus, also presented his compliments to the bishop and solicited his advice, if only to receive a disappointing reply.[19] Stilicho's deferential treatment of the bishop was therefore typical of a widespread pattern of behaviour.

Ambrose's position must have been further enhanced by the petitioners and office-seekers who arrived from Rome during this period, in greater numbers than ever before, to reinforce what had always been one of the principal axes of his authority.[20] His fame had spread even to the barbarian north, where the Germanic tribes seem to have been temporarily quiescent. Queen Fritigil of the Marcomanni learned of the bishop's fame from an Italian Christian who was visiting her people, and she was immediately persuaded to believe in Christ.[21] She sent an embassy laden with gifts to Milan, to ask Ambrose for instructions, and received in reply a catechetical letter urging her to persuade her husband to make peace with the Romans. This she did, then set out on a pilgrimage to Milan.

It was thus a time of rare stability. During the first years of Stilicho's administration, the alliance between the senatorial aristocrats of Rome, the *viri militares* of the court, and the church of Milan worked better perhaps than ever before.[22] The same period saw Ambrose hard at work redrawing the ecclesiastical map of northern Italy. During the two years after Theodosius' death he traversed the region, creating new sees and filling vacant ones with like-minded candidates. In effect, Ambrose was supervising the passing of his own generation: the 'bitter tears' with which he greeted news of each new death instilled in the inheritors a chastening sense of their own inferiority.[23] His tears also served notice, like those he had shed almost twenty years earlier at Satyrus' funeral, of his own impatience to be gone. This time the threat was real. The strain of another journey, to install a successor to the veteran Eventius of Pavia in early 397, finally broke the bishop's health.[24]

Ambrose departed on his own terms. He even negotiated the de-

19. Cf. above, p. 259. For the date, see *PLRE* 1, p. 672 (*contra* Palanque, *Saint Ambroise*, 546).

20. See Matthews, *Western Aristocracies and Imperial Court* (1975), 264–266, on Symmachus' extensive dealings with Milan during these years.

21. Paulin. *V. Amb.* 36: note the unofficial status of the visitor, 'qui ad illam forte de Italiae partibus advenerat'.

22. For the background, see Matthews, *Western Aristocracies*, 264–270. Palanque's argument for a *decline* in Ambrose's influence (*Saint Ambroise*, 302–312) reflects an exaggeration of his previous ascendancy.

23. Paulin. *V. Amb.* 40 describes Ambrose lecturing the clergy of Milan (who included several future bishops) on the difficulty of finding worthy candidates.

24. *V. Amb.* 45.1.

tails, solemnly informing his clergy that God had agreed to grant him his 'liberty' ahead of schedule: he would be with them only until Easter.[25] A formal petition that he arrange an extension was firmly rebuffed. Ambrose retained his authority until the very end. So instinctive was it for his disciples to find oracular significance in the bishop's every word that an exclamation from his sickbed, duly interpreted, secured the nomination of the venerable Simplicianus as his successor.[26]

As good as his word, Ambrose died on Easter Saturday. Paulinus' loving narrative of his final days assembles an impressive supporting cast, from an anxious Stilicho to the tearful ex-courtier Nicentius.[27] Bishops, too, abandoned their own churches during the most sacred festival in the Christian calendar to be beside him. Paulinus mentions Bassianus of Lodi and Honoratus of Vercelli; others can be surmised.[28] In death as in life, Ambrose provided his colleagues with an example to follow. Attended by ever stronger intimations of the divine, he passed gently into 'the company of Elijah'.[29]

Ambrose was carried to his cathedral, where he too had spoken out against kings and potentates, and triumphed over another Jezebel. Now his corpse became the focus of the Easter vigil, and as baptisms began excited neophytes reported visions of him mounting the dais in the apse or seated there upon his *cathedra*. The Easter service blended seamlessly into the bishop's funeral, as Ambrose was borne across the city and out, past the circus, to the tomb he had long since prepared for himself at the Basilica Ambrosiana. The procession accompanying him embodied in its most complete form the Christian Milan that he had first adumbrated at his brother's funeral. 'Innumerable crowds' participated, of men and women of all ages and every rank, and even Jews and pagans; but at their head, proceeding 'with greater grace', was the white-robed cohort of the newly baptized.[30] Another face of Ambrose's church—one which he had celebrated in 386—was in evidence at the actual

25. *V. Amb.* 40.2.

26. *V. Amb.* 46.

27. *V. Amb.* 44–45.

28. *V. Amb.* 47 (Bassianus and Honoratus). Paulinus' remark about Ambrose's baptismal work, that 'quinque postea episcopi, tempore quo decessit, vix inplerent' (*V. Amb.* 38.3), makes much better sense both logically and grammatically as a specific reference to Easter 397 than as a claim that four neighbouring bishops were regularly involved in conducting baptisms at Milan after Ambrose's death.

29. *V. Amb.* 47. Ambrose's influence is apparent at another famous deathbed scene: see Poss. *V. Aug.* 27.6–8.

30. *V. Amb.* 48.3: 'maiore tamen gratia ordo praecedebat eorum qui fuerant baptizati'.

burial, where crowds scrambled amid the 'unbearable' screams of the possessed to press their handkerchiefs against the corpse.[31] The symbolic order thus superimposed upon scenes of tumult made the occasion an entirely fitting conclusion to the episcopate of Ambrose.

AFTERLIFE

Augustine had once judged Ambrose 'fortunate'. He was lucky, too, in the timing of his death; for the peaceful interlude in which he spent his final years would not last. Stilicho was juggling with pressures, both external and internal, that would eventually overwhelm him. In the year that Ambrose died, he set off for the Balkans to do battle with Alaric a second time, but again he found it impossible to pin the Goths down in a decisive battle and succeeded only in confirming the eastern court in its suspicious enmity towards him. The same year, conflict with Gildo (a loyal servant of the 'legitimate' government of Constantinople) began to drive a wedge between Stilicho and his friends in the Roman senate. Such differences became critical a few years later when the Goths irrupted into Italy, turning the Po valley into a battlefield and menacing the walls of Milan. Irremediable fissures opened in the alliance over which Stilicho had presided, and in 408 he was lured from the sanctuary of a church at the behest of an ungrateful emperor, and butchered. Two years later, Alaric and his Goths poured into the sacred city of Rome.[32]

Had Ambrose lived as long as did Augustine (whose health was just as fragile as his), he would have had to endure all this—not only the destruction of so much that had seemed secure, but also the collapse of the political order that had given him his strength. In the winter of 402/3 Honorius and his court left Milan for Ravenna and the security of its marshes, never to return. Far more difficult for Ambrose than the trials of defeat and loss, one suspects, would have been the abrupt severance of his contacts with the empire's chief sources of power and influence. Death spared him the slow pains of obsolescence. Instead, the emergencies that followed his passing helped foster a legend. In 398, when Mascezel was campaigning for the Milanese government in Africa against his brother Gildo, the bishop appeared to him in a dream to identify the

31. *V. Amb.* 48.2–3. The apparent quotation from Ambrose's Hymn 11.30, 'iactata semicinctia', suggests that Paulinus himself made the connexion between Ambrose's burial and the *inventio* of 386.

32. For the events of these years, see Matthews, *Western Aristocracies*, 270–306.

time and place at which he would win his decisive victory. Such at least was the story disseminated among the bishops of Africa and pious circles in Milan; it is not unduly cynical to suspect the efforts of an opportunist to ingratiate himself.[33] But there were many others to take up the theme. When Radagaisus and his Goths beset Florence in 406, Ambrose appeared to one of the citizens in a dream and promised that the city's safety would be assured the following day. Those Florentines who rushed expectantly to the walls were rewarded with the sight of Stilicho and his army.[34] The general himself had contributed to the myth: it was recalled that he had foretold, before Ambrose's death, that the bishop's departure was bound to mean ruin for Italy.[35]

Ambrose lived on, above all, in Milan. His protégés continued to dominate the church;[36] his memory offered them and the community some compensation for the inexorable decline of the city's importance in both imperial and ecclesiastical politics. Ambrose looms particularly large in an event that occurred at Milan several months after his death. Fresh relics arrived, after the martyrdom of three missionaries in the Alpine hinterland of Trent, for installation in one of Ambrose's suburban basilicas. The cult was then marketed across Italy (and beyond) with a vigour that recalls Ambrose's distribution of the relics of his 'own' martyrs, and has persuasively been explained as an attempt to assert Milan's continuing status.[37] The bishop would doubtless have approved and indeed have made his own contribution to the campaign.[38] As in 386, a blind man was healed by touching the casket that contained the relics. This time, however, he was a stranger to the city. He had come from the Dalmatian coast after a dream: he had seen a ship approaching the shore, and a crowd of men dressed in white disembarking from it. Asking one of them who they were, he learned that it was 'Ambrose and his companions': even in death, it seems, the bishop retained his retinue. The man then presented a petition to Ambrose (a scene that the Milanese who heard the story could no doubt easily imagine), asking for his sight to be restored. 'Go to Milan and meet my brothers who are to come', he was told, being given a precise date, 'and you will see again'.

33. Paulin. *V. Amb.* 51; Orosius *Hist. adv. paganos* 7.36.7.

34. *V. Amb.* 50.2.

35. *V. Amb.* 45.1.

36. Simplicianus was succeeded as bishop by Ambrose's deacon Venerius; two other deacons, 'nutriti ab Ambrosio', were still serving in Milan when Paulinus wrote his biography: *V. Amb.* 46.2.

37. R. Lizzi, *Vescovi e strutture ecclesiastiche nella città tardoantica* (1989), 86–96.

38. *V. Amb.* 52.

Ambrose continued to work for his city, recruiting pilgrims and spreading its fame across the Roman world.

Various factors, therefore, assured the bishop an enduring fame, even as the world he had known crumbled into ruin. A younger generation turned eagerly to his writings, expecting to find their own concerns reflected there and seeking his authority to justify their own teachings. Both sides in the Pelagian controversy, which gathered force in the decade after the sack of Rome, made constant reference to the bishop of Milan. Pelagius seems to have sought to emulate Ambrose in his literary style, and he applauded the 'Roman faith' he discerned shining forth from his writings. To counter this, Augustine organized a battery of selective quotations to show Ambrose at the very heart of an 'orthodox' tradition, speaking 'as a catholic bishop, according to the catholic faith'.[39]

The competition for his mantle could only enhance Ambrose's reputation. Augustine was also responsible for a more direct attempt to promote the bishop. It was at his request that Paulinus, who had been Ambrose's secretary and was in Africa to supervise the estates held there by the Milanese church as *defensor et procurator*, undertook a biography that set out to match the popular classics of Latin hagiography, the lives of the desert monks Paul and Antony and Sulpicius Severus' recent account of Martin of Tours. Although the exact circumstances in which the project was conceived remain unclear, a connexion with the Pelagian conflict is plausible; Paulinus was involved from the outset, having denounced Pelagius' friend Caelestius at Carthage as early as 411.[40] But Paulinus' Ambrose was no mere peg upon which to hang the controversies of the day; nor, perhaps, was he the figure whom Augustine, with his memories of erudite *suavitas*, had expected. Only in the opening episode of the book is there a brief nod to Ambrose's eloquence, with the swarm of bees who descended upon his cradle portending 'the hives

39. P. Brown, 'Pelagius and His Supporters', *JThS*, n.s., 19 (1968), 108–109. Augustine quotes Pelagius on Ambrose's 'Romana fides' at *De nuptiis* 1.40 and hails him 'ut episcopus catholicus' at *De peccato originali* 47.

40. The date of the *Vita Ambrosii* is disputed. Paulinus wrote during the prefecture of John (*V. Amb.* 31.4), who held office in 412/3 and possibly again in 422. The biography is conventionally dated to this second term: see A. Paredi, 'Paulinus of Milan', *SE* 14 (1963), 206–230. I am nevertheless inclined to accept the case persuasively made for 413 by E. Lamirande, 'La datation de la "Vita Ambrosii"', *REAug* 27 (1981), 44–55. Lamirande's translation of the *Vita*, *Paulin de Milan et la 'Vita Ambrosii'* (1983), includes an excellent survey of what can be inferred of Paulinus' own outlook. See also Aug. *Ep.* 29* (*Lettres 1*–29*, ed. J. Divjak [1987]), with commentary by Y.-M. Duval at pp. 573–580.

of his writings, which announced the gifts of heaven and raised up the minds of men from earthly things to higher ones'.[41] Paulinus' hero is a man of relatively few words, expressing himself characteristically in a terse rebuke or oracular epigram; he makes his mark not by his words but by his merits. It is not quite correct, on the other hand, to call him a man of action,[42] for he is rarely shown in motion. He towers instead over the great conflicts of his day, a rock of stability in the turbulent seas that heaved around him.

The years since Ambrose's death had only accentuated the distance that had separated Paulinus from his master. Ambrose is already frozen in majesty, with few of the warm and human touches that quicken Sulpicius' portrait of Martin or Possidius' of Augustine. When Possidius' Augustine cries, we see the anguish of a young man being dragged away from the life he had planned for himself, or the pain of an old man broken by the destruction of all he had worked to build.[43] The *Vita Ambrosii* is also spangled by its hero's tears: 'he wept with those who wept', shed bitter tears when his colleagues died and groaned at the avarice he saw overwhelming Italy.[44] But these were public tears, like those which lent so powerful an emotional weight to the funerals of Satyrus and Valentinian, or to the bishop's protestations in the basilica during the 'siege' of 386. The difference is made plain in the bishop's response to Paulinus and his follow-clergymen when they tried to console him: he lectured them upon the real significance of his weeping.[45] Without any intimacy to modulate the biography, Ambrose's whole life is played in a major key. Even a boyhood prank saw the 'spirit of the Lord' speaking in him and portended the authority he would wield as a bishop.[46]

In this respect Paulinus' biography brought to a logical conclusion Ambrose's own careful editing of his writings. Put another way, the biographer's work had been done for him. This helps give the *Vita* a certain looseness of form, as if it were a tour of a grand cathedral conducted by a well-informed and helpful but slightly overawed guide. Above all, Paulinus has lost sight of the dangers that necessitated the

41. *V. Amb.* 3.5.

42. Thus P. Brown, *Augustine of Hippo* (1967), 409, remarking upon the heavy casualties among the ranks of the bishop's enemies; but Ambrose is never present at the scene of an opponent's death.

43. Poss. *V. Aug.* 4.2; 28.4–13.

44. *V. Amb.* 39.1; 40.1; 41.1.

45. *V. Amb.* 40.

46. *V. Amb.* 4.

massive fortifications which made of Ambrose a 'wall of the church against its enemies and a tower of David against the face of Damascus'.[47] The bishop had succeeded only too well; pressures against which he had struggled for years are reduced in retrospect to petulant and random outbursts of spite. There is thus no real urgency in Paulinus' biography, no sense that a case needed to be argued on his subject's behalf.

Only at the conclusion does Paulinus allow himself a brief sally at Ambrose's critics. These challengers operate, however, at a very different level than had those against whom the bishop had fought his greatest battles. It was around the dinner table, when men relaxed and bantered about their more famous contemporaries, that questions were asked about Ambrose's achievements. The great set-pieces of his career lent themselves only too well to gossip: how *had* he emerged so spectacularly from disgrace to persuade Theodosius to repent? Was his triple success at discovering hidden martyrs due only to the grace of God? Had he been as innocent as he claimed of the charge of inciting riot against Valentinian? And what of that other riot, all those years ago, which had propelled him to office? At Milan, some pious officers of Honorius' army were scandalized during a dinner party to hear disparaging remarks about the late bishop from one Donatus, a presbyter who was perhaps drawing upon inside information; but Paulinus reports how the offender was immediately smitten with a stroke and died soon after being carried from the table to his bed.[48] When Paulinus, now in Africa, was at supper with a group of bishops and deacons at the house of the Carthaginian deacon Fortunatus, he had to endure further belittlement of his hero, from a certain bishop Muranus. He quoted the fate of Donatus as a warning; Muranus thereupon himself suffered a seizure, was carried back to his lodgings and died.[49] It is unlikely that these exemplary punishments stifled all further chatter about Ambrose, but Paulinus was correct to consign the matter to an appendix. However irritating, these sceptics were doomed to failure. Too much had been invested in Ambrose by too many organizations, from the churches of Milan and northern Italy to the theological standard-bearers of the new Augustinian orthodoxy, to permit his reputation to be subjected to any real scrutiny from within the ecclesiastical establishment.

Paulinus' complacency was nevertheless slightly premature. Ambrose was not yet entirely secure, in the early fifth century, from external

47. *V. Amb.* 8.1.
48. *V. Amb.* 54.1.
49. *V. Amb.* 54.2.

threats. As the empire grew more dependent upon its barbarian allies and lost its edge over their less tractable cousins, it became impossible to ignore the claims of the priests, predominately Arian, who served the Christians among these peoples. Doctrines that Ambrose had once dismissed with a brusque anathema were once more in the air. In extreme old age, Augustine was distracted from his grim fight against the Pelagians by spokesmen of the resurrected heresy, confident of their immunity from the sanctions that Theodosius, in laws of increasingly repressive stridency, had devised against them during his latter years. At Carthage he confronted one Pascentius, a court official whose theological position seems to have consisted in unwavering adherence to the memory of Ambrose's old enemy Auxentius; the discussion broke up in ill temper and recriminations which cannot have reflected well upon either party. Even upon his home ground in Hippo, Augustine was unable to force a debate with Bishop Maximinus, in Africa with the Gothic troops of the *comes* Sigisvult, to a decisive conclusion.[50]

This Maximinus was already an old man when he met Augustine in 427/8; more than a decade later, however, he took up his pen against the other great champion of Latin Catholicism. The record of the council of Aquileia—forty years after Ambrose's death and a full sixty after the event itself—was finally to be set straight. Maximinus assembled a collection of texts to damn the bishop of Milan.[51] Palladius' *Apology* forms the centrepiece, but Maximinus introduced it with a series of extracts from the council's *Acta*, with his own pungent commentary, and then (as an example of a 'true' exposition of the faith) with a letter on the life and teachings of the Arian 'Apostle of the Goths', Ulfila, written by the Auxentius who had clashed in his turn with Ambrose.[52] Maximinus' work is more valuable for the documents it incorporates and so preserves than for the editor's own contributions. After adding some footnotes to the text of the *Acta*, he breaks off in sudden exasperation. 'If

50. These episodes, recounted by Possidius at *V. Aug.* 17, are conveniently summarized by G. Bonner, *Saint Augustine of Hippo*, 2d ed. (1986), 141–144; for Pascentius and Auxentius, see Aug. *Ep.* 238.

51. The identity between Augustine's opponent and the author of the commentary on Aquileia is demonstrated by Gryson, *Scolies Ariennes*, 63–75; cf. 97–100, for the dependence of the *Commentary* upon the Theodosian Code, published in 438.

52. The work is divided as follows (with chapters numbered as in Gryson's *SCh* edition; his edition in the *Corpus Christianorum* series follows a different system): Maximinus, *Commentary on Aquileia* (1–41); Auxentius, *Letter on Ulfila* (42–63); Maximinus, *Commentary on Auxentius* (64–80); (gap of fifteen folios); Palladius, *Apology* (81–140); Maximinus, *Note* (141–143).

anyone wants to read what follows, how haphazardly and foolishly they [the bishops at Aquileia] proceeded, let him read it in the full text, which he will find in the present collection, in order that he might see that what the holy Palladius maintained is correct'.[53] The remark draws attention to the fact that Maximinus was writing in the margins of a manuscript that contained (after Hilary's *De trinitate*) the first two books of Ambrose's *De fide* and the *Acta:* a compendium of the fourth-century Latin church's opposition, in thought and deed, to Arianism. There is a powerful symbolism in this cramming of Ambrose's greatest foes, Palladius and Auxentius, into the margins of the oldest testimony to his work.[54] The symbolism would have appealed to Ambrose: against the clear, even uncials that fill the columns of each page with his own words, the untidy scrawl of his enemies can only scream its impotent rage. How closely this corresponds to contemporary reality we can only speculate: nothing is known of how Maximinus' challenge was presented, or to what audience and with what effect. It seems, however, to have been a last throw. At the very end of the fifth century, Palladius' criticisms of Ambrose still remained in circulation and required refutation, but the conflict had lost its vitality. It was surmised that the bishop of Ratiaria had composed his polemic after Ambrose's death.[55] That Ambrose could have been so roughly handled by a contemporary seemed, a century after the event, incredible; an assumption of invincibility had already become established.

Maximinus' scholia already betray Ambrose's status as a classic. Palladius had used his commentary upon *De fide* as a springboard for a discursive treatment of his opponent's beliefs, actions and character; Maximinus shows his respect for the bishop by his myopic attentiveness to the text. His constant refrain is *ecce*—'look!'—as he pounces upon yet another inconsistency in Ambrose's words as evidence of trickery.[56] Ambrose's last enemy can in this respect be paired, paradoxically, with the bishop's ardent biographer. For Paulinus too was a scholiast: the *Vita*, as we have seen, consists largely of paraphrase, with revisions added where appropriate. The third longest episode of the book (after the election and the *inventio* of Gervasius and Protasius) is the confrontation with Theodosius over Callinicum and comprises a summary of the two relevant letters of Ambrose, with a discreet correction upon a point of

53. Max. *Comm.* 35.
54. There are some reflections upon this aspect of the text in A. d'Haenens, 'De la trace hétérodoxe', *RThL* 12 (1981), 212–228.
55. Vigilius of Thapsus *Contra Arianos* 2.50 (*PL* 62, 230A).
56. Max. *Comm.* 3, 9, 11, 19.

detail and the addition, in the interests of clarity, of a few inferences by the biographer.[57] Paulinus scrutinized his master's texts in a more sympathetic spirit than Maximinus, but his approach was basically the same.

There are limits to what such methods can yield. We thus return to the problem outlined at the very beginning of this book: the ancient sources on Ambrose had little more information than the modern historian and had, mostly like us, to draw what conclusions they could from the self-sufficient texts bequeathed by the bishop. Paulinus and Maximinus offer a melancholy lesson in the scope for error in this approach. It is hard to tell which is the worse offender. Maximinus does not hesitate to hold Ambrose personally responsible for a corruption in the text of the *Acta* which made one of Palladius' responses look 'ridiculous';[58] but Paulinus, being so much closer to Ambrose, perhaps has less excuse for his garbling of the altar of Victory dispute so that Symmachus addresses his third *relatio* to Valentinian in Gaul, circa 391 rather than in 384, and Eugenius finally capitulates to a phantom petition from Arbogast and Flavianus.[59] It is only too likely that the present work will have committed similar errors, whether scrutinizing an innocent text too critically or drawing unduly concrete conclusions from Ambrose's rhetoric. But it would be misplaced, I believe, to dwell upon these inevitable failings. More important is the fact that they *are* inevitable, for Ambrose owed much of his contemporary success to the same qualities that so frustrate the modern historian.

It has often been remarked that the fourth-century empire was a stage. The figure is usually employed to convey the artificially ceremonious tone of public life; but the pressures that were also involved, and the demands imposed upon the actors by the tableaux that constituted the main theatrical fare, should not be forgotten. Performances were examined carefully and were lent excitement by the possibility of failure.

57. *V. Amb.* 22–23, giving thirty as the number of deities worshipped by the Valentinians in place of Ambrose's thirty-two; the statement (22.1) that Theodosius was in Milan and Ambrose at Aquileia is evidently inferred from Amb. *Ep. extra coll.* 1 [41].1. Paulinus also adds a stage direction at 23.2.

58. Max. *Comm.* 24 (citing *Acta conc. Aquil.* 11). Cf. 142–143, adducing in relation to the council and attributing to Ambrose's malign influence not only a law issued by Theodosius from the Balkan city of Stobi seven years later, but also *CTh* 16.1.4, Valentinian's law of January 386: Maximinus thus becomes the first of the many historians who have misused the evidence of the Theodosian Code.

59. *V. Amb.* 26. Cf. *V. Amb.* 19.2, inferring (from Ambrose's report of his refusal to share communion with the Gallic bishops in 386) that he had excommunicated Maximus.

When the emperor Constantius II drove into Rome, men looked to see whether he would betray his common humanity by spitting or wiping his nose. He did not: he proceeded 'as if his head were clamped in a vice', standing stiff and immobile 'like a dummy'.[60] One grudging critic saw here only affectation; but even he had to admit that the emperor's poise made it seem that he possessed a special quality of endurance, granted to him alone.[61]

The aura that surrounded Ambrose had a similar effect. The studied calm of his demeanour defeated even those trained to see through the tricks by which such images were projected. A rhetorician confessed that his curiosity was baffled: 'What hopes he nourished, what struggles he endured against the temptations that his very excellence brought or what solace he found in adversity, and what joys he felt upon the inner face that was kept hidden in his heart when he tasted your bread: these things I could neither guess nor discover' (*Conf.* 6.3.3). Ambrose defied analysis; his audiences had to remain content with what was presented to them.

This poise was maintained only with considerable effort, for the bishop's career proceeded much more erratically than the chorus of reverent admirers, from Augustine and Paulinus to the present day (or for that matter the critics who, following Palladius and Maximinus, have seen him as a Machiavellian genius), have allowed. I have suggested some missed cues and fumbles, and characterized the overall tone of his career as hectic improvisation. But the fact remains that Ambrose's improvisations worked; the vast majority of contemporaries were willing to give him the benefit of any doubt. 'For no matter what his reason', as Augustine and his companions consoled themselves in their disappointment at the bishop's failure to include them in his reading programme, 'it was a good one'.[62] These words bring us as close to Ambrose as we will ever come. They reveal him, yet again, as a public figure, and again show men scrutinizing his behaviour, confident that there was a positive message to be extracted. The sympathetic attentiveness that even his silences commanded reveals the full measure of the bishop's sway over his audience. His true greatness resides here in his stagecraft, in his ability to control the interpretation that was given to his actions.

The deeper springs of Ambrose's personality therefore remain hid-

---

60. Amm. Marc. 16.10.10 ('tamquam figmentum hominis').
61. Amm. Marc. 16.10.11: 'Quae licet affectabat, erant tamen haec . . . patientiae non mediocris indicia, ut existimari dabatur, uni illi concessae'.
62. *Conf.* 6.3.3.

den. Historians might nevertheless be forgiven their speculations as they weigh the different traits they discern in his works against one another: an aristocrat's masterful temper against the passionate otherworldliness of a Platonist; a Roman's instinctive conservatism against a Christian's evangelical fervour; narrow and inflexible bigotry against alert sensitivity to contemporary social conditions. Or we might propose an Ambrose who found his most authentic expression, after all, in the bluffing and opportunism described in the preceding pages: the restless and anxious figure who would emerge, less resolute behind the imposing facade than has conventionally been suspected, is implausible neither psychologically nor in his fourth-century context. But the argument of this book does not depend upon so full a delineation of the bishop's character; nor, ultimately, are the superb political reflexes whose workings have been our principal concern incompatible with the pastor, philosopher or poet of other accounts. The 'real' Ambrose will in any case elude us. The polished surface of his writings will defeat our efforts to penetrate them as surely as his presence defeated Augustine; our inferences, like those which Augustine finally made in the *Confessions*, will reveal as much of ourselves as of our subject.

We should not unduly regret the lack of a key to Ambrose's inner life. What matters is his performance upon the public stage, enfolded in the dignity of his priestly office. We must look to his outward behaviour if we are to appreciate his historical significance—not only to his famous confrontations with authority but also to the more humdrum patterns of conduct within which these grand gestures belong and which alone make sense of them. What matters are details like the courteous welcome he extended to a stranger 'in proper episcopal style'. It was noted at the very beginning of this book how little Augustine's famous description of his reception at Milan actually reveals about Ambrose, but this small phrase—*satis episcopaliter*—nevertheless encapsulates beautifully what the bishop of Milan meant to his generation. In Ambrose they saw the very model of a late antique bishop; it was he who at last 'created' an episcopal role for the stage of the Christian empire.

BIBLIOGRAPHY

1. ANCIENT SOURCES

i. Works of Ambrose

De apologia David: SCh 239 (*Apologie de David,* ed. P. Hadot, 1977).

De bono mortis: CSEL 32.1 (ed. C. Schenkl, 1897), pp. 703–753.

Epistulae: CSEL 82.1 (ed. O. Faller, 1968; books 1–6); *CSEL* 82.2 (ed. M. Zelzer, 1990: books 7–9); *CSEL* 82.3 (ed. M. Zelzer, 1982: book 10 and *Epistulae extra collectionem*).

De excessu fratris: CSEL 73 (ed. O. Faller, 1955), pp. 207–325.

Exhortatio virginitatis: PL 16, 335–364.

De fide: CSEL 78 (ed. O. Faller, 1962).

De Helia et Ieiunio: CSEL 32.2, pp. 411–465.

Hexameron: CSEL 32.1, pp. 1–261.

Hymni: Hymnes, texte établi, traduit et annoté sous la direction de J. Fontaine (Paris, 1992).

De incarnationis dominicae sacramento: CSEL 79 (ed. O. Faller, 1964), pp. 223–281.

De institutione virginis: PL 16, 305–334.

De interpellatione Iob et David: CSEL 32.2, pp. 211–296.

De Ioseph: CSEL 32.2, pp. 71–122.

De Isaac vel anima: CSEL 32.1, pp. 639–700.

Expositio evangelii secundum Lucam: CCL 14 (ed. M. Adriaen, 1957).

De mysteriis: SCh 25 bis (*Des sacraments; Des mystères,* ed. B. Botte, 2d. ed., 1980), pp. 156–193.

De Nabuthae historia: CSEL 32.2, pp. 467–516.

De obitu Theodosii: CSEL 73, pp. 369–401.

De obitu Valentiniani: CSEL 73, pp. 327–367; cf. *Liber de consolatione Valentiniani,*
    ed. T. A. Kelly (Washington, D.C., 1940).
De officiis: Les devoirs, ed. M. Testard. Collection des universités de France. Paris,
    1984–1992.
De paradiso: CSEL 32.1, pp. 263–336.
De poenitentia: CSEL 73, pp. 117–206.
Expositio psalmi 118: CSEL 62 (ed. M. Petschenig, 1913).
Explanatio psalmorum: CSEL 64 (ed. M. Petschenig, 1919).
De sacramentis: SCh 25 bis, pp. 60–155.
De spiritu sancto: CSEL 79, pp. 15–222.
De Tobia: CSEL 32.2, pp. 517–573.
De viduis: PL 16, 233–262.
De virginibus: ed. E. Cazzaniga. Turin, 1948.
De virginitate: ed. E. Cazzaniga. Turin, 1952.

ii. Other Ancient Sources

Only those editions, translations and commentaries referred to in the notes are
included.

Council of Aquileia:
Gesta concili Aquileiensis (Epp. 1–2; *Acta*), ed. M. Zelzer. *CSEL* 82.3 (1982),
    pp. 313–368.

Arian Literature:
Scolies Ariennes sur le concile d'Aquilée, ed. R. Gryson. *SCh* 267. Paris, 1980.
Scripta Arriana Latina I, ed. R. Gryson. *CCL* 87 (1982).
Urkunden fur Geschichte der arianischen Streites 318–328, ed. H.-G. Opitz. Berlin,
    1934–1935.

Augustine:
Augustine: Confessions, ed. J. J. O'Donnell. Oxford, 1992.
Lettres 1*–29*, ed. J. Divjak. Bibliothèque Augustinienne: Oeuvres de saint Au-
    gustin 46B. Paris, 1987.

Ausonius:
The Works of Ausonius, ed. R. P. H. Green. Oxford, 1991.

Basil:
Saint Basile: Lettres, ed. Y. Courtonne. Collection des universités de France.
    Paris, 1957–1961.

Claudian:
Claudian's In Rufinum: An Exegetical Commentary, ed. H. L. Levy. APA Philological
    Monograph, 30. Cleveland, 1971.

Cyprian:
The Letters of Saint Cyprian of Carthage, trans. G. W. Clarke. Volume 1. Ancient Christian Writers, 43. New York, 1984.

'Euphemia':
Euphemia and the Goth: With the Acts of Martyrdom of the Confessors of Edessa, ed. F. C. Burkitt. London, 1913.

Gregory of Nazianzus:
Grégoire de Nazianze: Discours 1–3, ed. J. Bernardi. *SCh* 247. Paris, 1978.
Grégoire de Nazianze: Discours 32–37, ed. and trans. C. Moreschino and P. Gallay. *SCh* 318. Paris, 1985.

Nicetas:
Niceta of Remesiana. His Life and Works, ed. A. E. Burn. Cambridge, 1905.

Origen:
Origène: Homélies sur saint Luc, ed. H. Crouzel, F. Fournier and P. Perichon. *SCh* 87. Paris, 1962.

Pacatus:
Pacatus: Panegyric to the Emperor Theodosius, trans. C. E. V. Nixon. Liverpool. 1987.

Paulinus of Milan:
Paolino di Milano: Vita di S. Ambrogio, ed. M. Pellegrino. Verba Seniorum, n.s., 1. Rome, 1961.

Severus of Antioch:
The Sixth Book of the Select Letters of Severus, Patriarch of Antioch, ed. and trans. E. W. Brooks. London, 1902–1904.

Sulpicius Severus:
Sulpice Sévère: Vie de saint Martin, ed. J. Fontaine. *SCh* 133–135. Paris, 1967–1969.

Symmachus:
Symmaque: Lettres, tome II (livres iii–iv), ed. J.-P. Callu. Collection des universités de France. Paris, 1982.
Commento storico al libro IX dell'epistolario di Q. Aurelio Simmaco, ed. S. Roda. Pisa, 1981.
Commento storico alle "Relationes" di Q. Aurelio Simmaco, ed. D. Vera. Pisa, 1981.

Theodoret:
Theodoret: Kirchengeschichte: ed. L. Parmentier. *GCS* 19 (1911). 2d ed., rev. F. Scheidweiler, 1954.

Zosimus:
Zosime: Histoire nouvelle, ed. F. Paschoud. Collection des universités de France. Paris, 1970–1989.

2. MODERN WORKS

Ambrosioni, A. 'Contributo alla storia della festa di S. Satiro in Milano'. *Archivio Ambrosiano* 23 (1972), 71–96.

Angelis d'Ossat, G. de. *Studi Ravennati: Problemi di architettura paleocristiana*. Collana di studi d'arte paleocristiana, bizantina ed altomedievale, 2. Ravenna, 1962.

Arslan, E. A. 'Osservazioni preliminari sulla chiesa di San Simpliciano a Milano'. *Archivio Storico Lombardo*, n.s., 10 (1947), 5–32.

———. 'Urbanistica di Milano Romana: Dall'insediamento Insubre alla capitale dell'Impero'. In *Aufstieg und Niedergang der römischen Welt* II 12.1 (Berlin, 1982), 179–210.

Atti del colloquio internazionale sul concilio di Aquileia del 381. Antichità altoadriatiche 21 (1981).

Baldus, H. R. 'Theodosius der Grosse und die Revolte des Magnus Maximus: Das Zeugnis der Münzen'. *Chiron* 14 (1984), 175–192.

Bardy, G. 'Le concile d'Antioche (379)'. *Revue Bénédictine* 45 (1933), 196–213.

Barnes, T. D. 'Constans and Gratian in Rome'. *Harvard Studies in Classical Philology* 79 (1975), 325–333.

———. *Constantine and Eusebius*. Cambridge, Mass., 1981.

———. 'Christians and Pagans in the Reign of Constantius'. In *L'église et l'empire au IVe siècle*, ed. A. Diehle, 301–337. Fondation Hardt, Entretiens sur l'Antiquité Classique, 34. Geneva, 1989.

———. 'Religion and Society in the Age of Theodosius'. In *Grace, Politics and Desire: Essays on Augustine*, ed. H. A. Meynell, 157–175. Calgary, 1990.

———. 'Augustine, Symmachus and Ambrose'. In *Augustine: From Rhetor to Theologian*, ed. J. McWilliam, 7–13. Waterloo, Ont., 1992.

Béranger, J. 'Le refus du pouvoir: Recherches sur l'aspect idéologique du principat'. *Museum Helveticum* 5 (1948–49), 178–196.

Bernardi, J. *La prédication des pères Cappadociens et son auditoire*. Paris, 1968.

———. 'Nouvelles perspectives sur la famille de Grégoire de Nazianze'. *Vigiliae Christianae* 38 (1984), 352–359.

Bikerman, E. 'Les Maccabées de Malalas'. *Byzantion* 21 (1951), 73–83.

Birley, A. R. 'Magnus Maximus and the Persecution of Heresy'. *Bulletin of the John Rylands Library* 66 (1982–83), 13–43.

Bloch, H. 'The Pagan Revival in the West at the End of the Fourth Century'. In *The Conflict between Paganism and Christianity in the Fourth Century*, ed. A. Momigliano, 193–218. Oxford, 1963.

Bonner, G. *Saint Augustine of Hippo: Life and Controversies*. 2d ed. Norwich, 1986.

Booth, A. D. 'The Chronology of Jerome's Early Years'. *Phoenix* 35 (1981), 237–259.

Borgehammar, S. *How the Holy Cross Was Found: From Event to Medieval Legend.* Stockholm, 1991.

Bovini, G. 'I mosaici di S. Vittore "in ciel d'oro" di Milano'. *Corsi di cultura sull'arte ravennate e bizantina* 16 (1969), 71–81.

———. *Antichità cristiane di Milano.* Bologna, 1970.

Brennecke, H.-C. *Hilarius von Poitiers und die Bischofsopposition gegen Konstantius II.* Göttingen, 1984.

———. *Studien zur Geschichte der Homöer: Der Osten bis zum Ende der homöischen Reichskirche.* Tübingen, 1988.

Brown, P. R. L. 'Aspects of the Christianisation of the Roman Aristocracy'. *Journal of Roman Studies* 51 (1961), 1–11.

———. *Augustine of Hippo: A Biography.* London, 1967.

———. 'Pelagius and His Supporters'. *Journal of Theological Studies,* n.s., 19 (1968), 93–114.

———. *Religion and Society in the Age of Saint Augustine.* London, 1972.

———. *The Cult of the Saints: Its Rise and Function in Latin Christianity.* Chicago, 1981.

———. *The Body and Society: Men, Women and Sexual Renunciation in Early Christianity.* New York, 1988.

———. *Power and Persuasion in Late Antiquity: Towards a Christian Empire.* Madison, Wis. 1992.

Bruggisser, P. 'Orator disertissimus: A propos d'une lettre de Symmaque à Ambroise'. *Hermes* 115 (1987), 106–115.

Busek, V. 'Der Prozess der Indicia'. *Zeitschrift der Savigny-Stiftung für Rechtgeschichte* (Kanonische Abteilung) 29 (1940), 447–461.

Cagiano d'Azevedo, M. 'Lo "hortus Philippi" di Mediolanum'. In *Atti del IX congresso internazionale di archeologia cristiana* (Vatican City, 1978), 2:133–40.

Calderini, A., G. Chierici, and C. Cecchelli. *La basilica di san Lorenzo maggiore in Milano.* Milan, 1951.

Cameron, A. 'Gratian's Repudiation of the Pontifical Robe'. *Journal of Roman Studies* 58 (1968), 96–102.

———. 'Theodosius the Great and the Regency of Stilicho'. *Harvard Studies in Classical Philology* 73 (1969), 247–280.

———. *Claudian: Poetry and Propaganda at the Court of Honorius.* Oxford, 1970.

———. *Circus Factions: Blues and Greens at Rome and Constantinople.* Oxford, 1976.

———. 'Paganism and Literature in Late Fourth Century Rome'. In *Christianisme et formes littéraires de l'Antiquité tardive en Occident,* ed. M. Fuhrmann, 1–30. Fondation Hardt, Entretiens sur l'Antiquité Classique, 23. Geneva, 1977.

Capitani d'Arzago, A de. *La chiesa maggiore di Milano, Santa Tecla.* Milan, 1952.

Cattaneo, E. 'San Dionigi: Basilica paleocristiana?' *Archivio Ambrosiano* 27 (1974), 68–84.

————. 'Il governo ecclesiastico nel IV secolo nell'Italia settentrionale'. *Antichità altoadriatiche* 22 (1982), 1 : 175–187.

Cavallera, F. *Le schisme d'Antioche (IVe–Ve siècle)*. Paris, 1905.

Chadwick, H. *Priscillian of Avila: The Occult and the Charismatic in the Early Church.* Oxford, 1976.

Charlet, J.-L. 'Théologie, politique et rhétorique: La célébration poétique de Pâques à la cour de Valentinian et d'Honorius, d'après Ausone (*Versus Paschales*) et Claudien (*de Salvatore*)'. In *La poesia tardoantica: Tra retorica, teologia e politica*, 259–287. Messina, 1984.

Chastagnol, A. *Le préfecture urbaine à Rome sous le bas-empire*. Paris, 1960.

Clauss, M. *Der Magister Officiorum in der Spätantike, 4–6 Jahrhundert*. Vestigia 32. Munich, 1980.

Consolino, F. E. *Ascesi e mondanità nella Gallia tardoantica*. Naples, 1979.

————. 'Modelli di compartemento e modi di sanctificazione per l'aristocrazia femminile d'Occidente'. In *Società romana e impero tardoantico*, ed. A. Giardini, 1 : 273–306. Bari, 1986.

————. 'Il monachesimo femminile nella tarda Antichità'. *Codex Aquilarensis* 2 (1989), 33–45.

Corbellini, C. 'Sesto Petronio Probo e l'elezione episcopale di Ambrogio'. *Rendiconti dell'Istituto Lombardo*, Classe di lettere, scienze morali e storiche 109 (1975), 181–189.

Courcelle, P. 'Quelques symboles funéraires du néo-platonisme latin: Le vol de Dédale: Ulysse et les Sirènes'. *Revue des Études Anciens* 46 (1944), 65–93.

————. *Histoire littéraire des grands invasions germaniques*. 3d ed. Paris, 1964.

————. *Recherches sur les "Confessions" de saint Augustin*. 2d ed. Paris, 1968.

Cracco Ruggini, L. *Economia e società nell' "Italia Annonaria": Rapporti fra agricoltura e commercio dal IV al VI secolo d.C.* Milan, 1961.

————. 'Ambrogio e le opposizioni anticattoliche fra il 383 e il 390'. *Augustinianum* 14 (1974), 409–449.

————. 'Ambrogio di fronte alla compagine sociale del suo tempo'. In *Ambrosius Episcopus*, ed. G. Lazzati, 1 : 230–265. Milan, 1976.

————. 'Fame laborasse Italiam: Una nuova testimonianza sulla carestia del 383 d.C.'. In *L'Italia settentrionale nell'età antica: Convegno in memoria di Plinio Fraccaro*, 83–98. *Athenaeum*, fasc. spec., 1976.

————. 'Il paganesimo romano tra religione e politica (384–394 d.C.): Per una reinterpretazione del "Carmen contra paganos"'. *Memorie dell'Accademia Nazionale dei Lincei*, Classe di scienze morali, storiche e filologiche, 8.23 (1979), 3–143.

Croke, B. 'Arbogast and the Death of Valentinian II'. *Historia* 25 (1976), 235–244.

Dagens, C. 'Autour de Pape Libère: L'iconographie de Suzanne et des martyrs romains sur l'arcisolium de Celerina'. *Mélanges d'archéologie et d'histoire de l'Ecole Français de Rome, Antiquité* 78 (1966), 327–381.

Dagron, G. *Naissance d'une capitale: Constantinople et ses institutions de 330 à 451.* Paris, 1974.

Dassmann, E. 'Ambrosius und die Märtyrer'. *Jahrbuch für Antike und Christentum* 18 (1975), 49–68.

David, M. 'Appunti per lo studio della pavimentazione tardoantica della basilica dei SS. Apostoli e Nazaro Maggiore a Milan'. *Sibrium* 15 (1980–81), 177–194.

De Clerq, V. C. *Ossius of Cordova: A Contribution to the History of the Constantinian Period.* Washington, 1954.

Delehaye, H. *Les origines du culte des martyrs.* 2d ed. Brussels, 1933.

Dell'Acqua, G. A., ed. *La basilica di san Lorenzo in Milano.* Milan, 1985.

Demandt, A. 'Der Tod des älteren Theodosius'. *Historia* 18 (1969), 598–626.

D'Haenens, A. 'De la trace hétérodoxe: (Paléo)graphie et (histoire de hétéro)-doxie dans les travaux de R. Gryson sur les scolies ariennes du concile d'Aquilée'. *Revue théologique de Louvain* 12 (1981), 212–228.

Dionisotti, C. 'From Ausonius' Schooldays? A Schoolbook and Its Relatives'. *Journal of Roman Studies* 72 (1982), 83–125.

Doignon, J. 'Perspectives ambrosiennes: SS. Gervais et Protais, génies de Milan'. *Revue des Etudes Augustiniennes* 2 (1956), 313–334.

———. *Hilaire de Poitiers avant l'exil.* Paris, 1971.

Dolbeau, F. 'Damase, le *Carmen contra paganos* et Hériger de Lobbes'. *Revue des Etudes Augustiniennes* 27 (1981), 38–43.

Doutreleau, L. 'Le prologue de Jérôme au *De spiritu sancto* de Didyme'. In *Alexandrina: Hellenisme, judaïsme et christianisme à Alexandrie: Mélanges offerts à Claude Mondésert,* 297–311. Paris, 1987.

Downey, G. *A History of Antioch in Syria from Seleucus to the Arab Conquest.* Princeton, 1961.

Dunphy, W. 'On the Date of St. Ambrose's *De Tobia*'. *Sacris Erudiri* 27 (1984), 27–36.

Durliat, J. *De la ville antique à la ville byzantine: Le problème des subsistences.* Collection de l'école français de Rome, 136. Rome, 1990.

Duval, N. 'Les palais impériaux de Milan et Aquilée: Réalité et mythe'. *Antichità altoadriatiche* 4 (1973), 151–158.

Duval, Y.-M. 'L'éloge de Théodose dans la *Cité de Dieu* (V, 26, 1): Sa place, son sens, et ses sources'. *Recherches augustiniennes* 4 (1966), 135–179.

———. 'La "manoeuvre frauduleuse" de Rimini: A la recherche du *Liber adversus Ursacium et Valentem*'. In *Hilaire et son temps: Actes du colloque de Poitiers,* ed. J.-R. Labande, 51–103. Paris, 1969.

———. 'Vrai et faux problèmes concernant le retour d'exil d'Hilaire de Poitiers et son action en Italie en 360'. *Athenaeum,* n.s., 48 (1970), 251–275.

———. 'L'influence des écrivains africains du IIIe siècle sur les écrivains chrétiens de l'Italie du nord dans la seconde moitié du IVe siecle'. *Antichità altoadriatiche* 5 (1974), 191–226.

———. 'L'originalité du "De virginibus" dans le mouvement ascetique occidental: Ambroise, Cyprien, Athanase'. In *Ambroise de Milan: Dix études,* ed. Y.-M. Duval, 9–66. Paris, 1974.

————. 'Ambroise, de son élection à sa consécration'. In *Ambrosius Episcopus*, ed. G. Lazzati, 2:243–283. Milan, 1976.

————. 'Aquilée et la Palestine entre 370 et 420'. *Antichità altoadriatiche* 12 (1977), 263–322.

————. 'Formes profanes et formes bibliques dans les oraisons funèbres de saint Ambroise'. In *Christianisme et formes littéraires de l'Antiquité tardive en Occident*, ed. M. Fuhrmann, 235–291. Fondation Hardt, Entretiens sur l'Antiquité Classique, 23. Geneva, 1977.

————. 'Aquilée et Sirmium durant la crise Arienne (325–400)'. *Antichità altoadriatiche* 26 (1985), 2:331–379.

Ensslin, W. *Die Religionspolitik des Kaisers Theodosius d. Gr.* Sitzungsberichte der Bayerischen Akademie der Wissenschaften, philosophisch-historisch Klasse, Jahrgang 1953, Heft 2. Munich, 1953.

Errington, R. M. 'The Praetorian Prefectures of Virius Nicomachus Flavianus'. *Historia* 41 (1992), 439–461.

Faller, O. 'La data della consacrazione vescovile di sant'Ambrogio'. In *Ambrosiana: Scritti di storia, archeologia ed arte pubblicati nel XVI centenario della nascità di Sant'Ambrogio, CCCXL–MCMXL*, 97–112. Milan, 1942.

Faure, E. 'Saint Ambroise et l'expulsion des pérégrins de Rome'. In *Etudes d'histoire du droit canonique dédiées à Gabriel le Bras*, 1:523–540. Paris, 1965.

Favez, C. *La consolation latine chrétienne*. Paris, 1937.

Ferrario, E. 'Una antica iscrizione scoperta a Milano nella basilica degli Apostoli'. *Epigraphica* 10 (1948), 62–68.

Fontaine, J. 'Prose et poésie: L'interférence des genres et des styles dans la création littéraire d'Ambroise de Milan'. In *Ambrosius Episcopus*, ed. G. Lazzati, 1:124–170. Milan, 1976.

————. *Naissance de la poésie dans l'occident chrétienne: Esquisse d'une histoire de la poésie latine chrétienne du IIIe au VIe siècle*. Paris, 1981.

Forlin Patrucco, M., and S. Roda. 'Le lettere di Simmaco ad Ambrogio: Vent'anni di rapporti amichevoli'. In *Ambrosius Episcopus*, ed. G. Lazzati, 2:284–297. Milan, 1976.

Frend, W. H. C. *The Donatist Church: A Movement of Protest in Roman North Africa.* Oxford, 1952.

————. 'The Two Worlds of Paulinus of Nola'. In *Latin Literature of the Fourth Century*, ed. J. W. Binns, 100–133. London, 1974.

Ganshof, F. L. 'Note sur l'élection des évêques dans l'empire romain au IVme et pendant la première moitié du Vme siècle'. *Revue internationale des droits de l'Antiquité* 4 (*Mélanges Visscher* 3, 1950), 467–498.

Garnsey, P. 'Economy and Society of Mediolanum under the Principate'. *Papers of the British School of Rome* 44 (1976), 13–27.

Gaudemet, J. *L'église dans l'empire romain. Histoire du droit et des institutions de l'église en Occident*, tome 3. Paris, 1958.

————. 'La condamnation des practiques païennes en 391'. In *Epektasis: Mélanges patristiques offerts au card. J. Daniélou*, ed. J. Fontaine and C. Kannengiesser, 597–602. Paris, 1972.

Giet, S. 'De saint Basile à saint Ambroise: La condamnation du prêt à interêt au IVe siècle'. *Recherches des Sciences Religieuses* 33 (1944), 95–128.

Gilliard, F. D. 'Senatorial Bishops in the Fourth Century'. *Harvard Theological Review* 77 (1984), 153–175.

Glaesener, H. 'L'empereur Gratien et saint Ambroise'. *Revue d'Histoire Ecclésiastique* 52 (1957), 466–488.

Gleason, M. W. 'Festive Satire: Julian's "Misopogon" and the New Year at Antioch'. *Journal of Roman Studies* 76 (1986), 106–119.

Gottlieb, G. *Ambrosius von Mailand und Kaiser Gratian*. Göttingen, 1973.

———. 'Les évêques et les empereurs dans les affaires ecclésiastiques du IVe siècle'. *Museum Helveticum* 33 (1976), 38–50.

———. 'Das Konzil von Aquileia (381)'. *Annuarium Historiae Conciliorum* 11 (1979), 287–306.

———. 'Der Mailänder Kirchenstreit von 385/386: Datierung, Verlauf, Deutung'. *Museum Helveticum* 42 (1985), 37–55.

Granger Taylor, H. 'The Two Dalmatics of Saint Ambrose'. *Bulletin de Liaison, Centre Internationale d'Etude des Textiles Anciens*, 57–58 (1983), 127–173.

Grattarola, P. 'La morte dell'imperatore Valentiniano II'. *Rendiconti dell'Istituto Lombardo*, Classe di lettere, scienze morali e storiche 113 (1979), 359–370.

Green, M. R. 'The Supporters of the Antipope Ursinus'. *Journal of Theological Studies*, n.s., 22 (1971), 531–538.

Grumel, V. 'L'Illyricum de la mort de Valentinian Ier (375) à la mort de Stilicon (408)'. *Revue des Etudes byzantines* 9 (1951), 5–46.

Gryson, R. *Le prêtre selon saint Ambroise*. Louvain, 1968.

———. 'Les élections épiscopales en Occident au IVe siècle'. *Revue d'Histoire Ecclésiastique* 75 (1980), 257–283.

———. *Scolies Ariennes sur le concile d'Aquilée*. SCh 267. Paris, 1980.

———. 'Origine et composition des "Scolies Ariennes" du manuscrit *Paris, B.N., Lat. 8907'. *Revue d'Histoire des Textes* 14–15 (1985), 369–375.

Hanson, R. P. C. *The Search for the Christian Doctrine of God: The Arian Controversy 318–381*. Edinburgh, 1988.

Harries, J. 'Prudentius and Theodosius'. *Latomus* 43 (1984), 69–84.

———. 'The Roman Imperial Quaestor from Constantine to Theodosius II'. *Journal of Roman Studies* 78 (1988), 148–172.

Heather, P. J. 'The Crossing of the Danube and the Gothic Conversion'. *Greek, Roman and Byzantine Studies* 27 (1986), 289–318.

———. *Goths and Romans 332–489*. Oxford, 1991.

Heather, P. J., and J. F. Matthews. *The Goths in the Fourth Century*. Liverpool, 1991.

Hendy, M. F. 'Aspects of Coin Production and Fiscal Administration in the Late Roman and Early Byzantine Period'. *Numismatic Chronicle* 7.12 (1972), 117–139.

Hess, H. *The Canons of the Council of Sardica, AD 343*. Oxford, 1958.

Hobbs, H. C., and W. Wuellner, eds., *The Role of the Christian Bishop in Ancient Society*. Protocol of the 35th Colloquy, Center of Hermeneutical Studies. Berkeley and Los Angeles, 1980.

Hoffmann, D. *Das spätrömische Bewegungsheer und die Notitia Dignitatum*. Epigraphische Studien 7. Dusseldorf, 1969.

Holum, K. G. *Theodosian Empresses: Women and Imperial Dominion in Late Antiquity*. Berkeley and Los Angeles, 1982.

Homes Dudden, F. *The Life and Times of Saint Ambrose*. Oxford, 1935.

Honoré, A. 'The Making of the Theodosian Code'. *Zeitschrift der Savigny-Stiftung für Rechtsgeschichte* (Romanistische Abteilung) 103 (1986), 133–222.

———. 'Scriptor Historiae Augustae'. *Journal of Roman Studies* 77 (1987), 156–176.

Honoré, A., and J. F. Matthews. 'Some Writings of the Pagan Champion Nicomachus Flavianus'. In *Xenia* 23, ed. W. Schiller, 9–48. Konstanz, 1989.

Hopkins, M. K. *Death and Renewal*. Sociological Studies in Roman History, 2. Cambridge, 1983.

Hunt, E. D. *Holy Land Pilgrimage in the Later Roman Empire, A.D. 312–460*. Oxford, 1982.

———. 'Did Constantius II Have "Court Bishops"?' *Studia Patristica* 19 (1989), 86–90.

Huskinson, J. H. *Concordia Apostolorum: Christian Propaganda at Rome in the Fourth and Fifth Centuries: A Study of Early Christian Iconography and Iconology*. British Archaeological Reports, International Series, 148. Oxford, 1982.

Ihm, M. *Studia Ambrosiana*. Leipzig, 1890.

Janson, T. *Latin Prose Prefaces: Studies in Literary Conventions*. Stockholm, 1964.

Jones, A. H. M. *The Later Roman Empire, 284–602: A Social, Economic and Administrative Survey*. Oxford, 1964.

Kelly, J. N. D. *Early Christian Creeds*. 3d ed. London, 1972.

———. *Jerome: His Life, Writings and Controversies*. London, 1975.

King, N. Q. *The Emperor Theodosius and the Establishment of Christianity*. London, 1961.

Kinney, D. '"Capella Reginae": S. Aquilino in Milan'. *Marsyas* 15 (1970–71), 13–35.

———. 'The Evidence for the Dating of San Lorenzo in Milan'. *Journal of the Society of Architectural Historians* 31 (1972), 92–107.

Klein, R. *Der Streit um den Victoriaaltar: Die dritte Relatio des Symmachus und die Briefe 17, 18 und 57 des Mailänder Bischofs Ambrosius*. Darmstadt, 1972.

Kleinbauer, W. 'Toward a Dating of San Lorenzo in Milan'. *Arte Lombarda* 13 (1968), 1–22.

Klingshirn, W. 'Charity and Power: Caesarius of Arles and the Ransoming of Captives in Sub-Roman Gaul'. *Journal of Roman Studies* 75 (1985), 183–203.

Kolb, F. 'Der Bussakt von Mailand: Zum Verhaltnis von Staat und Kirche in der Spätantike'. In *Geschichte und Gegenwart: Festschrift für K. D. Erdmann*, ed. H. Boockmann, K. Jürgensen and G. Stottenberg, 41–74. Neumünster, 1980.

Krautheimer, R. *Three Christian Capitals: Topography and Politics*. Berkeley and Los Angeles, 1983.

Lamirande, E. 'La datation de la "Vita Ambrosii" de Paulin de Milan'. *Revue des Etudes Augustiniennes* 27 (1981), 44–55.

————. *Paulin de Milan et la "Vita Ambrosii"*. Paris, 1983.

Lane Fox, R. *Pagans and Christians*. Harmondsworth, 1986.

Lanzoni, F. *Le diocesi d'Italia: Dalle origini al principio del secolo VII (an. 604). Studi e Testi* 35. Faenza, 1927.

Larson, C. W. R. 'Theodosius and the Thessalonian Massacre Revisited—Yet Again'. *Studia Patristica* 10 (1970), 297–301.

Lécrivain, C. 'Note sur le recrutement des avocats dans la période du bas empire'. *Mélanges de l'Ecole français de Rome* 5 (1885), 276–283.

Lenox-Conyngham, A. 'The Judgement of Ambrose the Bishop on Ambrose the Roman Governor'. *Studia Patristica* 17 (1982), 62–65.

————. 'The Topography of the Basilica Conflict of A.D. 385/6 in Milan'. *Historia* 31 (1982), 353–363.

————. 'Juristic and Religious Aspects of the Basilica Conflict of A.D. 386'. *Studia Patristica* 18 (1985), 1:55–58.

Lewis, S. 'Function and Symbolic Form in the Basilica Apostolorum at Milan'. *Journal of the Society of Architectural Historians* 28 (1969), 83–98.

————. 'The Latin Iconography of the Single-Naved Cruciform Basilica Apostolorum in Milan'. *Art Bulletin* 51 (1969), 205–219.

————. 'San Lorenzo Revisited: A Theodosian Palace Church at Milan'. *Journal of the Society of Architectural Historians* 32 (1973), 197–222.

Liebeschuetz, J. H. W. G. *Antioch: City and Imperial Administration in the Later Roman Empire*. Oxford, 1972.

————. *Barbarians and Bishops: Army, Church and State in the Age of Arcadius and Chrysostom*. Oxford, 1990.

Lieu, S. N. C. *Manichaeism in the Later Roman Empire and Medieval China: A Historical Survey*. Manchester, 1985.

Lippold, A. *Theodosius der Grosse und seine Zeit*. 2d. ed. Munich, 1980.

Lizzi, R. 'Codicilli imperiale e *insignia* episcopali: Un'affinità significativa'. *Rendiconti dell'Istituto Lombardo*, Classe di lettere, scienze morali e storiche 122 (1988), 3–13.

————. 'Una società esortata all'ascetismo: Misure legislative e motivazioni economiche nel IV–V secolo d.C.' *Studi Storici* 30 (1989), 129–153.

————. *Vescovi e strutture ecclesiastiche nella città tardoantica (L' 'Italia Annonaria' nel IV–V secolo d.C.)*. Como, 1989.

————. 'Ambrose's Contemporaries and the Christianization of Northern Italy'. *Journal of Roman Studies* 80 (1990), 156–173.

————. 'Ascetismo e monachesimo nell'Italia tardoantica'. *Codex Aquilarensis* 5 (1991), 55–76.

MacCormack, S. G. *Art and Ceremony in Late Antiquity*. Berkeley and Los Angeles, 1981.

McCormick, M. *Eternal Victory: Triumphal Rulership in Late Antiquity, Byzantium and the Early Medieval West*. Cambridge, 1986.

Machielsen, L. 'Fragments patristiques non-identifiés du manuscrit Vatican palimpseste 577'. *Sacris Eruditi* 12 (1961), 488–539.

McKinnon, J. *Music in Early Christian Literature*. Cambridge, 1987.

McLynn, N. B. 'The "Apology" of Palladius: Nature and Purpose'. *Journal of Theological Studies*, n.s., 42 (1991), 52–76.

———. 'Christian Controversy and Violence in the Fourth Century'. *Kodai* 3 (1992), 15–44.

MacMullen, R. *Soldier and Civilian in the Later Roman Empire*. Cambridge, Mass., 1963.

———. *Corruption and the Decline of Rome*. New Haven, 1988.

———. 'The Preacher's Audience (A.D. 350–400)'. *Journal of Theological Studies*, n.s., 40 (1989), 503–511.

Madec, G. *Saint Ambroise et la philosophie*. Paris, 1974.

Maier, H. O. 'Private Space as the Social Context of Arianism in Ambrose's Milan'. *Journal of Theological Studies*, n.s., 45 (1994).

Maillé de la Tour-Landry, Marquise Marie Jeanne L. G. Aliette de. *Recherches sur les origines de Bordeaux chrétienne*. Paris, 1960.

Marinone, N. 'Il medico Disario in Simmaco e Macrobio'. *Maia*, n.s., 25 (1973), 344–345.

Marrou, H. I. 'Ammian Marcellin et les "Innocents" de Milan'. *Recherches de Science Religeuse* 40 (1952), 179–190.

Martroye, M. 'Un passage d'Ammian Marcellin: XXVII, 7, 5'. *Bulletin de la société nationale des antiquaires de France*, 1922, 165–172.

———. 'L'affaire "Indicia": Une sentence de saint Ambroise'. In *Mélanges P. Fournier*, 503–510. Paris, 1929.

———. 'Une sentence arbitrale de saint Ambroise'. *Revue Historique de Droit français et étranger* 4.8 (1929), 300–311.

Matthews, J. F. 'Gallic Supporters of Theodosius I'. *Latomus* 30 (1971), 1073–1099.

———. 'Symmachus and the *Magister Militum* Theodosius'. *Historia* 20 (1971), 122–128.

———. 'Symmachus and the Oriental Cults'. *Journal of Roman Studies* 63 (1973), 175–95.

———. *Western Aristocracies and Imperial Court, AD 364–425*. Oxford, 1975. Repr. 1990.

———. 'Symmachus and His Enemies'. In *Colloque genevois sur Symmaque, à l'occasion du mille six centième anniversaire du conflit de l'autel de la Victoire, 1984*, ed. F. Paschoud, 163–175. Paris, 1986.

———. *The Roman Empire of Ammianus*. London, 1989.

Mazzarino, S. *Storia sociale del vescovo Ambrogio*. Rome, 1989.

Menis, G. C. 'Le giurisdizioni metropolitiche di Aquileia e di Milano nell'antichità'. *Antichità altoadriatiche* 4 (1973), 271–294.

Merkle, S. 'Die ambrosianischen Tituli'. *Römische Quartalschrift* 10 (1896), 185–222.

Meslin, M. *Les Ariens d'Occident, 335–430*. Paris, 1967.

———. 'Hilaire et la crise arienne'. In *Hilaire et son temps. Actes du colloque de Poitiers*, ed. E.-R. Labande, 19–42. Paris, 1969.

Mesot, J. *Die Heidenbekehrung bei Ambrosius von Mailand*. Schöneck-Beckenried, 1958.

Mirabella Roberti, M. 'Contributi della ricerca archeologica all'architettura ambrosiana milanese'. In *Ambrosius Episcopus*, ed. G. Lazzati, 1:335–362. Milan, 1976.

———. *Milano Romana*. Milan, 1984.

Mossay, J. 'Note sur Héron-Maxime, écrivain écclesiastique'. *Analecta Bollandiana* 100 (1982), 229–236.

Murphy, F. X. *Rufinus of Aquileia (345–411): His Life and Works*. Washington, D.C., 1945.

Musso, L. 'Il *praefectus* del *carmen contra paganos:* Tra vecchie e nuove interpretazioni'. *Archaeologia Classica* 31 (1979), 185–240.

Nauroy, G. 'La méthode de composition d'Ambroise de Milan et la structure du *De Iacob et beata vita*'. In *Ambroise de Milan: Dix études*, ed. Y.-M. Duval, 115–153. Paris, 1974.

———. 'La structure du *De Isaac vel Anima* et la cohérence de l'allégorèse d'Ambroise de Milan'. *Revue des Etudes Latines* 63 (1985), 210–236.

———. 'L'écriture dans la pastorale d'Ambroise de Milan'. In *La monde latin antique et la Bible*, ed. J. Fontaine and E. Pietri (*Bible de tous les temps*, tome 2), 371–408. Paris, 1985.

———. 'Le fouet et le miel: Le combat d'Ambroise en 386 contre l'arianisme milanais'. *Recherches augustiniennes* 23 (1988), 3–86.

Nautin, P. 'Les premières relations d'Ambroise avec l'empereur Gratien: Le "De fide" (livres I et II)'. In *Ambroise de Milan: Dix études*, ed. Y.-M. Duval, 229–244. Paris, 1974.

Norman, A. F. 'Notes on Some Consulares of Syria'. *Byzantinische Zeitschrift* 51 (1958), 73–77.

Novak, D. M. '*Anicianae domus culmen, nobilitatis culmen*'. *Klio* 62 (1980), 473–493.

Oberhelman, S. M. *Rhetoric and Homiletics in Fourth-Century Christian Literature: Prose Rhythm, Oratorical Style and Preaching in the Works of Ambrose, Jerome and Augustine*. APA, American Classical Studies, 26. Atlanta, 1991.

O'Donnell, J. J. 'The Career of Nicomachus Virius Flavianus'. *Phoenix* 32 (1978), 129–149.

———. 'The Demise of Paganism'. *Traditio* 35 (1979), 43–88.

O'Meara, J. J. *The Young Augustine*. London, 1954.

———. 'Augustine and Neo-Platonism'. *Recherches augustiniennes* 1 (1958), 91–111.

Pabst, A. *Divisio Regni: Der Zerfall des Imperium Romanum in der Sicht der Zeitgenossen*. Bonn, 1986.

Palanque, J.-R. 'Un episode des rapports entre saint Ambroise et Gratien: A propos de la lettre I de saint Ambroise'. *Revue des Etudes Anciennes* 30 (1928), 291–301.

———. 'Famines à Rome à la fin du IVe siècle'. *Revue des Etudes Anciennes* 33 (1931), 346–356.

————. *Saint Ambroise et l'empire romain: Contribution à l'histoire des rapports de l'église et l'état à la fin du quatrième siècle*. Paris, 1933.

Palestra, A. 'La prima visita pastorale della basilica di S. Nazaro compiuta da S. Carlo Borromeo'. In *La basilica degli apostoli e Nazaro martire nel culto e nell'arte*, 81–95. Milan, 1969.

————. 'I cimiteri paleocristiani Milanesi'. *Archivio Ambrosiano* 28 (1975), 23–47.

Paredi, A. *S. Ambrogio et la sua età*. 2d ed. Milan, 1960.

————. 'Paulinus of Milan'. *Sacris Erudiri* 14 (1963), 206–30.

————. 'S. Gerolamo e S. Ambrogio'. *Studi e Testi* 235 (1964; *Mélanges Eugene Tisserant* 5), 183–198.

————. *Saint Ambrose*. Trans. J. M. Costelloe. Notre Dame, 1964.

————. 'Ambrogio, Graziano, Teodosio'. *Antichità altoadriatiche* 22 (1982), 1:17–49.

Paschoud, F. *Roma Aeterna: Etudes sur le patriotisme romain dans l'occident latin a l'époque des grands invasions*. Rome, 1967.

————. 'Zosime 2,29 et la version païenne de la conversion de Constantin'. *Historia* 20 (1971), 334–353.

————. *Cinq etudes sur Zosime*. Paris, 1975.

Pearce, J. W. C. *The Roman Imperial Coinage*. Vol. 9. London, 1951.

Petit, P. *Libanius et la vie municipale à Antioch au IVe siècle après J.-C*. Paris, 1955.

Picard, J.-C. *Le souvenir des évêques: Sépultures, listes épiscopales et culte des évêques en Italie du nord des origines au Xe siècle*. Bibliothèque des écoles françaises d'Athènes et de Rome 268. Rome, 1988.

Pietri, C. 'Concordia apostolorum et renovatio urbis (culte des martyrs et propaganda pontificiale)'. *Mélanges d'archéologie et d'histoire de l'Ecole Français de Rome, Antiquité* 73 (1961), 275–322.

————. *Roma Christiana: Recherches sur l'église de Rome, son organisation, sa politique, son idéologie, de Miltiade à Sixte III (311–440)*. Bibliothèque des écoles françaises d'Athènes et de Rome 224. Rome, 1976.

————. 'Une aristocracie provinciale et la mission chrétienne: L'exemple de la Venetia'. *Antichità altoadriatiche* 22 (1982), 1:89–138.

————. 'Damase, évêque de Rome'. In *Saecularia Damasiana* (Coll. Studi di antichità cristiana 39), 31–58. Vatican City, 1986.

Piganiol, A. *L'empire chrétien (325–395)*. 2d ed. Paris, 1972.

Pincherle, A. 'Ambrogio ed Agostino'. *Augustinianum* 14 (1974), 385–407.

Pizzolato, L. F. 'La Sacra Scrittura fondamento del metodo esegetico di sant' Ambrogio'. In *Ambrosius Episcopus*, ed. G. Lazzati, 1:393–426. Milan, 1976.

Ratti, A. 'Il più antico ritratto di S. Ambrogio'. In *Ambrosiana: Scritti vari pubblicati nel XV centenario dalla morte di sant'Ambrogio*, 5–74. Milan, 1897.

Rebenich, S. 'Gratian, a Son of Theodosius, and the Birth of Galla Placidia'. *Historia* 34 (1985), 372–385.

————. *Hieronymus und sein Kreis: Prosopographische und sozialgeschichtliche Untersuchungen*. Historia Einzelschriften 72. Stuttgart, 1992.

Reggiori, F. *La basilica Ambrosiana: Ricerche e restauri 1929–40*. Milan, 1941.

Richard, M. 'Saint Basile et la mission du diacre Sabinus'. *Analecta Bollandiana* 67 (1949), 178–202.

———. 'La lettre *Confidimus Quidem* du pape Damase'. *Annuaire de l'Institut de Philologie et d'Histoire Orientales et Slaves de l'Université Libre de Bruxelles* 11 (1951), 323–340.

Ritter, A. M. *Das Konzil von Konstantinopel und sein Symbol.* Göttingen, 1965.

Rogers, B. S. 'Merobaudes and Maximus in Gaul'. *Historia* 30 (1981), 82–105.

Rosso, G. 'La "lettera alla vergini": Atanasio e Ambrogio'. *Augustinianum* 23 (1983), 421–452.

Roueché, C. 'Acclamations in the Later Roman Empire: New Evidence from Aphrodisias'. *Journal of Roman Studies* 74 (1984), 181–199.

Rousseau, P. *Ascetics, Authority and the Church in the Age of Jerome and Cassian.* Oxford, 1978.

Ruggini, L. *See* L. Cracco Ruggini.

Salzman, M. R. *On Roman Time: The Codex-Calendar of 354 and the Rhythms of Urban Life in Late Antiquity.* Berkeley and Los Angeles, 1990.

Savio, F. *Gli antichi vescovi d'Italia dalle origini al 1300 descritti per regioni: Il Piemonte.* Turin, 1898.

———. *Gli antichi vescovi d'Italia dalle origini al 1300 descritti per regioni: La Lombardia, Parte 1: Milano.* Florence, 1913.

Savon, H. 'Maniérisme et allégorie dans l'oeuvre d'Ambroise de Milan'. *Revue des Etudes Latines* 55 (1977), 203–221.

———. *Saint Ambroise devant l'exégèse de Philon le juif.* Paris, 1977.

———. 'La première oraison funèbre de saint Ambroise et les deux sources de la consolation chrétienne'. *Revue des Etudes Latines* 58 (1980), 370–402.

Scheidweiler, F. 'Besitzen wir das lateinische Original der römischen Synodalschreibens vom Jahr 371?'. *Annuaire de l'Institut de Philologie et d'Histoire Orientales et Slaves de l'Université Libre de Bruxelles* 13 (1955), 572–586.

Schieffer, R. 'Von Mailand nach Canossa: Ein Beitrag zur Geschichte der christlichen Herrscherbusse von Theodosius d. Gr. bis zu Heinrich IV'. *Deutsches Archiv für die Erforschung des Mittelalters* 28 (1972), 333–370.

Seeck, O. *Geschichte des Untergangs der antiken Welt.* Band 5. Berlin, 1913.

———. *Regesten der Kaisern und Päpste für die Jahre 311 bis 476 n.Chr: Vorarbeit zu einer Prosopographie der christlicher Kaiserzeit.* Stuttgart, 1919.

Selb, W. 'Episcopalis audientia von der Zeit Konstantins bis zur Novelle XXXV Valentinians III'. *Zeitschrift der Savigny-Stiftung fur Rechtsgeschichte* (Romanistische Abteilung) 84 (1967), 162–217.

Shaw, B. D. 'The Family in Late Antiquity: The Experience of Augustine'. *Past and Present* 115 (1986), 3–51.

Sieben, H. J. *Die Konzilsidee der alten Kirchen.* Konziliengeschichte Reihe B: Untersuchungen. Paderborn, 1979.

Simon, M. *Verus Israel: A Study of the Relations between Christians and Jews in the Roman Empire.* Trans. H. McKeating. Oxford, 1986.

Simonetti, M. *Studi sull'arianesimo.* Rome, 1965.

Sivan, H. *Ausonius of Bordeaux: Genesis of a Gallic Aristocracy*. London, 1993.

Snee, E. R. 'Gregory Nazianzen's Constantinopolitan Career'. Ph.D. diss., University of Washington, 1981.

Speller, L. A. 'A Note on Eusebius of Vercelli and the Council of Milan'. *Journal of Theological Studies*, n.s., 36 (1985), 157–165.

Stancliffe, C. *St. Martin and His Hagiographer: History and Miracle in Sulpicius Severus*. Oxford, 1983.

Steidle, W. 'Beobachtung zu des Ambrosius Schrift *De officiis*'. *Vigiliae Christianae* 38 (1984), 18–66.

———. 'Beobachtung zum Gedankedang im 2. Buch von Ambrosius, *De officiis*'. *Vigiliae Christianae* 39 (1985), 280–298.

Szidat, J. 'Die Usurpation des Eugenius'. *Historia* 28 (1979), 487–508.

Testard, M. 'Etude sur la composition dans le *De officiis ministrorum* de saint Ambroise'. In *Ambroise de Milan: Dix études*, ed. Y.-M. Duval, 155–197. Paris, 1974.

———. 'Observations sur le rhétorique d'une harangue au peuple dans le *Sermo contra Auxentium* de saint Ambroise'. *Revue des Etudes Latines* 63 (1985), 193–209.

Thélamon, F. *Païens et chrétiens au IVème siècle: L'apport de l' "Histoire ecclésiastique" de Rufin d'Aquilée*. Paris, 1981.

Toynbee, J. M. C. *Death and Burial in the Roman World*. London, 1971.

Treucker, B. 'A Note on Basil's Letters of Recommendation'. In *Basil of Caesarea: Christian, Humanist, Ascetic: A Sixteen-Hundredth Anniversary Symposium*, ed. P. J. Fedwick, 1:405–410. Toronto, 1981.

Truzzi, C. 'La liturgia di Verona al tempo di San Zeno'. *Studia Patavina* 27 (1980), 539–564.

———. *Zeno, Gaudenzio, Cromazio: Testi e contenuti della predicazione cristiana per le chiese di Verona, Brescia e Aquileia (360–410 ca.)*. Brescia, 1985.

Van Andel, G. K. *The Christian Concept of History in the Chronicle of Sulpicius Severus*. Amsterdam, 1976.

Van Dam, R. *Leadership and Community in Late Antique Gaul*. Berkeley and Los Angeles, 1985.

Van der Meer, F. *Augustine the Bishop: The Life and Work of a Father of the Church*. Trans. B. Battershaw and G. R. Lamb. London, 1961.

Van Haeringen, J. H. 'De Valentiniano II et Ambrosio: Illustrantur et digeruntur res anno 386 gestae'. *Mnemosyne* 3.5 (1937), 152–158; 28–33; 229–40.

Van Ommeslaeghe, F. 'Jean Chrysostome et le peuple de Constantinople'. *Analecta Bollandiana* 99 (1981), 329–349.

Vasey, V. R. *The Social Ideas in the Works of Saint Ambrose: A Study on "De Nabuthe"*. Rome, 1982.

Vera, D. 'I rapporti fra Magno Massimo, Teodosio e Valentiniano II nel 383–384'. *Athenaeum*, n.s., 53 (1975), 267–301.

———. 'Le statue del senato di Roma in onore di Flavio Teodosio e l'equilibrio dei potere imperiali in età teodosiana'. *Athenaeum*, n.s., 57 (1979), 381–403.

Vermes, G. *Scripture and Tradition in Judaism: Haggadic Studies.* Studia Post-Biblica 4. Leiden, 1961.

Vessey, M. 'Jerome's Origen: The Making of a Christian Literary Persona'. *Studia Patristica* 25 (1993), 134–145.

Villa, E. 'Un autografo di Sant'Ambrogio'. *Ambrosius* 30 (1954), 65–68.

———. 'Come risolse Sant'Ambrogio il problema delle chiese alla periferia di Milano'. *Ambrosius* 32 (1956), 22–45.

———. 'Il culto agli Apostoli nell'Italia settentriole alla fine del sec. IV'. *Ambrosius* 33 (1957), 245–264.

———. 'La basilica ambrosiana degli Apostoli attraverso i secoli'. In *Quaderni di Ambrosius, Ambrosius* 39 suppl. (1963), 15–74.

Von Campenhausen, H. *Ambrosius von Mailand als Kirchenpolitiker.* Berlin, 1929.

Waldstein, W. 'Zur Stellung der Episcopalis audientia im spätrömischen Prozess'. In *Festschrift für Max Kaser zum 70. Geburtstag,* ed. D. Medicus and H. H. Seiler, 533–556. Munich, 1976.

Ward-Perkins, B. *From Classical Antiquity to the Middle Ages: Urban Public Building in Northern and Central Italy, A.D. 300–850.* Oxford, 1984.

Wightman, E. *Roman Trier and the Treviri.* London, 1970.

———. *Gallia Belgica.* London, 1985.

Wilcken, R. L. *John Chrysostom and the Jews: Rhetoric and Reality in the Late Fourth Century.* Berkeley and Los Angeles, 1983.

Wormald, P. 'The Decline of the Western Empire and the Survival of Its Aristocracy'. *Journal of Roman Studies* 66 (1976), 217–226.

Zangara, V. 'L'*inventio* dei corpi dei martiri Gervasio e Protasio: Testimoniaze di Agostino su un fenomeno di religiosità popolare'. *Augustinianum* 21 (1981), 119–133.

Zeiller, J. *Les origines chrétiennes dans les provinces danubiennes de l'Empire Romain.* Bibliothèque des écoles françaises d'Athènes et de Rome 112. Paris, 1918.

———. 'La date du concile d'Aquilée (3 septembre 381). *Studi Bizantini e Neoellenici* 5 (1939), 327–332.

Zelzer, K. 'Zur Beurteilung der Cicero-Imitatio bei Ambrosius'. *Wiener Studien* 90 (n.f. 11, 1977), 168–191.

Zelzer, M. 'Zum Osterfestbrief des hl. Ambrosius und zur römischen Osterfestberechnung des 4 Jh.'. *Wiener Studien* 91 (n.f. 12, 1978), 187–204.

———. '*Plinius Christianus:* Ambrosius als Epistolograph'. *Studia Patristica* 23 (1989), 203–208.

Zovatto, P. L. 'L'urnetta argentea di S. Ambrogio nell'ambito della rinascenza teodosiana'. *Critica d'Arte* 13–14 (1956), 2–14.

INDEX